Handbook of Contemporary Learning Theories

To G. Robert Grice and Frank A. Logan,
two professors who inspired my ongoing
appreciation for classical learning theory.
—R. R. M.

To Michael D'Amato and Norman E. (Skip) Spear,
both of whom have had a positive influence
on my career as a psychologist.
—S. B. K.

Contents

Preface

*T*heoretical interpretations of the learning process have concerned experimental psychologists since the late 1800s and have been a dominant force in psychology in general. Many of the initial theories, such as those of Hull and Tolman, attempted to capture the entire essence of learned behavior—the age of global theories of learning. Since the mid 1970s, theoretical concepts of the way in which human and nonhuman organisms learn or acquire information have undergone a dramatic metamorphosis. This change has involved moving from the broad, all-encompassing theories of Hull, Tolman, Guthrie, and Thorndike to more specific, focused theories.

Most learning texts available to upper-level students reviewing various theories of learning cover the traditional theories in detail, while only casually addressing more contemporary theories. Detailed treatment of the modern theories is available but can be found only by searching through a variety of sources (i.e., book chapters, review articles, or a series of research articles). Feeling that there was a definite need to put all of these ideas into a single, easily accessible medium, 11 years ago we contacted many noted modern learning theorists who graciously agreed to provide a discussion of their most recent research and theorizing. The result was a two-volume text published in 1989 by Lawrence Erlbaum describing contemporary conceptualizations of the learning process. The first volume described the views of 16 psychologists concerning Pavlovian conditioning and modifications of traditional learning theory. The second volume presented the ideas of 17 psychologists on instrumental conditioning and biological constraints on learning.

ix

It has been over a decade since we edited the two-volume contemporary learning theories text. A considerable amount of research has been published during that time on the nature of learning. It seemed clear to us that an update on the status of contemporary learning theories was needed. To this end, the *Handbook of Contemporary Learning Theories* contains 14 chapters that describe the most up-to-date perspectives on the learning process. The material in this text is appropriate for several different audiences. It could be used in an upper division learning theories course, a graduate learning theories class, or as a reference text for researchers. We hope that the ideas of these noted psychologists will be as enlightening and stimulating to you as they have been to us.

—*Robert R. Mowrer*
—*Stephen B. Klein*

chapter 1

The Transitive Nature of Contemporary Learning Theory

Robert R. Mowrer
Angelo State University

Stephen B. Klein
Mississippi State University

T his volume provides discussions of select learning processes and the theories developed to explain them. The definition of learning varies in wording and detail from source to source. A brief perusal of some of the more popular learning texts reveals several definitions of learning: "a relatively permanent change in an organism's potential for responding that results from prior experience or practice" (Gordon, 1989, p. 6); "an enduring change in the mechanisms of behavior involving specific stimuli and/or responses that results from prior experience with similar stimuli and responses" (Domjan, 1998, p. 13); "a ... more or less permanent change in behavior potentiality which occurs as a result of repeated practice" (Flaharty, 1985, p. 7, citing Kimble, 1961); "the change in a subject's behavior or behavior potential to a given situation brought about by the subject's repeated experiences in that situation, provided that the behavior change cannot be explained on the basis of the subject's native response tendencies, maturation or temporary states" (Bower & Hilgard, 1981, p. 11); and "an experiential process resulting in a relatively permanent change in behavior that cannot be explained by temporary states, maturation, or innate response tendencies." (Klein, 1996, p. 2).

All of these definitions seem to share the common theme that learning is a relatively permanent change in the probability of exhibiting a certain behavior resulting from some prior experience (successful or unsuccessful). Just as the definition of learning varies, theoretical approaches to studying and explaining the learning process have varied throughout the years.

Although theoretical approaches to learning can be traced back as far as Descartes, significant experimental studies began only a little more than 100 years ago. Much of the impetus for the early interest in learning was due to the paradigm shift from functionalism to behaviorism and as a result many different views of learning were generated. From the early studies of Thorndike and Pavlov in the late 19th and early 20th centuries through the 1960s, behavior theorists developed "global" theories of learning; that is, theories that attempted to explain all aspects of the learning process. Although a significant understanding of the learning phenomenon resulted from these general process models, more contemporary theorists investigate and explain specific aspects of the learning process. In this chapter, we briefly examine the traditional global learning theories, the reasons why contemporary learning theorists abandoned global learning theories that led to our earlier two-volume publication on contemporary learning theory (see Klein & Mowrer, 1989a, 1989b), and finally, the rationale behind the production of this volume.

This volume presents the conceptualizations and research of noted contemporary learning theorists. The chapters in this volume address a wide range of topics in Pavlovian conditioning, instrumental conditioning, and the biological aspects of learning. (The following sections represent only a thumbnail sketch of traditional learning theory. For an excellent treatment of traditional theoretical perspectives, see Bower & Hilgard, 1981.)

GLOBAL LEARNING THEORIES

Behaviorism, first clearly defined by Watson (1913), is a school of psychology that focuses on the role of experience in governing behavior.

Watson was born in 1878 in Traveler's Rest, South Carolina. He received his bachelor's and master's degrees from Furman University, graduating in 1899. He received the first doctorate offered in psychology from the University of Chicago in 1903 working primarily under James Angell. He remained at the University of Chicago as a faculty member until 1908. From 1908 until 1920, Watson was a member of the faculty at Johns Hopkins University. In 1920 he left Johns Hopkins and joined the J. Walter Thompson advertising agency, becoming vice president in 1924 and finally retiring in 1945. His last psychology publication was his revision of "Behaviorism" in 1930.

According to Watson and the behaviorist perspective, although we possess instinctive behavior and motives, the more important determinants of our behavior are learned. Traditionally, behaviors are considered to be learned through either classical conditioning (also known as Pavlovian or respondent conditioning) or instrumental or operant conditioning.

In the typical classical conditioning paradigm, an innocuous stimulus such as a tone is paired with a biologically significant stimulus such as a weak electric shock to the paraorbital region of a rabbit's eye. The electric shock or unconditioned stimulus (UCS) elicits an inherent or unconditioned response (UR), closure of the nictitating membrane. As tone–shock pairings continue, the tone or conditioned stimulus (CS) becomes capable of eliciting the nictitating membrane response in the absence of the UCS. The previous "UR" has now become a conditioned response (CR). (Note that not all CRs are the same as the corresponding UR.)

Classical conditioning is an involuntary or mechanistic type of learning that serves an adaptive purpose. It is important that an organism learn about signals in the environment (CSs) that predict biologically significant events (UCSs) and allow the organism to prepare for them (CRs).

Instrumental or operant conditioning is somewhat different than classical conditioning. The primary distinction can be summarized by the terms *elicited* and *emitted*. In classical conditioning, the behavior (response) is elicited by the UCS, automatically and involuntarily, whereas in instrumental or operant conditioning the behavior (response) is emitted voluntarily, and the organism experiences some consequence to that behavior. For example, a hungry rat in a T-maze voluntarily leaves the start chamber and after turning left (behavior) finds food in the goal box (consequence). The rat will subsequently learn that its behavior (turning left) will result in reward (consequence).

These two types of learning are not necessarily isolated in terms of governing behavior. In many learning situations, such as avoidance conditioning, both classical and instrumental conditioning are likely involved (see Levis & Brewer, chap. 14, this volume).

Even the drives that motivate us are typically acquired and our behavior based on these motives is usually learned through past experience. Specifically, according to Watson, "we can write a psychology ... in terms of stimulus and response, in terms of habit formation, habit integrations and the like [learning]" (Benjamin, 1988, p. 405). One main goal of the behaviorist is to determine the laws governing the learning process, a concern that has dominated the discipline of psychology for decades and continues to do so to this day. As stated previously, much of this effort has involved the development of global explanations of learning—a single view that could account for all learned behaviors. We briefly examine five representative global learning theories.

Edward L. Thorndike was born in 1874 and received his undergraduate degree in English at Wesleyan College in 1894. He earned his master's degree from Harvard under William James and his doctoral degree from Columbia University in 1898, "officially" supervised by James Cattell. The publication of his doctoral thesis, *Animal Intelligence*, in 1898 established for nearly 50 years "one learning theory [that] dominated all others in America" (Bower & Hilgard, 1981, p. 21). Thorndike spent most of his career in the Teacher's College at Columbia University.

Thorndike's dominance was rivaled only by that of Clark L. Hull, who was born in 1884 and intended a future as a mining engineer while attending Alma College in Michigan. Struck with polio after 2 years of college, he transferred to the University of Michigan to finish his undergraduate education in psychology. Hull received his bachelor's degree in 1913. After teaching for a year, Hull worked with Joseph Jastrow at the University of Wisconsin where he received his doctorate in 1918. He spent most of his life at Yale University in the Institute of Human Relations where he developed much of his theoretical perspective on learning. Hull's hypothetico-deductive theorizing reflects his early interests in engineering and mechanics. After his death, Hull's theoretical perspective continued to evolve through the work of his close colleague, Kenneth Spence and their students.

Two other theorists, Edward Tolman and Edwin Guthrie, continue to be appreciated in many contemporary approaches to learning. Tolman was born in 1886 and received his undergraduate degree in 1911 at the Massachusetts Institute of Technology, majoring in electrochemistry. He received his doctoral degree in 1915 from Harvard University in psychology. While a graduate student, he traveled to Germany and was exposed to the notions of Gestalt psychology through his relationship with Kurt Koffka. This Gestalt influence clearly shows in his theoretical approach to learning. After 3 years at Northwestern, he spent the rest of his career at the University of California–Berkeley.

Guthrie was born in 1886 and majored in mathematics at the University of Nebraska. He received his doctoral degree in philosophy from the University of Pennsylvania in 1912. Guthrie spent his entire career at the University of Washington (the Psychology Department is now housed in Guthrie Hall). Of all the classic behaviorists, Guthrie's model was probably closest to Watson's original position in terms of learning (Hill, 1997).

Finally, it would be impossible to discuss classic behavioristic approaches to learning without including B. F. Skinner, even though he did not consider himself a theorist. Skinner was born in 1904 and studied English as an undergraduate at Hamilton College, where he graduated in 1927. After several unsuccessful attempts at writing (despite encouragement from Robert Frost), he enrolled in the graduate program at Harvard and received his PhD in psychology in 1931. Skinner remained at Harvard as a research fellow until 1936, when he went to the University of Minnesota. In 1945, Skinner joined the faculty of Indiana University. He returned to Harvard in 1948, where he subsequently spent most of his career. Skinner's perspective on learning is much like that of Thorndike in terms of his definition of and emphasis on reinforcement.

Connectionism and Thorndike

Puzzle Boxes and Trial-and-Error Learning. Thorndike is probably best known for his work using cats and the infamous puzzle box. The impetus for this work derived from Thorndike's distaste for the anecdotal explanations of animal behavior predominant at the time. These explanations assumed that animals were intelligent and solved problems via reasoning and deliberation. Thorndike set out to provide a mechanistic explanation for animal learning, one that did not require the use of mentalistic terms.

In a typical case, a hungry cat was confined in a box that included some manipulandum (lever, pedal, knob, etc.) that would allow the cat to escape (open a door) and obtain the food placed just outside the door. On initial placement into the box, the cat would engage in various behaviors related to confinement—clawing, biting, meowing, rubbing, and so on—before accidentally activating the release mechanism (e.g., pushing the lever) and escaping to consume the food. When replaced into the box, the cat would again engage in a series of behaviors, one of which would again accidentally activate the release mechanism.

Thorndike noted that over successive trials, the time between initial placement and escape decreased, albeit slowly. This produced a typical learning curve in which the time elapsed before a correct response decreased. Thorndike assumed that the cat, when confronted with the puzzle box, engaged in several unsuccessful responses in an attempt to escape before happening on the correct one. In other words, the cat tried (trial) and erred (error) before it engaged in the correct response. Thus, Thorndike concluded that cats learned by way of trial and error (or, as he called it, selecting and connecting).

Stimulus–Response Connections. The gradual nature of the learning curve led Thorndike to believe that the cat was not really aware of how it was escaping but rather that learning consisted of the gradual "stamping in" of correct responses and the "stamping out" of incorrect responses. This stamping in consisted of the formation of a *connection* between the stimulus (puzzle box) and response (push lever), thereby producing stimulus–response bonds. The more times the cat was exposed to the stimulus (S) and made the correct response (R), the stronger the S–R connection became. Further, the stamping-in process was automatic (i.e., did not require awareness) and therefore allowed a "mechanistic" explanation for the animal's behavior. According to Bower and Hilgard (1981), Thorndike's "is the original stimulus–response, or S–R, psychology of learning" (p. 21).

Law of Effect. Thorndike replicated his puzzle box findings with numerous other species and variations of the puzzle box. As a result of these diverse experiments, he felt that animal learning consisted mainly of the association between a stimulus situation and some response. Up to this point we have neglected to mention the role of the food in establishing the S–R connection. The principle of frequency proposed by Watson argued that S–R connections can be established by pure repetition (or contiguity between S and R; see the discussion of Guthrie later). Although Thorndike did not totally reject this notion (law of exercise), his primary law of learning became known as the *law of effect*. Put simply, if a response is followed by a "satisfying" state of affairs, the S–R connection is strengthened; if a response is followed by an "annoying" state of affairs, the S–R connection is weakened. Thorndike (1913) operationally defined these states of affairs in the following quote:

> By a satisfying state of affairs is meant one which the animal does nothing to avoid, often doing things which maintain or renew it. By an annoying state of affairs is meant one which the animal does nothing to preserve, often doing things which put an end to it. (p. 2)

Thorndike later modified the law of effect to render the effect of a punisher (annoyer) less critical than the effect of a reward (satisfier). Specifically, a reward strengthens the S–R connection directly, whereas a punisher weakens the S–R connection indirectly (see Thorndike, 1932). Thus Thorndike's approach relied on reward (satisfying state), S–R bonds, and motivation (law of readiness). One theorist who provided an elaborate theory of learning that was also based on the concept of reward, S–R connections, and motivation was Hull.

Hull and Drive Reduction

The Concept of Drive.   Woodworth defined the concept of drive in 1918 as an intense internal force that motivates behavior. Hull's model (also known as the Hull–Spence model) was based on the notion that drive, learned or innate, automatically motivates behavior (Hull, 1943). Unlearned or innate sources of drive include deprivation of a biologically important substance such as food, water, or oxygen. Such a deficit threatens the organism's survival and drives the organism to make an adjustment to restore the biological system to normal (homeostasis). That is, the organism is motivated to reduce the deficit (or drive), thereby reestablishing homeostasis.

In addition to deprivation, intense environmental events also represent innate sources of drive. These might include electric shock or a loud noise, which activate an internal drive state. Although electric shock or a loud noise may not necessarily threaten survival, they may be aversive and again the organism is motivated to reduce the internal drive state. Thus, drive may be induced by intense circumstances that are aversive but not life threatening.

Besides innate sources of drive, Hull suggested that environmental stimuli can acquire the ability to produce a comparable drive state through classical conditioning. According to this position, environmental cues that are associated with the antecedent conditions that produce an innate drive state acquire the ability to induce that drive state by themselves. As a result, these cues can cause an internal arousal, thereby motivating behavior without the presence of innate drive-inducing stimuli.

Drive Reduction and Habit Strength.   When an organism is aroused, either by innate or learned sources of drive, it is motivated to reduce the drive. According to Hull, drive reduction is rewarding and any behavior that reduces the drive is likely to be associated with that drive state. As a behavior consistently serves to reduce a drive, its habit strength increases. Hull symbolized habit strength as $_sH_R$ to emphasize the S–R nature of habit strength. When an organism is confronted with a stimulus situation that induces a drive, it will engage in certain responses in an attempt to reduce the drive. If a given response is successful (reduces the drive) the bond between the stimulus situation and the response increases and consequently so does habit strength.

For Hull, habit strength was permanent; it can only increase not decrease. How then does an organism change its behavior when its "habitual" behavior becomes unsuccessful? According to Hull, unsuccessful behavior causes the drive to persist and activity is suppressed—a process he called *reactive inhibition*. As the drive state persists and reactive inhibition dissipates, the unsuccessful behavior occurs again. Continued failure of the habit to reduce the drive results in a permanent state called *conditioned inhibition*. Conditioned inhibition is specific to the unsuccessful habit and serves to counter its excitatory strength. As a result of conditioned inhibition, the second strongest response in the organism's habit hierarchy becomes the dominant habit. If this behavior is successful in reducing the drive state, its habit strength is enhanced and thus it will be elicited the next time the organism is motivated. If the second habit is also unsuccessful, this process will continue until a successful response is discovered.

The Role of Incentive Motivation.　　In Hull's (1943) model, the value of reward was assumed to influence the strength of the S–R bond; the larger or more valuable the reward, the greater the drive reduction and, therefore the greater the habit strength. Once a behavior was established, the probability of the behavior being exhibited depended on the organism's drive level, not reward value. This assumption was challenged by several studies, most notably that of Crespi (1942), who found that changes in reward magnitude produced a rapid change in rats' runway performance for food, too rapid to be accounted for by changes in habit strength. The rapid increase or decrease in running speed as a result of changes in reward magnitude indicated that the rats' behavior was modified due to changes in motivation rather than habit strength.

As a result of these findings, Hull (1952) altered his model to include the concept of incentive motivation (K), which was based on reward magnitude. Incentive motivation combined with drive motivation to influence the intensity of instrumental behavior. Many of the specifics of incentive motivation were provided by his close colleague, Kenneth Spence (Hull died shortly before his 1952 book was published). According to Spence (1956), when a reward is obtained, the reward elicits an internal goal response (Rg) such as salivation to food. This internal response elicits an internal stimulus state (Sg) that motivates consummatory behavior causing the animal to eat the food.

Spence believed that during the initial experiences, environmental cues present during the reward became associated with reward and acquire the ability to elicit a conditioned or anticipatory goal response (rg). This in turn causes internal stimulus changes (sg) that motivate behavior toward the goal stimulus. Once the association of the rg with the goal box has been established, the sight of the goal box elicits the rg–sg mechanism, motivating the organism to approach the goal box. The strength of the rg–sg mechanism increases on each reinforced trial producing corresponding increases in motivation. The formation of the rg–sg mechanism follows the basic principles of Pavlovian conditioning. The goal box stimuli serve as the CS, the food as the UCS and salivation as the UR (CR or rg). In Pavlovian conditioning, the stronger the UCS the stronger the CR. Thus, a larger reward (UCS) results in a larger or stronger CR or rg. The stronger rg elicits a stronger sg and an overall increase in incentive motivation (rg–sg). Likewise, small reward results in a weaker rg and thus a decrease in incentive motivation.

Spence's anticipatory goal mechanism suggests that Pavlovian conditioning is responsible for the effect of reward magnitude on the intensity of instrumental appetitive behavior. Others (see Amsel, 1958; D'Amato, 1970) have adopted this perspective on conditioning to explain an organism's motivation to avoid frustrating or painful situations.

Both Thorndike's and Hull's S–R positions relied heavily on the concept of reward. One classic theorist who eschewed the necessity for reward in establishing S–R associations was Guthrie.

Guthrie and the Sufficiency of Contiguity

The Necessity for Reward.   Guthrie (1935, 1959) proposed that contiguity between a stimulus and response was sufficient to establish an S–R association. In Guthrie's view, if a response occurs in a particular stimulus situation, the stimulus and response will automatically become associated; reward is not a requirement. To paraphrase Guthrie, if a response occurs in the presence of a particular stimulus, it will likely be repeated when confronted with that stimulus again. However, we make many responses in various stimulus situations; which one becomes associated? According to Guthrie, the last one, because that is the one that changes the stimulus situation such that the organism is now confronted with a different stimulus situation. That is not to say that reward had no effect, just that it was not necessary. Why then does reward increase responding? For Guthrie, once the required response (the one that produces reward) is expressed, the reward changes the stimulus context (internal or external) that was present prior to reward. Any actions following reward will become associated with a new stimulus context, therefore allowing the rewarded response to be exhibited when the old stimulus circumstance is presented again. In essence, reward acts to prevent further associations from being conditioned to that stimulus situation, rather than strengthening the S–R association. This notion, however, was directly challenged by Seward (1942), who attempted to train hungry rats to press a lever for either food or removal from the chamber. Given that removal from the chamber was a greater change in the stimulus configuration, it should produce the most effective learning—obviously it did not. To account for this, Guthrie proposed the concept of maintaining stimuli (such as hunger). Changes in these maintaining stimuli were more important for learning than general changes in the stimulus environment.

What about the magnitude of reward? To account for the effect of reward magnitude, Guthrie could again appeal to the notion of maintaining stimuli: Behavior continues to occur until a response changes these maintaining stimuli. For example, a hungry animal will continue to make responses until the maintaining stimulus (hunger) is changed. A large reward produces a greater change in the maintaining stimulus relative to a small reward. What if reward is delayed? According to Guthrie, reward must immediately follow the appropriate response for that response to occur on the next stimulus exposure. With delayed reward, behaviors occurring after the appropriate response but before the reward will become associated with the stimulus situation. Immediate reward prevents the acquisition of competing S–R associations. Consider arriving home from work and rewarding your dog for not defecating in the house. Rather than associating nondefecation with the reward, the dog will associate whatever behavior it had been engaging in (sleeping perhaps) just prior to reward. The same holds true if you were to punish the dog for chewing up the furniture. Punishment, however, poses a new issue for Guthrie: Doesn't punishment change the stimulus situation and shouldn't this result in the preceding behavior increasing?

The Function of Punishment. How did Guthrie explain the effect of punishment on behavior? Punishment, by definition, decreases the likelihood that the punished behavior will be repeated. In Guthrie's view, punishment, similar to reward, changes the stimulus situation, but its behavioral effect is a decrease, not an increase, in the preceding behavior. Unlike reward, Guthrie assumed that punishment serves as a stimulus—a UCS that elicits a number of responses incompatible with the punished behavior. If the response elicited by the punishment reduces or terminates the aversive event, it will become conditioned to the stimulus context in which the punishment occurred. When that stimulus situation is encountered again, the CR will occur.

Learning Is All or None. In Guthrie's view, learning occurs in a single trial; the S–R association is at full strength following the initial pairing of a stimulus and a response. This view seems inconsistent with the well-established finding that the efficiency and strength of a behavior improve with subsequent successful experience. Guthrie did not deny that behavior improves over successful experience; however, he did not ascribe to the Hullian (or Thorndikian) view that the strength of the S–R bond increases slowly with successful experience.

Guthrie provided three reasons for the gradual improvement in performance. First, there are many stimuli present during initial conditioning and only a portion of these stimuli will be active or attended to. The portion of stimuli present (attended to) when an animal or human responds will vary from trial to trial. For a stimulus attended to during a particular trial to produce a response, it must also have been attended to on the previous trial. In this case, changes in attention produce changes in behavior despite prior conditioning. Thus, changes in behavior from trial to trial reflect an attentional process rather than a learning process. Second, many different stimuli may become associated with a particular response. As more and more stimuli become associated with a response, the strength of the response will increase. This increased intensity is not due to a stronger S–R connection, but rather is due to an increase in the number of stimuli able to elicit the response. Finally, a complex behavior consists of many separate responses (movements). These movements then combine to produce the behavior (acts). For an act to be efficient, each response element must become conditioned to the stimulus. As this process continues, the behavior becomes more efficient and an improvement in behavior will be evidenced. According to Guthrie, the greater the complexity of the behavior, the more that practice will be necessary for efficient behavior.

The three preceding traditional theorists viewed learning as a mechanistic or robotic phenomenon. None hinted at the possibility that the organism actually understood what was going on. Thorndike even emphasized that his cats did not "know" they were learning; the stamping in of the S–R association was automatic and nonconscious. One traditional theorist, Edward Tolman, rejected this view and took a cognitive stance.

An Early Cognitive Perspective

Goals, Purposes, and Expectancies.   Tolman's (1932, 1959) perspective on learning was in direct contrast to the mechanistic views already described. He did not see behavior as reflecting an automatic response to some environmental stimulus but rather that behavior has direction and purpose in terms of obtaining some desired goal (or avoiding some unwanted consequence). Beyond this, organisms are capable of understanding the structure of their environment. He was careful however, in his use of the terms *purpose* and *expectation*; he never stated explicitly that organisms are aware of their purpose or expectancies, just that they behaved "as if" a particular action will lead to a particular outcome or goal.

In Tolman's view, not only is behavior goal directed, but specific behaviors are expected to produce specific outcomes. For example, a sports fan expects to sit down on a Saturday afternoon and enjoy a sporting event on the television. If that goal is not obtained (the event is canceled), that person will not accept any television program but will seek out a suitable alternative (this is especially true if the person has the 100-sport-channel cable package). In addition, certain cues in the environment provide information as to the location of various goals. Tolman felt that these goals could only be obtained after the organism has learned the environmental cues leading to reward or punishment. Thus, you know the location of your favorite rhythm and blues club and use cues in the environment to lead you there.

Somewhat similar to Guthrie, Tolman suggested that reward is not necessary for learning. However, expectations will not be evidenced unless the individual is motivated. Tolman assumed that motivation served two functions: (a) It produces an internal state of tension that creates a demand for the goal object, and (b) it focuses the individual on particular environmental features relevant to attaining the desired goal. For example, if you are not thirsty, you are less likely to learn the location of the drinking fountain as compared to "dying of thirst."

Although Tolman's concept of tension is similar to Hull's drive motivation, it does not possess the mechanistic quality that it does in Hull's postulations. In Tolman's view, expectations control the direction the organism will follow to reduce the state of tension. In this sense, behavior is not a fixed, automatic, or stereotyped series of responses in an attempt to reduce a drive (tension), but a flexible mechanism by which a goal may be obtained.

Cognitive Maps and Reward Magnitude. Tolman (1948) proposed that human and nonhuman animals expect reinforcement to occur in a certain location and they follow "paths" leading to that place. As the environment is explored, organisms form a mental representation, a cognitive map, of their environment; this map guides their exploration through the environment to the location of reward. In direct contrast, Hull proposed that environmental cues elicit certain motor responses that have led to reward in the past.

In a sense, Tolman says "head over that way" while Hull says "turn left, left, then right." Who is more accurate? It depends. When general environmental cues are not available to direct behavior, Hull is correct. However, when cues are available that indicate the location of a goal in a more general sense, Tolman is correct. To clarify, in a darkened cave you might find your way out by recalling specific turns in response to specific stimuli (turn left, left, then right). Under a different circumstance, one in which more general environmental cues are available, you might head in a general direction toward a goal (to get to the shopping mall, head toward the university and then head west). It is interesting to note that Hull tended to use enclosed mazes and Tolman used elevated mazes (limited general cues vs. many general cues).

How did Tolman handle the influence of reward magnitude? Fairly simply: The value of the goal affects the intensity of motivation; motivation is greater for a large or more valued reward than a small, lesser valued reward. Similar to Hull, Tolman referred to the motivational qualities of reward as *incentive motivation*. Not only are organisms motivated to obtain reward, but they also expect to obtain a particular reward. They will not accept a lesser reward when expecting to receive a more desirable one.

Tinkelpaugh (1928) demonstrated this nicely in his work with primates. Animals were taught to obtain a banana by choosing the container that had a banana under it. When the banana was replaced by lettuce (a less desirable reward) the animals refused to eat it and continued to search for the banana, shrieking at the experimenters to indicate displeasure.

Both Hull and Thorndike relied heavily on reward in their theorizing, whereas Tolman and Guthrie downplayed its importance. Our final traditional position, that of B. F. Skinner, focused almost exclusively on the role of reinforcement in the process of learning.

Skinner's Behaviorism

Theory versus Behavior Analysis. Skinner's behaviorism is quite different from that of Hull, Thorndike, Tolman, or Guthrie. In his text, *The Behavior of Organisms* (Skinner, 1938), Skinner asserted that the goal of behaviorism should be to identify and isolate the environmental factors that govern behavior. Further, he also indicated that a particular behavior can only be understood if it can be predicted and controlled, which can only be accomplished by understanding the circumstances governing the occurrence of the behavior. His analysis of a rat's behavior while pressing a lever for food, or that of a pigeon pecking a lighted key for grain, explained the environmental factors controlling the rats' responding.

Skinner subsequently expanded this analysis to include other animals, situations, and behaviors. For example, in his book *Verbal Behavior*, Skinner (1957) argued that people do not have an instinctive capacity for "expressing our ideas" but rather that verbal behavior is similar to any other operant response, controlled by reinforcement and punishment.

So how is Skinner different from the behaviorists described earlier? Skinner (1938) did not see the necessity for theory or theoretical constructs. He did not feel that they contributed to our understanding of behavior and in fact detracted from the progress of understanding learning. He felt that searching for and attempting to validate intervening variables interferes with the functional analysis of the variable controlling the behavior, namely the environment.

Consider the following example to illustrate Skinner's approach. A number of traditional learning theorists have proposed that the S–R connection is strengthened as a result of reinforcement and have spent years trying to validate this view. In Skinner's mind, understanding the theoretical nature of the construct underlying the effect of reward on S–R connections is useful only in that it demonstrates that reinforcement is one of the environmental variables controlling how frequently a specific behavior occurs in a particular context.

Even given the preceding, Skinner was still a connectionist. In fact, Skinner might be considered the "best-known exemplar of the connectionist tradition" (Hill, 1997, p. 68). The connection he studied involved stimuli and responses without reference to habit strength or S–R bonds, but it was still a connection.

Environment, Behavior, and Consequence.   Skinner (1938) spoke about two types of learning: respondent and operant conditioning. *Respondent conditioning* refers to classical conditioning, the learning situation investigated by Pavlov; the CS and UCS are paired, and the CS subsequently comes to elicit the CR. In this type of learning the response is elicited by the UCS, so the animal or human has no choice but to respond (involuntary). These responses are most commonly internal responses such as emotional or glandular reactions to stimuli. Skinner was much more concerned with *operant conditioning,* a situation in which the organism emits some response and experiences some consequence. The response is not elicited by any particular stimulus, rather it is emitted by the organism (voluntary). Skinner called the relation between behavior and its consequence a *contingency.* Skinner focused primarily on reinforcement as the consequence of a given behavior. The environment establishes the contingencies, and the animal or human must perform the appropriate behavior to obtain reinforcement.

A contingency does not necessarily represent a perfect relation between a behavior and a consequence. An individual may have to exhibit a number of responses or wait a certain amount of time before a response is reinforced. Effective responding requires that the organism be sensitive to the relation between behavior and reinforcement (or schedule of reinforcement). The concept of schedule of reinforcement was based on the observation that organisms respond differently when confronted with different schedules or contingencies (see Ferster & Skinner, 1957). When organisms are confronted with a situation in which there is no relation between behavior and consequence, they may experience helplessness and, in humans, additional feelings of depression (see LoLordo & Taylor, chap. 12, this volume).

CONTEMPORARY LEARNING THEORIES

Dissatisfaction With Global Learning Theories

Can a Single Theory Encompass the Entire Learning Process? In 1989 we were editors of a two-volume text entitled *Contemporary Learning Theories* (Klein & Mowrer, 1989a, 1989b). This text was based on the premise that since the 1960s contemporary learning theories, rather than attempting a global explanation for all learning, focused on specific aspects of the learning process. In fact, Tolman (1959) seemed to anticipate this shift in the third sentence of his opening statement from *Psychology: A Study of Science*: "I think the days of such grandiose, all-covering systems in psychology as mine attempted to be are, at least for the present, pretty much passe" (p. 93). We surmised that there were probably many reasons for this change in the learning research, including the question as to whether the fundamental nature of learning could ever be completely answered (Bolles, 1979).

A majority of the global learning theories of the 1930s through the 1950s focused on instrumental conditioning to the exclusion of classical or Pavlovian conditioning. This emphasis was indicative of the belief that classical conditioning was a fairly simple form of learning and that the mechanisms underlying the acquisition of the conditional response were fairly well understood. In addition, Hull, Tolman, and others demonstrated that many responses were not subject to modification via classical conditioning, leading to the conclusion that classical conditioning applied only to certain behaviors (reflexes; Mowrer, 1947; Skinner, 1938). Hull (1943) even questioned the necessity for a separation of classical conditioning from instrumental learning. He argued that in the typical classical conditioning paradigm involving salivation, it was impossible to determine whether the dog salivated in response to the bell because the bell was associated with food delivery (classical conditioning) or because food delivery reinforced salivation (instrumental conditioning).

Currently, most researchers assume there are at least two distinct paradigms (classical and instrumental conditioning) or three if you separate operant conditioning from instrumental, each with different efficacies in modifying behavior. Recognition of several forms of learning may create difficulties in developing a single, unitary explanation to account for the entire range of learned behavior. Finally, it has been argued that these paradigms interact in a number of learning situations leading to positions that entail a combination of paradigms (e.g., Mowrer, 1960).

A Greater Interest in Specific Learning Processes

Renewed Interest in Classical Conditioning. In our previous endeavor, we identified three reasons for the reinvestigation of classical conditioning: (a) the realization that classical conditioning may have much wider application than originally assumed (e.g., autoshaping or sign-tracking), (b) the precision inherent to the classical conditioning paradigm, and (c) a renewed interest in inhibitory conditioning.

More recent and gaining in importance is the relation between classical conditioning and health-related issues. The two most prominent are drug abuse (e.g., development and maintenance of drug abuse, conditioned withdrawal response, accidental overdose), and cancer therapy (conditioned immunosuppression or enhancement, conditioned nausea). One of the fastest growing disciplines is that of psychoneuroimmunology—the interaction among the brain, the immune system, and behavior, much of which is based on classical conditioning. (See Tomie, chap. 10, and Riley & Simpson, chap. 13, this volume, for the role of conditioning in drug-taking behavior.) Finally, classical conditioning has formed the basis for the discovery of the neurophysiological underpinnings of learning and memory (e.g., the role of the cerebellum in the establishment of the rabbit's nictitating membrane response). (See DeSousa & Vaccarino, chap. 11, this volume, for the biological basis for incentive motivation.)

The Return of Cognition

As previously briefly detailed, Tolman (1932, 1959) rejected the mechanistic viewpoint of many traditional learning theorists. He argued that behavior has both direction and purpose in our understanding of the environment. Tolman's view did not gain wide acceptance until the late 1960s.

One of the leading contemporary cognitive theorists was the late Robert Bolles (1972, 1979). He argued that based on our interaction with the environment, we form at least two types of expectancies that allow us to obtain reinforcement or avoid punishment. According to Bolles, whenever a biological significant event occurs (e.g., presentation of water, food, pain), it occurs in a particular environmental context. The stimuli or cues in that environment may or may not become associated with obtaining food or water or the presence of shock. Bolles labeled the biologically significant event S^* and the environmental cue(s) S. For the environmental stimuli to cause the animal to expect food, water, or pain (i.e., $S–S^*$ association), S must reliably predict S^*. Contiguity is a necessary but not sufficient condition for an expectancy to develop. The events (S and S^*) must occur consistently together for an $S–S^*$ expectancy to be established. In the case of multiple environmental cues, the most reliable S becomes associated with S^*.

The second type of expectancy is called an $R–S^*$ expectancy. In this case, the expectancy refers to an understanding on the part of the organism that certain responses (R) are associated with certain outcomes (S^*). In Bolles' model, $S–S^*$ expectancies predict the occurrence of a biologically significant event and $R–S^*$ expectancies direct behavior. (See Baker, Murphy, & Vallée-Tourangeau, chap. 7, this volume, for an analysis of causal attributions and Balleine, chap. 8, this volume, for an analysis of incentive motivation.)

Another example of the acceptance of a more cognitive view was provided by Wagner (1976, 1978, 1981, 1989). Wagner modified the original Rescorla–Wagner model (1972) to fit a more cognitive interpretation of learning in which the animal is an active information processor. (Wagner's more recent theorizing is presented in chap. 2, this volume.)

The preceding represent earlier transitions to a cognitive model of the learning process. More recently, Miller and his colleagues provided us with another distinctive model in which the organism is presented as an active information processor, in this case comparing stimuli to determine which is the best predictor of a significant event—the comparator model. Miller presents his most recent revision of this model in chapter 3 of this volume (see also Hall, chap. 9, this volume).

Biological Constraints on Learning

Possibly the single most important factor in the transition from global learning theories to the more specific, contemporary learning theories was the realization that our biological systems constrain what we do or do not learn about. Traditional learning theory was premised on the assumption of the generality of the laws of learning across all stimuli, responses, and situations. This position is best summarized by Pavlov and Skinner. According to Skinner (1938); "the general topography of the operant behavior is not important, because most if not all specific operants are conditioned. I suggest that the dynamic properties of operant behavior may be studied with a single reflex" (pp. 45–46). In a similar manner Pavlov (1928) stated: "Any natural phenomenon chosen at will may be converted into a conditioned stimulus ... any visual stimulus, any desired sound, any odor and the stimulation of any part of the skin" (p. 86).

There are many research findings that are at odds with these assumptions but the classic example was provided by Garcia and Koelling (1966). Briefly, they found that if an exteroceptive CS, light + noise, was paired with an interoceptive UCS, radiation or lithium chloride (LiCl) which produced a UR of illness, little or no conditioned responding was observed. A similar result was obtained when an interoceptive CS, flavor, was paired with an exteroceptive UCS, shock, producing a pain UR. This finding did not hold when light and noise was paired with shock or flavor was paired with illness; the expected CR was established. A similar result was found in an operant avoidance situation in which rats were to press a lever to avoid shock. Rats had a difficult time learning to press the lever to avoid (or even escape) footshock (Mowrer, 1960). These findings directly contradict the assumptions of traditional learning theory and those of Pavlov and Skinner in particular.

As a result of these findings, Seligman (1970) proposed the notion of *preparedness*. He suggested that the ecological niche and hence biological predispositions of a given species will determine what will be learned or not learned. Seligman mentioned three levels of preparedness: prepared when the biological predisposition facilitates learning, unprepared when it neither facilitates nor retards learning, and contraprepared when it retards learning. It is clear to see how this applies to Garcia and Koelling's (1966) findings. Rats were prepared to associate flavor with illness but contraprepared to associate light and noise with illness. Further, rats easily learn to avoid the taste or odor of a food when its consumption is followed by illness but are unprepared or contraprepared to associate the color of food with illness (rats primarily use odor and taste when seeking food). The situation is quite the opposite with certain birds, such as the hawk, that locate food visually; they are prepared to associate the visual aspect of the food source with illness but unprepared or contraprepared to associate smell or taste. Thus it is clear that our biological underpinnings influence the process of learning and call into question the concept of general laws of learning.

The Ever Changing Nature of Contemporary Learning Theory

This volume represents an update of our previous endeavor to compile a collection of selected contemporary learning theories (Klein & Mowrer, 1989a, 1989b). As such we have tried to include as many of the original authors as possible. As the reader will see, some of the authors have continued their focus with updates of their previous work (e.g., Church & Kirkpatrick, chap. 6; Denniston, Savastano, & Miller, chap. 3; Hall, chap. 9; Levis & Brewer, chap. 14; Wagner & Brandon, chap. 2) whereas others have taken a somewhat different focus (e.g., Baker, Murphy, & Vallée-Tourangeau, chap. 7; Balleine, chap. 8; De Sousa & Vaccarino, chap. 11; LoLordo & Taylor, chap. 12; Riley & Simpson, chap. 13; Timberlake, chap. 5; Tomie, chap. 10). Each chapter, however, contains evidence that contemporary learning theory continues to evolve and change.

REFERENCES

Amsel, A. (1958). The role of frustrative nonreward in noncontinuous reward situations. *Psychological Bulletin, 55*, 102–119.

Benjamin, L. T. (1988). *A history of psychology: Original sources and contemporary research*. New York: McGraw-Hill.

Bolles, R. C. (1972). Reinforcement, expectancy and learning. *Psychological Review, 79*, 394–409.

Bolles, R. C. (1979). *Learning theory* (2nd ed.). New York: Holt, Rinehart & Winston.

Bower, G. H., & Hilgard, E. R. (1981). *Theories of learning* (5th ed.). Englewood Cliffs, NJ: Prentice Hall.

Crespi, L. P. (1942). Quantitative variation of incentive and performance in the white rat. *American Journal of Psychology, 55*, 467–517.

D'Amato, M. R. (1970). *Experimental psychology: Methodology, psychophysics, and learning*. New York: McGraw-Hill.

Domjan, M. (1998). *The principles of learning and behavior* (4th ed.). Pacific Grove, CA: Brooks/Cole.

Ferster, C. B., & Skinner, B. F. (1957). *Schedules of reinforcement*. New York: Appleton-Century-Crofts.

Flaharty, C. (1985). *Animal learning and cognition*. New York: Knopf.

Garcia, J., & Koelling, R. A. (1966). Relation of cue to consequence in avoidance learning. *Psychonomic Science, 4*, 123–124.

Gordon, W. C. (1989). *Learning and memory*. Pacific Grove, CA: Brooks/Cole.

Guthrie, E. R. (1935). *The psychology of learning*. New York: Harper.

Guthrie, E. R. (1959). Association by contiguity. In S. Koch (Ed.), *Psychology: A study of a science* (Vol. 2, pp. 158–195). New York: McGraw-Hill.

Hill, W. F. (1997). *Learning: A survey of psychological interpretations* (6th ed.). New York: Addison-Wesley.

Hull, C. L. (1943). *Principles of behavior*. New York: Appleton.

Hull, C. L. (1952). *A behavior system.* New Haven, CT: Yale University Press.

Kimble, G. A. (1961). *Hilgard and Marquis' conditioning and learning* (2nd ed.). New York: Appleton-Century-Crofts.

Klein, S. B. (1996). *Learning: Principles and applications (3rd ed).* New York: McGraw-Hill.

Klein, S. B., & Mowrer, R. R. (Eds.). (1989a). *Contemporary learning theories: Instrumental conditioning and the impact of biological constraints on learning.* Hillsdale, NJ: Lawrence Erlbaum Associates.

Klein, S. B., & Mowrer, R. R. (Eds.). (1989b). *Contemporary learning theories: Pavlovian conditioning and the status of traditional learning theory.* Hillsdale, NJ: Lawrence Erlbaum Associates.

Mowrer, O. H. (1947). On the dual nature of learning—A reinterpretation of "conditioning" and "problem solving". *Harvard Educational Review, 17,* 102–148.

Mowrer, O. H. (1960). *Learning theory and behavior.* New York: Wiley.

Pavlov, I. P. (1928). *Lectures on conditioned reflexes: The higher nervous activity of animals* (Vol. 1, H. Gantt, Trans.). London: Lawrence & Wishart.

Rescorla, R. A., & Wagner, A. R. (1972). A theory of Pavlovian conditioning: Variations in the effectiveness of reinforcement and non-reinforcement. In A. H. Black & W. F. Prokasy (Eds.), *Classical conditioning II* (pp. 64–99). New York: Appleton-Century-Crofts.

Seligman, M. E. P. (1970). On the generality of the laws of learning. *Psychological Review, 44,* 406–418.

Seward, J. P. (1942). An experimental study of Guthrie's theory of reinforcement. *Journal of Experimental Psychology, 30,* 247–256.

Skinner, B. F. (1938). *The behavior of organisms: An experimental analysis.* New York: Appleton-Century-Crofts.

Skinner, B. F. (1957). *Verbal Behavior.* New York: Appleton.

Spence, K. W. (1956). *Behavior theory and conditioning.* New Haven, CT: Yale University Press.

Thorndike, E. L. (1898). Animal intelligence: An experimental study of the associative process in animals. *Psychological Review.* [Monograph supplement, 2, No. 8].

Thorndike, E. L. (1913). *The psychology of learning.* New York: Teachers College Press.

Thorndike, E. L. (1932). *The fundamentals of learning.* New York: Teachers College Press.

Tinkelpaugh, O. L. (1928). An experimental study of representative factors in monkeys. *Journal of Comparative Psychology, 8,* 197–236.

Tolman, E. C. (1932). *Purposive behavior in animals and men.* New York: Century.

Tolman, E. C. (1948). Cognitive maps in rats and men. *Psychological Review, 55,* 189–208.

Tolman, E. C. (1959). Principles of purposive behavior. In S. Koch (Ed.), *Psychology: A study of a science* (Vol. 2, pp. 92–157). New York: McGraw-Hill.

Wagner, A. R. (1976). Priming in STM: An information processing mechanism for self-generated or retrieval-generated depression in performance. In T. J. Tighe & R. N. Leaton (Eds.), *Habituation: Perspectives from child development, animal behavior and neuropsychology* (pp. 95–128). Hillsdale, NJ: Lawrence Erlbaum Associates.

Wagner, A. R. (1978). Expectancies and the priming of STM. In S. H. Hulse, H. Fowler, & W. K. Honig (Eds.), *Cognitive processes in animal behavior* (pp. 177–289). Hillsdale, NJ: Lawrence Erlbaum Associates.

Wagner, A. R. (1981). SOP: A model of automatic memory processing. In R. R. Miller & N. E. Spear (Eds.), *Information processing in animals: Memory mechanisms* (pp. 5–47). Hillsdale, NJ: Lawrence Erlbaum Associates.

Wagner, A. R. (1989). Evolution of a structured connectionist model of Pavlovian conditioning (AESOP). In S. B. Klein & R. R. Mowrer (Eds.), *Contemporary learning theories: Pavlovian conditioning and the status of traditional learning theory* (pp. 149–189). Hillsdale, NJ: Lawrence Erlbaum Associates.

Watson, J. B. (1913). Psychology as the behaviorist views it. *Psychological Review, 20,* 158–177.

Watson, J. B. (1930). *Behaviorism* (2nd ed.). Chicago: University of Chicago Press.

Woodworth, R. S. (1918). *Dynamic Psychology.* New York: Columbia University Press.

chapter 2

A Componential Theory of Pavlovian Conditioning

Allan R. Wagner
Susan E. Brandon
Yale University

M ost modern theories of Pavlovian conditioning have been so-called S–S theories; that is, to have supposed that Pavlovian conditioning involves the development of associations between representations of the stimuli encountered in training. Pavlov's (1927) original interpretation was of this form, presuming the formation of new functional connections between centers for the conditioned stimulus (CS) and unconditioned stimulus (UCS) in the animal's brain. On such perspective, many of the fundamental theoretical questions about Pavlovian conditioning center around how one should construe the conditioning stimuli as being coded or processed. A common theoretical device for describing such stimulus processing is through the assumption that CSs and UCSs activate representative elements or components that have prescribed occasions of occurrence. The theories of Pavlovian conditioning to which we have contributed

(Rescorla & Wagner, 1972; Wagner, 1981; Wagner & Brandon, 1989) have used this device, as does the theory we present here. Much of the substance of such theory, as shown, is in the theoretical rules that relate elemental activity to the conditions of stimulation.

In the collection that preceded this volume (Klein & Mowrer, 1989), we offered a quantitative model of Pavlovian conditioning labeled AESOP (Wagner & Brandon, 1989) that focused on the way in which UCSs are represented. The model formalized Konorski's (1967) reasoning that UCSs are generally multiattribute events and that Pavlovian CSs form independent associations with the emotive and the sensory-perceptual components—the former leading to conditioned emotional responses (CERs) and the latter to discrete conditioned responses (CRs). We argued that many observations concerning the lack of covariation of these response measures with variations in the conditions of training (see, e.g., Lennartz & Weinberger, 1994; Schneiderman, 1972) might be due to parametric differences in the temporal processing of the different stimulus components. For example, that extending a CS beyond the termination of the UCS can facilitate acquisition of the CER at the same time that it interferes with acquisition of the eye-blink CR (Betts, Brandon, & Wagner, 1996) was predicted by AESOP on the assumption that the elemental activity occasioned by the emotive properties of the UCS decays more slowly than does the elemental activity occasioned by the sensory properties of the UCS. We further argued that although the learning of CRs and CERs may follow different courses, the performance of discrete CRs, such as the conditioned eye blink, is linked to CERs by virtue of being subject to emotional modulation in the same fashion as is the performance of instrumental behaviors (Rescorla & Solomon, 1967; Trapold & Overmier, 1972). A substantial literature now bears this out (Betts et al., 1996; Bombace, Brandon, & Wagner, 1991; Brandon, Bombace, Falls, & Wagner, 1991; Brandon & Wagner, 1991).

In this chapter we present some theoretical ideas concerning how CSs can be conceived to be represented. The motivation for the work stemmed from the fact that the elementistic trial-level model of Rescorla and Wagner (1972; Wagner & Rescorla, 1972) and our more recent real-time models, SOP and AESOP (Wagner, 1981; Wagner & Brandon, 1989), have not dealt in depth with how conjunctions of stimuli might be represented. How should we deal theoretically with so-called configural cues? We first discuss such cues in relation to some simple Pavlovian phenomena of generalization and discrimination. We indicate how a range of theoretical alternatives that have been proposed can be construed as different elementistic models and present some evidence that encourages a relatively novel possibility. In the second section of the chapter, we address a Pavlovian phenomenon that has been of great recent interest, namely, occasion setting, which can be largely understood by appreciating how configural cues operate within a dynamic real-time model. In the final section, we try to illustrate some of the further utility of the approach by showing how it can address various phenomena that have been taken to show a contextual control of stimulus meaning.

GENERALIZATION AND DISCRIMINATION

Elementistic representation has had a long and distinguished presence in Pavlovian theory. Panel (a) of Fig. 2.1 presents a figure originally drawn by Sherrington (1929) that Konorski (1948) employed to describe the representation produced by two different CSs, A and B. It was meant to show that the two stimuli can be presumed to activate populations of neural elements that are different from each other but are partially overlapping. Konorski used the device to rationalize the phenomenon of stimulus generalization. Suppose that CS A is paired with a UCS in a manner effective for Pavlovian conditioning. Then it can be assumed that all of the neural elements activated by CS A will develop connections to the elements activated by the UCS, and that this will be seen in the exhibition of a CR when these neural elements are activated again. If the animal is presented for the first time with CS B, some CR may also occur, because B activates some of the same elements activated by A. One should expect more of a CR the greater the overlap. Burke and Estes (1957) used the same form of reasoning to explain stimulus generalization within stimulus-sampling theory, and so do we in our theorizing.

Rescorla and Wagner (1972) made this overlapping-elements approach work better than it otherwise might. Bush and Mosteller (1951) pointed out that according to the conventional linear-operator learning rule shown in Panel (b) of Fig. 2.1, if any stimuli, A and B, show any generalization due to overlapping elements, it should not be possible by reinforcing one of the stimuli and nonreinforcing the other to produce errorless discrimination performance. The overlapping elements would sometimes be reinforced and sometimes nonreinforced and always serve to produce errors as they occurred on either kind of trial. The learning rule that Rescorla and Wagner proposed, shown in Panel (c), provides one solution to this problem. This rule supposes that the learning to each element of the CS depends not on the current connection weight of that component alone, V_i, but on the total connection weight of all of the components on that trial, ΣV_i. By this account, those elements that are unique to the nonreinforced B and are never reinforced can be made to have negative associative loadings. Errorless discrimination learning can eventually occur because the negative associative

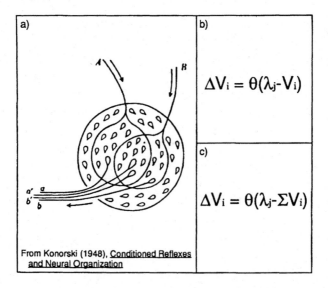

FIG. 2.1. (a) The partial convergence of allied reflexes. A and B are two afferent nerve paths; a, a′, b, and b′ are efferent paths. Taken from Sherrington (1929) and copied from Konorski (1948), Fig. 7 (p. 110). Reprinted by permission of Cambridge University Press. (b) The linear operator rule for learning used by Hull (1943), Spence (1956), and Estes (1950). Associative strength, V_i, is modified according to the difference between the asymptotic level of strength attainable with that reinforcement, λ_j, and the current associative strength of that same cue; that is, $\lambda_j - V_i$). θ is a learning rate parameter. (c) The learning rule proposed by Rescorla and Wagner (1972). All terms are the same as in (b), except that the difference term is computed with ΣV_i, which is the sum of the associative strengths of all cues present on that learning trial.

loadings of the elements unique to CS B will offset any positive associative loadings of the common elements.

Biconditional Discrimination and Configural Cues

A further challenge for such elemental representation of the CS is that animals can learn not only to respond to one stimulus, A, and not to another stimulus, B, but to respond differently to different patterns made up from the same components. Fig. 2.2 presents the results of an eyelid conditioning experiment conducted in our laboratory by Saavedra (1975). Saavedra used rabbit subjects and compound CSs, made up of simultaneous combinations of 1–sec auditory, visual, and vibrotactual stimuli, designated as A, B, C, and D, either reinforced with a paraorbital shock UCS (+) or nonreinforced (–).[1] One group received training on a biconditional discrimination of the form indicated, AC+, BC–, AD–, BD+. By this training the constituent stimuli—A, B, C, and D—were all equally often reinforced and nonreinforced over the several compounds so that each should have gained equivalent associative strength. On this basis, the reinforced compounds, AC and BD, should have become no stronger with discrimination training than the nonreinforced compounds, AD and BC. But, as may be seen, the rabbits solved the problem, responding more frequently to the reinforced compounds than to the nonreinforced compounds. They did not solve it as easily as they solved a comparison problem that Saavedra called a "component" problem, using the same compounds but arranged such that the two that included one of the cues (A) were consistently rein-

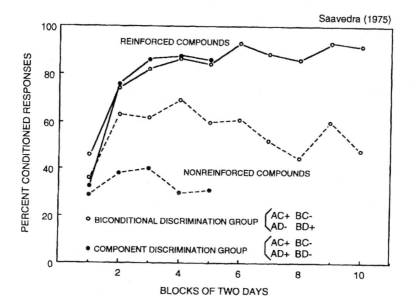

FIG. 2.2. Mean percentage conditioned responses in 2-day training blocks, corresponding to the biconditional discrimination group and the component discrimination group. Redrawn from Saavedra (1975), Fig. 1 (p. 318). Reprinted by permission of Academic Press. The training cues for the two groups are indicated.

---

[1]In this and all other experiments reported from our laboratory, the reader may assume that the assignment of specific stimuli to the experimental conditions was counterbalanced across different subjects or within subjects to remove the possibility that differential responding was due to stimulus differences.

forced and the two that included an alternative cue (B) were consistently nonreinforced. However, they solved it.

The question is, how did they solve it? Wagner and Rescorla (1972) proposed one solution. Pearce (1987, 1994) proposed a very different solution. An alternative that we have recommended (Brandon & Wagner, 1998), and elaborate here, might be seen as a compromise between the two.

Added Unique Elements.   Wagner and Rescorla (1972) adopted a simple solution proposed by Spence (1952) some years earlier. They supposed that there are configural elements that behave just like any other elements, except that they are active not when a single stimulus is present, but when there is a particular conjunction of two or more stimuli. The essence of this reasoning is depicted in Fig. 2.3a. Any CS, i, is assumed to activate one set of elements, another CS, j, to activate another set of elements. The configural assumption is that CS i and CS j, when presented in conjunction, also activate an additional, unique element. Thus, if the four stimuli, A, B, C, and D, were each represented in isolation by the sets of elements shown in Fig. 2.3b, the compounds AC, AD, BC, and BD would be represented by the sets indicated in Fig. 2.3c.

It should be obvious that given the representations of the four compounds shown in Fig. 2.3c, subjects should be able to learn to associate any of the compounds with reinforcement versus any others with nonreinforcement, but that some discriminations should be easier than others. To discriminate those compounds including A from those including B, as in Saavedra's (1975) component discrimination, should be relatively easy because of the large number of unique versus common elements. To discriminate AC and BD from AD and BC, as in Saavedra's biconditional discrimination, should be possible because of the configural elements unique to each compound. However, it should be relatively difficult because of the much larger number of elements common to both the reinforced and nonreinforced compounds.

Inhibited Elements.   Pearce (1987) had a more radical reaction to data such as those of Saavedra (1975). He suggested that we give up an elementistic view of the stimulus and suppose that association is always between the stimulus configurations that stand in the place of the CS and UCS on each trial. In such a case, the learning of the biconditional discrimination would not be seen as a problem because each compound is presumed to be a different configuration. The challenge in this case is to explain why the two problems investigated by Saavedra, each involving two reinforced and two nonreinforced compounds made from the same stimuli, were not equally difficult. Pearce (1987, 1994) presented a quantitative generalization model that did this

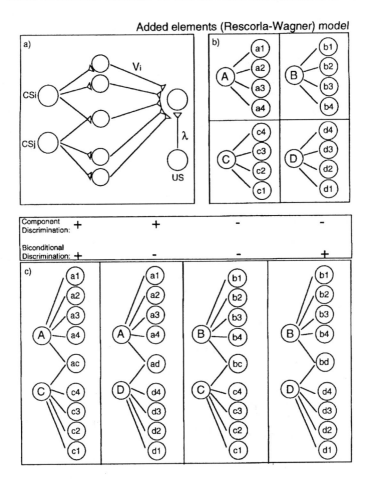

FIG. 2.3.   The added elements model. Panel (a) shows how CS_i and CS_j are assumed by this model to form a compound consisting of the original and added elements. The elements of this compound, via associative connections V_i, activate an adaptive unit that also can be activated by the UCS; the strengths of the connections are modified according to the difference term $(\lambda - \Sigma V_i)$. Panel (b) shows the elements that are assumed to comprise the CSs A, B, C, and D, for purposes of illustration of a component and biconditional discrimination, as shown in Panel (c). See text for details.

nicely. This configural conception has been quite provocative against the prevailing background of elementistic theory and has gained considerable attention. We think it is instructive to appreciate that the Pearce view can be equally construed as an elementistic model, albeit one that is different from that of Rescorla and Wagner (1972).

Pearce (1987) made two essential assumptions. One was that the salience of all configurations is equal. The other was that the similarity between any pair of configurations, which dictates the degree of generalization between them, is as indicated in Equation 1.

$$S_{i,j} = nc_i / nt_i \times nc_j / nt_j \qquad (1)$$

Equation 1 specifies that the similarity, S, between configurations i and j is equal to the proportion of the total elements in configuration i that are common to the two configurations, multiplied by the proportion of the total elements in configuration j that are common to the two configurations. For example, stimulus A is, thus, said to have a similarity of ½ with both stimulus AC and stimulus AD, but AC and AD are said to have only a similarity of ¼ with each other. This similarity reasoning appropriately predicts the greater difficulty of the biconditional discrimination as compared to the component discrimination in the Saavedra (1975) experiment. To appreciate this, notice that in the component case, the mean similarity, $S_{i,j}$, is greater between those compounds that were similarly reinforced than between those that were differentially reinforced, whereas in the biconditional case the opposite obtains; $S_{i,j}$ is less between like-treated compounds than between unlike-treated compounds.

An interesting fact is that one can devise an elemental model that is generally isomorphic to Pearce's (1987) configural model. In elemental terms, the assumption that the salience of all configurations is the same translates into saying that the total number of theoretical elements in any compound is a constant. In this case, if A, B, and C are equivalent experimental stimuli, each represented by n elements when presented alone, it would follow that the number of elements representing stimuli A and B would each be ½n when presented in an AB compound, and the number representing stimuli A, B, and C would each be ⅓n when presented in an ABC compound. With such a constraint, it is generally possible to construct elemental representations for any set of configurations that share nominal components, such that the proportion of overlapping elements in any pair is equivalent to (or closely approximates) the similarity, S, computed for that pair according to Equation 1. For example, considering the set of configurations A, AC, and AD, their elemental representation need provide that half of the elements in configurations A and AC be in common, half those in A and AD be in common, but only one quarter of the elements in AC and AD be in common. The rule that works in this instance is one that stipulates that the subset of theoretical elements representing stimulus i that is active when i is in compound with one stimulus, j, is statistically independent of the subset that is active when i is in compound with another stimulus, k.

Figure 2.4 illustrates how this elemental version of Pearce's (1987) theory works, in application to the Saavedra (1975) comparisons, as previously shown for the Rescorla–Wagner added elements view. What is depicted in Fig. 2.4a is that CS i alone is represented by a number of elements (here, two), CS j alone by the same number of elements, and CS i in compound with CS j, also by the same number of elements. The rule is that if CS j is coactive with CS i, it inhibits half of the elements otherwise activated by CS i. Likewise, if CS i is coactive with CS j, it inhibits half of the elements otherwise activated by CS j. If one assumes, again, that stimuli A, B, C, and D alone are each represented by four elements as depicted in Fig. 2.4b, it can be seen in Fig. 2.4c how the statistical independence specification produces the similarity relations of Equation 1. In the case of each compound, we have indicated with shading, which of the elements said to be activated by each stimulus alone are not active in the compound. Notice in these examples that AC and AD each share half of their theoretical elements with A alone, in agreement with Pearce's computation of 50% generalization between A and each of the two compounds. However, also notice that because only half of the A elements left active in compound with C and D are the same, AC and AD share only ¼ of their theoretical elements with each other. This is consonant with Pearce's computation of 25% generalization between the two.

This inhibited elements model accounts for the Saavedra (1975) data just as well as does the added elements model. It predicts that the biconditional discrimination can be learned because there are active elements that are unique to each compound (e.g., a2 and c2 in the reinforced AC and b2 and d2 in the reinforced BD). However, the biconditional discrimination should not be learned as rapidly as the component discrimination, where the reinforced AC and AD compounds have a common element, a1, and the nonreinforced compounds BC and BD have a common element, b1. The differential discrimination learning is predicted for reasons of the differential common elements: In the component discrimination there are more elements in common between compounds that are similarly reinforced than between those that are differentially reinforced, whereas in the biconditional case the opposite obtains; there are fewer elements in common between like-treated compounds than between unlike-treated compounds.

Replaced Elements.   We have proposed (Brandon & Wagner, 1998) an alternative to the Rescorla–Wagner and the Pearce views that might have advantages over each. The Rescorla–Wagner view is that representation of a compound of stimuli includes the addition of unique configural elements. The Pearce theory corresponds to the view that representation of a compound of stimuli involves the inhibition of elements otherwise activated by the constituent stimuli. The possibility

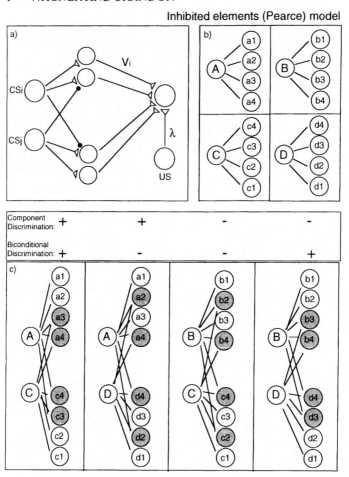

FIG. 2.4. The inhibited elements model. Panel (a) shows how CS_i and CS_i are assumed by this model to form a compound by inhibiting elements otherwise expressed. The elements of this compound, via associative connections V_i, activate an adaptive unit that also can be activated by the UCS; the strengths of the connections are modified according to the difference term $(\lambda - \sum V_i)$. Panel (b) shows the elements that are assumed to comprise the CSs A, B, C, and D, for purposes of illustration of a component and biconditional discrimination, as shown in Panel (c). The inhibited elements are indicated with shading. See text for details.

to which we have been led is that the representation of a compound of stimuli involves both the addition of unique configural elements and the inhibition of elements otherwise activated. In effect, the view is that representation of a compound of stimuli involves the replacement of some elements otherwise contributed by the constituent stimuli in isolation.

Figure 2.5 presents a diagram of the replaced elements notion and illustrates its application to the Saavedra (1975) comparisons, in a manner similar to the characterizations of the added elements and inhibited elements notions presented in Figs. 2.3 and 2.4. What is meant to be shown in Panel (a) of Fig. 2.5 is that CS i alone is represented by a number of elements (here, two), CS j alone by the same number of elements and CS i in compound with CS j by the total of the number of elements representing CS i and CS j alone (four). An important point is that although the number of elements activated by the compound is assumed to be the sum of the number of elements activated by the constituents, the identity of the elements activated by the compound is not assumed to be the same as that of the elements activated by the constituents. It is suggested that the presentation of CS j along with CS i activates a conjunctive element that is not activated by CS i alone, but at the same time inhibits the activation of an element that is activated by CS i alone. Likewise, the presentation of CS i along with CS j activates a conjunctive element that is not activated by CS j alone, but inhibits an element that is activated by CS j alone.

One way to think of this replacement notion is as a way to make Hull's (1943, 1945) historically influential notion of *afferent neural interaction* computational. It expresses how the representation of one stimulus is different in the presence versus the absence of another stimulus: The representation of CS i is changed, one might say, by the afferent neural interaction with CS j, to include one element (or set of elements) rather than another.

In implementing this view, we have made the assumption that each stimulus with which a CS can be compounded engenders the replacement of different elements (and that such pairwise replacement is adequate to produce the necessary discriminable representations in any n-term compounds). Panels (b) and (c) of Fig. 2.5 show how this would work in the case of the Saavedra (1975) comparisons. As in Figs. 2.3 and 2.4, Panel (b) assumes that each of the stimuli—A, B, C, and D—alone activates four elements. And, as in Fig. 2.4, Panel (c) indicates by shading, those elements, otherwise activated by a stimulus, that are replaced when that stimulus is in compound with each other stimulus. The compounding of A with C is depicted as leading to the replacement of the conjunctive a_c for one of the elements of A and the replacement of the conjunctive c_a for one of the elements of C. In comparison, the compounding of A with D and of C with B are depicted as leading to the replacement of the conjunctives a_d and c_b for different elements of A and C, respectively. With these and the other indicated results of compounding, animals should learn the biconditional discrimination because there are elements that are unique to the reinforced AC and BD compounds. However, they should not learn the task as quickly as the com-

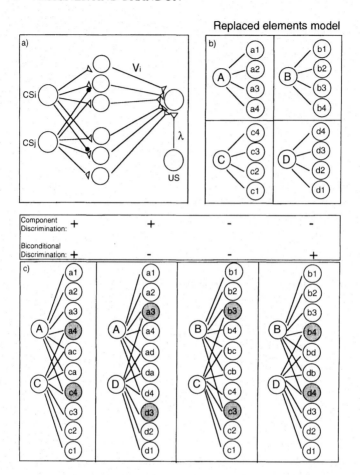

FIG. 2.5. The replaced elements model. Panel (a) shows how CS_i and CS_j are assumed by this model to form a compound by replacing elements otherwise expressed. The elements of this compound, via associative connections V_i, activate an adaptive unit that also can be activated by the UCS; the strengths of the connections are modified according to the difference term $(\lambda - \Sigma V_i)$. Panel (b) shows the elements that are assumed to comprise the CSs A, B, C, and D, for purposes of illustration of a component and biconditional discrimination, as shown in Panel (c). The replaced elements are indicated with shading. See text for details.

ponent discrimination for the same reasons as specified by the previous accounts. In the component discrimination there are more elements in common between compounds that are similarly reinforced than between those that are differentially reinforced, whereas in the biconditional case the opposite obtains; there are fewer elements in common between like-treated compounds than between unlike-treated compounds.

A Generalization Test

All three of the foregoing conceptions of how to deal with configural cues can account for biconditional discrimination, along with the greater ease of acquiring a component discrimination. A number of studies (Aydin & Pearce, 1994; Darby & Pearce, 1995, 1997; Pearce, Adam, Wilson, & Darby, 1992; Pearce, Aydin, & Redhead, 1997; Pearce & Redhead, 1993, 1995; Pearce & Wilson, 1990; Redhead & Pearce, 1995a, 1995b) have tested various differential predictions of the Rescorla–Wagner added elements view versus those of the Pearce account. In relation to these studies, we can say that our simulations confirm the equivalence of an inhibited elements approach to that of Pearce's original formulation, and the replaced elements view generally sides with that of Rescorla and Wagner (1972). Unfortunately, conclusions about relative theoretical adequacy concerning this literature are denied at this writing by the fact that some of the most interesting formal comparisons have led to different outcomes in studies of autoshaping using combinations of visual components (Aydin & Pearce, 1994; Pearce et al., 1997; Pearce & Redhead, 1993, 1995; Pearce & Wilson, 1990; Redhead & Pearce, 1995a) than they have in other studies of autoshaping (e.g., Rescorla & Coldwell, 1995) using combinations of stimuli from different modalities and in studies of rabbit eye-blink conditioning, with either stimuli in the same modality or stimuli from different modalities (e.g., Bahçekapili, 1997; Myers, Vogel, Shin, & Wagner, in press).

A recently reported study from our laboratory by Brandon, Vogel, and Wagner (2000) assessed a rather fundamental difference in the expectations from the three theories. The study was addressed to the differential predictions that are made when subjects are trained to respond to one CS configuration and then are tested for generalization on a new stimulus that is formed from either removing one of the nominal stimuli or from adding a new stimulus.

Consider once again the Rescorla–Wagner reasoning as depicted in the stimulus representations of Panels (b) and (c) of Fig. 2.3. Suppose that a subject were trained on the compound AC and then tested on A alone, or were trained with A alone and then tested on the compound AC. According to the Rescorla–Wagner analysis, training on AC and then testing on A should lead to a considerable generalization decrement: Whatever associative strength had developed to the c elements and the ac configural element during training of AC should be lost in the test of A that does not include these elements. In contrast, training on A and then testing on AC should lead to no decrement: Whatever associative strength had developed to the a elements during training should still be accessible in test, and because the added c and ac configural elements should be associatively neutral, they should have no predicted effect. Pearce (1987) had good reason to seize on this prediction as problematic for the Rescorla–Wagner view: Investigators as early as Pavlov (1927), and including Reiss and Wagner (1972), reported a decrement as a result of the adding of novel stimuli in test. Pearce (1987) claimed it as one of the advantages of his theoretical conception that it avoided the Rescorla–Wagner prediction. His similarity rule embodies the premise that the generalization decrement from adding a cue (e.g., from testing AC after training on A) is identical to the decrement from removing a cue (e.g., from testing A after training on AC). It is instructive to see how identical computation comes about by the inhibited elements representation of the stimuli shown in Panels (b) and (c) of Fig. 2.4. Suppose, again, that a subject were trained on the compound AC and then tested on A alone, or were trained with A alone and then tested on the compound AC. By this schema, like the Rescorla–Wagner view, training on AC and then testing on A should lead to a generalization decrement: Whatever associative strength had developed to the c elements that make up half of the representation of AC should be lost in the test with A. The notable difference from the Rescorla–Wagner view is that training on A and then testing of AC should lead to an equivalent decrement: Whatever associative strength had been developed to that half of the a components that are active during A alone but are inhibited during the AC compound should be lost in the test. If the distinguishing prediction of the Rescorla–Wagner view is that there should be no generalization decrement from adding a stimulus in test, the distinguishing prediction of the Pearce view is that there should be an equal decrement from the adding as from the removal of a cue.

The replaced element view has an opportunity to do what all compromises are designed to do, and that is to be more acceptable than the alternatives. Consider the representations of A and AC contained in Panels (b) and (c) of Fig. 2.5, presenting the replaced elements view. If a subject were trained on the AC compound and then tested on A, there should be considerable generalization decrement due to the loss of the c elements and the ac element that are in the AC representation but not in the A representation. If a subject were trained on the A stimulus and then tested on the AC compound, there should also be some, albeit a smaller, generalization decrement, due to the loss of the associative strength commanded by that a element that is in the A representation but is replaced by the ac element in the AC compound. The replaced element view, unlike the Rescorla–Wagner view, but like the Pearce view, predicts that there will be a generalization decrement as a result of either the addition or the withdrawal of a stimulus. On the other hand, like the Rescorla–Wagner view, but unlike the Pearce view, it predicts that the generalization decrement as a result of adding a stimulus should be less than that as a result of removing a stimulus.

Brandon et al. (2000) tested these alternatives in an eyelid conditioning experiment using the simple design described in Fig. 2.6. Three groups of rabbits were employed with 1-sec auditory, visual, and vibrotactual stimuli in counterbalanced identification as CSs A, B, and C, and a paraorbital shock as the UCS. One group was trained with a single stimulus (A) as the CS, another with a compound of two stimuli (AB), and the third with a compound of three stimuli (ABC). After training that was sufficient to bring all three groups to similar stable levels of eye-blink responding to the training stimulus, all three groups were administered equivalent test trials on all three of the stimuli (A, AB, and ABC).

The results are described in Fig. 2.7. The bar graphs display separately for each of the three groups the percentage of eye-blink CRs to the training stimulus and the two generalization test stimuli during the test series. As may be seen, there was less responding to the two novel stimuli than to the training stimulus in each group, whether the novel stimuli involved the removal of stimuli, as it did in the case of the ABC group; the addition of stimuli, as it did in the case of the A group; or either the removal or addition of stimuli, as it did in the case of the AB

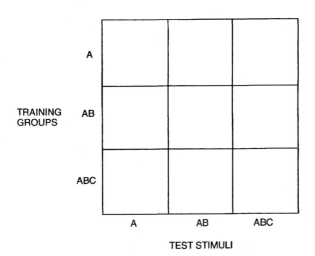

FIG. 2.6. The design of an experiment testing the different predictions of the added elements, inhibited elements, and replaced elements models. Three groups of rabbits were trained with three cues, A, AB, or ABC, and then each group was tested with A, AB, and ABC.

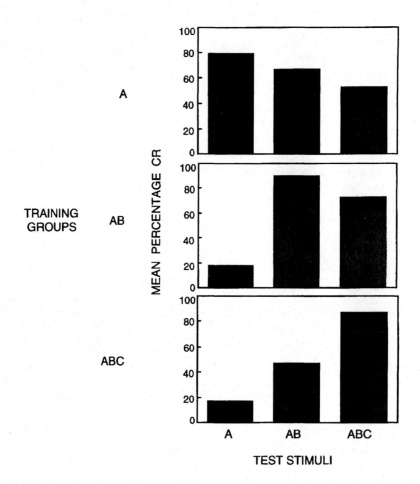

FIG. 2.7. The mean percentage eyelid CRs to each of the test stimuli, A, AB, and ABC, by each of the training groups A, AB, and ABC for the experiment described by Fig. 2.6. Redrawn from Brandon, Vogel, and Wagner (2000).

group. That there was a decrement due to the adding of stimuli is clearly contrary to the Rescorla–Wagner view. As also may be seen, however, the effects of adding or withdrawing a stimulus were not symmetrical, as predicted by Pearce. In all of the direct comparisons there was a reliably greater decrement produced by the withdrawal of a stimulus than by its addition: There was more of a decrement in conditioned responding when B was withdrawn from the trained AB compound than when B was added to the trained A cue; there was more of a decrement in conditioned responding when C was removed from the trained ABC compound than when C was added to the trained AB; and there was more of a decrement in conditioned responding when BC was removed from the trained ABC compound than when BC was added to the trained A cue.

The pattern of test data observed by Brandon et al. (2000) is in much better accord with the replaced elements view than either the Rescorla–Wagner added elements view or the Pearce configural (inhibited elements) conception. It must be mentioned, however, that those partial to the Rescorla–Wagner or the Pearce view might avoid this judgment by appealing to an additional mechanism that has long been considered as a possible contributor to the response decrements that occur in response to novel stimuli. Pavlov (1927) noted that novel stimuli can lead to investigatory behavior, which, if antagonistic to the measured CR, would produce a decrement in conditioned responding. Konorski (1948) argued that such a process, rather than a generalization decrement, is responsible for those response decrements that occur with an added stimulus. Based on such reasoning, adherents to the Rescorla–Wagner view might argue that the relatively small response decrement observed by Brandon et al. (2000) with the addition of a stimulus was due to the elicitation of incompatible orienting responses, whereas the larger response decrement with the withdrawal of a stimulus was due to a genuine associative decrement. This is possible.

Since Pearce (1987) pointed to the decrement in responding following the addition as well as the subtraction of stimuli as favoring his theory, as compared to that of Rescorla and Wagner, one might assume that he should necessarily accept the inequality of the two decrements reported by Brandon et al. (2000) as indicating an advantage of the replaced element view. However, one might again argue that competing orienting responses complicate the matter. The deletion of a stimulus from a familiar compound is known to produce evidence of an orienting reaction just as is the addition of a stimulus (see, e.g., Konorski, 1967; Sokolov, 1975; Wagner, 1979). Thus, it would be possible to conjecture that the larger response decrement observed by Brandon et al. with the withdrawal as compared to the addition of a stimulus is indicative of the orienting response being greater to a novel configuration formed from the withdrawal of a usual component than one formed from the addition to a usual stimulus. The fact is that little is known about whether orienting responses are differentially associated with the withdrawal versus the addition of stimuli, or whether they are responsible in either case for CR decrements, independent of generalization.[2] Until there is a more secure

---

[2]Whatever the merits of the orienting response reasoning, it should not be thought that the CR decrement that occurs with the addition of a stimulus is produced only by unfamiliar stimuli. Using stimuli similar to those of Brandon et al. (in press), Reiss and Wagner (1972) observed a decrement in the eye-blink CR with the addition of a stimulus that had been preexposed more than 1,000 times prior to CS training.

empirical foundation, one can only point to the greater decrement due to the withdrawal than the adding of a stimulus as encouraging the replaced elements view more than either the Rescorla–Wagner or the Pearce view.

OCCASION SETTING

No finding in Pavlovian conditioning since the mid-1980s has generated as much research as has the phenomenon of occasion setting as brought to our attention by Holland (1985; Holland & Ross, 1981) and Rescorla (1985). The phenomenon is observed in certain discrimination learning tasks with compound stimuli, in which the constituent stimuli are presented successively rather than simultaneously. Figure 2.8 presents the findings from two different eye-blink conditioning experiments from our laboratory that exemplify the basic contrast. Both experiments involved what is called a *feature positive discrimination*, in which a compound of a feature (A), and a common cue (X) is reinforced and the common cue (X) by itself is nonreinforced. In one case the compound involved the 1-sec simultaneous presentation of A and X; in the other case the compound involved the successive presentation of a 10-sec A followed by, and terminating with a 1-sec X. In both cases the subjects learned to respond on the reinforced compound trials and not to respond to the nonreinforced common cue alone. The interesting observation is what happened on test occasions in which A was presented alone. In the simultaneous case the subjects responded to A nearly as much as they did to the AX compound. This is what one might expect from the trial-level Rescorla–Wagner learning rule. In contrast, in the successive case, the subjects did not respond at all to A alone. This is what characterizes occasion setting: The animal comes to respond robustly to A and X together, but little to either X or A alone. The feature A does not appear to elicit a CR, but does somehow, it is said, set the occasion for responding to X. How does this happen?

Interpretation: Control by Configural Cues?

By virtue of the extensive research on this question in many laboratories, we now know that there is probably more than one contributor to occasion setting (see Brandon & Wagner, 1998; Schmajuk, Lamoureux, & Holland, 1998). However, one of the first possibilities that Holland (1985) considered, and that we would emphasize, is that, perhaps, in the successive case the subject learns to respond to the configuration of AX, rather than to A or X. One of the attractive features of this interpre-

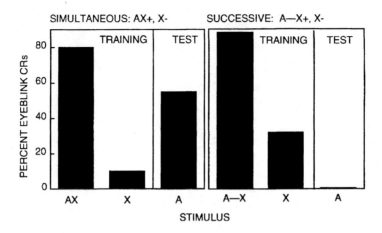

FIG. 2.8.   The mean percentage of eyelid CRs after training with simultaneous AX+, X– (left graph) and successive A–X+, X– (right graph) training, and in tests with A alone following such training, in each condition.

tation is that beyond allowing for the facts of responding to the conjunction AX and not to A or X, it would predict another thing that frequently has been demonstrated (Holland, 1989; Rescorla, 1986): Following sequential feature positive training, the A feature can be extinguished alone or even trained as a negative feature with a different common cue, and still retain much of its ability to act as an occasion setter with X. If behavioral control is by the configuration of AX, the only extinction or antagonistic training that should matter would be that to the AX configuration, not to A.

The reluctance of investigators to accept a configural account of occasion setting was largely for lack of understanding why the same findings did not obtain in simultaneous discriminations. Indeed, several investigators (e.g., Bonardi, 1996; Bouton & Swartzentruber, 1986; Holland, 1983, 1992) rejected a configural interpretation of occasion setting because the phenomenon does not occur with simultaneous training that maximizes the physical conjunction of the feature and target, but does occur with serial nonoverlapping stimuli.[3] What was lacking was a real-time account that would compute how one result should happen with sequential compounds and a different result with simultaneous

---

[3]There is at least one published exception to this generalization, and that is a report by Holland (1989) of occasion setting with simultaneous compounds. In this instance, an occasion-setting-like outcome was dependent on a disparity between the salience of the target and the feature.

compounds. Brandon and Wagner (1998) proposed a variation on the model SOP (Wagner, 1981) that does this in a principled way, using the replaced elements conception as introduced in the preceding section. We present a simplified rendition of that proposal.

A Real-Time Model

There are different ways to build a real-time model. An approach that is followed by many models (Gluck, Reifsnider, & Thompson, 1990; Schmajuk & DiCarlo, 1992; Wagner, 1981) is to divide trial episodes into a series of small "moments" of time and compute the moment-by-moment learning and performance in a manner analogous to the way in which they would be computed on a trial-by-trial basis by trial-level models such as that of Rescorla and Wagner (1972) or Pearce and Hall (1980). A crude model might do no more than this, treating any moment that includes the occurrence of both the CS and the UCS like a reinforced trial, and any moment that includes only the CS like a nonreinforced trial, which is to assume that stimuli have consequences only when physically present, and of equal consequence whenever present.

More sophisticated real-time models attempt to address, in some fashion, the temporal dynamics of what Hull (1943) called the *stimulus trace* of any CS and UCS. A genuine real-time model must deal with moment-to-moment variation in stimulus processing, that is, with systematic variation in CS and UCS parameters as a function of temporal variables such as the time since stimulus onset and termination. An elemental conception must do this by specifying when representative elements are active and inactive in relation to the presence and absence of the provoking stimuli. Among the requirements of any configural representation, as previously introduced, is that of specifying how context-dependent elements are active and inactive under various temporal arrangements of stimulus and context.

The Stimulus Trace

A variety of data, including a set of so-called priming studies by Whitlow (1975), Terry (1976), Pfautz (1980), and Donegan (1981) in our laboratory, encouraged Mazur and Wagner (1982; Wagner, 1981) to offer the general characterization of stimulus processing illustrated in Fig. 2.9. We supposed that the molar stimulus trace resulting from a temporally defined stimulus application, as exemplified by the graphic function in Fig. 2.9, reflects the summed activity of a large, but finite, collection of elements, with activity courses such as those depicted in the com-

puter-generated rastor plot that the trace overlays. In general, it was assumed that each element probabilistically passes among the states of
being inactive, active, and refractory, as indicated in Panel (b): The
probability of elemental activation from the inactive state is taken to
have a stimulus-determined value of p1 in the presence of an adequate
stimulus and a value of 0 in its absence; the probabilities of transition
from active to refractory and from refractory to inactive, defined as pd1

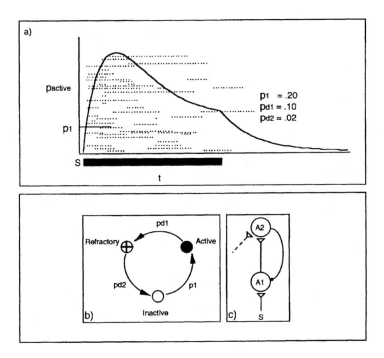

FIG. 2.9. (a) The activity of the individual elements of a CS_{A1} node in SOP
across real time. These elements were assumed to be generated by the CS
whose duration is indicated by the black bar, given the p1, pd1, and pd2 parameters listed. The solid line represents the sum of the activity of the individual elements. (b) The three activity states possible for an individual element of stimulus
representation assumed by SOP. Presentation of the stimulus prompts elements
from an inactive state to an active state according to the parameter p1, for as
long as the stimulus is present. Once active, the elements decay to a refractory
state and then to inactivity, according to the passive decay parameters pd1 and
pd2. (c) A connectionist view of the stimulus representation assumed by SOP.
The active state of Panel (b) is represented by the A1 node, and the refractory
state of Panel (b) is represented by the A2 node. There is a recurrent inhibition
between elements active in the A2 state on elements in the A1 state. The acquired connection is indicated by the dashed line: An associatively linked stimulus elicits activity in the A2 node of the stimulus representation with which it is
associated.

and pd2, respectively, were taken to be independent of the presence or absence of the stimulus. The refractory state, from which an element is incapable of being activated, could be attributed to various mechanistic processes, but Donegan and Wagner (1987) supposed that it was due to a recurrent inhibition process cartooned in Panel (c) of Fig. 2.9. The sense of this notion is that the activity of the node labeled A1 is initiated by its stimulus, S, but is actively inhibited when A1 is effective in activating a second node, A2, and continues to be inhibited until the activity in A2 dissipates. We ignore this part of our theorizing in this chapter to simplify the exposition, but mention it because the A2 process is essential to many of the predictions of our models, SOP and AESOP, beyond the focus here (see, e.g., Kim, Krupa, & Thompson, 1998; McNish, Betts, Brandon, & Wagner, 1996; Wagner, 1981; Wagner & Brandon, 1989).

The state-transition assumptions lead to characteristic temporal patterns of element activity during and following stimulus exposure that depend on the several parameters that have been mentioned and the temporal course of the stimulus. The first-increasing-and-then-decreasing stimulus trace, with gradual decay after stimulus termination, as shown in Fig. 2.9a, follows from the parameters and stimulus duration indicated. Different functions, for example, with longer or shorter recruitment phases or more or less prominent adaptation, would be generated with different assumptions, but Mazur and Wagner (1982) supposed that the trace shown in Fig. 2.9 is relatively characteristic of that generated by Pavlovian CSs. We make use of similar parameters in this discussion.

There is ample precedent for assuming a pattern of afferent activity such as that depicted in Fig. 2.9. Hull (1943) proposed a nonmonotonic stimulus trace based on the data of Adrian, showing the change in the frequency of impulses recorded in the optic nerve of the eel during continuous light stimulation, as shown in the top panel of Fig. 2.10. More abundant reason to attach significance to the pattern has come from research in human psychophysics. The function in the bottom panel of Fig. 2.10 is copied from Marks (1974). It summarizes the general results of a large number of studies in which human observers were presented with stimuli of varying durations and asked to judge their sensory magnitude. The function was meant to illustrate what Marks (1974) concluded to be two general principles of sensory magnitude judgment: "Given a stimulus intensity that remains constant over time, sensation first increases in magnitude (temporal integration) and then declines (adaptation)" (p. 100). Marks noted that the integration and adaptation phases are more or less prominent and take place over different durations of time with stimuli in different sensory modalities. For example, he characterized temporal integration as occurring over a duration of about .5 sec for visual stimuli in comparison to about 3 to 6 sec for taste stimuli, and adaptation as being more modest for visual stimuli than for taste stimuli. However, he emphasized that temporal integration and adaptation "appear to be nearly universal sensory phenomenon" (p. 126). Our three-state stochastic conception provides a simple computational means for producing an approximation to this fundamental sensory processing regularity.

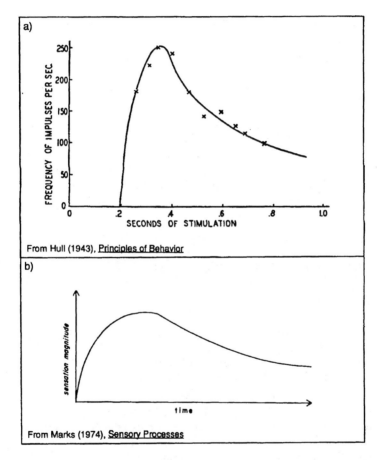

FIG. 2.10.   (a) The rise and gradual decay in the frequency of impulses emitted by the eye of an eel during continuous stimulation by a light of 830-m candles. Adapted from Adrian (1928) and copied from Hull (1943), Fig. 4 (p. 42). Reprinted by permission of Ms. Ruth Hull Low. (b) A graph showing how human subjects reported sensation magnitude as a function of the presentation of stimuli from a variety of modalities across time. Copied from Marks (1974), Fig. 4.1 (p. 100). Reprinted by permission of Academic Press.

Context-Dependent Components

Brandon and Wagner (1998) made the general assumption, within this framework, that context-dependent elements that represent conjunctions of stimuli are just like any other elements in being governed by the parameters p1, pd1, and pd2. However, they assumed that the activation parameter, p1, in the case of such elements is not dependent on the simultaneous occurrence of two stimuli, but on the conjunction of the physical presence of a represented stimulus and the trace state of its contextual influence. Figure 2.11 summarizes the assumptions and illustrates their consequences as applied to the replaced elements conception, assuming two stimuli, A and X, that can occur together or apart from each other.

It is assumed that X is represented in part by a pool of context-independent elements, designated x_i, whose opportunity for occurrence is independent of any other experimental stimuli. The element activation rule for such elements, shown in Panel (a), is that p1 is a constant, k, in any moment in which X is present, and 0 in any moment in which X is absent. It is also assumed that X is represented by two complimentary pools of context-dependent elements, ones designated x_a that represent X in the context of A, and ones designated x_{-a} that represent X in the absence of A. The element activation rule for the x_a elements is that p1 is a constant, k, in any moment in which X is present and the proportion of active elements representing stimulus A is suprathreshold, whereas the rule for the x_{-a} elements is that p1 is a constant, k, in any moment in which X is present and the proportion of active elements representing stimulus A is not suprathreshold.

With these rules, and analogous rules for the corresponding elements representing stimulus A, one can compute the trace consequences for various arrangements of stimulus X in temporal relation to stimulus A. Plot (i) shows, in the same manner as in Fig. 2.9, the trace activity of the elements that represent X when X is presented alone, assuming that the context-independent elements, x_i, are more numerous than the context-dependent elements, x_{-a}. Plot (ii) shows the trace activity presumed to occur when X is presented in simultaneous compound with A. Here the context-independent and context-dependent components of A are concurrent with those of X, and the conjunctive elements x_a and a_x occur rather than x_{-a} and a_{-x}. Plot (iii) shows the trace activity when A precedes X in successive, overlapping compound. The important thing to see here is how the A components that are activated independent of the presence or absence of X, x_i, and the context-dependent components of A that are activated in the absence of X, a_{-x}, occur prior to the occurrence of X, and that X activates not only x_i components, but the a_x and x_a components. Plot (iv) shows the trace activity when A and X are in a serial compound in which A terminates prior to the onset of X. Among the notable features here are that the x_a elements are activated, representing X in the context of A, even though the two stimuli do not physically overlap, but that the a_x elements, representing A in the context of X, do not similarly occur, because there was no (contextual) trace of X during the presentation of A.

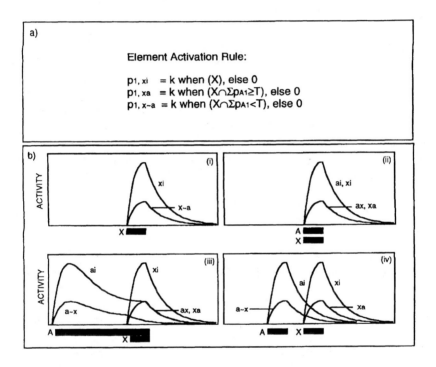

FIG. 2.11.   (a) The rules for element activation in the replaced elements model. The parameters are as assumed in SOP; that is, p1 is a parameter determined by the intensity of the eliciting stimulus, where $0 \leq p1 \leq 1$ as long as the stimulus is present, and p_{A1} is the proportion of elements that are active in the A1 state. T is a threshold value. (b) The activity generated in the components of various stimuli as a function of time and stimulus element conjunctions. The first instance (i) is the activity generated by a single stimulus, X; both context-independent (x_i) and context-dependent (x_{-a}) elements are shown. The subsequent graphs show the activity of components generated by the simultaneous presentation of A and X (ii), the successive presentation of A and X (iii), and a serial presentation of the same cues (iv). In each instance, context-independent elements—weighted by a factor of four—are shown along with presumed context-dependent elements.

Real-Time Computations

Figure 2.12 illustrates how real-time computation would work with traces as have been described. The lefthand panels in Fig. 2.12b describe the CS traces that would be assumed to be encountered on either a simultaneous AX compound trial or a successive A–X compound trial. Each of the panels also includes a UCS trace that should occur if the trials were each reinforced by a momentary UCS, overlapping and terminating with the compound. With these traces one can compute moment-by-moment changes in associative strength using an extension of the Rescorla–Wagner learning rule shown in Fig. 2.12a: V_i is computed, in each moment of time, t, for each CS element that is active in that moment, using the parenthetical quantity, $(\lambda_t - \Sigma V_t)$, where λ_t is a measure of the number of UCS elements that are active and ΣV_t is the aggregate V of all of the CS elements that are active. By this computation, there will generally be an increment in associative strength to those CS elements that are active during the trace of the UCS, and a decrement to those CS elements that are active prior to the UCS. In moment-by-moment application, there will be competition among the components for ΣV just as there is through the familiar trial-level application of the Rescorla– Wagner rule.[4]

Simulations using the traces shown for the simultaneous and successive compounds in Fig. 2.12 produced asymptotic distributions of associative strength to the several cues and their separable components as indicated in the histograms to the left in Panel (b). After reinforcement of the simultaneous compound, the more numerous context-independent x_i and a_i components each gained substantial and equal associative strengths, which would be evident in conditioned responding if the A and X cues were presented alone. The elements representing the conjunction of A and X, a_x and x_a, also gained some lesser strength, which would summate with that of the context-independent elements to increase conditioned responding if the stimuli were presented in AX compound. After reinforcement of the successive compound, there was a

---

[4]It need be emphasized again that this real-time extension of the Rescorla–Wagner rule is inadequate to deal with certain temporal phenomena, such as the variations in inhibitory backward conditioning (see Larew, 1986; McNish et al., 1996; Wagner & Larew, 1985), for which the more complex rules of SOP (Wagner, 1981) and AESOP (Wagner & Brandon, 1989) were developed. However, most workers in the field are conversant with the trial-level Rescorla–Wagner model and, we think, will be better prepared to appreciate the sense of our representational proposals within the approximate adequacy of its real-time extension. Because the representational proposals are developed in SOP terms, those familiar with this model will find them immediately applicable therein.

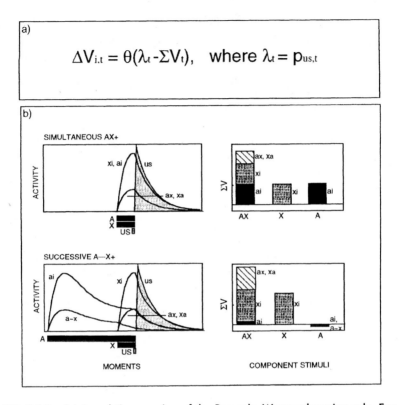

FIG. 2.12. (a) A real-time version of the Rescorla–Wagner learning rule. For each moment of time, ΔV_i is calculated as the weighted difference between the proportion of UCS elements active at that moment (λ_t), and the summed activity of all CSs also active at that moment (ΣV_t). (b) Panel (b) shows that application of the rule described in Panel (a) to the CS traces generated by the simultaneous (top) and successive (bottom) reinforced presentations of two cues, A and X, generates the predicted asymptotic associative strengths for each element. Stimulus representation traces are those assumed by the replaced elements SOP model. Context-independent elements (x_i, a_i) are weighted by a factor of four relative to the context-dependent elements (a_x, x_a, a_{-x}). Also shown is the activity generated by presentation of the UCS.

different distribution of strengths: The most obvious result is that the association to the context-independent A components, a_i, was rendered inconsequential by the extended periods of nonreinforcement of A, so that there would be no associative strength evident if A were presented alone. Also, with the contribution of A removed, both the context-independent elements of X, x_i, and the elements representing the conjunction of A and X, a_x and x_a, gained more strength. One should notice that, by this account, a substantial part of the occasion setting phenomenon does not require discrimination training involving nonreinforced trials with X. The differential responding to A can result from the differential learning to that stimulus that occurs within the reinforced compounds formed from successive as compared to simultaneous presentations of A and X.

Figure 2.13 depicts the stimulus traces that would be presumed to be present during a simultaneous feature positive discrimination (in the top panels), as contrasted with a successive feature positive discrimination (in the bottom panels), according to the replaced elements view and the simplified representational conventions in the preceding figures. What is different in this figure, as compared to Fig. 2.12, is that these simulations include the nonreinforced trials with X alone that occur in each discrimination. What the nonreinforced trials with X should do is decrease the associative strength to the context-independent components, x_i. The results of theoretical simulations show that when this is accomplished in the simultaneous case, it leaves a distribution of elemental strengths as shown in the adjacent right panel: Comparing the strengths here with those shown to the same components in Fig. 2.12 indicates that the decrease in associative strength of x_i is accompanied by a notable gain in the associative strength of the context-independent elements of A, a_i, and a small gain in the associative tendencies to the conjunctive cues, a_x and x_a. The results of the theoretical simulations in the successive case are quite different. Because the context-independent A components are rendered

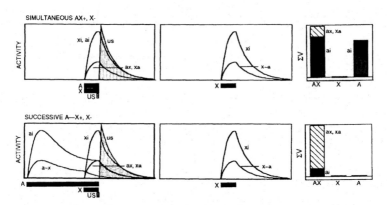

FIG. 2.13. Application of the real-time version of the Rescorla–Wagner learning rule, as indicated in Fig. 2.12, to an instance of a simultaneous (top) and successive (bottom) feature positive problem, AX+, X–, using the stimulus element representation traces assumed by the replaced elements SOP model. The predicted asymptotic associative strengths for each element are shown for each instance. Context-independent elements (x_i, a_i) are weighted by a factor of four relative to the context-dependent elements (a_x, x_a, a_{-x}). Also shown is the activity generated by presentation of the US.

noncompetitive by their nonreinforcement within the compound trials, when the context-independent components of the X cue are extinguished on the nonreinforced X trials, the way is left for the consistently reinforced conjunctive elements, a_x and x_a, to acquire the majority of the associative strength. These are the results that may be observed in the simulations shown in the panel to the right.

An Experimental Confirmation

The simulations depicted in Figs. 2.12 and 2.13 give interpretation to the eyelid findings from our laboratory shown in Fig. 2.8, which we have portrayed as being characteristic of the phenomenon of occasion setting. The real-time model predicts essentially the same results as would be expected from the trial-level Rescorla–Wagner model when applied to reinforced training with a simultaneous AX compound: The majority of the associative loadings accrue to the context-independent components of A and X, so that both of these stimuli are predicted to be responded to in isolation, and to produce summative responding to the AX compound. In contrast, the real-time model predicts very different results when applied to reinforced training with a successive A–X compound: Associative loadings accrue to the context-independent components of X, but not of A, so that the subject should come to respond more to A–X than to X only because of the associative learning to the conductive elements. To test this reasoning, Anh Chung and Karyn Myers in our laboratory conducted an unpublished eye-blink conditioning study that proceeded in the same sequence of reinforced compound training followed by discrimination training depicted in Figs. 2.12 and 2.13. That is, rabbits were initially trained over a series of five conditioning sessions with either a simultaneous 1-sec compound, AX, or a successive compound, A–X, with a 10-sec A cue overlapping and terminating with a 1-sec X, all consistently reinforced. They were then tested over a series of nonreinforced trials for their eye-blink responding to the elements and the compound. After the completion of this phase of training and testing, the rabbits were given five additional training sessions with the same simultaneous or successive compounds, reinforced, but now interspersed with nonreinforced trials with X alone; that is, they were given either simultaneous or successive feature positive training. The two groups were then tested again for their response to their training compound and its components.

The data are shown in Fig. 2.14. As may be seen, the pattern of data is essentially identical to that simulated in Figs. 2.12 and 2.13. The major difference resulting from the simultaneous and successive training—which is the occurrence of responding to A in the simultaneous case but not in the successive case—was evident after simple reinforced training. The further effect of discrimination training with X nonreinforced was primarily to reduce the responding to X in both groups. As predicted, discrimination training also increased the responding to A in the simultaneous group, as previously observed by Wagner (1969) in comparisons of responding to A after equivalent amounts of AX+/X– versus AX+ training.

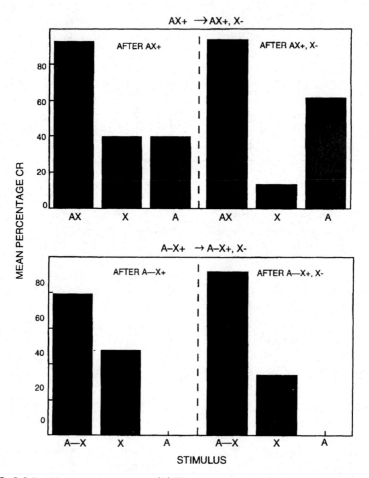

FIG. 2.14.   Mean percentage eyelid CRs to a compound CS AX and to each of the elements A and X, after training with the compound only (left graphs) or with the same compound in a feature positive problem, AX+, X– (right graphs). The data depicted in the top graphs were after training with a simultaneous AX compound, and those depicted in the bottom graphs were after training with a successive A–X compound.

Transfer From Feature Positive to Biconditional Discrimination.

There has been a voluminous amount of research on the phenomenon of occasion setting. Much of it shows just what one would expect if sequential training caused behavior to come under the control of the configuration of feature and target stimulus rather than the isolable components, as in our simulations. One of the most obvious predictions that one would make from our configural interpretation of occasion setting was tested recently by Karyn Myers in an unpublished study in our laboratory.

Myers reasoned that, if sequential feature positive training brings behavior under the control of configural cues in a way that simultaneous training does not, as suggested by the simulations in Figs. 2.12 and 2.13, then sequential discrimination training should lead to more positive transfer of training, if subjects were shifted to a new discrimination that requires the use of the same configural cues. Figure 2.15 shows the design of the study. Two groups of rabbits were trained on two concurrent feature positive discriminations, one designated as AX+, X–, the other as BY+, Y–. In one group the two reinforced compounds involved the 1-sec simultaneous presentation of the feature and common cue; in the other group the two compounds involved the successive presentation of a 10-sec feature that preceded and overlapped with a 1-sec common cue. After both groups learned the two feature positive discriminations, they were shifted to the same kind of biconditional discrimination that Saavedra (1975) employed, using the stimuli from the two feature positive tasks in simultaneous compounds. That is, all rabbits were trained with the simultaneous com-

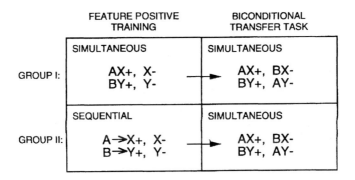

	FEATURE POSITIVE TRAINING	BICONDITIONAL TRANSFER TASK
	SIMULTANEOUS	SIMULTANEOUS
GROUP I:	AX+, X– BY+, Y–	AX+, BX– BY+, AY–
	SEQUENTIAL	SIMULTANEOUS
GROUP II:	A→X+, X– B→Y+, Y–	AX+, BX– BY+, AY–

FIG. 2.15.   The design of a two-group study where rabbits were trained with either two simultaneous or two successive feature positive problems, and then all were switched to a biconditional problem with the same cues as in the previous problems.

pounds, AX+, BX–, AY–, and BY+, in which discrimination requires association to the AX and BY configurations.

Figure 2.16 summarizes the results, using a nonparametric discrimination index that was calculated as the percentage of blocks of trials in which the conditioned responding to each of the positive stimuli was superior to that of the two negative stimuli. As shown in the left panel, both groups reached high levels of performance on the initial feature positive discriminations, although the sequential group made somewhat more errors. The findings of major interest are shown in the right panel. As shown, the group with a history of sequential, as compared to simultaneous, feature positive training performed better on the biconditional discrimination. This difference, which was statistically reliable, makes it the more plausible that feature positive training with a sequential arrangement of feature and common cue brings behavior under the control of configural cues, in a way that similar training with simultaneous compounds does not.

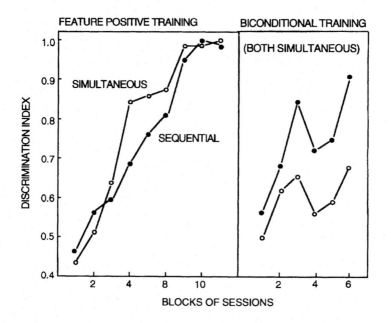

FIG. 2.16. The outcome of the study described in Fig. 2.15. Performance in the training problems with the simultaneous or successive arrangement of cues is shown in the left panel, and performance in the simultaneous biconditional problem is shown in the right panel. The discrimination index was calculated as the percentage of trials in which the conditioned responding to the positive stimuli was superior to that to the negative stimuli.

Contextual Control of Stimulus Meaning

In a recent symposium, Bouton (1999) titled his comments "What Makes Learning Context Specific?" What Bouton was concerned with was a wealth of observations in which it appears that an association that is learned in one context is especially detectable in that context, beyond what might be attributable to the context simply acting as an additional retrieval cue. Independent studies by Bonardi (1992), Gewirtz, Brandon, and Wagner (1998), and Hall and Honey (1989) demonstrate the essential observation. In each of these studies animals had one CS paired with a UCS in one experimental context (an extended stimulus or distinctive environment within which the CS and UCS could occur) and had another CS paired with the same UCS in a different context. By this arrangement both of the contexts were equally paired with the UCS so that any tendency for direct associations between the contexts and the UCS to facilitate responding to either CS, for example, by summation or emotive modulation (Wagner & Brandon, 1989), should have been equated. However, in each study there was a substantial advantage in conditioned responding to the two CSs when they were tested in their training context as compared to the alternate context. What causes this to be the case?

Many current theorists (e.g., Bonardi, 1998; Bouton & Nelson, 1998; Hall & Mondragon; 1998) would guess that what causes learning to appear context specific in instances such as these is likely to be the same mechanism that is responsible for the principle observation of occasion setting; that is, that a target CS is especially responded to in the context of a preceding feature, without that feature independently eliciting responding. They would not necessarily agree with our judgment that the common mechanism is the associative control that is acquired by context-dependent elements. Our position is simply that this possibility is sufficiently plausible on the basis of existing theoretical machinery that it should not be rejected for less determinant accounts.

What is necessary, of course, for any theoretical analysis of the contextual specificity of learning is a real-time account that naturally distinguishes between contextual stimuli and discrete CSs by virtue of their temporal characteristics. Wilson and Pearce (1989, Experiment 1) reported an experiment that closely bridged the gap between studies of occasion setting and the contextual specificity of learning and concluded that a configural cue account based on a Pearce conception would be adequate to explain the results. It is instructive to see that the form of real-time account that we have offered for occasion setting, which includes an alternative configural conception to that of Pearce, predicts the same kind of findings. In their study, using rats and a food magazine approach response, Wilson and Pearce periodically presented separate 10-sec target stimuli, X and Y, within each of two 2-min background stimuli, A and B. When X was presented within A it was reinforced with the delivery of food; when it was presented within B it was nonreinforced. When Y was presented within A it was nonreinforced; when it was presented within B it was reinforced. This arrangement presented the opportunity for the animals to learn a biconditional discrimination similar to that studied by Saavedra (1975), but with the important procedural difference that one pair of cues had the temporal characteristic of background stimuli and the other pair of cues had the temporal characteristics of discrete CSs, analogous to the difference between the extended features and brief target stimuli in studies of occasion setting with successive compounds. Suffice it to say that the animals in the Wilson and Pearce study learned the discrimination, responding more to X than to Y when the stimuli were presented within the A background, but responding more to Y than to X when the stimuli were presented within the B background.

Panel (a) of Fig. 2.17 depicts the theoretical stimulus traces that would be expected in an episode of the Wilson and Pearce (1989) study in which the X stimulus was presented within the A background and reinforced. Different but similar traces would be expected involving the Y stimulus reinforced within the B background, and the two CSs each nonreinforced in the alternate background. Panel (b) of Fig. 2.17 summarizes the results using the moment-by-moment application of the Rescorla–Wagner equation to these traces, as described in previous simulations. What is shown is that the context-independent elements representing both X and Y are predicted to become moderately excitatory, and that these tendencies are augmented or inhibited by the tendencies that accrue to the context-dependent elements. Responding to X is augmented by the tendencies to a_x and x_a, that occur in context A and is inhibited by the tendencies to b_x and x_b that occur in context B; responding to Y is augmented by the tendencies to b_y and y_b that occur in context B, and inhibited by the tendencies to a_y and y_a that occur in context A.

It remains to be seen whether this manner of account will be adequate to deal with the range of circumstances under which there is apparent contextual control of stimulus meaning, as there was in the Wilson and Pearce (1989) study. The reasoning can easily be extended to deal with instances in which the same CSs are associated with different UCSs, and come to elicit different CRs, in different contexts, as in the study by Asratyan (1965) in which tactile stimulation signaled shock and a buzzer signaled food in one room, whereas this relation was reversed in a second room. The situations that are likely to be more puzzling to understand are those like simple reinforced training with sequential compounds, as commented on in Figs. 2.12 and 2.14, in which training is not

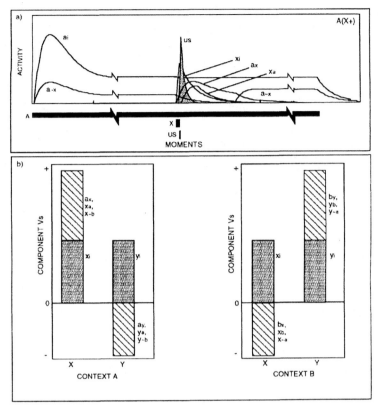

FIG. 2.17. (a) Application of the real-time version of the Rescorla–Wagner learning rule, as indicated in Fig. 2.12, to an instance of contextual specificity of learning, using the stimulus representation traces assumed by the replaced elements SOP model, as shown in Panel (a). The top graph shows the elements activated when a discrete cue X is reinforced in context A: Context-independent elements (x_i, a_i) are weighted by a factor of four relative to the context-dependent elements (a_x, x_a, a_{-x}). Also shown is the activity generated by presentation of the UCS. (b) The predicted asymptotic associative strengths for elements, as represented in Panel (a), after differential training with X and Y in two contexts, that is, A(X+), A(Y–), B(X–), B(Y+).

so clearly designed to bring the behavior under the exclusive control of configural cues, but in which some control still occurs as part of the associative learning involved. The so-called renewal effect is an example.

The *renewal effect* is said to occur when a CS that is reinforced in one distinctive experimental environment and is subsequently extinguished in a different environment shows recovery of the CR when tested back in the training context. Bouton and his students (e.g., Bouton & King, 1983; Bouton & Swartzenruber, 1986), who have extensively investigated this effect, eliminated the possibility that the recovery they observed was due only to direct context-UCS associations that could summate with or modulate the CS–UCS association. For example, there was no similar modulating influence of the acquisition and extinction contexts on the test responding to a different CS for the same UCS that had been trained in yet a third context. Arguing against a simple associative summation account was also the fact that the acquisition context maintained its ability to enhance responding to a CS that had been trained in it, even after numerous sessions of nonreinforcement of that context alone. It appears as though the CS–UCS, reinforcement learning, and the CS–no UCS, extinction learning, were to some degree context specific. Our analysis would expect that in simple acquisition and extinction, some associations develop to context-dependent elements as well as to the context-independent elements of the CS, and whereas the latter should be expressed on presentation of the CS in any context, the former should be expressed only if the CS were presented in the training context.

CONCLUDING COMMENTS

The supposition with which we began this chapter is that many of the issues in association theory can be stated as problems about how to represent the stimuli involved. Consistent with that notion, we have tried to show how some fundamental issues become less mysterious when formulated in componential fashion.

Spence (1952) pointed to Pavlov's (1927) demonstration of differential conditioning to stimulus compounds involving the same stimuli in different orders as evidence that for animals to solve certain discrimination problems they must learn to respond on the basis of the different "patterns" of stimulus components. However, in his theorizing, Spence (1952) assumed that one could generally ignore such associations to stimulus patterns, saying that "discrimination will involve such patterning ... only when no one of the cue members is systematically reinforced more than the others" (p. 90). Wagner and Rescorla (1972) were aware of the data of Saavedra (1975), as well as the negative patterning data of Woodbury (1943), to agree with Spence, that in such situations configural cues must play an important role, and to specifically state that configural cues "should be treated like any other component contributing to ΣV" (Wagner & Rescorla, 1972, p. 306). But, again like Spence, Wagner and Rescorla went on to say that the available evidence suggested that configural cues were probably "relatively inconsequential" (p. 306) in the kinds of studies they would discuss.

The major conclusion that might be drawn from the work we have described is that configural cues cannot be ignored in Pavlovian conditioning, whether one is concerned with the simplest and, presumably, best understood, of phenomena, or one is groping for understanding of relatively new findings. We have presented evidence that the associative loadings to configural cues importantly determine the generalization decrement that occurs when a reinforced CS is altered as a result of either removal of one of its components or the addition of like components. We have attempted to make the case that the different associative loadings acquired by configural cues are responsible for the different results of simultaneous versus successive feature positive discrimination learning—where the latter, but not the former, is said to involve occasion setting. We discussed how the associative control acquired by the configuration of contextual cues and CSs is likely to be responsible for a range of findings that are said to exhibit the contextual control of CS meaning.

If this change in evaluation of the significance of configural cues turns out to be correct, much of the credit must go to the configural theory of Pearce (1987, 1994) for forcing the issue to better appraisal. We are more comfortable with the inhibited elements version of Pearce's theory that we present here, rather than the original version, for the ease with which it can reside within the developed structure of elementistic theory (Bush & Mosteller, 1951; Estes, 1950; Konorski, 1948; Pearce & Hall, 1980; Rescorla & Wagner, 1972; Spence, 1936; Wagner, 1981; Wagner & Brandon, 1989). Indeed, the capturing of the substance of Pearce's configural theory in an inhibited elements formulation is a good reminder of the power of the elementistic conception as Estes (1951) and others developed it, which should not be lightly dismissed. As it turns out, an alternative replaced elements notion appears to have greater advantage. However, much remains to be evaluated.

The phenomena of occasion setting and the contextual control of CS meaning are phenomena that involve variations in the temporal distribution of stimuli. They require real-time models for their explanation. When quantitative models addressed closely to the circumstances of Pavlovian conditioning were developed in the 1970s (e.g., Rescorla & Wagner, 1972), they greatly spurred the conduct of informative studies. Real-time models addressed to what are arguably the most striking and potentially illuminating facts of Pavlovian conditioning were first introduced in the 1980s (e.g., Sutton & Barto, 1981; Wagner 1981), but, probably because they are more complex than their trial-level predecessors, have been slow to have as significant an influence on research efforts. We hope that the simplified real-time model that we have employed here, adapting the trace reasoning from SOP (Wagner, 1981) to a moment-by-moment application of the Rescorla–Wagner rule, will prove accessible enough to encourage further theoretical development.

ACKNOWLEDGMENTS

Portions of this chapter were presented by Allan R. Wagner in Inaugural Address to the X Congress of the Spanish Society of Comparative Psychology, Almeria, Spain, September 1998, and in the Distinguished Scientific Contribution Award Address to the Annual Meeting of the American Psychological Association, Boston, August 1999, and by Susan E. Brandon in invited address to the Annual Meeting of the Pavlovian Society, Dusseldorf, Germany, October 1998. We gratefully acknowledge the contribution of Hasan Bahekapili and Karyn Myers. Both conducted theoretical simulations relating to the work presented and provided instructive discussions of the ideas involved. Portions of the research reported were supported by National Science Foundation grant IBN 97–28896 to Allan R. Wagner.

■ REFERENCES

Asratyan, E. A. (1965). *Conditioned reflex and compensatory mechanisms.* Oxford, UK: Pergamon.

Aydin, A., & Pearce, J. M. (1994). Prototype effects in categorization by pigeons. *Journal of Experimental Psychology: Animal Behavior Processes, 20,* 264–277.

Baçhekapili, H. G. (1997). *An evaluation of Rescorla & Wagner's elementistic model versus Pearce's configural model in discrimination learning.* Unpublished doctoral dissertation, Yale University, New Haven, CT.

Betts, S. L., Brandon, S. E., & Wagner, A. R. (1996). Differential blocking of the acquisition of conditioned eyeblink responding and conditioned fear with a shift in UCS locus. *Animal Learning & Behavior, 24,* 459–470.

Bombace, J. C., Brandon, S. E., & Wagner, A. R. (1991). Modulation of a conditioned eyeblink response by a putative emotive stimulus conditioned with hindleg shock. *Journal of Experimental Psychology: Animal Behavior Processes, 17,* 323–333.

Bonardi, C. (1992). Occasion setting without feature-positive discrimination training. *Learning & Motivation, 23,* 343–367.

Bonardi, C. (1996). Transfer of occasion setting: The role of generalization decrement. *Animal Learning & Behavior, 24,* 277–289.

Bonardi, C. (1998). Conditional learning: An associative analysis. In N. A. Schmajuk & P. C. Holland (Eds.), *Occasion setting: Associative learning and cognition in animals* (pp. 37–68). Washington, DC: American Psychological Association.

Bouton, M. E. (1999, August). What makes learning context specific? In M. Domjan (Chair), *Contemporary learning theory—Mind, brain, and behavior series.* Symposium conducted at the annual meeting of the American Psychological Association, Boston.

Bouton, M. E., & King, D. A. (1983). Contextual control of the extinction of conditioned fear: Tests for the associative value of the context. *Journal of Experimental Psychology: Animal Behavior Processes, 9,* 374–389.

Bouton, M. E., & Nelson, J. B. (1998). Mechanisms of feature-positive and feature-negative discrimination learning in an appetitive conditioning paradigm. In N. A. Schmajuk & P. C. Holland (Eds.), *Occasion setting: Associative learning and cognition in animals* (pp. 69–144). Washington, DC: American Psychological Association.

Bouton, M. E., & Swartzentruber, D. (1986). Analysis of the associative and occasion-setting properties of contexts participating in a Pavlovian discrimination. *Journal of Experimental Psychology: Animal Behavior Processes, 12,* 333–350.

Brandon, S. E., Bombace, J. C., Falls, W. T., & Wagner, A. R. (1991). Modulation of unconditioned defensive reflexes via an emotive Pavlovian conditioned stimulus. *Journal of Experimental Psychology: Animal Behavior Processes, 17,* 312–322.

Brandon, S. E., Vogel, E. H., & Wagner, A. R. (2000). A componential view of configural cues in generalization and discrimination in Pavlovian conditioning. *Behavioural Brain Research. 110,* 67–72.

Brandon, S. E., & Wagner, A. R. (1991). Modulation of a discrete Pavlovian conditioned reflex by a putative emotive Pavlovian conditioned stimulus. *Journal of Experimental Psychology: Animal Behavior Processes, 17,* 299–311.

Brandon, S. E., & Wagner, A. R. (1998). Occasion Setting: Influences of conditioned emotional responses and configural cues. In N. Schmajuk (Ed.), *Occasion setting: Associative learning and cognition in animals* (pp. 343–382). Washington, DC: American Psychological Association.

Burke, C. T., & Estes, W. K. (1957). A component model for stimulus variables in discrimination learning. *Psychometrika, 22,* 133–245.

Bush, R. R., & Mosteller, F. (1951). A mathematical model for simple learning. *Psychological Review, 58,* 313–323.

Darby, R. J., & Pearce, J. M. (1995). Effects of context on responding during a compound stimulus. *Journal of Experimental Psychology: Animal Behavior Processes, 21,* 143–154.

Darby, R. J., & Pearce, J. M. (1997). The effect of stimulus preexposure during a compound stimulus. *The Quarterly Journal of Experimental Psychology, 50B,* 203–216.

Donegan, N. H. (1981). Priming-produced facilitation or diminution of responding to a Pavlovian unconditioned stimulus. *Journal of Experimental Psychology: Animal Behavior Processes, 7,* 295–312.

Donegan, N. H., & Wagner, A. R. (1987). Conditioned diminution and facilitation of the UR: A sometimes-opponent-process interpretation. In I. Gormezano, W. F. Prokasy, & R. F. Thompson (Eds.), *Classical conditioning III* (pp. 339–369). Hillsdale, NJ: Lawrence Erlbaum Associates.

Estes, W. K. (1950) Toward a statistical theory of learning. *Psychological Review, 57,* 94–104.

Gewirtz, J. C., Brandon, S. E., & Wagner, A. R. (1998). Modulation of the acquisition of the rabbit eyeblink conditioned response by conditioned contextual stimuli. *Journal of Experimental Psychology: Animal Behavior Processes, 24,* 106–117.

Gluck, M. A., Reifsnider, E. S., & Thompson, R. F. (1990). Adaptive signal processing and the cerebellum: Models of classical conditioning and VOR adaptation. In M. A. Gluck & D. E. Rumelhart (Eds.), *Neuroscience and connectionist theory* (pp. 131–185). Hillsdale, NJ: Lawrence Erlbaum Associates.

Hall, G., & Honey, R. C. (1989). Contextual effects in conditioning, latent inhibition, and habituation: Associative and retrieval functions of contextual cues. *Journal of Experimental Psychology: Animal Behavior Processes, 15,* 232–241.

Hall, G., & Mondragon, E. (1998). Contextual control as occasion setting. In N. A. Schmajuk & P. C. Holland (Eds.), *Occasion setting: Associative learning and cognition in animals* (pp. 199–222). Washington, DC: American Psychological Association.

Holland, P. C. (1983). Occasion-setting in Pavlovian feature positive discriminations. In M. L. Commons, R. J. Herrnstein, & A. R. Wagner (Eds.), *Quantitative analyses of behavior: Discrimination processes* (Vol. 4, pp. 182–206). New York: Ballinger.

Holland, P. C. (1985). The nature of conditioned inhibition in serial and simultaneous feature negative discriminations. In R. R. Miller & N. E. Spear (Eds.), *Information processing in animals: Conditioned inhibition* (pp. 267–297). Hillsdale, NJ: Lawrence Erlbaum Associates.

Holland, P. C. (1989). Feature extinction enhances transfer of occasion setting. *Animal Learning & Behavior, 17,* 269–279.

Holland, P. C. (1992). Occasion setting in Pavlovian conditioning. In D. L. Medin (Ed.), *The psychology of learning and innovation, 28* (pp. 69–125). New York: Academic Press.

Holland, P. C., & Ross, R. T. (1981). Within-compound associations in serial compound conditioning. *Journal of Experimental Psychology: Animal Behavior Processes, 7,* 228–241.

Hull, C. L. (1943). *Principles of Behavior.* New York: Appleton-Century-Crofts.

Hull, C. L. (1945) The discrimination of stimulus configurations and the hypothesis of afferent neural interaction. *Psychological Review, 53,* 133–142.

Kim, J. J., Krupa, D. J., & Thompson, R. F. (1998). Inhibitory cerebello-olivary projections and blocking effect in classical conditioning. *Science, 279,* 570–573.

Klein, S. B., & Mowrer, R. R. (1989). *Contemporary learning theories: Pavlovian conditioning and the status of traditional learning theory.* Hillsdale, NJ: Lawrence Erlbaum Associates.

Konorski, J. (1948). *Conditioned reflexes and neuron organization.* Cambridge, UK: Cambridge University Press.

Konorski, J. (1967). *Integrative activity of the brain: An interdisciplinary approach.* Chicago: University of Chicago Press.

Larew, M. B. (1986). *Inhibitory learning in Pavlovian backward procedures involving a small number of UCS-CS trials.* Unpublished doctoral dissertation, Yale University, New Haven, CT.

Lennartz, R. C., & Weinberger, N. M. (1994). A comparison of nonspecific and nictitating membrane conditioned responses: Additional support for two-factor theories. *Psychobiology, 22,* 5–15.

Marks, L. E. (1974). *Sensory processes.* New York: Academic.

Mazur, J. E., & Wagner, A. R. (1982). An episodic model of associative learning. In M. Commons, R. Herrnstein, & A. R. Wagner (Eds.), *Quantitative analyses of behavior: Acquisition* (Vol. 3, pp. 3–39). Cambridge, MA: Ballinger.

McNish, K., Betts, S. L., Brandon, S. E., & Wagner, A. R. (1996). Divergence of measures of conditioned eyeblink and conditioned fear in backward Pavlovian training. *Animal Learning & Behavior, 25,* 43–52.

Myers, K. M., Vogel, E. H., Shin, J., & Wagner, A. R. (in press). A comparison of the Rescorla–Wagner and Pearce models in a negative patterning and a summation problem. *Animal Learning and Behavior.*

Pavlov, I. P. (1927). *Conditioned reflexes.* Oxford, UK: Oxford University Press.

Pearce, J. M. (1987). A model for stimulus generalization in Pavlovian conditioning. *Psychological Review, 94,* 61–75.

Pearce, J. M. (1994). Similarity and discrimination: A selective review and a connectionist model. *Psychological Review, 101,* 587–607.

Pearce, J. M., Adam, J., Wilson, P. N., & Darby, R. J. (1992). Effects of discrimination training on responding during a compound conditioned stimulus. *Journal of Experimental Psychology: Animal Behavior Processes, 18,* 379–386.

Pearce, J. M., Aydin, A., & Redhead, E. S. (1997). Configural analysis of summation in autoshaping. *Journal of Experimental Psychology: Animal Behavior Processes, 23,* 84–94.

Pearce, J. M., & Hall, G. (1980). A model for Pavlovian learning: Variations in the effectiveness of conditioned but not unconditioned stimuli. *Psychological Review, 87,* 532–552.

Pearce, J. M., & Redhead, E. S. (1993). The influences of an irrelevant stimulus on two discriminations. *Journal of Experimental Psychology: Animal Behavior Processes, 19,* 180–190.

Pearce, J. M., & Redhead, E. S. (1995). Supernormal conditioning. *Journal of Experimental Psychology: Animal Behavior Processes, 21,* 155–165.

Pearce, J. M., & Wilson, P. N. (1990). Feature-positive discrimination learning. *Journal of Experimental Psychology: Animal Behavior Processes, 16,* 315–325.

Pfautz, P. L. (1980). *Unconditioned facilitation and diminution of the unconditioned response.* Unpublished doctoral dissertation, Yale University, New Haven, CT.

Redhead, E. S., & Pearce, J. M. (1995a). Similarity and discrimination learning. *The Quarterly Journal of Experimental Psychology, 48B,* 46–66.

Redhead, E. S., & Pearce, J. M. (1995b). Stimulus salience and negative patterning. *The Quarterly Journal of Experimental Psychology, 48B,* 67–83.

Reiss, S., & Wagner, A. R. (1972). CS habituation produces a "latent inhibition effect" but no active conditioned inhibition. *Learning and Motivation, 3,* 237–245.

Rescorla, R. A. (1985). Inhibition and facilitation. *Information processing in animals: Conditioned inhibition* (pp. 299–326). Hillsdale, NJ: Lawrence Erlbaum Associates.

Rescorla, R. A. (1986). Extinction of facilitation. *Journal of Experimental Psychology: Animal Behavior Processes, 12,* 16–24.

Rescorla, R. A. (1997). Summation: Assessment of a configural theory. *Animal Learning & Behavior, 25,* 200–209.

Rescorla, R. A., & Coldwell, S. E. (1995). Summation in autoshaping. *Animal Learning & Behavior, 23,* 314–326.

Rescorla, R. A., & Solomon, R. L. (1967). Two-process learning theory: Relationships between Pavlovian conditioning and instrumental learning. *Psychological Review, 74,* 151–182.

Rescorla, R. A., & Wagner, A. R. (1972). A theory of Pavlovian conditioning: Variations in the effectiveness of reinforcement and nonreinforcement. In A. H. Black & W. F. Prokasy (Eds.), *Classical conditioning II* (pp. 64–99). New York: Appleton-Century-Crofts.

Saavedra, M. A. (1975). Pavlovian compound conditioning in the rabbit. *Learning and Motivation, 6,* 314–326.

Schmajuk, N. A., & DiCarlo, J. J. (1992). Stimulus configuration, classical conditioning, and hippocampal function. *Psychological Review, 99,* 268–305.

Schmajuk, N. A., Lamoureux, J. A., & Holland, P. C. (1998). Occasion setting: A neural network approach. *Psychological Review, 105,* 3–32.

Schneiderman, N. (1972). Response system divergencies in aversive classical conditioning. In A. H. Black & W. F. Prokasy (Eds.), *Classical conditioning II: Current theory and research* (pp. 313–376). New York: Appleton-Century-Crofts.

Sherrington, C. S. (1929). Ferrier lecture. *Proceedings of the Royal Society, B, 55,* 332.

Sokolov, E. N. (1975). The neuronal mechanisms of the orienting reflex. In E. N. Sokolov & O. S. Vinogradova (Eds.), *Neuronal mechanisms of the orienting reflex.* Hillsdale, NJ: Lawrence Erlbaum Associates.

Spence, K. (1936). The nature of discrimination learning in animals. *Psychological Review, 43,* 427–449.

Spence, K. W. (1952). The nature of the response in discrimination learning. *Psychological Review, 59,* 89–93.

Spence, K. (1956). *Behavior theory and conditioning.* New Haven, CT: Yale University Press.

Sutton, R. W., & Barto, A. G. (1981). Toward a modern theory of adaptive networks: Expectation and prediction. *Psychological Review, 88,* 135–170.

Terry, W. S. (1976). The effects of priming UCS representation in short-term memory on Pavlovian conditioning. *Journal of Experimental Psychology: Animal Behavior Processes, 2,* 354–370.

Trapold, M. A., & Overmier, J. B. (1972). The second learning process in instrumental learning. In A. H. Black & W. F. Prokasy (Eds.), *Classical conditioning II: Current theory and research* (pp. 427–452). New York: Appleton-Century-Crofts.

Wagner, A. R. (1969). Incidental stimuli and discrimination learning. In R. M. Gilbert & N. S. Sutherland (Eds.), *Animal discrimination learning* (pp. 83–111). London: Academic Press.

Wagner, A. R. (1979). Habituation and memory. In A. Dickinson & R. A. Boakes (Eds.), *Mechanisms of learning and motivation: A memorial to Jerzy Konorski* (pp. 53–82). Hillsdale, NJ: Lawrence Erlbaum Associates.

Wagner, A. R. (1981). SOP: A model of automatic memory processing in animal behavior. In N. E. Spear & R. R. Miller (Eds.), *Information processing in animals: Memory mechanisms* (pp. 5–47). Hillsdale, NJ: Lawrence Erlbaum Associates.

Wagner, A. R., & Brandon, S. E. (1989). Evolution of a structured connectionist model of Pavlovian conditioning (SOP). In S. B. Klein & R. R. Mowrer (Eds.), *Contemporary learning theories: Pavlovian conditioning and the status of traditional learning theory* (pp. 149–189). Hillsdale, NJ: Lawrence Erlbaum Associates.

Wagner, A. R., & Larew, M. B. (1985). Opponent processor and Pavlovian inhibition. In R. R. Miller & N. E. Spear (Eds.), *Information processing in animals: Conditioned inhibition* (pp. 233–265). Hillsdale, NJ: Lawrence Erlbaum Associates.

Wagner, A. R., & Rescorla, R. A. (1972). Inhibition in Pavlovian conditioning: Application of a theory. In R. A. Boakes & M. S. Haliday (Eds.), *Inhibition and learning* (pp. 301–336). New York: Academic.

Whitlow, J. W., Jr. (1975). Short-term memory in habituation and dishabituation. *Journal of Experimental Psychology: Animal Behavior Processes, 1,* 189–206.

Wilson, P. N., & Pearce, J. M. (1989). A role for stimulus generalization in conditional discrimination learning. *Quarterly Journal of Experimental Psychology, 418,* 243–273.

Woodbury, C. B. (1943). The learning of stimulus patterns by dogs. *Journal of Comparative Psychology, 35,* 29–40.

chapter 3

The Extended Comparator Hypothesis:
Learning by Contiguity, Responding by Relative Strength

James C. Denniston
Appalachian State University

Hernán I. Savastano
Ralph R. Miller
State University of New York at Binghamton

In recent years, acquisition-deficit accounts of cue competition (e.g., Rescorla & Wagner, 1972) have been challenged by expression-deficit accounts of cue competition (e.g., the comparator hypothesis; Miller & Matzel, 1988). The comparator hypothesis was originally proposed as a response rule for the expression of Pavlovian associations that posits that associative learning is determined by

65

spatiotemporal contiguity, whereas expression of that learning is determined by relative associative strengths. The comparator hypothesis has received support from studies of posttraining deflation and (with qualification) inflation of the competing cues that yield retrospective revaluation of responding to target stimuli. However, recent models of associative learning that also predict retrospective revaluation have revitalized acquisition-deficit accounts of cue competition (e.g., Dickinson & Burke, 1996; Van Hamme & Wasserman, 1994), such that the comparator hypothesis is no longer unique in predicting recovery from cue competition. This chapter reviews studies that are supportive of both the comparator hypothesis and retrospective revaluation models of cue competition, as well as recent studies that differentiate between acquisition-focused models that predict retrospective revaluation and the comparator hypothesis. An extended multilayer version of the comparator hypothesis is presented, and the importance of encoded temporal information for the comparator process is discussed.

One of the most influential findings in the history of associative learning was the phenomenon of *blocking* (Kamin, 1969). Kamin demonstrated that the effectiveness of a conditioned stimulus (CS) in acquiring behavioral control is influenced by other stimuli that are present during training of the target CS. That is, a CS (X) comes to control less conditioned responding when trained in the presence of another CS (A) that had previously been established as a signal for the unconditioned stimulus (US), relative to subjects that lack such pretraining with CS A. According to Kamin, the blocking deficit is a consequence of CS A fully predicting the outcome, thereby preventing CS X from acquiring any predictive value in signaling the US. Blocking and other so-called cue competition effects, as well as a renewed interest in inhibitory conditioning, inspired a new family of associative models (e.g., Pearce & Hall, 1980; Rescorla & Wagner, 1972).

THE RESCORLA–WAGNER MODEL

The Rescorla–Wagner (1972) model has proven to be the dominant theory of associative learning for nearly three decades (see Miller, Barnet, & Grahame, 1995; Siegel & Allan, 1996). According to the Rescorla–Wagner model, the effectiveness of a CS–US pairing in changing the strength of the CS–US association is determined not only by the current strength of the CS–US association, but also by the associative strength of other stimuli present during the pairing. This latter feature allows the model to account for cue competition effects such as overshadowing (Pavlov, 1927) and blocking. Formally stated, the Rescorla-Wagner model posits that:

$$\Delta V_x = \alpha_x \beta_{US} (\lambda_{US} - V_{\Sigma}^{n-1}) \tag{1}$$

where ΔV_x " is the change in the associative strength (V) of CS X as a result of a pairing with US on Trial n, α_x and β_{US} are learning rate parameters closely related to stimulus saliency and represent the associability of CS X and the US, respectively, λ_{US} is the maximum associative strength supportable by a US ($\lambda > 0$ for a presented US and $\lambda = 0$ for an omitted US), and V_{Σ}^{n-1} is the sum of the associative strengths of all stimuli present on that trial. Thus, changes in the associative strength of a target CS (ΔV_x) reflect the discrepancy between the US actually presented on a trial and the magnitude of the US predicted by all stimuli present on that trial ($\lambda_{US} - V_{\Sigma}$). Thus, the Rescorla–Wagner model formalized Kamin's idea that blocking is the result of CS A (the competing stimulus), having already been established as a signal for the US, leaving less "surprise" value (i.e., less of a discrepancy between the US expected based on all stimuli present on the trial and the US actually presented) to support further acquisition of an association to the target stimulus (CS X). As such, the Rescorla–Wagner model accounts for the response deficit following cue competition treatments such as blocking as a failure of CS X to acquire appreciable associative strength.

Several years after publication of the Rescorla–Wagner (1972) model, the acquisition deficit view of cue competition was challenged by studies showing that responding could be influenced through posttraining changes in the associative status of the competing cue. For example, Kaufman and Bolles (1981; see also Matzel, Schachtman, & Miller, 1985) questioned whether overshadowing was the result of a deficit in the acquisition of an association between the overshadowed CS and the US. Following overshadowing training (in which the presence of salient cue A during CS X–US pairings interferes with subsequent conditioned responding to X), Kaufman and Bolles extinguished the overshadowing stimulus (CS A) and observed increased responding to the overshadowed stimulus (CS X). They interpreted this result as suggesting that the normally poor behavioral control by an overshadowed stimulus results from an expression, rather than an acquisition deficit. Other findings were equally problematic for the Rescorla–Wagner model. For example, Matzel, Brown, and Miller (1987) found that massive posttraining extinction of the training context could also attenuate the US preexposure deficit, which is the retarded behavioral control that occurs when the CS–US pairings are preceded by preexposure of the US in the training context (Randich, 1981; Randich & LoLordo, 1979; Tomie, 1976). The Rescorla–Wagner model explains the US preexpo- sure deficit in a manner analogous to blocking, with the context, rather than a punctate cue, serving as the blocking stimulus. Much like recovery from overshadowing through posttraining extinction of the overshadowing stimulus, posttraining extinction of the context attenuated the response deficit that was otherwise observed following US preexposure and training. Again, these findings suggested that cue competition reflects a failure to express acquired information, rather than a failure to learn a CS–US association.

THE COMPARATOR HYPOTHESIS

The observation that cue competition deficits could be alleviated through posttraining extinction of the competing cue was a major inspiration for the comparator hypothesis (Miller & Matzel, 1988; Miller & Schachtman, 1985). The comparator hypothesis can be viewed as a descendent of Rescorla's (1968) contingency model and Gibbon and Balsam's (1981) scalar expectancy theory. Rescorla's contingency model followed from the observation that degrading the CS–US contingency by presenting the US in the absence of the CS decreased excitatory responding to the CS. Thus, Rescorla viewed the CS–US contingency as a critical determinant of whether conditioned responding would be observed. Similarly, scalar expectancy theory states that the probability of responding to a CS is based on a comparison of the rate of reinforcement in the presence of the CS with the overall rate of reinforcement in the context. When the rate of reinforcement in the presence of the CS relative to the overall rate of reinforcement in the context exceeds some threshold, excitatory responding will be observed. Notably, both Rescorla's contingency theory and Gibbon and Balsam's scalar expectancy theory are devoid of the construct of associations. Both models assume that acquired behavior arises from assessment of a direct, largely veridical representation of past experience with the CS, US, and background, and that animals compute the CS–US contingency (Rescorla, 1968) or rates of reinforcement of the CS and the background (Gibbon & Balsam, 1981) to determine conditioned responding. Notably, the domains of both of these models are limited to situations with a single CS. Thus, in their original form they were not able to account for cue competition (other than degraded contingency, which some researchers regard as a form of cue competition with the context functioning as the competing cue).

The comparator hypothesis (Miller & Schachtman, 1985) differs from Rescorla's (1968) contingency model and Gibbon and Balsam's (1981) scalar expectancy theory in that the comparator hypothesis assumes that associations are formed according to a simple associative acquisition mechanism that is directly dependent on the salience of each of the two associates and the spatiotemporal contiguity between them (e.g.,

Bush & Mostellar, 1955). That is, the comparator hypothesis, unlike the Rescorla–Wagner model, assumes that there is no competition between cues in acquiring associative strength during training. Instead, cue competition effects arise from competition at the time of testing. That is, the response deficits observed at test following blocking or overshadowing training reflect a failure to express an acquired association, rather than a deficit in associative acquisition.

According to the comparator hypothesis, at least three associations are learned during the course of Pavlovian training, all of which are presumably governed by the principles of spatiotemporal contiguity and stimulus salience (see Fig. 3.1). The first association is the traditional one between the target CS and the US (Link 1). The second association is between the target CS and the most salient stimulus (other than the target CS and US) present during training (Link 2). This stimulus we call the *comparator stimulus* for the target CS. The third association is between the comparator stimulus and the US (Link 3). In the case of simple Pavlovian conditioning in which a target CS (X) is paired with the US, the most salient stimulus present during training of the CS (other than the CS and the US) is the context, which will act as CS X's comparator stimulus. The strength of the directly activated US representation is determined by the absolute associative strength of the target CS (Link 1), whereas the strength of the US representation activated indirectly through the comparator stimulus is determined by the product of the strengths of Links 2 and 3. Given the multiplicative relation in determining the strength of the indirectly activated US representation, this representation will only be strongly activated when both Links 2 and 3 are relatively strong. Therefore, weakening either Link 2 or 3 will result in reduced strength of the indirectly activated US representation.

Essential to this performance model is the comparator process. At test, conditioned responding is assumed to reflect a comparison of the US representations directly and indirectly activated by the target CS. Excitatory behavioral control is presumed to increase (and inhibitory behavioral control to decrease) as the strength of the directly activated US representation increases relative to the indirectly activated US representation. In other words, excitatory responding to a CS is directly related to the increases signaled by the CS in the likelihood of the US from the likelihood of the US in the training context without the CS. Hence, not only is excitatory conditioned responding anticipated, but so too is the trial-spacing effect (i.e., weaker responding with massed trials; e.g., Yin, Barnet, & Miller, 1994). Conversely, as the strength of the indirectly activated US representation increases relative to the directly activated US representation, excitatory behavioral control by the CS will decrease.

The Comparator Hypothesis

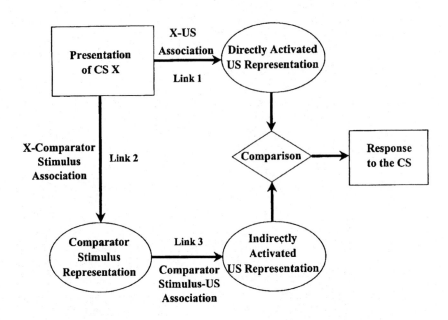

FIG. 3.1. The original comparator hypothesis (Miller & Matzel, 1988; Miller & Schachtman, 1985). CS = conditioned stimulus; US = unconditioned stimulus. Conditioned responding to CS X is directly related to the magnitude of the US representation that is directly activated by CS X and is inversely related to the magnitude of the US representation that is indirectly activated by CS X (i.e., mediated by CS X's comparator stimulus through conjoint action of the X–comparator stimulus and comparator stimulus–US associations).

According to the comparator hypothesis, associations are always of positive strength (with zero strength denoting a complete absence of association). Behavior indicative of conditioned inhibition is explained as a response phenomenon arising from the interaction of exclusively excitatory associations, rather than associations of negative strength or associations to no-US representations (e.g., Konorski, 1967; Rescorla & Wagner, 1972). Inhibitory behavior is predicted to increase with increases in the strength of the indirectly activated US representation relative to the strength of the directly activated US representation (i.e., as the product of the strengths of Links 2 and 3 increases relative to the strength of Link 1). For example, following negative contingency training, in which a CS is infrequently reinforced in the presence of an excitatory context, behavior indicative of conditioned inhibition is observed

(Schachtman, Brown, Gordon, Catterson, & Miller, 1987). This effect is presumed to be the result of a strong target CS–context association (Link 2) and a strong context–US association (Link 3) indirectly activating a robust representation of the US relative to that directly activated by the target CS. Additionally, Schachtman et al. (1987) found that reducing the strength of the indirect activated US representation, through posttraining exposure to the context, reduced inhibitory behavioral control at test. The comparator approach is entirely consistent with the passage of summation and retardation tests (Rescorla, 1969) for behavior indicative of conditioned inhibition (also see Lysle & Fowler, 1985; Savastano, Cole, Barnet, & Miller, 1999, for a review of the comparator hypothesis account of conditioned inhibition).

Notably, the nature of the comparator process has not been stated in formal mathematical terms. That is, although we have acknowledged that the indirectly activated representation of the US is a direct function of the product of the strengths of Link 2 and Link 3, we have not precisely specified a mathematical rule by which to calculate the comparison of the directly and indirectly activated US representations (i.e., whether the comparator process is sensitive to ratios, differences, or some other mathematical contrast). Although commitment to a formal rule would reduce ambiguity, extensive pilot work in our laboratory has failed to identify a single mathematical relation that could consistently account for most of the observed variance in behavior across subjects and tasks. Additionally, although subscribing to either a ratio or a difference rule would lead to a more precise model that in principle could predict quantitative differences in behavior rather than mere ordinal relations, we feel that this would distract from what we believe is centrally important, the relativity of associations in eliciting conditioned responding. Moreover, most associative models that are stated in mathematical terms (e.g., Rescorla & Wagner, 1972) ultimately fall back on ordinal predictions because they lack a precise transformation between associative strength and behavior; thus, their quantitative precision is illusionary. At this time, we see no merit in being theoretically more precise than is justified by available data. (Gibbon & Balsam [1981] made a strong case for the use of a ratio comparison rule, but their argument is based almost exclusively on data from autoshaping studies in pigeons.)

Through a single mechanism—the comparator process—the comparator hypothesis can account for many of the important phenomena in the Pavlovian literature, including various cue competition and stimulus preexposure deficits. Essentially, any treatment that enhances the strength of the indirectly activated US representation relative to the strength of the directly activated US representation is expected to reduce excitatory responding to the target CS. For example, the US preexposure deficit discussed earlier is viewed as a consequence of a strong context–US association (Link 3) established during US preexposure. During subsequent CS–US pairings, both the target CS–US (Link 1) and the target CS–context (Link 2) associations are strengthened, just as would have occurred without US preexposure. However, for subjects that received pretraining exposure to the US, there is a strong context–US association (Link 3) already in place at the start of training. Thus, according to the comparator hypothesis, the US–preexposure effect reflects an expression (rather than an acquisition) deficit. The response deficit observed as a result of CS preexposure (also called *latent inhibition;* Lubow, 1973; Lubow & Moore, 1959) is similarly explained, except that it is Link 2, the CS–context association, that is established prior to the CS–US pairings by the preexposure treatment. The profound retardation of stimulus control that arises from random presentations of a CS and the US (i.e., the so-called learned-irrelevance effect) is simply a potentiated CS preexposure effect perhaps summating with the US preexposure effect (Bonardi & Hall, 1996). Moreover, cue competition deficits such as blocking and overshadowing are assumed to arise from an analogous process, except that a punctate stimulus (the blocking or overshadowing CS), rather than the context, serves as the comparator stimulus for the target CS (presumably because punctate stimuli are ordinarily more salient and temporally contiguous to the target CS than is the background context). Thus, blocking and overshadowing treatments presumably establish strong target CS–comparator (Link 2) and comparator–US (Link 3) associations relative to conventional control conditions.

As mentioned earlier, the view that the response deficit observed as a consequence of US preexposure treatment is the result of a strong context–US association is supported by studies that have provided context extinction either prior to (Randich, 1981) or following (Matzel et al., 1987) CS–US pairings. In these studies, weakening the effective context–US association (Link 3) should reduce the strength of the indirectly activated representation of the US. Additionally, the CS preexposure effect can be attenuated by changes in physical context between CS preexposure and CS–US pairings (Channell & Hall, 1983; Honey & Hall, 1989), and through extensive posttraining extinction of the context (Grahame, Barnet, Gunther, & Miller, 1994). Again, the comparator hypothesis predicts both of these effects. Changes in context between CS preexposure and the CS–US pairings should prevent the preexposure context (which is well established as the CS's comparator stimulus due to the CS preexposure treatment) from acquiring a strong context–US association (Link 3), and posttraining extinction of the context should reduce the effective strength of Link 3 (and possibly the CS-context association [Link 2]).

Central to the comparator hypothesis is the prediction that posttraining changes in the associative strength of the companion stimulus in a cue competition procedure should influence responding to the target CS. For example, posttraining extinction (i.e., associative deflation) of the comparator stimulus should enhance responding to the target CS by reducing the strength of the indirectly activated US representation. Conversely, posttraining inflation of the associative strength of the competing cue, through additional comparator stimulus–US pairings, should reduce responding to the target CS by enhancing the strength of the indirectly activated US representation. The effects of posttraining deflation have been largely confirmed with a variety of procedures, tasks, and species. For example, Dickinson and Charnock (1985) reported alleviation of cue competition through posttraining extinction of the overshadowing stimulus in instrumental responding; Kaufman and Bolles (1981) and Matzel et al. (1985) in Pavlovian overshadowing; Blaisdell, Gunther, and Miller (1999) in Pavlovian blocking; Shanks (1985) and Wasserman and Berglan (1998) in blocking of causal judgment; Cole, Barnet, and Miller (1995) in the relative stimulus validity effect; Blaisdell, Denniston, and Miller (1999b) in the overexpectation effect; Best, Dunn, Batson, Meachum, and Nash (1985), Kasprow, Schachtman, and Miller (1987), and Lysle and Fowler (1985) in Pavlovian conditioned inhibition; Miller, Hallam, Hong, and Dufore (1991) in differential conditioned inhibition; and Friedman, Blaisdell, Escobar, and Miller (1998) and Schachtman et al. (1987) in negative contingency conditioned inhibition.[1]

The predicted decrement in conditioned responding as a result of posttraining inflation of the comparator stimulus (i.e., comparator stimulus–US pairings) has been more difficult to observe. For quite some time, we have failed to observe decrements in conditioned responding to a stimulus as a result of inflating the associative strength of its comparator stimulus (Grahame, Barnet, & Miller, 1992; Miller, Hallam, & Grahame, 1990; also see Larkin, Aitken, & Dickinson, 1998). One potential explanation for the asymmetry in the effects of posttraining

---

[1]Notably, not all investigators have observed posttraining deflation effects (e.g., Rescorla & Holland, 1977). However, across studies one critical factor that often differentiates failure from success in obtaining a posttraining deflation effect is the amount of deflation (extinction) treatment that is given. Our laboratory has repeatedly found that massively more extinction treatment is needed than is necessary simply to eliminate direct conditioned responding to the comparator stimulus (e.g., Blaisdell, Gunther, & Miller, 1999). One possible reason that posttraining deflation effects require so much extinction is that the shift in the temporal context between training and extinction produces considerable stimulus generalization decrement between the comparator stimulus perceived during training and the comparator stimulus perceived during extinction, thus requiring substantially more extinction treatment to compensate for the stimulus generalization decrement (Yin, Grahame, & Miller, 1993).

inflation and deflation is provided by the comparator hypothesis. Posttraining deflation of the associative status of the comparator stimulus operationally consists of presenting the comparator stimulus by itself. This should effectively weaken the CS–comparator stimulus association (Link 2) as well as the comparator stimulus–US association (Link 3). This should have a catastrophic consequence on the product of Links 2 and 3, thereby greatly reducing the strength of the indirectly activated US representation and enhancing responding to the CS. In contrast, posttraining inflation of the comparator stimulus–US association through additional comparator stimulus–US presentations should increase the strength of Link 3, but simultaneously reduce the effective strength of Link 2 (as a result of the comparator stimulus being presented in the absence of the target CS). Therefore, much or the entire potential enhancement of the strength of the indirectly activated US representation as a consequence of strengthening Link 3 will be offset by reductions in the strength of Link 2. Whether decreased or increased responding to the target CS will be observed will presumably depend on the relative increases and decreases in the strengths of Links 3 and 2, respectively. Although this difference in contribution of weakening Link 2 likely contributes to the relative difficulty of obtaining posttraining inflation effects, it cannot be the whole story because inflation effects are relatively easy to obtain when treatment is embedded in a sensory preconditioning procedure (Miller & Matute, 1996).

A second factor that apparently also influences the effectiveness of inflation and deflation procedures and can account for the ease of obtaining posttraining inflation effects in sensory preconditioning is *biological significance* (Denniston, Miller, & Matute, 1996; Miller & Matute, 1996). A biologically significant stimulus is one that controls (or has controlled) behavior, either inherently (e.g., food, water, painful or intense stimulation, or sex), or through association with another biologically significant event (e.g., a CS that has been paired with an inherently biologically significant stimulus). One example of associative inflation that can be modulated by the biological significance of the target CS is backward blocking. In a typical backward blocking experiment, a compound consisting of two stimuli is reinforced in Phase 1 (i.e., AX-US), followed by reinforcement of one of the elements in Phase 2 (i.e., A-US). The phenomenon consists of weaker responding to CS X than is observed if CS A is not associatively inflated in Phase 2. Thus, backward blocking is procedurally identical to forward blocking except that the phases of training are reversed. Traditionally, backward blocking has been more easily demonstrated in studies involving human participants (Chapman, 1991; Shanks, 1985; Van Hamme, 1994; D. A. Williams, Sagness, & McPhee, 1994), than in studies using nonhuman subjects (e.g., Miller et al., 1990; Schweitzer & Green, 1982). One possible explanation for the greater ease in demonstrating backward blocking in human participants relative to nonhuman subjects is the biological significance of the outcomes used during training (Denniston et al., 1996; Miller & Matute, 1996). That is, studies with humans typically use outcomes of low biological significance (e.g., fictitious allergic reactions to foods experienced by hypothetical patients), whereas studies involving nonhuman subjects typically use biologically significant outcomes (e.g., electric shock or food). Miller and Matute (1996) examined whether this difference in biological significance was responsible for the discrepant findings.

In their studies, Miller and Matute (1996) manipulated the biological significance of the competing cues in a backward blocking experiment by embedding backward blocking training within a sensory preconditioning procedure (e.g., Brogden, 1939; Rizley & Rescorla, 1972). Two neutral CSs (A and X) were compounded and followed by a third neutral stimulus that served as the outcome (O) in Phase 1 (i.e., AX-O). Then, in Phase 2, A alone was followed by the outcome (i.e., A-O). Prior to testing, O was paired with the US to provide a motivational basis for responding to CSs A and X. Miller and Matute observed reduced responding to CS X as a result of CS A having received additional pairings with the surrogate US in Phase 2, relative to control subjects lacking equivalent Phase 2 training. These results demonstrated that inflation of a target CS's comparator stimulus–US association through additional pairings of the comparator stimulus with the US (or a surrogate for the US) could result in reduced conditioned responding to the target CS at test. Therefore, the comparator hypothesis' predictions of the effects of posttraining associative inflation as well as deflation have been confirmed experimentally. However, the effectiveness of inflation appears to be limited to situations in which the target CS is of relatively low biological significance during training (i.e., does not elicit any sort of vigorous responding at any time before or during the cue competition treatment, as in sensory preconditioning training). Based on these findings, it appears that biologically significant stimuli are relatively immune to cue competition effects. That is, once a stimulus elicits a vigorous response, posttraining inflation effects are exceedingly difficult to obtain (see Blaisdell, Denniston, Savastano, & Miller, 1999; Oberling, Bristol, Matute, & Miller, 1999). However, if the stimulus does not yet control behavior (i.e., is of low biological significance), then posttraining inflation effects can be obtained. Notably, unlike the greater difficulty in obtaining inflation than deflation effects due to inflation of Link 3 also deflating Link 2, the protection afforded biologically significant cues against cue competition is a constraint that appears to delimit the domain of the comparator hypothesis.

Notably, the comparator hypothesis emphasizes the relativistic nature of behavior that is evident across many areas of experimental psychology. The cue competition, trial spacing, and contigency (Rescorla, 1968) effects discussed previously are common examples of the notion of *relativity* in Pavlovian conditioning, as is Gibbon and Balsam's (1981) scalar expectancy theory of Pavlovian conditioning. Analogous concepts are found in the matching law (Herrnstein, 1970) of instrumental conditioning, the notion of *marginal utility* in motivation, economics, and decision-making theory (e.g., Kahneman & Tversky, 1979), Fechner's Law in psychophysics (e.g., Gamer, 1954), and optimal foraging theory (e.g., Charnov, 1976; Kamil & Roitblat, 1985). Common to all of these examples is the inverse relationship between the probability or magnitude of the target response and the base rate or value of other stimuli or responses in the situation.

RETROSPECTIVE REVALUATION MODELS

Although the comparator hypothesis predicts many frequently observed phenomena such as cue competition and stimulus preexposure deficits, these phenomena are also anticipated by many acquisition-focused models (e.g., Pearce & Hall, 1980; Wagner, 1981). However, for several years the comparator hypothesis was unique in being supported by studies of posttraining deflation of companion stimuli (e.g., recovery from overshadowing through extinction of the overshadowing stimulus, and uniquely predicted the effect of posttraining inflation (e.g., backward blocking). Recently, however, acquisition-deficit models of cue competition have been proposed that account for the effects of posttraining inflation and deflation (e.g., Dickinson & Burke, 1996; Tassoni, 1995; Van Hamme & Wasserman, 1994).

Through one simple, yet clever modification of the Rescorla–Wagner model, Van Hamme and Wasserman (1994) were able to explain many of the effects that were previously inexplicable by associative acquisition models of cue competition. This change was in how nonpresented cues are treated in the Rescorla–Wagner equation. Recall that in the Rescorla–Wagner model, only cues present on a given trial are eligible for increments or decrements in associative strength as a result of that trial (see Equation 1). That is, α for a nonpresented CS was assumed to equal zero (which prevents any change in associative strength regardless of the value of the discrepancy term $[\lambda - V_{\Sigma}]$), whereas α for a presented cue was assumed to have a positive value (which allowed for increments or decrements in associative strength depending on the sign and value of the discrepancy term).

Applied to overshadowing, the original Rescorla–Wagner model predicts that extinction of the overshadowing cue should have no effect on the associative strength of the overshadowed cue because the overshadowed cue was not present on these extinction trials. According to the original Rescorla–Wagner model, the only way to increase responding to the overshadowed cue is through additional pairings of the overshadowed cue with the US (with the $[\lambda - V_\Sigma]$ parenthetical term being greater than zero). However, Van Hamme and Wasserman (1994) proposed that α for an absent cue has a negative value (on trials during which some element that previously occurred in the company of that cue is presented). The consequence of this modification is that a cue can receive increases or decreases in associative strength (depending on the sign of the discrepancy term), even when that cue is absent on a given trial. That is, further training or extinction of a competing cue can result in associative retrospective revaluation of the absent target cue.

By allowing α for an absent cue to vary between 0 and –1, the revised Rescorla–Wagner model of Van Hamme and Wasserman (1994) predicts posttraining deflation and inflation effects. For example, consider recovery from overshadowing through posttraining extinction of the overshadowing cue. According to Van Hamme and Wasserman, presentation of the overshadowing CS A in the absence of the US should result in the weakening of the CS A–US association. This is the result of CS A being assigned a positive α value, while the discrepancy term $(\lambda - V_\Sigma)$ takes on a negative value (as a result of λ equaling zero and the total associative strength of all stimuli present on the trial being greater than zero). More important, on these nonreinforced trials the overshadowed CS X is assigned a negative α value. The product of this negative α value multiplied by the negative discrepancy term results in an *increment* in associative strength to the overshadowed CS X, thereby explaining recovery from overshadowing. Similarly, Van Hamme and Wasserman readily accounted for inflation effects such as backward blocking. Following AX-US training, additional pairings of CS A with the US should decrease the associative strength to CS X because CS X takes on a negative α value and the value of the discrepancy term $(\lambda - V_\Sigma)$ is positive, resulting in a negative change in associative strength to CS X. Therefore, the revised Rescorla–Wagner model can readily account for the backward blocking deficit. However, it is challenged by the observation that posttraining inflation effects are more difficult to obtain than posttraining deflation effects (e.g., Larkin et al., 1998), an asymmetry that is anticipated by the comparator hypothesis (and the revised SOP model, see later).

Dickinson and Burke (1996) recently revised Wagner's (1981) SOP model to account for posttraining deflation and inflation effects. In

Wagner's original model, there are three states in which an event representation can exist, A1 (high activation), A2 (low activation), and I (inactive). Representations normally reside in the I state. Presentation of an event activates part or all of the event representation into A1. Presentation of an associate of the event activates part or all of the event representation into A2. The excitatory association between two stimuli increases when representations of the two stimuli are simultaneously in the A1 state. For example, pairing a CS with a US results in both the CS and US being temporarily represented in the A1 state, thereby strengthening the excitatory association between the CS and the US. Following extended training, presentation of the CS prior to the US activates a representation of the US from the I state into the A2 state. This leaves fewer US elements eligible for activation to the A1 state when the US is subsequently presented (transitions from A2 to A1 are prohibited), resulting in less new learning on each subsequent trial (i.e., a negatively accelerating acquisition curve). According to Wagner, excitatory associations are formed when two stimulus representations simultaneously occupy the A1 state, but no learning occurs when two stimulus representations simultaneously occupy the A2 state. Similarly, an inhibitory CS–US association is formed when a CS is represented in the A1 state and the US is activated to the A2 state, but no inhibitory (or excitatory) CS–US learning occurs when a CS is represented in the A2 state and the US is represented in the A1 state.

Dickinson and Burke (1996) modified Wagner's (1981) SOP model by allowing the simultaneous activation of two stimulus representations in the A2 state to result in the strengthening of an excitatory association between the stimuli, albeit less so than when the two stimuli are both in the A1 state. This activation of stimuli from the I state into the A2 state is presumably dependent on within-compound associations by which a presented stimulus activates the representation of a target stimulus into the A2 state. Moreover, Dickinson and Burke postulated a growth in the inhibitory association between a CS represented in A2 and a US represented in A1.

Now consider, for example, recovery from overshadowing as a result of extinction of the overshadowing stimulus. According to the revised SOP model, extinction of the overshadowing CS (A) following overshadowing training results in CS A being excited into the A1 state (because it is physically present), and activation of both the representations of the overshadowed stimulus (X) and the US to the A2 state (as a result of the A–X within-compound association and the A–US association, respectively). According to Dickinson and Burke (1996), because simultaneous activation of two stimulus representations in the A2 state should strengthen the excitatory association between those elements, the strength of the X–US association, and consequently conditioned responding to CS X, should increase.

Dickinson and Burke (1996) can also account for backward blocking (i.e., posttraining inflation of a companion stimulus). During the first phase of backward blocking training, a compound of CSs A and X is followed by the US. This training strengthens both the A–US and the X–US associations. Then in Phase 2, A–US pairings further increase the associative strength of CS A, but more important, they also build an inhibitory X–US association. The formation of an inhibitory X–US association occurs because the presentation of CS A activates a representation of CS X into the A2 state. With CS X represented in A2, presentation of the US places much of the US representation in the A1 state, permitting an inhibitory association to be formed between CS X and the US, thus attenuating conditioned responding to CS X at test. To summarize, Dickinson and Burke proposed that deflation of the associative status of a companion cue results in the strengthening of the excitatory target CS–US association, whereas inflation of a companion cue results in the formation of an inhibitory target CS–US association. (Notably, with select parameters Dickinson and Burke also accounted for instances in which posttraining inflation effects are not observed, and can even predict increases in the X–US excitatory associative strength following posttraining A–US pairings [depending on the learning rate parameter for A2–A1 learning and decay rates from A1 to A2]. This great flexibility as a function of parameters is a potential weakness of the Dickinson and Burke model, in that many of its predictions are too ambiguous to allow for empirical tests of the model.)

As a result of the revisions of the Rescorla–Wagner (1972) model and Wagner's (1981) SOP model, these new retrospective revaluation models can account for much of the data that were previously uniquely predicted by the comparator hypothesis. That is, the models of Van Hamme and Wasserman (1994) and Dickinson and Burke (1996) allow acquisition-deficit models of cue competition to explain the effects of posttraining associative inflation and deflation of a target CS's companion (comparator) stimulus on responding to the target CS. Thus, although the comparator hypothesis posits that the reduced conditioned responding to a CS following cue competition training reflects an expression rather than an acquisition deficit (as supported by the potential for recovery of responding through posttraining changes in the status of the competing cue), the ability of the retrospective revaluation models to explain the same effects through an acquisition-deficit mechanism questions the veracity of the expression-deficit accounts of cue competition. What is needed, then, are experiments that differentiate between these two families of models.

BEYOND THE ORIGINAL COMPARATOR HYPOTHESIS

Blaisdell, Bristol, Gunther, and Miller (1998) performed an initial series of experiments aimed at differentiating the retrospective revaluation models of Dickinson and Burke (1996) and Van Hamme and Wasserman (1994) from the comparator hypothesis. In these experiments, Blaisdell, Bristol, et al. investigated whether the combined effects of CS preexposure treatment and overshadowing treatment would summate or counteract each other. According to the comparator hypothesis, CS preexposure establishes a strong CS–context association (Link 2; see Fig. 3.1) that enhances the strength of the indirectly activated US representation at test (Grahame et al., 1994). Therefore, the comparator hypothesis accounts for the CS preexposure effect as a deficit in expressing, rather than acquiring a CS–US association.

In contrast, both the original (Wagner, 1981) and revised (Dickinson & Burke, 1996) versions of SOP view the effect of CS preexposure as a deficit in associative acquisition. That is, presentation of the CS in the training context during preexposure treatment builds a context–CS association. During subsequent CS–US training, the context has already activated a representation of the CS into the A2 state, leaving fewer CS element representations eligible for activation to the A1 state when the CS and US are paired, thereby attenuating acquisition of the CS–US association.

As previously described, the overshadowing deficit is explained by the comparator hypothesis as an expression deficit arising from strong associations between the overshadowed and the overshadowing CSs (Link 2) and between the overshadowing CS and the US (Link 3). SOP (both the original and revised versions) explains overshadowing as a failure to acquire a strong overshadowed CS–US association because the overshadowing CS, due to its greater saliency, formed an association to the US on the first few AX-US trials, which then allows A to retrieve much of the representation of the US into the A2 state, making it unavailable to move into the A1 state when it is presented immediately after AX presentations.

However, consider what would happen if CS preexposure were followed by overshadowing treatment. Intuitively, one might expect the two treatments, which separately result in response deficits, to summate when presented successively. SOP predicts that when preexposure to CS X is followed by AX-US overshadowing treatment, the context will retrieve the representation of X into the A2 state and A will retrieve the US into the A2 state; hence, even fewer X and US elements are available for activation to the A1 state, resulting in a greater acquisition deficit. That is, according to the original SOP model, the detrimental effects of CS preexposure treatment and overshadowing treatment should summate. However, Dickinson and Burke's (1996) revised SOP model potentially predicts some facilitation of responding relative to either treatment alone as a result of simultaneous activation of the representations of CS X and the US in the A2 state, a condition that results in the strengthening of the X–US association. Thus, the revised SOP predicts that the combined treatments of CS preexposure and overshadowing should be less than the sum of the two effects, and quite possibly less than either effect alone, but importantly, Dickinson and Burke failed to predict complete prevention of both the CS preexposure effect and the overshadowing effect. This follows from Dickinson and Burke's assumption that learning as a result of simultaneous activation of representations in the A1 state is more effective than learning as a result of simultaneous activation of representations in the A2 state. (Neither Rescorla and Wagner [1972] nor Van Hamme and Wasserman [1994] accounted for the basic CS preexposure effect, much less the interaction of latent inhibition treatment and overshadowing treatment; consequently, here we focus on Dickinson and Burke and the comparator hypothesis.)

Although the comparator hypothesis can explain either the CS preexposure effect or the overshadowing effect, it us unable to account for the possibility of the two effects counteracting each other. This follows from the comparator hypothesis predicting either the CS preexposure effect or the overshadowing effect depending on which stimulus serves as the comparator stimulus for the target CS X (the context or the overshadowing stimulus A, respectively). As a result of preexposure treatment (many X–context pairings), the context is well established as CS X's comparator stimulus, and the subsequent overshadowing treatment (few AX–US pairings) is insufficient for CS A to displace the context as the comparator stimulus for CS X. Thus, given the greater CS preexposure experience, relative to the amount of overshadowing training, the comparator hypothesis would predict a strong CS preexposure effect.

However, Blaisdell, Bristol, et al. (1998) suggested an extension of the comparator hypothesis that could account for the potentially counteractive effects of CS preexposure treatment and overshadowing. Their extension of the comparator hypothesis proposed that the effectiveness of a comparator stimulus in modulating responding to its target stimulus is determined by higher order comparator stimuli. By this account, the presence of the highly salient CS A on the AX–US trials interferes with (or, in a sense, overshadows) what would otherwise be an effective association between the context and the US, resulting in an attenuation of the CS preexposure effect.[2] In the absence of overshadow-

---

[2]Effective associative strength differs from absolute associative strength in that the degree of activation, relative to the absolute associative strength, can be attenuated by other (comparator) stimuli.

ing treatment, a stronger effective context–US association is formed, thereby increasing the strength of the indirectly activated US representation at test, which should result in the response deficit normally observed following CS preexposure treatment alone. Conversely, had CS preexposure treatment not been provided, the formation of strong effective X–A and A–US associations would be expected to increase the strength of the indirectly activated US representation at test, resulting in the response deficit normally observed following overshadowing treatment alone. Providing both treatments should establish the context as the comparator stimulus (i.e., a strong effective X–context association), but the effective context–US association would be weakened by the presence of the overshadowing stimulus, A, thereby preventing strong indirect activation of the US at test, and, as a result, generating stronger conditioned responding relative to that observed following either treatment alone.

To test these predictions, Blaisdell, Bristol, et al. (1998) provided thirsty rats with CS preexposure treatment consisting of either preexposure to the target CS X, or a control CS Y. Then in Phase 2, subjects received either overshadowing treatment with AX (i.e., AX–US with A more salient than X), or elemental training of X (i.e., X–US), with X, Y, and A being highly discriminable audiovisual cues and the US being a mild foot shock. The design of this experiment is depicted in Table 3.1. Groups OV and LI received overshadowing or CS preexposure treatments alone, respectively, whereas Group LI + OV received both CS preexposure and overshadowing treatments. Group Acq received preexposure to an irrelevant stimulus followed by X–US pairings to provide a baseline level of conditioned responding, reduction from

TABLE 3.1   Design Summary From Blaisdell, Bristol, Gunther, and Miller (1998)—Experiment 1

Group	Phase 1	Phase 2	Test
LI + OV	X	AX–US	X?
OV	Y	AX–US	X?
LI	X	X–US	X?
Acq	Y	X–US	X?

Note. LI and OV = latent inhibition (i.e., CS preexposure) treatment and overshadowing treatment, respectively; Acq = an acquisition control group; CSs X and Y were counterbalanced auditory cues; CS A was a bright flashing light intended to be more salient than CSs X and Y. All CSs were 10 sec in duration. The US was a brief, mild foot shock.

which would be evidence of CS preexposure or overshadowing. (Control subjects not described here indicated that overshadowing in this preparation was not due to stimulus generalization decrement.) The conditioned suppression data for CS X are depicted in Fig. 3.2. Groups OV and LI both showed weaker conditioned responding than Group Acq at test, separately demonstrating the overshadowing and CS preexposure deficits, respectively. However, conditioned responding in Group LI + OV did not differ from that observed in Group Acq, demonstrating that the combined effects of CS preexposure and overshadowing counteract the effect of either treatment alone. Surprisingly, administration of both treatments appears to have completely eliminated the two deficits.

These results challenge all current models of acquired behavior including the original comparator hypothesis, Van Hamme and Wasserman's (1994) revision of the Rescorla–Wagner model, and Dickinson and Burke's (1996) revision of SOP. However, Blaisdell, Bristol, et al.'s (1998) proposed extension of the comparator hypothesis can account for their results. According to this modification of the comparator hypothesis, the joint effects of CS preexposure and overshadowing should counteract each other as a result of the context being established as the primary comparator stimulus and the overshadowing stimulus (CS A) preventing the context–US association from being expressed, thereby preventing strong activation of the indirect US representation. As predicted, omitting either of these treatments resulted in overshadowing (Group OV) or the CS preexposure effect (Group LI).

THE EXTENDED COMPARATOR HYPOTHESIS

The original comparator hypothesis (Miller & Matzel, 1988; Miller & Schachtman, 1985) posited that the sole comparator stimulus for a CS was that stimulus (other than the US) with the strongest within-compound association with the CS. However, Blaisdell, Bristol, et al. (1998) discussed the potential role played by higher order comparator stimuli in determining the effectiveness of a primary (first-order) comparator stimulus as one means of accounting for the interaction of CS preexposure and overshadowing treatment. Here, as the *extended comparator hypothesis*, we elaborate the process through which stimuli compete for primary comparator stimulus status. Figure 3.3 depicts a generic representation of the extended comparator hypothesis. Whereas the original comparator hypothesis (see Fig. 3.1) has long stated that Links 2 and 3 modulate responding based on the strength of Link 1, the extended comparator hypothesis posits that (higher order) comparator processes also modulate the effectiveness of Links 2 and 3.

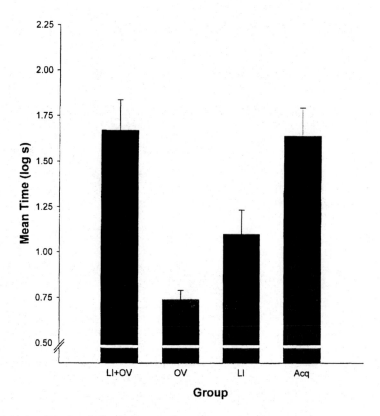

FIG. 3.2. Results of Blaisdell, Bristol, et al.'s (1998) Experiment 1. See Table 3.1 for group treatments. Bars represent mean times (log s) to complete 5 cumulative sec of drinking in the presence of the target CS. All groups were tested for conditioned suppression to CS X. Higher scores are indicative of stronger stimulus control. Brackets represent standard errors of the mean. From "Overshadowing and Latent Inhibition Counteract Each Other: Support for the Comparator Hypothesis," by A. P. Blaisdell, A. S. Bristol, L. M. Gunther, & R. R. Miller, 1998, *Journal of Experimental Psychology: Animal Behavior Processes, 24,* p. 339. Copyright 1998 by the American Psychological Association. Adapted with permission.

That is, the value of Link 2 no longer mirrors the absolute strength of the target CS–comparator stimulus association. Rather, the target CS–comparator stimulus association (now called Link 2.1) is modulated by the comparator stimulus for Link 2.1, which is any and all other stimuli with a strong within-compound association to the target CS excluding the immediate first-order comparator stimulus and the US. This stimulus is hereafter referred to as the second-order comparator stimulus for Link 2. To the extent that Links 2.2 and 2.3 are weak relative to the

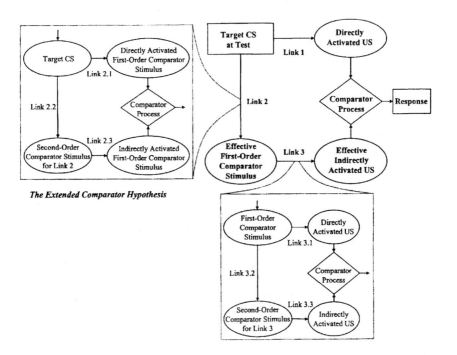

FIG. 3.3. The extended comparator hypothesis for one first-order comparator stimulus. The model is to be applied simultaneously to all potential first-order comparator stimuli. Comparator processes within dashed rectangles represent comparator processes for Link 2 and Link 3. Ovals depict stimulus representations; solid rectangles depict physical events; diamonds represent comparator process.

strength of Link 2.1 (as would be the case in a typical overshadowing experiment in which the context is likely to serve as the second-order comparator stimulus for Link 2), the activation of the effective first-order comparator stimulus will not be attenuated. However, any treatment that produces strong Links 2.2 and 2.3 should attenuate Link 2.1's activation of the first-order comparator stimulus (i.e., the consequence of the original Link 2).

A similar comparator process modulates the effectiveness of the comparator stimulus–US association (now called Link 3.1), with the second-order comparator stimulus being any and all other stimuli with a strong within-compound association to the first-order comparator stimulus (excluding the target CS and the US). Alternatively stated, Link 2.1 is effective only to the extent that the target CS predicts an increase in the likelihood of the occurrence of the first-order comparator stimulus over that in the absence of the target CS; and Link 3.1 is effective only to the extent that the first-order comparator stimulus predicts an increase in the likelihood of the occurrence of the UCS relative to the second-order comparator stimulus. (Presumably higher-order comparator stimuli [i.e., beyond second order] exist, but their contribution in modulating responding to the target stimulus would be expected to be reduced through a dampening factor that increases with the order of the comparator process.)

Importantly, the extended comparator hypothesis, unlike the original comparator hypothesis, does not posit that the comparator stimulus for a target CS will be the stimulus with the strongest within-compound association with the target CS. Instead, the extended comparator hypothesis merely applies the comparator process to all relevant associations. The typical result is that a single stimulus functions as the predominant first-order comparator stimulus. This is a consequence of stimuli with strong within-compound associations with the target CS not only being effective first-order comparator stimuli in their own right, but simultaneously being effective second-order comparator stimuli that down modulate the effectiveness of other stimuli as first-order comparator stimuli to the target CS.

The extended comparator hypothesis can fully explain the counteractive effects of CS preexposure and overshadowing treatment (Blaisdell, Bristol, et al., 1998). Figures 3.4a and 3.4b depict this account. Following CS preexposure and overshadowing treatments, responding to CS X at test will be determined by the strength of Link 1 relative to the product of the effective strengths of Links 2 and 3, which are each modulated by their own (higher order) comparator processes. For example, the effective activated representation of each potential first-order comparator stimulus (the output of Link 2) will be determined by the strength of its Link 2.1 relative to the product of the strengths of its Links 2.2 and 2.3. Both the context (Fig. 3.4a) and CS A (Fig. 3.4b) simultaneously serve as first-order comparator stimuli with their potential to modulate responding to the target CS determined by higher order comparator stimuli. The context is a strong candidate first-order comparator stimulus for CS X (Fig. 3.4a), as a result of the animals having received extensive target CS X preexposures in that context, which is represented in Fig. 3.4a as a much stronger Link 2a.1 (in boldface) than would exist without preexposure to CS X. The second-order comparator stimuli for this CS X–context link would be all stimuli possessing within-compound associations to the context (excluding the target CS and the US). In the present case, CS A would serve as the second-order comparator stimulus as a result of the X–A pairings during overshadowing training. The comparator process for Link 2a should strongly ac-

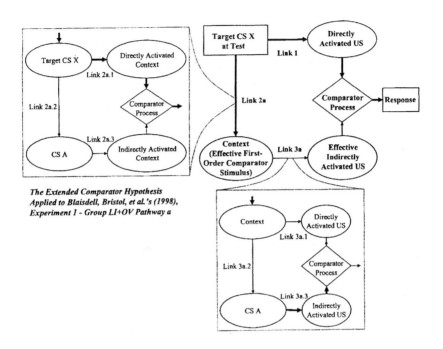

FIG. 3.4a. The extended comparator hypothesis applied to the results of Blaisdell, Bristol, et al.'s (1998) Experiment 1. This figure depicts Pathway a, in which the context serves as a first-order comparator stimulus. The target CS is CS X; the first-order comparator stimulus is the context; the second-order comparator stimulus is CS A. Ovals depict stimulus representations. Importantly, the processes depicted in this figure and Fig. 3.4b are assumed to occur concurrently. Bold arrows represent strong associations; solid, nonbold arrows represent relatively weak associations.

tivate the context as a first-order comparator stimulus. This is the result of the effective strength of Link 2a.1 being large relative to the product of the strengths of Links 2a.2 and 2a.3. The product of these links will be relatively weak despite a strong X–A association (Link 2a.2) because the A–context association (Link 2a.3) is only of moderate strength, given the amount of time spent in the context in the absence of A (e.g., between trials and during CS preexposure).

The effectiveness of Fig. 3.4a's Link 3a in indirectly activating a representation of the US will be determined by Link 3a's comparator process in which CS A serves as a second-order comparator stimulus for Link 3 be-

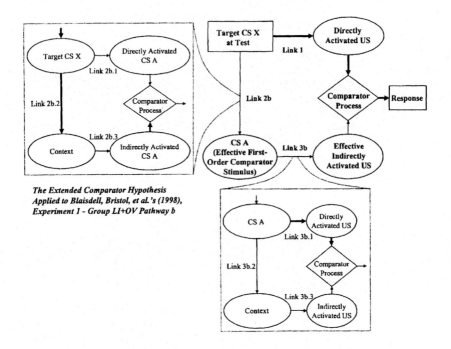

FIG. 3.4b. The extended comparator hypothesis applied to the results of Blaisdell, Bristol, et al.'s (1998) Experiment 1. This figure depicts Pathway b, in which CS A serves as a first-order comparator stimulus. The target CS is CS X; the first-order comparator stimulus is CS A; the second-order comparator stimulus is the context. Ovals depict stimulus representations. Importantly, the processes depicted in this figure and Fig. 3.4a are assumed to occur concurrently. Bold arrows represent strong associations; solid, nonbold arrows represent relatively weak associations.

cause CS A has a within-compound association to the context (CS X and the US are excluded as second-order comparator stimuli). In this case, the product of Links 3a.2 and 3a.3 is expected to be relatively large. This follows from the CS A–US association (Link 3a.3) being strong due to CS A being a highly salient stimulus and having been present during all reinforced trials, and the context–A association (Link 3a.2) being of moderate strength. Therefore, the product of the moderate strength Link 3a.2 and the strong Link 3a.3 will be strong relative to Link 3a.1, which itself is presumably weak as a result of considerable exposure to the context in the absence of the US. This results in a weak effective indirectly activated US representation. In summary, for the context as a first-order comparator stimulus for CS X, presentation of CS X will activate a relatively weak indirectly activated representation of the US as a result of CS preexposure and overshadowing treatments.

In addition to the context, CS A can also serve as a potential first-order comparator stimulus for CS X. As illustrated in Fig. 3.4b, the potential of CS A to modulate responding to the target CS will be determined by CS A's higher order comparator stimuli. Analysis of the comparator process for Link 2b reveals that the context, the most salient stimulus excluding CSs X, A, and the US, will serve as a second-order comparator stimulus for the target CS X. The product of the strong CS X–context association (Link 2b.2) and the moderately strong context–A association (Link 2b.3) is expected to be relatively large, resulting in a weak effective representation of CS A as a first-order comparator stimulus. The effectiveness of Link 3b in indirectly activating the US representation will be determined by its own comparator process, in which the context serves as the second-order comparator stimulus. The product of the strengths of the moderate A–context association (Link 3b.2) and the moderate context–US association (Link 3b.3) will be small relative to the strong A–US association (Link 3b.1), resulting in a relatively strong effective Link 3b. However, the product of a weak Link 2b with a strong Link 3b will be small, allowing for a weak indirectly activated US representation. Because the US representation indirectly activated by presentation of CS X that is mediated by either the context (Fig. 3.4a) or CS A (Fig. 3.4b) is weak, and the X–US association is strong (Link 1), robust responding to CS X is anticipated. Thus, the strong X–context association not only facilitates the context's serving as a first-order comparator stimulus for CS X (Fig. 3.4a), but the context also acts as a second-order comparator stimulus for CS A's serving as a first-order comparator stimulus (Fig. 3.4b). In this latter role, the strong X–context association acts to disable CS A from serving as a critical first-order comparator stimulus for CS X. (If there had been appreciably more AX–US pairings, presumably CS A would have begun to displace the context as the primary first-order comparator stimulus for CS X. This would occur as a consequence of the increasing X–A association both strengthening CS A's role as a first-order comparator stimulus and its down modulating the context's role as a first-order comparator stimulus).

In the preceding account of the interaction between CS preexposure and overshadowing, one of the factors responsible for the strong responding to CS X at test was the relatively weak context–US association (Link 3a.1; Fig. 3.4a) compared to the CS A–US association (Link 3a.3). In other words, CS A effectively overshadowed the context's potential to activate a representation of the US. Had the context–US association (Link 3a.1) been stronger or the context–A (Link 3a.2) or A–US (Link

3a.3) associations weaker, then the indirectly activated representation of the US would have been enhanced, resulting in a reduction of conditioned responding to CS X at test relative to simple acquisition groups. Blaisdell, Bristol, et al.'s (1998) Experiment 3 provided empirical support for this prediction of the extended comparator hypothesis. They inflated the associative value of the context by presenting unsignaled USs after completion of the CS preexposure and overshadowing treatments.[3] At test, they observed reduced conditioned responding to X in the group that received the dual treatment followed by associative inflation of the context. This finding is anticipated as a result of strengthening Link 3a.1 (in Fig. 3.4a) relative to the product of Links 3a.2 and 3a.3. Therefore, the now enhanced effective Link 3a led to a stronger indirectly activated US representation relative to the US representation directly activated by the target CS X, circumstances that are predicted by the extended comparator hypothesis to produce a loss of excitatory conditioned responding to CS X.

ASSESSMENT OF THE EXTENDED COMPARATOR HYPOTHESIS

The expression-deficit explanation of cue competition provided by the comparator hypothesis has recently been challenged by B. A. Williams (1996; also see Rauhut, McPhee, & Ayres, 1999). In his study, Williams examined the potential of a blocked stimulus (X) to subsequently serve as a blocking stimulus for a novel CS (Y). Following blocking treatment (A–US trials in Phase 1 and AX–US trials in Phase 2), Williams presented subjects with XY–US pairings in Phase 3 and then examined responding to CS Y. According to acquisition-deficit models of cue competition (e.g., Rescorla & Wagner, 1972), the blocked stimulus X, which presumably has acquired little associative strength, should be unable to block associative acquisition to CS Y. In contrast, the comparator hypothesis posits that an X–US association was formed during Phase 2, but that strong X–A and A–US associations prevented expression of the X–US association. Therefore, in Phase 3, the X–US association, although latent in terms of direct response elicitation, was well learned. Consequently, Williams reasoned that according to the comparator hypothesis, CS X should have blocked expression of the Y–US association during testing. In contrast, Williams found no evidence of blocking of CS Y when CS X

---

[3]As in the studies by Miller and Matute (1996), Blaisdell, Bristol, et al. (1998) used a sensory preconditioning procedure to enhance the effectiveness of the inflation treatment. Therefore, their inflation treatment actually consisted of unsignaled presentations of the surrogate for the US, which was subsequently paired with a foot shock US.

had been blocked, relative to a group in which CS A had not been paired with the US in Phase 1. That is, pairing the blocked CS X with the target CS Y did not prevent CS Y from acquiring behavioral control.

These findings are problematic for the original comparator hypothesis if the comparator process is assumed to modulate response generation rather than the activation of event representations (i.e., retrieval). However, they are entirely consistent with the extended comparator hypothesis. Fig. 3.5 depicts the extended comparator hypothesis explanation of B. A. Williams's (1996) results. According to the extended comparator hypothesis, conditioned responding to CS Y (the target stimulus) at test will depend not only on the strength of Y's first-order comparator stimulus (CS X), but also on the relative strength of Y's second-order comparator stimuli (CS A and the context). CS X functions as the primary first-order comparator stimulus because it was the most salient stimulus (other than the US) present during training of CS Y (see Fig. 3.5). (The context is also a potential first-order comparator stimulus for CS Y, but the Y–X and X–context associations would conjointly down modulate the first-order comparator stimulus role of the context.) In Link 2, the context, as the primary second-order comparator stimulus for CS Y (Link 2.2) fails to down modulate the potential of CS Y to activate a representation of CS X, resulting in strong activation of CS X as a first-order comparator stimulus for CS Y. (CS A fails to function as an effective comparator stimulus for CS Y because CSs A and Y were never paired. Furthermore, CS Y and the US are precluded because they are the associates being assessed). However, the effective indirectly activated representation of the US will be weak, despite a relatively strong Link 2, because Link 3 is relatively weak. The weak effective Link 3 is the result of strong Links 3.2 (the X–A association) and 3.3 (the A–US association) relative to the strength of link 3a (the X–US association). (Note the difference in second-order comparator stimuli in Links 2 and 3. This difference arises from the context being the most salient stimulus present during training of CS Y [excluding CS X and the US], whereas CS A is the most salient stimulus present during training of CS X [excluding CS Y and the US].) In other words, the strong conditioned responding to CS Y at test is the result of CS X failing to modulate conditioned responding to CS Y as a result of CS A having been established as a better predictor of the US than CS X. Alternatively stated, CS A in a sense blocked the potential of CS X to function as an effective first-order comparator stimulus for CS Y.

The extended comparator hypothesis uniquely predicts that associative deflation of CS A following training such as that provided by B. A. Williams (1996) should both increase responding to CS X and decrease responding to CS Y. That is, extinction of CS A should produce not only retrospective unblocking of responding to CS X, but also retrospective blocking of responding to CS Y. This prediction follows from the comparator process for Link 3 (see Fig. 3.5). Posttraining deflation of the A–US association should not influence Link 2 for CS Y because there was no Y–A association (Link 2.2) formed during initial training. However, deflation of the A–US association should effectively weaken Link 3.3 (and possibly Link 3.2; see Rescorla & Freberg, 1978) relative to Link 3.1, resulting in a stronger effective indirectly activated representation of the US. Therefore, extinction of CS A should increase the effectiveness of Link 3, enhancing the indirectly activated representation of the US relative to the US representation directly activated by CS X (Link 1), thereby reducing excitatory behavioral control by CS Y at test.

In contrast, the models of Van Hamme and Wasserman (1994) and Dickinson and Burke (1996) predict that extinction of CS A either should have no effect on responding to CS Y (due to the lack of an A–Y

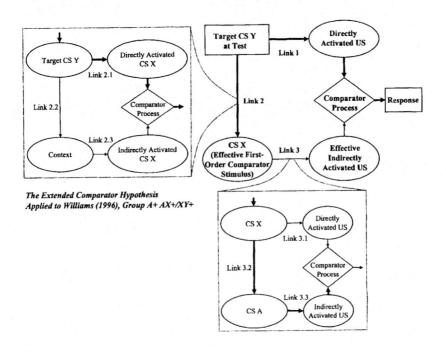

The Extended Comparator Hypothesis
Applied to Williams (1996), Group A+ AX+/XY+

FIG. 3.5. The extended comparator hypothesis applied to the results of B. A. Williams (1996). The target CS is CS Y; the first-order comparator stimulus is CS X; the second-order comparator stimulus for Link 2 is the context; the second-order comparator stimulus for Link 3 is CS A.

within-compound association; see Wasserman & Berglan, 1998) or should increase conditioned responding to CS Y (if one assumes that CS A activates a representation of CS X, which in turn activates a representation of CS Y). If nonreinforced presentations of CS A were assumed to activate a representation of CS Y (mediated by CS X, a possibility not directly addressed by Van Hamme and Wasserman), then Van Hamme and Wasserman would predict that the negative discrepancy term ($\lambda - V_\Sigma$) of the Rescorla–Wagner model multiplied by the negative α of the absent CS Y should increase the associative strength of CS Y, resulting in greater conditioned responding to CS Y at test. On the other hand, Dickinson and Burke predicted that presentation of CS A in the absence of the US will activate both CS X and the US into the A2 state, thereby strengthening the X–US excitatory association. If presentation of CS A can also activate a representation of CS Y into the A2 state (an issue not directly addressed by Dickinson & Burke), this too should strengthen, rather than weaken, responding to CS Y at test. Without this added assumption of second-order activation, both models predict no change in responding to CS Y. Therefore, only the extended comparator hypothesis predicts decreased responding to CS Y as a result of posttraining deflation of CS A.

To test this prediction, Denniston, Savastano, Blaisdell, and Miller (1999) provided rats with overshadowing treatment followed by blocking treatment, with the overshadowed CS serving as the blocking stimulus. The question was whether blocking would prove sensitive to posttraining associative deflation of the overshadowing CS (A; see Table 3.2). In Phase 1, the OV groups (i.e., Groups OV-A and OV-Cxt) received a compound of CSs A and X followed by the outcome (i.e., AX–O), whereas control subjects (Groups Con-A and Con-Cxt) received X paired with the outcome in the absence of A (i.e., X–O).[4] In Phase 2, all

---

[4]Two aspects of the experimental design warrant comment. First, we used a sensory preconditioning procedure because prior studies (e.g., Denniston et al., 1996; Miller & Matute, 1996) have found that posttraining inflation procedures are less effective in first-order conditioning than in sensory preconditioning. Although this experiment used posttraining deflation, the rationale from the inflation studies is the same because we were attempting to decrease responding to the target CS (Y). That is, once a stimulus already controls conditioned responding (as in backward blocking, or in this study without deflation of CS A), it is difficult to reduce responding to that stimulus through changes in the effective value of its comparator stimulus. Second, we used an overshadowing rather than a blocking procedure to degrade the effective associative status of CS X because recovery from blocking through posttraining deflation of the blocking stimulus requires substantially more extinction than does recovery from overshadowing (Blaisdell, Gunther, et al., 1999). Presumably, the same results would be observed had we used a blocking rather than an overshadowing procedure and administered more extinction treatment of CS A.

TABLE 3.2 Design Summary From Denniston, Savastano, Blaisdell, and Miller (1999)—Experiment 2

Group	Phase 1	Phase 2	Phase 3	Phase 4	Test
OV-A	AX-O	XY-O	A-	O-US	Y?
OV-Cxt	AX-O	XY-O	Context	O-US	Y?
Con-A	X-O	XY-O	A-	O-US	Y?
Con-Cxt	X-O	XY-O	Context	O-US	Y?

Note. CS A was a tone; CS X was white noise; CS Y was a click train; O (the outcome) was a buzz stimulus. CS A was more intense than CSs X and Y, which were of equal salience. CSs A, X, and Y were 10 sec in duration; O was 5 sec in duration; the US was a brief, mild foot shock.

subjects received blocking training consisting of pairings of the overshadowed stimulus X and a novel stimulus Y paired with the outcome (i.e., XY–O). In Phase 3, subjects in the A groups (i.e., OV-A and Con-A) received massive posttraining associative deflation of CS A (i.e., extinction of A), whereas subjects in the Cxt groups received equivalent exposure to the experimental context. Finally in Phase 4, subjects received the second stage of sensory preconditioning training, during which stimulus O was paired with the US to provide a motivational basis for responding to Y. As discussed earlier, in the framework of the comparator hypothesis, extinction of CS A should result in retrospective blocking of CS Y. At test, the ability of CS Y to disrupt baseline-drinking behavior was assessed. As illustrated in Fig. 3.6, posttraining deflation of CS A resulted in decreased conditioned responding to CS Y in Group OV-A.[5]

Let us summarize the nature of the prediction that differentiates between the extended comparator hypothesis and the acquisition-focused

---

[5]In a companion experiment by Denniston et al. (1999), rats received training on two separate sets of CSs (i.e., AX–O and BY–O) followed by extinction of either overshadowing stimulus A or B. A and B were counterbalanced, and X and Y were counterbalanced. At test, conditioned responding to the overshadowed CS X was low (indicative of overshadowing) in subjects that received extinction of B, whereas responding to X was strong (indicative of recovery from overshadowing) in subjects that received extinction of A. This companion experiment demonstrates that (a) the procedures used in the overshadowing–blocking study described earlier were appropriate for producing overshadowing; (b) the recovery from overshadowing was stimulus specific; and (c) the loss of responding to Y in the overshadowing–blocking study was not the result of generalized extinction from A to Y.

models capable of anticipating the phenomenon of retrospective revaluation. All of these models agree in their predictions concerning the consequences of posttraining revaluation of a first-order comparator stimulus. That is, there should be an inverse effect on responding to the target CS. However, the extended comparator hypothesis is unique among these three models in predicting that posttraining revaluation of a second-order comparator stimulus will have a direct effect on responding to the target CS, as opposed to no effect or an inverse effect. That is, associative deflation or inflation of a second-order comparator stimulus should, respectively, retrospectively enhance or diminish the comparator effectiveness of the first-order comparator stimulus, which in turn should, respectively, diminish or enhance the response potential of the target CS. Thus, revaluation of first-order and second-order comparator stimuli should have opposite effects on responding to the target CS.

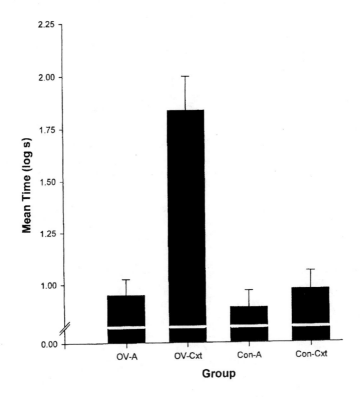

FIG. 3.6. Results of Denniston et al.'s (1999) Experiment 2. See Table 3.2 for group treatments. Bars represent mean times (log s) to complete 5 cumulative sec of drinking in the presence of target CS Y. Higher scores are indicative of stronger stimulus control. Brackets represent standard errors of the means.

As a further test of the extended comparator hypothesis, Savastano, Escobar, and Miller (1999) examined the CS preexposure deficit. One important characteristic of the CS preexposure effect is that the response deficit normally observed following CS preexposure can be alleviated if the target CS is preexposed in the presence of another stimulus (Honey & Hall, 1989; Lubow, Schnur, & Rifkin, 1976; Lubow, Wagner, & Weiner, 1982; Matzel, Schachtman, & Miller, 1988). This attenuation of the CS preexposure deficit has been conventionally explained through perceptual processes (e.g., Honey & Hall, 1989), specifically, stimulus generalization decrement. That is, following preexposure to two CSs presented serially or in simultaneous compound (i.e., AX), X–US training results in less of a deficit in responding to the CS than does preexposure to CS X alone because X is perceived as being perceptually different than the preexposed compound AX. This generalization decrement from AX to X presumably results in less of a preexposure effect than if CS X had been preexposed alone.

The extended comparator hypothesis, however, provides an alternative account in which preexposure to the compound AX establishes CS A, rather than the context (as would be the case following preexposure to CS X alone) as the primary comparator stimulus for CS X. Recall that according to the comparator hypothesis, the standard CS preexposure deficit is the result of the strong X–context association facilitating the indirectly activated US representation, relative to subjects that did not receive CS preexposure. However, compound preexposure establishes CS A as the primary comparator stimulus for CS X (Link 2). However, because CS A has never been paired with the US, the A–US association (Link 3) is nonexistent. Thus, although CS X strongly activates a representation of CS A as its first-order comparator stimulus (strong Link 2), CS A fails to activate a strong (indirect) representation of the US, thereby allowing for expression of the X–US association at test.

To test this account of the compound preexposure effect, Savastano, Escobar, and Miller (1999) examined the effects of massive nonreinforced exposure to CS A following both compound preexposure and training. In their Experiment 3, rats received preexposure to both an AX compound and to an element (either Y or B; see Table 3.3). Then in Phase 2, subjects received both CS X and CS Y paired separately with the outcome (O). In Phase 3, subjects in the A groups received massive nonreinforced presentations of CS A, whereas subjects in the None groups received equivalent exposure to the context (of sufficiently brief duration to prevent appreciable changes in the comparator value of the context, on the basis of preliminary studies). Prior to testing, all subjects received O–US pairings in Phase 4 to provide a motivational basis for responding. At test, the potentials of CSs X and Y to disrupt baseline levels of bar pressing were assessed. Based on the

TABLE 3.3   Design Summary From Savastano, Escobar, and Miller (1999)—Experiment 3

Group	Phase 1	Phase 2	Phase 3	Phase 4	Test 1	Test 2
CP/LI-A	AX- / Y-	X-O / Y-O	A-	O-US	X?	Y?
CP/LI-None	AX- / Y-	X-O / Y-O	Context	O-US	X?	Y?
CP/AQ-A	AX- / B-	X-O / Y-O	A-	O-US	X?	Y?
CP/AQ-None	AX- / B-	X-O / Y-O	Context	O-US	X?	Y?

Note. CS A was a buzzer; CSs X, Y, and B were either a click train, white noise, or tone, counterbalanced; O (outcome) was a 5-sec flashing light that served as a surrogate for the US. Trials on either side of the slash were interspersed within a session. CS A was 65 sec in duration; CSs X, Y, and B were 60 sec in duration; US was a brief, mild foot shock. Nonreinforcement is denoted by -.

extended comparator hypothesis, Savastano et al. expected to observe the compound preexposure effect (an attenuation of the CS preexposure effect) in Group CP/LI-None when subjects were tested for conditioned responding to CS X and the standard CS preexposure effect when subjects were tested for conditioned responding to CS Y. The results of their Experiment 3 are depicted in Fig. 3.7 (lower numbers represent more conditioned responding). At test, responding to CS X in Group CP/LI-None was stronger than that observed to CS Y, demonstrating the compound preexposure effect when the target CS was preexposed in the presence of another stimulus (A), relative to conventional CS-alone preexposure. More important, posttraining extinction of CS A in Group CP/LI-A attenuated the compound preexposure effect. That is, conditioned responding to CS X was reduced as a result of massive posttraining extinction (deflation) of CS A. Moreover, this attenuation of responding was specific to the target CS; extinction of CS A had no effect on responding to CS X in Group CP/AQ-A, presumably because the context rather than A was the critical comparator stimulus for CS Y.

The extended comparator hypothesis uniquely predicts that posttraining extinction of CS A will result in a retrospective CS preexposure effect with respect to CS X. That is, extinguishing CS X's companion stimulus A should result in a reinstatement of the CS preexposure effect. This prediction is based on the following reasoning. Because CS A had never been paired directly with the US during training, the A–US association was of zero strength, and consequently ex-

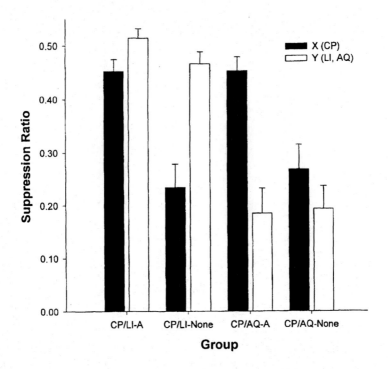

FIG. 3.7.   Results of Savastano, Escobar, and Miller's (1999) Experiment 3. See Table 3.3 for group treatments. Bars represent Kamin suppression ratios for CSs X and Y (0.5 = no suppression; 0 = total suppression; thus, lower numbers indicate more stimulus control). Open bars represent conditioned suppression to CS X; closed bars represent conditioned suppression to CS Y. Brackets represent standard errors of the mean.

tinction of A could not further weaken Link 3. Instead, sufficient presentation of CS A alone should effectively extinguish the X–A within-compound association. This should diminish CS A's own effectiveness as a first-order comparator as well as its potential to down modulate the effectiveness of the context as a first-order comparator stimulus. As a consequence, the relatively excitatory context now serving as CS X's primary comparator stimulus should down modulate responding to CS X. (Holland [1983] and Hall [1996] proposed models that predict this outcome, but their models fail to account for many of the other data presented in this chapter, e.g., Denniston et al., 1999, Experiment 2.)

The extended version of the comparator hypothesis is again necessary to fully appreciate the competition between CS A and the context in serving as CS X's comparator stimulus. Both the context and CS A can potentially serve as first-order comparator stimuli for CS X, but their contributions in modulating responding to CS X will each in turn be modulated by the other. First, let us consider the context's role as a first-order comparator stimulus for CS X. Presumably, without extinction of CS A, CS A will down modulate the potential of the context to function as an effective first-order comparator, thereby attenuating the CS preexposure deficit. In Fig. 3.8, preexposure of CSs A and X in the training context results in a strong X-context association (Link 2.1). However, following extinction of CS A in Phase 3, the X–A association (Link 2.2) will be weakened. Therefore, despite a strong A–context association (Link 2.3), the weak X–A association (Link 2.2) will result in the product of Links 2.2 and 2.3 being relatively weak compared to the strength of Link 2.1. That is, the indirectly activated representation of

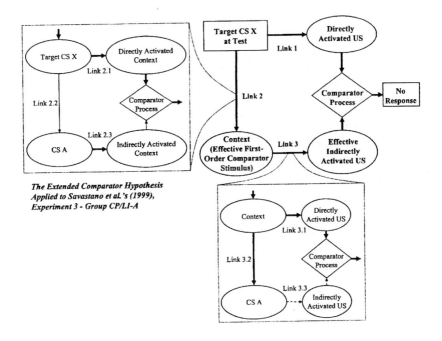

The Extended Comparator Hypothesis Applied to Savastano et al.'s (1999), Experiment 3 - Group CP/LI-A

FIG. 3.8.   The extended comparator hypothesis applied to Savastano, Escobar, and Miller (1999) Experiment 3. The target CS is CS X; the first-order comparator stimulus is the context; the second-order comparator stimulus is CS A. Ovals depict stimulus representations. Bold arrows represent strong associations; solid nonbold arrows represent moderately strong associations; dashed arrows represent weak associations.

the context as a first-order comparator stimulus will be substantially weaker than the strength of the directly activated representation of the context as a first-order comparator stimulus, resulting in a strong effective Link 2 of the context as X's first-order comparator stimulus (output of Link 2). As a consequence of the comparator process for Link 3, in which CS A serves as the second-order comparator stimulus for CS X, the weak Link 3.3, despite a strong Link 3.2, results in the strength of the indirectly activated representation of the US being weak relative to the strength of the representation of the US activated directly by the context (Link 3.1). In summary, CS A will fail to down modulate the effectiveness of the first-order comparator stimulus (the context), thereby resulting in diminished conditioned responding to CS X at test, constituting a retrospective CS preexposure effect.

As previously discussed, CS A and the context can simultaneously serve as a first-order comparator stimulus for CS X. However, the effectiveness of CS A in this role is reduced as a result of both the massive posttraining extinction of CS A and down modulation by the context. That is, strong X–context and context–A associations down modulate the effectiveness of CS A as a first-order comparator stimulus. Thus, despite both CS A and the context serving as first-order comparator stimuli for the target CS X, they potentially can down modulate each other's role as a comparator stimulus. This interaction is a central feature of the extended comparator hypothesis.

To summarize the results of Savastano, Escobar, and Miller's (1999) Experiment 3, massive posttraining extinction of CS A enhanced the potential of the context to serve as a first-order comparator stimulus for CS X and simultaneously enhanced the potential of the context to down modulate the effectiveness of CS A in serving as a first-order comparator stimulus for CS X. Therefore, the potential first-order comparator stimulus with the strongest association to the target CS not only asserts itself, but it turns off competing comparator stimuli. This explains why multiple potential first-order comparator stimuli do not appear to simply summate the individual products of their Links 2 and 3. That is, each link for each potential first-order comparator stimulus is subject to down modulation by other comparator stimuli. Importantly, we see here again that with the extended comparator hypothesis, we need no longer postulate that the first-order comparator stimulus for a target CS will be the stimulus with the strongest within-compound association to that CS. Instead all stimuli with within-compound associations to the target CS will serve as first-order comparator stimuli for the target CS. However, not all such stimuli will have an influence on responding to the target CS (i.e., they will not all be effective first-order comparator stimuli). The extended comparator stimulus provides a mechanism for this to happen as a by-product of Links 2 and 3 themselves being subject to comparator processes.

Van Hamme and Wasserman (1994) could not account for the results of Savastano, Escobar, and Miller (1999) because their model fails to explain both the basic CS preexposure and the compound preexposure effects. Dickinson and Burke (1996) had difficulty explaining the effect of posttraining extinction of CS A because CS A was never paired with the outcome. Consequently, in their framework, posttraining nonreinforced presentations of A should have activated a representation of X (to State A2) but not the outcome (which should have remained in State I). Thus, according to Dickinson and Burke, presentation of A alone should have had no effect on behavioral control by CS X. Alternatively, if one were to extend the Dickinson and Burke model by positing that A had a first-order association to X and therefore a second-order association to the outcome, presentation of CS A alone in Phase 3 might be expected to activate representations of both CS X and the US into State A2. According to Dickinson and Burke, this should have increased rather than decreased the excitatory value of CS X. Thus, the extended comparator hypothesis and the two retrospective revaluation models generate highly divergent predictions in this case, and the findings of Savastano et al. are consistent only with the predictions of the extended comparator hypothesis.

One of the major successes of the Rescorla–Wagner model (1972) was its a priori prediction of the phenomenon of superconditioning. *Superconditioning* refers to the enhancement in conditioned responding to a CS (X) as a consequence of that CS having been paired with the US in the presence of a conditioned inhibitor (i.e., AX–US, where A was trained as a conditioned inhibitor), relative to subjects that received X–US pairings in the presence of a neutral stimulus B (i.e., BX–US). However, Navarro, Hallam, Matzel, and Miller (1989) demonstrated that the increased responding to CS X as a result of having been trained in the presence of the inhibitor A was actually the result of a prevention of overshadowing of X by A, rather than enhanced conditioning of CS X. That is, conditioned responding to CS X following AX–US pairings was no greater than responding by subjects that merely received X–US pairings.

Navarro et al. (1989) interpreted their results as being consistent with the Pearce and Hall (1980) model, in that the prior inhibitory training of CS A results in decreased processing of CS A, which in turn reduces the potential of CS A to overshadow CS X during subsequent AX–US pairings. The extended comparator hypothesis provides an alternative explanation of the prevention of overshadowing following superconditioning treatment. According to the extended comparator hypothesis, the explicitly unpaired conditioned inhibition treatment used to establish CS A as a conditioned inhibitor produces a strong context–US association. This strong context–US association can then down modulate the comparator status of CS A. That is, the context serves as CS A's comparator stimulus (second-order to CS X) and allows the X–US association to be expressed at the time of testing.

An additional empirical finding that is readily accommodated by the extended comparator hypothesis is the prevention of the degraded contingency effect by using a cue (other than the CS) to signal the added outcomes (e.g., Durlach, 1983). The original comparator hypothesis explains the degraded contingency effect as arising from the context serving as the target CS's comparator stimulus and the added unsignaled outcomes making the context more excitatory. The signaling effect can be readily explained by the extended comparator hypothesis in terms of the signal for the added outcomes serving as the comparator stimulus for the context (i.e., the signal is the second-order comparator stimulus for the target CS), thereby undermining the effectiveness of the context as the first-order comparator stimulus for X. Notably, most acquisition-focused models can also explain both of these effects in terms of blocking of the CS–US association by the context–US association, and the signal–US association overshadowing the context–US association. However, the comparator hypothesis account of the two effects is unique in focusing on whether the added outcomes inflate the target CS's comparator stimulus.

THE ROLE OF TEMPORAL VARIABLES
IN THE COMPARATOR PROCESS

This chapter has largely focused on how a change in the associative strength of comparator stimuli affects responding to the target CS at test. Both the extended and the original comparator hypotheses reasonably assume that the effectiveness of an indirectly activated US representation in modulating responding to a target CS is a direct function of the similarity of the directly and indirectly activated US representations in all attributes (except strength of activation, which is what is compared). This assumption follows from the comparator process serving to down modulate responding to a CS when the CS fails to predict a change in the US relative to the US expected in the absence of the CS. Thus, variables other than the associative strengths of comparator stimuli can also influence responding to the target CS. For example, Blaisdell, Denniston, and Miller (1997; also see Bakal, Johnson, & Rescorla, 1974; but see B. A. Williams, 1994) found that blocking could be prevented with qualitative changes in US in Phase 2. In their study, rats were exposed to CS A–foot shock pairings in Phase 1, followed by either CS AX–foot shock pairings or CS AX–ice water dunking in Phase

2, with the aversiveness of the foot shock and dunking equated. They observed that blocking was reduced in subjects that received a shift in the qualitative features of the US. Based on these results, Blaisdell et al. (1997) concluded that maximal cue competition would be observed when, above and beyond the role of magnitude of the indirectly activated US representation, the comparator stimulus conveys the same information about the US as does the target CS.

Another potential attribute of the CS–US association that could be the same or different for the target CS and the competing cue is their temporal relation to the US. That is, the greatest cue competition should be observed when both the target CS and the competing cue predict qualitatively similar USs at the same points in time. (See Matzel, Held, & Miller, 1988; Miller & Barnet, 1993; Savastano & Miller, 1998, for reviews of evidence indicating that Pavlovian associations include information concerning the temporal relation between the CS and the US.) Differences in any attribute between the comparator stimulus–US association and the CS–US association, including the temporal relation, should reduce cue competition. To test this prediction, Blaisdell, Denniston, and Miller (1998) investigated the influence of temporal variables on the magnitude of the overshadowing effect (also see Barnet, Grahame, & Miller, 1993, for a demonstration of the role of temporal variables in blocking). In conventional overshadowing studies, the overshadowing stimulus (CS A) and the overshadowed stimulus (CS X) share common onsets and terminations (i.e., both CSs predict the US at the same temporal location). Given Blaisdell et al.'s (1997) finding that blocking was maximal when the blocking and blocked stimuli conveyed similar qualitative information about the US, Blaisdell, Denniston, and Miller (1998) questioned whether overshadowing would be maximal when the two CSs shared the same temporal relation with the US. In their experiments, the overshadowing stimulus was trained as either a forward, simultaneous, or backward CS, and the overshadowed stimulus was trained with respect to the US as either a forward, simultaneous, or backward CS. Blaisdell, Denniston, et al., using a second-order conditioning procedure to obtain sensitivity to simultaneous and backward associations, observed maximal overshadowing when the overshadowing and overshadowed stimulus shared the same temporal relation to the US. When the overshadowing and overshadowed stimuli possessed different temporal relations to the US, overshadowing was reduced (see Table 3.4).

In a related study, Blaisdell, Denniston, and Miller (1999a) investigated whether overshadowing could be alleviated through posttraining shifts in the overshadowing stimulus–US temporal relation. Their rationale was that if overshadowing could be reversed through deflation of the overshadowing CS–US association, then

TABLE 3.4   The Role of Temporal Variables in Overshadowing—
Blaisdell, Denniston, and Miller (1998): Conditioned
Suppression (M log s) to the Overshadowed Stimulus
as a Function of the Overshadowing CS–US and the
Overshadowed CS–US Temporal Relations

Overshadowing CS–US Relation	Overshadowed CS–US Relation		
	Forward	Simultaneous	Backward
Forward	**0.92**	1.73	1.70
Simultaneous	1.59	**1.00**	1.70
Backward	1.70	1.52	**0.86**

Note. Suppression scores reflect the mean time to complete 5 cumulative sec of drinking
(log s) in the presence of the overshadowed stimulus; thus, lower scores are indicative of
overshadowing. Scores indicative of overshadowing are in bold.

posttraining shifts in the overshadowing CS–US temporal relation
should also reduce cue competition as a result of the competing cues no
longer conveying the same information about the US. To test this prediction, Blaisdell et al. provided overshadowing training with the two
competing cues sharing the same temporal relation to the US in Phase 1
(i.e., AX-^{5}→US, in which A and X were followed by the US 5 sec following termination of CSs A and X, see Table 3.5). Then in Phase 2, the temporal relation between the overshadowing stimulus and the US was
either maintained or shifted (i.e., CS A was either followed by the US 5
sec following termination of A or immediately following termination of
A). More specifically (see Table 3.5), in Phase 1 control subjects in the
Acq condition (i.e., Groups Acq-Same and Acq-Diff) received elemental
training of CS X (the overshadowed CS) with the US, which was presented 5 sec following termination of CS X (i.e. X-^{5}→US), whereas subjects in the OV and Update conditions (i.e., Groups OV-Same, OV-Diff,
Update-Same, and Update-Diff) received overshadowing training with
the US presented 5 sec following termination of CSs A and X (i.e.,
AX-^{5}→US). In Phase 2, subjects in the Same groups (i.e., Groups
Acq-Same, OV-Same, and Update-Same) received either A–US or B–US
pairings with the US presented 5 sec following termination of CS A or B,
whereas subjects in the Diff conditions (i.e., Groups Acq-Diff, OV-Diff,
and Update-Diff) received either A–US or B–US pairings with the UCS
presented immediately following termination of CS A or B. At test, con-

ditioned response suppression to CS X was assessed by presenting these test stimuli to the subjects while they were drinking. Greater times to complete 5 cumulative sec of drinking in the presence of these stimuli was taken as evidence of reduced overshadowing (i.e., stronger conditioned responding).

Blaisdell et al. (1999a) expected to observe strong conditioned responding in the Acq and GenDec control groups, and weak conditioned responding to X in the OV groups, indicative of overshadowing. The two critical groups were Groups Update-Same and Update-Diff. Weak conditioned responding was expected in Group Update-Same because the further training of CS A with the US was anticipated to result in no change in the US expectations provided by either CS A or X. That is, cue competition was expected to be strong as a result of CS A and CS X activating strong representations of the US at the same temporal location. However, changing the A–US temporal relation in Group Update-Diff through a posttraining shift in the CS A–US temporal relation was expected to produce recovery from overshadowing by establishing the overshadowing and overshadowed CSs as predictors for the US at different temporal locations.

TABLE 3.5 Design Summary From Blaisdell, Denniston, and Miller (1999)—Experiment 1

Group	Phase 1	Phase 2	Test
Acq-Same	$X\text{-}^5{\to}US$	$A\text{-}^5{\to}US$	X?
Acq-Diff	$X\text{-}^5{\to}US$	$A\text{-}^0{\to}US$	X?
OV-Same	$AX\text{-}^5{\to}US$	$B\text{-}^5{\to}US$	X?
OV-Diff	$AX\text{-}^5{\to}US$	$B\text{-}^0{\to}US$	X?
Update-Same	$AX\text{-}^5{\to}US$	$A\text{-}^5{\to}US$	X?
Update-Diff	$AX\text{-}^5{\to}US$	$A\text{-}^0{\to}US$	X?

Note. Acq = acquisition control group; OV = overshadowing treatment (with updating of an irrelevant stimulus CS–US temporal relation in Phase 2); Update = overshadowing treatment with updating of the overshadowing CS–US temporal relation in Phase 2; Same = the temporal relation in Phase 2 was the same as that in Phase 1; Diff = the temporal relation in Phase 2 was different from that in Phase 1. CSs A and B were a tone and a noise, counterbalanced; CS X was a click train. CSs A and B were of equal intensity and more salient than CS X. All CSs were 10 sec in duration; the US was a brief, mild foot shock. Additional groups not presented here demonstrated that the present overshadowing was not due to stimulus generalization decrement between training and test.

The results of Blaisdell et al.'s (1999a) Experiment 1 are depicted in Fig. 3.9. At test, reduced behavioral control by CS X was evident in Groups OV-Same and OV-Diff, relative to Groups Acq-Same and Acq-Diff, demonstrating the basic overshadowing effect and that the further training of (irrelevant) CS B in the OV groups had no effect on responding to CS X. Of greatest interest, overshadowing was attenuated in Group Update-Diff, for which the A–US temporal relation was changed between Phases 1 and 2, but not in Group Update-Same, for which the CS A–US temporal relation was maintained between Phases 1 and 2.[6] This suggests that the comparator process is sensitive to temporal expectancies as well as associative strengths. That is, any change in the indirectly activated US representation, either through changes in the comparator stimulus associative strength, its qualitative attributes, or its temporal relation to the US can reduce the effectiveness of that stimulus in serving as a comparator stimulus.

The comparator hypothesis prediction of Blaisdell et al.'s (1999a) results can be contrasted with those generated by the acquisition-focused models of Dickinson and Burke (1996) and Van Hamme and Wasserman (1994). According to both of these latter models, reinforced presentations of CS A should result in activation of the representation of the overshadowed stimulus prior to presentation of the US, which should result in decreased conditioned responding to the target CS X, rather than the observed recovered responding, following changes in the A–US temporal relation. Alternatively, one might view a posttraining shift to a longer A–US interval as a nonreinforced presentation of CS A if the new interval was sufficiently long. This assumption leads to a prediction of increased responding to CS X given a posttraining shift to a longer A–US interval and decreased responding to CS X given a posttraining shift to a shorter A–US interval, which is still contrary to the increase in responding to CS X that was observed with both posttraining manipulations.

In a related series of experiments, Blaisdell et al. (1999b) examined whether the overexpectation effect (Rescorla, 1970) is the result of an associative acquisition or expression deficit. The *overexpectation effect* refers to the decreased conditioned responding to a CS following compound conditioning of two CSs with a US, when the CSs had been previously trained as independent signals for the US (i.e., A–US / X–US pairings in

---

[6]In Blaisdell et al.'s (1999a) Experiment 2, they used delay conditioning in Phase 1 and either delay or trace conditioning in Phase 2 (i.e., they reversed the temporal intervals throughout the experiment relative to Experiment 1) and obtained the same pattern of results. Thus, a second-order conditioning explanation, in which the reduced CS A–US interval in Group Update-Diff strengthened the CS A–US association, which in turn mediated stronger responding to CS X, is not tenable.

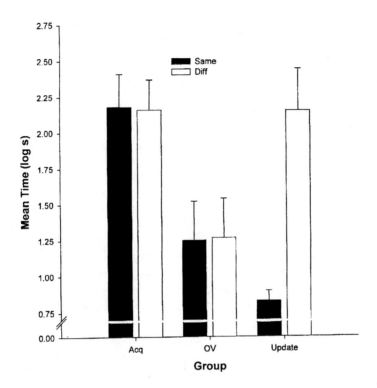

FIG. 3.9. Results of Blaisdell et al.'s (1999a) Experiment 1. See Table 3.5 for group treatments. Bars represent mean times (log s) to complete 5 cumulative sec of drinking in the presence of the target CS. Higher scores are indicative of stronger stimulus control. Brackets represent standard errors of the means. From "Posttraining Shifts of the Overshadowing Stimulus–Unconditioned Stimulus Interval Alleviates the Overshadowing Deficit," by A. P. Blaisdell, J. C. Denniston, & R. R. Miller, 1999, *Journal of Experimental Psychology: Animal Behavior Processes, 25,* p. 22. Copyright 1999 by the American Psychological Association. Adapted with permission.

Phase 1 and AX–US pairings in Phase 2). Acquisition models of associative learning (e.g., Rescorla & Wagner, 1972) describe the reduced responding to CS X following compound training of CSs A and X as a consequence of the anticipated US being greater than the actual US presented on the compound trials. As a consequence of this overexpectation of the US relative to the US that is delivered, the associative strengths of CSs A and X are reduced until the expected US (based on CS A and CS X) matches the intensity of the US actually presented.

In contrast, the comparator hypothesis predicts that with sufficient compound training, CS A should replace the context as the most effective comparator stimulus for CS X, and the strong X–A and A–US associations (Links 2 and 3 of Fig. 3.1) should activate a strong (indirect) representation of the US when CS X is presented at test, conditions that should reduce conditioned responding to CS X. Using the same strategy as in the Blaisdell et al. (1999a) overshadowing experiments, Blaisdell et al. (1999b) investigated whether changing the temporal relation between the CS A and the US (after Phase 2 of overexpectation treatment) would attenuate the overexpectation effect. Following separate delay conditioning of CSs A and X and subsequent delay conditioning of the AX compound, Blaisdell et al. (1999b) provided either additional delay or trace conditioning of CS A. Their results indicated that additional training of CS A with a different temporal relation than had been used during overexpectation training attenuated the response deficit normally observed as a result of overexpectation training. (As in the overshadowing studies, a parallel experiment was conducted that provided trace overexpectation training followed by either trace or delay CS A–US training. That experiment replicated the results of the experiment described earlier). Thus, the overexpectation effect appears to be similar in nature to other cue competition effects (e.g., overshadowing) and seemingly reflects an expression deficit that is readily accounted for by the comparator hypothesis.

SOME WEAKNESSES

As might be expected, the extended comparator hypothesis fails to address some rather important phenomena in the learning literature. Here we briefly review these issues.

Extinction

The model has no compelling means of accounting for experimental extinction. Within the comparator framework, one might view extinction as analogous to latent inhibition and attribute it to the extinction treatment increasing the strength of the target CS–comparator stimulus (context) association (Link 2). We could leave extinction to be explained by the Bush and Mostellar (1955) mechanism for decrementing associations, also found in the models of Rescorla and Wagner (1972) and Van Hamme and Wasserman (1994). However, there is considerable evidence contrary to this view of extinction, including spontaneous recovery (Pavlov, 1927), external disinhibition, and renewal. Hence, we prefer to account for extinction through the kind of competition for retrieval between multiple memories that has been proposed by Bouton (e.g., 1993) to account for renewal and related phenomena.

Trial Order

The comparator hypothesis assumes that trial order is not relevant, whereas at least in some situations it clearly influences behavior. For example, forward blocking is usually stronger than backward blocking (i.e., less responding to CS X is observed when A–US pairings are followed by AX–US pairings than when AX–US pairings are followed by A–US pairings; e.g., Chapman, 1991). Such an effect is outside the domain of the comparator hypothesis and an explanation for it must found elsewhere. One potential explanation for this trial-order effect can be cast in terms of the partial protection against cue competition that is provided by the target cue being biologically significant (which we previously discussed in this chapter).

Mediated Learning

Under select conditions, posttraining deflation of a comparator stimulus decreases responding to the target CS (mediated extinction) and posttraining inflation of a comparator stimulus increases responding to the target CS (e.g., sensory preconditioning). In recent years, these effects have been investigated by Hall (1996) and Holland (1983). Neither the comparator hypothesis nor the acquisition-focused retrospective revaluation models of Dickinson and Burke (1996) and Van Hamme and Wasserman (1994) can account for these observations. Closely related is the observation by Dwyer, Mackintosh, and Boakes (1998) that simultaneous presentation of CSs A and B following pairings of A–X and B–US facilitates responding to CS X. Although this sort of finding is problematic to the comparator hypothesis and explicable in the frameworks of either Dickinson and Burke or Van Hamme and Wasserman, we anticipate that it will also be explicable in terms of whatever mechanism is ultimately identified to explain the mediated learning reported by Holland and Hall, which is problematic to all contemporary models of acquired behavior.

SUMMARY

Since the 1970s, interest in the mechanisms underlying cue competition has flourished. One of the primary reasons for the initial surge of interest was the highly influential Rescorla–Wagner (1972) model, which provided a simple and clear mechanism for describing cue competition effects and further generated several counterintuitive predictions, some of which have been confirmed and others of which have been refuted (see Miller et al., 1995). Central to the Rescorla–Wagner model is the assumption that cue competition effects reflect an associative acquisition deficit, in which the reduced responding to a CS following cue competition treatment is the result of the CS failing to acquire an association to the UCS as a consequence of a more predictive (blocking) or more salient (overshadowing) cue having been present during training of the target CS. This view, that cue competition is the result of a learning deficit, was widely accepted until studies revealed that cue competition effects could be reversed through posttraining extinction of the competing cue (e.g., Kaufman & Bolles, 1981).

Studies of the effects of posttraining associative deflation of the competing cue called into question the acquisition-deficit explanation put forth by the Rescorla–Wagner (1972) model as well as other acquisition-focused models of acquired behavior. Such studies led to the formulation of the comparator hypothesis (Miller & Matzel, 1988; Miller & Schachtman, 1985). According to the comparator hypothesis, conditioned responding to a CS is determined not only by the absolute CS–US associative strength, but also by the associative strength to the US of other (comparator) stimuli present during training of the target CS. When the associative strength of the other stimuli present during training of the target CS is great, the comparator hypothesis predicts that excitatory conditioned responding to the target CS will be attenuated despite no difference in the absolute strength of the target CS–US association. This prediction has been largely confirmed through studies of posttraining deflation of the competing cue (e.g., Best et al., 1985; Blaisdell et al., 1999b; Blaisdell, Gunther, et al., 1999; Cole et al., 1995; Dickinson & Charnock, 1985; Grahame et al., 1994; Kasprow et al., 1987; Kaufman & Bolles, 1981; Matzel et al., 1985; Miller et al., 1991; Shanks, 1985; Wasserman & Berglan, 1998).

More difficult to obtain have been the effects of posttraining inflation of the competing cue. That is, the comparator hypothesis predicts that additional training of the competing cue with the US should further reduce responding to the target CS (e.g., backward blocking). However, recent studies by Miller and colleagues (e.g., Denniston et al., 1996; Miller & Matute, 1996; Savastano, Escobar, and Miller, 1999; also see Wasserman & Berglan, 1998) have confirmed the comparator hypothesis predicted effect of posttraining inflation. However, an important qualifier is needed. Once a CS has come to control robust responding it appears relatively immune to inflation manipulations. However, if a procedure is used in which the inflation manipulation is implemented without the CS ever having come to control behavior (as is possible with a sensory preconditioning procedure), the anticipated effect of posttraining associative inflation of the CS's comparator stimulus can be obtained. Alternatively stated, if the CS acquires biological significance prior to associative inflation of its comparator stimulus, or is inherently biologically significant, attempts to reduce responding to the target CS through further pairings of the comparator cue with the US will have relatively little effect on responding to the target CS (Denniston et al., 1996). Although this effect of biological significance is not directly predicted by the comparator hypothesis, the finding that inflation effects can be obtained under select circumstances is supportive of the mechanism posited by the comparator hypothesis.

Recently, the comparator hypothesis has been challenged by modified associative acquisition-deficit models of cue competition (e.g., Dickinson & Burke, 1996; Van Hamme & Wasserman, 1994). These models have provided an alternative explanation for the inflation and deflation effects that were heretofore uniquely predicted by the comparator hypothesis. Van Hamme and Wasserman (1994) modified the Rescorla–Wagner (1972) model by positing that nonpresented cues take on a negative α value, which results in increments in the associative strength of the CS when its comparator stimulus is extinguished. Similarly, Dickinson and Burke (1996) modified Wagner's (1981) SOP model, allowing for the development of excitatory associations between representations of stimuli simultaneously active in the A2 state.

In response to these modified associative acquisition models as well as new data inexplicable in terms of the original comparator hypothesis (e.g., Blaisdell, Bristol, et al., 1998; B. A. Williams, 1996), we here presented an extension of the comparator hypothesis. This elaboration of the original comparator hypothesis has led to several counterintuitive predictions that have pitted the predictions of the extended comparator hypothesis against those of the retrospective revaluation models of Dickinson and Burke (1996) and Van Hamme and Wasserman (1994; e.g., Blaisdell, Bristol, et al., 1998). According to the extended comparator hypothesis, responding to a target CS is not only determined by the associative strength of the target stimulus, as modulated by the strength of the target CS–comparator stimulus association and comparator stimulus–US association, but is additionally determined by higher order comparator stimuli that modulate the effectiveness of these two latter associations. That is, the effectiveness of a comparator stimulus in modulating responding to a target CS is modulated by its own comparator stimuli. In other words, just as strengthening the US representation indirectly activated through the first-order comparator stimulus attenuates conditioned responding to the target CS, strengthening the representation of the first-order comparator stimulus indirectly activated through the second-order comparator stimulus attenuates the effectiveness of the first-order comparator stimulus in modulating responding to the target CS. Thus, deflation and inflation of a CS's second-order comparator stimulus will result in decreased and increased responding, respectively, to the target CS.

The predictions of the extended comparator hypothesis can be directly contrasted with those of the retrospective revaluation models of cue competition (i.e., Dickinson & Burke, 1996; Van Hamme & Wasserman, 1994). Both Dickinson and Burke (1996) and Van Hamme and Wasserman (1994) predicted that posttraining deflation of a second-order comparator stimulus either will have no effect on responding to the target CS or will increase responding to the target CS. Conversely, the extended comparator hypothesis predicts that the change in behavior to the target CS will normally mirror the change in responding to the second-order comparator stimulus following either posttraining inflation or deflation treatment. For example, following overshadowing training (i.e., AX–US) in Phase 1 and blocking training in Phase 2 (XY–US), both Dickinson and Burke and Van Hamme and Wasserman predicted that extinction of CS A should result in increased conditioned responding to CS X (as does the extended comparator hypothesis). However, both of the acquisition-focused models either fail to predict any change in conditioned responding to CS Y following extinction of CS A (as a result of the absence of an A–Y within-compound association) or predict increases in responding to both CSs X and Y (provided that CS A activates the representation of CS X, which in turn activates the representation of CS Y). Denniston et al.'s (1999) results support the prediction of the extended comparator hypothesis that massive extinction of CS A should decrease conditioned responding to CS Y.

In summary, the challenge of the retrospective revaluation models has stimulated an extension of the comparator hypothesis as well as several new techniques for pitting the predictions of the associative acquisition-focused models of retrospective revaluation against the extended comparator hypothesis. We hope that the extended comparator hypothesis will be as successful as the associative acquisition-focused models have proven in inspiring new research and theories.

ACKNOWLEDGMENTS

Support for this research was provided by National Institute of Mental Health Grant 33881. We would like to thank Francisco Arcediano, Aaron Blaisdell, Daniel Burger, Raymond Chang, Martha Escobar, and Philippe Oberling for their critical contributions to the development of this model and for critiquing an earlier version of this chapter.

REFERENCES

Bakal, C. W., Johnson, R. D., & Rescorla, R. A. (1974). The effect of change in US quality on the blocking effect. *Pavlovian Journal of Biological Science, 9*, 97–103.

Barnet, R. C., Grahame, N. J., & Miller, R. R. (1993). Temporal encoding as a determinant of blocking. *Journal of Experimental Psychology: Animal Behavior Processes, 19*, 327–341.

Best, M. R., Dunn, D. P., Batson, J. D., Meachum, C. L., & Nash, S. M. (1985). Extinguishing conditioned inhibition in flavour aversion learning: Effects of repeated testing and extinction of the excitatory element. *Quarterly Journal of Experimental Psychology, 37B*, 359–378.

Blaisdell, A. P., Bristol, A. S., Gunther, L. M., & Miller, R. R. (1998). Overshadowing and latent inhibition counteract each other: Support for the comparator hypothesis. *Journal of Experimental Psychology: Animal Behavior Processes, 24*, 335–351.

Blaisdell, A. P., Denniston, J. C., & Miller, R. R. (1997). Unblocking with qualitative change of unconditioned stimulus. *Learning and Motivation, 28*, 268–279.

Blaisdell, A. P., Denniston, J. C., & Miller, R. R. (1998). Temporal encoding as a determinant of overshadowing. *Journal of Experimental Psychology: Animal Behavior Processes, 24*, 72–83.

Blaisdell, A. P., Denniston, J. C., & Miller, R. R. (1999a). Posttraining shifts of the overshadowing stimulus–unconditioned stimulus interval alleviates the overshadowing deficit. *Journal of Experimental Psychology: Animal Behavior Processes, 25*, 18–27.

Blaisdell, A. P., Denniston, J. C., & Miller, R. R. (1999b). *Recovery from the overexpectation effect: Contrasting acquisition and performance models of retrospective revaluation effects.* Manuscript submitted for publication.

Blaisdell, A. P., Denniston, J. C., Savastano, H. I., & Miller, R. R. (1999). *Counterconditioning of an overshadowed cue attenuates overshadowing.* Manuscript submitted for publication.

Blaisdell, A. P., Gunther, L. M., & Miller, R. R. (1999). Recovery from blocking through deflation of the block stimulus. *Animal Learning & Behavior, 27*, 63–76.

Bonardi, C., & Hall, G. (1996). Learned irrelevance: No more than the sum of CS and US preexposure effects? *Journal of Experimental Psychology: Animal Behavior Processes, 22*, 183–191.

Bouton, M. E. (1993). Context, time, and memory retrieval in the interference paradigms of Pavlovian learning. *Psychological Bulletin, 114*, 80–99.

Brogden, W. J. (1939). Sensory preconditioning. *Journal of Experimental Psychology, 25*, 323–332.

Bush, R. R., & Mosteller, F. (1955). *Stochastic models for learning.* New York: Wiley.

Channell, S., & Hall, G. (1983). Contextual effects in latent inhibition with an appetitive conditioning procedure. *Animal Learning & Behavior, 11*, 67–74.

Chapman, G. B. (1991). Trial order affects cue interaction in contingency judgment. *Journal of Experimental Psychology: Learning, Memory, and Cognition, 17*, 837–854.

Charnov, E. L. (1976). Optimal foraging: The marginal value theorem. *Theoretical Population Biology, 9*, 129–136.

Cole, R. P., Barnet, R. C., & Miller, R. R. (1995). Effect of relative stimulus validity: Learning or performance deficit? *Journal of Experimental Psychology: Animal Behavior Processes, 21*, 293–303.

Denniston, J. C., Miller, R. R., & Matute, H. (1996). Biological significance as a determinant of cue competition. *Psychological Science, 7*, 325–331.

Denniston, J. C., Savastano, H. I., Blaisdell, A. P., & Miller, R. R. (1999). *Cue competition as a performance deficit.* Manuscript submitted for publication.

Dickinson, A., & Burke, J. (1996). Within-compound associations mediate the retrospective revaluation of causality judgements. *Quarterly Journal of Experimental Psychology, 49B,* 60–80.

Dickinson, A., & Charnock, D. J. (1985). Contingency effects with maintained instrumental reinforcement. *Quarterly Journal of Experimental Psychology, 37B,* 397–416.

Durlach, P. J. (1983). The effect of signaling intertrial USs in autoshaping. *Journal of Experimental Psychology: Animal Behavior Processes, 9,* 374–389.

Dwyer, D. M., Mackintosh, N. J., & Boakes, R. A. (1998). Simultaneous activation of the representations of absent cues results in the formation of an excitatory association between them. *Journal of Experimental Psychology: Animal Behavior Processes, 24,* 163–171.

Friedman, B. X., Blaisdell, A. P., Escobar, M., & Miller, R. R. (1998). Comparator mechanisms and conditioned inhibition: Conditioned stimulus preexposure disrupts Pavlovian conditioned inhibition but not explicitly unpaired inhibition. *Journal of Experimental Psychology: Animal Behavior Processes, 24,* 453–466.

Garner, W. R. (1954). Context effects and the validity of loudness scales. *Journal of Experimental Psychology, 48,* 218–224.

Gibbon, J., & Balsam, P. (1981). Spreading association in time. In C. M. Locurto, H. S. Terrace, & J. Gibbon (Eds.), *Autoshaping and conditioning theory* (pp. 219–253). New York: Academic Press.

Grahame, N. J., Barnet, R. C., Gunther, L. M., & Miller, R. R. (1994). Latent inhibition as a performance deficit resulting from CS-context associations. *Animal Learning & Behavior, 22,* 395–408.

Grahame, N. J., Barnet, R. C., & Miller, R. R. (1992). Pavlovian conditioning in multiple contexts: Competition between contexts for comparator status. *Animal Learning & Behavior, 20,* 329–338.

Hall, G. (1996). Learning about associatively activated stimulus representations: Implications for acquired equivalence in perceptual learning. *Animal Learning & Behavior, 24,* 233–255.

Hernstein, R. J. (1970). On the law of effect. *Journal of the Experimental Analysis of Behavior, 13,* 243–266.

Holland, P. C. (1983). Representation-mediated overshadowing and potentiation of conditioned aversions. *Journal of Experimental Psychology: Animal Behavior Processes, 9,* 1–13.

Honey, R. C., & Hall, G. (1989). Attenuation of latent inhibition after compound preexposure: Associative and perceptual explanations. *Quarterly Journal of Experimental Psychology, 41B,* 355–368.

Kahneman, D., & Tversky, A. (1979). Prospect theory. *Econometrica, 47,* 263–292.

Kamil, A. C. & Roitblat, H. L. (1985). The ecology of foraging behavior: Implications for animal learning and memory. *Annual Review of Psychology, 36,* 141–169.

Kamin, L. J. (1969). Predictability, surprise, attention, and conditioning. In B. A. Campbell & M. R. Church (Eds.), *Punishment and aversive behavior* (pp. 279–296). New York: Appleton-Century-Crofts.

Kasprow, W. J., Schachtman, T. R., & Miller, R. R. (1987). The comparator hypothesis of conditioned response generation: Manifest conditioned excitation and inhibition as a function of relative excitatory associative strengths of CS and conditioning context at the time of testing. *Journal of Experimental Psychology: Animal Behavior Processes, 13,* 395–406.

Kaufman, M. A., & Bolles, R. C. (1981). A nonassociative aspect of overshadowing. *Bulletin of the Psychonomic Society, 18,* 318–320.

Konorski, J. (1967). *Integrative activity of the brain: An interdisciplinary approach.* Chicago: University of Chicago Press.

Larkin, M. J. W., Aitken, M. R. F., & Dickinson, A. (1998). Retrospective revaluation of causal judgments under positive and negative contingencies. *Journal of Experimental Psychology: Learning, Memory, and Cognition, 24,* 1331–1352.

Lubow, R. E. (1973). Latent inhibition. *Psychological Bulletin, 79,* 398–407.

Lubow, R. E., & Moore, A. V. (1959). Latent inhibition: The effect of nonreinforced exposure to the conditioned stimulus. *Journal of Comparative and Physiological Psychology, 52,* 415–419.

Lubow, R. E., Schnur, P., & Rifkin, B. (1976). Latent inhibition and conditioned attention theory. *Journal of Experimental Psychology: Animal Behavior Processes, 2,* 163–174.

Lubow, R. E., Wagner, M., & Weiner, I. (1982). The effects of compound stimulus preexposure of two elements differing in salience on the acquisition of conditioned suppression. *Animal Learning & Behavior, 10,* 483–489.

Lysle, D. T., & Fowler, H. (1985). Inhibition as a "slave" process: Deactivation of conditioned inhibition through extinction of conditioned excitation. *Journal of Experimental Psychology: Animal Behavior Processes, 11,* 71–94.

Matzel, L. D., Brown A. M., & Miller, R. R. (1987). Associative effects of US preexposure: Modulation of conditioned responding by an excitatory training context. *Journal of Experimental Psychology: Animal Behavior Processes, 13,* 65–72.

Matzel, L. D., Held, F. P., & Miller, R. R. (1988). Information and expression of simultaneous and backward conditioning: Implications for contiguity theory. *Learning and Motivation, 19,* 317–344.

Matzel, L. D., Schachtman, T. R., & Miller, R. R. (1985). Recovery of an overshadowed association achieved by extinction of the overshadowing stimulus. *Learning and Motivation, 16,* 398–412.

Matzel, L. D., Schachtman, T. R., & Miller, R. R. (1988). Learned irrelevance exceeds the sum of the CSpreexposure and USpreexposure deficits. *Journal of Experimental Psychology: Animal Behavior Processes, 14,* 311–319.

Miller, R. R., & Barnet, R. C. (1993). The role of time in elementary associations. *Current Directions in Psychological Science, 2,* 106–111.

Miller, R. R., Barnet, R. C., & Grahame, N. J. (1995). Assessment of the Rescorla–Wagner model. *Psychological Bulletin, 117,* 363–386.

Miller, R. R., Hallam, S. C., & Grahame, N. J. (1990). Inflation of comparator stimuli following CS training. *Animal Learning & Behavior, 19,* 434–443.

Miller, R. R., Hallam, S. C., Hong, J. Y., & Dufore, D. S. (1991). Associative structure of differential inhibition: Implications for models of conditioned inhibition. *Journal of Experimental Psychology: Animal Behavior Processes, 17,* 141–150.

Miller, R. R., & Matute, H. (1996). Biological significance in forward and backward blocking: Resolution of a discrepancy between animal conditioning and human causal judgment. *Journal of Experimental Psychology: General, 125,* 370–386.

Miller, R. R., & Matzel, L. D. (1988). The comparator hypothesis: A response rule for the expression of associations. In G. H. Bower (Ed.), *The psychology of learning and motivation* (Vol. 22, pp. 51–92). San Diego, CA: Academic Press.

Miller, R. R., & Schachtman, T. R. (1985). Conditioning context as an associative baseline: Implications for response generation and the nature of conditioned inhibition. In R. R. Miller & N. E. Spear (Eds.), *Information processing in animals: Conditioned inhibition* (pp. 51–88). Hillsdale, NJ: Lawrence Erlbaum Associates.

Navarro, J. I., Hallam, S. C., Matzel, L. D., & Miller, R. R. (1989). Superconditioning and overshadowing. *Learning and Motivation, 20,* 130–152.

Oberling, P., Bristol, A. S., Matute, H., & Miller, R. R. (1999). *Biological significance attenuates overshadowing, relative validity, and degraded contingency effects.* Manuscript submitted for publication.

Pavlov, I. P. (1927). *Conditioned reflexes.* London: Oxford University Press.

Pearce, J. M., & Hall, G. (1980). A model for Pavlovian conditioning: Variations in the effectiveness of conditioned but not unconditioned stimuli. *Psychological Review, 87,* 332–352.

Randich, A. (1981). The US preexposure phenomenon in the conditioned suppression paradigm: A role for conditioned situational stimuli. *Learning and Motivation, 12,* 321–341.

Randich, A., & LoLordo, V. M. (1979). Preconditioning exposure to the unconditioned stimulus affects the acquisition of a conditioned emotional response. *Learning and Motivation, 10,* 245–277.

Rauhut, A. S., McPhee, J. E., & Ayres, J. J. B. (1999). Blocked and overshadowed stimuli are weakened in their ability to serve as blockers and second-order reinforcers in Pavlovian fear conditioning. *Journal of Experimental Psychology: Animal Behavior Processes, 25,* 45–67.

Rescorla, R. A. (1968). Probability of shock in the presence and absence of CS in fear conditioning. *Journal of Comparative and Physiological Psychology, 66,* 1–5.

Rescorla, R. A. (1969). Pavlovian conditioned inhibition. *Psychological Bulletin, 72,* 77–94.

Rescorla, R. A. (1970). Reduction in the effectiveness of reinforcement after prior excitatory conditioning. *Learning and Motivation, 1,* 372–381.

Rescorla, R. A., & Freberg, L. (1978). The extinction of within-compound flavor associations. *Learning and Motivation, 9,* 411–427.

Rescorla, R. A., & Holland, R. C. (1977). Associations in Pavlovian conditioned inhibition. *Learning and Motivation, 8,* 429–447.

Rescorla, R. A., & Wagner, A. R. (1972). A theory of Pavlovian conditioning: Variations in the effectiveness of reinforcement and nonreinforcement. In A. H. Black & W. F. Prokasy (Eds.), *Classical conditioning II: Current research and theory* (pp. 64–99). New York: Appleton-Century-Crofts.

Rizley, R. C., & Rescorla, R. A. (1972). Associations in second-order conditioning and sensory preconditioning. *Journal of Comparative and Physiological Psychology, 81,* 1–11.

Savastano, H. I., Cole, R. P., Barnet, R. C., & Miller, R. R. (1999). Reconsidering conditioned inhibition. *Learning and Motivation, 30,* 101–127.

Savastano, H. I., Escobar, M., & Miller, R. R. (1999). *A comparator hypothesis account of the CS-preexposure effects.* Manuscript submitted for publication.

Savastano, H. I., & Miller, R. R. (1998). Time as content in Pavlovian associations. *Behavioural Processes, 44,* 147–162.

Schachtman, T. R., Brown, A. M., Gordon, E., Catterson, D., & Miller, R. R. (1987). Mechanisms underlying retarded emergence of conditioned responding following inhibitory training: Evidence for the comparator hypothesis. *Journal of Experimental Psychology: Animal Behavior Processes, 13,* 310–322.

Schweitzer, L., & Green, L. (1982). Reevaluation of things past: A test of the "retrospective hypothesis" using a CER procedure in rats. *Pavlovian Journal of Biological Science, 17,* 62–68.

Shanks, D. R. (1985). Forward and backward blocking in human contingency judgement. *Quarterly Journal of Experimental Psychology, 37B,* 1–21.

Siegel, S., & Allan, L. G. (1996). The widespread influence of the Rescorla-Wagner model. *Psychonomic Bulletin & Review, 3,* 314–321.

Tassoni, C. J. (1995). The least mean squares network with information coding: A model of cue learning. *Journal of Experimental Psychology: Learning, Memory, and Cognition, 21,* 193–204.

Tomie, A. (1976). Interference with autoshaping by prior context conditioning. *Journal of Experimental Psychology: Animal Behavior Processes, 2,* 323–334.

Van Hamme, L. J. (1994). *Associative and statistical accounts of cue competition in causality judgments.* Unpublished doctoral dissertation, University of Iowa, Iowa City.

Van Hamme, L. J., & Wasserman, E. A. (1994). Cue competition in causality judgments: The role of nonpresentation of compound stimulus elements. *Learning and Motivation, 25,* 127–151.

Wagner, A. R. (1981). SOP: A model of automatic memory processing in animal behavior. In N. E. Spear & R. R. Miller (Eds.), *Information processing in animals: Memory mechanisms* (pp. 5–47). Hillsdale, NJ: Lawrence Erlbaum Associates.

Wasserman, E. A., & Berglan, L. R. (1998). Backward blocking and recovery from overshadowing in human causality judgment: The role of within-compound associations. *Quarterly Journal of Experimental Psychology, 51B,* 121–138.

Williams, B. A. (1994). Blocking despite changes in reinforcer identity. *Animal Learning & Behavior, 22,* 442–457.

Williams, B. A. (1996). Evidence that blocking is due to associative deficit: Blocking history affects the degree of subsequent associative competition. *Psychonomic Bulletin & Review, 3,* 71–74.

Williams, D. A., Sagness, K. E., & McPhee, J. E. (1994). Configural and elemental strategies in predictive learning. *Journal of Experimental Psychology: Learning, Memory, and Cognition, 20,* 694–709.

Yin, H., Barnet, R. C., & Miller, R. R. (1994). Trial spacing and trial distribution effects in Pavlovian conditioning: Contributions of a comparator mechanism. *Journal of Experimental Psychology: Animal Behavior Processes, 20,* 123–134.

Yin, H., Grahame, N. J., & Miller, R. R. (1993). Extinction of comparator stimuli during and after acquisition: Differential effects on Pavlovian responding. *Learning and Motivation, 24,* 219–241.

chapter 4

Experimental Extinction

Robert A. Rescorla

University of Pennsylvania

O ne of the most widely known phenomena in the field of associative learning is that of experimental extinction. Any discussion of the acquisition of responding as a result of arranging a contingent relation, either between two stimuli or between responding and a stimulus, includes the observation that disrupting that contingency results in the loss of responding. Curves describing extinction feature as prominently in our textbooks as do curves of acquisition. Yet our understanding of the processes underlying those curves remains very primitive.

One might have thought that such a ubiquitous phenomenon would have attracted increasing experimental attention. Yet interest seems only to have declined in recent years. Historically important texts, such as Hilgard and Marquis (1940), Kimble (1961), and Mackintosh (1974) all devoted full chapters to the discussion of extinction, allocating to it between 10% and 15% of their total pages. By contrast, a sampling of recent texts finds that extinction rarely merits either a chapter or anything like 10% of the pages (e.g., Domjan, 1998; Lieberman, 1993; Schwartz & Robbins, 1995).

The heyday of the study of extinction was in the 1950s and 1960s, when the investigation of the partial reinforcement extinction effect (PRE) absorbed much of the field's attention. The finding of slower extinction following partial reinforcement so dominated our thinking that its study became virtually coextensive with the study of extinction itself. Investigation of the PRE spawned two of our best known theoretical formulations, the frustration theory of Amsel (1958, 1967, 1992) and the sequential theory of Capaldi (1967). In spite of sometimes being cast as rivals for explaining extinction, each of these theories points to important, and essentially complementary, contributors to the changes in performance that occurred in extinction. Indeed, it may have been the perception of their joint success, together with a waning interest in distinguishing the finer points of their positions, that has led to reduced interest in extinction.

This is an especially unfortunately conclusion because, as Mackintosh (1974) rightly pointed out, neither of these approaches focuses on the learning that occurs in extinction. Approaches to the PRE call attention to the generalization between learning and extinction, pointing to the importance of viewing extinction in terms of the transfer from acquisition. They note, in one language or another, how different conditions of acquisition bear different similarity relations to the circumstances of extinction. They depend on the observation that treatments that encourage learning about features of the acquisition that would also be present in extinction will result in the most behavior during extinction. However, they provide little discussion of the learning that might occur during extinction itself.

Yet there is little doubt that the removal of a contingency provides conditions for new learning on the part of the animal. The performance changes during extinction are not all attributable to failure of transfer from acquisition. In the remainder of this chapter, I focus on the analysis of the nature of such learning. In doing so I depart from the typical extinction study in which one examines responding during the course of extinction itself. Instead I focus on examining behavior in a subsequent test, comparing stimuli or responses that have been subjected to extinction with those that have been spared extinction. The question of interest will be how the differing opportunities to learn during extinction yield differences measured in a subsequent test. This parallels the procedure that I have elsewhere advocated for the study of acquisition—comparison of the test performance of two groups as a function of their different opportunities to learn in acquisition (e.g., Rescorla & Holland, 1976).

CONSEQUENCES OF NONREINFORCEMENT

There is no doubt that if previously trained stimuli or responses are subjected to nonreinforcement, there will be a depression of their ability to exhibit their original learning. The question of initial interest is what the nature of the process is that produces the depression.

Erasure of Initial Learning

The most obvious account of the observation that breaking the original contingency results in the loss of subsequently tested behavior is that doing so removes some portion of what was originally learned. Indeed, a variety of theoretical approaches appear to make this assumption because they attribute the effects of reinforcement and nonreinforcement to variations in the strength of a single set of underlying associations. Early implementation of error correction models, such as Bush and Mosteller (1951) and Estes (1950), spoke of changes in a single probability. Successors, such as Rescorla and Wagner (1972), made that assumption at the level of theoretical associative strengths. Current connectionist models frequently share that assumption (e.g., Rumelhart, Hinton, & Williams, 1986). However, as textbook authors invariably point out, we have known since Pavlov (1927) about a variety of phenomena in which extinguished behavior appears to be restored, implying that breaking the contingency does not simply remove the original learning. Four phenomena deserve particular mention.

Restoration of Extinguished Behavior

Spontaneous Recovery. Perhaps the most powerful such result is spontaneous recovery, the return of responding with the simple passage of time after extinction. Many authors have argued that if the behavioral depression produced by extinction partially dissipates with time, then that implies that extinction did not fully reverse the effects of initial acquisition. Many instances of such recovery have been described over the years.

Figure 4.1 shows two recent examples of spontaneous recovery observed in our laboratory, one from extinction following instrumental learning and one from extinction following Pavlovian conditioning (Rescorla, 1996c, 1997b). Both of these examples employed a within-subject procedure in which differential recovery was observed either to two stimuli or to two responses, as a function of time following

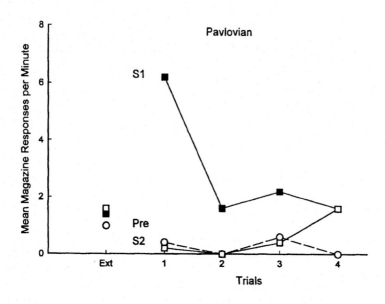

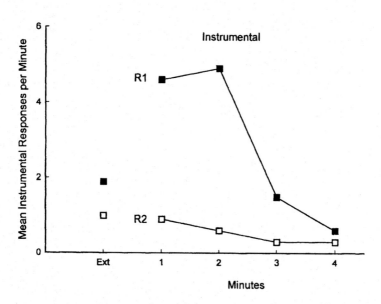

FIG. 4.1. Spontaneous recovery after extinction in Pavlovian conditioning and instrumental training. The top panel shows responding in a test session prior to any stimulus presentation and then for two stimuli tested either 5 days (S1) or 1 (S2) day after extinction. The bottom panel shows comparable data for two responses tested either 5 days (R1) or 1 (R2) day after extinction (after Rescorla, 1996c, 1997b).

their extinction. In each case, responding was assessed at the same point in time for the same animal for target associations that had been extinguished at different points in the past. I have argued elsewhere that such a design allows a more precise identification of the spontaneous recovery as being specific to a particular association (Rescorla, 1996c).

The top panel of Fig. 4.1 shows Pavlovian conditioned magazine approach responding in rat subjects during auditory and visual stimuli that had both signaled the delivery of food pellets and then had both been extinguished. S1 had been extinguished 5 days previously and S2 immediately before the test. The greater test responding to S1 shows highly stimulus-specific spontaneous recovery with the passage of time. The bottom panel of Fig. 4.1 shows the results of an analogous procedure in which two instrumental responses were first trained and then extinguished. R1 had been extinguished 5 days prior to the test and R2 was extinguished immediately before the test. Again recovery is highly specific to the response that had been extinguished in the more distant past.

Apparently the substantial depression of responding observed during extinction, and remaining in an immediate test, does not represent the full erasure of the original learning in either of these preparations. Nevertheless, it is important to note that neither does behavior recover fully in these experiments, or in the majority of other published reports of spontaneous recovery. The initial level of responding after recovery typically falls short of that prior to extinction and the effects of recovery are dissipated after a few trials, far fewer than necessary for original extinction. In the absence of a fully developed theory of the basis of recovery, it is difficult to know whether to attribute this incomplete recovery to partial loss of the original learning or to incompleteness of the removal of the depressive process with the passage of time. In either case, however, it suggests that just as the effects of acquisition are not fully removed by the extinction procedure, so the effects of extinction are not fully removed by the passage of time.

Disinhibition. A second phenomenon originally described by Pavlov, and regularly listed by textbooks as a companion to spontaneous recovery, is disinhibition, the restoration of extinguished responding as a result of the presentation of a novel, but neutral, stimulus. The fact that this is typically described together with spontaneous recovery has given the impression that it is just as easily observed and equally robust. However, a search of the literature reveals very few demonstrations of disinhibition that do not admit of ready alternative interpretation (cf. Brimer, 1972). Repeated attempts to observe disinhibition in our laboratory have been without success. Consequently, it may be incautious to lean heavily on this phenomenon to support the inference that extinction leaves substantial portions of original training intact.

Reinstatement. A less frequently cited observation made by Pavlov was that extinguished behavior could also be restored by the simple reexposure to the original unconditioned stimulus (US), in the absence of further presentations of the conditioned stimulus (CS; Pavlov, 1927). This observation of "reinstatement" has been repeated for the case of instrumental behavior and thoroughly studied for Pavlovian fear conditioning (e.g., Bouton & Bolles, 1979; Rescorla & Heth, 1975). A recent example from a Pavlovian conditioned magazine approach setting was reported by Delamater (1997). He measured approach to the locus of the US delivery during two different CSs, paired with similarly valued, but qualitatively different USs: food pellets and liquid sucrose. Both stimuli were then extinguished; but prior to testing, the US previously paired with one of the stimuli was given noncontingently. He found greater reinstatement of responding for the CS whose US had been presented in a noncontingent fashion. Clearly the animal retained sufficient information about the original training to allow US-specific reinstatement. As in the case of spontaneous recovery, the selective restoration of performance implies that extinction did not destroy all of the original learning.

Contextual Renewal. Another postextinction manipulation that appears to restore responding is moving the animal to a new context. In an extensive series of studies in a variety of conditioning preparations, Bouton and his colleagues (e.g., Bouton, 1991, 1993) found that if extinction is conducted in one context, then behavior is partially restored when the stimulus is tested in another context. It appears as though the context of extinction somehow controls the animal's memory of the extinction experience itself. One possibility is that the context plays the role of a conditional stimulus that signals the nonreinforcement contingency. Although this observation does not specify the nature of the learned decremental process, it does point to the failure of extinction to remove all of the original learning.

These four "unmasking" phenomena all demonstrate that associative learning that is not evident in responding following extinction has nevertheless been partially preserved through extinction. They represent various manipulations that can be conducted to unmask those associations to partly restore the extinguished performance.

More Direct Measures of the Association After Extinction

Although unmasking procedures have historically figured prominently in discussions of extinction, they are limited in the inferences they permit. They allow one to conclude that extinction did not fully wipe out the original associative learning. However they are not especially powerful in estimating the strength of that association, relative to associations that have not undergone extinction. Moreover, they are sometimes poorly understood themselves, so that it is difficult to know to what degree to attribute incomplete restoration to incomplete unmasking or to some partial loss of the original association. Consequently, it would be very useful to have an alternative way of assessing the state of the original associations after extinction so as to compare it with associations that have not undergone extinction..

Two recently developed general strategies for measuring the strength of associations seem promising in this regard. The first of these is a devaluation procedure. In both instrumental training and Pavlovian conditioning, the associations that develop with a particular outcome include information about the qualitative properties of that outcome. The result is that should the outcome be devalued following the completion of acquisition (e.g., by its pairing with the toxin lithium chloride [LiCl], then there is a specific adverse effect on stimuli and responses that have signaled that particular outcome (e.g., Adams & Dickinson, 1981; Colwill & Motzkin, 1994; Colwill & Rescorla, 1985; Rescorla, 1996a). Consequently, one can use sensitivity to outcome devaluation as an index of the strength of the association with that outcome. The second strategy involves transfer of Pavlovian and instrumental stimuli to the control of novel instrumental responses. There is good evidence that a Pavlovian stimulus, or an instrumental discriminative stimulus, that signals the coming of a particular outcome will also control selectively new responses that have themselves earned that same outcome (e.g., Colwill & Rescorla, 1988). This allows one to use transfer as a measure of the state of the stimulus–outcome or the response–outcome association.

Outcome Devaluation. Figure 4.2 shows an example of the application of the devaluation procedure to the study of extinction following Pavlovian conditioning in a magazine approach situation (Rescorla, 1996a). As schematized in the top portion of the figure, the rats initially received Pavlovian conditioning with two auditory and two visual stimuli (S1 and S2 as well as S3 and S4). One stimulus within each modality signaled solid pellets and the other signaled liquid sucrose, counterbalanced as O1 and O2. Then each animal received extinction with both of the stimuli in one of the modalities. Following this, one outcome, O1, received devaluation by pairing with LiCl and the animals were tested for their responding to all of the stimuli. The intention was to look for evidence of the S–O associations in terms of greater responding to S2 and S4, compared with that to S1 and S3. This should result because the outcome that had reinforced S1 and S3 had been devalued. The comparison between S3 and S4 gives information about the state of

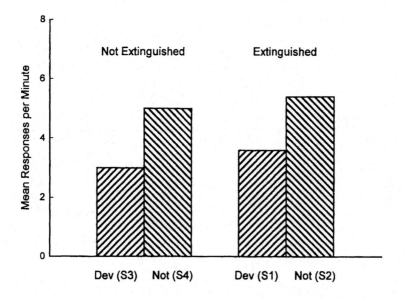

Phase 1	Ext	Phase 2	Devaluation	Test
S1--O1	S1--	S1--O3		S1
S2--O2	S2--	S2--O3		S2
			O1--LiCl	
S3--O1		S3--O3		S3
S4--O2		S4--O3		S4

FIG. 4.2. Design and results of a Pavlovian experiment assessing the effects of outcome devaluation for stimuli that had been subjected to extinction or not. Initially four stimuli (S1–S4) were paired with two outcomes (O1 and O2). Then two stimuli received extinction, all stimuli were retrained with a third outcome (O3), one outcome was paired with LiCl, and all stimuli were tested. Responding is shown separately for the nonextinguished (S3 and S4) and extinguished (S1 and S2) stimuli when the outcome paired with those stimuli had been devalued (Dev) or not (after Rescorla, 1996a). Adapted with permission of Experimental Psychology Society.

those associations in the absence of extinction; that between S1 and S2 gives an estimate of those associations after extinction.

However, we anticipated that the overall levels of responding to S1 and S2 would be substantially below those of S3 and S4 because of the response depression produced by the extinction procedure; this would greatly complicate a comparison of the size of the devaluation effect in the two cases. Consequently, between extinction and devaluation all stimuli were given simple Pavlovian conditioning with another outcome, O3 (polycose, a substance discriminably different from both sucrose and pellets), to ensure substantial levels of responding to all stimuli. We knew from other work (see later) that using this third outcome would not, in itself, undermine the associations with O1 and O2, but it would allow the stimuli to produce similar response levels, permitting a meaningful comparison between extinguished and nonextinguished stimuli.

As illustrated in the bottom portion of Fig. 4.2, test presentations of S3 and S4, the stimuli spared extinction, show the typical selective impact of outcome devaluation. The stimulus whose outcome had been paired with LiCl (S3) elicited substantially less magazine approach than did the stimulus whose outcome had not been devalued (S4). Of more interest, the same pattern of results occurred for the stimuli that had been subjected to extinction. Despite this extinction, and the loss of behavior it entailed, devaluation selectively depressed responding to the stimulus that had earned the outcome paired with LiCl (S1). Indeed, the magnitude of the devaluation effect is indistinguishable from that observed with stimuli that had not received extinction. This suggests that there is excellent preservation of the S–O associations through an extinction procedure.

Figure 4.3 shows the results of an analogous experiment in instrumental learning (Rescorla, 1993b). The design is like that of the previous experiment, except that four instrumental responses (lever press, chain pull, nose poke, and handle pull) replaced the four Pavlovian stimuli. These four different responses were organized in two pairs, within each of which the responses signaled two different outcomes. Then one pair of responses was extinguished, all responses were given retraining with polycose, and one of the outcomes paired with LiCl. In agreement with earlier data, the nonextinguished responses (R3 and R4) were differentially affected by the differential treatment of their outcomes; that indicates the coding of R–O associations in the absence of extinction (e.g., Colwill & Rescorla, 1985). More interesting, the same differential effect occurred for the pair of responses that had been extinguished (R1 and R2). As in the case of Pavlovian conditioning, the magnitude of the effect of devaluation was comparable for extinguished and nonextinguished

Phase 1	Ext	Phase 2	Devaluation	Test
R1--O1	R1--	R1--O3		R1 v R2
R2--O2	R2--	R2--O3	O1--LiCl	
R3--O1		R3--O3		R3 v R4
R4--O2		R4--O3		

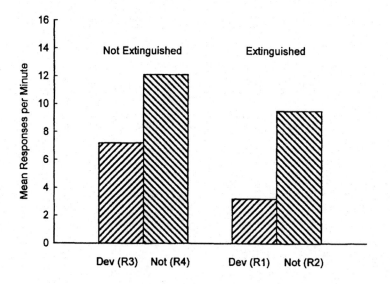

FIG. 4.3. Design and results of an instrumental learning experiment assessing the effects of outcome devaluation for responses that had been subjected to extinction or not. Initially four responses (R1–R4) were paired with two outcomes (O1 and O2). Then two responses received extinction, all responses were retrained with a third outcome (O3), one outcome was paired with LiCl, and all responses were tested. Responding is shown separately for the nonextinguished (R3 and R4) and extinguished (R1 and R2) responses when the outcome paired with those responses had been devalued (Dev) or not, (after Rescorla, 1993b).

responses, suggesting excellent preservation of the R–O associations through extinction.

Outcome-Based Transfer. Another technique for assessing the state of various associations is a transfer procedure, in which S–O and R–O associations are measured in terms of the selective transfer of S to the control of a new R, based on their separate histories of pairing with a shared O. That technique provides confirmatory data on the preservation of associations through extinction. Figure 4.4 shows the results of a representative experiment examining extinction of the R–O associations formed in instrumental learning (Rescorla, 1991b). As illustrated in the top portion of that figure, the design was similar to that of the devaluation experiment described in Fig. 4.3. Like that experiment, the animals were trained with four instrumental responses, earning different outcomes. Then two of the responses were extinguished and the state of the R–O associations was assessed after intervening training with a common outcome to guarantee similar response levels. However, in this experiment the assessment procedure involved transfer rather than devaluation. Prior to the training and extinction of the instrumental responses, all animals had received discriminative instrumental training in which a light and noise signaled the availability of different outcomes for a common response (manipulating a joystick). We knew from earlier work (e.g., Colwill & Rescorla, 1988) that those stimuli would transfer their control to the separately trained R1, R2, R3, and R4 responses to the degree that those responses signaled the availability of the same outcomes as the stimuli.

Consequently, in this experiment, the results of which are shown in bottom portion of Fig. 4.4, the light and noise were superimposed on those trained instrumental responses, two of which had previously received extinction. The leftmost set of bars describes the results for the nonextinguished responses (R3 and R4) in the absence of any stimulus and then during stimuli that signaled the same or different outcomes. Those data show the characteristically greater elevation of the same-outcome response. The rightmost set of bars describes the comparable data from the responses that had been extinguished (R1 and R2). The interesting feature of the data is that the same pattern of results emerged, greater elevation of the same-outcome response. Although the general level of responding is somewhat lower for the extinguished responses, the overall patterns are remarkably similar.

These results provide further evidence for the preservation of the R–O association through extinction. Comparable results have been obtained for the case of the S–O associations in instrumental learning (e.g., Rescorla, 1992) and in Pavlovian conditioning (e.g., Delamater, 1996).

Discrimination	Training	Ext	Retraining	Transfer Test
S1: Rc–O1	R1–O1	R1--	R1–O3	S1, S2: R1 v R2
	R2--O2	R2–	R2--O3	
S2: Rc–O2	R3–O1		R3–O3	S1, S2: R3 v R4
	R4–O2		R4--O3	

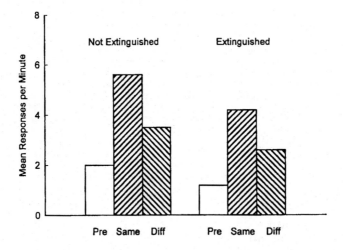

FIG. 4.4.   Design and results of an instrumental learning experiment assessing the effects of extinction on transfer. Initially two stimuli (S1 and S2) signaled that a common response (Rc) would earn different outcomes (O1 and O2). Then four responses were trained with these outcomes and one pair of responses was extinguished. After retraining of all the responses, transfer of S1 and S2 was assessed. Responding is shown prior to any stimulus presentation (Pre) and during stimuli that signaled either the same or a different outcome from that which the responses had earned (after Rescorla, 1991b). Copyright ©1991 by the American Psychological Association. Adapted with permission.

One advantage of the devaluation and transfer procedures is that they seem to provide a way of approaching the question of whether or not the associations formed in acquisition are fully preserved through extinction. As noted earlier, the historically important unmasking phenomena, such spontaneous recovery, allow one to conclude that extinction did not fully wipe out the associations; but one cannot use them to draw the further inference that there is no attenuation of those associations. By contrast, the transfer and devaluation procedures can provide concurrent assessments of the S–O and R–O associations for instances in which extinction has and has not been conducted. By allowing that comparison, they encourage one to ask the question of whether all of the initial learning is preserved. The preliminary answer suggested by the experiments just described is affirmative.

The establishment of behavior as a result of acquisition surely involves an extended chain of components. Disruption of any portion of that chain could be expected to undermine performance. This discussion has focused on the S–O and R–O associations, but it seems likely that the animal also learns about the individual, S, R, and O events. Moreover, in the case of discriminated instrumental learning it seems likely that more hierarchical relations are developed in which the stimulus signals the relation between the response and the outcome (e.g., Colwill & Rescorla, 1990; Rescorla, 1991a). Given this array of consequences of acquisition, it is not surprising that several authors have suggested that extinction might affect the state of the outcome (e.g., Rescorla & Cunningham, 1978) or the stimulus (e.g., Robbins, 1990) representations. Although the preceding discussion has emphasized that the experimental results demonstrate the preservation of the simple R–O and S–O associations through extinction, they also suggest that the learning about the individual elements is preserved. The continued ability of the animal to base transfer on the identities of the S, R, and O events, as well as the ability of devaluation of O to selectively act on particular S and R events, suggests that there must be excellent coding of those elements. Moreover, direct assessment (e.g., Rescorla, 1998) of the state of the hierarchical relation learned in instrumental learning also suggests that it survives extinction. Consequently, it seems increasingly plausible to consider the possibility that extinction leaves intact the major consequences of acquisition. We are well advised to look elsewhere for the basis of the decrement in performance induced by extinction.

WHAT THEN PRODUCES THE DECREMENT?

Stimulus Generalization Decrement

As already noted, the conventional study of extinction focuses on the loss of performance over the course of nonreinforcement itself. It seems clear that a major contributor to that decrement is the changed stimulus situation in which the animal is asked to exhibit its learning. There are many ways—some obvious, some more subtle—in which the context of extinction differs from that in which original learning took place. Consider the most frequently employed extinction procedure, simply omitting the O altogether. Deleting the outcome clearly removes from the situation a major stimulus in the presence of which initial training took place. With continued extinction, the extensive exposure without the outcome must make the situation increasingly different from initial acquisition. Capaldi (1967) argued very effectively that this change in stimulus environment may account for a large portion of the loss of responding during the application of an extinction procedure. He exposed detailed and subtle ways in which the pattern of nonreinforcement in acquisition shows differential generalization to the pattern experienced in extinction. Similarly, the repeated occurrence of nonreinforcement in extinction has been documented to give rise to novel emotional states, such as frustration. To the degree that these states were absent in acquisition, and the animal has been denied the opportunity to learn to respond in their presence, we can expect their appearance to disrupt performance. Amsel (1967) effectively highlighted the power of attending to such an emotional change in accounting for the details of response decrements during the course of extinction.

It seems unlikely, however, that one could account for the impact of nonreinforcement entirely in terms of these effects on performance. There are surely some forms of new learning that occur under nonreinforcement and leave a permanent impact on the animal. The simple observation that extinction can be specific to one stimulus or one response, rather than another, within a single subject, suggests that overall changes from acquisition to extinction are an incomplete account. The specificity of nonreinforcement to particular stimuli and responses suggests that extinction invokes some associative changes.

Associative Changes in Extinction

In thinking about what the animal might learn in the course of extinction, it may be useful to begin with the events that the animal actually experiences. In a typical Pavlovian extinction experiment, some signal is presented, which because of its associative history, evokes a response on the part of the animal; but then no further stimuli occur. The trial sequence consists of an externally applied stimulus that is followed by nothing beyond the animal's own response to it. The animal's response will commonly contain several components, most notably the overt behavior we measure (e.g., magazine entry, lever pressing, or general activity) as well as the internal emotional consequences of the omission of an anticipated reward. The latter have been variously characterized as the discrepancy that generates inhibition (e.g., Rescorla & Wagner,

1972), a fall in excitation in the UScenter (e.g., Konorski, 1948), a negative affective opponent process (e.g., Solomon & Corbit, 1974; Wagner, 1981), and a frustration reaction (e.g., Amsel, 1958). In any case, the primary events that are paired with the stimulus in extinction are the animal's own overt and emotional responses. There are no powerful sensory events.

In the absence of stimulus events, it would not be surprising if the animal's learning were dominated by the coding of these response events. The situation is not unlike that used to characterize some cases of second-order conditioning (e.g., Rescorla, 1973). In a second-order conditioning procedure, a relatively neutral S1 is first paired with a US, giving it the ability to evoke a strong conditioned response. Then S2 is paired with S1, with the result that S2 also evokes a response. In many cases, however, detailed analysis shows that the association with S2 has encoded relatively little information about the sensory features of S1, but a great deal of information about the response to S1. One interpretation is that the organism learns about the high-salience emotional and peripheral responses evoked by S1 but not about the low-salience stimulus features of S1 itself. This analogy suggests that in extinction the animal learns primarily about the high-salience responses that follow the stimulus.

Viewed this way, the previously described results showing the preservation of information about the sensory features of the outcomes are not at all surprising. The techniques of devaluation and transfer are designed to be sensitive to encoding of differential sensory information about different outcomes. Indeed, Rescorla (1990, 1994) found that transfer can readily be obtained based on neutral features of outcomes or on whole outcomes that have been subjected to devaluation. The fact that no new stimulus occurs at the end of the trial in extinction means that prior learning about the stimulus features of the outcome is not subjected to new differential information. Hence, one might well expect techniques that are sensitive to such information to continue to detect its presence.

By contrast, extinction does arrange for a new emotional response to occur following the stimulus, one that is quite different from that which normally occurs in acquisition. Because that new emotional response depends on the affective properties of the outcome, it is common to the various same-valued original outcomes. However, it can be expected to function to produce various associative changes. First, the negative emotional response may well serve as a Pavlovian conditioning event that generates new associative learning in the manner described by such theorists as Amsel, Konorski, and Wagner. It would be natural to think of this new learning as primarily affective and of opposite value to the affective learning that occurs during acquisition. The resultant counterconditioning would effectively undermine the emotional and motivational learning that took place in acquisition. To the degree that this motivational learning is essential for the performance of the original response, one would anticipate that this would produce a deterioration in performance. Second, because the animal continues to produce a variety of overt responses in extinction, this emotional response will occur in conjunction with those responses. One might then expect that emotional response to serve as a punisher for any of those overt responses that are sensitive to their consequences. For instance, if an instrumental response such as lever pressing should be nonreinforced, that response would be followed by the affective reaction, resulting in new instrumental learning about that lever pressing. The resultant associative changes might take a variety of forms, but one might conceive of the formation of a hierarchical associative structure of the form S–(R–O), like that frequently described for initial acquisition. In the case of extinction, the outcome would be a negative affective event, such as frustration.

It has sometimes been suggested that in extinction the animal learns that the CS is paired with the "no-US", by analogy with its learning about the US in acquisition (e.g., Konorski, 1967). However, unlike an explicitly presented US, which presumably contains sensory, affective, and response components, the absence of the US contains little sensory information and is dominated by responses generated by the animal itself. The previously described results agree with the implication that there should be relatively little new sensory learning in extinction. It is then of interest to ask what evidence supports the further implication that extinction involves important learning about the responses that occur.

The Involvement of Emotional Responses.   No one who has ever handled rats immediately after their initial experiences with nonreinforcement can doubt the presence of negative emotional effects of extinction. It is a common experience for instructors of laboratory courses to find that their students are most at risk for bites when they subject their rats to an extinction procedure. Such negative emotional responses to nonreinforcement have been demonstrated to have a variety of effects. Azrin, Hutchinson, and Hake (1966) found that extinction enhanced the likelihood of aggression against conspecifics. Amsel (1958) carefully documented the motivational consequences of omission of anticipated reward in his studies of the so-called frustration effect. Extensive studies by Daly (1974), following up on the earlier work by Wagner (1963), document the aversiveness of nonreinforcement by demonstrating that animals learn a response to escape from it. This same result occurs when the reward level is reduced to a nonzero level that is below that normally administered.

More directly relevant to this discussion, there is substantial evidence that these emotional responses themselves condition stimuli paired with them. Both Wagner (1963) and Daly (1974) found that neutral stimuli present during the time of omission of an anticipated reward take on aversive properties, becoming themselves capable of promoting escape learning. Indeed, such conditioned consequences of frustration are an integral part of one of the most successful accounts of the partial reinforcement extinction effect (e.g., Amsel, 1967). Moreover, the potential for such emotional responses to serve as punishers for instrumental behavior was explicitly noted some years ago by Wagner (1966). Overall, there seems to be little doubt that during extinction a negative emotional response occurs and leads to important learned consequences.

This is not to say, however, that such learning replaces that of acquisition. The counterconditioning of frustration likely reduces the overall emotional and motivational value of the stimulus by superimposition on the consequences of original learning. Indeed, the assumption of a parallel existence of conditioned frustration and conditioned positive motivation is an implicit part of the frustration account of the PRE.

Evidence for the Involvement of Overt Responses. The possibility that overt responding might be involved in the associative changes that take place in extinction is suggested by a common general observation: The decremental impact of a nonreinforcement is positively correlated with the amount of responding that was nonreinforced. This kind of observation contributed to Skinner's (1938) appeal to the notion of the reflex reserve. A useful rule of thumb is that procedures that enhance the likelihood of a response to a stimulus during extinction also enhance the changes produced by nonreinforcement of that stimulus, whereas those that reduce the response likelihood reduce the changes produced by a nonreinforcement of the stimulus. Examples of the former are high levels of motivation (e.g., Holland & Rescorla, 1975) and the copresence of another excitatory stimulus (e.g., Wagner, 1969). Examples of the latter are low levels of motivation, prior devaluation of the outcome (e.g., Holland & Rescorla, 1975), and the copresence of an inhibitory stimulus (e.g., Chorazyna, 1962).

That the frequency of nonreinforced instrumental responding might affect the associative change is hardly surprising. The more frequent the instrumental response, the greater the exposure to the contingency of central importance. More interesting is the finding that manipulations that depress the Pavlovian response to a stimulus also depress the decremental impact of nonreinforcing that stimulus. Figure 4.5 shows the results of two early experiments displaying this result for a conditioned general activity response that results from the pairing of audi-

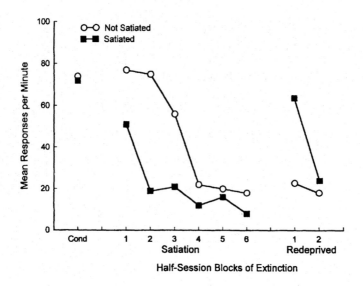

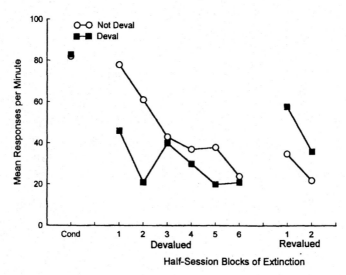

FIG 4.5. Extinction and testing of responses originally paired with a pellet reinforcer. Responding is shown at the end of conditioning, during an initial extinction phase, and then during a final test extinction phase. Initial extinction was carried out either under deprivation or satiation (top panel) or when the original outcome had been devalued or not (bottom panel). Final testing took place after redeprivation or revaluation of the outcomes (after Holland & Rescorla, 1975). Copyright © 1975 by the American Psychological Association. Adapted with permission.

tory stimuli with food in rat subjects (Holland & Rescorla, 1975). In both experiments, rats received nonreinforced presentations of a tone that had previously been paired with food. However, in each experiment half of the animals received these nonreinforcements at a time when the food had been devalued, either by satiation (top panel) or pairing with high-speed rotation (bottom panel). It is clear that in each case devaluation depressed responding during extinction. More interesting is the observation that when the value of the food was restored during a subsequent test (by redeprivation or extinction of the food–rotation association), responding was greater in the animals that had exhibited lower responding during the prior extinction period. These results suggest that nonreinfocement had less impact on those animals. Of course, it is difficult to know whether to attribute this difference to the lower occurrence of the peripheral response or to the reduced negative emotional response that presumably occurred with the omission of an outcome of lower current value. However, such results are not easily dismissed in terms of the stimulus changes induced by satiation or devaluation. These same manipulations did not affect the likelihood of responding to other stimuli also extinguished and tested—second-order conditioned stimuli whose response was not affected by virtue of their having signaled a different outcome.

In recent years, the clearest proposal for the involvement of learning about responses in extinction was made by Colwill (1991), who suggested that learning not to make a particular response might contribute importantly to the decrement observed during extinction. She argued that extinction might result in an inhibitory association between stimuli and a particular response. One observation that has encouraged this proposal is that under some circumstances the depressive process involved in extinction seems highly specific to particular responses. For instance, Rescorla (1993a) reported that the presence of a neutral stimulus at a time when an instrumental response was extinguished gave that stimulus the specific ability to inhibit that particular response, rather than other responses equivalently treated in the presence of other stimuli.

Indeed, one may argue that the simple ability of an extinguished Pavlovian CS to augment a transfer response at the same time that it has lost its ability to elicit its originally trained response suggests some response specificity. For instance. Delamater (1996) reported that an extinguished stimulus, unable to provoke its original magazine-approach response, nevertheless showed undiminished ability to transfer to new instrumental responses. One interpretation of that finding is that the occurrence of the magazine response, but not the transfer responses, during nonreinforcement of the stimulus led to effects that were highly restricted to the magazine response.

A similar observation was recently made, in an unpublished experiment in our laboratory, for the extinction of an instrumental discriminative stimulus. In that experiment, rats were given instrumental training in which lever pressing and chain pulling led to different outcomes. Then they received instrumental discriminative training in which a light and noise signaled the availability of one or the other of those outcomes for nose poking. That was followed by extinction of the nose poke in either the light or the noise and a final test in which the light and noise were transferred to the lever and chain. During that transfer test the nose poke was also available.

Figure 4.6 shows the results of the test. To the right are the results of the transfer to lever and chain, separated for the extinguished and nonextinguished stimuli. It is clear that highly successful selective transfer occurred. The occurrence of outcome-based transfer for the nonextinguished stimulus is unremarkable. Of more interest is the equally successful transfer for the stimulus that had been extinguished. These results replicate those in Fig. 4.2 in documenting the preservation of the S–O associations through extinction. Of more interest are the results of nose poking during the extinguished and nonextinguished stimulus, shown to the left. It is clear that the extinguished and nonextinguished stimuli differed substantially in their ability to produce the nose poke response. The observation that during the same test the stimuli transferred equally to the other responses but differed in their ability to control their original nose poke response suggests a high degree of response specificity. It also implies that the ability to show continued transfer can occur even in the absence of any contextual change that would be sufficiently large to restore the originally trained response. One possible interpretation is that extinction was relatively specific to the response that was allowed to occur during nonreinforcement.

A recent series of experiments conducted in our laboratory has pushed the notion of response involvement a step further (Rescorla, 1997a). The idea of these experiments was deliberately to bias a stimulus to produce one, rather than another, of two equally possible responses during its extinction. If a stimulus were inherently equally capable of producing either of two responses, but it were arranged that one of these occurred with greater frequency during extinction, then a response-specific mechanism might produce greater extinction of that response. To examine this possibility, we exploited the ability of an instrumental discriminative stimulus especially to augment transfer responses with which it shares an outcome. The design is shown at the top of Fig. 4.7. Initially, the animals received discriminative instrumental training with two different stimuli, S1 and S2, signaling the availability of different outcomes, O1 and O2 (pellets and sucrose). Then, they received instrumental training of two responses, R1 and R2 (lever press-

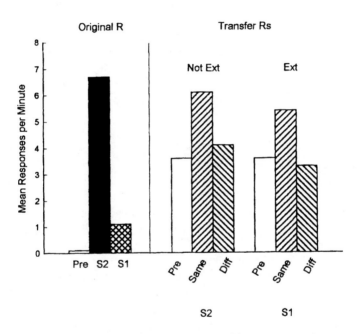

R train	Cond	Ext	Test
R1–O1	S1: Ro–O1		S1: Ro, **R1**, R2
		S1: Ro-	
R2–O2	S2: Ro–O2		S2: Ro, R1, **R2**

FIG. 4.6. Design and results of an instrumental learning experiment concurrently measuring the originally trained and extinguished response at a time of transfer to new responses. Initially two responses (R1 and R2) earned different outcomes. Then each of two stimuli (S1 and S2) signaled the availability of those outcomes for a common response (Ro). After extinction of S1, both S1 and S2 were tested for their ability to produce the original Rc and the transfer R1 and R2 responses. The responses underlined and in bold are those that shared a common outcome with the transfer stimulus. Responding is shown for the original Ro (left panel) and for the extinguished and nonextinguished stimulus when it was transferred to a response earned the same or a different outcome (right panel).

ing and chain pulling). In Phase 1, one set of response–outcome contingencies was in effect and then in Phase 2 those contingencies were reversed. We knew from other experiments that this sequence of response training would result in each response being fully associated with each outcome (see later). Consequently, in the absence of other treatments, we could expect S1 and S2 to both augment R1 and R2 equally in the test. However, between the two phases of response training, the animals were given extinction of S1 and S2 at a time when they could make nonreinforced choices between R1 and R2. It was anticipated that during this extinction the responses would occur with different frequencies during the stimuli. During S1, R1 should be especially likely to occur (and be nonreinforced) whereas during S2, R2 should be especially likely to occur (and be nonreinforced). To the degree that there is response specificity to the extinction of the stimuli, this should specifically diminish the ability of S1 to evoke R1 and S2 to evoke R2. That in turn should result in the inverse likelihood of the stimuli evoking those responses in the ultimate test.

The bottom portion of Fig. 4.7 shows the results of this experiment. That figure shows responding over the course of extinction and then in the final test. Responding is shown separately during a pre-CS period as well as during stimuli signaling the same or a different outcome from that which the responses had earned in Phase 1. During extinction, the responses that had the same outcome as the stimuli occurred at an especially high rate. This means that each stimulus had one response (its same-outcome response) occur with a higher frequency in its presence. It was anticipated that this would yield an especially large amount of response-specific inhibition for that stimulus. The final test shows results that confirm that expectation. By the time of that test, each response had earned each outcome; consequently one would anticipate that the stimuli would evoke the responses equally. Instead, however, each stimulus more successfully evoked the response it had evoked less successfully during extinction. This suggests that each stimulus had developed inhibition specific to its same-outcome response. That is, the effects of extinction were highly response specific. This same result has been observed for the case of Pavlovian CSs and occurs in experiments that control for the order of training of the responses per se (Rescorla, 1997a).

Recent studies have extended that conclusion in two ways. First, they have shown more clearly what is implied in this last experiment, that the specificity is actually to stimulus–response combinations. A stimulus and response that have been extinguished together are each capable of continuing to control responding to other responses and stimuli with which they share outcomes. Second, the spontaneous recovery that follows extinction also appears to be specific to those combinations (e.g., Rescorla, 1997c).

Discrimination	Phase 1	Extinction	Phase 2	Test
S1: Rc–O1	R1–O1	S1:	R1–O2	S1:
		R1 v R2		R1 v R2
S2: Rc–O2	R2–O2	S2:	R2–O1	S2:

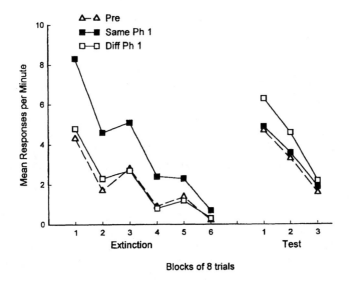

FIG. 4.7.   Design and results of an instrumental learning experiment measuring transfer to R1 and R2 after extinction had been conducted with those same responses at a time when each should have been more likely during one stimulus. Stimulus and response identifications are as in previous figures (after Rescorla, 1997a). Adapted with permission from Experimental Psychology Society.

These observations lend credence to the possibility that learning about the response is a part of what happens in extinction. Of course, such learning might be independent of information about the outcomes. Suppression at the level of responding itself might allow preservation of the initial outcome associations, permitting their detection with techniques like transfer and devaluation.

OTHER CHANGES IN THE CONTINGENCY

Random Outcome Presentation

Although simple removal of the outcome is the standard extinction procedure, and by far the one most frequently employed, there are other ways of changing the contingency that are of interest. For instance, many authors have pointed out the advantages of disrupting the contingency by arranging for the outcome to continue to occur but to do so independently of the stimulus or response. As noted earlier, the importance of the outcome as a stimulus event leads to the anticipation that its removal would produce stimulus generalization decrement. Often, one would like to minimize such generalization decrement to explore other changes that occur with removal of the contingency. Consequently, many experiments have investigated the changes that take place when the contingency is disrupted by continuing the outcome in a noncontingent manner (e.g., Boakes, 1973; Rescorla & Skucy, 1969; Uhl & Garcia, 1969). Typically, such experiments have found that behavior still deteriorates, although sometimes at a slower rate compared with that observed during an extinction procedure involving outcome removal.

There is reason to believe that the associative changes that result from such random delivery are similar to those that result from a conventional extinction procedure. For instance, the decrement produced by random reinforcement can frequently give way to substantial spontaneous recovery if the reinforcement is removed entirely (e.g., Lindblom & Jenkins, 1981). Moreover, recent experiments suggest that the strength of the original S–O associations may be left intact by such a procedure. Delamater (1996) reported that Pavlovian S–O associations remain intact through a procedure in which O is delivered independently of S. Using a Pavlovian conditioned magazine approach preparation like that described earlier, he found that a random contingency depressed magazine approach but left intact the ability of S to transfer to new responses based on a shared outcome.

In addition, there is some evidence of response specificity to the decrement produced by a random contingency. A previously unpublished experiment in our laboratory recently replicated for, random reinforcement, the result reported by Rescorla (1993a) for extinction—that a neutral stimulus present during the decremental procedure develops the specific ability to decrease the response undergoing the decrement. In that experiment, two responses were both trained for six 20-min sessions on a variable interval (VI) 1-min schedule with a pellet reinforcer. Then both responses were subjected to random deliveries of the pellet on a variable time (VT) 1-min schedule. A light was present for this treatment of one response and a noise present for the treatment of the other. After six 20-min sessions of this treatment, the responses were retrained with two VI sessions and then each tested in an 8-min extinction session during which both stimuli occurred for 30-sec periods. Figure 4.8 displays the results of responding during the test, showing responding in the absence of any stimulus, during the stimulus present at the time of a particular response's random treatment, and during the stimulus present at the time when the other response had been given the random treatment. Presenting the stimulus that had been present when a response was given random reinforcement depressed the response relative both to that in the nonstimulus period, Wilcoxon $T(15) = 25, p < .05$, and to that during the presentation of the other stimulus given the same treatment with another response, $T(15) = 13, p < .01$. The rates did not differ reliably during the latter two periods. These results suggest that the decremental process active during a random treatment has the same kind of response specificity previously observed following a standard extinction treatment.

Taken together, these results begin to suggest that, as in the case of extinction, response depression produced by a random relation to the out-

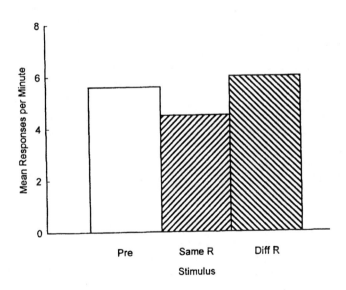

FIG. 4.8.   Test responding for a stimulus that had been present when the same R was subjected to a random procedure. Another stimulus had been present when the different R was likewise subjected to that procedure.

come is accomplished by a mechanism that leaves outcome associations intact but importantly involves the response.

Replacement of One Outcome by Another

Another alteration in the contingency that has been of some historical interest is the replacement of the original outcome by another. The most frequently studied case, so-called "counterconditioning," involves using a second outcome that is affectively the opposite of that used initially. For instance, one might replace a food pellet with a shock or vice versa. Not surprisingly, this procedure produces marked changes in behavior, typically taking the form of a loss in the originally trained response. Because one can view the replacement of O1 by O2 as concurrently carrying out extinction of the S–O1 or R–O1 association together with training of the S–O2 or R–O2 association, this result is to be expected if O1 and O2 support different behaviors. Recent experiments by Bouton and his collaborators suggest, however, that this loss in behavior does not involve loss of the S–O1 association any more than does simple extinction (e.g., Peck & Bouton, 1990). They found that after such counterconditioning, the response that S evokes is heavily dependent on the context in which it is tested. Of particular interest, testing in the original conditioning context produces evidence of preservation of the original association with O1.

In our laboratory we have been investigating a somewhat different case of counterconditioning, in which O1 and O2 are similarly valued but qualitatively different events, sucrose and pellets. This is a particularly interesting case because it involves changing the sensory aspects of the outcome while leaving its motivational, affective, and response components relatively unchanged. Our results indicate that replacing one of these outcomes by the other results in little change in responding either in Pavlovian magazine responding or in instrumental responding (e.g., Rescorla, 1996b). Yet more detailed analysis of the associations that result from this procedure, using transfer and devaluation techniques, reveals that associations with the sensory aspects of both outcomes have developed fully and remain intact. Moreover, it appears as though both associations remain concurrently active.

This is illustrated in Fig. 4.9, which shows the results of one instrumental learning experiment using the devaluation procedure to explore the associative structure after one outcome replaces another (Rescorla, 1995). In this experiment several responses successively earned O1 and then O2. Then devaluation was conducted with O1, O2, or neither outcome. The results of the test show that devaluation of either the first or second earned outcome depressed responding. Moreover, the degree of that depression was similar in each case, suggesting that both outcomes continue to contribute to performance, and to about the same extent. It appears as though current performance depends on the integrity of both associations.

It is worth noting that this equivalent dependence on the state of both outcomes in the test is not due to initial replacement of an R–O1 association with an R–O2 association from which the animal shows spontaneous recovery during the period when the devaluation takes place. In a parallel series of experiments, we have attempted to monitor such recovery by "tagging" the periods during which O1 and O2 were used with the concurrent presence of another discrimination and its reversal (Rescorla, 1996b). This allows one to inspect which of those other discriminations dominates at the time of the test following devaluation, the discrimination present during the use of O1 or that present during the use of O2. The results clearly showed the domination of the more recently trained discrimination despite the equivalence of sensitivity to devaluation of O1 and O2.

The fact that replacing O1 with O2 establishes a new association with O2 while leaving the original with O1 in place might lead one to expect that responding would increase. We know that such a procedure does

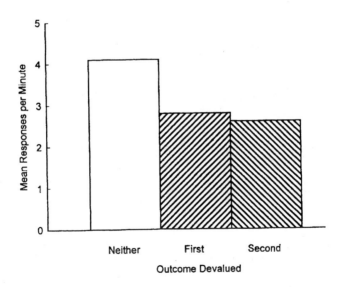

FIG 4.9. Effects of devaluation on responses successively trained with two outcomes. Either the first-earned, second-earned, or neither outcome was devalued prior to the test (after Rescorla, 1995). Adapted with permission from Experimental Psychology Society.

increase the number of associations with a valued outcome. Moreover, the results of experiments like that displayed in Fig. 4.9 suggest that both associations remain concurrently functional. It is natural to anticipate that these associations would sum to generate increased performance. This seems especially plausible because we have recently observed summation responding to two stimuli that were separately paired with these same pellet and sucrose outcomes (Rescorla, 1999). Yet when one outcome replaces another in either an instrumental or Pavlovian procedure, we have often found little evidence for increased responding (e.g., Rescorla, 1995, 1996b).

Investigation of a less frequently studied decremental procedure, "overexpectation," may provide some helpful insight into this result. It has been known for some years that if two stimuli are separately conditioned by an outcome, then presenting them in compound followed by the same outcome results in a decrement of the response that each controls (e.g., Rescorla, 1970). Lattal and Nakajima (1998) recently reported a careful series of experiments documenting this overexpectation result in the magazine approach preparation. This phenomenon has typically been interpreted in terms of an extinction-like process in which the outcome delivered is inadequate to the outcome expected on the basis of the summed associations (e.g., Rescorla & Wagner, 1972). It has implicitly been thought of as reducing the strength of the association established in initial conditioning.

However, in the light of the previously described results with other decremental procedures, it is natural to ask whether overexpectation instead superimposes some outcome-independent decremental process while leaving the original associations with outcomes in place. If that were to happen, then the replacement of O1 by O2 might allow the growth of the S–O2 association alongside of the S–O1 association, with the resulting emergence of overexpectation because of the summed associations. If the consequence of that overexpectation were an outcome-independent depressive process, then the final result might be concurrent presence of both S–O1 and S–O2 associations as well as of a depressive process that prevents the exhibition of greater responding.

A recent series of experiments provides some encouragement for that account (Rescorla, 1999). Those experiments found not only summation, but also overexpectation, when two stimuli signaling different outcomes are combined. Of more interest, the behavioral decrement produced by reinforcing the compound with only one outcome did not result from changes in the S–O associations. At the same time that exhibition of the original behavior declined, transfer experiments showed continued integrity of the S–O associations.

Figure 4.10 shows one example of this result. In this experiment two auditory and two visual stimuli received conditioning using different

Response Training	Conditioning	Overexpectation	Test
R1–O1	A1–O1	V2A1--O1	A1:
	A2–O2		R1, R2, Rm
R2--O2	V1--O1	A2--O2	A2:
	V2--O2		

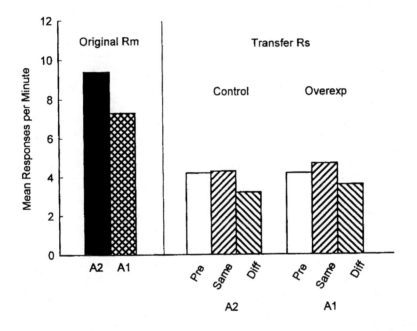

FIG. 4.10. Design and results of an overexpectation experiment. Initially two transfer responses (R1 and R2) earned different outcomes (O1 and O2). Then two auditory stimuli (A1 and A2) and two visual (V1 and V2) stimuli were paired with those outcomes in Pavlovian fashion, resulting in magazine responding (Rm). One auditory stimulus (A1) was subjected to overexpectation and then both were tested for their transfer to R1 and R2 as well as their ability to evoke the original Rm. Results are shown during A1 and A2 in terms of their abilities to evoke magazine responding and to transfer to responses that previously earned the same or different outcomes (after Rescorla, 1999).

outcomes. Then one of the auditory stimuli was subjected to an overexpectation procedure in which it was presented concurrently with a visual stimulus that had signaled the alternative outcome. That compound was followed by the outcome previously used to train the auditory stimulus alone. The other auditory stimulus simply received continued training and hence serves as a point of comparison. When the two auditory stimuli were then transferred to responses that had earned these same outcomes, two results were observed. First, the rate of magazine approach was lower during the auditory stimulus that had been subjected to additional reinforcement in compound. Decrement in that response (i.e., overexpectation) indeed occurred. Second, both the control and the treated auditory stimulus showed selective augmentation of responses with which they shared outcomes. This suggests the continued presence of outcome associations for both. Indeed, the magnitude of the transfer, although characteristically small for Pavlovian CSs, was similar in the two cases. Although overexpectation had diminished the ability of the stimulus to control the magazine approach, it did not affect its ability to transfer.

These results from overexpectation are quite similar to those observed in extinction by Delamater (1996), as well as those shown in Fig. 4.6. There was a depression of the original response accompanied by a preservation of the underlying outcome associations. As in the case of extinction, a plausible account is that the depression was produced by a response-specific process rather than one tied to outcomes.

The similarity in the results encourages one to ask whether one could find other evidence that the depressive process is the same with outcome replacement as in extinction. One recent series of experiments identifies one other commonality of interest—spontaneous recovery. Although replacement of one outcome by another of equal value does not diminish behavior, the account given earlier suggests that it does engage the same depressive process as extinction in preventing the growth of behavior. If that is the case, then one might expect to observe the same dissipation of that depressive process with the passage of time. That is, even though replacing O1 with O2 does not immediately change performance, it may be that allowing time to pass would nevertheless produce "spontaneous recovery." In several recent experiments, we have found evidence for such an effect in instrumental learning and in Pavlovian conditioning (Rescorla, 1996c, 1997b, 1997c).

Figure 4.11 shows one example of this taken from a Pavlovian magazine approach experiment, modeled after the spontaneous recovery experiments described in Fig. 4.1. Initially two stimuli received Pavlovian conditioning with different outcomes. They each then received additional training with the other outcome and were tested for responding in a final test. However, for one stimulus (S1) the training with the second outcome was given at a temporal distance from the test, whereas for the other stimulus (S2) it came immediately prior to the test. Figure 4.11 shows the level of magazine performance to those two stimuli at the end of treatment with the second outcome and then in the test. It is clear that there was greater responding to S1, the stimulus that was allowed more time for recovery after its training with the second outcome. Despite the fact that this second training had no immediate impact on responding, if time were allowed to elapse before the test, there was considerable elevation.

This basic result has been replicated for instrumental R–O and S–O associations. Moreover, there is some evidence that the growth in responding with time does not reflect growth in the outcome-based associations themselves. Transfer does not change with time (e.g., Rescorla, 1997c). In some ways this is unsurprising because earlier work had shown that replacing O1 with O2 did not diminish the outcome associations; hence they might not be expected to recover. However, it does confirm the view that the depressive process here and in extinction may be response-based and may show the same temporal dynamics.

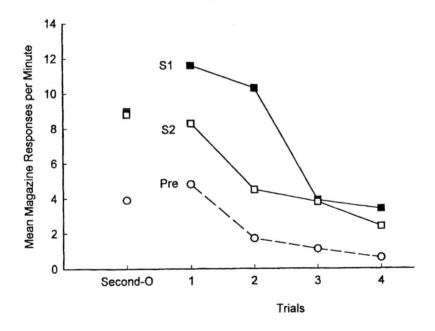

FIG. 4.11. Spontaneous recovery after successive pairing with two different outcomes. The second pairing took place either at a temporal distance (S1) or immediately prior to the test (S2). Responding during the pairing with the second outcome is shown at the left.

CONCLUSION

I have reviewed a number of different procedures that undermine previously learned performance. One way to think about all of the instances that produce behavioral depression is that they result from an associative structure producing behavior that is inappropriately large for the outcome that actually occurs. In all of these cases the animal has a total expectation that is greater than that warranted by the result of the trial. In extinction, its prior learning leads to the expectation of an outcome that is deleted. When outcomes are uncorrelated with stimuli or responses, this should result in additional conditioning to situational cues and behaviors. That additional conditioning may then summate with the original learning to produce a similar discrepancy. Moreover, when one outcome is replaced by another, the joint presence of both associations results in a total expectation that exceeds the value of the single outcome that is delivered.

A natural way to think about such results is in terms of the negative emotional reaction that might result from the discrepancy between the value of the outcome anticipated and that received. As noted previously, the occurrence of such an emotional reaction, such as frustration, might have a number of consequences. By counteracting the positive affect of the outcomes, it would act to limit the total affective reaction and presumably undermine performance. However, to the degree that frustration depends only on the affective nature of the outcomes it would not differentially undermine sensory information, instead leaving intact information about the sensory features of the outcomes. As a result, the conditioning of frustration might limit the ability of the stimuli to motivate their original behaviors while allowing transfer and devaluation procedures to continue to detect knowledge about the sensory properties of the outcomes. Moreover, it could provide a mechanism for changes in performance with time, such as spontaneous recovery from extinction or from the decrements involved in replacing one outcome by another, if the separate frustration process were partially to dissipate with time. Finally, frustration might also be conditioned to the particular responses that are evoked when it occurs, providing a means to account for the high degree of response specificity reported here.

Although relatively neglected in recent years, extinction remains a central phenomenon in the study of associative learning. In agreement with historical views, recent evidence suggests that extinction leaves in place the associations developed during acquisition. Extinction superimposes on that learning some depressive process that interferes with performance. The finding that extinction allows excellent preservation of the details of the originally used outcomes suggests that this depressive process is relatively outcome independent. One candidate with some promise is that the responses that occur during extinction enter into new learning.

ACKNOWLEDGMENT

The research reported in this chapter was made possible by a series of generous grants from the National Science Foundation.

REFERENCES

Adams, C., & Dickinson, A. (1981). Actions and habits: Variations in associative representations during instrumental learning. In N. E. Spear & R. R. Miller (Eds.), *Information processing in animals: Memory mechanisms* (pp. 143–166). Hillsdale, NJ: Lawrence Erlbaum Associates.

Amsel, A. (1958). The role of frustrative nonreward in noncontinuous reward situations. *Psychological Bulletin, 55*, 102–119.

Amsel, A. (1967). Partial reinforcement effects on vigor and persistence. In K. W. Spence & J. T. Spence (Eds.), *The psychology of learning and motivation* (Vol. 1, pp. 1–65). New York: Academic Press.

Amsel, A. (1992). *Frustration theory.* Cambridge, UK: Cambridge University Press.

Azrin, N. H., Hutchinson, R. R., & Hake, D. F. (1966). Extinction-induced aggression. *Journal of the Experimental Analysis of Behavior, 9*, 191–204.

Boakes, R. A. (1973). Response decrements produced by extinction and by response-independent reinforcement. *Journal of the Experimental Analysis of Behavior, 19*, 293–302.

Bouton, M. E. (1991). Context and retrieval in extinction and in other examples of interference in simple associative learning. In L. W. Dachowski & C. F. Flaherty (Eds.), *Current topics in animal learning: Brain, emotion, and cognition* (pp. 25–53). Hillsdale, NJ: Lawrence Erlbaum Associates.

Bouton, M. E. (1993). Context, time, and memory retrieval in the interference paradigms of Pavlovian learning. *Psychological Bulletin, 114*, 8–99.

Bouton, M. E., & Bolles, R. C. (1979). Role of conditioned contextual stimuli in reinstatement of extinguished fear. *Journal of Experimental Psychology: Animal Behavior Processes, 5*, 368–378.

Brimer, C. J. (1972). Disinhibition of an operant response. In R. A. Boakes & M. S. Halliday (Eds.), *Inhibition and learning* (pp. 225–227). New York: Academic Press.

Bush, R. R., & Mosteller, F. (1951). A mathematical model for simple learning. *Psychological Review, 58*, 313–323.

Capaldi, E. J. (1967). A sequential hypothesis of instrumental learning. In K. W. Spence & J. T. Spence (Eds.), *Psychology of learning and motivation* (Vol. 1, pp. 67–156). New York: Academic Press.

Chorazyna, H. (1962). Some properties of conditioned inhibition. *Acta Biologiae Experimentalis, 22*, 5.

Colwill, R. M. (1991). Negative discriminative stimuli provide information about the identity of omitted response-contingent outcomes. *Animal Learning and Behavior, 19*, 326–336.

Colwill, R. M., & Motzkin, D. K. (1994). Encoding of the unconditioned stimulus in Pavlovian conditioning. *Animal Learning and Behavior, 22,* 384–394.

Colwill, R. M., & Rescorla, R. A. (1985). Post-conditioning devaluation of a reinforcer affects instrumental responding. *Journal of Experimental Psychology: Animal Behavior Processes, 11,* 120–132.

Colwill, R. M., & Rescorla, R. A. (1988). The role of response–reinforcer associations in creases throughout extended instrumental training. *Animal Learning and Behavior, 16,* 105–111.

Colwill, R. M., & Rescorla, R. A. (1990). Evidence for the hierarchical structure of instrumental learning. *Animal Learning and Behavior, 18,* 71–82.

Daly, H. B. (1974). Reinforcing properties of escape from frustration aroused in various learning situations. In G. H. Bower (Ed.), *The psychology of learning and motivation* (Vol. 8, pp. 187–232). New York: Academic Press.

Delamater, A. R. (1996). Effects of several extinction treatments upon the integrity of Pavlovian stimulus-outcome associations. *Animal Learning and Behavior, 24,* 437–449.

Delamater, A. R. (1997). Selective reinstatement of stimulus–outcome associations. *Animal Learning and Behavior, 25,* 400–412.

Domjan, M. (1998). *The principles of learning and behavior* (4th ed.). New York: Brooks/Cole.

Estes, W. K. (1950). Toward a statistical theory of learning. *Psychological Review, 57,* 94–107.

Hilgard, E. R., & Marquis, D. G. (1940). *Conditioning and learning.* New York: Appleton-Century.

Holland, P. C., & Rescorla, R. A. (1975). Second-order conditioning with food unconditioned stimulus. *Journal of Comparative and Physiological Psychology, 88,* 459–467.

Kimble, G. A. (1961). *Hilgard and Marquis' conditioning and learning.* New York: Appleton-Century-Crofts.

Konorski, J. (1948). *Conditioned reflexes and neuron organization.* Cambridge, UK: Cambridge University Press.

Konorski, J. (1967). *Integrative activity of the brain.* Chicago: University of Chicago Press.

Lattal, K. M., & Nakajima, S. (1998). Overexpectation in appetitive Pavlovian and instrumental conditioning. *Animal Learning and Behavior, 26,* 351–360.

Lieberman, D. A. (1993). *Learning: Behavior and cognition* (2nd ed.). Pacific Grove, CA: Brooks/Cole.

Lindblom, L. L., & Jenkins, H. M. (1981). Responses elicited by noncontingency or negatively contingent reinforcement recover in extinction. *Journal of Experimental Psychology: Animal Behavior Processes, 7,* 175–190.

Mackintosh, N. J. (1974). *The psychology of animal learning.* New York: Academic Press.

Pavlov, I. P. (1927). *Conditioned reflexes.* Oxford, UK: Oxford University Press.

Peck, C. A., & Bouton, M. E. (1990). Contest and performance in aversive-to-appetitive and appetitive-to-aversive transfer. *Learning and Motivation, 21,* 1–31.

Rescorla, R. A. (1970). Reduction in the effectiveness of reinforcement after prior excitatory conditioning. *Learning and Motivation, 1,* 372–381.

Rescorla, R. A. (1973). Second-order conditioning: implications for theories of learning. In F. J. McGuigan & D. Lumsden (Eds.), *Contemporary approaches to learning and conditioning* (pp. 127–150). New York: Winston.

Rescorla, R. A. (1990). Instrumental responses become associated with reinforcers differing in one feature. *Animal Learning and Behavior, 18,* 206–211.

Rescorla, R. A. (1991a). Association relations in instrumental learning: The Eighteenth Bartlett memorial lecture. *Quarterly Journal of Experimental Psychology, 43B,* 1–23.

Rescorla, R. A. (1991b) Associations of multiple outcomes with an instrumental response. *Journal of Experimental Psychology: Animal Behavior Processes, 17,* 465–474.

Rescorla, R. A. (1992). Association between an instrumental discriminative stimulus and multiple outcomes. *Journal of Experimental Psychology: Animal Behavior Processes, 18,* 95–104.

Rescorla, R. A. (1993a). Inhibitory associations between S and R in extinction. *Animal Learning and Behavior, 21,* 327–336.

Rescorla, R. A. (1993b). Preservation of response–outcome associations through extinction. *Animal Learning and Behavior, 21,* 238–245.

Rescorla, R. A. (1994). Transfer of instrumental control mediated by a devalued outcome. *Animal Learning and Behavior, 22,* 27–33.

Rescorla, R. A. (1995). Full preservation of a response–outcome association through training with a second outcome. *Quarterly Journal of Experimental Psychology, 48B,* 252–261.

Rescorla, R. A. (1996a). Preservation of Pavlovian associations through extinction. *Quarterly Journal of Experimental Psychology, 49B,* 245–258.

Rescorla, R. A. (1996b). Response–outcome associations remain functional through interference treatments. *Animal Learning and Behavior, 24,* 450–458.

Rescorla, R. A. (1996c). Spontaneous recovery after training with multiple outcomes. *Animal Learning and Behavior, 24,* 11–18.

Rescorla, R. A. (1997a). Response-inhibition in extinction. *Quarterly Journal of Experimental Psychology, 50B,* 238–252.

Rescorla, R. A. (1997b). Spontaneous recovery after Pavlovian conditioning with multiple outcomes. *Animal Learning and Behavior, 25,* 99–107.

Rescorla, R. A. (1997c). Spontaneous recovery of instrumental discriminative responding. *Animal Learning and Behavior, 25,* 485–497.

Rescorla, R. A. (1998). Instrumental learning: Nature and persistence. In M. Sabourin, F. I. M. Craig, & M. Roberts (Eds.), *Proceedings of the XXVI International Congress of Psychology: Vol. 2. Advances in psychological science: Biological and cognitive aspects* (pp. 239–258). London: Psychology Press.

Rescorla, R. A. (1999). Summation and overexpectation with qualitatively different outcomes. *Animal Learning and Behavior, 27,* 50–62.

Rescorla, R. A., & Cunningham, C. L. (1978). Recovery of the US representation over time during extinction. *Learning and Motivation, 9,* 373–391.

Rescorla, R. A., & Heth, C. D. (1975). Reinstatement of fear to an extinguished conditioned stimulus. *Journal of Experimental Psychology: Animal Behavior Processes, 1,* 88–96.

Rescorla, R. A., & Holland, P. C. (1976). Some behavioral approaches to the study of learning. In E. Bennett & M. R. Rosenzweig (Eds.), *Neural mechanisms of learning and memory* (pp. 165–192). Cambridge, MA: MIT Press.

Rescorla, R. A., & Skucy, J. C. (1969). The effect of response-independent reinforcers during extinction. *Journal of Comparative and Physiological Psychology, 67,* 381–389.

Rescorla, R. A., & Wagner, A. R. (1972). A theory of Pavlovian conditioning: Variations in the effectiveness of reinforcement and nonreinforcement. In A. Black & W. F. Prokasy (Eds.), *Classical conditioning II* (pp. 64–99). New York: Appleton-Century-Crofts.

Robbins, S. J. (1990). Mechanisms underlying spontaneous recovery in autoshaping. *Journal of Experimental Psychology: Animal Behavior Processes, 16,* 235–249.

Rumelhart, D. E., Hinton, G. E., & Williams, R. J. (1986). Learning internal *representations* by error propagation. In D. E. Rumelhart & J. McClelland (Eds.), *Parallel distributed processing: Explorations in the microstructure of cognition* (Vol. 1, pp. 318–362). Cambridge, MA: MIT Press.

Schwartz, B., & Robbins, S. J. (1995). *Psychology of learning and behavior* (4th ed.). New York: Norton.

Skinner, B. F. (1938). *The behavior of organisms.* New York: Appleton-Century-Crofts.

Solomon, R. L., & Corbit, J. D. (1974). An opponent-process theory of motivation. *Psychological Review, 81,* 119–145.

Uhl, C. N., and Garcia, E. E. (1969). Comparison of omission with extinction in response elimination in rats. *Journal of Comparative and Physiological Psychology, 73,* 556–564.

Wagner, A. R. (1963). Conditioned frustration as a learned drive. *Journal of Experimental Psychology, 66,* 142–148.

Wagner, A. R. (1966). Frustration and punishment. In R. N. Haber (Ed.), *Current research in motivation* (pp. 229–239). New York: Holt, Rinehart, & Winston.

Wagner, A. R. (1969). Stimulus selection and a "modified continuity theory." In G. H. Bower & J. T. Spence (Eds.), *The psychology of learning and motivation* (Vol. 3, pp 1–41). New York: Academic Press.

Wagner, A. R. (1981). SOP: A model of automatic memory processing in animal behavior. In N. E. Spear & R. R. Miller (Eds.), *Information processing in animals: Memory mechanisms* (pp. 5–47). Hillsdale, NJ: Lawrence Erlbaum Associates.

chapter 5

Motivational Modes in Behavior Systems

William Timberlake
Indiana University

A recent development in the study of learning and behavior is the emergence of a behavior systems approach, based on both the laboratory and field behavior of animals (Domjan, 1994; Fanselow, 1994; Hogan, 1994; Shettleworth, 1994; Timberlake, 1994). The behavior systems approach combines an ethologist's emphasis on the evolutionary foundation of the form and control of functional behavior with a psychologist's concern with the role of learning in creating new responses and controlling stimuli.

The importance and potential power of integrating ethological and laboratory approaches to learning and behavior has been argued with persuasiveness (e.g., Kamil, 1988; D. B. Miller, 1977; Tinbergen, 1951). Unfortunately, differences between the two approaches have proved surprisingly difficult to reconcile (Timberlake & K. M. Silva, 1995). For example, even though laboratory research on memory for stored food in birds has both face validity and rigor (e.g., Brodbeck, 1994; Kamil &

Balda, 1985; Krebs, Healy, & Shettleworth, 1990; Olson, Kamil, Balda, & Nims, 1995; Sherry, 1984), a given piece of research rarely satisfies both field biologists interested in foraging and psychologists concerned with the traditional concepts and procedures of laboratory learning. In short, although more has been discovered about how learning contributes to solving specific functional problems, there remains surprisingly little contact between the study of functional behavior in animals and the laboratory learning research accumulated over the last 100 years (e.g., Hearst, 1988; Kimble, 1961; Mackintosh, 1974).

BEHAVIOR SYSTEMS

The behavior systems approach has worked toward resolving the separation between laboratory learning and ethological analysis by relating all behavior to a common functional behavior system. A behavior system is constructed initially by integrating observations of the sensorimotor organization and motivational processes of a species in both the laboratory and field (Timberlake, 1999). Then the system is tested and developed further using the procedures and phenomena of laboratory learning. Assumptions underlying the behavior systems approach include: (a) the same systems organize behavior and stimulus processing in all circumstances, no matter how "natural" or "artificial"; and (b) the effect of an experimental manipulation is rarely direct or simple, but results from interactions among the manipulation, the supporting stimulus environment, and the mechanisms and ongoing processes of the relevant behavior systems.

A behavior system is composed of multiple levels of stimulus and response structures and motivational processes (see Fig. 5.1). The system level accounts for the organization of processing and control around important functions such as feeding (Timberlake, 1983a, 1983b, 1983c; Timberlake & Lucas, 1989), reproduction (Baerends & Drent, 1982; Domjan & Hollis, 1988), defense (Bolles, 1970; Fanselow, 1994; Fanselow & Lester, 1988), and body care (Fentress, 1973). *Subsystems* refer to a coherent subset of stimulus sensitivities, response components, and regulatory strategies that relate to the system function. Figure 5.1 shows an example of a predatory subsystem of the feeding system in rats. This hypothesized organization is culled from observations of relatively unconstrained laboratory rats and free-ranging wild rats (Barnett, 1975; Blanchard & Blanchard, 1990; Calhoun, 1962; Ewer, 1971; Galef, 1990; Steininger, 1950; Telle, 1966; Timberlake & F. J. Silva, 1994).

The vertical column of modes near the center of Fig. 5.1 represents a sequence of motivational substates ranging from a general search mode at the top of the column to a consummatory search mode at the bottom.

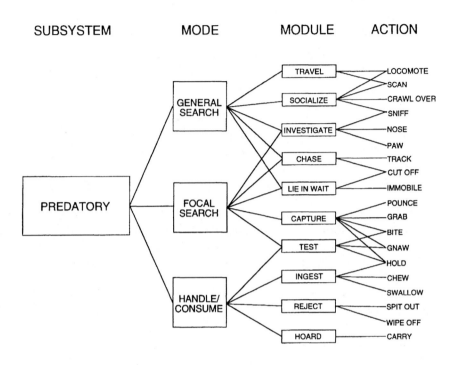

FIG 5.1.   There are four levels of a behavior system: the system, subsystems, motivational modes, and perceptual-motor modules. This figure focuses on the motivational modes and perceptual-motor modules of the predatory subsystem of the feeding system of a rat. The actions potentially controlled by the system components in conjunction with the environment are shown on the far right. Note there is overlap in the relation of modules to specific modes.

Engaging a mode engages a repertoire of preorganized perceptual-motor modules (shown to the right) that increase sensitivities to particular stimuli (e.g., Baerends & Kruijt, 1973; Barlow, 1977) and tendencies to respond with particular motor components (Fentress, 1976; Hogan, 1988; Tinbergen, 1951). These perceptual-motor units are dubbed *preorganized* because they have been both selected over generations and modified by previous individual experience to increase the possibilities of successful search behavior in a variety of circumstances.

A typical feeding sequence begins with a rat in general search mode, showing locomotor search and increased sensitivity to spatial and social stimuli that are likely to lead closer to food. The sight of a small moving object at a distance readily elicits chasing. As the prey becomes proximate, a focal search mode is elicited, engaging a repertoire of perceptual-motor units related to capturing and subduing the prey. Tactual and olfactory cues from the prey should then evoke the handling-consuming mode and sensitize a repertoire of biting, manipulation, chewing, and swallowing. Following consumption of a small prey item, a postfood focal search mode predominates as the animal engages in area-restricted search; then, if food is not forthcoming, the general search mode and repertoire will reemerge. (For a similar analysis of modes in a defensive system, see Fanselow, 1994.)

Returning to Fig. 5.1, a combination of system, subsystem, mode, and module, in conjunction with the environment, facilitates and coordinates individual responses (*action patterns*). It is worth noting that the levels and units of organization within a behavior system are functional concepts based on characteristic combinations of determinants and classes of outcome rather than on known neural mechanisms (although connections between these levels of analysis would be expected to emerge; e.g., Fanselow, 1991, 1994; Tinsley, Rebec, & Timberlake, 1999). Finally, the interface of the system with the environment by means of specific action patterns and environmental support stimuli is at the far right of the diagram.

Behavior Systems and Learning

Learning in a behavior system is potentially complex and extensive, including changes in perceptual processing, responses, modes, and systems and their relation to each other and to the environment. Such a view seems at variance with the traditional tendency to conceptualize Pavlovian and operant conditioning as strengthening simple associations or responses. In a behavior systems view, Pavlovian and operant conditioning are better viewed as experimental procedures than as fundamental building blocks of behavior. These procedures interact with aspects of the environment system structures and processes to produce behavior and many sorts of learning (Timberlake, 1995), including: learning about the timing of daily sessions and subsequent feedings in both local and circadian frames (e.g., Timberlake, Gawley, & Lucas, 1987; White & Timberlake, 1999), the adaptation of novelty and stress reactions to the apparatus, differentiating and generalizing stimuli on the basis of available modules, the conditioning of systems and modes, and the incorporation of food intake into the overall regulation of energy. Conceptualizing these changes using the elements and processes of a behavior system seems preferable to modeling outcomes using only a single response strengthening process, or a small set of associative links.

This is not to say that distinctions are lacking among the outcomes of Pavlovian and operant conditioning procedures, but differences that arise result from more than the procedures. Because responding is created at the interface of the procedure, the supporting environment, and the system, the result will depend on their interaction. An additional critical determinant of the outcome of a conditioning procedure is the experimenter's choice of a response measure. To the extent that operant and Pavlovian procedures interact differently with the organism's structures and processes, and the experimenter's measures highlight those differences, the procedures will produce different outcomes. To the extent that interactions are similar despite differences in experimenter manipulations, and the experimenter's measures bring out these similarities, the results will be similar.

THIS CHAPTER

The initial emphasis of research on behavior systems and learning was to explore the contribution of preorganized perceptual-motor modules to the form of learned behavior in the laboratory (e.g., Timberlake & Lucas, 1989). The importance of such modules is particularly apparent in the Pavlovian conditioning paradigm (as well as under minimal response requirements in the operant paradigm) because animals are not required to perform a specific response to produce food. Instead they "fill in" with response forms from their available repertoire. The interested reader should consult Timberlake and Lucas (1989) and Timberlake (1983b, 1990, 1994) for reviews of these studies. I briefly mention a few examples here.

Based on prey consumed in the field and the reactions of laboratory-reared animals to live crickets, Timberlake and Washburne (1989) hypothesized differences among six rodent species in preorganized perceptual-motor units relevant to predation. Based on these observations we predicted the relative probability and form with which prey-naive members of each species would interact with a prey surrogate (a moving ball bearing related to food) in the laboratory. As predicted, the more predatory species contacted the ball bearings more frequently and all species showed responses to the bearings similar to those occurring during interaction with the live crickets. For example, the species *Peromyscus californicus* attacked both crickets and ball bearings by lunging toward them, sliding along the substrate with paws outstretched on either side of the prey item and mouth open to bite.

We confirmed several more predictions of the relevance of preorganized perceptual-motor organization to learned behavior, including differences in rats' interactions with a moving bearing predicting food versus water (Timberlake, 1986), differences between the behavior of rats versus hamsters to conspecifics predicting food (Timberlake, 1983b; Timberlake & Grant, 1975), and difference in the type of behavior directed toward a ball bearing predicting acceptable versus poisoned food (Timberlake & Melcer, 1988). Similar evidence for the importance of preorganized perceptual-motor units in other species included differences in the autoshaped key pecking of pigeons as a function of food versus water reward (Jenkins & Moore, 1973), aggressive behavior directed at conspecifics by territorial gouramis (Hollis, 1990), and sexual behavior directed by male quail at models (Domjan, 1994).

The purpose of this chapter is to extend the work on behavior systems by focusing primarily on the contribution of search modes to learned behavior in the feeding system of the rat. As noted previously, search modes are motivational states involving particular repertoires of modules (response components and stimulus sensitivities). There appear to be four types of mode: general search, focal search, handling and consuming, and postfood focal search. Activation of a search mode increases the probability that perceptual-motor structures comprising it will be evoked by appropriate environmental stimuli or conditioned by appropriate environmental contingencies. Most important, we assume that search modes themselves can be conditioned to cues that are related to receipt of an unconditioned stimulus (US; a reward). Unlike the conditioning of specific stimuli and responses, the conditioning of search modes should produce a more general motivational quality that supports their entire repertoire of perceptual-motor modules.

This chapter explores evidence for search modes and their characteristics, how they are produced, and how they combine with specific cues and contextual support to determine learning. We will continue to focus on Pavlovian conditioning procedures and phenomena for the same reasons we used Pavlovian procedures to explore the existence of characteristic perceptual-motor (module) organization. The animal must "fill in" behaviors related to the system of the US, the environmental support, and the relation of the CS to the US. As a result, the behaviors that emerge can be used to identify the dominant search modes present.

In the first section of this chapter, I consider whether we can account for both naturally occurring and learned strings of appetitive responses using only a sequence of stimulus–response units (perceptual-motor modules), or if an extra layer of causation in the form of search modes is required. In the second section, I evaluate the ways in which the characteristics of the conditioned stimulus (CS)–US relation in a Pavlovian procedure can influence the dominant search mode. In the third section,

I explore the temporal characteristics of search modes in interfood intervals. In the fourth section, I consider how search modes may contribute to complex Pavlovian conditioning phenomena, such as backward conditioning, context blocking, and conditioned inhibition. I conclude with a discussion of the usefulness and coherence of search modes as revealed in these data and their possible relation to other conceptions of motivational states (Brown & Jenkins, 1968; Hearst & Jenkins, 1974; Konorski, 1967; Rescorla & Solomon, 1967; Solomon & Corbit, 1974).

POSSIBLE DIFFICULTIES

To some researchers it may seem unlikely that an ethologically based model like behavior systems can account for phenomena occurring within the artificial environments and seemingly arbitrary problems of laboratory learning research. Several arguments, however, support this attempt. First, laboratory experimenters have invested considerable time in tuning (iteratively changing and checking the effects of) their apparatus and procedures to produce reliable and vigorous responding (Timberlake, 1990). I assume that such tuning engages the existing appetitive organization of the animal (e.g., Timberlake, 1990, 1997). As evidence for this view, note that the dominant learning responses—manipulation and locomotion in rats, and pecking in pigeons—are important parts of naturally occurring foraging behavior in these species.

Second, because animals have not been selected to deal with artificial laboratory environments, they must necessarily fall back on the same stimulus processing and response repertoire engaged in more natural settings. As Tinbergen (1951) and Lorenz (1981) so artfully documented, artificial stimuli and controlled environments can be of great advantage in revealing the causation of naturally occurring behavior. Finally, the laboratory rat, presumably an artificial creature perverted by domestication, has been shown to have the same perceptual-motor repertoire as its wild cousins, but with altered thresholds for expression (e.g., Blanchard & Blanchard, 1990; Boice, 1972; Galef, 1990).

BEHAVIOR CHAINS AND SEARCH MODES

A major focus in both ethology and laboratory learning has been on the production of behavior chains, a sequence of perceptual-motor modules leading to a consummatory response. Ethologists such as Tinbergen (1951) showed how courtship behavior in sticklebacks and bee hunting in wasps could be explained as a sequence of releaser/fixed-action-pattern units. Psychologists have created similar complex chains of behavior by conditioning a sequence of novel discriminative-stimulus/operant-response units. For example, Skinner (1937) trained the rat, Pliny, to pull a long chain to obtain a marble, which the rat then carried across the cage and deposited down a chimney before returning to the food tray to obtain food. In both types of behavior chain the observed sequence of responses is presumed to be linked by the fact that the performance of one pattern places the animal in position to receive the stimulus controlling the next response.

A basic premise of the behavior systems approach is that underlying and supporting a behavior chain is a sequence of search modes, each related to a large repertoire of perceptual-motor organization on the basis of both learning and natural selection. A critical assumption is that each search mode can be conditioned to environmental stimuli and internal timing cues related to the US. The major question to be answered in this section is whether there is a need to assume the existence of a sequence of modes underlying behavior chains, or if behavior can be explained completely without this assumption. I examine this question separately within the approaches of ethology and laboratory learning. This analysis is based on noting that behavior chains are not so stereotyped as may have been first thought, and that this variability in responding appears to occur in clumps that fall within the temporal purview of different modes.

Ethology

The view that appetitive behavior can be accounted for strictly in terms of chains of sensorimotor units probably began with the study by physiologists of chained reactions like the peristalsis that occurs in swallowing or regurgitation. The chain reaction concept was used to account for more complex repetitive behavior like swimming in eels (Fearing, 1930; Hinde, 1970). Then, despite data supporting more central control of repetitive behaviors (e.g., von Holst, 1937/1973), the concept of reaction chains was extended to complex behavior such as reproduction (Tinbergen, 1951) and hunting (Leyhausen, 1979).

The extension of behavior chains to ethology involved positing independent releaser/fixed-action-pattern units that were linked by the environmentally based result that one response led to receipt of the next releasing stimulus. For example, Tinbergen (1951) used a reaction chain of releaser/fixed-action-pattern units to account for courtship behavior in sticklebacks. When the female appeared, the male swam toward her, which released a head-up posture in the female, which released nest-leading behavior on the part of the male, following by the female, nest-showing by the male, entry by the female, quivering by the male, spawning by the female, milting (fertilization) by the male, the exit of the female, and the return to guard duty by the male. In each case, the action pattern response to one releaser put the animal in position to receive the releasing stimulus for the next action pattern.

At first glance such behavior chains do not appear to require the presence of an underlying sequence of motivational modes and their repertoires. However, on closer examination, evidence for underlying modes and repertoires of stimulus sensitivities and motor components seems more compelling. One type of evidence is that responses in a behavior chain appear to drop out in a sequence of groupings as overall motivation decreases. Leyhausen provided a particularly clear qualitative account of the organized waning of hunting behavior in a cat (recounted in Lorenz, 1981). When placed in a room full of mice, a cat initially hunted captured, killed, and ate them. After a time, the cat would chase and capture but not kill the mice. Finally, the cat would simply lie still and follow the moving mice with its eyes. Such data support the presence of a series of motivational substates that require successively higher levels of motivation and/or stimulus support to make the transition to the next mode in the sequence and related responses (see also Tugendhat, 1960).

A second form of evidence for specific motivational modes and repertoires lies in the local flexibility of appetitive strings. A hunting cat shows many variations in its specific sequences of responses. The variation is often particularly striking in the early stages of prey finding, although variable responding accompanies and follows prey capture as well. Most important, the variation appears to occur within general repertoire classes, like locating prey, stalking or chasing prey, capturing and dispatching prey, and consuming prey. Within a repertoire class, behaviors repeat and change with the environment, while transitions between classes are related to single behaviors like sighting or capturing the prey. Hinde (1970) reviewed data showing similar constrained interchangeability and transitions in a variety of appetitive strings and species.

Related evidence arises from carefully examining strings of behavior in the courtship behavior of sticklebacks. Tinbergen (1951) outlined a prototypical behavior chain leading the animals from start to finish of an egg-laying and fertilization sequence. However, Morris (1958) analyzed actual strings of behaviors, revealing an initial clump of appearing and dancing on the part of the male accompanied by presenting and orienting on the part of the female. Male leading was a transitional behavior for the female from dancing to behaviors related to approaching and entering the nest, which in turn were accompanied by a "clump" of nest-related behaviors by the male. Finally, once the female was in position, the male "trembled" with his snout near her tail, precipitating spawning and a transition to another set of behaviors by each.

The existence of such "clumps" of variable and interchangeable behaviors, separated by transitional responses, suggests a relatively small number of underlying motivational modes in both feeding and reproduction behavior chains. Each mode and its accompanying repertoire, combined with environmental support, allow repetitions and loops of behavior within them. Pivotal behaviors and changes in the environment and levels of motivation appear to mark transitions to a different mode.

Laboratory Learning

Like ethology, the laboratory study of learning also focused on stereotyped stimulus–response chains, but of the sort apparently acquired by the sequential conditioning of individual units. This view emerged first in the study of maze learning in which animals were hypothesized to learn a chain of motor responses that allowed them to choose the appropriate sequence of turns (Hull, 1932; Munn, 1950). A more general chaining approach was articulated by Skinner (1937) and used by him to train complex sequences of responses, such as the slot machine behavior of the rat Pliny that was featured in the national press.

Variability in the Context of Trained Stereotypy. There seems little question that stereotyped units of behavior can be trained by consistent reward and then combined with other units to form stereotyped chains, yet this is not the complete story. That variation still occurs in both individual responses and in overall chains suggests the existence of more complex underlying repertoires associated with search modes. A clear illustration of the presence of underlying repertoires occurs in the misbehavior examples of Breland and Breland (1961). For example, using operant procedures with food reward, the Brelands carefully trained a pig to perform a chain of responses; picking up, transporting, and depositing a surrogate coin in a container (a "piggy" bank). However, when they lengthened the chain by requiring the pig to deposit two coins in the bank, the previously unexpressed foraging response of rooting (applied to the coin) suddenly emerged. This sudden intrusion of an obviously preorganized response into a carefully trained operant chain is readily explained by positing the existence of alternative perceptual-motor units related to an underlying mode.

Misbehavior is only a particularly arresting example of a larger repertoire of alternative responses in conditioning. In a more standard procedure, Muenzinger (1928) observed guinea pigs operate a lever for food on more than 700 trials and documented a complex set of behaviors used to operate the lever that slowly varied over trials, including pressing with the paw, moving the bar with the head, biting the bar, and so on (see also

Stokes & Balsam, 1991). In the case of mazes, researchers have reported that in a single-choice maze rats tend to alternate choices (Hughes, 1998), in a Dashiell maze they routinely alter their route to food (Munn, 1950), and in a radial maze they tend to enter arms in an unpredictable order whether food is present or not (Timberlake & White, 1990).

In short, constrained variability is often the rule rather than the exception, and such a rule makes sense as a means of ensuring successful foraging in an environment that is similar but not identical from day to day. That such variability is not more obvious in conditioning experiments is in part a tribute to the ability of experimenters to tune their apparatus, manipulanda, and response measures to maximize apparent stability. B. F. Skinner (personal communication, 1977) appears to have been keenly aware of the importance of altering the environment to produce tighter control over behavior. He told me that he had grave difficulty in shaping the rat Pliny to carry a marble over to a chimney and drop it cleanly in. Instead, the rat would manipulate the marble, hesitate to release it, and then try to retrieve it as it disappeared down the chimney. To reduce this problem, Skinner simply made the chimney taller so that the rat could not see or feel with its whiskers the bearing disappear.

In a better known example of how the environment can support stereotyped learned behavior, Skinner (1938, 1956) recounted how he successively modified his operant chamber and lever to promote lever pressing, including lowering the ceiling, moving the lever higher on the wall and closer to the feeder, and, eventually, rounding the end of a lever that barely protruded from the wall. The importance of Skinner's efforts for the reliability of lever pressing can best be appreciated by attempting to manufacture your own lever, as we did. By slightly changing the lever's dimensions and location, we could (inadvertently) support nosing underneath, biting, grasping, shaking, or two- and one-handed presses. Together, these results support the existence of an underlying repertoire of perceptual-motor units that can emerge and change, tracking changes in the stimulus conditions despite a long history of reinforcement for the previous response in this context.

Temporal Patterns of Variability. In addition to examples of alternative responses, there are also data that suggest transitions between different repertoires, points at which the animal moves from one group of responses and stimulus sensitivities to another. Delivering small amounts of reward at a fixed time in the absence of response requirements or environmental signals provides a particularly rich source of data for such transitions. The curves in Fig. 5.2 illustrate how search modes are hypothesized to map onto the interfood interval between deliveries of food. Repeated food deliveries at the point shown in the middle of the horizontal axis should organize a sequence of overlapping search modes preceding and following food. The dominance of a particular search mode at a particular time will depend probabilistically on its relative strength (height on the vertical axis), and the response shown will depend on the supporting stimulus environment as well as the strength of the mode selected.

For example, researchers commonly treat the results of the *superstition procedure*, in which food is presented each 12 to 15 sec (regardless of responding), as evidence for the arbitrary effectiveness of proximate reward in strengthening a response (Skinner, 1948). However, when behavior in the superstition procedure is examined more carefully, further points emerge that are compatible with a version of Fig. 5.2 compressed horizontally so that general search has relatively little time for expression.

First, responding appears to involve several inflection points. Following eating, there is a postfood set of behaviors by the bird (postfood focal search), followed frequently by turning away from and then back toward the wall (more general search), followed typically by a pattern of stepping or pecking focused near the feeder (this focus is more obvious in a large box than in a small one). The transitions between these different repertoires become even clearer when the interval between food presentations grows longer (Innis, Simmelhag-Grant, & Staddon, 1983). In particular the turning response develops into much more extensive walking and pacing.

Second, the behavior shown within each repertoire has some variability in it and can be altered by the nature of the supporting stimuli around the hopper (Timberlake & Lucas, 1985). In other words, there is constrained variability within and between trials. The typical interpretation of superstitious behavior as accidental strengthening of responding can account for the (surprisingly sparse) individual differences (Staddon & Simmelhag, 1971; Timberlake & Lucas, 1985), but it has a much harder time with the regular temporal transitions between repertoires and the less regular changes within them.

The *adjunctive behavior procedure* differs from the superstition procedure in that the interval between food deliveries is generally much longer, and the subjects typically are rats. Again, however, there is ample evidence of constrained variability in responding falling within repertoires organized by transitions from one repertoire to another (Lucas, Timberlake, & Gawley, 1988; Staddon, 1977; Timberlake & Lucas, 1991). The first repertoire of behavior after food is consumed consists of postfood focal search represented by head in feeder, local restless activity, and rearing around the food hopper. A second large repertoire extends across a great deal of the interval and involves running in the wheel, passing in and out of the nest, and locomotion about the chamber, behaviors that appear related to general search. Preceding food is a

CONTINUUM OF SEARCH MODES

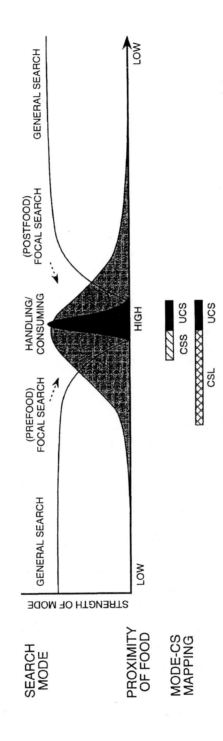

FIG 5.2. A representation of how the periodic presentation of a US entrains a distribution of search modes, and how the strength of these modes (shown along the vertical axis) is related to the proximity of the US (along the horizontal axis). The proximity dimension is multiply determined by the spatial, temporal, correlational, and evolutionary relation of the CS and US. The precise distribution of modes should vary with the characteristics of CS–US relatedness, the presence and duration of any CSs, and the support of any environmental stimuli.

focal search repertoire, the majority of which consists of head in feeder and inspection around it.

Our classification of interfood repertoires into general search, focal search, and postfood focal search reflects, expands, and integrates classification schemes by Staddon (1977) and Cohen, Looney, Campagnoni, and Lawler (1985). Two questions, though, arise for all these models. The first is why highly excessive drinking occurs primarily at interfood intervals of greater than 90 sec, and the second concerns how to explain the variability in particular response sequences. I consider these questions at a little length to show how a behavior systems framework can integrate both general and specific mechanisms underlying behavior.

Four observations support a unique transitional status for drinking between postfood focal search and the general search repertoire. First, drinking resembles the postfood focal search repertoire in peaking at a relatively fixed time after food (Lucas et. al., 1988). Second, at shorter interfood intervals neither drinking nor general search occur with much frequency. Only as the interfood interval increases do both sorts of response emerge and take over increasing parts of the interval. Third, the amount of drinking relative to the regulatory demands of eating is, to say the least, excessive. Fourth, the occurrence of such excessive behavior does not occur with other rewards, like water (Timberlake & Lucas, 1991)

Additional relevant evidence was provided by Lucas et al. (1988), who showed that the interfood interval at which excess drinking starts to emerge is close to the interval at which free-feeding rats start to drink following their voluntary termination of a meal. Postmeal water intake is usually attributed to its ability to lower the cost of metabolizing the food by substituting for water that would otherwise be retrieved from the intercellular and intracellular stores, requiring additional energy to withdraw and later replace (Mook, 1996). Evidence for the critical importance of postmeal drinking is provided by observations that rats rarely drink in the middle of a meal, and by the experimental demonstration that rats are unable to drink before meals in anticipation of reduced in postmeal water availability (Lucas, Timberlake, & Gawley, 1989).

Together these data suggest that rats have a mechanism eliciting water intake that begins to act if food is interrupted for longer than approximately a minute. This explanation requires the meal terminating mechanism to operate at the same time the rat is expecting more food at a later point, but such independence is not unusual in a complex system. Given the cost of bringing water out of the intracellular store (Mook, 1996), a mechanism that evoked drinking after a certain period without food makes sense. Whether fully correct or not, this hypothesis invites further testing and relates closely to the structure and mechanisms of foraging behavior and energy regulation rather than to mysterious side-effects of reinforcement.

A second issue for theories positing motivational substates underlying interfood behavior was raised by the report of Reid, Bacha, and Moran (1993). They reported that although the average sequence of behaviors in the interfood interval is stable, the sequence of responses within individual interfood intervals is quite variable. I have similar data that are not published. Actually, the predictability of average sequences and the variability of sequences of individual responses appears to fit reasonably with the present hypothesis of a sequence of overlapping search modes entrained to the period of the interfood interval. If there are probabilistic aspects to the time at which a mode is evoked and which behavior within a mode is sampled, we should expect stable distributions of response repertoires in time, but not necessarily stable sequences of particular responses within intervals.

Other Paradigms. Evidence potentially compatible with the distinction between general and focal search states also occurs in self-control paradigms (Logue, 1988). Self-control procedures offer subjects a choice between responding for a temporally proximate but smaller reward and responding for a more temporally distant but larger reward. When food on average is imminent, the animal predominantly responds for the closer but smaller reward with rapid strong responding. However, when food on average is more distant, the choices are more frequently directed to the more distant, larger reward, and the rate and intensity of responding is considerably lower. These differences can be explained by the difference between search states conditioned to different delays to food (Timberlake, 1988). For proximate rewards the subject is in a focal search state in which less choice flexibility is possible, whereas the distant rewards initially heighten a general search state in which more choice flexibility exists.

Stereotyped Response Chains. None of this evidence is intended to deny the existence of stereotypy in learned chains of behavior. For example consider the reports of mice running into runway walls when they are moved, or plowing by piles of pellets on the way to the goal box (Olton, 1979). It seems, though, that the majority of such stereotypy occurs when the organism is very close to reward or to the receipt of a stimulus that has been closely correlated with reward in time and space; in other words, when the focal search mode is likely to be well engaged. In support of this view, even when an animal is being rewarded for variability in responding, the degree of variation decreases with proximity of reward (Cherot, Jones, & Neuringer, 1996).

Summary

In short, there seems to be considerable evidence that a sequence of search modes and repertoires underlies both naturally occurring and trained sequences of behavior. Evidence for constrained variability both within repertoires and across repertoires and differences in flexibility of responding exists in naturally occurring sequences such as courtship in sticklebacks and in conditioned behavior produced by the periodic delivery of food in laboratory rats. Interestingly, even well-trained operant responses appear to show transitions in response patterns across the intertrial interval. For example, animals performing on fixed-interval schedules show no responding following food, then low response rates, followed by rapid acceleration to a higher rate as food approaches (Ferster & Skinner, 1957).

CS CHARACTERISTICS AND SEARCH MODES

Prototypic examples of laboratory work on Pavlovian conditioning traditionally focused on autonomic responses (like salivation or eye blinks) to neutral CSs using short CS–US intervals of a few seconds or less. Doubt was cast on the completeness of this view by a number of phenomena, including the ready conditioning of skeletal avoidance responses (Liddell, 1934), and operant conditioning of autonomic responses (N. E. Miller, 1969). However, the most generally bothersome problem has been the phenomenon of autoshaping—the acquisition of extensive skeletal responding in freely moving animals using CS–US intervals much longer than usual, (e.g., 5–20 sec; Hearst & Jenkins, 1974).

In contrast to attempts made to separate autoshaping phenomena from "true" Pavlovian conditioning (e.g., Gormezano, 1966), the behavior systems analysis views both "forms" of conditioning as part of the same appetitive sequence, attributing their apparent differences to a combination of different underlying modes and repertoires, environmental support, and measurement choices by the experimenter. Figure 5.2 can be used to illustrate how motivational modes are assumed to relate to each other and to the procedures of Pavlovian conditioning. For our purposes here the abscissa represents the relatedness of the CS and the US in dimensions such as time, spatial proximity, correlation, and evolutionary association. Examples of how short and long forward CSs relate to motivational modes are shown below the abscissa.

The ordinate corresponds to the strength of the mode. It can be seen that the modes have characteristic distances from the US along the relatedness dimension, but overlap considerably. A CS that falls predominantly within one search mode would be expected to most strongly condition that mode. One or more perceptual-motor units in the repertoire comprising the search mode and supported by the nature of the CS and the environment should be conditioned as well.

This view of Pavlovian procedures raises the intriguing possibility of using manipulations of the CS–US relation to test and provide evidence for the nature of motivational search modes and related perceptual-motor repertoires. At the same time, this view makes clear that traditional Pavlovian experiments typically use only a small part of the possible space of relations between the CS and US, namely short CS–US intervals, high spatial proximity, high correlation, and low evolutionary relatedness. In the first part of this section, I look at evidence for differences in response repertoires as a function of the interval between the CS and the US. In the second part of this section, I look at the role of spatial proximity between the CS and US. The third part briefly examines how the correlation between CS and US affects behavior, and the fourth part tests how the qualities (evolutionary relatedness) of a CS and a given US influence the effects of the CS–US interval.

CS–US Interval and Response Measures

A basic prediction of the behavior systems approach as represented in Fig. 5.2 is that different CS–US intervals should differentially condition different modes along with examples of their repertoires of stimulus sensitivities and response components. Several experiments have provided supporting evidence for the behavior systems view. For example, Schneiderman (1972) showed that the optimal intertrial interval for conditioning varied with the response being measured. CSs predicting a puff of air to the eye of a rabbit showed an optimal CS–US interval of less than 1 sec for the eye blink response, but an optimal CS–US interval of 5 to 6 sec for a change in heart rate. Timberlake, Wahl, and King (1982), using the CS of a rolling ball bearing to predict food for hungry rats, showed that when the ball bearing was presented more than 6 sec before food, rats typically engaged in responses first related to general search, namely attending to the emergence of the bearing, then chasing and capturing it. However, when the same ball bearing was presented just 2 sec before food, rats in that group responded to the bearing as a signal for behavior related to focal search alone, such as nosing in the food tray.

Similar evidence of different response repertoires under different CS–US intervals comes from the work of Holland (1980) and Hilliard, Domjan, Nguyen, and Cusato (1998). A particularly clear example is found in the work of Akins, Domjan, and Gutierrez (1994), who presented a light CS of 30 or 1,200 sec to a male quail as a predictor of access to a receptive female US. The CS was presented near the alcove where the female was to appear. The 30-sec CS produced approach and attention to the alcove with the light CS. A 1,200-sec CS failed to increase approach, but considerably increased locomotion about the apparatus compared to that shown by a yoked control group. This finding is compatible with the existence of a focal search mode conditioned to the shorter CS and a general search mode conditioned to the longer CS.

Matthews and Lerer (1987) used yet another technique to test the effects of CS–US interval on conditioning in pigeons. They introduced a sequence of three 10-sec clock stimuli (three different colored key lights) that completely filled a 30-sec interfood interval, and showed that the behavior of the pigeons varied during each 10-sec segment. The pigeons predominantly turned around the chamber during the first segment, paced near the hopper wall during the second, and key pecked during the final segment. Strong stimulus control of these effects was demonstrated when the segments of the interfood clock were randomized or extended in duration; in all cases the pigeons showed behavior more appropriate to the typical location of the cue than to the current postfood interval.

Taken together, such data strongly indicate that a major determinant of the traditional results of Pavlovian conditioning is the combination of the CS, the CS–US interval, and the choice of what response is measured. It appears that the view of Pavlovian conditioning as related to autonomic responses with maximum conditioning at short CS–US intervals was based primarily on the choice of responses and CSs. To see conditioned responses at longer intervals with a food US it is necessary to remove physical and temporal constraints and focus on search responses related to discovering and capturing food and CSs that should support them. It follows that if Pavlov had allowed his dogs to roam free in the presence of the CS he would have discovered begging behavior to longer CSs, similar to that shown by Jenkins, Barrera, Ireland, and Woodside (1978), and seemingly to that reported by Zener (1937) and perhaps Konorski (1967).

The behavior systems view of the conditioning of search modes and related perceptual-motor units makes good sense of these data, yet learning researchers are typically quite cautious in extending traditional views further than necessary. Thus, it is possible to attribute many of these results simply to the empirical fact that different CS–US intervals condition different responses, without any need to presume the additional conditioning of a search mode. Although this empirical use of the traditional view does not explain why the same CS should best condition different responses at different intervals (or for that matter predict the occurrence and form of autoshaping, superstitious behavior, misbehavior, and adjunctive behavior), nonetheless this empirical interpretation highlights the absence of an explicit separate test for the motivational search states presumably being conditioned and supporting the conditioning of the perceptual-motor unit. The data in the next section attempt to test more directly for the presence of a general search mode.

Unconditioned Probes of the General Search Mode. A classic way to test for the conditioning of a motivational state like a search mode is to first present a CS to evoke or prime the state and then present an unconditioned probe stimulus that elicits a response presumably related to the state. That a response to the unconditioned probe stimulus is facilitated relative to its baseline level by the presentation of a conditioned CS strongly supports the existence of a motivational state tied to the CS. An example of this procedure is to compare the unconditioned startle response to a loud sound with and without the prior presentation of a putative fear CS. If the startle response following presentation of the CS is enhanced relative to baseline and the presentation of other CSs, one assumes the presence of a fear state related to the CS.

Our studies first paired presentations of a tone CS with the delivery of food to condition a motivational mode, and in a subsequent test condition we used a rolling ball bearing as an unconditioned probe stimulus related primarily to general search. To the extent that prior pairings of the CS with food condition a general search state, then presenting the CS prior to the ball bearing should facilitate bearing contact relative to baseline levels, in the absence of any possibility of second-order conditioning. To the extent that prior pairings conditioned a focal search state, we expected no increase (or a decrease) in bearing contact as a function of presentation of the CS prior to the ball bearing.

K. M. Silva and Timberlake (1997) presented separate groups of animals with a tone CS with a duration either long (16 or 18 sec) or short (2 or 4 sec). Following training, the animals were first exposed to 6 days of 12 presentations of unconditioned presentations of a rolling ball bearing to reliably assess the unconditioned strength of the probe as well as extinguish responding to the context of the food tray; then the CS was presented 2 sec before the bearing to see its effect on bearing contact. The results (shown in the top of Fig. 5.3) supported the existence of a general search state conditioned to the CS under the longer interval but not the short interval. Contact with the bearing increased significantly over baseline only in the case of the long CS–US interval. In contrast, the bottom of Fig. 5.3 shows that both long and short groups increased nosing in the feeder following presentation of the CS, though, as would be expected, the short group increased more.

In sum, there is considerable evidence compatible with the behavior systems prediction that search modes and parts of their repertoires can

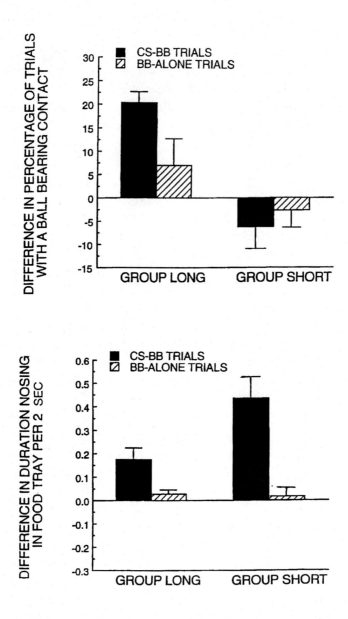

FIG 5.3. (Top) Average change from baseline level in percentage trials with a contact of an unconditioned ball bearing probe during an extinction test in which the bearing was presented either alone or 2 sec after the onset of a long or short CS. (Bottom) Average change from baseline duration of nosing in the food tray per 2 sec during presentation of a bearing in an extinction test either alone or 2 sec after the onset of a long or short CS (K. M. Silva & Timberlake, 1997).

be conditioned to a CS, and that the modes most strongly conditioned will vary with the CS–US interval. Longer CS–US intervals appear to differentially condition a general search mode and related general search behaviors, whereas shorter CS–US intervals appear to differentially condition a focal search mode and related behaviors. The use of a ball bearing as an unconditioned probe for a general search state strongly supported our conclusion that long CS–US intervals condition a motivational mode rather than only a stimulus–response unit.

CS–US Spatial Proximity

Given that motivational modes can be mapped to the temporal separation between the CS and the US, it would seem reasonable that the mapping of motivational modes may also be a function of the spatial separation of the CS and the US. The view presented here predicts that both a spatially distant CS and a temporally distant CS should better condition a general search mode and related responses, whereas both a spatially and a temporally proximate CS should better condition a focal search mode and related responses. To understand the following experiment it is also necessary to assume that a serial CS can differentially condition different modes to different elements of the CS.

Consider the case of a two-element forward serial CS consisting of an 8-sec sequence of lever insertions, one lever on each side of the food tray and at different distances from it. Temporally the first lever should differentially condition a general search mode and the second lever should differentially condition a focal mode. Spatially, the farther lever should differentially condition general search mode and the closer lever should differentially condition focal mode (see F. J. Silva, Timberlake, & Koehler, 1996). Both of these predictions can be seen from Fig. 5.2 by imagining a sequence of two CSs preceding the food, and assigning the dimension of either space or time to the abscissa.

F. J. Silva, Timberlake, and Gont (1998) tested these predictions by presenting rats with either congruent or incongruent combinations of temporal and spatial characteristics of the elements of a serial CS. Two levers were presented in succession for 4 sec each followed by food. In the congruent (far–near) case the far lever was followed by the near lever to predict food (the spatial dimension and the temporal dimension for Fig. 5.2 predict the same outcome). In the incongruent (near–far) case the near lever was first, followed by the far lever and food (the spatial dimension and the temporal dimension predict opposite outcomes). At an intuitive level we expected the animal to "follow" the levers to food in the far–near case because both the temporal and spatial cues supported the appropriate sequence of search modes, more general followed by focal. In the near–far case, the animal could not "follow" the levers to food spatially because the far lever in the second position lead them away from food, so we expected less contact of the far lever. (We previously had discovered that rats were extremely sensitive to the relative spatial differences between two levers near food.)

The results supported our predictions, showing that the congruent (far–near) sequence of Group FN evoked attention to each element of the CS sequence followed by nosing in the food site just prior to food (see Fig. 5.4, top and bottom). In contrast, rats in Group NF, receiving the near–far sequence, attended to the first lever but then to the food site, skipping the second (far) lever almost entirely; they even spent more time nosing during the first lever than Group FN.

It is possible again to argue (after the fact) that this outcome occurred because of the particular stimuli presented, not because any modes were involved. However, a further prediction was made also based on the assumption of the presence of underlying modes. Assume the reason for minimal contact with the second lever by Group NF was that the contradiction between its relative spatial and temporal positions resulted in a conflict between general and focal search modes resolved in favor of the dominance of the focal search mode and nosing in the hopper. Then it should be possible to resolve this conflict in favor of the general search mode and contact with the lever by increasing the temporal distance of the second lever onset to food.

Increasing the duration of the second lever should increase the relative strength of the general search mode and produce more contact with the second lever and less nosing in the feeder. This prediction that responding to the spatially far lever in the near temporal position (the incongruent, near–far sequence) should be increased markedly by increasing its duration was confirmed (F. J. Silva, Timberlake, & Gont, 1998, Experiments 3 & 4). In short, both spatial and temporal proximity to reward appear important in determining the conditioning of search modes.

CS–US Correlation (Partial Reinforcement)

We realize that based on the work of Kamin (1969) and Rescorla (1967) the concept of correlation has expanded considerably beyond the manipulation of partial reinforcement (percent CSs followed by a US). However, the testing of mode predictions seems clearest and the potential complexities fewest if we limit our concern to partial reinforcement. To this end we presented food on either 100%, 50%, 25%, or 12.5% of the CS presentations. Our question was to what extent the partial reinforcement correlation between the CS and US would map differentially to search modes, producing responding above baseline levels. We as-

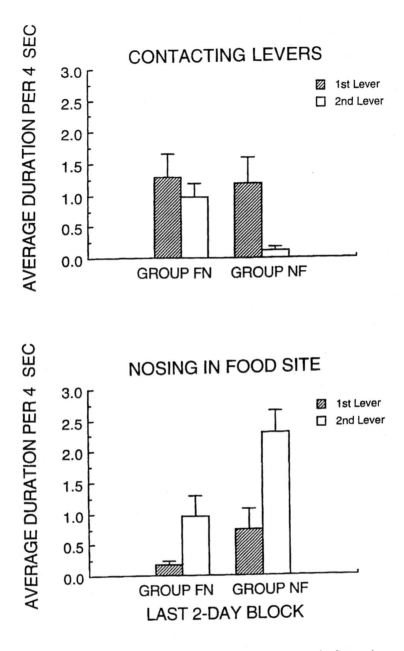

FIG 5.4. (Top) Average duration of contact per 4-sec access to the first and second levers for Group FN (far–near order of levers) and Group NF (near–far order of levers. (Bottom) Average duration per 4-sec lever access for nosing in the feeder during the first and second levers for Group FN (far–near order of levers) and Group NF (near–far order of levers; F. J. Silva, Timberlake, & Gont, 1998).

sumed that other things being equal, partial correlations would map onto the abscissa of Fig. 5.2 such that a high positive correlation would act like a short CS–US interval in differentially conditioning a focal search mode and related behavior. In contrast, a low positive correlation between CS and US should act more like a long CS–US interval and differentially condition a general search mode.

The behavior system view was tested more completely by using four CSs: ball bearings, an insertable rat, an insertable lever, and a jewel light proximate to the food tray. Supported by our observations and previous data, we predicted an interaction between CS type and percentage reward. In essence when the CS and the percentage reward both predict differential conditioning of the same search mode, the result should be the maximum expression of that mode. When the CS and the percentage reward predict differential conditioning of different search modes an intermediate level of responding should occur.

Translated into the current experiment, we predicted that ball bearings, because of their shared characteristics with moving prey items, would differentially condition a general search mode (and, thus, maximum responding at a lower percentage reward), whereas a punctate jewel light proximate to the feeder should differentially condition a focal search mode (and, thus, show maximum responding at the highest reward percentages). Levers and rats should condition general and focal search more evenly, and, thus, show peaks of attentional responding at intermediate percentages of reward. Finally, nosing in the hopper (a focal search behavior) should be maximal at the highest reward percentages and fall off rapidly at lower levels.

Rats were divided into 16 groups of six rats each formed by crossing the four CSs (light, insertable lever, rat, and ball bearing), and the four percentage reward levels (100%, 50%, 25%, and 12.5%). Baselines to the CSs alone were collected prior to conditioning for each group. The results shown in the top of Fig. 5.5 for the last 2-day block of acquisition and the first 2-day block of extinction are compatible with our predictions, most clearly on the two extinction test trials. Extinction trials have the advantage of no direct conflict with food or handling behaviors; they also tend to highlight general search behaviors because in the absence of food the focal search mode begins to weaken and the general search mode to predominate.

The ball bearing groups peaked at the lowest reward percentages, still contacting on more than 80% of the trials at 12.5% reward. The light groups peaked at 100% reward (extinction data). The rat group had very high responding through 25% reward and the lever had highest responding at 50% reward. The bottom of Fig. 5.5 shows that (except for the rat CS groups) head in feeder at the end of acquisition showed highest responding at 100% reward, falling rapidly from there. Lever and

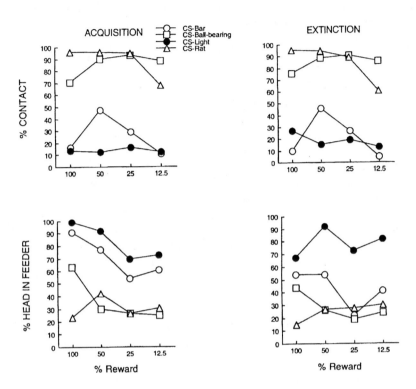

FIG 5.5.   (Top) Average percentage trials with a CS contact for percentage reward varying from 100% to 12.5% during one of four CSs: proximal jewel light,
insertable lever, ball bearing, or rat. The data shown were averaged over the
last two trials of acquisition and the first two trials of extinction. (Bottom) Average percentage trials nosing in the food tray for percentage reward varying
from 100% to 12.5% during one of four CSs: proximal jewel light, insertable lever, ball bearing, or rat. The data were averaged over the last two trials of acquisition or the first two trials of extinction

light CS groups also showed greater levels of nosing than the rat and
ball bearing groups.

   In short, both percentage reward and presumed evolutionary relatedness of the CS appeared to map to motivational modes. In general,
high reward percentage was related to focal search modes and lower reward percentages to general search modes. Most interesting, CSs presumed to differentially condition a general search mode showed higher
responding to the CS at lower reward percentages relative to groups
with higher reward percentages with the same CS and to the responding

of other CS groups at the same reward percentages. Similarly, CSs presumed to differentially condition a focal search mode showed higher at higher responding reward percentages.

Evolutionary Relatedness of the CS and US and the CS–US Interval

The previous results showed a strong relation between the presumed evolution-based tendency of particular CS types to condition general and focal search and the manipulation of the relation between the CS and the US in terms of partial reinforcement. This study examines the possibility of a similar relation between the CS type and the CS–US interval. Again our general hypothesis was that to the extent that the CS type and the CS–US interval conditioned the same mode, the behavior demonstrated would be either the strongest focal search or the strongest general search behavior. In contrast, if the CS type and the CS–US interval predicted the conditioning of different modes, responding would be more of a compromise between general and focal search behaviors.

Given the previously established CS–US interval data, we expected the ball bearing CS to peak at the longest CS–US interval where both conditioned a general search mode and related responding. In contrast, the jewel light should peak at a shorter CS–US interval where both the light and the interval should lead to the differential conditioning of focal search. The peak of responding for the rat should fall more toward the ball bearing, and for the lever more toward the light.

The experiment involved 16 groups of six rats each. We used the same CSs as in the percentage reward study discussed earlier (ball bearing, light, lever, and rat). Four groups were assigned to each CS with CS–US intervals of 2, 6, 12, or 24 sec. It is important to note that all CSs were approximately 6 sec long (the duration of the ball bearing presentation was ultimately determined by how much the rat interacted with it). This means that in the 2-sec condition the CS continued past the US, which should make it a weaker conditioner of prefood focal search behaviors. We measured approach responses as movement to within 5 cm of the object with the nose pointed at the object. The stimuli were presented on a VT 72-sec schedule and the US consisted of one 45-mg pellet. Approach responses were coded by an observer unfamiliar with the hypotheses under test and checked for reliability (Timberlake & F. J. Silva, 1994).

The results for percentage trials with a contact with a CS are shown in the top of Fig. 5.6 averaged on the left over the last two trials of acquisition and on the right over the first two trials of extinction, both plotted by CS type and CS–US interval. The results are similar in both graphs, differing primarily in the undifferentiated responding to the light at the end of acquisition, possibly interfered with by the high levels of nosing in the feeder. The peak of responding occurred at the shortest CS–US interval for the light, at intermediate CS–US intervals for the lever and rat, and at the longest CS–US intervals for the ball bearing. The bottom of Fig. 5.6 shows the expected pattern of head in feeder peaking only at the shortest intervals. The peak likely would have been pronounced if the length of the CS had not been 6 sec, so that at the 2-sec CS–US interval it extended past the US.

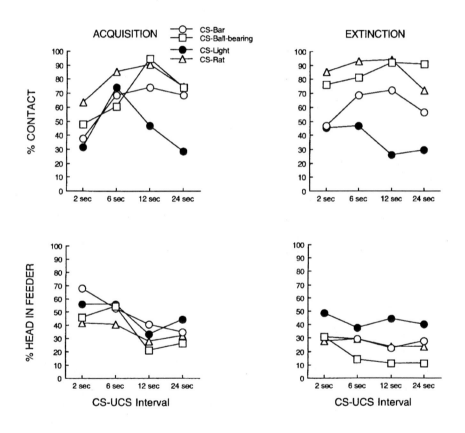

FIG 5.6.   (Top) Average percentage trials with a CS contact during CS–US intervals of 2, 6, 12, and 24 sec with one of four CSs: proximal jewel light, insertable lever, ball bearing, or rat. The data were averaged over the last two trials of acquisition or the first two trials of extinction. (Bottom) Average percentage trials nosing in feeder during CS–US intervals of 2, 6, 12, and 24 sec with one of four CSs: proximal jewel light, insertable lever, ball bearing, or rat. The data shown were averaged over the last two trials of acquisition or the first two trials of extinction.

These results provide support for the prediction that different CSs may ultimately be most readily related to particular modes, and thus, should be differentially conditionable at different CS–US intervals. The light CS, which should have most readily evoked a focal search mode, peaked at a shorter interval than any other CS. The lever and rat essentially peaked at the same interval and showed the same levels of responding at longer intervals as well. The ball bearing stimulus peaked a little later and was sustained. It appears that even a lower degree of association between the ball bearing and food may be necessary to outline the distant limits of the general search mode.

Summary

In short, it appears that four dimensions of the CS–US relation (temporal proximity, spatial proximity, correlation, and evolutionary relatedness) share sufficient attributes to have reasonably similar effects on responding. Although I propose no clear and precise common metric of relatedness, these CSs share at least a common qualitative relation to the hypothesized sequence of search modes. In almost every case high relatedness between the CS and US produced evidence for the differential conditioning of a focal search mode, and low relatedness between the CS and US produced evidence for the differential conditioning of general search modes. These predictions can be contrasted with a traditional associative view that would have focused on short CS–US intervals, the light stimulus, and the response of nosing in the feeder.

THE TEMPORAL CHARACTERISTICS OF MOTIVATIONAL MODES

The research and observations outlined in the preceding sections provide considerable support for the presence of search modes along with some evidence of their temporal extent. The research in this section attempts to get a clearer idea of the temporal characteristics of the different search modes including the extent to which they show absolute timing versus scalar timing (timing proportional to the interreward interval), how dependent the effects of timing are on CS characteristics, and how flexible the relative timing of the modes is. The first part of this section considers briefly a series of experiments performed by Silva for her PhD thesis (K. M. Silva & Timberlake, 1998a, 1998b, 1999) that makes use of an interfood clock procedure to cast light on the temporal characteristics of search states. The second part of this section examines the results of a procedure that structures the time before and after delivery of a pellet by repeatedly delivering the CS (e.g., 10 times before the US and 10 times after the US).

Interfood Clocks and the Timing of Motivational Modes

A major advantage of the laboratory is that one can control precisely the time at which reward is delivered. To the extent that this timing is predictable, but no response is required, the simple delivery of reward provides an opportunity for the animal to organize its behavior in time, thereby indirectly casting light on how motivational modes are organized in time. The work on adjunctive behavior considered earlier in this chapter (Lucas et al., 1988) suggested that the timing of modal organization is to a great extent scalar. In other words, the time spent in a particular mode (except for the postfood focal search mode) appears to be a relatively constant proportion of the interval between rewards.

The purpose of the first experiment here was to determine the extent to which behaviors associated with particular modes did show scalar performance, and how it was associated with the elements of a four-element interfood clock, each element of which occupied 25% of the interval between food deliveries. We chose four elements for the clock in part to provide the opportunity to test if there might be four discrete search modes instead of the three we had considered (handling and consuming aside). The second experiment used an unconditioned ball bearing probe to test for the conditioning of a state rather than a response, whereas the third experiment showed that the search modes had only so much flexibility in tracking the elements of the interfood clock.

Interfood Clocks and Scalar Search Modes. K. M. Silva and Timberlake (1998b) compared the effects of presenting an interfood clock ending with food delivery with the effects of no clock during interfood intervals (IFIs) ranging from 12 to 196 sec. Each four-clock element was one fourth of the length of the IFI, so that in a 60-sec interval, for example, each clock element was 15 sec in duration. Our purpose was to determine whether different conditioned responses (and inferred underlying modes) showed absolute or scalar timing characteristics (scalar timing occurs when the proportion of the interval at or during which a response appears is constant across different IFIs). Figure 5.7 shows that for all rats and IFIs, the first postfood quarter was dominated by checking and remaining near the food site; the second postfood quarter was dominated by locomotion around the cage; the third quarter combined aspects of locomotion with nosing in the feeder; the final quarter was dominated by nosing in the feeder.

With the exception of postfood behavior during the first quarter of the interval, behavior from different clock intervals showed scalar (proportional) timing; that is, the same proportion of total responding was shown in each clock element by animals with different IFIs. Animals with either interfood clock stimuli or no clock stimuli increased time spent near the feeder during the last two quarters of the interval, but the clock animals showed a sharper discrimination and higher levels of nosing in the feeder during the last two clock elements. The latter finding supported stimulus control of nosing in the feeder by clock cues. In general the data supported the existence of three motivational modes,

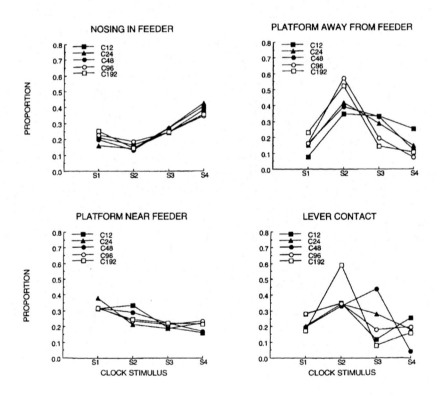

FIG 5.7. Average proportion of total responding shown during each of the four equal elements of an interfood clock. Data are shown separately for interfood intervals ranging from 12 to 192 sec and by one of four responses: nosing in the feeder, contacting the platform near the feeder, contacting the platform away from the feeder, and lever contact (K. M. Silva & Timberlake, 1998b).

postfood focal search, general search, and focal search, each compromising different response repertoires.

Clocks and Probes. The results of the previous study supported the hypothesis that general and focal search modes showed scalar timing distributions, whereas postfood focal search showed a fixed timing. However, it seemed worthwhile to test more directly for the general search mode while trying to distinguish between a general search mode and a simple arousal effect. To this end rats were first trained to asymptotic performance using a 48-sec interfood clock with 12-sec elements, then probe stimuli were presented once in each element per day with no food following that interval. The remaining trials remained the same. For one group the probe was a rolling ball bearing that was expected to serve as a probe for the presence of a general search mode. For a second group the probe was the opening of a 4.5 in. × 9 in. door in the wall of the chamber, which provided access to a wire mesh screen for 5 sec. This manipulation was designed to test the possibility that the bearing produced a nonspecific arousal that interacted with the conditions present in the different clock elements to produce the results.

The results showed very strong facilitation of ball bearing contact in the second CS element (see Fig. 5.8) and no difference among these elements in reaction to the moving door (see K. M. Silva & Timberlake, 1998a). These data strongly suggest that an excitatory general search state not based solely on nonspecific arousal produced by the bearing is relatively most strongly conditioned to the second time period.

Mode Flexibility. Taken together, the previous two studies suggest modes have predominantly scalar timing, although there were also modifying effects based on CS presence and duration. The point of this next study (K. M. Silva & Timberlake, 1999) was to explore the possibility that the temporal distribution of the stimuli of an interfood clock could facilitate or interfere with the conditioning of particular modes and the expression of particular response repertoires. We assumed that although there should be flexibility in terms of responding following temporal durations, some distributions of clock elements in time should be closer to "naturally" occurring temporal patterning of search modes than other distributions.

To test this temporal distribution hypothesis, this study presented one group of rats (decreasing) with a four-element interfood clock that successively decreased the size of the elements in a trial (24, 12, 8, and 4 sec); a second group (increasing) received clock elements that increased in size (4, 8, 12, and 24 sec). A third (basic) group received four equal elements (12, 12, 12, and 12 sec). Presumably the more compatible the distribution of clock elements with the flexibility of the underlying modes and response repertoires, the more clearly distributed and vigorous should be the distribution of the index responses we used, namely remaining on a platform in front of the hopper (postfood focal search), crossing a platform along the back wall (general search), and nosing in the feeder (focal search). Based on the data from our adjunctive behavior studies, we assumed that the decreasing group should be most compatible on average, the increasing group the least compatible, and the basic (equal) group should be intermediate.

Figure 5.9 shows clear differences in our three index responses as a function of the temporal distribution of the clock elements. When the clock elements increased, postfood focal search responses were facilitated by the short elements at the beginning of the interval, and other responses showed little or no change in responding with time. When the clock elements decreased, prefood focal search responses were facilitated at the end of the interval and general search responses were facilitated in the middle of the interval.

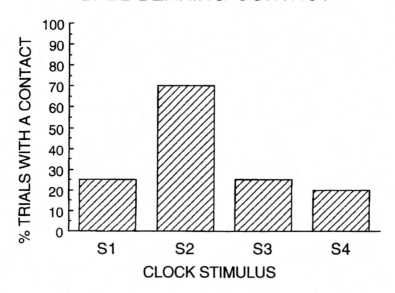

FIG 5.8. Average percentage trials with contact of an unconditioned ball bearing probe when it was presented during each of four equal elements of an interfood clock (K. M. Silva & Timberlake, 1998a).

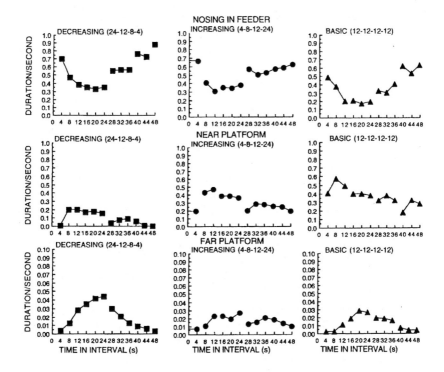

FIG 5.9. Mean duration of head in feeder per second of presentation of a four-element clock stimulus during a 48-sec interfood interval at asymptote. In the different conditions the size of the element of the interfood clock either decreased from 24 sec to 4 sec across the interfood interval, increased from 4 sec to 24 sec, or remained at 12 sec across the interfood interval (after K. M. Silva & Timberlake, 1999).

In short, the temporal distribution of responses associated with postfood focal, general, and prefood focal search modes is sensitive to the distribution of clock cues within the IFI. Shorter clock elements, whether at the beginning or the end of the IFI showed the most articulated responding that remained relatively constant within each element.

Periodic Probes Using Different CSs

The focus of the previous studies in this section was on the temporal distribution of responding within an interfood "space" defined by periodic presentations of food during the experimental session. In contrast, this study focused on the temporal extent (the "envelope") of the effects of a single presentation of a food US (two 45-mg pellets) on repeated unrewarded CS probes presented before and after the single CS–US pairing on the 10th min of a 20-min session. In the initial phase of the experiment there was only the single CS presentation in the middle of the session. In subsequent phases the CS was delivered first 6 additional times a session (3 before and 3 after the food pairing) and then 19 additional times a session (9 times before and 10 after the food pairing).

Three types of CS probe were used: a ball bearing, an insertable lever, and a jewel light mounted within 2 in. of the feeder. We expected the probes to reveal the temporal limits of a general search mode around the US produced by a single CS–US pairing and as revealed by reactions to the CS probes. As in previous experiments, the ball bearing was assumed to be the best probe for a general search mode and the light the worst. Thus, we predicted the largest envelope of general reactivity to CS probes should occur in the case of the ball bearing, the next for the lever, and the least for the light.

The behavior to the CS probes of the paired group (receiving the pairing between the CS and US in the 10th min) was compared to that of an unpaired group and a CS-only group. The unpaired group received the same pattern of presentation of the CSs except the CS was omitted on the 10th min when food was delivered so that no proximate pairing occurred. The CS-only group received all presentations of the CS but never was presented with food. To the extent that behavior to the CS depends on the pairing with food, we would expect more frequent and intensive interaction with the CS in the paired group than the unpaired or CS-only groups.

Two further questions arise in this design. The first is whether responding should be related to the number of CSs presented. A simple associative account would seem to argue that the most intense excitation should occur under conditions of perfect predictability of the US given the CS—namely the one-CS phase when the single CS in the 10th min predicts food perfectly. For the other two phases for the paired group either 6 out of 7 CSs or 19 out of 20 CSs never predict food. Following this logic predicts that the average excitation should be highest for the 1-CS phase, followed by the 7-CS phase and the 20-CS phase. For a variety of reasons having to do with the learning of a discrimination, one would also expect no responding to CSs that follow food because food never occurs past the midpoint of the session.

From a behavior systems view, to the extent that a cue is related to the repertoire of the general search state, presentation of the CS alone may facilitate a general search state particularly if the CS predicts food (see the partial reinforcement results earlier in the chapter). On these grounds we would expect that when responding to a cue is related to response components that characterize and even evoke a general search state, the animal should respond to most of the CSs, including some of those after the US. Thus, we would expect the general search state to be actually enhanced by presentation of multiple ball bearings, less so by lever insertions, and very little, if at all, by multiple lights.

Results are shown in Fig. 5.10. Following the 1-CS phase in which all stimuli showed significant levels of contact in the paired group, the introduction of 7 or 20 CSs resulted in significant increases in contact in the paired condition for all CS types. For the bar and light the increase was primarily (although not exclusively) before the presentation of food. For the ball bearing high levels of contact again occurred across the entire session. The unpaired group for the ball bearing, and to a lesser extent in the 7-CS phase for the bar, showed higher levels of contact than the baseline group, although it was differential before and after the CS.

Several points are raised by these data. First, regular, repeated presentations of a probe stimulus at regular intervals preceding and following the presentation of a single pairing between that stimulus and food elicits behavior despite the fact that none of the extra presentations are ever followed by food. Second, the probe stimuli showed both excitatory and suppressive effects of number. In the multiple CS (probe) phases, the average contacts were greatest in the 20-CS phase for the lever, roughly the same in the 7- and 20-CS conditions for the lever, and higher in the 7-CS phase for the light. In short, number of probes was most excitatory for the ball bearing, next for the lever, and least (but still present) for the light.

Third, the light and lever stimuli showed increased contact predominantly, although by no means exclusively, in the 10 min preceding the food. In contrast, the ball bearing showed increased contact with their CS throughout the 20-min session. However, in the unpaired ball bearing group the contact was greater before than after the presentation of the food. Fourth, the ball bearing group, and to a lesser extent the lever group, showed strong excitatory effects of presenting the probes on responding in the unpaired condition. The ball bearing particularly showed striking effects in the 20-CS condition. It is important to note that this effect is particular to this paradigm; it is not characteristic of a random relation between ball bearings and food (Timberlake et al., 1982) or of responding in random interfood clock intervals during an IFI of 48 sec (K. M. Silva & Timberlake, 1998a), or in using ball bearing probes in tests with no food present. It might be that a 1-min interval balances the excitatory effects of the bearing presentation against the consummatory aspects of interacting with it, with food adding to the excitatory qualities. This might also account for the unusually high baseline of contacting ball bearings in the CS-only group.

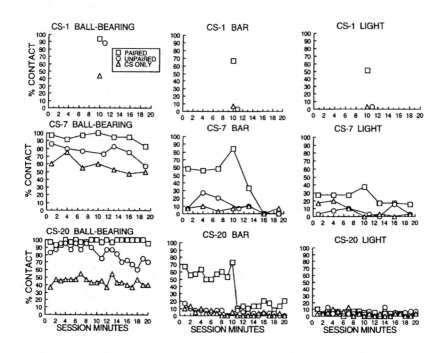

FIG 5.10. Mean percentage contact with either a ball bearing CS, insertable lever CS, or light CS averaged at asymptote (four trials) over a 20-min session. Results are shown separately by CS type and within CS type by number of CS presentations (from top to bottom, 1, 7, and 20 presentations). Curves are shown separately in each plot for a paired group receiving a single pairing of the CS and two food pellets at the midpoint of the session, an unpaired group that received the same two pellets at the midpoint of the session but in the absence of a CS at that point, and a CS-only group that received only the CS presentations.

These data appear to be a puzzle for theories emphasizing an associative view. It is not clear how to explain why, given that the animals appear to know the reward is in the middle of the interval (based both on a tendency to scallop in responding to the prefood CSs for the lever and light and on the peak in head-in-feeder data—not shown), they continue to respond to the CS probes before and even after the single pairing.

The behavior systems approach receives support from the relative amounts of contact frequency to the different CSs and the enhancement effects of multiple CS presentations on CS contact. The data also provide good evidence for postfood search states that produce interaction with CSs that are never followed by food. The data also point out the unique qualities of the ball bearing to sustain interest and contact despite multiple presentations and even when there is not a forward pairing with food. This sort of sensitivity and persistence would be expected for behavior related to an unconditioned general search mode important in a species' niche. One last thing worth noting is that the bearing contacts in the unpaired group, despite being nearly as high as in the paired group, differed considerably in intensity. A measure of carrying the bearing showed a significant difference between the paired and unpaired groups, and the unpaired group did not differ from the baseline group.

CONDITIONED MODES AND TRADITIONAL PAVLOVIAN PHENOMENA

This section briefly examines the preliminary relevance of search modes to a number of traditional Pavlovian phenomena: backward conditioning, context blocking, and conditioned inhibition. I do not argue that these phenomena are completely explained by the conditioning of search modes and modules. I do argue that focusing on the potential contribution of search modes provides a number of novel predictions and considerations that appear to be important in a complete theory of Pavlovian conditioning.

Backward Conditioning: Conditioning Modes Versus Responses

The behavior systems framework posits that postfood focal search modes follow the delivery and consumption of food and can be conditioned to postfood stimuli reliably present (see Fig. 5.2 and picture a CS presented following food). F. J. Silva et al. (1996) provided evidence for a two-part hypothesis: Backward pairing of a CS and US at short intervals will condition a focal search mode on the basis of proximity, but will not condition focal perceptual-motor units because the latter requires the prediction of proximate food. Postfood focal responses, though, will likely appear, evoked by the presentation of food, the stimulus support present, and the presence of the postfood focal search mode.

F. J. Silva et al. (1996) obtained evidence for this hypothesis by training different groups of rats with either forward or backward pairings of food with a three-equal-element serial light CS (a total of 24 sec in duration). (Superimpose a three-element CS either preceding or following food on the modes shown in Fig. 5.2). Following initial conditioning, different groups of animals were tested under forward pairings between a compound CS and food. For each group the compound was formed by combining one of the 8-sec elements of the previous serial light CS with a new lever stimulus. Thus, there were three compound groups that first received backward serial training and three compound groups that first received forward training.

The purpose of using the lever was to see whether previous training with the serial CS had conditioned focal perceptual-motor units that interfered with conditioning of approach to the lever or focal search modes that facilitated contact with the lever. Thus, in both the backward and forward conditioning of the three-element serial CS, the 8-sec element most proximal to food should have differentially conditioned a focal search mode, but in addition the forward near element should have strongly conditioned focal search responses to the light (approaching and nosing in the food tray), whereas the backward near element may have facilitated the expression of, but should not have conditioned, specific focal search responses. The most distant CS element in both backward and forward should have differentially conditioned a general search mode, with slightly better conditioning of general search responses in the forward group. The intermediate CS element should fall between the near and distant elements.

On these grounds we can predict that for the backward groups, responding to the lever should be highest in the compound with the near element because the near element should have most strongly conditioned a focal search mode but without potentially interfering perceptual-motor units. In contrast, in the forward group the near element should show lowest initial responding to the lever because in addition to the presence of a conditioned focal search mode there should be conditioned focal responses that interfere with attention to the lever. Figure 5.11 (top) supports both of these predictions. In the backward conditioned groups, responding to the lever in compound with either the near or intermediate elements is far higher than in the far element backward compound group or the near element forward group. Considering the forward groups only, responding to the lever in the near element group is somewhat lower than in the intermediate element group and considerably lower than the far element group. The bottom of Fig. 5.11 shows approximately inverse effects for the groups in terms of entries to the food tray.

In short, the data support the hypothesis that CSs proximal to a food US condition a focal search mode whether presented before or after the US. In addition, however, forward CSs condition focal perceptual-motor units, whereas backward CSs, although they evoke focal perceptual-motor units, do not appear to condition them. Follow-up

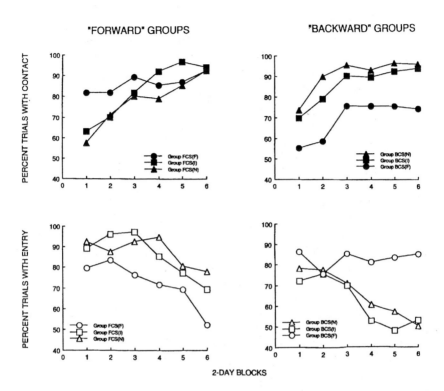

FIG 5.11. Mean percentage trials with contact of a lever CS presented in compound with an element of a previously conditioned serial CS, over 2-day blocks. During previous conditioning the elements of the serial CS were presented either near the US (N), far from the US (F), or intermediate with respect to the US (I). Also during previous training the serial CSs received either forward pairings with the US (FCS group) or backward pairings with the US (BCS group; after F. J. Silva, Timberlake, & Koehler, 1996).

experiments support this view as well (e.g., F. J. Silva & Timberlake, 2000; F. Silva, Timberlake, & Cevik, 1998). These results show some promise in making sense out of the complex results of backward conditioning (e.g., Tait & Saladin, 1986).

Conditioned Inhibition

As previously noted, in the behavior systems view the time between regular presentations of food is presumed to be divided among postfood focal search, general search, and prefood focal search. At a conceptual level this appears to leave no place for conditioned inhibition, (the accrual of negative associative strength between CS and US that is presumed to occur when backward or unpaired CSs are presented along with food (Rescorla, 1967). It is possible that the current behavior systems approach is simply incomplete in this area by not subscribing to an inhibitory associative relation that applies to the strength of particular types of learning. Another possibility, though, is that at least sometimes the phenomenon of conditioned inhibition reflects the results of conditioning a general search mode to the CS, the expression of which is not indexed by a measure of focal search like nosing in the food tray, and may, in fact, initially interfere with that response.

To test the possibility that a negative CS (CS–) may condition a general search mode, Tinsley and I first conditioned a discrimination between paired and unpaired CSs on a Fixed-Time (FT) schedule in which every 90 sec food was presented following a 4-sec positive CS (CS+). At the 45-sec midpoint of each interval a 4-sec CS– was presented. One set of animals receiving this training was then exposed to tests of conditioned inhibition: The summation test compared responding to a compound of CS+ and CS– with that to a compound of CS+ and novel CS (CSN). The retardation test compared the effects of presenting the CS– and food with the presentation of a CSN with food. As would be expected from both the traditional conditioned inhibition view and the conditioned general search view, the CS– significantly reduced acquisition of nosing in the food tray in the retardation test, and decreased (although not quite significantly) the expression of nosing in the feeder in the summation test.

The second set of animals receiving CS+/ CS– discrimination training was then exposed to the combination of stimuli used in the summation and retardation tests (with the addition of the CS+ alone), but instead of being followed by nothing or by food, each CS or CS compound was followed only by a ball bearing probe stimulus overlapping the CS, beginning 2 sec after CS onset. In this way the ball bearing served as an unconditioned probe for a general search mode (see K. M. Silva & Timberlake, 1997), predicting an increase in contact with the bearing following a CS–, and no increase or a decrease in the case of the other CSs. In contrast, the conditioned inhibition view should predict either no effect or a suppression of contact of the bearing following the CS–.

Figure 5.12 shows that only presentation of the CS– significantly enhanced ball bearing contact relative to baseline, thereby supporting the argument that the CS– should control a general search mode. Presentation of the CSN and CS+/CS– had no effect on baseline ball bearing contact, and presentation of the CS+ alone and the CS+/CSN decreased contact with the bearing, presumably because of the conditioned mode and modules related to focal search.

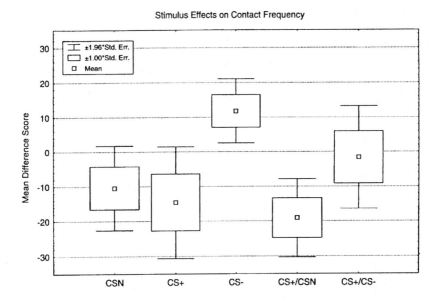

FIG 5.12. Average change from baseline level in percentage trials with a contact of an unconditioned ball bearing probe during extinction tests in which the bearing was presented 2 sec after the onset of CSN(ovel), CS+, or CS– alone, or compounds of the CS+ and the CSN or the CS+ and the CS–.

Context Blocking

Context blocking refers to the effect of multiple presentations of the US prior to conditioning in markedly reducing acquisition of responding to the CS (Balsam, 1985). The typical explanation of this phenomenon is that multiple presentations of the US condition the context stimuli, which then block subsequent conditioning of a predictive CS. The behavior systems view argues that at least some aspects of the blocking effects may be based on a combination of competition between modes and their potential repertoires.

For example, Timberlake (1986) showed that multiple presentations of a food US prior to conditioning interfered with subsequent conditioning of approach to a ball bearing CS only when the animal received the US presentations while nosing in the feeder; that is, only when a focal search mode was strongly conditioned. The same number of presentations occurring when the animal was away from the feeder had little or no suppressive effect on subsequent conditioning. These results suggest that context blocking can relate not only to interference at the level of the perceptual-motor unit, but at the level of modes as well, a possibility suggesting blocking is more complicated than suggested by traditional models.

Higher Order Conditioning

In this section, I report no data but provide further examples of how a behavior systems approach can generate predictions related to complex Pavlovian phenomena. Higher order conditioning is a procedure in which animals are first trained with a CS1 paired with food and then receive pairings of a CS2 with CS1; these higher order pairings are frequently interspersed with continued pairings of the CS1 and food. We suspect that the surprisingly mixed success of this procedure has been due in part to a lack of relation between the modes conditioned and the responses measured.

In our view, if the initial conditioning trials produce a focal search mode controlled by CS1 (as would be the case if a 4-sec light CS1 preceded food), then following a CS2 (such as a 4-sec tone) with the CS1 should produce little transfer of the focal search mode and behavior to the CS2 because it precedes the focal search mode. However, the CS2–CS1 sequence should differentially condition a general search mode and response to CS2 based on predicting the focal search mode related to the CS1. However, if the experimenter measures only focal search responses to CS2, there should be little or no apparent effect.

This procedure could be changed to test the behavior systems analysis a variety of ways. For example, the original CS1 training could be simultaneous rather than delayed, thus differentially conditioning a handling and consuming mode to CS1. Subsequently, when CS2 is presented 4 sec before CS1, CS2 is in the temporal and sequential relation to the handling and consuming mode evoked by CS1 that is appropriate to condition a focal search mode to CS2. In this case, measuring a focal search behavior to CS2 like nosing in the feeder should reveal conditioning.

A second example of procedure to reveal mode conditioning would be to keep the original CS1 interval to the US at 4 sec and the subsequent CS2 interval to CS1 at another 4 sec, but use a CS2 and a conditioning measure more related to general search (such as a ball bearing CS2 and a measure of contacting the bearing). One would predict conditioning of a general search mode to the CS2 ball bearing revealed by increased contact.

These examples should make clear that a variety of combinations of training and testing could easily be proposed to test the contribution of modes to higher order conditioning. In many of these tests I find myself in agreement with the recent analysis of R. R. Miller and Barnet (1993) and Barnet, Cole, and Miller (1997) based on the assumption that animals learn the timing of the CS–US interval as well as characteristics of the CS and US. I simply assume that the timing information is encoded primarily by the conditioning of different search modes. The behavior systems approach adds to the timing hypothesis the importance of measuring appropriate response repertoires, and that CS–US relations other than timing may be important also, including spatial, correlational, and evolutionary dimensions.

DISCUSSION

The data reviewed in this chapter provide considerable support for the hypothesis that a sequence of several motivational modes underlies predatory foraging behavior in rats. Modes appear to consist of repertoires of perceptual-motor organization involving stimulus sensitivities and related response components. This organization arises from unlearned and learned sources in combination with the particular environmental circumstances in effect. Perhaps most important, modes can be conditioned to environmental cues, including the passage of time (K. M. Silva & Timberlake, 1998a, 1998b).

Data from both ethological analyses of naturally occurring appetitive behavior and laboratory construction and analysis of strings of instrumental behavior support the conclusions that appetitive and instrumental behavior is more than an invariant string of stimuli and response units, and that multiple modes (and their repertoires) support multiple transitions within a repertoire and less frequent transitions between repertoires. In addition, the data support the existence of more differentiated repertoires than suggested by the traditional contrast between appetitive and consummatory behavior. In fact the majority of data suggest a minimum of four modes—general search, prefood focal search, handling and consuming, and postfood focal search. Of the four, pre- and postfood focal search are most similar in repertoire, differing primarily in the absence of conditioned postfood modules and the different temporal characteristics in periodic schedules (scalar timing for prefood focal search and a relatively fixed time for postfood focal search; K. M. Silva & Timberlake, 1998b).

Data from many laboratory studies by F. Silva and K. Silva and myself reviewed earlier support the hypothesis that motivational modes can be conditioned to predictive stimuli on the basis of the temporal, spatial, and correlational separation of the CS and the US. Even for the same CS, a small temporal, spatial, or correlational separation between the CS and the US tends to condition a focal search mode and related behavior. A larger temporal, spatial, or correlational separation between CS and US tends to condition a general search mode and related behavior. No separation between the CS and US should produce conditioning of handling and consuming mode and related behaviors. In addition, it appears possible to make predictions based on the observed ecological (and presumed evolutionarily based) correlation between some stimuli and food (e.g., Timberlake & Washburne, 1989).

An increasing amount of laboratory data argues that the conditioning of motivational modes plays an important part in many of the phenomena of Pavlovian conditioning. The most striking contribution of the mode concept is the notion of mode-related repertoires of stimulus sensitivities and response components. This is of critical relevance to the choice of a conditioned response measure. Choosing a single measure can mislead the experimenter as to what is occurring (see also Holland, 1980, 1984). In conjunction with the idea of separate conditioning of the response mode and the responses, the mode concept has obvious potential relevance to phenomena such as backward conditioning, blocking, higher order conditioning, and perhaps occasion setting. Data briefly summarized earlier suggest the importance of both mode and perceptual-motor unit conditioning.

In sum, the phenomena discussed in this chapter are simplest to predict and integrate using the behavior systems concept of conditionable sequential search modes. Any single example undoubtedly can be explained on the basis of specific linked stimulus–response units in combination with others of the many concepts developed within associative theory. However, I think we are at the point where the array of specific assumptions and hypothesized associative and nonassociative processes has become, if not too plentiful, then too disorganized and unpredictable in application. The framework of a behavior system seems to provide a consistent heuristic organization of mechanisms of learning and behavior that can be built on in subsequent work. There are compelling reasons not to abandon all forms of acquired associations among stimuli and responses, but there are compelling reasons to stop trying to explain everything by these links. An advantage of embedding the study of learning within a behavior systems framework is that the framework calls attention to a grammar of modes in which to realize and clarify behavioral results. Such a framework can be modified and built on rather than discarded as particular interpretations and procedures fall from favor (Timberlake, 1993). Once you begin looking at appetitive behavior in general, and Pavlovian conditioning procedures in particular, within the framework of a behavior system, many anomalous findings (ranging from adjunctive behavior and misbehavior to backward and higher order conditioning) become more understandable and predictable. Perhaps most important, many of the predictions that arise from considering how a behavior systems framework should interact with learning procedures have not evolved from traditional learning models.

Related Views

The behavior systems approach is by no means the first to hypothesize the existence of motivational states or substates. In the first part of this century Sherrington (1906) and Craig (1918) proposed a distinction between appetitive and consummatory behavior, a distinction built on by Tinbergen and Lorenz. Within the learning tradition Rescorla and Solomon (1967) highlighted two-factor theory, and Konorski argued for a distinction between a preparatory (drive) state and a consummatory (goal) state. The preparatory state supported the conditioning of diffuse excitatory responses at relatively long CS–US intervals, whereas the consummatory state supported the conditioning of precise focused responses at short CS–US intervals. Wagner developed Solomon and Corbit's (1974) opponent process idea within the context of Pavlovian conditioning, separating motivation into two processes: an anticipatory process before presentation of the US and an opposing process following presentation of the US (e.g., Wagner & Brandon, 1989). Holland and his co-workers (1980, 1984) pointed out transitions among different components of conditioning. More recently Killeen (1998) applied the concept of increasing arousal underlying the development of an appetitive string of behavior.

A careful analysis of the similarities and differences among these theories and a contrast with behavior systems is beyond the scope of this chapter. There are many similarities and each theory has its own strengths. The behavior systems approach differs from any one of these theories largely in completeness and specificity. It argues for more than two classes of motivational modes: general, focal, handling/consuming, and postfood focal search. Most previous approaches appear to fail to discriminate these modes or do not consider their influence in deciding on CS presentations and response measures to test their theories. The behavior systems approach also attempts to specify the large repertoire of stimulus sensitivities and response components available to the animal in each mode.

A second difference is that most previous approaches treat appetitive behavior as consisting only of variable and diffuse excitatory responses, most often controlled by relatively contextual stimuli. The behavior systems approach is more empirical. For example, for many predators, forms of specific general search appear evoked by moving cues of a certain size; consider the actions of the rat with respect to moving stimuli of around ⅝-in. diameter (Timberlake et al., 1982), and the reactions of several species of rodents to smaller bearings (Timberlake & Washburne, 1989). Further, the general search behavior of many predatory birds, such as kestrels, consists of systematically searching general areas of potential prey (Daan, 1981).

Third, in contrast with the ethological approach, behavior systems makes clear how laboratory learning circumstances interact with the system framework and can be used to explore it. In contrast to laboratory approaches, behavior systems theory assumes a good deal of specific perceptual-motor and motivational preorganization that the animal brings to the circumstances. Although the physiology of the body and the physics of gravity and momentum set limits and windows on the functioning of sensory apparatus and motor output, there is no theory that as yet predicts precise response form or stimulus sensitivities a priori. At present these data must be entered for each species, system, mode, and module on the basis of observation and structural, neural, and chemical analysis. However, when such a theory arises, it should be possible to incorporate it into a behavior system framework that probably already contains aspects of its predictions (see Domjan, 1994; Fanselow, 1994; Hogan, 1994).

Characteristics of Motivational Modes

It should be apparent that the concept of modes and repertoires is sufficiently clear to make predictions and account for a considerable amount of data. However, it should be equally obvious that the behavior system approach, and especially the concept of motivational modes, is neither settled nor complete. There are several issues of importance that need further development and resolution.

One issue is the number of modes. As previously indicated, I think it is evident that there are more than two modes in the case of feeding: a general search mode, prefood focal search, and handling/ consuming modes. There are also several reasons to believe that postfood focal search differs sufficiently from prefood focal search to make a total of four modes (e.g., F. J. Silva et al., 1986; K. M. Silva & Timberlake, 1998b). My intuitive reaction is that three to four modes is sufficient, particularly if, as Fig. 5.2 indicates, modes overlap along the dimensions of CS–US relatedness, including time, space, correlation, and evolutionary function. Exactly how these dimensions relate to each will require a model of some complexity, but the implied flexibility allows a given CS the potential to condition and evoke more than one mode and more than one behavior.

However, it is worth considering an alternative model in which there are no discrete modes or separate dimensions of relatedness to the US. Instead there simply are modules arranged on a continuum of arousal that can be conditioned in relatively discrete segments (F. Silva has argued this case in several presentations). It is clear, however, that such a continuum would still effectively locate modules in clumps of increased interchangeability within a range of arousal values that can be conditioned, a not dissimilar picture. Also, it may be difficult to argue that arousal will do all the work of the dimensions of temporal, spatial, correlational, and evolutionary relatedness to the US. The choice of a model may well come down to factors of flexibility and ease of representation.

A second issue about modes is their distribution in time, especially relative to USs and CSs. It appears from free response data that, other things equal, the temporal extent of the prefood modes is scalar relative to the IFI and the temporal extent of the postfood focal search is fixed for a particular reward amount. However, it makes sense that the temporal extent should be flexible and should vary with the presence of the CSs present and the CS–US relations. The data of K. M. Silva and Timberlake (1999) indicate both a tendency toward a particular temporal distribution of modes across an interval and a temporal flexibility in tying modes to stimuli. Data from the multiple CS "envelope" study suggest a temporal range of effects from a single US far beyond what might be expected from typical Pavlovian results.

Further, data from serial CS studies (e.g., F. J. Silva, Timberlake, & Cevik, 1998; F. J. Silva, Timberlake, & Gont, 1998; F. J. Silva et al., 1996) suggest that the temporal extent of a mode can be quite flexible. Apparently, at least some aspects of the timing of modes can be conditioned to different elements of fixed-length serial CSs, and short elements at that. An interesting consideration is that time judgments may differ within different modes. The underlying "clock" may run faster in focal search mode than in general search modes. Similarly, because the postfood focal search mode has the unique quality of following rather than preceding food, there is no particular reason to assume that the animal is judging an interval as it might be in anticipating food. The question of timing is far from resolved.

A third question relates to what determines the strengths of modes, and, in fact, whether we should think of modes as having a coherent strength that affects their repertoire of modules equally. For simplicity, I assume that modes have a basic strength reflecting system variable that may be affected directly by specific neurophysiological conditions and by CS and US that activate perceptual-motor structures. A related issue concerns the mechanisms of learning that operate for modes. For example, to what extent can modes be associated with each other and with the environment, the US, and components of perceptual-motor organization, and are these possible associations similar for all modes (see Hilliard et al., 1998)?

A final set of issues revolves around the contributions of system and species differences to the influence of motivational modes. The great majority of research on behavior systems has focused on the feeding system of rats. Evidence from fear systems suggests that the equivalent of a focal search mode (seeking to remain unseen in the presence of a predator) may be considerably longer in duration than a food-related focal search mode (Fanselow, 1994). Similar differences appear to be present in the courtship system in quail (Domjan, 1994).

Even the operation of the feeding system of a particular species may differ according to the density of prey, its location, and the potential difficulty in acquiring it. Clearly the probability of different repertoire components of focal search may differ with the type of prey and its potential resistance. It is equally reasonable that the length and relative extent of general and focal search and even their potential differentiation into a larger number of modes should vary with the ecological niche of the animal. Bell (1991) and Roche and Timberlake (1999) suggested that the physical food niches in an environment can affect the number and form of available repertoires. Pecoraro, Timberlake, and Tinsley (1999) suggested how a behavior system might serve as a framework for combining changes in foraging repertoires and the psychological concept of frustration in dealing with downshifts in food availability. A key to using a behavior system well is to carefully ground it in the repertoires and environments available for each system and species.

SUMMARY

The behavior systems approach brings together and extends historical ideas about the sequence of motivational states underlying appetitive strings of behavior. In practice search modes appear to encompass differing repertoires based on both US and CS sensitivities and response components. The strength of a search mode as well as the individual stimulus sensitivities and response components expressing it reflect both the overall system motivation and specific contributions of stimulus environment. Data supporting the importance of motivational modes come from the analysis of appetitive strings of behavior in both the field and the laboratory; research investigating the effects of temporal, spatial, correlational, and evolutionary relations between CS and US on conditioned behavior; temporal characteristics of modes; and several traditional phenomena of Pavlovian conditioning, including backward conditioning. Modes should provide a long-term basis for the study of purposive behavior in general and should facilitate the understanding and control of behavior in both laboratory and field settings.

ACKNOWLEDGMENTS

Preparation of this chapter was supported by National Science Foundation IBN #17175 and National Institute of Drug Abuse #11092. Thanks to Gary Lucas, John Pearce, Norman Pecoraro, Matthew Tinsley, and Ron Villarreal for their comments, to Joe Leffel, Don Gawley, and Gary Lucas for their help, and special thanks to Francisco and Kathleen Silva for their extensive research contributions and comments.

REFERENCES

Akins, C. A., Domjan, M., & Gutierrez, G. (1994). Topography of sexually conditioned behavior in male Japanese quail (Coturnix japonica) depends on the CS–US interval. *Journal of Experimental Psychology: Animal Behavior Processes, 20,* 199–209.

Baerends, G. P., & Drent, R. H. (1982). The herring gull and its eggs. *Behaviour, 82,* 1–416.

Baerends, G. P., & Kruijt, J. P. (1973). Stimulus selection. In R. A. Hinde & J. Stevenson-Hinde (Eds.), *Constraints on learning: Limitations and predispositions* (pp. 23–50). New York: Academic Press.

Balsam, P. (1985). The functions of context in learning and performance. In P. D. Balsam & A. Tomie (Eds.), *Context and learning* (pp. 1–21). Hillsdale, NJ: Lawrence Erlbaum Associates.

Barlow, G. W. (1977). Modal action patterns. In T. A. Sebeok (Ed.), *How animals communicate* (pp. 98–134). Bloomington: Indiana University Press.

Barnet, R. C., Cole, R. P., & Miller, R. R. (1997). Temporal integration in second-order conditioning and sensory preconditioning. *Animal Learning & Behavior, 25,* 221–233.

Barnett, S. A. (1975). *The rat: A study in behavior.* Chicago: University of Chicago Press.

Bell, W. J. (1991). *Searching behavior: The behavioural ecology of finding resources.* London: Chapman Hall.

Blanchard, D. C., & Blanchard, R. J. (1990). The colony model of aggression and defense. In D. A. Dewsbury (Ed.), *Contemporary issues in comparative psychology* (pp. 410–430). Sunderland, MA: Sinauer.

Boice, R. (1972). Some behavioral tests of domestication in Norway rats. *Behaviour, 42,* 198–231.

Bolles, R. C. (1970). Species-specific defense reactions and avoidance learning. *Psychological Review, 77,* 32–48.

Breland, K., & Breland, M. (1961). The misbehavior of organisms. *American Psychologist, 16,* 681–684.

Brodbeck, D. R. (1994). Memory for spatial and local cues: A comparison of a storing and a nonstoring species. *Animal Learning & Behavior, 22,* 119–133.

Brown, P. L., & Jenkins, H. M. (1968). Auto-shaping of the pigeon's key-peck. *Journal of the Experimental Analysis of Behavior, 11,* 1–8.

Calhoun, J. B. (1962). *The ecology and sociology of the Norway rats.* Bethesda, MD: U. S. Department of Health, Education, and Welfare.

Cherot, C., Jones, A., & Neuringer, A. (1996). Reinforced variability decreases with approach to reinforcers. *Journal of Experimental Psychology: Animal Behavior Processes, 22,* 497–508.

Cohen, P. S., Looney, T. A., Campagnoni, F. R., & Lawler, C. P. (1985). A two-state model of reinforcer-induced motivation. In F. R. Brush & J. B. Overmier (Eds.), *Affect, conditioning, and cognition: Essays on the determinants of behavior* (pp. 281–297). Hillsdale, NJ: Lawrence Erlbaum Associates.

Craig, W. (1918). Appetites and aversions as constituents of instincts. *Biological Bulletin of Marine Biology, Woods Hole, MA, 34,* 91–107.

Daan, S. (1981). Adaptive daily strategies in behavior. In J. Aschoff (Ed.), *Handbook of behavioral neurobiology: Vol. 4. Biological rhythms* (pp. 275–298). New York: Plenum.

Domjan, M. (1994). Formulation of a behavior system for sexual conditioning. *Psychonomic Bulletin & Review, 1,* 421–428.

Domjan, M., & Hollis, K. L. (1988). Reproductive behavior: A potential model system for adaptive specializations in learning. In R. C. Bolles & M. D. Beecher (Eds.), *Evolution and learning* (pp. 213–237). Hillsdale, NJ: Lawrence Erlbaum Associates.

Ewer, R. F. (1971). The biology and behaviour of a free-living population of black rats (Rattus rattus). *Animal Behaviour Monographs, 4*(3).

Fanselow, M. S. (1991). The midbrain periaqueductal gray as a coordinator of action in response to fear and anxiety. In A. Depaulis & R. Bandler (Eds.), *The midbrain periaqueductal grey matter: Functional, anatomical and immunohistochemical organization* (pp. 151–173). New York: Plenum.

Fanselow, M. S. (1994). Neural organization of the defensive behavior system responsible for fear. *Psychonomic Bulletin & Review, 1,* 429–438.

Fanselow, M. S., & Lester, L. S. (1988). A functional behavioristic approach to aversively motivated behavior: Predatory imminence as a determinant of the topography of defensive behavior. In R. C. Bolles & M. D. Beecher (Eds.), *Evolution and learning* (pp. 185–211). Hillsdale, NJ: Lawrence Erlbaum Associates.

Fearing, F. (1930). *Reflex action: A study in the history of physiological psychology.* New York: Hafner.

Fentress, J. C. (1973). Specific and nonspecific factors in the causation of behavior. In P. P. G. Bateson & P. H. Klopfer (Eds.), *Perspectives in ethology* (Vol. 1, pp. 155–224). New York: Plenum.

Fentress, J. C. (1976). Dynamic boundaries of patterned behavior: Interaction and self-organization. In P. P. G. Bateson & R. A. Hinde (Eds.), *Growing points in ethology* (pp. 135–169). Cambridge, UK: Cambridge University Press.

Ferster, C. B., & Skinner, B. F. (1957). *Schedules of reinforcement.* Englewood Cliffs, NJ: Prentice Hall.

Galef, B. G. (1990). An adaptionist perspective on social learning, social feeding, and social foraging in Norway rats. In D. A. Dewsbury (Ed.), *Contemporary issues in comparative psychology* (pp. 55–79). Sunderland MA: Sinauer Associates.

Gormezano, I. (1966). Classical conditioning. In J. B. Sidowski (Ed.), *Experimental methods and instrumentation in psychology* (pp. 385–420). New York: McGraw-Hill.

Hearst, E. (1988). Fundamentals of learning and conditioning. In R. C. Atkinson, R. J. Herrnstein, G. Lindzey, & R. D. Luce (Eds.), *Stevens' handbook of experimental psychology: Vol. 2. Learning and cognition* (2nd ed., pp. 3–109). New York: Wiley.

Hearst, E., & Jenkins, H. M. (1974). *Sign tracking: The stimulus–reinforcer relation and directed action.* Austin, TX: Psychonomic Society.

Hilliard, S., Domjan, M., Nguyen, M., & Cusato, B. (1998). Dissociation of conditioned appetitive and consummatory sexual behavior: Satiation and extinction tests. *Animal Learning & Behavior, 26,* 20–33.

Hinde, R. A. (1970). *Animal behaviour: A synthesis of ethology and comparative psychology.* New York: McGraw-Hill.

Hogan, J. A. (1988). Cause and function in the development of behavior systems. In E. M. Blass (Ed.), *Developmental psychobiology and behavior ecology: Handbook of behavior neurobiology* (Vol. 9, pp. 63–106). New York: Plenum.

Hogan, J. A. (1994). Structure and development of behavior systems. *Psychonomic Bulletin and Review, 1,* 439–450.

Holland, P. C. (1980). CS–US interval as a determinant of the form of Pavlovian appetitive conditioned responses. *Journal of Experimental Psychology: Animal Behavior Processes, 6,* 155–175.

Holland, P. C. (1984). Origins of Pavlovian conditioned behavior. In G. H. Bower (Ed.), *The psychology of learning and motivation* (Vol. 18, pp. 129–173). Englewood Cliffs, NJ: Prentice Hall.

Hollis, K. L. (1990). The role of Pavlovian conditioning in territorial aggression and reproduction. In D. A. Dewsbury (Ed.), *Contemporary issues in comparative psychology* (pp. 197–219). Sunderland, MA: Sinauer.

Hughes, R. N. (1998). Spontaneous alternation behavior in animals: Mechanisms, motives, and applications. In R. R. Hoffman & M. F. Sherrick (Eds.), *Viewing psychology as a whole: The integrative science of William N. Dember* (pp. 269–286). Washington, DC: American Psychological Association.

Hull, C. L. (1932). The goal-gradient hypothesis and maze learning. *Psychological Review, 39,* 25–43.

Innis, N. K., Simmelhag-Grant, V. L., & Staddon, J. E. R. (1983). Behavior induced by periodic food delivery: The effects of interfood interval. *Journal of the Experimental Analysis of Behavior, 39,* 309–322.

Jenkins, H. M., Barrera, C., Ireland, C., & Woodside, B. (1978). Signal-centered action patterns of dogs in appetitive classical conditioning. *Learning and Motivation, 9,* 272–296.

Jenkins, H. M., & Moore, B. R. (1973). The form of the auto-shaped response with food or water reinforcers. *Journal of the Experimental Analysis of Behavior, 20,* 163–181.

Kamil, A. C. (1988). A synthetic approach to animal intelligence. In D. W. Leger (Ed.), *Nebraska symposium on motivation, 1987: Comparative perspectives in modern psychology* (pp. 257–308). Lincoln: University of Nebraska Press.

Kamil, A. C., & Balda, R. (1985). Cache recovery and spatial memory in "Clark's nutcrackers" (*Nucifraga columbiana*). *Journal of Experimental Psychology: Animal Behavior Processes, 11,* 95–111.

Kamin, L. J. (1969). Predictability, surprise, attention, and conditioning. In B. A. Campbell & R. M. Church (Eds.), *Punishment and aversive behavior* (pp. 279–296). New York: Appleton-Century-Crofts.

Killeen, P. R. (1998). The first principle of reinforcement. In C. D. L. Wynne & J. E. R. Staddon (Eds.), *Models of action: Mechanisms for adaptive behavior* (pp. 127–156). Mahwah, NJ: Lawrence Erlbaum Associates.

Kimble, G. A. (1961). *Hilgard and Marquis' conditioning and learning* (2nd ed.). New York: Appleton-Century-Crofts.

Konorski, J. (1967). *Integrative activity of the brain: An interdisciplinary approach.* Chicago: University of Chicago Press.

Krebs, J. R., Healy, S. D., & Shettleworth, S. J. (1990). Spatial memory of Paridae: Comparison of a storing and a nonstoring species, the coal tit, *Parus ater,* and the great tit, *P. major. Animal Behavior, 39,* 1127–1137.

Leyhausen, P. (1979). *Cat behavior: The predatory and social behavior of domestic and wild cats.* New York: Garland.

Liddell, H. S. (1934). The conditioned reflex. In F. A. Moss (Ed.), *Comparative psychology* (pp. 247–296). New York: Prentice Hall.

Logue, A. W. (1988). Research on self-control: An integrating framework. *Behavioral and Brain Sciences, 11,* 665–709.

Lorenz, K. (1981). *The foundations of ethology.* New York: SpringerVerlag.

Lucas, G. A., Timberlake, W., & Gawley, D. J. (1988). Adjunctive behavior in the rat under periodic food delivery in a 24-hr environment. *Animal Learning & Behavior, 16,* 19–30.

Lucas, G. A., Timberlake, W., & Gawley, D. J. (1989). Learning and meal-associated drinking: Meal-related deficits produce adjustments in post prandial drinking. *Physiology & Behavior, 46,* 361–367.

Mackintosh, N. J. (1974). *The psychology of animal learning.* London: Academic Press.

Matthews, T. J., & Lerer, B. E. (1987). Behavior patterns in pigeons during autoshaping with an incremental conditioned stimulus. *Animal Learning & Behavior, 15,* 69–75.

Miller, D. B. (1977). Roles of naturalistic observation in comparative psychology. *American Psychologist, 32,* 211–219.

Miller, N. E. (1969). Learning of visceral and glandular responses. *Science, 163,* 434–445.

Miller, R. R., & Barnet, R. C. (1993). The role of time in elementary associations. *Current Directions in Psychological Science, 2,* 106–111.

Mook, D. G. (1996). *Motivation: The organization of action.* New York: Norton.

Morris, D. (1958). The reproductive behavior of the ten-spined stickleback (*Pygosteus pungitius L.*). *Behaviour, 61* (Suppl.), 1–154.

Muenzinger, K. F. (1928). Plasticity and mechanization of the problem box habit in guinea pigs. *Journal of Comparative Psychology, 8,* 45–69.

Munn, N. L. (1950). *Handbook of psychological research on the rat: An introduction to animal psychology.* Boston: Houghton Mifflin.

Olson, D. J., Kamil, A. C., Balda, R. P., & Nims, P. J. (1995). Performance of four-seed caching corvid species in operant test of nonspatial and spatial memory. *Journal of Comparative Psychology, 109,* 173–181.

Olton, D. S. (1979). Maps, mazes, and memory. *American Psychologist, 34,* 483–506.

Pecoraro, N., Timberlake, W., & Tinsley, M. (1999). Incentive downshifts evoke search behavior in rats (*Rattus norvegicus*). *Journal of Experimental Psychology: Animal Behavior Processes, 25,* 153–167.

Reid, A. K., Bacha, G., & Moran, C. (1993). The temporal organization of behavior on periodic food schedules. *Journal of the Experimental Analysis of Behavior, 59,* 1–27.

Rescorla, R. A. (1967). Pavlovian conditioning and its proper control procedures. *Psychological Review, 74,* 71–80.

Rescorla, R. A., & Solomon, R. L. (1967). Two-process learning theory: Relations between Pavlovian conditioning and instrumental learning. *Psychological Review, 74,* 151–182.

Roche, J., & Timberlake, W. (1999). *Refining foraging theory: How do search-mode sequences and the structure of the environment influence prey path selection.* Manuscript submitted for publication.

Schneiderman, N. (1972). Response system divergences in aversive classical conditioning. In A. H. Black & W. F. Prokasy (Eds.), *Classical conditioning II: Current research and theory* (pp. 341–376). New York: Appleton-Century-Crofts.

Sherrington, C. S. (1906). *The integrative action of the nervous system.* New York: Scribner.

Sherry, D. F. (1984). Food storage by black-capped chickadees: Memory for the location and contents of caches. *Animal Behavior, 32,* 451–464.

Shettleworth, S. J. (1994). What are behavior systems and what use are they? *Psychonomic Bulletin and Review, 1,* 451–456.

Silva, F. J., & Timberlake, W. (2000). A clarification of the nature of backward excitatory conditioning. *Learning and Motivation, 21,* 67–80.

Silva, F. J., Timberlake, W., & Cevik, M. O. (1998). A behavior systems approach to the expression of backward associations. *Learning and Motivation, 29,* 1–22.

Silva, F. J., Timberlake, W., & Gont, R. S. (1998). Spatiotemporal characteristics of serial CSs and their relation to search modes and response form. *Animal Learning & Behavior, 26,* 299–312.

Silva, F. J., Timberlake, W., & Koehler, T. L. (1996). A behavior systems approach to bidirectional excitatory conditioning. *Learning and Motivation, 27,* 130–150.

Silva, K. M., & Timberlake, W. (1997). A behavior systems view of response form during long and short CS–US intervals. *Learning and Motivation, 28,* 465–490.

Silva, K. M., & Timberlake, W. (1998a). A behavior systems view of responding during an interfood clock. *Animal Learning & Behavior, 26,* 313–325.

Silva, K. M., & Timberlake, W. (1998b). The organization and temporal properties of appetitive behavior in the rat. *Animal Learning & Behavior, 26,* 182–195.

Silva, K. M., & Timberlake, W. (1999). Rats' behavior during an interfood clock is altered by the temporal pattern of the clock stimuli. *Learning and Motivation, 30,* 183–200.

Skinner, B. F. (1937, May 31). Rat works slot machine for a living. *Life, 2,* pp. 80–81.

Skinner, B. F. (1938). *The behavior of organisms.* New York: Appleton-Century-Crofts.

Skinner, B. F. (1948). "Superstition" in the pigeon. *Journal of Experimental Psychology, 38,* 168–172.

Skinner, B. F. (1956). A case history in the scientific method. *American Psychologist, 11,* 221–233.

Solomon, R. L., & Corbit, J. D. (1974). An opponent-process theory of motivation: I. The temporal dynamics of affect. *Psychological Review, 81,* 119–145.

Staddon, J. E. R. (1977). Schedule-induced behavior. In W. K. Honig & J. E. R. Staddon (Eds.), *Handbook of operant behavior* (pp. 125–152). Englewood Cliffs, NJ: Prentice Hall.

Staddon, J. E. R., & Simmelhag, V. L. (1971). The "superstition" experiment: A reexamination of its implications for the principles of adaptive behavior. *Psychological Review, 78,* 3–43.

Steininger, F. von. (1950). Beitrage zur soziologie und sonstigen biologie der wanderratte [Contributions to the Sociology and other biology of Rattus norvegicus,]. *Zeitschrift fur Tierpsychologie, 7,* 356–379.

Stokes, P. D., & Balsam, P. D. (1991). Effects of reinforcing preselected approximations on the topography of the rat's bar press. *Journal of the Experimental Analysis of Behavior, 55,* 213–232.

Tait, R. W., & Saladin, M. E. (1986). Concurrent development of excitatory and inhibitory associations during backward conditioning. *Animal Learning & Behavior, 14,* 133–137.

Telle, H. J. (1966). Beitrage zur kenntnis der verhaltensweise von ratten, vergleichend dargestellt bei, *Rattus norvegicus and Rattus rattus*. [Contribution to knowledge of the behavior of rats, a comparative study of *Rattus norvegicus* and *Rattus rattus*.] *Zeitschrift fur Angewandte Zoologie, 53,* 129–196.

Timberlake, W. (1983a). Appetitive structure and straight alley running. In R. Mellgren (Ed.), *Animal cognition and behavior* (pp. 165–222). Amsterdam: North Holland.

Timberlake, W. (1983b). The functional organization of appetitive behavior: Behavior systems and learning. In M. D. Zeiler & P. Harzem (Eds.), *Advances in the analysis of behavior: Vol. 3. Biological factors in learning* (pp. 177–221). Chichester, UK: Wiley.

Timberlake, W. (1983c). The rat's response to a moving object related to food or water: A behavior systems analysis. *Animal Learning & Behavior, 11,* 309–320.

Timberlake, W. (1986). Unpredicted food produces a mode of behavior that affects rats' subsequent reactions to a conditioned stimulus: A behavior system approach to "context blocking." *Animal Learning & Behavior, 14,* 276–286.

Timberlake, W. (1988). Evolution, behavior systems, and "self-control:" The fit between organism and test environment. *Behavioral and Brain Sciences, 11,* 694–695.

Timberlake, W. (1990). Natural learning in laboratory paradigms. In D. A. Dewsbury (Ed.), *Contemporary issues in comparative psychology* (pp. 31–54). Sunderland, MA: Sinauer.

Timberlake, W. (1993). Behavior systems and reinforcement: An integrative approach. *Journal of the Experimental Analysis of Behavior, 60,* 105–128.

Timberlake, W. (1994). Behavior systems, associationism, and Pavlovian conditioning. *Psychonomic Bulletin & Review, 1,* 405–420.

Timberlake, W. (1995). Reconceptualizing reinforcement: A causal system approach to reinforcement and behavior change. In W. O'Donohue & L. Krasner (Eds.), *Theories in behavior therapy* (pp. 59–96). Washington, DC: American Psychological Association.

Timberlake, W. (1997). An animal-centered, causal-system approach to the understanding and control of behavior. *Applied Animal Behaviour Science, 53,* 107–129.

Timberlake, W. (1999). Biological behaviorism. In W. O'Donohue & R. Kitchener (Eds.), *Handbook of behaviorism* (pp. 243–283). New York: Academic Press.

Timberlake, W., Gawley, D. J., & Lucas, G. A. (1987). Time horizons in rats foraging for food in temporally separated patches. *Journal of Experimental Psychology: Animal Behavior Processes, 13,* 302–309.

Timberlake, W., & Grant, D. L. (1975). Auto-shaping in rats to the presentation of another rat predicting food. *Science, 190,* 690–692.

Timberlake, W., & Lucas, G. A. (1985). The basis of superstitious behavior: Chance contingency, stimulus substitution, or appetitive behavior? *Journal of the Experimental Analysis of Behavior, 44,* 279–299.

Timberlake, W., & Lucas, G. A. (1989). Behavior systems and learning: From misbehavior to general principles. In S. B. Klein & R. R. Mowrer (Eds.), *Contemporary learning theories: Instrumental conditioning theory and the impact of biological constraints on learning* (pp. 237–275). Hillsdale, NJ: Lawrence Erlbaum Associates.

Timberlake, W., & Lucas, G. A. (1991). Periodic water, interwater interval, and adjunctive behavior in a 24-hour multi-response environment. *Animal Learning and Behavior, 19,* 369–380.

Timberlake, W., & Melcer, T. (1988). A laboratory simulation of predatory behavior in rats: Effects of poisoning. *Journal of Comparative Psychology, 102,* 182–187.

Timberlake, W., & Silva, F. J. (1994). Observation of behavior, inference of function, and the study of learning. *Psychonomic Bulletin & Review, 1,* 73–88.

Timberlake, W., & Silva, K. M. (1995). Appetitive behavior in ethology, psychology, and behavior systems. In N. Thompson (Ed.), *Perspectives in ethology* (pp. 211–253). New York: Plenum.

Timberlake, W., Wahl, G., & King, D. (1982). Stimulus and response contingencies in the misbehavior of rats. *Journal of Experimental Psychology: Animal Behavior Processes, 8,* 62–85.

Timberlake, W., & Washburne, D. L. (1989). Feeding ecology and laboratory predatory behavior toward live and artificial moving prey in seven rodent species. *Animal Learning & Behavior, 17,* 1–10.

Timberlake, W., & White, W. (1990). Winning isn't everything: Rats need only food deprivation not food reward to traverse a radial arm maze efficiently. *Learning and Motivation, 21,* 153–163.

Tinbergen, N. (1951). *The study of instinct.* New York: Oxford University Press.

Tinsley, M., Rebec, G. V., & Timberlake, W. (1999). *Facilitation of behavior in an artificial prey paradigm by D1 dopamine receptor activation.* (Manuscript submitted for publication).

Tugendhat, B. (1960). The disturbed feeding behavior of the three-spined stickleback: I. Electric shock is administered in the food area. *Behaviour, 16,* 159–187.

von Holst, E. (1973). On the nature of order in the central nervous system. In *The behavioral physiology of animals and man: Selected papers of E. von Holst* (Vol. 1, R. D. Martin, Trans.). Coral Gables, FL: University of Miami Press. (Original work published 1937).

Wagner, A. R., & Brandon, S. E. (1989). Evolution of a structured connectionist model of Pavlovian conditioning (AESOP). In S. B. Klein & R. R. Mowrer (Eds.), *Contemporary learning theories: Pavlovian conditioning and the status of traditional learning theory* (pp. 149–189). Hillsdale, NJ: Lawrence Erlbaum Associates.

White, W., & Timberlake, W. (1999). Meal-engendered circadian ensuing activity in rats. *Physiology and Behavior, 65,* 625–642.

Zener, K. (1937). The significance of behavior accompanying conditioned salivary secretion for theories of the conditioned response. *American Journal of Psychology, 50,* 384–403.

chapter 6

Theories of Conditioning and Timing

Russell M. Church
Kimberly Kirkpatrick
Brown University

T heories of conditioning and timing were developed independently, and they have been used to explain different phenomena. Theories of conditioning are designed to account for differential strengths of responding in the presence of different stimulus configurations. For example, they explain the acquisition of a higher response rate in the presence than in the absence of a light if reinforcement occurs during the light. In contrast, theories of timing are designed to account for differential responding as a function of the time from a stimulus transition. For example, they explain differences in response rate and response choice as a function of time since the onset of a stimulus. The separate goals of theories of conditioning and timing are reflected in two chapters of the previous edition of this book (Klein & Mowrer, 1989): The chapter "Theories of Timing Behavior" (Church, 1989) did not refer to conditioning literature or theory, and the chapter "Perceptual and Associative Learning" (Hall & Honey, 1989) did not refer to timing literature or theory. Textbooks on animal cognition and learning (e.g., Roberts, 1998; Schmajuk, 1997) typically describe theories of conditioning and timing in separate chapters with minimal cross-referencing. In an excellent review of recent research on associative learning that was put in historical context, Wasserman and Miller (1997) described various types of theories (contiguity, contingency, rule-based, and associative), but not the timing theories or real-time conditioning theories described in this chapter. In the last decade there has been an increasing convergence of theories of conditioning and timing, and it is no longer clear that separate theories are required (Kirkpatrick & Church, 1998). This chapter describes some of these developments.

DATA TO BE EXPLAINED BY THEORIES OF CONDITIONING AND TIMING

Although theories of conditioning and timing have normally been evaluated on the basis of different experimental procedures, they may be able to account for the results of the same experimental procedures.

One standard conditioning procedure is called delay conditioning. In this procedure, after a random duration, a stimulus is presented for a fixed duration, reinforcement is presented at the end of the stimulus, and then the cycle repeats (Fig. 6.1, bottom panel). For example, in a goal-tracking experiment with rats, after a random interval of 75 sec, a white noise stimulus is presented for 15 sec with food delivered at the end of the stimulus, and the cycle repeats. Each time the rat puts its head into the food cup a photobeam is interrupted. The rate of head entries in the presence of the stimulus (p) and in the absence of the stimulus (a) is calculated, and a discrimination ratio is defined as $p / (a + p)$. If the rate of head entries is equal in the presence and the absence of the white noise ($a = p$), the discrimination ratio would be 0.5; if head entries are only made during the presence of the white noise ($p = 1, a = 0$), the discrimination ratio would be 1.0. Six rats were trained on this procedure for 10 2-hr sessions. The mean discrimination ratio (plus or minus the standard error of the mean) is shown as a function of session number in the top panel of Fig. 6.1. This is a standard learning curve in which the discrimination ratio was about 0.6 on the first session, and it gradually increased to a level of about 0.9 on the 10th session. If a theoretical fit to the acquisition curve in Fig. 6.1 was desired, a conditioning theory such as the Rescorla–Wagner model would be the natural choice.

This same procedure is also a standard timing procedure in which a reinforcement is presented at some fixed time after stimulus onset. The

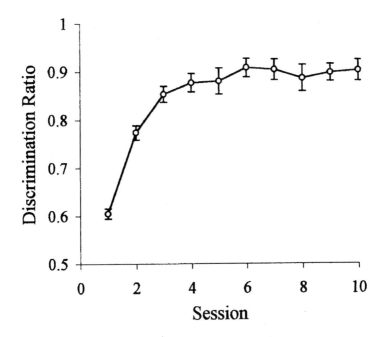

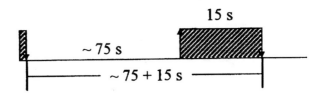

FIG. 6.1. Strength of response in the presence of the stimulus. The mean discrimination ratio, and the standard error of the mean, as a function of sessions of training (top panel). The bottom panel shows the procedure in which, following a random interval with a mean of 75 sec, noise occurs for 15 sec, and a pellet of food is delivered in the last 0.1 sec of the noise. The noise is indicated by the striped pattern; the reinforcement is indicated by the vertical line at the end of the noise; random intervals are indicated by ∼.

time (to the nearest .01 sec) of the onset of each noise and each head entry was recorded, and the rate of head entries in each 1-sec interval in the 60 sec prior to the stimulus and each 1-sec interval during the stimulus was calculated. (The calculations of response rate prior to stimulus onset excluded any times during which a previous stimulus or reinforcement occurred.) The mean response rate as a function of time since stimulus onset is shown in the top panel of Fig. 6.2. This is a standard temporal gradient; the response rate was low and relatively constant at about 4 responses per minute prior to stimulus onset and then increased as a function of time since stimulus onset to a rate over 50 responses per minute. If a theoretical fit to the response rate gradient in Fig. 6.2 was desired, a timing theory such as scalar timing theory would be the natural choice.

In conditioning theories (e.g., Mackintosh, 1975; Pearce & Hall, 1980; Rescorla & Wagner, 1972), the current condition is specified by a state, which is defined as a stimulus configuration. The perceptual represen-

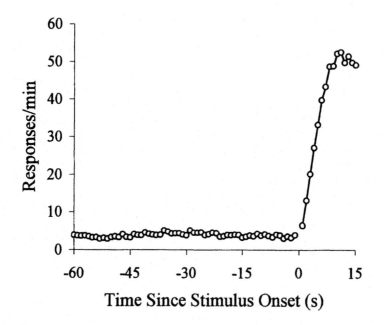

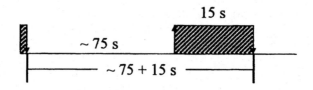

FIG. 6.2.   Response gradient as a function of time since stimulus onset. The mean response rate as a function of time relative to signal onset (top panel). The procedure in the bottom panel is the same as the one in Fig. 6.1.

tation of the white noise in the top panel of Fig. 6.3 is at one level when
the white noise is present and at another level when the white noise is
absent. In conditioning theories, reinforcement operates on a representa-
tation of the state (present or absent) and produces acquisition of responding in the presence (vs. the absence) of the stimulus.

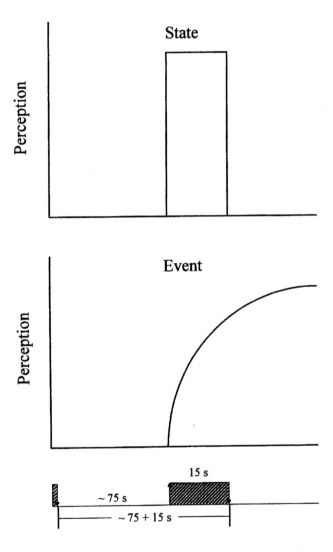

FIG. 6.3.   Definitions of state and event: A state is a configuration of physical
stimuli; an event is a transition between states. Perception may be a function of
state (top panel) or a function of time since an event (bottom panel).

In timing theories (e.g., Gibbon & Church, 1984; Killeen & Fetterman, 1988), the current condition is specified by the time from an event (a state transition). These events include stimulus onset, stimulus termination, response, and food delivery. One example of a perceptual representation of time is shown in the bottom panel of Fig. 6.3. The perceptual representation increases as a function of time from stimulus onset. In timing theories, reinforcement operates on a representation of time from an event and produces an increasing response rate gradient.

SIMULATIONS

Simulations were conducted using seven different models: one pure conditioning model, one pure timing model, and five hybrid models. Three of the hybrid models are generally considered to be timing models and two are considered to be conditioning models. The predictions made by each of the models are based on simulations of the delay conditioning procedure shown in the bottom panel of Figs. 6.1, 6.2, and 6.3. Explicit solutions of some of the models are available for some behavioral indexes in some procedures, but simulations of any of the models can be readily conducted for any behavioral index in any procedure. The same procedure was used for the simulation of the data and for the training of the rats; the same information was recorded, and the same data analysis routines were used to calculate discrimination ratios and response rate gradients.

All simulation programs were written in Matlab in a modular form (Church, 1997). That is, a single procedure program was written that was used by all seven of the theory programs. This guarantees that the same procedure was used for all of the theories. The organization of the calling program was:

```
Initialize_procedure
Initialize_model
for Time = 1 to N
    Procedure
    Model
end

Record_data
```

The simulation of a model began by setting the values of the parameters of the procedure and initializing variables of the model. Unless otherwise noted, all model variables were initialized at 0. Then at each 1-sec time step during a 1,000-min simulated session (at 60,000 time steps), the simulation program implemented anything that needed to be done by the procedure (turn the white noise on or off, or deliver food) and anything that needed to be done by the model (update the perception or memory values, or make a head entry response). The type of event that occurred (stimulus, reinforcement, or response) and its time of occurrence was recorded in a time–event code format. An example of such a time–event code would be 3045.008, where the number before the decimal point is the integer number of seconds since the session began and the number after the decimal point is a code for the type of event (in this case, a head entry).

At the end of the session the list of time–event codes was saved in a file with a unique name indicating the procedure, the model, and the run number (e.g., delayrwm.005 for the fifth run of the delay procedure on the Rescorla–Wagner model). The 1,000-min simulated session was broken down into 10 100-min blocks (containing approximately 65 reinforcements each) and the discrimination ratio in each block was calculated in the same manner as the data from the rats. Response rate as a function of time since stimulus onset was calculated for the simulated data with the same analysis routines that were used for the analyses of the behavioral data.

In simulation of all models, an operant level of responding was added that consisted of an exponential waiting time distribution with a mean of 15 sec, yielding a mean response rate of 4 responses per minute. The results of the simulations of the seven models (in Figs. 6.4–6.10) were based on an informal hill-climbing procedure that attempted to find a set of parameters that minimized the sum of squared deviations of the model predictions from two measures of the observed data: the discrimination ratio as a function of session and the response rate as a function of time since stimulus onset. These parameters, used for the simulations in Figs. 6.4–6.10, are listed in Table 6.1. They may not be the best possible quantitative fit that could be obtained with an exhaustive search of the parameter space.

In this chapter the terms *model* and *theory* are used interchangeably; we adhere to the standard conventions such as Rescorla–Wagner model and scalar timing theory, but refer to them collectively either as models or theories. Models of conditioning and timing may be described in terms of three processes: perception, memory, and decision. The remaining seven figures provide a description of seven different models. Each of them are divided into the three processes, so that the different assumptions of the various theories about perception, memory, and decision processes can be readily compared.

The generic terms, *stimulus, reinforcement,* and *response* were used in both the conditioning and timing models to facilitate comparisons. They should be considered to be equivalent to the terms *conditioned*

TABLE 6.1   Parameter Values Used in the Model Simulations Displayed in Figs. 6.4 Through 6.10. Parameters Are Categorized According to the Modular Framework (Perception, Memory, and Decision).

Model/Theory	Perception		Memory			Decision
	λ	s_λ	β	γ	α	B
Rescorla–Wagner			0.020		0.110	0.625
Scalar timing	5.0	1.25				0.650[a]
Multiple-oscillator	p^b	0.25p	0.001			0.500
Behavioral timing	0.6		0.001[c]			0.025
Spectral timing[d]			0.010			0.075
Sutton–Barto	0.1		0.003	0.0		2.500
Temporal difference	0.9		1.000	0.9	0.025	0.035

Note.   Symbols for the parameters are defined as follows: λ = clock speed; s_λ = standard deviation of clock speed; β = learning rate; γ = discount weight; α = stimulus salience; B = mean response threshold.

[a]In scalar timing theory, the threshold was normally distributed with $SD = 0.195$. In all other models, thresholds were uniformly distributed between 0 and B.

[b]Oscillators with different periods (p) were used: 1, 2, 4, 8, 16, 32, 64, 128, 256, and 512 sec.

[c]β was the incremental learning rate. A decremental learning rate of 0.01 was applied at all times, except the time of reinforcement.

[d]The parameters for the spectral timing perceptual representation were $a = 0.5$, $b = 1$, $c = 0.0001$, $d = 0.125$, $e = 0.8$, and $n = 8$.

stimulus, unconditioned stimulus, and *conditioned response,* respectively, which are often used in the description of a conditioning theory. The notation in the equations that specify the theories is slightly different from that used in the original references. Some of the models were originally described in terms of differential equations, and these have been changed to difference equations. The equations for each of the models have been explicitly divided into perception, memory, and decision processes, and a consistent notation has been adopted to facilitate comparison among the theories.

CONDITIONING THEORIES

In a theory of conditioning, reinforcement is associated with a particular configuration of stimuli (a state) and results in a particular level of associative strength in each state. The most influential theory of conditioning was developed by Rescorla and Wagner (1972). It was based on the earlier models of learning as the development of response strength (e.g., Hull, 1943) and as a stochastic process (e.g., Bush & Mosteller, 1955).

From the mid-1940s until the mid-1950s Hull's (1943) deductive behavior theory was most prominent. It consisted of definitions, axioms, postulates, and theorems, such that the deductions from the theory could be compared with data from experiments. The central concept was *habit strength,* an intervening variable that was determined by various independent variables and determined various dependent variables. Reinforcement of a state led to an increase in habit strength that was characterized by a negatively accelerating exponential function.

A major simplification of this type of theory was provided by the stochastic models of learning (Bush & Mosteller, 1955). The central dependent variable was probability of response. The major equation was $p_{n+1} = p_n + \beta (Y - p_n)$, where p_n is the probability of a response on trial n, β is the learning rate parameter, and Y is the asymptotic probability of a response. At the end of each trial, the probability of a response was updated by the application of this equation. The value of Y depended on the nature of the outcome (normally 1 for reinforcement and 0 for nonreinforcement); the value of β (which varied between 0 and 1) depended on such factors as the salience of the stimulus. The probability of a response could be estimated from many individuals or many trials, and this could be used to estimate the parameters β and Y. Based on these parameter estimates, predictions could be made about dependent variables other than those that had been used for the parameter estimates. For example, predictions could be made about the number of trials to a criterion level of performance.

The Rescorla–Wagner model modified Bush and Mosteller's stochastic model in three ways. First, it replaced the concept of probability of response (p) with the concept of strength of response (V), a critical intervening concept in Hull's theory. The Rescorla–Wagner model did not describe how the strength of a response should be mapped onto behavioral observations and permitted any order-preserving transformation. Thus, the predictions of the Rescorla–Wagner model are only ordinal. The second modification was that it replaced the single learning rate constant (β) of the Bush and Mosteller model with two constants (α and β), with α subscripted for each stimulus (such as light or noise) and β subscripted for each reinforcement (such as food or water). The third, and most important, modification was that the change in strength of a particular stimulus was not necessarily proportional to the discrepancy between asymptotic strength and strength of that stimulus; it was proportional to the discrepancy between asymptotic strength and the strength of all stimuli currently present. The details of this feature are shown in Equations 2a and 2b. The theory is normally described as a modified version of a traditional learning theory with a single intervening variable (V).

In the reference experiment (shown in the bottom panels of Figs. 6.1–6.3), a white noise stimulus was presented for 15 sec followed by food. In the Rescorla–Wagner model, the perception of a stimulus is 1 when the stimulus is present and 0 when it is absent. $Y_{i,t}$ is the perception of stimulus i at time t.

$$Y_{i,t} = 1 \text{ if stimulus } i \text{ is present at time } t \qquad (1a)$$

$$Y_{i,t} = 0 \text{ if stimulus } i \text{ is absent at time } t \qquad (1b)$$

Thus, the perception is based on the current configuration of stimuli (see Fig. 6.4, top left panel). Equations 1a and 1b apply to the reinforcement ($i = 0$) as well as to the n stimuli ($1 \leq i \leq n$).

At reinforcement, memory is updated according to the following equation:

$$V_{i,t} = V_{i,t-1} + \beta(Y_{0,t} - P_t)\, \alpha_i\, Y_{i,t} \qquad (2a)$$

where, $V_{i,t}$ is the strength of memory of the i_{th} stimulus at time t, α_i is the salience of the i_{th} stimulus, β is a learning rate parameter (between 0 and 1), and P_t is the combined strength of all stimuli present at time t.

$$P_t = \Sigma_i(Y_{i,t}\, V_{i,t-1}) \qquad (2b)$$

P_t is the summation of strength over the i stimuli, beginning with $i = 1$. $Y_{0,t}$ refers to the perception of reinforcement at time t: It is 1 when reinforcement occurs and 0 at other times. β affects the rate at which asymptotic strength (of 1) is reached. α_i affects the weight given to each stimulus. With a single stimulus, as in the reference experiment, the summation of strength $\Sigma_i(Y_{i,t}V_{i,t-1})$ is simply the product $Y_{1,t}V_{1,t-1}$. The strength of the memory of the noise stimulus after the last reinforcement delivery in the 1,000-min simulated session is shown in the top right panel of Fig. 6.4. (See Table 6.1 for parameter values used in the simulations.)

If reinforcement is not presented at the end of a trial ($Y_{0,t} = 0$), the strength of memory is decreased. A decremental parameter δ can be used in Equation 2 instead of the incremental parameter β, typically with δ much lower than β. In the procedure here, with reinforcement on each cycle, there is no need for this extinction operation.

In the Rescorla–Wagner model there is no formal decision rule for responding. The strength of the tendency to respond is equal to the strength of all stimuli present at time t.

$$S_t = \Sigma_i (Y_{i,t}\, V_{i,t-1})$$ (3a)

To convert this strength to an observable value, such as probability of a response, response rate during the stimulus, or discrimination ratio, the model permits any order-preserving transformation. To convert the response strength (S_t) to a thresholded response (R_t) we used the following equation:

$$R_t = 1 \text{ if } S_t > b$$ (3b)

$$R_t = 0 \text{ if } S_t \le b$$ (3c)

where b is a variable threshold that was uniformly distributed between 0 and B.

The Rescorla–Wagner model is normally expressed as a deterministic model that should lead to identical behavior by all animals exposed to the same classical conditioning procedure: If a deterministic basis for transforming response strength into a response were used, and if there were no random baseline responding, observed responding would be a monotonically increasing function of the number of reinforcements. With the variable threshold and random baseline responding, there are bases for individual differences and irregular acquisition functions.

The discrimination ratio produced by the simulation increased as a function of training in a manner similar to the discrimination ratio observed in the data (Fig. 6.4, bottom left panel). The simulated results, however, were not consistent with the gradually increasing temporal gradient (Fig. 6.4, bottom right panel). The simulated response rate was a step function that was approximately constant at all times prior to the stimulus, and then abruptly increased to another approximately constant response rate during the stimulus.

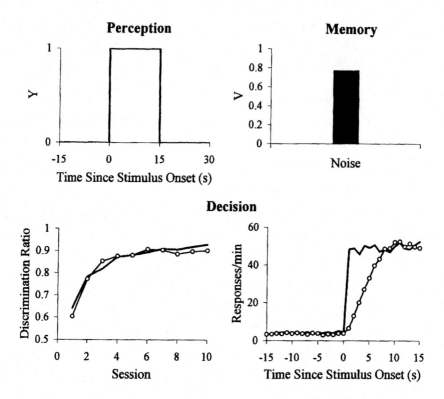

FIG. 6.4.   Rescorla–Wagner model. Perception is a function of the presence or absence of a state as a function of time since stimulus onset (top left panel); memory strength (**V**) is a function of the noise state (top right panel). The observed discrimination ratio of the rats (open circles) and the simulated discrimination ratio (line) is shown as a function of session (bottom left panel). The observed response rate of the rats (open circles) and the simulated response rate (line) is shown as a function of time since stimulus onset (bottom right panel). See text for equations.

The main success of the Rescorla–Wagner model has been to provide a well-specified process for several observed effects of stimulus competition. The most thoroughly studied of these is *blocking*, in which prior training with a stimulus (such as reinforced noise) followed by training with a compound stimulus (such as reinforced noise and light) led to reduced responding to the added stimulus (in this case, light).

The Rescorla–Wagner model was not designed to account for the observed effects of temporal intervals on conditioning, and it cannot do so because the perceptual representation of the stimulus does not change as a function of time since stimulus onset. One modification that was considered was to segment the temporal stream into intervals of fixed length and consider the configuration of stimuli present in each of these segments as different states, and analyze them with Equations 1, 2, and 3. For example, in one experiment (Rescorla, 1968), a tone was present for 2 min, then was absent for 8 min repeatedly throughout a session. A shock was delivered according to one random schedule in the presence of the tone and according to another random schedule in the absence of the tone. The session can be considered to be a sequence of 2-min intervals that may contain both tone and shock, tone but no shock, shock but no tone, or neither tone nor shock. With the use of much shorter segments, there would be no problem of differing numbers of shocks during a single tone, and there would be no problem with tones of random, rather than fixed, durations. However, the approach does not provide a basis for generating temporal gradients of responding in a delay conditioning procedure, such as the one shown in the bottom panels of Figs. 6.1, 6.2, and 6.3, because there is no representation of the time since stimulus onset. (See Fig. 6.4, top left panel, and Equation 1.)

A standard view is that conditioning theories are designed to account for whether or not an animal will respond to a particular stimulus, and that a timing theory is necessary to account for when the animal will respond during a stimulus.

TIMING THEORIES

The most extensively used timing theory has been scalar timing theory (Gibbon, 1977). An information processing version of the theory explicitly describes separate modules for perception, memory, and decision (Gibbon, 1991; Gibbon & Church, 1984; Gibbon, Church, & Meck, 1984). This version of the theory uses the style of analysis of cognitive psychology in which separate modules each have input, intervening variables, and output. The input can come from stimuli or from the output of other modules, the output can go to other modules or to a response generator, and multiple intervening variables within a module have transformation rules.

In scalar timing theory, a pacemaker is assumed to emit pulses according to some distribution, a switch determines whether or not the pulses reach an accumulator, and the number of pulses in the accumulator is the perception of time. In the full model there is a variable latency to start and stop the clock.

In the reference experiment (shown in the bottom panels of Figs. 6.1–6.3), when white noise begins, a switch is closed and pulses emitted by the pacemaker enter the accumulator. An essential feature of this theory is that the perception of time since an event is represented by a quantity in an accumulator. Such counter models have been used extensively in models of human reaction time (Luce, 1986), and were developed for models of animal timing by Triesman (1963). The equation used in scalar timing theory is:

$$n_t = \lambda\, d_t \qquad\qquad (4)$$

where n_t is the number of pulses in the accumulator at time t, d_t is the duration that the switch has been closed at time t, and λ is the number of pulses emitted by the pacemaker during each particular stimulus. The top left panel of Fig. 6.5 shows the output of this pacemaker–switch–accumulator clock, under the assumption that stimulus onset initiates pulses at a rate determined by a single random sample from a normal distribution of rates with a mean of 5 pulses per sec and a standard deviation of 1.25 pulses per sec (Gibbon et al., 1984). The ratio of the standard deviation to the mean, called the *coefficient of variation*, is the critical variable. Smaller coefficients of variation result in more stable timing from cycle to cycle.

An alternative process is a pacemaker that emits pulses according to an exponentially distributed waiting-time distribution (Creelman, 1962; Gibbon et al., 1984). This is a simple process that is fully specified by a single parameter, and it results in the probability of a pulse being constant regardless of the time since the last pulse. Other assumptions have been used (e.g., Reid & Allen, 1998; Staddon & Higa, 1999) but, in the range of seconds to minutes, it is difficult to discriminate empirically among the predictions (Gibbon, 1992).

In scalar timing theory, at reinforcement, the number of pulses in the accumulator is multiplied by a memory storage variable k^*, this product is stored as a single value in memory, and the number of pulses in the accumulator is reset to zero. This exemplar representation of temporal memory is illustrated in the top right panel of Fig. 6.5, which plots the frequency distribution of remembered values in reference memory. The storage equation is:

$$m^*_{s+} = k^* n_{s+} \qquad\qquad (5)$$

where k^* is a memory storage value that transforms the number of pulses in the accumulator to a remembered value in reference memory,

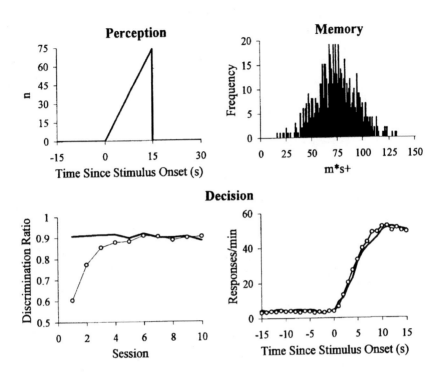

FIG. 6.5. Scalar timing theory. Perception is the number of pulses from a pacemaker as a function of time since stimulus onset (top left panel). Memory is a distribution of the number of pulses at the time of reinforcement (top right panel). The observed discrimination ratio of the rats (open circles) and the simulated discrimination ratio (line) is shown as a function of session (bottom left panel). The observed response rate of the rats (open circles) and the simulated response rate (line) is shown as a function of time since stimulus onset (bottom right panel). See text for equations.

n_{S+} is the number of pulses in the accumulator at the time of reinforcement, and m^{*}_{S+} is the value that is stored in reference memory. The assumption is that there is a normal distribution of memory storage values with some mean and standard deviation and, at reinforcement, one of the values is randomly selected. In the simulation, the mean of k^{*} was set at 1.0 and the standard deviation was set at 0, so that the number of pulses in the accumulator are stored in reference memory without distortion. Because the expected mean pacemaker rate was 5 pulses per sec and the time from stimulus onset to reinforcement was 15 sec, the observed mean value that was stored in reference memory was about 75 pulses; because the expected standard deviation was about 1.25 pulses per sec, the standard deviation of the values stored in reference memory was about 18.75 (1.25 × 15). Each of the individual exemplars in memory is preserved, and there is no organization to the set of values. The use of an exemplar memory is a distinctive feature of scalar timing theory.

In scalar timing theory, the measure of relative proximity of the accumulator value to the sample from memory is calculated with a ratio rule shown in Equation 6.

$$S_t = \mid (m^{*} - n_t) / m^{*} \mid \qquad (6a)$$

When the stimulus begins, a random sample of a single value from memory (m^{*}) is selected and, at each interval of time, it is compared to the current perception of time (n_t). If the absolute difference between these values, expressed as a ratio of the sample from memory, is less than the variable threshold (b), a response is made; otherwise, no response is made at that time (see Equations 6b and 6c). The variable threshold is a single random sample from a normal distribution of threshold values with a mean of B and a standard deviation of $0.3\,B$ that is taken at stimulus onset.

$$R_t = 1 \text{ if } S_t < b \qquad (6b)$$

$$R_t = 0 \text{ if } S_t \geq b \qquad (6c)$$

There were two sources of variance in this version of scalar timing theory: clock and threshold. The simulation produced an increasing response rate as a function of time since stimulus onset with a maximum near the time that reinforcement was delivered, as illustrated in the bottom right panel of Fig. 6.5. The discrimination ratio produced by the simulation, however, was relatively constant at about 0.9 over sessions (left panel of Fig. 6.5). The number of examples of the remembered time of reinforcement in reference memory increases as a function of training, but the expected mean and standard deviation of the distribution remains constant. A single item in memory is sufficient to produce a temporal gradient in a subsequent occurrence of the stimulus. Thus, there was no basis for change in response strength with additional training.

DUAL THEORIES

Standard state-based theories of conditioning, such as the Rescorla–Wagner model, provide an explanation of the acquisition of differential responding in the presence of different configurations of stimuli, but they do not explain differential responding as a function of time from stimulus transitions or the influence of temporal variables on performance. Standard event-based theories of timing, such as scalar timing theory, have the opposite problem. They provide explanations of the effect of temporal variables, and temporal gradients of responding, but they do not provide explanations for the development of differential responding to different stimuli.

One possibility is that a theory of conditioning is necessary to explain some phenomena, and a theory of timing is necessary to explain others. Therefore, a dual theory that contains both mechanisms may be able to explain many more facts of conditioning and timing than either type of theory alone. Such dual theories have been proposed. For example, Gibbon and Balsam (1981) showed that a dual theory involving a combination of scalar timing theory and a rate-expectancy theory of conditioning can account for many of facts of autoshaping experiments (conditioning experiments that involve presentation of food to pigeons in the presence of a lighted disk). The broad applicability of a dual theory of conditioning and timing was described by Gallistel and Gibbon (2000). This dual theory first applies a conditioning module to determine whether or not to respond to a stimulus, and then, if the decision is to make a response, it applies a timing module to determine when to respond. For example, in the delay conditioning experiment shown in the bottom panels of Figs. 6.1, 6.2, and 6.3 the rat first determines whether the rate of reinforcement in the presence of the stimulus (as a state) is substantially greater than the overall rate of reinforcement (the conditioning module). If the global rates of reinforcement are substantially different, the animal then uses the principles of scalar timing theory to determine the time of occurrence of the response.

The strength of dual theories is that they have the potential to explain facts that either of two theories can explain. A problem for a dual theory is to specify which of the theories to apply in any specific situation or, if both theories are applicable to the same situation, how to resolve any conflicts.

HYBRID THEORIES

An alternative approach to a dual theory, which employs separate mechanisms for conditioning and timing, is a hybrid theory. Hybrid theories use a single mechanism to account for behavior as a function of stimulus configuration (state) and time since stimulus change (event). All of them include a perceptual representation that changes as a function of time since an event, and they all include elements that are strengthened with reinforcement. As a consequence, they provide a basis for the acquisition of stimulus discrimination as well as for timing. Three of the models to be described are generally regarded as timing models (the multiple-oscillator model of timing, the behavioral theory of timing, and the spectral theory of timing); the final two models are generally regarded as conditioning models (the Sutton–Barto model

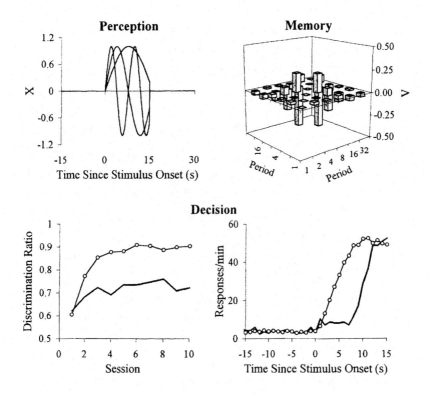

FIG. 6.6. Multiple-oscillator model. The onset of a stimulus initiates periodic functions with different periods (top left panel); memory strength (**V**) is an autoassociation matrix (top right panel). The observed discrimination ratio of the rats (open circles) and the simulated discrimination ratio (line) is shown as a function of session (bottom left panel). The observed response rate of the rats (open circles) and the simulated response rate (line) is shown as a function of time since stimulus onset (bottom right panel). See text for equations.

and the temporal difference model). These real-time theories of conditioning are explicit attempts to explain both conditioning and timing with a common mechanism.

Multiple-Oscillator Model of Timing

Any theory of timing requires a process that changes as a function of time since an event. This process may be referred to as a *clock*. In scalar timing theory, the clock was a pacemaker-accumulator system, but there are many alternatives. For example, circadian rhythms appear to be based on a cyclic clock with a period of about 24 hr. It is plausible that periodic processes, such as the phase of various neural or other bodily periodic processes, are also involved in the timing of shorter intervals (e.g., Gluck, Reifsnider, & Thompson, 1990; Miall, 1989).

In the multiple-oscillator model of timing (Church & Broadbent, 1990), the perceptual representation of time is based on patterns that change with time. The assumption is that there are multiple oscillators, each with a distinctive period. The top left panel of Fig. 6.6 shows three of the oscillators. In the simulation, 10 oscillators were set to zero at the onset of the stimulus, and then ran with mean periods of $1, 2, 4, 8, \ldots,$ 512 sec. The equation is:

$$X_{i,j,t} = \sin[(2\pi/p_{i,j})\, t] \tag{7a}$$

where the subscripts refer to the j_{th} oscillator of the i_{th} stimulus at time t, and $p_{i,j}$ refers to the period (in sec). When an event occurred, the set of periods was varied by multiplying them by a constant coefficient of variation (ratio of standard deviation to mean) that was randomly sampled from a normal distribution with a mean of 1.0.

The output of the oscillators for a particular stimulus i was thresholded in a vector (f) of +1s or −1s, as follows:

$$f_{i,j,t} = +1 \text{ if } X_{i,j,t} > 0 \tag{7b}$$

$$f_{i,j,t} = -1 \text{ if } X_{i,j,t} \leq 0 \tag{7c}$$

This thresholding operation transformed the exact phase information available in $X_{i,j,t}$ into the rough half-phase information available in $f_{i,j,t}$. The primary purpose for the development of this model was to determine if this binary representation of the status of each oscillator was sufficient to account for performance.

Working memory consists of an autoassociation of the perception vector to create a matrix of +1s and −1s. The equation is:

$$W_{i,j,t} = f_{i,j,t} f_{i,j,t}^{\mathrm{T}} \tag{8a}$$

This matrix of weights is the product of the perceptual vector and its transpose (the outer product). Working memory is an autoassociation matrix. The assumption is made that the oscillators are not connected to themselves, so the resulting matrix is a 10 × 10 array of +1s and –1s with a positive diagonal of zeros. The weights encode which pairs of oscillators are in the same half-phase (+1s) or in different half-phases (–1s). The primary purpose of the use of an autoassociation matrix, rather than a vector representation of memory, was to facilitate temporal generalization. An example of the failure of the vector f to provide a smooth generalization can be seen in the top left panel of Fig. 6.6. Shortly before 16 sec the phase of the slowest oscillator is positive and the phases of the other two oscillators are negative; immediately after 16 sec, the phase of the slowest oscillator is negative and the phases of the other two oscillators are positive. Thus, the pattern of half-phases of these three oscillators changes abruptly at this time, but the autoassociation of the oscillators is stable. The half-phase of the slowest oscillator multiplied by the half-phase of the other two oscillators remains at –1 before and after 16 sec, and the product of the half-phases of the two faster oscillators remains at +1 before and after 16 sec.

At the time of reinforcement, the working memory matrix, **W**, is combined with a reference memory matrix, **V**, of the same dimensions according to Equation 8b.

$$V_{i,j,t} = V_{i,j,t-1} + \beta\,(W_{i,j,t} - V_{i,j,t-1}) \tag{8b}$$

where the subscripts refer to the j_{th} oscillator of the i_{th} stimulus at time t. β is the learning rate parameter that can be set between 0 and 1. The amount of change in reference memory is proportional to the discrepancy between working and reference memory. An alternative way to interpret Equation 8b is as a linear averaging of working memory and reference memory. This is most easily seen by rearranging the terms in Equation 8b to be $V_{i,j,t} = \beta\,W_{i,j,t} + (1 - \beta)\,V_{i,j,t-1}$.

The values in reference memory are constrained to be between +1 and –1. In the simulation, the reference memory matrix was initialized at zero at the beginning of the experiment, but there is no need to initialize reference memory if multiple experiments are done: The values in reference memory gradually adjust with new times of reinforcement represented in working memory, with a learning rate determined by β.

The strength of reference memory after the last reinforcement in the simulated session is shown in the top right panel of Fig. 6.6. The X and Y axes identify the first 6 of the 10 different oscillators by their periods (1,

2, 4, 8, 16, and 32 sec). The vertical axis (V) shows the strength of weights for each pair of oscillators. The remembered time of reinforcement (in this case, 15 sec) is stored as a pattern of activation weights. For example, there is a high positive weight on some oscillator pairs (such as 4 sec and 8 sec) that indicates that they are typically at the same half-phase 15 sec after stimulus onset; there is a high negative weight on other oscillator pairs (such as 8 sec and 16 sec and, to a lesser extent, 4 sec and 16 sec) that indicates that they are typically at the opposite half-phase 15 sec after stimulus onset; and there is a near-zero weight on other oscillator pairs, such as (1 and 32 sec) that indicates that they convey little information regarding the reinforced interval. The amount of information about the time of reinforcement is contained in the absolute value of the weights. In general, oscillators with periods much faster than the duration are not informative because they are in a random phase; oscillators with periods much slower than the duration are not informative because they are in a constant phase; but oscillators with periods similar to the duration are informative.

A decision to respond is made based on a comparison of the current perception and reference memory. The output from reference memory is:

$$g_{i,j,t} = V_{i,j,t} f_{i,j,t} \tag{9a}$$

In the original model, independent vectors were used for storage and retrieval. This provided a mechanism to account for some memory biases. For simplicity, this description of the model (and the simulation) uses the same vector, $\mathbf{f}$ for storage and retrieval.

A cosine similarity rule is used for the comparison:

$$S_t = \cos \theta \tag{9b}$$

where θ is the angle between the vectors $\mathbf{f}$ and $\mathbf{g}$. The similarity measure is the inner product of the two vectors, normalized by the lengths of the vectors. The equation is:

$$S_t = f^T_{i,j,t} g_{i,j,t} / [(f^T_{i,j,t} f_{i,j,t})(g^T_{i,j,t} g_{i,j,t})]^{\frac{1}{2}} \tag{9c}$$

This is the same as a Pearson product–moment correlation: the ratio of the covariance to the square root of the product of the variances. Like the correlation coefficient, the similarity value (S_t) varies between +1 and –1, with 0 indicating the absence of a linear relation.

If similarity of perception of current time and the memory of reinforced time at time t is greater than a threshold value (b), a response will be made:

$$R_t = 1 \text{ if } S_t > b \qquad (9\text{d})$$

$$R_t = 0 \text{ if } S_t \leq b \qquad (9\text{e})$$

As in earlier models, b is a variable threshold that is a random value from a uniform distribution between 0 and B. The discrimination ratio produced by the simulation increased as a function of training, but the asymptotic value was lower (Fig. 6.6, bottom left panel). The temporal gradient of responding increased as a function of time since stimulus onset, but the increase began later and was more abrupt (Fig. 6.6, bottom left panel). Other values of the parameters provided an excellent quantitative fit to the temporal gradient, but they produced very rapid acquisition of the stimulus discrimination. It may not be possible to find a single set of parameter values that provides good fits to both of these dependent variables.

Although the original motivation for the multiple-oscillator model was simply to determine whether the coding of times as patterns rather than amounts could account for performance in the standard timing procedures, such as the peak procedure (Church & Broadbent, 1990), subsequent use of this model revealed its ability to capture local irregularities in responding in variable interval schedules of reinforcement (Church, Lacourse, & Crystal, 1998), in the perception of temporal intervals (Crystal, 1999), and in timed performance of human participants (Collyer & Church, 1998).

Behavioral Theory of Timing

The behavioral theory of timing developed by Killeen and Fetterman (1988) uses a behavioristic style of analysis with emphasis on observable stimuli, responses, and reinforcement. The onset of a stimulus initiates a sequence of behavioral states that serve as the perceptual representation of time. In some versions of the model, a pacemaker with a variable rate drives the system through these various states. However, unlike scalar timing theory, there is no accumulation process: The perceptual representation of time is the current state, not the number of pulses in an accumulator. This section uses Machado's (1997) version of the theory because it provides specific equations for the processes that are essential for simulations. To facilitate comparison with other theories of timing and conditioning, this theory is described in terms of a discrete process (difference equations rather than differential equations) and it is described with the same three parts: perception, memory, and decision.

In the behavioral theory of timing, the onset of a stimulus initiates a cascade of functions that can be described by the following equations:

$$X_{i,1,t} = (1 - \lambda) X_{i,1,t-1} \tag{10a}$$

$$X_{i,j,t} = (1 - \lambda) X_{i,j,t-1} + \lambda X_{i,j-1,t-1} \tag{10b}$$

where $X_{i,j,t}$ is the perceptual representation of the j_{th} function of the i_{th} stimulus transition (event) at time t since stimulus onset and λ is a rate of change. The number of functions, n, is a parameter of the model. At the time of stimulus onset, Function 1 is initialized at 1 and Functions 2 through n are initialized at 0. The level of activation for Function 1 is determined by Equation 10a and the level of activation for Functions 2 through n is determined by Equation 10b. At each successive time step after stimulus onset, there will be a spread of activation to a new function; this produces a cascade of functions, shown in the top left panel of Fig. 6.7. The cascade continues until reinforcement delivery, a new stimulus onset event, or activation flows completely out of the system (when the maximum number of functions is reached). At any given time step, the perceptual representation of time is a vector of the activation strengths for each of the functions at that time. The change in activation of any particular function (except Function 1) at successive time steps is a linear combination of the strength of that function on the previous time step and the strength of the previous function on the previous time step. The rate of spread of activation through the set of functions is determined by the parameter λ, which can range between 0 and 1; larger values of λ produce faster rates of flow in the cascade of functions. A large value of λ (e.g., 0.9) produces a set of closely spaced functions that are effective for timing short intervals (less than 10 sec), whereas a small value of λ (e.g., 0.1) produces a set of widely spaced functions that are effective for timing much longer intervals (in the range of minutes). The range of intervals that can be timed may also be increased by increasing the number of functions.

At reinforcement, the vector representing the current perception of time is combined with the vector representing the memory of the time of reinforcement, according to the following equation:

$$V_{i,j,t} = V_{i,j,t-1} + \beta[X_{i,j,t-1} (Y_{0,t} - V_{i,j,t-1})] \tag{11a}$$

where $V_{i,j,t}$ is the memory representation of the j_{th} function of the i_{th} stimulus at time t since stimulus onset. The parameter β, which is set be-

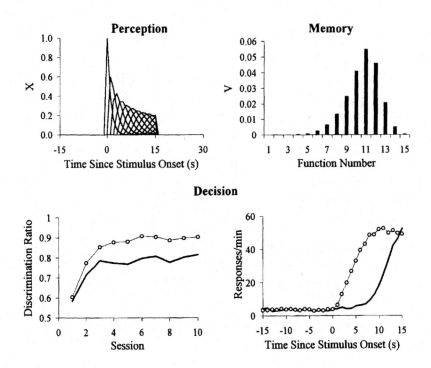

FIG. 6.7. Behavioral theory of timing. The onset of a stimulus initiates a cascade of functions such that perception is a vector of values (top left panel); memory strength (**V**) is a distribution of strengths of each of the functions (top right panel). The observed discrimination ratio of the rats (open circles) and the simulated discrimination ratio (line) is shown as a function of session (bottom left panel). The observed response rate of the rats (open circles) and the simulated response rate (line) is shown as a function of time since stimulus onset (bottom right panel). See text for equations.

tween 0 and 1, determines the rate of learning. The increment to each function produced by the onset of a stimulus is a product of the learning rate parameter (β), the perceptual strength of the stimulus ($X_{i,j,t-1}$), and the difference between the presence of the reinforcement ($Y_{0,t}$, normally set to 1.0) and the memory strength of the stimulus ($V_{i,j,t-1}$).

The strength of memory, $V_{i,j,t}$, cannot exceed the asymptotic strength. When the first reinforcement occurs, the strength of a function is equal to $\beta X_{i,j,t-1}$, the level of activation for that function at the time of reinforcement. In essence, the incremental learning rule is a method of storing the vector of activation strengths at the time of reinforcement; functions that are most active at the time of reinforcement will receive the greatest strength weight. This can be seen in the top right panel of Fig. 6.7, which plots the strength of each function after the last reinforcement in the simulated session. Functions 10, 11, and 12 were most active at the time of reinforcement, 15 sec, and these functions received the greatest strength weight.

At time intervals when reinforcement is not present, the vector representing the current perception of time is combined with the vector representing the memory of the time of reinforcement according to the following equation:

$$V_{i,j,t} = V_{i,j,t-1} + \delta[X_{i,j,t-1} (Y_{0,t} - V_{i,j,t-1})] \tag{11b}$$

This equation produces a decrement in strength at all times, except the time of reinforcement, that is a product of the decremental learning rate parameter (δ), the perceptual strength of the stimulus ($X_{i,j,t-1}$), and the current memory strength ($V_{i,j,t-1}$); $Y_{0,t}$, the absence of reinforcement, is normally set to 0. The only difference between Equation 11a (which is applied only at the time of reinforcement) and Equation 11b (which is applied at all other time steps) is the learning rate parameters (β and δ). The decremental operation produces extinction by reducing memory strength toward zero; the δ/β ratio determines the effective rate of acquisition.

In the behavioral theory of timing, the decision to respond is based on a combination of the perceptual vector ($X_{i,j,t}$) and the memory vector ($V_{i,j,t}$) according to Equation 12a:

$$S_t = \Sigma_i \Sigma_j (X_{i,j,t} V_{i,j,t}) \tag{12a}$$

Thus, for any given stimulus at any given time, the perceptual strength of each function is multiplied by the memory strength of the corresponding function and summed across functions, and these are summed across stimuli to provide a measure of response strength. Responding occurs if S_t exceeds a variable threshold, according to Equations 12b and 12c.

$$R_t = 1 \text{ if } S_t > b \tag{12b}$$

$$R_t = 0 \text{ if } S_t \leq b \tag{12c}$$

where b is a threshold that is a random variable from a uniform distribution between 0 and B. (See Table 6.1 for parameter values.)

The discrimination ratio produced by the simulation increased as a function of training in a manner similar to the discrimination ratio observed in the data, but the asymptotic value was lower (Fig. 6.7, bottom left panel). The temporal gradient of responding as a function of time since stimulus onset increased in a manner similar to the temporal gradient observed in the data, but the increase began later and was more abrupt (Fig. 6.7, bottom right panel). Although the fits of either of these two functions could be improved, it may not be possible to find a single set of parameter values that provides good fits to both of these dependent variables.

Spectral Theory of Timing

The spectral theory of timing is a neural model that may be described in terms of biological mechanisms (e.g., cellular response rates and habituative transmitter gates), psychological mechanisms (e.g., short-term memory and long-term memory), or neural architecture (e.g., gated dipoles and adaptive resonance theory architecture). It has also been fully specified in terms of equations, and the following is a description of this formal model.

In the spectral theory of timing (Grossberg & Schmajuk, 1989; Schmajuk, 1997), the onset of a stimulus initiates a series of functions. The perceptual representation of time (which is referred to as the gated signal spectrum in the original article) is shown, for the parameter settings used in the simulation, in the upper left panel of Fig. 6.8, based on the following equation:

$$X_{i,j,t} = g_{i,j,t}\, h_{i,j,t} \tag{13a}$$

The terms in this equation are defined as follows:

$$g_{i,j,t} = f_{i,j,t}{}^{n} / (e^{n} + f_{i,j,t}{}^{n}) \tag{13b}$$

$$f_{i,j,t} = f_{i,j,t-1} + \{.2/i\,[-a\,f_{i,j,t-1} + (1 - bf_{i,j,t-1})\,Y_{i,t}]\} \tag{13c}$$

$$h_{i,j,t} = h_{i,j,t-1} + [c\,(1 - h_{i,j,t-1}) - d\,g_{i,j,t}\,h_{i,j,t-1}] \tag{13d}$$

These equations have 7 parameters (a, b, c, d, e, n, and the length of time the step function $Y_{i,t}$ remains active following stimulus onset). The maximum number of functions is an additional parameter: 80 functions were used in the simulation. Because of the large number of parameters, the perceptual representation may take many different shapes. In the model $Y_{i,t}$ is set to 1.0 at stimulus onset, and it is reset to 0.0 at some fixed time after stimulus termination. In the simulations here, the reset occurs at the time of stimulus termination. All variables were initialized at 0, except $h_{i,j,t}$, which was initialized at 1.0.

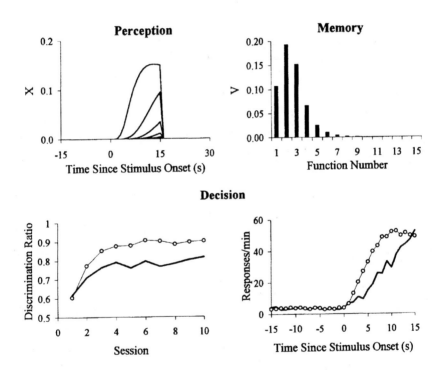

FIG. 6.8.   Spectral theory of timing. The onset of a stimulus initiates a series of functions that increase during the stimulus and decrease in the absence of the stimulus (top left panel). Memory (**V**) is represented by the strength of each of the functions (top right panel). The observed discrimination ratio of the rats (open circles) and the simulated discrimination ratio (line) is shown as a function of session (bottom left panel). The observed response rate of the rats (open circles) and the simulated response rate (line) is shown as a function of time since stimulus onset (bottom right panel). See text for equations.

At reinforcement, the vector representing the current perception of time (X) is combined with the vector representing the memory of the time of reinforcement (V), according to the following equation:

$$V_{i,j,t} = V_{i,j,t-1} + \beta[X_{i,j,t} (Y_{0,t} - V_{i,j,t-1})] \qquad (14)$$

The strength of each function after the last reinforcement in the simulated session is shown in the top right panel of Fig. 6.8. The pattern of weights in memory is similar to the pattern of the perceptual functions at the time of reinforcement, but with some distortion (e.g., Function 2 received the most weight, but Function 1 was slightly more active at the time of reinforcement.

In the spectral theory of timing, the decision to respond is based on a combination of the perceptual vector (X) and the memory vector (V) according to the following equations:

$$S_t = \Sigma_i \Sigma_j (X_{i,j,t} V_{i,j,t}) \qquad (15a)$$

To translate the strength of the tendency to respond, S_t, into a probability of responding, this value was compared to a variable threshold, b, according to Equations 15b and 15c.

$$R_t = 1 \text{ if } S_t > b \qquad (15b)$$

$$R_t = 0 \text{ if } S_t \leq b \qquad (15c)$$

where b is a variable threshold that was uniformly distributed between 0 and B.

The discrimination ratio produced by the simulation increased as a function of training in a manner similar to the discrimination ratio observed in the data, but the asymptotic value was lower (Fig. 6.8, bottom left panel). The temporal gradient of response rate as a function of time since stimulus onset increased in a manner similar to the temporal gradient observed in the data, but the increase began later and was more abrupt (Fig. 6.8, bottom right panel). Although the fits of either of these two functions could be improved, it may not be possible to find a single set of parameter values that provides good fits to both of these dependent variables.

Sutton–Barto Model

State-based theories of conditioning, such as the Rescorla–Wagner model, provide predictions about behavior as a function of the present configuration of stimuli; real-time theories of conditioning, such as the Sutton–Barto model, make predictions about behavior as a function of time in small units (usually fractions of a second or a second). The Sutton–Barto real-time theory of conditioning contains a representation of time from an event (a clock). It is sensitive to the configuration of stimuli, and it uses a learning rule similar to the Rescorla–Wagner model.

The real-time theories of conditioning do not require the use of the "trial" concept, which has caused confusion because it has acquired many incompatible meanings. In procedures in which all stimuli end with reinforcement, there is general agreement that memory should be updated at the time of reinforcement. In other procedures, however, the time when updating should occur is not well-specified. Although there is agreement that memory should be updated at the end of a trial, the term *trial* is not used consistently. Historically, the term referred to a single episode in a complex maze or puzzle box in which an experimenter placed an animal in the apparatus, and the animal escaped from the apparatus. In free-responding procedures, such as those of a rat in a lever box, there may be a repeating cycle of events that may be referred to as a trial. Or, there may be a repeating cycle of events that consists of a part in which the animal may receive reinforcement and a part in which it cannot receive reinforcement. The former may be called the trial, and the latter referred to as the intertrial interval. Alternatively, a stimulus may be presented for some duration and this may be referred to as a trial, whereas the interval between stimuli is called the intertrial interval (Gibbon & Balsam, 1981). Finally, the time may be divided into arbitrary units, such as 2-min intervals, during a stimulus and in the absence of a stimulus and these 2-min intervals may be regarded as trials (Rescorla, 1968). Because there is no generally accepted definition of trial in the conditioning and timing literature, and it is not clear that any particular definition is appropriate for all procedures, it is meaningless to conclude that memory is updated at the end of a trial. The substantive question, of course, is not what is a trial, but when is memory updated. One of the advantages of time-based rather than trial-based theories of conditioning and timing is that it is possible to consider memory updates that occur continuously or at the times of well-defined events.

In the Sutton–Barto real-time theory of conditioning (Barto & Sutton, 1982; Sutton & Barto, 1981), the three processes of perception, memory, and decision may be identified. The equations are based on those presented by Barto and Sutton (1982), but the notation has been slightly changed to be more consistent with the description of other models in this chapter.

The perceptual representation of time since stimulus onset is a stimulus trace, shown in the top left panel of Fig. 6.9. The trace of the stimulus gradually increases as a function of time that the stimulus has been pres-

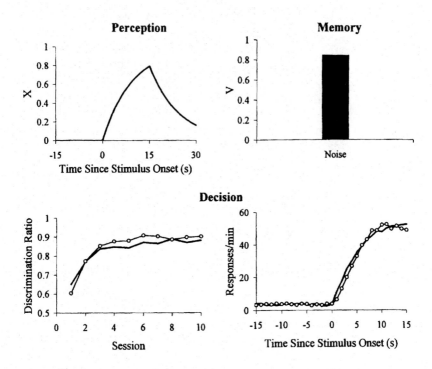

FIG. 6.9. Sutton–Barto model. The onset of a stimulus initiates an increasing exponential function, and the termination of a stimulus initiates a decreasing exponential function that serves as the perception of time since stimulus onset (top left panel); memory strength (**V**) is updated at the time of reinforcement (top right panel). The observed discrimination ratio of the rats (open circles) and the simulated discrimination ratio (line) is shown as a function of session (bottom left panel). The observed response rate of the rats (open circles) and the simulated response rate (line) is shown as a function of time since stimulus onset (bottom right panel). See text for equations.

ent and it gradually decreases as a function of time that the stimulus has been absent. (This trace is often called an *eligibility trace* because it represents the extent to which the physical stimulus is available for conditioning, not the degree to which the trace of the stimulus is confused with the physical stimulus.) The value of the trace is a linear combination of the value of the trace at the previous time step and a 1 or 0 representing the presence or absence of the stimulus ($Y_{i,t-1}$). The equation is:

$$X_{i,t} = (1 - \lambda) X_{i,t-1} + \lambda Y_{i,t-1} \tag{16}$$

This equation results in an exponentially increasing growth during the stimulus, and then an exponential decay beginning at stimulus termination. The value of λ determines the rate of growth of the trace in the presence of the stimulus and the rate of decay in the absence of the stimulus. Larger values of λ produce faster rates of growth and decay of the trace. At the maximum value of 1, the perceptual representation follows the stimulus. Thus, with $\lambda = 1$, the perceptual representation of the stimulus becomes a state ($Y_{i,t-1}$; see Equations 1a and 1b).

The strength of the memory of the noise stimulus after the last reinforcement in the simulated session is shown in the top right panel of Fig. 6.9. The strength of memory is updated according to the following equation:

$$V_{i,t} = V_{i,t-1} + \beta (P_t - P_{t-1}) X_{i,t-1} \tag{17a}$$

The equation for the strength of all stimuli present at time t, P_t, is:

$$P_t = \phi Y_{0,t} + \Sigma_i (Y_{i,t} V_{i,t-1}) \tag{17b}$$

ϕ is a parameter for the salience of the reinforcement, set to 1 in the simulation. Thus, P_t is greater than zero at time t if a reinforcement occurs ($Y_{0,t} = 1$) or if a stimulus is present with some memory strength ($Y_{i,t} = 1$ and $V_{i,t-1} > 0$).

The difference between P_t and P_{t-1} serves as an event detector, producing a positive change in **V** at stimulus onset and reinforcement, and a negative change at stimulus termination. This difference is multiplied with β, the learning rate parameter, and with **X**, the strength of the eligibility trace.

P_t is the sum of strength of all stimuli currently present rather than the strength of a particular stimulus separately from the others. This is the same competitive feature that was the hallmark of the Rescorla–Wagner model, and it permits the model to account for such phenomena as blocking.

The Sutton–Barto model also includes an output trace (**O**) that was defined in the same way as a stimulus trace:

$$O_t = \gamma O_{t-1} + (1 - \gamma) P_{t-1} \tag{17c}$$

In their simulations, and in the present analysis, $\gamma = 0$, so that $O_t = P_{t-1}$. With an output trace ($\gamma > 0$), the memory representation of any stimulus present at any time is updated according to the following equation:

$$V_{i,t} = V_{i,t-1} + \beta \, (P_t - O_t) \, X_{i,t-1} \tag{17d}$$

However, with $\gamma = 0$, this becomes the transition detector equation given in Equation 17a.

The determination of whether a response will occur is based on a combination of the perceptual vector (X) and the memory vector (V) according to the following equations:

$$S_t = \Sigma_i (X_{i,t} \, V_{i,t}) \tag{18a}$$

$$R_t = 1 \text{ if } S_t > b \tag{18b}$$

$$R_t = 0 \text{ if } S_t \leq b \tag{18c}$$

where b is a variable threshold that was uniformly distributed between 0 and B.

The discrimination ratio produced by the simulation increased as a function of training in a manner similar to the discrimination ratio observed in the data (Fig. 6.9, bottom left panel). The Sutton–Barto learning rule results in a gradual increase in the strength of memory of a particular stimulus, so it is easy to obtain good fits to a gradually increasing discrimination ratio. The simulated results were also consistent with the gradually increasing temporal gradient (Fig. 6.9, bottom right panel). The temporal gradient is produced by the combination of the stimulus trace, which increases gradually as a function of time since stimulus onset, with the strength of memory, which is relatively constant at asymptote. This yields a temporal gradient that has the same shape as the stimulus trace function.

Temporal Difference Model

The perceptual representation of time in one version of the temporal difference model is a series of functions that continue to occur while the stimulus is present (Sutton & Barto, 1990). The assumption in this complete serial compound version is that a continuous stimulus consists of many short components as follows:

$$Y_{i,j,t} = 1 \text{ if component } j \text{ of stimulus } i \text{ is present} \tag{19a}$$

$$Y_{i,j,t} = 0 \text{ if component } j \text{ of stimulus } i \text{ is absent} \qquad (19b)$$

Each component is equivalent to an identifiably different stimulus. The size of a component is the same as the size of a time step (t) which was 1 sec in the simulation. The time (t) is an index that increments from the start of the session until the end of the session; the component j is an index that increments from the start of a stimulus to the end of the stimulus. Each component of a given stimulus is active (i.e., set to 1) for only one time step during each stimulus presentation. The series of stimulus traces is:

$$X_{i,j,t} = (1 - \lambda) X_{i,j,t-1} + \lambda Y_{i,j,t-1} \qquad (19c)$$

Each of these j functions is initiated by the presence of the stimulus and functions continue to be generated as long as the stimulus is present (the final term is $\lambda Y_{i,j,t-1}$).

This produces a series of functions shown in the upper left panel of Fig. 6.10, each based on the same equation as the perceptual representation in the Sutton–Barto model (Equation 16). Because the components were on for only a single time unit, there was an initial magnitude that was followed by a decay. Larger values of λ produce faster rates of decay of the stimulus trace.

The strength of memory of each component of each stimulus is determined by Equations 20a and 20b.

$$V_{i,j,t} = V_{i,j,t-1} + \beta (Y_{0,t} + \gamma P_t - P_{t-1}) \alpha_i X_{i,j,t} \qquad (20a)$$

$$P_t = \Sigma_i \Sigma_j (Y_{i,j,t} V_{i,j,t-1}), \text{ if } \Sigma_i \Sigma_j (Y_{i,j,t} V_{i,j,t}) \geq 0, \text{ otherwise } P_t = 0 \qquad (20b)$$

P_t is the combined strength of all stimuli present at time t, which is the competitive feature found in other conditioning models, such as the Rescorla–Wagner and Sutton–Barto models. β is the learning rate parameter, and α_i is the parameter for the salience of the i_{th} stimulus. $V_{i,j,t}$ is the strength of the j_{th} component of the i_{th} stimulus at time t, and $X_{i,j,t}$ is the eligibility trace of the j_{th} component of the i_{th} stimulus. γ is a discounting parameter that slightly alters the shape of the memory structure; without it memory would be the same shape as the perceptual vector at the time of reinforcement. The strength of the memory of the set of components after the last reinforcement in the simulated session is shown in the top right panel of Fig. 6.10. The strength of memory was greater for components that were activated shortly before reinforcement. Thus, like the behavioral theory of timing and spectral timing theory, the most active components at the time of reinforcement receive the greatest weight in memory.

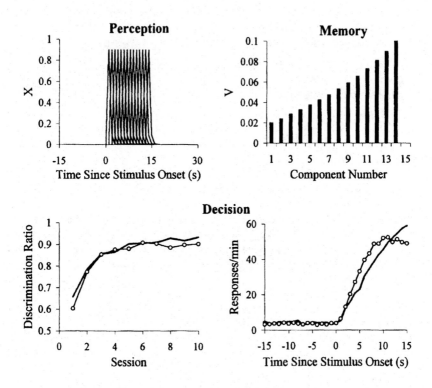

FIG. 6.10. Temporal difference model. A stimulus is composed of multiple components, each component initiates a decreasing function, and these functions serve as the perception of time since stimulus onset (top left panel); memory strength (**V**) is a distribution of strengths of each of the components (top right panel). The observed discrimination ratio of the rats (open circles) and the simulated discrimination ratio (line) is shown as a function of session (bottom left panel). The observed response rate of the rats (open circles) and the simulated response rate (line) is shown as a function of time since stimulus onset (bottom right panel). See text for equations.

The response at any time is determined by a combination of the strength of the memory and the presence of a particular component of a stimulus.

$$S_t = \Sigma_i \, \Sigma_j \, (Y_{i,j,t-1} \, V_{i,j,t-1}) \tag{21a}$$

$$R_t = 1 \text{ if } S_t > b \qquad (21b)$$

$$R_t = 0 \text{ if } S_t \leq b \qquad (21c)$$

where b is a variable threshold that was uniformly distributed between 0 and B.

The discrimination ratio produced by the simulation increased as a function of training in a manner similar to the discrimination ratio observed in the data (Fig. 6.10, bottom left panel). The simulated results were also consistent with the increasing temporal gradient (Fig. 6.10, bottom right panel), although the shape of the gradient was sharper than the rat data. The temporal difference learning rule always produces a maximum rate of responding during the last time step before reinforcement delivery.

SUMMARY AND CONCLUSION

Theories of conditioning and timing have been developed to account for behavior as a function of past experience and the current situation. In conditioning theories, the current situation is specified by a state, which is defined as a stimulus configuration. In timing theories, the current situation is specified by the time from some event. Dual theories have been proposed that consider conditioning and timing to be separate processes. In contrast, hybrid theories have been developed that use the same mechanism to account for behavior as a function of stimulus configuration and time since stimulus change. This chapter described three quantitative theories of conditioning and four quantitative theories of timing, applied them to the same experimental data, and compared these alternative approaches to the explanation of conditioning and timing.

Historically, there were clear distinctions between a theory of conditioning and a theory of timing. A conditioning theory, such as the Rescorla–Wagner model, had a representation of the stimulus that was related to the presence or absence of the stimulus (the state), and this representation increased in strength as a function of training. However, such a theory had no representation of the time since stimulus onset (an event). The emphasis of conditioning theories on states rather than events was clear from the standard notation that was employed. For example, the delay conditioning procedure that was used for the simulations in this chapter would be indicated as A+, where A would refer to the presence of the noise, and + would refer to the reinforcement. This notation did not identify such factors as (a) the time from stimulus onset to reinforcement, (b) the duration of the stimulus or the interval between stimuli, and (c) the constant or random duration of the stimulus or the interval between stimuli. In contrast, a timing theory, such as scalar timing theory, had a representation of the time since stimulus onset, but it had no basis for the acquisition of a tendency to respond in the presence of a stimulus as a function of training.

Converging empirical studies have demonstrated critical interrelations between timing and conditioning. Three examples of the close empirical connections between conditioning and timing are the following:

1. The number of reinforcements to reach a criterion of acquisition is a function of the ratio of the stimulus duration to the cycle duration (Gibbon & Balsam, 1981).
2. The apparent duration of a stimulus is a function of the prior contingencies of reinforcement (Holder & Roberts, 1985).
3. The temporal relation between a stimulus and a reinforcement, or between two different stimuli, plays a role in such conditioning phenomena as backward conditioning, higher order conditioning, blocking, the conditioned stimulus preexposure effect, and conditioned inhibition (Barnet, Grahame, & Miller, 1993; Savastano & Miller, 1998).

The clear distinction between a theory of conditioning and timing can no longer be made. Real-time conditioning theories have been developed in which the perceptual representation of the stimulus changes as a function of time since stimulus onset. Timing theories have been developed in which the memory of a reinforced condition increases as a function of training. Although the verbal descriptions of conditioning and timing theories continue to make them appear to be quite different, a close inspection of the actual theories (i.e., the equations) reveals the underlying similarities. The seven models may be compared with respect to perception, memory, and decision rules. In Table 6.2, equations for different models are shown in different rows, and equations for different processes are shown in different columns. For comparison of the models with respect to a particular process, one should examine the equations in a particular column.

The hybrid models shown in Figs. 6.6 through 6.10 all have a perceptual representation of time that changes as a function of time since an event, and all of them have a memory of reinforced conditions that is strengthened with increasing training. All five of these hybrid models were able to produce qualitatively correct fits to both a standard measure of conditioning (the acquisition of differential responding in the presence of a reinforced stimulus) and timing (the increasing response rate as a function of time to reinforcement). The models differ in their

TABLE 6.2 Equations for the Seven Models, Divided Into the Components of Perception, Memory, and Decision (Equation Number Is Indicated in Parentheses)

Model/Theory	Perception	Memory	Decision
Rescorla–Wagner	(1a) $Y_{i,t} = 1$ if stimulus i is present at time t (1b) $Y_{i,t} = 0$ if stimulus i is absent at time t	(2a) $V_{i,t} = V_{i,t-1} + \beta\,(Y_{0,t} - P_t)\alpha_i Y_{i,t}$ (2b) $P_t = \Sigma_i(Y_{i,t} V_{i,t-1})$	(3a) $S_t = \Sigma_i(Y_{i,t}\, V_{i,t-1})$
Scalar timing	(4) $n_t = \lambda d_t$	(5) $\overset{\cdot}{m}_{s*} = \overset{\cdot}{k}\,n_{s*}$	(6a) $S_t = \lvert\,(\overset{\cdot}{m} - n_t)/\overset{\cdot}{m}\,\rvert$
Multiple-oscillator	(7a) $X_{ij,t} = \sin[(2\pi/p_{ij})\,t]$ (7b) $f_{ij,t} = +1$ if $X_{ij,t} > 0$ (7c) $f_{ij,t} = -1$ if $X_{ij,t} < 0$	(8b) $V_{ij,t} = V_{ij,t-1} + \beta(W_{ij,t} - V_{ij,t-1})$ (8a) $W_{ij,t} = f_{ij,t} f_{ij,t}$	(9b) $S_t = \cos\theta$
Behavioral timing	(10b) $X_{ij,t} = (1-\lambda)X_{ij,t-1} + \lambda X_{ij-1,t-1}$	(11a) $V_{ij,t} = V_{ij,t-1} + \beta[X_{ij,t-1}\,(Y_{0,t} - V_{ij,t-1})]$ (11b) $V_{ij,t} = V_{ij,t-1} + \delta[X_{ij,t-1}\,(Y_{0,t} - V_{ij,t-1})]$	(12a) $S_t = \Sigma_i\Sigma_j(X_{ij,t}\, V_{ij,t})$

(continued on next page)

TABLE 6.2. (continued from previous page)

Model/Theory	Perception	Memory	Decision
Spectral timing	(13a) $X_{i,j,t} = g_{i,j,t}\, h_{i,j,t}$ (13b) $g_{i,j,t} = f_{i,j,t}^{\,n} / (e^{n} + f_{i,j,t}^{\,n})$ (13c) $f_{i,j,t} = f_{i,j,t-1} + \{.2/i\,[-af_{i,j,t-1} + (1 - bf_{i,j,t-1})\, Y_{i,t}]\}$ (13d) $h_{i,j,t} = h_{i,j,t-1} + [c(1 - h_{i,j,t-1}) - dg_{i,j,t}\, h_{i,j,t-1}]$	(14a) $V_{i,j,t} = V_{i,j,t-1} + \beta[X_{i,j,t}\,(Y_{0,t} - V_{i,j,t-1})]$	(15a) $S_t = \Sigma_i \Sigma_j (X_{i,j,t}\, V_{i,j,t})$
Sutton–Barto	(16) $X_{i,t} = (1 - \lambda)X_{i,t-1} + \lambda Y_{i,t-1}$	(17a) $V_{i,t} = V_{i,t-1} + \beta(P_t - P_{t-1})\, X_{i,t-1}$ (17b) $P_t = \phi Y_{0,t} + \Sigma_i (Y_{i,t}\, V_{i,t-1})$	(18a) $S_t = \Sigma_i (X_{i,t}\, V_{i,t})$
Temporal difference	(19c) $X_{i,j,t} = (1 - \lambda)X_{i,j,t-1} + \lambda Y_{i,j,t-1}$	(20a) $V_{i,j,t} = V_{i,j,t-1} + \beta(Y_{0,t} + \gamma P_t - P_{t-1})\, \alpha X_{i,j,t}$ (20b) $P_t = \Sigma_i \Sigma_j (Y_{i,j,t}\, V_{i,j,t-1})$	(21a) $S_t = \Sigma_i \Sigma_j (Y_{i,j,t-1}\, V_{i,j,t-1})$

representation of time, the factors responsible for the strengthening of memory, and the basis for the decision to respond.

Three of the models use a single function for perception: In the Rescorla–Wagner model it is a step function, in scalar timing theory it is a linearly increasing function, and in the Sutton–Barto model it is an exponentially increasing process. The increasing functions provide a changing perceptual representation of the time from a stimulus; the step function, however, does not. Both the Rescorla–Wagner model and the Sutton–Barto model provide a way to represent the state. In the Sutton–Barto model, the function rises toward an asymptotic level during the stimulus and falls to zero in the absence of the stimulus. With a fast rise and fall time, the function approaches a step function.

The other four models use multiple functions for perception: In the multiple-oscillator model, periodic functions are used. In the behavioral theory of timing and the spectral timing theory a cascade of functions is used. In the temporal difference model, a sequence of functions continues to be initiated during the stimulus. The models differ with respect to the form of the multiple but, in each case, a particular time since stimulus onset (within some range) is uniquely determined by a vector of values of the functions at that time. Despite large differences in the form and number of functions used in the different models, all of the models that contain a perception of time since stimulus onset produced increasing temporal gradients.

Four of the models (Rescorla–Wagner, Sutton–Barto, temporal difference, and spectral theory of timing) have a perceptual representation of the state ($Y_{i,j,t}$); three other models do not (scalar timing, multiple-oscillator model, and behavioral timing). The spectral theory of timing has a state representation if Y becomes zero immediately at stimulus termination, the assumption made in these simulations, but not if Y remains 1.0 for a fixed time after stimulus termination, a parameter of the model.

At the time of reinforcement, all of the models provide a way to update reference memory. In scalar timing theory this consists of the storage of another example of the time of reinforcement; in all the other models it consists of an increase in strength that is affected by current perception and memory strength. The three conditioning models (Rescorla–Wagner, Sutton–Barto, and temporal difference) use the competitive rule introduced by Rescorla and Wagner (P_t); the others do not. These models are, therefore, capable of predicting stimulus competition effects, such as blocking. All of the models (other than scalar timing theory) produce acquisition of a discrimination, although timing models generally produce it too rapidly if the parameters are set to be appropriate for the form of the temporal gradient.

Although the conditioning models have a competitive rule and the timing models do not, there is an additional difference in the memory module that does not divide along these lines. The three models that contain a single function for perception, two conditioning models (Rescorla–Wagner model and Sutton–Barto model) and one timing model (scalar timing theory), all store a single quantity in memory at the time of reinforcement. In the two conditioning models, there is a single quantity that combines with a prior value to increase or decrease the strength of memory. In scalar timing theory, the single quantity is added to a set of quantities (of pulse numbers) from previously reinforced occasions.

In contrast, the four models that contain multiple functions for perception, one conditioning model (temporal difference model) and three timing models (multiple-oscillator model, behavioral theory of timing, and spectral timing theory), all store a pattern of quantities in memory. In all of these models, the pattern of weights in memory is similar to the pattern of perception at the time of reinforcement, but with some translation (as in the autoassociation matrix of the multiple-oscillator model) or distortion (as in the other three models).

The decision to respond is based on a similar process in all models: There is a comparison of perception with memory that produces a magnitude and a thresholding of that magnitude to determine whether or not there is a response. Thus, the key differences among these models appears to be in the perception and memory modules.

The purpose of the simulations was to clarify the exposition of the models, not to provide an evaluation of them. The simulations were only for one procedure (delay conditioning) with one set of time intervals. It is quite possible a model that provided a good fit of behavior in this procedure would fail to do so in many other procedures, and models that did not provide a good fit of behavior in this procedure might succeed in many other procedures. Only two dependent variables were used (the discrimination ratio and the mean response rate as a function of time since stimulus onset). It is quite possible a model that provided a good fit of these indexes of behavior might fail to do so for other indexes of behavior, such as the distribution of interresponse times. Finally, a more thorough search of the parameter space could reveal improved fits of some of the models.

The procedures and response measures in the domain of theories of conditioning and timing are becoming broader. Ideally, a single model would account for all measures of behavior in all procedures in a large and well-defined set of procedures. A theory that accounts for the time of occurrence of responses necessarily accounts both for discrimination ratios and temporal gradients. The next generation of conditioning and timing models undoubtedly will strive to achieve the goal of an integrated theory of conditioning and timing. Because of the modularity of current models (perception, memory, and decision), improvements can be made either in single parts of a current theory or by unique combinations of parts (Church, 1997).

ACKNOWLEDGMENT

Preparation of this chapter was supported by a grant from the National Institute of Mental Health (RO1–MH44234).

■ REFERENCES

Barnet, R. C., Grahame, N. J., & Miller, R. R. (1993). Temporal encoding as a determinant of blocking. *Journal of Experimental Psychology: Animal Behavior Processes, 19,* 327–341.

Barto, A. G., & Sutton, R. S. (1982). Simulation of anticipatory responses in classical conditioning by a neuron-like adaptive element. *Behavioural Brain Research, 4,* 221–235.

Bush, R. R., & Mosteller, F. (1955). *Stochastic models for learning.* New York: Wiley.

Church, R. M. (1989). Theories of timing behavior. In S. B. Klein & R. Mowrer (Eds.), *Contemporary learning theory* (pp. 41–69). Hillsdale, NJ: Lawrence Erlbaum Associates.

Church, R. M. (1997). Quantitative models of animal learning and cognition. *Journal of Experimental Psychology: Animal Behavior Processes, 23,* 379–389.

Church, R. M., & Broadbent, H. A. (1990). Alternative representations of time, number, and rate. *Cognition, 37,* 55–81.

Church, R. M., Lacourse, D. M., & Crystal, J. D. (1998). Temporal search as a function of the variability of interfood intervals. *Journal of Experimental Psychology: Animal Behavior Processes, 24,* 291–315.

Collyer, C. E., & Church, R. M. (1998). Interresponse intervals in continuation tapping. In D. A. Rosenbaum & C. E. Collyer (Eds.), *Timing of behavior* (pp. 63–87). Cambridge, MA: MIT Press.

Creelman, C. D. (1962). Human discrimination of auditory duration. *Journal of the Acoustical Society of America, 34,* 582–593.

Crystal, J. D. (1999). Systematic nonlinearities in the perception of temporal intervals. *Journal of Experimental Psychology: Animal Behavior Processes, 25,* 3–17.

Gallistel, R., & Gibbon, J. (2000). Time, rate and conditioning. *Psychological Review, 107,* 289–344.

Gibbon, J. (1977). Scalar expectancy theory and Weber's law in animal timing. *Psychological Review, 84,* 279–325.

Gibbon, J. (1991). Origins of scalar timing. *Learning and Motivation, 22,* 3–38.

Gibbon, J. (1992). Ubiquity of scalar timing with a Poisson clock. *Journal of Mathematical Psychology, 36,* 283–293.

Gibbon, J., & Balsam, P. (1981). Spreading association in time. In C. M. Locurto, H. S. Terrace, & J. Gibbon (Eds.), *Autoshaping and conditioning theory* (pp. 219–254). New York: Academic Press.

Gibbon, J., & Church, R. M. (1984). Sources of variance in an information processing theory of timing. In H. L. Roitblat, T. G. Bever, & H. S. Terrace (Eds.), *Animal cognition* (pp. 465–488). Hillsdale, NJ: Lawrence Erlbaum Associates.

Gibbon, J., Church, R. M., & Meck, W. H. (1984). Scalar timing in memory. *Annals of the New York Academy of Science, 423,* 52–77.

Gluck, M. A., Reifsnider, E. S., & Thompson, R. F. (1990). Adaptive signal processing and the cerebellum: Models of classical conditioning and VOR adaptation. In M. Gluck & D. E. Rumelhart (Eds.), *Neuroscience and connectionist theory* (pp. 131–185). Hillsdale, NJ: Lawrence Erlbaum Associates.

Grossberg, S., & Schmajuk, N. A. (1989). Neural dynamics of adaptive timing and temporal discrimination during associative learning. *Neural Networks, 2,* 79–102.

Hall, G., & Honey, R. (1989). Perceptual and associative learning. In S. B. Klein, & R. R. Mowrer (Eds.), *Contemporary learning theories* (pp. 117–147). Hillsdale, NJ: Lawrence Erlbaum Associates.

Holder, M. D., & Roberts, S. (1985). Comparison of timing and classical conditioning. *Journal of Experimental Psychology: Animal Behavior Processes, 11,* 172–193.

Hull, C. L. (1943). *Principles of behavior.* New York: Appleton-Century-Crofts.

Killeen, P. R., & Fetterman, J. G. (1988). A behavioral theory of timing. *Psychological Review, 95,* 274–295.

Kirkpatrick, K., & Church, R. M. (1998). Are separate theories of conditioning and timing necessary? *Behavioural Processes, 44,* 163–182.

Klein, S. B., & Mowrer, R. R. (Eds.). (1989). *Contemporary learning theories: Pavlovian conditioning and the status of traditional learning theory.* Hillsdale, NJ: Lawrence Erlbaum Associates.

Luce, D. (1986). *Response times: Their role in inferring elementary mental organization.* New York: Oxford.

Machado, A. (1997). Learning the temporal dynamics of behavior. *Psychological Review, 104,* 241–265.

Mackintosh, N. J. (1975). A theory of attention: Variations in the associability of stimuli with reinforcement. *Psychological Review, 82,* 276–298.

Miall, R. C. (1989). The storage of time intervals using oscillating neurons. *Neural Computation, 1,* 359–371.

Pearce, J. M., & Hall, G. (1980). A model for Pavlovian learning: Variations in the effectiveness of conditioned but not unconditioned stimuli. *Psychological Review, 87,* 532–552.

Reid, A. K., & Allen, D. L. (1998). A parsimonious alternative to the pacemaker/accumulator process in animal timing. *Behavioural Processes, 44,* 119–125.

Rescorla, R. A. (1968). Probability of shock in the presence and absence of CS in fear conditioning. *Journal of Comparative and Physiological Psychology, 66,* 1–5.

Rescorla, R. A., & Wagner, A. R. (1972). A theory of Pavlovian conditioning: Variations in the effectiveness of reinforcement and nonreinforcement. In A. H. Black & W. F. Prokasy (Eds.), *Classical conditioning II: Current research and theory* (pp. 64–99). New York: Appleton-Century-Crofts.

Roberts, W. A. (1998). *Principles of animal cognition.* Boston: McGraw-Hill.

Savastano, H. I., & Miller, R. R. (1998). Time as content in Pavlovian conditioning. *Behavioural Processes, 44,* 147–162.

Schmajuk, N. A. (1997). *Animal learning and cognition: A neural network approach.* Cambridge, UK: Cambridge University Press.

Staddon, J. E. R., & Higa, J. J. (1999). Time and memory: Toward a pacemaker-free theory of interval of timing. *Journal of the Experimental Analysis of Behavior, 71,* 215–251.

Sutton, R. S., & Barto, A. G. (1981). Toward a modern theory of adaptive networks: Expectation and prediction. *Psychological Review, 88,* 135–170.

Sutton, R. S., & Barto, A. G., (1990). Time-derivative models of Pavlovian reinforcement. In M. Gabriel & J. Moore (Eds.), *Learning and computational neuroscience: Foundations of adaptive networks* (pp. 497–537). Cambridge, MA: MIT Press.

Triesman, M. (1963). Temporal discrimination and the indifference interval: Implications for a model of the "internal clock." *Psychological Monographs, 77* (Whole No. 576).

Wasserman, E. A., & Miller, R. R. (1997). What's elementary about associative learning? *Annual Review of Psychology, 48,* 573–607.

chapter 7

Contingency Learning and Causal Reasoning

A. G. Baker
McGill University

Robin A. Murphy
Frédéric Vallée-Tourangeau
University of Hertfordshire

Rick Mehta
McGill University

F rom at least Ferster and Skinner's (1957) early work documented in *Schedules of Reinforcement* there has been a great deal of interest in contingencies of reinforcement. The relation between the conditional stimulus (CS) and the unconditional stimulus (US) in Pavlovian conditioning and between the response and the outcome or reinforcer has long been known to exert subtle control over animal behavior. Moreover, students of causal reasoning consider the correlation or contingency between cause and effect to be one of the crucial empirical determinants of the causal reasoning process (e.g.,

255

Einhorn & Hogarth, 1986). Recently there have been attempts to analyze how humans judge contingencies in causal reasoning scenarios and in categorization tasks in terms of contingency sensitivity. Much of this research has been motivated by associative models derived directly from experiments on animal learning (e.g., Baker, Mercier, Vallée-Tourangeau, Frank, & Pan, 1993; Shanks, 1991; Wasserman, Elek, Chatlosh, & Baker, 1993)

It is puzzling, that, following a burst of interest generated by Rescorla's (1968) seminal work on contingency learning in Pavlovian conditioning, there has been relatively little analysis of the mechanisms by which animals represent contingencies. This has partly been due to what we believe to be a rather naive empirical and theoretical analysis of the issue. This simplistic analysis has led many to deny that the correlation or contingency between the CS and the US is even an important concept in animal learning, or even if it is, that there is strong prima facie evidence against the argument that animals learn these contingencies (see Papini & Bitterman, 1990). Much of this chapter deals with an empirical and theoretical response to this position. In fairness it must be recognized that the motivation behind this "simpler" analysis of the mechanism underpinning learning in animals is at least partly driven by the traditional desire for parsimony. The argument that animals might actually learn the correlation or contingency between events and then retrospectively base their decisions on this information seems to imply a homunculus located inside the animal that has within itself all the cognitive capacities we wish to explain with our science. We argue that a modern theoretical analysis maintains the parsimony of the traditional associative position yet still has a place in it for the representation of, or sensitivity to, event contingencies or correlations.

Recently a more complete formal analysis of event contingencies than that offered in the animal literature has been offered by students of human causal inference (e.g., Baker, Murphy, & Vallée-Tourangeau, 1996; Cheng, Park, Yarlas, & Holyoak, 1996; Spellman, 1996; Waldmann & Holyoak, 1992). We feel that this more complete analysis clarifies a number of issues and renders the claim that animals represent, or at least are sensitive to, event contingencies much less controversial. It could also lead to a reevaluation of the analysis of certain selective learning phenomena that are now referred to as deficits in learning or performance (e.g., Cole, Barnet, & Miller, 1995; Denniston, Savastano, & Miller, chap. 3, this volume). These include blocking (Kamin, 1969) and the relative validity effect (Wagner, Logan, Haberlandt, & Price, 1968). Rather then being a failure to learn, this analysis would argue that these phenomena suggest causal learning effects.

A final conceptualization that will help reconcile traditional animal learning models and the notion that animals might learn contingencies arises from modern cognitive science (e.g., Marr, 1982) but is very similar to one that has been espoused by radical behaviorists and other animal learners (e.g., Church, 1997). The force of this argument is that theoretical analyses are done at several levels. Only two levels concern us here, using Marr's terminology; these are the levels of *computation* and *algorithm*. When trying to understand an empirical phenomenon, one first needs to know what the organism computes. The computational analysis includes a formal analysis of the structure of the problem in the environment and any behavioral solution that the animal might offer. An important issue with respect to a normative analysis is to determine the correct solution to the problem, and then to determine whether the animal conforms to this normative analysis, and if not, to identify the errors that it might make. This may inform the choice of algorithm that the animal may actually use to solve the problem.

As an example, students of timing behavior might postulate that an animal maintains a continuous timer of life events and a second timer that can be started and stopped. This would describe the computational requirements of this problem. If an appropriate psychophysical analysis showed that the animal behaves as if it had such a timer, then the researcher would develop an associative or connectionist model or some other theoretical solution or algorithm that generates this behavior. This associative model would represent an analysis at the algorithmic level.

It is clear that neither analysis contradicts the other or eliminates the need for the other. Moreover the claim that the animal has an interval timer does not imply that the animal has a small stopwatch in its head. Likewise the claim that the animal calculates correlations or contingencies does not imply that there is a small but animate version of Rodin's "The Thinker" in the animal's head constantly pondering a record of past history. A proper computational model or analysis of a cognitive function serves several useful functions:

1. It provides an accurate computational logical and normative analysis of the process.
2. It provides a useful framework to guide research.
3. It provides a formal set of guidelines for evaluating the resulting behavior.
4. If the analysis is normative and behavior conforms to it then it implies that the function might be adaptive and the various empirical phenomena are less likely to be uninteresting epiphenomena.

In the remainder of this chapter we first outline a computational analysis of contingency learning. We then discuss some theoretical, or algorithmic, approaches to this problem. Finally we describe several experiments using humans and animals that outline the utility of this approach. The first experiments deal with simple contingency learning and the later ones extend this analysis to include cue competition and relative validity effects.

COMPUTATIONAL ANALYSIS OF CONTINGENCIES

Traditional associative analyses of learning focused on event contiguity and thus on event pairings or the probability of reinforcement. For example, schedules of reinforcement were defined in terms of response-reinforcer probability or temporal relations. Indeed, even schedules in which the contingency involved reinforcement in the absence of the target response were defined in terms of pairing between the reinforcement and putative other responses (e.g., differential reinforcement of other behaviors). Rescorla (1968) pointed out that the true logical contingency in Pavlovian conditioning included not only some measure of the likelihood or frequency of CS–US pairings but also included the likelihood or frequency of occurrence of the US in the absence of the CS. Moreover, Rescorla pointed out that this bias toward pairings led to a similar bias in experimental design. Rescorla's (1967) advocacy of the truly random control procedure was a reaction to this incomplete computational approach to contingency. This example illustrates how an incomplete computational analysis can lead to possibly inappropriate experimental designs. In sum, Rescorla's position might be summarized by arguing that it is not the number of CS–US pairings that determines the strength of a conditioned response, but whether the CS provides unique information about the occurrence or nonoccurrence of the US.

Allan (1980) is identified with initiating a similar computational approach to contingencies in the field of human causal reasoning. She, as do we, restricted her computational analysis to binary events rather than the temporally extended events in conditioning. However the computational principles she describes, whereby events in the presence and absence of the predictor must be considered, are more general. Allan pointed out that there were four possible conjunctions of two binary events in a causal or conditioning scenario (say the CS and the US): either the CS and US could occur together, the CS could occur alone, the US could occur alone, or neither could occur. A two-way contingency table representing this relation is shown in the top portion of Fig. 7.1. In addition, this figure shows several contingencies used in our subsequent experiments. The rows of the table represent the presence and absence of the cause (or CS) and the columns represent the presence and absence of the outcome (or US). The contents of the cells are the frequency of the various conjunctions just mentioned. For example, Cell A contains the number of CS–US pairings. Although humans often attribute more importance to some conjunctions than to others (e.g., Kao & Wasserman, 1993) each conjunction provides equally valid information for the relation between the two events. When one event is the predictor and the other is a consequence, such as when a cause leads to an effect, Allan suggested that the appropriate measure of contingency is ΔP, the one-way contingency between events. ΔP is the difference between the conditional probability of the US in the presence and absence of the CS:

$$\Delta P = P(\text{US} \mid \text{CS}) - P(\text{US} \mid \text{no CS}) = A/(A+B) - C/(C+D) \qquad (1)$$

where $A, B, C,$ and D are the frequencies of the event conjunctions from the two-way contingency table.

This computational formula emphasizes that contingency is a relative concept. For example, a positive contingency between a CS and US occurs when the presence of the CS signals a higher probability of outcome than its absence (e.g., contingencies H.5, M.5, and L.5 of Fig. 7.1). There is an important problem in imposing this arbitrary scheme on a natural cognitive system. The computation requires the organism to keep track of the frequency of events in the four cells of the contingency table. There is no problem, at least conceptually, for the top row, in which the conditional probability of outcomes in the presence of the cause or CS is assessed. The CS is present on all these trials and thus marks clearly the number of trials on which the US does and does not occur. It is also important to note that this row is the crucial one for the traditional analysis of contingencies in terms of pairings.

The bottom row is not so simple. Although Cell C, the presence of the US, marks those trials on which the CS does not occur but the US does, Cell D is a problem. Because Cell D involves the conjunction of no CS and no US, it has no events to mark its occurrence. Although the experimenter might try and assign a frequency to Cell D, the important question concerns how many times the organism believes a Cell D conjunction to have occurred. There are two ways in which the perception of Cell D may depart from that arbitrarily set up by the experimenter. First the animal might differ from the experimenter in its perception of how often the conjunction of no CS and no US occurs during the actual programmed D trials or within the temporal D period. Alternatively, the organism might recruit more of its experience from outside the trial context (i.e., from the intertrial interval [ITI] or less formally defined extra trial experience). Thus the actual contingencies perceived by the animal might be very different from the programmed

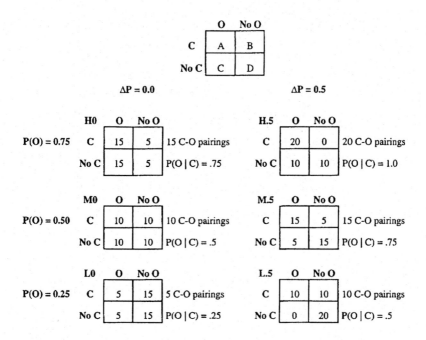

FIG 7.1.   At the top is a 2 × 2 table containing the four event conjunctions that define the ΔP contingency between O = Outcome and C = Cause. ΔP is the difference between the probability of the outcome given the presence of the cause, $P(O \mid C) = A/(A + B)$, and the probability of the outcome given the absence of the cause, $P(O \mid \text{no } C) = C / (C + D)$. The outcome density, $P(O)$, is the sum of the frequencies in Cells A and C divided by the total number of frequencies, that is, $(A + C)/(A + B + C + D)$. Shown are six contingencies that represent the positive and zero contingencies used in the first two experiments described here.

contingency yet still be consistent with a computational contingency analysis. For example consider the H0 zero contingency from Fig. 7.1 in which the conditional probabilities of an outcome in the presence and absence of the CS are both .75. $P(US \mid \text{no } CS)$ is based on a Cell D frequency of 5. If extra trials or other experience are added into Cell D then the ratio $C/(C+D)$ will become smaller and will gradually approach 0. Therefore depending on the animal's perception of Cell D, the perceived ΔP will vary from the experimenter's planned zero to one that is equivalent to $p(US \mid CS)$ (for H0 the contingency would vary from 0 to .75). The normative computational analysis recognizes this problem by referring to the focal set over which ΔP might be calculated (e.g., Baker

& Mercier, 1989; Cheng & Novick, 1992). The experimenter's arbitrary set of trials represents one focal set and that involving the ITI represents another. Remembering always that contingencies are conditional or relative, a given CS or causal candidate may have several ΔPs depending on which set of conditionalizing cues are considered to be the focal set. This has several implications:

1. In both animal research and human research in causal reasoning and categorization, judgments should be monotonically related to the contingency but need not conform to an arbitrary "normative" contingency defined by the experimenter. We should remain unmoved by data that indicate that judgments map extremely accurately onto the experimenter's arbitrary ΔP (e.g., Wasserman et al., 1993). This accurate output does not necessarily reflect an internal mechanism that is based on a computation of ΔP. Conversely, this "absolute" accuracy should not be the benchmark for determining contingency sensitivity. Failure to be normative in this absolute sense in no way eliminates a contingency analysis as a viable theoretical analysis.

2. There are many normative computational solutions to an individual problem.

3. Certain results that have been considered to be inconsistent with a contingency learning perspective, such as the tendency for animals to judge certain zero contingencies to be positive, may well be normative (e.g., Quinsey, 1971; see Papini & Bitterman, 1990).

THE RESCORLA–WAGNER MODEL PROVIDES A SIMPLE ALGORITHM THAT COMPUTES CONTINGENCY

As we mentioned above, an algorithm is a theoretically based system that might generate the values that a computational-level framework demands. The Rescorla–Wagner (1972) model is a traditional associative model developed to account for selective associations. Selective association experiments have shown the level of behavior controlled by a CS is determined not only by the number of pairings between that CS and the US but also by the associative status of other cues that are present during training. The model describes a mechanism involving cue competition in which stimuli compete for a limited amount of associative strength. Thus, just as the computation of contingency involves a relative comparison of two cues, selective associations demonstrate that conditioning involves relative comparisons and the Rescorla–Wagner model is one algorithmic formalization of this process (for ΔP the comparison is between CS and no CS trials).

It has long been known that the Rescorla–Wagner model's competitive learning process can account for rat contingency learning (e.g., Rescorla, 1968) data if the cue competition is conceived of as being between the CS and the experimental context. The *experimental context* is the galaxy of all uncontrolled cues that make up the situation in which the animal is trained or sometimes, more narrowly, those cues that mark the time in the session in which a trial might occur (the trial context or trial marker). In terms of computations, the context includes all the cells in the contingency table shown in Fig. 7.1 (i.e., Cells A, B, C, and D). Thus computationally this model is slightly different from ΔP which uses Cells C and D in its comparison [i.e., in $P(\text{US} \mid \text{no CS})$]. The model generates associative strength to the two cues. When there are positive contingencies (i.e., contingencies H.5, M.5, and L.5 from Fig. 7.1) the CS gets relatively more associative strength and the context gets less. When there are zero contingencies (i.e., contingencies H0, M0, and L0 from Fig. 7.1) the CS ends up with very little associative strength and the context relatively more. Many others and we have pointed out that associative models provide certain advantages over the computational model we consider here (e.g., Baker et al., 1996; Shanks, 1995). Associative models predict the course of learning whereas the simple computational model only predicts asymptotic performance. Furthermore associative models do not have problems with situations (e.g., simple schedules of reinforcement) in which some cells of the contingency table are not defined and thus either $P(\text{US} \mid \text{CS})$ or $P(\text{US} \mid \text{no CS})$ are undefined. However, we restrict ourselves in this chapter to considering a computational solution to asymptotic performance in situations in which reasonable assumptions about the cells of the contingency tables may be made.

Chapman and Robbins (1990) provided an analytic solution of the Rescorla–Wagner model. They showed that, with certain assumptions about learning rate parameters, asymptotic associative strengths for the CS reduce to ΔP. In collaboration with Wasserman and his colleagues, we showed that, with more conventional assumptions concerning the learning rate parameters, this analytic solution was slightly biased but still correlated highly with ΔP. This computation correlated even more highly with human participants' estimates of contingency in an operant contingency judgment task than did ΔP (see Baker et al., 1996; Wasserman et al., 1993). Finally, Cheng (1997) provided a more general analytic solution of the Rescorla–Wagner model for situations like blocking and overshadowing where there is more then one cue. It is ironic that the Rescorla–Wagner model, which itself computes ΔP, has been offered as evidence against the utility of contingency in conditioning.

EVIDENCE THAT HUMANS AND OTHER ANIMALS COMPUTE CONTINGENCIES

As we have mentioned, Rescorla (1968) demonstrated that animals were sensitive to the contingency between the CS and the US and not just the number of CS–US pairings. He varied the temporal density of the shock US during the presence and the absence of a tone CS. The experimental design allowed him to compare several groups receiving a fixed US density during the CS [a constant $P(US \mid CS)$] but with varying US densities in the absence of the CS [varying $P(US \mid No\ CS)$]. The findings were quite clear: When the temporal density of the US was the same in the presence and the absence of the CS [$P(US \mid CS) = P(US \mid no\ CS)$] the CS controlled little responding. Furthermore, when the density of outcomes was higher during the CS than during its absence, the CS came to control a conditioned response. This response was greater the greater the difference between densities (i.e., with increased ΔP).

The availability of the Rescorla–Wagner model as an explanation of contingency learning probably reduced interest in contingency learning because it provided a simple explanation using the traditional principle of temporal contiguity. However, although the Rescorla–Wagner model does provide an algorithm that computes contingencies, it postulates a very specific mechanism to do so—namely a competition between the CS and the experimental context. It reflects the general, and perhaps complacent, acceptance of this model, that the role of the context during simple contingency learning experiments was never fully analyzed (Hallam, Grahame, & Miller, 1992; Odling-Smee, 1975; Tanner, Rawlins, & Mellanby, 1987). The Rescorla–Wagner model and alternative algorithms make specific predictions concerning the level of associative strength controlled by the context. If these theories are to be accepted as an algorithm for contingency learning, more must be known about the role of the context during contingency learning.

To this end, over the past several years we have been evaluating the utility of several associative algorithms in understanding human causal reasoning (Murphy & Vallée-Tourangeau, 1999; Vallée-Tourangeau, Murphy, & Baker, 1998; Vallée-Tourangeau, Murphy, Drew, & Baker, 1998). The experiments are very closely analogous to Wagner et al.'s (1968) demonstration of the relative validity effect in which animals show conditioned responses based on cues' relative validity as predictors of a US. We chose a discrete trial protocol because all the trials are marked, distinct, and countable. This increases the likelihood that our arbitrary choice of event frequencies for the cells of the contingency table match closely with the participants' perceptions of event frequency. The six contingencies from the experiment we describe are shown in Fig. 7.1 (see Vallée-Tourangeau, Murphy, Drew, & Baker, 1998). The experiment used a factorial design in which two levels of contingency (ΔP = 0 and ΔP = .5) were crossed with three levels of outcome density [P(outcome) = .75, .5, .25]. This design includes treatments that allow a direct comparison of computational versions of the traditional pairings account of conditioning (in this case P(US | CS) or CellA frequency) with ΔP.

The scenario in this experiment is typical of recent experiments designed to model causal induction from contingency information presented in a trial-by-trial manner much as in conditioning. Individuals were asked to take part in a medical diagnosis task. Each trial they were presented with information about the medical profile of a fictitious patient. Specifically they were provided information about the presence or absence of two fictitious viruses (e.g., threbagia) and the presence or absence of one disease (e.g., voldusis). One virus (X) was present in all patients and therefore assumed the role of the context for the presence of a second virus (A) that covaried with the outcome in one of the two ΔP relations. The participants were informed that the viruses could be positively correlated, negatively correlated, or uncorrelated with the disease and thus might predict increases, decreases, or no change in disease likelihood.

Participants saw six samples of 40 patients with each sample corresponding to one of the six treatments shown in Fig. 7.1. The information about the patients was presented on a computer screen one patient at a time. Each screen showed the patient number and which viruses were present. At this point the participants were asked to provide a diagnosis by pressing the 1 or the 0 key on the keyboard. One second later, information about whether the patients had the disease appeared. The diagnoses were made to engage the participants' attention and to monitor their progress. The critical data for our analysis was obtained after 20 trials and after the full 40 trials when the participants were asked to judge the causal status of the constant virus (X) and the variable virus (A) independently. The judgments were made on a scale that ranged from –100 to 100 with 100 representing a perfect facilitative cause, –100 representing a perfect inhibitory cause, and 0 representing a possible cause with neither facilitative nor inhibitory power.

Participants' terminal judgments of the contingency of the variable cue (A) and of the constant contextual cue (X) are shown, respectively, in the two panels of Fig. 7.2. The results of this experiment are quite clear cut and at a superficial level are consistent with the Rescorla–Wagner model. For each outcome density, when A was moderately correlated with the outcome ($\Delta P = .5$) judgments were greater than when A was not correlated with the outcome ($\Delta P = 0$). Furthermore, the context X was judged to have more causal power in the zero contingency treatment than in the positive treatment at each density level. This is consistent with the claim that A and X compete for associative strength. However, in addition to a reliable effect for contingency, there was also a clear effect of overall outcome density. Judgments of both causes at both contingencies were positively related to the outcome density. This result is not easily reconciled with the Rescorla–Wagner model as an overall algorithm for contingency sensitivity but we return to that issue shortly.

We mentioned earlier that the criterion for contingency sensitivity was not that the participants be normative; that is, that they judge all $\Delta P = .5$ contingencies to be the same and all $\Delta P = 0$ contingencies to be the same. Indeed, because of the density effect, the data on judgments of A in the lefthand panel of Fig. 7.2 do not meet this strict criterion. The more modest goal of the computational approach is that, other things being equal, judgments be monotonic with contingency. The judgments in Fig. 7.2 meet this criterion at least with respect to density. There is, however, another computational conceptualization of conditioning. This is that the associative strength of a cue is a function of the number or proportion of cue–outcome pairings [i.e., of $P(US \mid CS)$]. This was the assumption of the Hull–Spence model (Hull, 1952; Spence, 1940) but it is not merely of historic interest. It is a common assumption of modern comparator and scalar expectancy models of conditioning (Gibbon & Balsam, 1981; Miller & Schachtman, 1985). We discuss these shortly but it is important empirically to distinguish between this simpler computational account that judgments were determined solely by $P(\text{Effect} \mid \text{Cause})$ and the notion that judgments are sensitive to the overall ΔP. To do this treatments having the same number and proportions of cause–effect pairings but different ΔPs must be compared. This comparison is also important to eliminate the alternative and quite parsimonious empirical hypothesis that when asked to make judgments of cause participants report $P(US \mid CS)$ or even frequency Cell A rather than some metric of contingency analogous to ΔP (cf. Baron, 1994, chap. 14).

In our design there are two comparisons in which $P(US \mid CS)$ is equal yet ΔP differs: Treatment H0 is compared with M.5 and treatment M0 with L.5. The comparisons are shown as dotted lines in Fig. 7.2. These lines show a modest positive slope indicating that given constant $P(US \mid CS)$, and competing against unequal outcome densities, participants ascribe higher causal value to the $\Delta P = .5$ than to the $\Delta P = 0$ contingency.

This is statistically reliable (see Vallée-Tourangeau, Murphy, Drew, & Baker, 1998). The empirical conclusion that must be drawn from this experiment is that at a computational level, humans are sensitive to event-outcome contingency and this sensitivity does not reduce to either of these simple alternative hypotheses (see Papini & Bitterman, 1990).

FIVE THEORETICAL ACCOUNTS OF THE DATA

Our participants' estimates of the causal status of A were influenced by A's contingency with the outcome and by outcome density. There was no statistical interaction. This analysis permits the possibility that the judgments result from two independent processes: one for contingency and the other for density. Before claiming that two processes might coexist, it is worth examining the more parsimonious alternative that both effects might emerge from a single computational or algorithmic account. Moreover, recall that one of the arguments used by Papini and Bitterman (1990) against the possibility that animals might be sensitive to the correlation between outcomes was that simple associative algo-

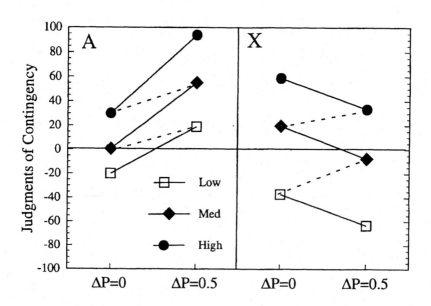

FIG 7.2. Mean human judgments of contingency for cues A (left panel) and X (right panel) in the simulated medical diagnosis experiment. Each participant received training with each of six treatments. The treatments fully cross two virus–disease contingencies ($\Delta P_A = 0.5$ and $\Delta P_A = 0$) with three disease density conditions (high, medium, and low: .75, .50, and .25, respectively).

rithms could account for the data. For this argument to have force, the models should accurately predict both the order of judgments of A and the order of judgments of X. This is important because the interaction with X is crucial for the predictions of the models concerning A. We outline how the computational ΔP theory can be modified to account for the density effect in judgments of X. We follow this with a description of the Rescorla–Wagner model simulations for judgments of A and X. Next we describe and evaluate the success of Pearce's generalization model at explaining our data. Finally we attempt a computational formalization of Miller's comparator theory. The predictions for A and X from each of these five approaches to contingency judgments are shown in Fig. 7.3. From Fig. 7.2 we can identify eight characteristics of our data that the various theories might account for. These include:

1. Individuals judge the contingency of A to be higher when ΔP = .5 than when ΔP = 0.
2. Individuals judge the contingency of X to be lower when ΔP = .5 than when ΔP = 0.
3. Judgments of A increase with density.
4. Judgments of X increase with density.
5. The density effect on A is not a consequence of the conditional probability P(Effect | A) because the comparisons H0 versus M.5 and M0 versus L.5 (Shown as dotted lines in Fig. 7.2) are reliable. We call this the *cross-density contrast* for contingency sensitivity.
6. The equivalent contrast for the context X is also reliable.
7. The order of means for A is H.5 > M.5 > H0 > L.5 > M0 > L0.
8. The order of means for X is H0 > H.5 > M0 > M.5 > L0 > L.5.

These eight points are not independent but they do represent a more or less increasing degree of specificity of theoretical predictions. Table 7.1 shows how our five approaches deal with these points.

Evaluation of ΔP

We have already described the predictions of ΔP for judgments of A and these are shown in Panel 1 (upper left) of Fig. 7.3. This computational account predicts that subjects will judge all ΔP = .5 contingencies to be higher than all ΔP = 0 contingencies but it predicts no effect of density on these predictions. Thus Table 7.1 shows that ΔP accounts for A's contingency and the cross-density contrast effect (because all positive contin-

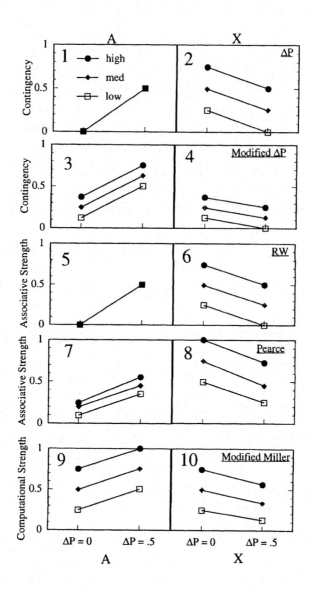

FIG 7.3. Simulations from five computational or algorithmic models for the data from Experiment 1 of Vallée-Tourangeau et al. (1998). The predictions for computation or associative strength of A are shown in the lefthand panels and X is shown in the righthand panels. Panels 1 and 2 show predictions from ΔP, Panels 3 and 4 from a modified version of ΔP that includes extra Cell D events, Panels 5 and 6 show the Rescorla–Wagner model (1972) predictions assuming equal betas, Panels 7 and 8 show predictions from Pearce (1987), and Panels 9 and 10 show predictions from a modified comparator hypothesis. The black squares in Panels 1 and 5 represent all these symbols falling on top of one another.

gencies are higher than all zero contingencies) but does not account for the density effect or the order of means. It predicts the order of the means to be H.5 = M.5 = L.5 > H0 = M0 = L0.

The contingency of X (ΔP_X) is not defined within our present frame because X is present on all trials and hence $P(US \mid no\ X)$ is not defined. Proponents of the normative computational approaches called *probabilistic contrast theory* and later, *PowerPC theory*, offered a simple solution to this problem (see Cheng, 1997; Cheng & Holyoak, 1995). They argued that judgments of any potential cause depend on the amount of information that that cause adds to other causes that are present. If there are several potential causes, subjects will focus on the most informative cue (that with the highest unconditional ΔP). It will then be determined if the cue of interest adds any information beyond that provided by the strong cue (i.e., does it predict a change in the likelihood of an outcome given the presence or absence of this strong cue?). Thus ΔP_X might be calculated over a focal set of experience conditionalized or influenced by the presence or absence of A. This is particularly true when A is correlated with the outcome in the $\Delta P = .5$ treatments. Moreover, PowerPC theory argues that the causal importance of X is best assessed in the absence of A. Thus the conditional probability of the outcome in the absence of A $[P(US \mid no\ A)]$ is one term in the formula for ΔP_X. For a constant cause X, the conditional probability of an outcome on the ITIs can be used as the second term in the calculation of ΔP_X. However in this experiment the probability of an outcome in the ITI is always zero so the computational formula for ΔP_X reduces to:

$$\Delta P_X = P(\ US \mid No\ A) \tag{2}$$

Panel 2 of Fig. 7.3 shows these values of ΔP_X for the six treatments of our experiment. These values of ΔP_X are consistent with the contingency effect and density effect on X in our data but they do not predict the cross contingency comparison difference on X or the order of means of X. The order of ΔP_X is H0 > H.5 = M0 > M.5 = L0 > L.5.

A Modified ΔP

ΔP_A does not provide a good account of the density effect on the judgments of A. However we mentioned earlier that frequency of events in Cell D can be thought of as somewhat arbitrary and described how differences in Cell D frequency might influence ΔP_A. If it is assumed that

TABLE 7.1. Tests of the Predictions From Five Computational or Algorithmic Models for the Data of Experiment 1 (Vallée-Tourangeau et al., 1998).

Theory	Contingency A	Contingency X	Density A	Density X	Cross-Contrast A	Cross-Contrast X	Mean Order A	Mean Order X
Raw data	Yes	Yes	Yes	Yes	Yes	Yes	Yes	Yes
ΔP	Yes	Yes	No	Yes	Yes	No	No	No
Rescorla–Wagner	Yes	Yes	No	Yes	Yes	No	No	No
Pearce	Yes	Yes	Yes	Yes	Yes	No	No	No
Modified ΔP	Yes	Yes	Yes	Yes	Yes	No	No	No
Modified comparator	Yes	Yes	Yes	Yes	No	Yes	No	Yes

Note. Yes = model is able to predict the observed pattern.

individuals overestimate Cell D, a density effect is generated. We assumed that participants overestimated the frequency of Cell D by 20 and the resulting modified ΔP_A values are plotted in Panel 3 of Fig. 7.3. These values for A mirror the density effect as well as the basic contingency effect found with the judgments of A. They also predict the cross-density contingency contrast. However they do not predict the order of means. The order of means predicted by the modified ΔP_A is H.5 > M.5 > L.5 > H0 > M0 > L0. It should be mentioned that if quite large values are chosen for Cell D (greater than the number of actual training trials) the modified ΔP does predict the ordering of the means.

The modified values of ΔP_X (assuming 20 extra trials) are shown in Panel 4 of Fig. 7.3. These values are of smaller magnitude but otherwise are qualitatively identical to those for the unmodified ΔP_X. Clearly, while modifying Cell D does generate a density effect on A it still provides an incomplete explanation of the interaction of outcome density and contingency.

The Rescorla–Wagner Model

In the introduction it was mentioned that associative strength from the Rescorla–Wagner model correlates very highly with ΔP_A so it is not surprising that the associative strengths for A shown in Panel 5 of Fig. 7.3 match ΔP from Fig. 7.1. These simulations were conducted with the assumption that the learning parameters for outcome presence and outcome absence (B_1 and B_0) were equal. One assumption often made (e.g., Rescorla & Wagner, 1972) is that outcome trials are relatively more effective at changing associative strength than no outcome trials (i.e., $B_1 > B_0$). With this assumption, the Rescorla–Wagner model does predict a small density effect (see Baker et al., 1996), although the effect is in the opposite direction to that found here, and only for nonzero contingencies. For nonzero contingencies, increasing outcome density produces weaker associations. The Rescorla–Wagner model does model the effects of some human operant causal judgments (e.g., Wasserman et al., 1993) but has similar difficulties to ΔP_A with the present data. Alternatively if the opposite assumption $B_0 > B_1$ is made (see Dickinson, Shanks, & Evenden, 1984) the model does predict that associative strength should increase with increases in outcome density, but again only for nonzero contingencies. These density effects are quite small.

It turns out, not surprisingly, that the associative strength for X comes very close to computing ΔP_X. So again, Panel 6 of Fig. 7.3, which shows the associative strength of X, is very similar to Panel 2, which shows

ΔP_X. Therefore the Rescorla–Wagner associative strength predicts a contingency and a density effect on X but no reliable cross-density contrast. The order of means is the same as that predicted by ΔP_X. In summary, the Rescorla–Wagner model provides a reasonable algorithm for computing ΔP but it does not account well for judgments in even this rather simple experiment. Thus the notion of competition between A and X does not provide a complete explanation of our participants' judgments. We have, however, recently begun to evaluate a different associative algorithm that more closely models this behavior.

The Pearce Generalization Model

The Pearce model (Pearce, 1987, 1994) is an associative model that is similar to stimulus sampling theory (Estes, 1959) and differs from the Rescorla–Wagner model in several important ways. Details of the model and our simulations are available elsewhere (Vallée-Tourangeau, Murphy, Drew, & Baker, 1998) but we outline differences between this model and the Rescorla–Wagner model here. In the Rescorla–Wagner model stimuli are treated as individual elements that are learned about separately. These elements compete for limited associative strength. In the Pearce model all stimuli on a trial make a single stimulus complex of many elements that is learned about as a whole. For example, a trial in which A and X are present would be conceptualized as being an A, X plus context trial. Over the course of training, this complex would acquire both inhibitory and excitatory associations (i.e., connections with outcome and no-outcome centers). Likewise the complex X plus context is learned about separately on other trials. The complexes do not compete directly for associative strength but on any trial the response to any complex is determined jointly by the associative strength of that particular complex and by associative strength that generalizes from other similar complexes. The similarity between complexes is determined by the number of common elements. For example an AX trial shares X and the context with an X trial but does not share A. This theory was designed to deal with discrimination learning but it does make clear predictions concerning our simple contingency learning preparations.

Panels 7 and 8 of Fig. 7.3 show the generalized associative strength for A and X from Pearce's model. This model does better than the Rescorla–Wagner model but still does not provide a complete account of our data. It produces both a density and a contingency effect on A and predicts the cross-density comparison. However, it does not predict the order of the means for A. Its predictions are similar to those of modified ΔP_A: H.5 > M.5 > L.5 > H0 > M0 > L0. The Pearce model also predicts both a density effect and a contingency effect on the contextual cue X. However, it does not predict the cross-density comparison or the order of means. The order of means was H0 > M0 $\geq$ H.5 > L0 $\geq$ M.5 > L.5. The Pearce model again is a better but not complete algorithm for our results. We now turn to a final approach in which we offer a computational formalization of a hypothesis generally attributed to Miller (e.g., Miller & Schachtman, 1985).

Computational Version of the Comparator Hypothesis

Miller and his colleagues (Denniston et al., chap. 3, this volume; Miller & Matzel, 1988; Miller & Schachtman, 1985) proposed a three-stage approach to Pavlovian learning. According to them animals first form associations. Then when asked to respond to a target stimulus (say A) the animal will compare the associative strength of the target with the strength of all other stimuli that were present during training (not just those present on that trial). Only if the target has more associative strength than any other will it generate a response; otherwise it will be "behaviorally silent" (Cole, Gunther, & Miller, 1997). Practically speaking, the theory states that each stimulus will be compared with the strongest stimulus and the strength of this comparison will influence the response generated by that stimulus. Miller did not propose a specific computational version of this theory but his recent writings seem to imply that this is an all-or-none process whereby only the strongest stimulus controls responding (Cole et al., 1995; Cole et al., 1997). If so, this theory would definitely have difficulties with our graded means. It is, however, entirely within the spirit of this theory that the comparisons might be relative rather than absolute (see Blaisdell, Bristol, Gunther, & Miller, 1998, for a revised version of the comparator theory that includes this assumption). Moreover, this assumption is a crucial aspect of the relative waiting time hypothesis of scalar expectancy theory (Gibbon & Balsam, 1981). Thus it seems worthwhile to generate a probabilistic computational version of this theory to account for the present results. To do so we need to generate (a) a rule for determining associative strength, (b) a rule for comparing associative strengths, and (c) a rule for combining the associative strength and the result of the comparisons.

Although at times Miller implied that a stimulus competition rule similar to that in the Rescorla–Wagner model would be appropriate for acquisition of associative strength, this is not the most parsimonious account because it provides two separate mechanisms for phenomena like the present and others (e.g., blocking, Kamin, 1969). Thus we follow the lead of Gibbon and Balsam (1981) and hypothesize that associative strengths are acquired independently to X and to A. Using our computational approach, the associative strength to A will be estimated by the conditional probability [P(US | A)]. The associative strength of X will be calculated by the conditional probability of the outcome on all X trials [i.e., P(US | (X & AX)]. Because X is present on all trials this probability is equivalent to the outcome density that is shown in Fig. 7.1. We chose a relative comparison rule. The conditional probability for each stimulus is compared with the strongest stimulus using the ratio P(US | compared stimulus) / P(US | strongest). Thus the comparison value for the strongest stimulus would be 1 and that for weaker stimuli would vary from 1 to 0. Our response rule is again straightforward. The response controlled by a stimulus should be a function of both its associative strength and the strength of its comparison with the strongest stimulus. We simulated this relation by multiplying the conditional probability of an outcome during the stimulus by the strength of its comparison with the strongest stimulus. Thus the predicted response generated by our computational model may be calculated by the following formula:

$$P(US \mid C)* [P(US \mid C) / P(US \mid S)] \qquad (3)$$

Here C represents the compared stimulus and S the strongest stimulus. It should be mentioned that, although the computations are different, the main assumptions of the comparator theory are very similar to those of the probabilistic contrast and PowerPC theory of human causal reasoning. Similar assumptions include the three-stage process described here whereby the strengths of stimuli are determined, rank ordered, and finally compared in some manner.

The predictions from the computational version of the comparator theory are shown in Panels 9 and 10 of Fig. 7.3. This theory has the most success of any model with the constant causal cue X. It correctly predicts each of the four empirical characteristics we identified including the order of the means. The predictions for the variable cue A are not so good. The theory does predict a reliable effect of density and contingency but does not predict the cross-density comparison or the ordering of the means. The ordering of means on A is H.5 > H0 = M.5 > M0 = L.5 > L0.

Conclusion: Individuals Judge Both Contingency and Outcome Density

This exercise has been somewhat tedious but some important conclusions have emerged. None of the algorithms can, from a single computational mechanism, generate both the density effects and the contingency effect we have reported. The reliable cross-density comparison on A clearly demonstrates that, although individuals' estimates are influenced by density, they are also influenced by contingency. If it is assumed that these two processes are independent and additive, the results of the initial analysis of variance imply that a weighted sum of the two factors could model the ordering of means we report here. We do not wish to be identified with this bipartite hypothesis because there are an infinite number of possible algorithms and surely one could model the ordering of the 12 means we report here. We do, however, wish to claim that the preceding analysis shows that a contingency learning mechanism is necessary.

CONTEXT–CS INTERACTION IN AN APPETITIVE PREPARATION IN RATS

In a casual reasoning preparation, humans were sensitive to the contingency when density and pairings were controlled. Moreover, none of the algorithms accounted for the observed pattern of density effects and sensitivity to covariation. Although there is much evidence that the theoretical traditions of animal associative learning have utility for understanding human causal reasoning, one might expect that associative models designed for conditioning would perhaps better model conditioning data than the human causal reasoning tasks described earlier. We sought to test these models as accounts of a conditioning task designed to investigate the interaction between context and CS in contingency learning in Pavlovian conditioning.

The goal of the previous experiment was to investigate the relation between sensitivity to the covariation of the variable cause with the outcome and responding controlled by the constant or contextual cause. Moreover it is important to use a design that as clearly as possible marks out the "events" in Cell D (the no-cause no-effect cell) of the contingency table. To do this, Murphy (1999) developed a discrete trial appetitive conditioning preparation in which all trials were marked by the occurrence of a trialmarker. Moreover, this trialmarker generated a unique conditioned response that could be measured independent of that generated by the CS. Holland (1977) demonstrated the utility of the strategy of measuring separate conditioned responses in multi-CS conditioning preparations.

The trial marker in these experiments was the insertion of a standard retractable response lever into the chamber. Because this is a Pavlovian conditioning preparation, responses on the lever had no programmed consequences. However Peterson, Ackil, Frommer, and Hearst (1972) showed that if insertion of the lever is paired with food it will elicit conditioned approach behavior. In our conditioning chambers, this behavior manifests itself as conditioned lever presses. Thus in Murphy's experiment the insertion of the lever was analogous to the constant virus in the previous experiment and acted as the conditioning trial context. Moreover, lever presses could be used to assess conditioning to the lever independent of conditioning controlled by the variable CS. The variable CS was a light in this first experiment and the conditioned response elicited by the light was entry of the food magazine. The design was very similar to that of the previous experiment. There were two contingencies between the variable light and the food US ($\Delta P = 0$ and $\Delta P = .5$) and three densities of food presentations [P(food) = .25, .5 and .75]. The conditional probabilities of an outcome in the presence and absence of the light were identical to those used in the human causal reasoning experiment (see Fig. 7.1). Only the number of trials per session and the length of the experiment differed. Some specific details of the experiment follow.

Method

Subjects. Thirty-six naive male Wistar rats were used. They weighed between 275 g and 300 g and were reduced to 80% of their free-feeding body weight and maintained at this weight for the duration of the experiment.

Apparatus. Six standard sound and light attenuating conditioning chambers were used. The opening to the food tray was located in the middle of one wall of the chamber, flush with the wall and covered by a transparent plastic flap. The animals could retrieve 45-mg food pellets by pushing the flap approximately 20° to 40° from the vertical exposing the food tray. Tray openings were recorded by closures of a microswitch. A standard retractable lever, which acted as the trial context (X), was located on the wall to the left of the food tray flap. The house light that acted as the variable cue (A) was located in the center of the ceiling.

Procedure. During a single 30-min session, rats were trained to retrieve food pellets delivered on a variable time 60-sec schedule. The lever was retracted for this session.

The following seven conditioning sessions consisted of 64 10-sec trials presented on a variable interval 30-sec schedule. The start of each trial was signaled by the entry of the retractable lever (X) into the chamber. On half these trials the light (A) was paired with the lever for the full 10-sec interval. There were 32 trials each of the light + lever (AX) and lever alone (X). All trials ended with the termination of the stimuli, coinciding on some trials with the delivery of a single food pellet into the tray. The distribution of the food deliveries during the two trial types was different in the six treatments. Six rats were assigned to each treatment that crossed two levels of light–food contingency (ΔP_A = .5 or 0) with three levels of food density (high [H], medium [M], or low [L]). The letter designation refers to the density or absolute number of food deliveries during the entire session (48, 32, or 16 food pellets, respectively; density = .75, .50, and .25). In the three positive contingency groups, AX trials signaled an increased likelihood of food compared with that signaled by X alone. For the three zero contingency groups both AX trials and X trials signaled the same likelihood of food. Therefore, there was a positive and zero A contingency treatment at each US density. The conditional probabilities for the occurrence of food on the AX and X trials for the three positive contingency groups were H.5: $P(US \mid AX) = 1.0$ and $P(US \mid X) = .50$; M.5: $P(US \mid AX) = .75$ and $P(US \mid X) = .25$; and L.5: $P(US \mid AX) = .50$ and $P(US \mid X) = 0$. The conditional probabilities for the occurrence of food on the AX and X trials for the three zero contingency groups were H0: $P(US \mid AX) = P(US \mid X) = .75$; M0: $P(US \mid AX) = P(US \mid X) = .5$; and L0: $P(US \mid AX) = P(US \mid X) = .25$. The exact trial frequencies and proportion of trials paired with the US are reported in Table 7.2.

Following training with the US there was a single extinction test session during which AX and X were presented but there were no US deliveries.

Results and Discussion

The results of this experiment, shown in Fig. 7.4 are similar to those of our human contingency experiment. The upper two panels show the frequency of magazine entries during the light (AX trials: the lever X is always present) and on the lever only (X) trials.

These data from magazine entries, which represent responding controlled by the light, are straightforward and are consistent with ΔP and the Rescorla–Wagner model. There are relatively few magazine entries in the absence of the light and, more important, there are a fairly equal number in all groups. The top lefthand panel shows a clear contingency effect. Unlike with our human data, there seems to be no density effect on magazine entries here. All groups exposed to a positive contingency responded more than all groups exposed to the zero light–food contingencies. Moreover for the $\Delta P = 0$ groups, adding the light to the lever caused no increase in magazine entries. Thus there is strong evidence that responding to the light is controlled largely by the light–food contingency with no density effect. This agrees completely with the ΔP and

TABLE 7.2. Trial Frequencies in the Six Treatments of Rat Density Experiment.

Trial Type	Positive Contingency ($\Delta P = 0.5$)			Zero Contingency ($\Delta P = 0.0$)		
	High (H.5)	Medium (M.5)	Low (L.5)	High (H0)	Medium (M0)	Low (L0)
AX→US	32	24	16	24	16	8
X→US	16	8	0	24	16	8
AX→ no US	0	8	16	8	16	24
X→no US	16	24	32	8	16	24
Total US	48	32	16	48	32	16
Total no US	16	32	48	16	32	48
P(US ǀ A)	1	.75	.5	.75	.5	.25
P(US ǀ no A)	.5	.25	0	.75	.5	.25
ΔP_A	.5	.5	.5	0	0	0

Note. Training involved either $\Delta P = .5$ or 0 between A and the food US at one of the three US densities. High, Medium, and Low refer to US densities of .75, .50, and .25, respectively. A = light; X = presence of lever.

the Rescorla–Wagner model's predictions for A in that there is a contingency effect, no density effect on A, the cross-density contrast is reliable, and the order of means is H.5 = M.5 = L.5 > H0 > M0 > L0. This ordering is not consistent with any of the other algorithms shown in Fig. 7.3 because they all predict a density effect on A.

Lever pressing, which reflects control by X, is shown in the bottom panels of Fig. 7.4. Although there is an interaction caused by a floor effect in Treatments H.5 and M.5, lever pressing to X shows contingency and density effects similar to those found in the previous experiment. In this experiment there was a reliable density and contingency effect and the cross contingency comparison was reliable but in the opposite direction. Although ΔP and the Rescorla–Wagner model provided a good description of the order of the means of magazine entries to A, they fail with X because they predict that lever presses will track $P(US \mid no\ A)$.

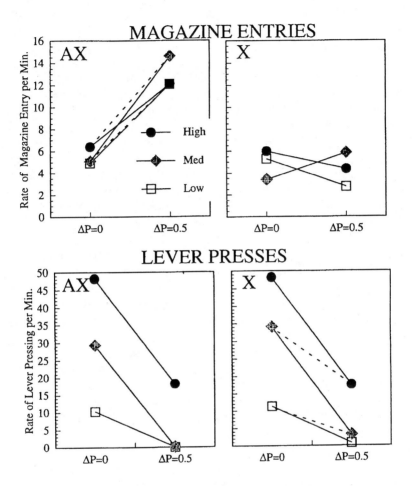

FIG 7.4. Mean tray entries per min on the final appetitive conditioning session shown separately for AX trials (top left panel) and X trials (top right panel). Mean lever presses per min are shown separately on AX trials (bottom left panel) and X trials (bottom right panel). There were six treatments: three positive (ΔP_A = 0.5) A–US contingency treatments and three zero contingency treatments (ΔP_A = 0). High, Medium, and Low refer to the US densities.

Responding controlled by the lever should be a function of the number or proportion of lever–food pairings in the absence of the light. This is the null hypothesis of the cross-density comparison for X and this comparison is reliable, thereby rejecting that null hypothesis that H0 = M.5 > M0 = L.5. The other algorithms also have problems with these data just as they had with the human contingency data. Although the computational comparator model accounted for the means of X in the human data, the different orderings of means here are not predicted by it.

To recap, the data in this experiment again show that subjects are sensitive to the A contingency and that there is a density effect but the effect of density is somewhat different than the one found in causal reasoning. The common feature of these two very different preparations was that subjects were sensitive to contingency and that none of the simple algorithms we studied accounted for both this contingency sensitivity and conditioning controlled by the context. There is, however, an alternative explanation of the contingency effect in this experiment. We chose to use a context and a CS that generated different responses so we could continuously assess which stimulus was controlling behavior. However when very different responses are elicited in a conditioning preparation, it is possible that the mechanism of contingency sensitivity is more peripheral. It is thus quite possible that the associations controlled by A in the $\Delta P = 0$ and $\Delta P = .5$ contingencies do not differ. However because X controls lever pressing, which is physically incompatible with simultaneous magazine entries, it is possible that the differential responding to A is a consequence of response competition between lever pressing and magazine entries.

It should be obvious that from a computational point of view this is not an important issue. Response competition is, after all, just another algorithm that might compute contingency although it is not a particularly subtle one. However, from the point of view of those who wish to champion associative algorithms, peripheral response competition is not particularly interesting. Close inspection of our data most certainly rules out this mechanism as a unitary explanation of our results. For example, the contingency H.5 generates both more lever presses and more magazine entries than the contingency L0. Moreover, although the lever pressing controlled by the three zero contingencies varies by a factor of five, all three contingencies control a very similar level of magazine entries. Nonetheless, proponents of theories that ascribe conditioning effects as artefacts of response competition are often immune to such empirical and logical arguments; indeed, the position approaches tautology. To provide further evidence against a competing response explanation of contingency sensitivity, Murphy (1999) carried out a second experiment in which responding controlled by the light was assessed in the absence of the lever.

This experiment included two groups that received treatments equivalent to M0 and M.5 of the previous experiment. During training these two groups acquired differential responding to the light and the lever. By the final day of training, the level of magazine responding controlled by the light was 13 responses per min in the $\Delta P = .5$ group and was 5 responses per min in the $\Delta P = 0$ groups. Conversely, the level of lever pressing controlled by X in the $\Delta P = .5$ group was 17 responses per min whereas lever pressing in the $\Delta P = 0$ group was 28 responses per min.

Other experiments (Murphy, Baker, & Fouquet, 1999; Murphy, McDonald, & Baker, 1998) have found that a contingent cue has two effects on simple conditioning. It controls more responding than a noncontingent cue and it blocks or reduces responding controlled by the context (in this case the general experimental context not our trial context—X). The results of our test in which the light was presented in the absence of the lever are shown in Fig. 7.5 and replicate this general finding. The left panel shows the rate of magazine entries during the light and during the 10-sec period before the light (pre-CS). The animals in $\Delta P = .5$ contingency respond more during the light and less during the pre-CS period. This interaction was reliable. The right panel of Fig. 7.5 shows elevation scores in which the pre-CS score was subtracted from the light score. The light, in the $\Delta P = .5$ group, controlled a much stronger response tendency even in an extinction test in a new (no lever) context. These results support the notion that the sensitivity to contingency with this preparation is a consequence of something learned about the light and not simple response competition with the lever on the test.

Summary of Simple Contingency Experiments

In summary, these experiments have shown sensitivity to both the contingency of cues and to the density of outcomes in two very different preparations involving different information processing systems. Contingency sensitivity cannot be explained by simple concepts such as sensitivity to the number of cue–outcome pairings. Rather, as implied by metrics such as ΔP, our subjects somehow integrate the likelihood of outcomes in the presence and the absence of the CS to make a "judgment" of the contingency. Moreover, closer analysis of responding controlled by the context and judgments shows that contrary to some claims (Papini & Bitterman, 1990) simple associative algorithms involving interacting associations for the context and the cue do not account for this sensitivity. Thus arguments that correlation learning can be eliminated as a fundamental principle of conditioning because they can be more "parsimoniously" explained by simple algorithms do not stand up to closer scrutiny. Papini and Bitterman (1990) claimed, "There is no dependence of conditioning on contingency qua contingency, … and

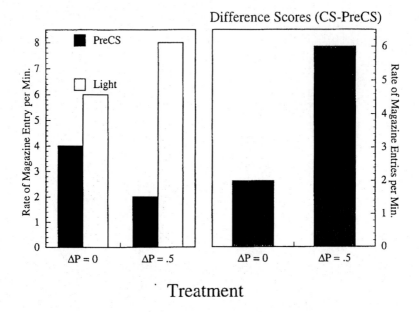

FIG 7.5. Mean tray entries per min during a test of the cue A. Training involved either ΔP = .5 or ΔP = 0 A–US training with X always present. This test involved A alone. The left panel shows responding during the pre-CS and to A separately. The right panel shows a measure of conditioning: CS-(pre-CS) responding.

many of the results that contradict the contingency view can be understood in terms of the Rescorla–Wagner theory" (p. 401). It is unduly glib to claim that these results on contingency learning reduce to a simple associative algorithm.

Again it must be emphasized that accepting sensitivity to contingency as a computational principle of conditioning does not necessarily imply that it is the algorithm that is used to compute this sensitivity. Our bias is that it is not. However, contingency learning is retrospective in the sense that to keep updating correlation judgments one must keep track of event frequencies (or something correlated with them) and use this information at the time of responding to inform the contingency learning process. At the time when one of us (e.g., Baker & Mackintosh, 1977) was first interested in correlation learning the argument that conditioning is retrospective was quite controversial. However, there are now several theories that are retrospective. These include the comparator theories (Denniston et al., chap. 3, this volume; Gibbon & Balsam, 1981), the Sometimes Opponent Process theory (Dickinson & Burke, 1996; Wagner, 1981) and associative theories (Van Hamme & Wasserman, 1994) that involve different mechanisms of association for events that are or are not present.

Cue competition between the context and the discrete cues is an important feature of explanations of contingency learning. We now turn to experiments investigating cue competition among discrete cues.

CONTINGENCY AND CUE COMPETITION

Kamin's (1969) blocking and Wagner et al.'s (1968) relative validity finding are among the most influential modern findings in Pavlovian conditioning. The common feature of these experiments is that they include treatments in which animals received equivalent numbers of pairings of one cue (X) and the US. The crucial difference between the treatments involves the number or proportion of pairings of other cues (A, B) with the US. The important result of these experiments was that responding controlled by X was an inverse function of the relation of A with the outcome. If A was a relatively good predictor of the outcome, X would control less responding and vice versa. The parallel between these experiments and simple contingency learning experiments is obvious. The critical comparison to demonstrate sensitivity to contingency involved demonstrating that animals responded more to X in spite of the fact that it had the same number or proportion of cue–outcome pairings as in a control group.

In the relative validity experiment (Wagner et al., 1968); rats or rabbits were exposed to two compounds. Each compound comprised a common visual element (X) and one of two auditory elements (A or B). Half of the compound trials were paired with an outcome (food or shock) and the other half were not. There were two treatments, but because X was present on all trials it was reinforced 50% of the time in both treatments ($[P(US \mid X) = .5]$). The critical difference between the groups was the correlation between A and B and the outcomes. In the correlated treatment (*correlated* and *uncorrelated* refer to the correlation of the individual compounds with the outcomes) all AX trials were reinforced and none of the BX trials was (AX$^+$, BX$^-$). In the uncorrelated treatment half of the AX and half of the BX trials were paired with the outcome (AX$^{+/-}$ and BX$^{+/-}$). The critical result of this experiment was that even though $P(US \mid X)$ was constant in the two treatments, X controlled a different level of responding. According to Wagner et al. (1968) the absolute validity of X as a predictor of the outcome was the same in both groups. However, because X controlled a different level of responding in the two treatments, the level of responding to it must have been determined by its relative validity compared to A and B.

Descriptions of this experiment in learning texts and in original research papers betray the simplistic analysis of contingency we discussed earlier (e.g., Domjan & Burkhard, 1993, Mackintosh, 1974, Tarpy, 1997). It is often argued that the validity of A, B, and X is the same in the uncorrelated groups (e.g., Cole et al., 1995; Cole et al., 1997; Wagner et al., 1968). However, this description reveals a bias toward confusing validity with pairings or proportion of reinforced trials. Although $P(US \mid A, B, \text{ or } X)$ is .5, the probability of the occurrence of outcomes in the absence A, B, and X is not the same. If we consider A and B in a focal set that includes all trials $P(US \mid \text{no A or no B})$ is .5. Therefore ΔP_A and ΔP_B are zero. It will be obvious that ΔP_X is not defined within the focal set of trials because there are no trials on which X is not present so $P(US \mid \text{no X})$ is undefined. It should however also be obvious that X is logically identical to the context from our earlier analysis of simple contingency learning. Just as for treatment H0 in those experiments, if $P(US \mid \text{no X})$ is calculated from the extra trial experience, ΔP_X will be .5.

From the perspective of contingency learning these experiments have also been thought to provide crucial negative evidence because, although the absolute contingency between X and the outcome is the same in the uncorrelated groups, X controls different levels of responding (see Papini & Bitterman, 1990). Commentators on human judgments of covariation and contingency have drawn similar conclusions. For example, Dickinson et al. (1984) wrote that selective attribution or blocking is "a finding that [can] not be explained in terms of the ΔP rule" (p. 47; see also Chapman & Robbins, 1990). Moreover, students of the relative validity effect and blocking have often described the low level of responding controlled by X as a failure to learn or to perform (e.g., Cole et al., 1995; Cole et al., 1997).

Starting with Waldmann and Holyoak (1992), proponents of a more complete contingency analysis have argued that cue competition effects do not necessarily represent a failure to learn. Rather they are a normative consequence of a contingency learning analysis (e.g., Baker et al., 1996; Cheng et al., 1996; Spellman, 1996). We have already mentioned that the critical point about the information processing in contingency learning is whether or not the CS is informative compared to other cues that may be present. When there are multiple cues, one normative analysis would argue that the organism first calculates the unconditional contingencies for all cues (ΔPs). Strong predictors are subsequently identified and then these are used to delineate the focal sets in which conditionalized contrasts (conditional ΔPs) are calculated. The process is closely analogous to experimental design and scientific reasoning. For example in the correlated group (AX$^+$ vs BX$^-$) from Wagner et al.

(1968), A is perfectly correlated with the outcome so it would be used to establish focal sets for determining the contingency of X. If a system is interested in attributing causal power to a cue, it is not particularly informative to query its contingency in the presence of strong predictors like A. This is true because the outcome may well be attributable to the contemporaneous presence of A rather than to the cue of interest. Therefore the best focal set for determining the contingency of X is the absence of A. This is exactly the analysis used earlier for determining the contingency of the context in simple contingency learning experiments. The conditional probability of the outcome in the presence of X and the absence of A (i.e., on the BX⁻ trials) is zero. The conditional probability of the outcome in the absence of X (i.e., from the ITIs) is also zero. Therefore $\Delta P_{X|no\,A}$ is zero. It follows from this analysis that the low level of responding controlled by X is a perfectly normative consequence of a contingency analysis. Certainly these results should not be argued to represent evidence against contingency learning (Papini & Bitterman, 1990). More important, the view that cue competition reflects failure to learn or perform can be replaced by the view that cue competition is a positive consequence of an adaptive contingency learning process. The view that sees cue competition as a failure to learn can be seen as a vestige of the traditional emphasis on CS–US pairings.

The original relative validity design is not ideal for studying contingency learning because the contingency of X is not defined in the set of learning trials. Several years ago as part of a series of experiments on causal reasoning we developed a modified version of the relative validity experiment in which the contingencies of both A and X were defined within the structure of the discrete learning trials. The original version of this procedure involved a video game in which humans attempted to protect tanks from land mines by camouflaging them (Baker et al., 1993). However, we describe it using a scenario developed in our laboratory by Mehta. Mehta replicated the important features of our earlier data. The scenario involves two possible chemicals (cues A and X) that are found in the stomach (e.g., ubitone, dichlorparylate). The outcome is the survival of a bacterial culture (e.g., *E. Chronismus*). According to the scenario the bacteria may have differential likelihoods of survival in the presence and absence of the chemicals. Moreover, it is possible that either or both chemicals may aid or hinder the survival of the bacteria. Therefore it is possible to arrange contingencies from −1 to +1 with survival of the bacterial culture for A and X. For example if the bacteria always survived in the absence of X [$P(US \mid no\,X) = 1$] but never survived in its presence [$P(US \mid X) = 0$] the contingency ΔP_X would be −1. If $P(US \mid no\,X) = .25$ and $P(US \mid X) = .75$ then $\Delta P_X = .5$. The critical feature of these experiments was that, unlike in the experiment by Wagner et al. (1968), we could program trials involving the presence and absence of both X and A so all four cells of the contingency table were defined within the focal set of trials. In our original experiments we paired both positive moderate, zero, and negative moderate contingencies of X ($\Delta P_X = -.5, 0,$ and .5) with either perfect positive, zero or perfect negative contingencies of A ($\Delta P_A = -1, 0,$ and 1). We found that perfect contingencies reduced judgments of X regardless of the polarity of either contingency (see Baker et al., 1996; Baker, Vallée-Tourangeau, & Murphy, 2000, for a discussion of one exception). These experiments were, we believe, the first demonstrations of the relative validity effect with positive and negative contingencies. Moreover they were the first demonstration of cue competition with contingencies involving outcomes in the presence and absence of A and X.

Deterministic Versus Probabilistic Cue Competition

Cue competition as already described can be seen empirically as a competition between contingencies and can be modeled computationally by conditional ΔPs. Moreover, this mechanism can be modeled with at least moderate success by any of the three algorithms we have been considering. However there is an important procedural difference between the treatments that has not been closely investigated. This can be illustrated by considering the original experiment by Wagner et al. (1968). In the jargon of casual reasoning a deterministic relation between a cue and an outcome is one in which the relation is perfect. For example, in the AX^+ versus BX^- discrimination each compound is deterministically related to the outcome. Every time subjects are presented with either compound they can be perfectly certain of the outcome. Moreover, compared to a probabilistic relation very little information must be retained to perfectly conceptualize the procedure. Only one exemplar trial for each compound need be maintained to respond perfectly to this contingency. However the relation in the $AX^{+/-}$ versus $BX^{+/-}$ treatment is probabilistic and the observer is never certain as to what the outcome on any given trial may be. Moreover, to discriminate various probabilistic contingencies from one another, more than one exemplar of each compound must be maintained. Therefore it is quite possible that cue competition might reflect the procedural difference between probabilistic and deterministic contingencies and not a direct competition of some sort between A and X contingency.

We have described the probabilistic versus deterministic dichotomy from a human casual reasoning perspective but thinking in animal learning has also reflected this distinction. For example, the attentional theory of Pearce and Hall (1980) stipulates that attention and learning to cues will be maintained as long as there is uncertainty concerning the outcome. Therefore attention will be maintained much longer on a partial reinforcement schedule (probabilistic) than on a continuous reinforcement schedule (deterministic). These differences in attention will generate different levels of learning about cues that are present.

If cue competition reflects a competition of contingencies and not this probabilistic versus deterministic distinction, it is important to investigate cue competition in a situation in which all the contingencies are probabilistic. We reported one experiment in which we did that. Baker et al. (1993) exposed subjects to a contingency of $\Delta P_X = .5$ for cue X and $\Delta P_A = .8$ for cue A and still found that the higher contingency to A reduced judgments of X. Although a contingency of $\Delta P_A = .8$ seems quite different from 1 it actually represents conditional probabilities of $P(US \mid A) = .9$ and $P(US \mid no\ A) = .1$. Thus it does not contain many disconfirming instances from the deterministic contingencies of $P(US \mid A) = 1$ and $P(US \mid no\ A) = 0$. Moreover because the actual frequencies of events were determined stochastically from the participants' own behavior, it is entirely possible that at least some of the participants were exposed to a deterministic relation for at least the first 20 trials. It is thus possible that the probabilistic A contingency was reacted to as if it was deterministic.

The preceding considerations led us to collaborate with Hirsch and Levine to carry out several experiments investigating cue competition in a probabilistic setting. We used Mehta's scenario involving the effect of chemicals on the survival of a bacteria culture. There were four treatments. In each treatment, participants were exposed to the same low but discriminable contingency for the target cue X ($\Delta P_X = .33$). This contingency was paired with four different A contingencies varying in equal steps from 0 to 1. The four treatments were labeled .33/0, .33/.34, .33/.67, and .33/1 where .33 was the moderately positive X contingency and the second number was the variable A contingency. The overall outcome density in all four treatments was constant at .5. The 24 undergraduate participants each observed all four treatments. Each treatment consisted of 48 trials. As in our earlier experiments the students were asked to predict whether the outcome would occur on each trial but again the critical data came after 24 trials and after 48 trials when they were asked to estimate the causal importance of A and X.

The second set of contingency estimates for the two chemicals A and X is shown in Fig. 7.6. This figure shows quite clearly that judgments of the moderate predictor X were influenced by the contingency of the second predictor A. The critical question in this experiment was whether we would find a relative validity effect in a probabilistic preparation. To test this the crucial comparison directly compares treatments .33/0 and .33/.67 and this comparison was reliable. A further empirical question was whether cue competition can be viewed as a competition of contingencies and not a function of contrasting probabilistic and deterministic treatments. The apparently linear trend in estimates of X contingency as a function of A contingency is consistent with this. The statistical analyses support this assumption because there was a large reliable linear trend. Closer inspection will show, however, that the difference between treatment .33/.67 and the deterministic treatment .33/1 was larger than any of the others. This observation was supported by the presence of a small reliable quadratic trend. Thus there may have been an effect of the deterministic treatment above and beyond the contrast between contingencies of A and X. However, an argument stipulating that the interaction of contingency information is not linear for high ΔP_A is equally justified. It might also be noted that the judgments of A, although very close to linear, also show the greatest difference between .33/.67 and .33/1. Al-

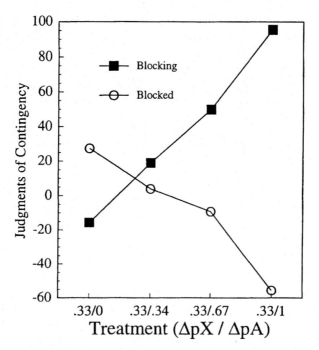

FIG 7.6. Mean judgments in the probabilistic blocking experiment. Judgments of the blocked stimulus represent the stimulus X that was always defined by a moderate .33 contingency. The blocking stimulus's contingency ranged from $\Delta P = 0$ to $\Delta P = 1$.

though not reliable, this difference is attenuated by a possible ceiling effect and could reflect a subjective enhancement of the perfect contingency. It must be emphasized that the statistical evidence for the preceding arguments is weak at best and that the main conclusion that can be drawn from this experiment is that cue competition can be robustly demonstrated in nondeterministic preparations (see also Van Hamme & Wasserman, 1993; Wasserman, 1974).

Four of our preceding theoretical analyses make predictions here and these predictions are shown in the four panels of Fig. 7.7. When compared with Fig. 7.6 it can be seen that all four agree with the general form of the data. They all predict that judgments of X will decline as A contingency increases and they all show that judgments of A will increase. Moreover each of the models predicts that the functions will cross at about the .33/.34 treatment. Nonetheless each of the theories fails to predict the magnitude of the cue competition. They each predict that judgments of X in the .33/1 contingency will be either at or somewhat above the judgments of X in the .33/0 contingency. Actual judgments of X in the .33/1 treatment were about 40 judgment scale points lower (i.e., one fifth the possible range) than were judgments of X in treatment .33/0. This is also shown in the relative ranges of judgments of X and A. The range of judgments of X as a proportion of judgments of A, which reflects the relative size of blocking compared to a 0 to 1 difference in actual contingency, is .75. With the exception of Pearce's model, which is quite accurate, the predicted size of the cue competition effect compared to the range of the stronger cue is much smaller for our algorithms. For the Rescorla–Wagner model this probably reflects the previously observed fact that in general it predicts quite small relative validity effects (Gallistel, 1990).

One other interesting feature is that both conditionalized ΔPs and the computational comparator model predict no difference between judgments of X in the .33/0 and the .33/.34 contingencies. They predict this because each reduces estimates of a contingency if there is a higher comparison stimulus around and in these cases $\Delta P_X = .33$ is either the highest or ties for the highest contingency. (See Table 7.3).

Summary of Probabilistic Cue Competition

The conclusions are similar to those of each of the previous sections. The concept of contingency is important for understanding cue competition effects and probabilistic cue competition. Although several of our possible simple algorithms make predictions that are somewhat congruent with this conclusion, none of them adequately accounts for

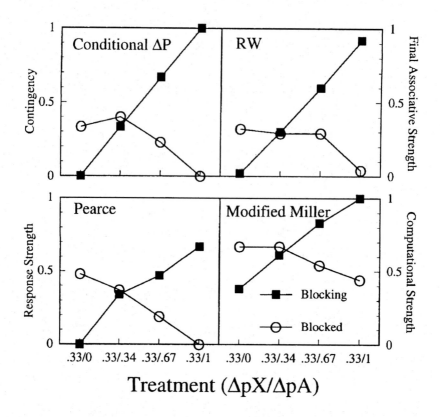

FIG 7.7. Predictions from four possible models of human contingency judgment for the probabilistic blocking experiment. The models are ΔP, Rescorla and Wagner (1972), Pearce (1987), and a modified version of Miller's comparator hypothesis.

the details of our students' judgments. Again we are left with the conclusion that, at a computational level, biological systems compute contingency. No simple algorithm can account for these computations.

CUE COMPETITION IN RATS

Because the original relative validity experiment by Wagner et al. (1968) was designed at a time when the emphasis in conditioning was on the conditional probability of outcomes in the presence of the CS [$P(US \mid CS)$] the design is not ideal for a contingency analysis. We have already mentioned that X was present on all trials so its contingency was unde-

TABLE 7.3. Trial Type Frequencies for Probabilistic Blocking Experiment.

Trial Type	33 | 0	33 | 34	33 | 67	33 | 100
AX→ O	8	11	13	16
X→ O	8	5	3	0
A→ O	4	7	7	8
No A and no X→O	4	1	1	0
AX→ no O	4	3	1	0
X→ no O	4	5	7	8
A→no O	8	7	3	0
No A and no X→ no O	8	9	13	16
Total O	24	24	24	24
Total no O	24	24	24	24
$P(O \mid X)$	0.67	0.67	0.67	0.67
$P(O \mid$ no X$)$	0.33	0.33	0.33	0.33
ΔP_x	0.33	0.33	0.33	0.33
$P(O \mid A)$	0.50	0.64	0.83	1.00
$P(O \mid$ no A$)$	0.50	0.30	0.17	0.00
ΔP_A	0	0.34	0.67	1.00

Note. Causal candidate X's contingency is 0.33 on all four treatments, and causal candidate A's contingency varies from 0 to 1. 0 = outcome.

fined. Also the contingencies for A, B, and X were not equal in the AX$^{+/-}$, BX$^{+/-}$ control group. Moreover because of the design of the experiment, there were twice as many X trials as there were A and B trials. Furthermore, the design of our human cue competition experiments allowed us to investigate the full set of contingencies between the outcome and A and X because it was possible to present outcomes in the presence and absence of X. No study using rats has investigated cue competition with outcomes occurring in the presence and absence of X. Moreover, the contextual control of responding in cue competition experiments has been the subject of little analysis. This is important because the context is a critical element that mediates cue sensitivity to covariation in the Rescorla–Wagner model. Finally in our human experiments a strong positive contingency would often reduce judgments of a zero contingency (e.g., Baker et al., 1993). This finding is of interest because it is difficult to reconcile with the Rescorla–Wagner model and the conditional ΔPs. There are few data on the influence of a positive contingency on a zero contingency in conditioning preparations.

We modified the design of our human contingency experiments to investigate some of these issues. In this experiment (Murphy, 1993) a visual stimulus served as the target stimulus X. It was present on half of the trials in each of six treatments. For two of the treatments X was involved in a moderate positive contingency with food [$P(US \mid CS) = .75$, $P(US \mid no\ food) = .25$, $\Delta P = .5$]. This is the treatment for X called M.5 in our earlier experiment. The four other treatments all had a zero contingency between X and the food. Two of the zero treatments used the moderate density zero contingency (M0) from the previous experiment [$P(US \mid CS) = P(US \mid no\ CS) = .5$]. The other two used the high-density zero contingency [H0; $P(US \mid CS) = P(US \mid no\ CS) = .75$]. The reason that there were two sets of zero contingencies was that M0 controls for the number and density of outcomes in the positive contingencies and H0 controls for the number of X–outcome pairings.

Two auditory stimuli served as analogues to the comparison stimuli (A and B) in the original relative validity experiment (Wagner et al., 1968). Either A or B was present on any trial. A and B were either perfectly correlated with the outcome (all A trials signaled food and all B trials signaled no food) or they were uncorrelated with food (each signaled the same proportion of food presentations). The correlated procedure is called a *true discrimination* (referred to as T in group designations) and the uncorrelated procedure is called a *pseudo-discrimination* (referred to as P). We used factorial design in which each A, B contingency was paired with the three X contingencies. The three treatments with correlated A, B (TM.5, TM0, and TH0) represent treatments in which A and B are relatively more valid than X. The three treatments PM.5, PM0, and PH0 all involve an A, B contingency that is either equal to or lower than the X contingency. Comparing the level of responding controlled by X in these treatments allows us to determine:

1. Whether cue competition can be observed in rats with moderate positive contingencies involving outcomes in the presence and absence of X (compare TM.5 with PM.5).

2. Whether cue competition can be observed in rats with zero X contingencies just as it is in our human data.

In addition to observing responding during the cues we also recorded magazine entries during the 10 sec before the trials (pre-CS period). This measure, which assesses contextual control of responding allows us to evaluate the possible relative validity effects of the A, B contingency and the X contingency on contextual conditioning. We have found such an effect in an operant experiment (Murphy et al., 1998). If such effects are robust they can pose problems for the Rescorla–Wagner model and for the interpretation of relative validity experiments in general. Furthermore, knowing the level of overall responding controlled by the context allows us to determine contingency effects even if possible density or cue competition effects influence the overall level of responding. A CS that is perceived as correlated with the US might well increase the level of responding above that controlled by the context regardless of the baseline level of responding.

Procedural Details. Sixty rats were divided into six equal groups. The duration of all stimuli was 10 sec. Stimulus X was the illumination of the house light and Stimuli A and B were a 2000-Hz tone and a 10-Hz string of clicks. The number of occurrences of each trial type as well as the calculation of the unconditional contingencies for A, B, and X is shown in Table 7.4. Discrimination training continued for 9 days. There were 80 trials each day. On each trial either Stimulus A or B occurred and on half of the trials X was compounded with Stimulus A or B. In the four medium-density contingencies (PM.5, TM.5, PM0, and PM0) there were equal numbers of A, B, and X trials. Food occurred on half of the trials. However, for A to predict all the outcomes in the high-density treatments there were 60 A, 20 B, and 40 X presentations. Sixty of these trials terminated with food.

Following the discrimination training all animals received an extinction test to the light. The light was presented 40 times without reinforcement. On the test, responding during the pre-CS and the CS periods was recorded and converted to log units.

Results

The animals in the three true discrimination groups (TM.5, TM0, and TH0) all learned the discrimination at an equivalent rate in spite of the different numbers of reinforced and nonreinforced trials in the moderate and high density conditions.

TABLE 7.4. Event Frequencies for the Relative Validity Experiment Using Rats.

Events	TM.5	PM.5	TM0	PM0	TH0	PH0
AX→US	30	15	20	10	30	15
A→US	10	5	20	10	30	15
BX→US	0	15	0	10	0	15
B→US	0	5	0	10	0	15
AX→no US	0	5	0	10	0	5
A→no US	0	15	0	10	0	5
BX→no US	10	5	20	10	10	5
B→no US	30	15	20	10	10	5
A table						
All A→US	40	20	40	20	60	30
Al A→no US	0	20	0	20	0	10
No A→US	0	20	0	20	0	30
N A→no US	40	20	40	20	20	10
$P(US \mid A) =$	1	0.5	1	0.5	1	0.75
$P(US \mid no\ A) =$	0	0.5	0	0.5	0	0.75
$\Delta P_A =$	1	0	1	0	1	0
B table						
All B→US	0	20	0	20	0	30
All B→no US	40	20	40	20	20	10
No B→US	40	20	40	20	60	30
No B→no US	0	20	0	20	0	10
$P(US \mid B) =$	0	0.5	0	0.5	0	0.75
$P(US \mid no\ B) =$	1	0.5	1	0.5	1	0.75
$\Delta P_B =$	−1	0	−1	0	−1	0

Events	TM.5	PM.5	TM0	PM0	TH0	PH0
Target cue X table						
All X→US	30	30	20	20	30	30
All X→no US	10	10	20	20	10	10
No X→US	10	10	20	20	30	30
No X→no US	30	30	20	20	10	10
$P(US \mid X) =$	0.75	0.75	0.5	0.5	0.75	0.75
$P(US \mid no\ X) =$	0.25	0.25	0.5	0.5	0.75	0.75
$\Delta P_x =$	0.5	0.5	0	0	0	0
$P(US \mid X\ no\ A) =$	0	0.75	0	0.5	0	0.75
$P(US \mid no\ X\ no\ a) =$	0	0.25	0	0.5	0	0.75
$\Delta P_{X \mid no\ A} =$	0	0.5	0	0	0	0

Note. A and B = auditory stimuli; X = target visual stimulus; T and D = true and pseudo-discrimination groups; M = moderate US density; H = high US density.

The results of the critical test to the light are shown in Fig. 7.8. This figure shows that the A, B contingency influenced the rate of lever pressing during the pre-CS and during X for all treatments. The fact that responding during X is reduced by the presence of a highly correlated cue that was present during training in both the contingent X group (TM.5) and the two zero contingency X groups replicates some of our earlier results in human causal reasoning. The significant difference in responding to X in Groups TM.5 and PM.5 is the traditional comparison of a relative validity experiment.

The main difference between performance-based theories like the comparator and cue competition theories is whether control of responding by X is reduced because the animals fail to learn the X–US association during training or because of a retrospective decision. Although there have been several quite elegant indirect experiments designed to investigate this question (Kauffman & Bolles, 1981; Miller & Schachtman, 1985) it has not been directly tested. However this experiment allows such a test. The information value of X can be measured in

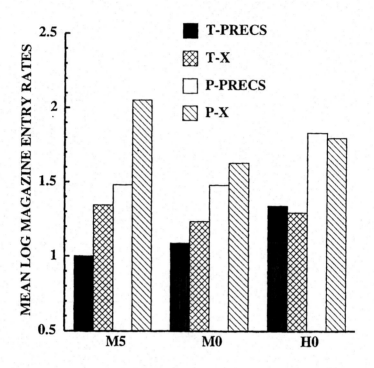

FIG 7.8. Mean responding during the pre-CS and to X in the relative validity experiment using rats. T and P refer to the true and pseudo-discrimination groups. M and H represent moderate and high US densities. The numbers represent ($\Delta P \times$ 100).

two ways. First, and this is what we have described up to this point, the absolute level of responding controlled by X may be assessed. According to this measure, responding to X was degraded in all three true discrimination treatments. However if we consider the results of the three pseudo-discrimination groups (these groups for which responding to X should not be affected by the A, B contingency), there is an effect of density on response rate. The high-density zero X correlation response rates are higher than all the medium-density zero correlation rates (compare M0 and H0). Moreover if we compare the response rates to X in the Groups PM.5 and PH0 it would appear that the response rates are very similar. Inspection of Table 7.4 will show that these two treatments have a similar number of X–US pairings. It could be concluded that the apparent sensitivity to the X contingency (i.e., $\Delta P_X = .5$ vs. $\Delta P_X = 0$) shown in the comparison of PM0 and PM.5 is simply a consequence of differences in X–US pairings. This is equivalent to a failed cross-density comparison from our earlier experiments.

However, the sensitivity to the information value or contingency of X can be assessed in a second way. If X is relatively informative, then adding it to the context should elevate responding. There is a large reliable difference in responding during the pre-CS and X in Group PM.5. This shows that the animals are, indeed, sensitive to the X contingency. No difference is observed in Groups PH0 and PM0. Therefore we can safely conclude that the rats are sensitive to the contingency between X and the outcome. Because the high level of responding in Group PH0 occurs in both the pre-CS and in X we can further conclude that this reflects the higher overall outcome density in this treatment.

We can now consider the true discrimination treatments in which the A, B contingency suppressed overall responding to X. Here the level of responding to X is similar in all three groups. This might be taken to imply that the presence of a highly contingent A, B suppressed sensitivity to contingency, but again if the X–pre-CS difference is considered a different picture emerges. Again in Treatment TH.5, X reliably elevates responding compared to the pre-CS but this does not occur in the zero X contingency groups. Just as in the pseudo-discrimination groups, the animals were sensitive to the X contingency. However, here this sensitivity occurred even in the presence of a strong cue competition effect from A, B. We can conclude that sensitivity to a moderate cue's contingency with the outcome is not entirely lost when a more contingent cue suppresses responding to that cue. This result is consistent with the performance-based accounts of cue competition. These include the comparator account as well as the similar probabilistic contrast theory and the PowerPC from human casual reasoning.

These data do not eliminate the argument that the strong A, B contingency might somewhat reduce sensitivity to the X contingency. For, although this difference is not reliable, the magnitude of the difference between X and the pre-CS is larger in Group PM.5 than in TM.5. Certainly, because the baseline level of responding differs in these two groups, it is possible that a different transformation of our data might generate a reliable difference between the two treatments. It is equally certain, however, that a different transformation might eliminate the difference. Another way to consider the X–pre-CS differences in the contingent X treatments is to argue that just as the strong A, B contingency suppresses the response rate to X and the pre-CS, so does the modest X contingency cause a relative suppression of context responding. Thus there is a cue competition effect of higher X contingency on the context just as there is a cue competition effect of A, B contingency on X and the context. Finally, it is important to note that the differences in responding to the pre-CS in the six treatments are of about the same magnitude as those to X. Moreover there is considerable overlap of absolute response rates to the pre-CS and X on the test. These latter two points are important for the theoretical analysis of these data that follows.

Theoretical Analysis.   Table 7.5 shows the predictions of Rescorla and Wagner (1972), Pearce (1987) and the computational comparator. Because the Rescorla–Wagner model sometimes computes correlations, its predictions are very close to those of unconditional ΔP. That is there are no large differences in predicted responding to X between any of the zero contingency groups. A large blocking effect is predicted in Group TM.5. This pattern of means to X is not close to the actual empirical means. It must be acknowledged that if the magnitude of means is ignored and only ordinal predictions are considered, then Rescorla–Wagner predicts a general effect of A, B contingency on X. For each X contingency the associative strengths for the correlated true discrimination group are lower than those for the comparable pseudo-discrimination group. However, to take this ordinal relation seriously, there would need to be an extreme nonlinear response rule. For example, Groups TH0 and PH0 differ by about .5 log units in response rate to X and the ratio of their associative strengths is 2, whereas Groups PH0 and PM.5 differ by .2 log units yet the ratio of habit strengths is 6. Certainly no reasonable data transformation or response rule could deal with this difference and maintain predictions concerning response magnitude in our earlier data.

The predictions of Pearce and the computational comparator for responding controlled by X provide a better fit than those of the Rescorla–Wagner model because they predict a realistic magnitude of differences between means and they predict the consistent effect of the true A, B discrimination on response rates to X. Moreover both predict a density effect (compare the two H0 groups with the two M0 groups). Pearce's model, however, because it does not have a direct response competition rule, is driven largely by density. Hence it predicts little difference in responding between the comparable M.5 and M0 groups and predicts that responding will be highest in Group PH0. This prediction does not agree well with the data. The predicted means from the computational comparator agree very well with the observed means of X.

Inspection of the predictions of each of the models for the pre-CS reveals a serious problem. In sharp contrast to the data there is no overlap of predicted strength of responding during X and the pre-CS in any of the models. Moreover, the ratios of ranges of the effect on X and the pre-CS vary from four to nine. When the range and considerable over-

TABLE 7.5. Predictions of the Rescorla–Wagner, Pearce, and Modified Comparator Models for Responding to X in the Relative Validity Experiment Using Rats.

	Rescorla–Wagner		Pearce		Comparator	
	PRECS	X	PRECS	X	PRECS	X
TM.5	0.06	0.20	0.02	0.63	0.06	0.56
PM.5	0.03	0.49	0.03	0.76	0.08	0.75
TM0	0.06	0.11	0.02	0.56	0.06	0.25
PM0	0.10	0.13	0.06	0.74	0.13	0.5
TH0	0.05	0.08	0.01	0.65	0.14	0.56
PH0	0.12	0.16	0.06	0.94	0.19	0.75

Note. T and P = true and pseudo-discrimination groups; M = moderate US density; H = high US density. Numbers represent X's contingency with the US, shown as $(\Delta P \times 100)$.

lap of the means of the empirical data mentioned earlier are considered, it is certain that no monotonic response generation rule or data transformation could allow the empirical data to fit these means.

However the large difference in predicted pre-CS and X response could in principle be accounted for by noting that different stimuli often generate very different conditioned responses. For example, X is a visual stimulus and Holland (1977) showed that lights can generate approach responses (rearing). These responses could compete with magazine entries and reduce the absolute effect of light associative strength on magazine entries. The context on the other hand might not generate responses that compete with magazine entries. Therefore if the context is a very much better substrate for magazine entries than the light, it is possible that this difference could cancel out the large predicted differences in response strength between X and the pre-CS. This is the sort of strategy that is sometimes used to rescue parsimonious associative predictions but it is very post hoc and this difference in response-generating properties would need to be considered in the analysis of our earlier rat experiments that used very similar parameters. Furthermore it would be a very fortuitous coincidence if this response competition would exactly cancel out the several-fold differences in response strength and bring X and pre-CS response tendencies into the same magnitude and range.

Conclusions

We are thus left with the conclusion that the animals are sensitive to the difference between $\Delta P = 0, .5$, and 1 contingencies and that this sensitivity is not lost in cue competition effects. Moreover we have found that a high cue contingency reduces responding to a modest positive contingency, to a zero contingency, and to the context. Finally the modest positive contingency to X suppresses relative responding to the context. Although the design of this experiment is different from the previous one on causal reasoning, we are left with the conclusion that blocking occurs in probabilistic scenarios. Finally, the computational comparator deals reasonably well with response rates during X and during the pre-CS. Nonetheless, the failure of the comparator and the other models to easily account for the similarity of pre-CS and X response rates suggests that these algorithms cannot be offered as simple accounts of the effect of contingency in this experiment.

SUMMARY AND CONCLUSIONS

Rescorla's (1968) early work on contingency learning was partly motivated by a desire to clear up a misunderstanding of contingency. He observed that a common control procedure for excitatory conditioning actually involved a negative correlation between the US and the CS. We have argued that errors such as this arose from the traditional bias toward treating $P(\text{US} \mid \text{CS})$ as the controlling variable in excitatory conditioning. This led psychologists to ignore the equally informative $P(\text{US} \mid \text{no CS})$. In spite of Rescorla's initial demonstration that animals were sensitive to both $P(\text{US} \mid \text{CS})$ and $P(\text{US} \mid \text{no CS})$, the Rescorla–Wagner (1972) model, which provided a rather appealing potential analysis to the problem in terms of traditional temporal contiguity and pairings, led researchers to discount the likelihood that animals "learned" these contingencies (see Papini & Bitterman, 1990). The model provided an account of contingency learning in terms of $P(\text{US} \mid \text{context})$ and $P(\text{US} \mid \text{CS and context})$.

We have argued that the belief that there is nothing left to explain with respect to contingency learning has led researchers to overlook a more complete account of learning contingencies and has led to errors. We have documented how research reports and textbooks have described the contingencies in cue competition experiments incorrectly (e.g., Domjan & Burkhard, 1993; Tarpy, 1997). Many researchers have even argued that cue competition represents a departure from contingency learning and have claimed that cue competition represents a failure to learn and provides evidence against contingency learning (Chapman & Robbins, 1990, Dickinson et al., 1984). Moreover, at the computational level, cue competition is one possible "normative" solution from an information processing perspective. This is encouraging when taken in a functional or evolutionary perspective. It suggests that one of the more important phenomena in associative learning is the success of information processing and not the failure to form associations. Cue competition is, therefore, a potentially adaptive information processing strategy.

Empirically, we have shown that rats and humans are sensitive to contingencies in a wide range of situations. We have replicated Rescorla's early finding that animals are sensitive to contingency and that this sensitivity cannot be discounted as being a consequence of the number of pairings or of outcome density. Nonetheless, animals are simultaneously and, perhaps, independently sensitive to these variables. We also provided evidence that cue competition is found in rats and humans using contingencies involving $P(US \mid CS)$ and $P(US \mid no\ CS)$. We have further shown that cue competition is well characterized as a graded competition between contingencies of the competing stimuli. Moreover, the results of the last relative validity experiment using rats imply that even though strong contingencies degrade responding to weaker ones (the comparison process we wrote about earlier), it seems that animals still maintain some representation of the weaker contingencies.

We also studied the role of the context in our preparations and found that contextual responding was sensitive to the contingencies of A and X and to outcome density. Even within cue selection procedures in which there was always a more valid predictor, the context showed cue selection effects.

One of the arguments offered against contingency sensitivity as an important determinant of conditioning is that theoretical algorithms that are only sensitive to $P(US \mid CS)$ could account for apparent contingency learning. We have argued that this may be a false parsimony, nevertheless, these algorithms rely on the context to modulate contingency sensitivity. This has been so widely accepted that there has been little experimental analysis of this fundamental mechanism. Throughout this chapter we have tested these algorithms. In addition, we have provided a formal computational version of comparator theory. It is clear that none of these algorithms provide a nearly complete description of the interaction between conditioning to the context and the CS. In spite of its apparent parsimony a modestly careful scrutiny of responding controlled by the context refutes this argument against contingency learning.

There is a sentiment against contingency learning that stems from both the traditional desire for parsimony in conditioning and the associationist tradition. This has led to a bias against retrospective reasoning. It is difficult for a research culture steeped in a positivist and eliminativist tradition to accept that an animal might store events and then think about them when they are not there, let alone calculate correlations. This concern should be allayed by the fact that associative structures like the Rescorla–Wagner model can compute correlations. Conditioned responses generated on a test show that animals can represent things that are not there (i.e., the US). Sensory preconditioning is a demonstration that animals can also represent neutral stimuli that are not there. Associative mechanisms do computations on these retrospections. Moreover, once the empirical fact that animals and, particularly, humans reason retrospectively in phenomena like backward blocking was accepted, creative associative solutions to this problem have been offered (e.g., Dickinson & Burke, 1996; Van Hamme & Wasserman, 1994). It is unfortunate that the original bias for $P(US \mid CS)$ delayed this work and the elegant experiments that followed it by 25 years.

Part of the blame can be laid on the doorstep of strong proponents of contingency learning, including ourselves (Baker & Mackintosh, 1977; Baker & Mercier, 1989). They confused the issue of whether contingency representation was a computational phenomenon or represented an actual algorithm for contingency sensitivity. This raised the specter of a homunculus calculating contingencies. The other implication of this research and our other work on causal reasoning is that retrospective contingency calculating algorithms such as modified ΔP, conditional ΔPs, and even PowerPC are not successful at accounting for our rather simple experiments (e.g., Vallée-Tourangeau, Murphy, & Baker, 1998; Vallée-Tourangeau, Murphy, Drew, & Baker, 1998)). Once these unsuccessful algorithms are eliminated we are left with one conclusion: Organisms compute contingencies.

ACKNOWLEDGMENTS

The research reported in this chapter was supported by a National Science and Engineering Research Council of Canada operating grant held by A. G. Baker, a United Kingdom Biotechnology and Biological Sciences Research Council project grant (310/S1093) to Robin A. Murphy, and a United Kingdom Economic and Social Research Council project grant (R000222542) to Frédéric Vallée-Tourangeau.

REFERENCES

Allan, L. G. (1980). A note on measurement of contingency between two binary variables in judgment tasks. *Bulletin of the Psychonomic Society, 15,* 147–149.

Baker, A. G., & Mackintosh, N. J. (1977). Excitatory and inhibitory conditioning following uncorrelated presentations of CS and UCS. *Animal Learning & Behavior, 5,* 315–319.

Baker, A. G., & Mercier, P. (1989). Attention, retrospective processing and cognitive representations. In S. Klein & R. Mowrer (Eds.), *Contemporary learning theories and Pavlovian conditioning and the status of general learning theory* (pp. 85–116). Hillsdale, NJ: Lawrence Erlbaum Associates.

Baker, A. G., Mercier, P., Vallée-Tourangeau, F., Frank, R., & Pan, M. (1993). Selective associations and causality judgments: Presence of a strong causal factor may reduce judgments of a weaker one. *Journal of Experimental Psychology: Learning, Memory, and Cognition, 19,* 414–432.

Baker, A. G., Murphy, R. A., & Vallée-Tourangeau, F. (1996). Associative and normative models of causal induction: Reacting to versus understanding cause. In D. R. Shanks, K. J. Holyoak, & D. L. Medin (Eds.), *The psychology of learning and motivation,* (Vol. 34, pp. 1–45). San Diego, CA: Academic Press.

Baker, A. G., Vallée-Tourangeau, F., & Murphy, R. A. (2000). Asymptotic judgment of cause in a relative validity paradigm. *Memory & Cognition, 28.* 466–479.

Baron, J. (1994). *Thinking and deciding* (2nd ed.). New York: Cambridge University Press.

Blaisdell, A. P., Bristol, A. S., Gunther, L. M., & Miller, R. R. (1998). Overshadowing and latent inhibition counteract each other: Support for the comparator hypothesis. *Journal of Experimental Psychology: Animal Behavior Processes, 24,* 335–351.

Chapman, G. B., & Robbins, S. I. (1990). Cue interaction in human contingency judgment. *Memory & Cognition, 18,* 537–545.

Cheng, P. W. (1997). From covariation to causation: A causal power theory. *Psychological Review, 104,* 367–405.

Cheng, P. W., & Holyoak, K. J. (1995). Complex adaptive systems as intuitive statisticians: Causality, contingency, and prediction. In J.-A. Meyer & H. Roitblat (Eds.), *Comparative approaches to cognition* (pp. 271–302). Cambridge, MA: MIT Press.

Cheng, P. W., & Novick, L. R. (1992). Covariation in natural induction. *Psychological Review, 99,* 365–382.

Cheng, P. W., Park, J., Yarlas, A. S., & Holyoak, K. J. (1996). A causal-power theory of focal sets. In D. R. Shanks, K. J. Holyoak, & D. L. Medin (Eds.), *The psychology of learning and motivation* (Vol. 34, pp. 313–355). San Diego, CA: Academic Press.

Church, R. M. (1997). Quantitative models of animal learning and cognition. *Journal of Experimental Psychology: Animal Behavior Processes, 23,* 379–389.

Cole, R. P., Barnet, R. C., & Miller, R. R. (1995). Effect of relative stimulus validity: Learning or performance deficit? *Journal of Experimental Psychology: Animal Behavior Processes, 21,* 293–303.

Cole, R. P., Gunther, L. M., & Miller, R. R. (1997). Spontaneous recovery from the effect of relative stimulus validity. *Learning and Motivation, 28,* 1–19.

Dickinson, A., & Burke, J. (1996). Within-compound associations mediate the retrospective revaluation of causality judgements. *Quarterly Journal of Experimental Psychology, 49B,* 60–80.

Dickinson, A., Shanks, D. R., & Evenden, J. L. (1984). Judgment of act-outcome contingency: The role of selective attribution. *Quarterly Journal of Experimental Psychology, 36A,* 29–50.

Domjan, M., & Burkhard, B. (1993). *The principles of learning and behavior* (3rd ed.). Pacific Grove, CA: Brooks/Cole.

Einhorn, H. J., & Hogarth, R. M. (1986). Judging probable cause. *Psychological Bulletin, 99,* 3–19.

Estes, W. K. (1959). The statistical approach to learning theory. In S. Koch (Ed.), *Psychology: A study of science* (Vol. 2, pp. 380–492). New York: McGraw-Hill.

Ferster, C. B., & Skinner, B. F. (1957). *Schedules of reinforcement.* New York: Appleton-Century-Crofts.

Gallistel, C. R. (1990). *The Organizations of Learning.* Cambridge: MIT Press.

Gibbon, J., & Balsam, P. (1981). Spreading association in time. In C. M. Locurto, H. S. Terrace, & J. Gibbon (Eds.), *Autoshaping and conditioning theory* (pp. 219–253). New York: Academic Press.

Hallam, S. C., Grahame, N. J., & Miller, R. R. (1992). Exploring the edges of Pavlovian contingency space: An assessment of contingency theory and its various metrics. *Learning and Motivation, 23,* 225–249.

Holland, P. C. (1977). Conditioned stimulus as a determinant of the form of the Pavlovian conditioned response. *Journal of Experimental Psychology: Animal Behavior Processes, 3,* 77–104.

Hull, C. L. (1952). *A behavior system.* New York: John Wiley.

Kamin, L. J. (1969). Selective associations and conditioning. In W. K. Honig & N. J. Mackintosh (Eds.), *Fundamental issues in associative learning* (pp. 42–64). Halifax, Canada: Dalhousie University Press.

Kao, S.-F., & Wasserman, E. A. (1993). Assessment of an information integration account of contingency judgment with examination of subjective cell importance and method of information presentation. *Journal of Experimental Psychology: Learning, Memory & Cognition, 19,* 1363–1386.

Kauffman, M. A., & Bolles, R. C. (1981). A nonassociative aspect of overshadowing. *Bulletin of the Psychonomic Society, 18,* 318–320.

Mackintosh, N. J. (1974). *The psychology of animal learning.* London: Academic Press.

Marr, D. (1982). *Vision: A computational investigation into the human representation and processing of visual information.* San Francisco: Freeman.

Miller, R. R., & Matzel, L. D. (1988). The comparator hypothesis: A response rule for the expression of associations. In G. H. Bower (Ed.), *The psychology of learning and motivation* (Vol. 22, pp. 51–92). San Diego, CA: Academic Press.

Miller, R. R., & Schachtman, T. R. (1985). The several roles of context at the time of retrieval. In P. D. Balsam & A. Tomie (Eds.), *Context and learning* (pp. 167 194). Hillsdale, NJ : Lawrence Erlbaum Associates.

Murphy, R. A. (1993). *Pavlovian conditioning is the consequence of more than just the number of CS–US pairings.* Unpublished master's dissertation, McGill University, Montréal, Canada.

Murphy, R. A. (1999). *Relative contingency learning in Pavlovian conditioning.* Unpublished doctoral dissertation, McGill University. Montréal, Canada.

Murphy, R. A., Baker, A. G.& Fouquet (2000). *Relative validity of the CS and context.* Manuscript submitted for publication.

Murphy, R. A., McDonald, R. J., & Baker, A. G. (1998). Lesions of the hippocampus or fornix do not interfere with the relative validity effect on a discrete stimulus or the context. *Behavioural Brain Research, 92,* 55–66 .

Murphy, R. A., & Vallée-Tourangeau, F. (1999). *Further tests of the Power PC theory of causal induction.* Manuscript submitted for publication.

Odling-Smee, F. J. (1975). The role of background during Pavlovian conditioning. *Quarterly Journal of Experimental Psychology, 27*, 201–209.

Papini, M. R., & Bitterman, M. E. (1990). The role of contingency in classical conditioning. *Psychological Review, 97*, 396–403.

Pearce, J. M. (1987). A model for stimulus generalization in Pavlovian conditioning. *Psychological Review, 94*, 61–73.

Pearce, J. M. (1994). Similarity and discrimination: A selective review and a connectionist model. *Psychological Review, 101*, 587–607.

Pearce, J. M., & Hall, G. (1980). A model for Pavlovian learning: Variations in the effectiveness of conditioned stimuli. *Psychological Review, 87*, 532–552.

Peterson, G. B., Ackil, J. E., Frommer, G. P., & Hearst, E. S. (1972). Conditioned approach and contact behavior toward signals for food or brain-stimulation reinforcement. *Science, 177*, 1009–1011.

Quinsey, V. L. (1971). Conditioned suppression with no CS–US contingency in the rat. *Canadian Journal of Psychology, 25*, 69–82.

Rescorla, R. A. (1967). Pavlovian conditioning and its proper control procedures. *Psychological Review, 74*, 71–80.

Rescorla, R. A. (1968). Probability of shock in the presence and absence of CS in fear conditioning. *Journal of Comparative and Physiological Psychology, 66*, 1–5.

Rescorla, R. A., & Wagner, A. R. (1972). A theory of Pavlovian conditioning: Variations in the effectiveness of reinforcement and non-reinforcement. In A. H. Black & W. F. Prokasy (Eds.), *Classical conditioning II: Current theory and research* (pp. 64–99). New York: Appleton-Century-Crofts.

Shanks, D. R. (1991). Categorization by a connectionist network. *Journal of Experimental Psychology: Learning, Memory, and Cognition, 17*, 433–443.

Shanks, D. R. (1995). *The psychology of associative learning.* Cambridge, UK: Cambridge University Press.

Spellman, B. A. (1996). Conditionalizing causality. In D. R. Shanks, D. L. Medin & K. J. Holyoak (Eds.), *The psychology of learning and motivation: Causal learning* (pp. 167–206). San Diego, CA: Academic Press.

Spence, K. W. (1940). Continuous versus noncontinuous interpretation of discrimination learning. *Psychological Review, 47*, 271–288.

Tanner, J., Rawlins, J. N. P., & Mellanby, J. H. (1987). Manipulation of CS–US conditional probability and of the CS–US trace interval on conditioning to the CS and to background stimulus in a CER situation. *Learning and Motivation, 18*, 371–391.

Tarpy, R. M. (1997). *Contemporary learning theory and research.* New York: McGraw-Hill.

Vallée-Tourangeau, F., Murphy, R. A. & Baker, A. G. (1998). Causal induction in the presence of a perfect negative cue: Contrasting predictions from associative and statistical models. *Quarterly Journal of Experimental Psychology, 51B*, 173–191.

Vallée-Tourangeau, F., Murphy, R. A., Drew, S., & Baker, A. G. (1998). Judging the importance of constant and variable candidate causes: A test of the power PC theory. *Quarterly Journal of Experimental Psychology, 51A*, 65–84.

Van Hamme, L. J., & Wasserman, E. A. (1993). Cue competition in causality judgments: The role of manner of information processing. *Bulletin of the Psychonomic Society, 31*, 457–460.

Van Hamme, L. J., & Wasserman, E. A. (1994). Cue competition in causality judgments: The role of nonpresentation of compound stimulus elements. *Learning and Motivation, 25*, 127–151.

Wagner, A. R. (1981). SOP: A model of automatic memory processing in animal behavior. In N. E. Spear & R. R. Miller (Eds.), *Information processing in animals: Memory mechanisms* (pp. 5–47). Hillsdale, NJ: Lawrence Erlbaum Associates.

Wagner, A. R., Logan, F. A., Haberlandt, K., & Price, T. (1968). Stimulus selection in animal discrimination learning. *Journal of Experimental Psychology, 76,* 171–180.

Waldmann, M. R., & Holyoak, K. J. (1992). Predictive and diagnostic learning within causal models: Asymmetries in cue competition. *Journal of Experimental Psychology: General, 121,* 222–236.

Wasserman, E. A. (1974). Stimulus-reinforcer predictiveness and selective discrimination learning in pigeons. *Journal of Experimental Psychology, 163,* 284–297.

Wasserman, E. A., Elek, S. M., Chatlosh, D. L., & Baker, A. G. (1993). Rating causal relations: Role of probability in judgments of response-outcome contingency. *Journal of Experimental Psychology: Learning, Memory and Cognition, 19,* 174–188.

chapter **8**

Incentive Processes in Instrumental Conditioning

Bernard W. Balleine
University of California, Los Angeles

*T*he shift from behavioral to more identifiably cognitive theories of learning in the 1960s produced two innocent casualties caught, as it were, in the crossfire of competing general approaches. The first casualty was the systematic study of what animals learn in instrumental conditioning and the second was then-burgeoning interest in the role that primary motivational processes play in learning. Nevertheless, although there has been a lack of general interest in these issues, systematic research efforts in the intervening decades have significantly advanced our understanding of them. These advances are described in this chapter as they emerge from investigations of the role that incentive processes play in instrumental conditioning.

Unavoidably, much of the research described in this chapter draws on theories that were current more than 50 years ago, a period that is now often considered "preenlightenment" in psychology. As such, the casual reader may be forgiven for feeling that there can be little of general relevance to contemporary theory and research arising from this approach. This view is, however, mistaken. Contemporary theories make two assumptions about the structure of basic learning processes: (a) that the representation of biologically significant events is innate or hard-wired within the biology, and (b) that motivational processes, in general, play only an ancillary role in learning through modulation of the output of learning processes in performance. As progressively revealed here, current research suggests that both of these assumptions are in need of reconsideration.

THE REPRESENTATIONAL ASSUMPTION

Contemporary theories of animal learning are essentially information processing theories; that is, the explanations of adaptive behavior that these theories generate refer to the formation of associations between event representations of one kind or another. As a consequence, contemporary research in animal learning has almost exclusively employed the Pavlovian conditioning paradigm, using which researchers can control both the kinds of perceptual events and the relations between those events to which the experimental subject is exposed. Nevertheless, although this theoretical and empirical program has been reasonably successful in elaborating the processes involved in learning predictive or signaling relations between events, of necessity, it has left unaddressed other forms of learning that are not easily studied within the Pavlovian paradigm.

Evaluative Conditioning

In common with Pavlov (1927), contemporary analyses of conditioning draw a distinction between classes of stimuli that he referred to as conditioned and unconditioned. However, in line with his rejection of the distinction between instinct and reflex, Pavlov distinguished these classes of stimuli solely in terms of the behavioral responses that they evoke on first presentation. Thus, unconditioned stimuli (or USs) evoke a specific inborn or innate reflex (the UR) on first presentation that conditioned stimuli (or CSs) do not (cf. Pavlov, 1927). Contemporary theorists (e.g., Gallistel, 1990; Mackintosh, 1975; McLaren, Kaye, & Mackintosh, 1989; R. R. Miller & Matzel, 1988; Pearce, 1994; Pearce & Hall, 1980; Rescorla & Wagner, 1972; Sutton & Barto, 1981; Wagner, 1981) typically defer to Pavlov or remain silent with respect to how these classes of stimuli are to be distinguished without recognizing that the information processing approach on which their theories are based adds an important assumption to Pavlov's analysis; that stimulus representation intervenes between stimulus presentation and the behavioral reaction. As illustrated in Fig. 8.1, in essence, this position assumes that behavioral effects, like the UR, are induced by the activation of specific representational structures (or nodes). Hence, from this perspective, to argue that the UR is innate means necessarily to assert that a perceptual representation of that US is innate also.

In fact Pavlov not only adhered to a behavioral definition of the US, he explicitly rejected the existence of innate US representations. In his book Conditioned Reflexes (Pavlov, 1927, Lecture 2) Pavlov's discussion of this issue revolves around a series of demonstrations. In a first demonstration he described the effect of presenting the sound of a metronome, previously paired with food, on the salivary secretion of a dog as follows: "When the sounds from a beating metronome are allowed to fall upon the ear, a salivary secretion begins after 9 seconds, and in the course of 45 seconds eleven drops have been secreted" (p. 22). He next describes the effect of showing food to a dog: "The salivary secretion begins after 5 seconds, and six drops are collected in the course of 15 seconds" (p. 22). These two demonstrations could be used to infer that the actual sight of food and the food recalled on presentation of the metronome increase activity in an innate representation of food and, therefore, consistent with most contemporary accounts, that the salivary secretion in both cases is a result of activation of this representation. Instead, Pavlov argued against this account as follows:

> That the effects of the sight and smell of food is not due to an inborn reflex, but to a reflex which has been acquired in the course of the animal's own individual existence, was shown by experiments carried out by Dr. Zitovich in the laboratory of the late Prof. Vartanov. Dr. Zitovich took several young puppies away from their mother and fed them for a considerable time directly on milk. When the puppies were a few months old he established fistulae of their salivary ducts, and was thus able to measure accurately the secretory activity of the glands. He now showed these puppies some solid food—bread or meat—but no secretion of saliva was evoked. It is evident, therefore, that the sight of food does not itself act as a direct stimulus to salivary secretion. *Only after the puppies have been allowed to eat bread and meat on several occasions does the sight or smell of these food stuffs evoke the secretion.* (p. 23, italics added)[1]

---

[1]This effect has recently been replicated in the study of the development of an appetite for water in weanling rats made thirsty by a subcutaneous injection of hypertonic saline. Although rats show physiological sensitivity to dehydration soon after birth, they appear to have to learn about the relation between fluids and dehydration before they will acquire the appetitive responses necessary to seek out, approach, and drink water. Thus, rats weaned onto a liquid diet are very slow to initiate water consumption when dehydrated although, after a single pairing of water and dehydration, they immediately begin drinking when they are subsequently dehydrated (cf. Hall, Arnold, & Myers, 2000).

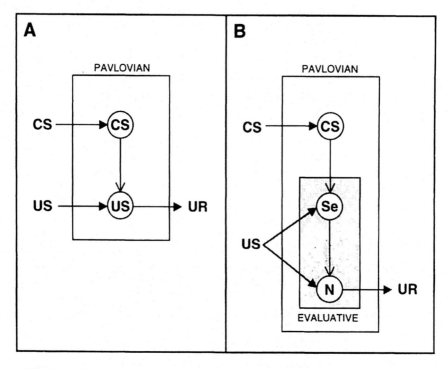

FIG. 8.1.   Two perspectives on Pavlovian conditioning. Fig. 8.1a is a characterization of contemporary views of conditioning and Fig. 8.1b illustrates how this
view could be modified by the inclusion of an evaluative process such as that envisaged by Pavlov (1927). Fixed excitatory connections are illustrated as blocked
arrows (→), acquired excitatory connections as open arrows (→).

By his own definition, Pavlov (1927) clearly did not regard the sight
and smell of food as a US for hungry dogs. Indeed, he obviously regarded the ability of these stimuli to evoke salivation as a learned response; that is, not something generated by an innate representation of
food but by the acquisition of an association between the perceptual features and, as he put it, the "chemical properties of the food itself acting
upon receptors in the mucous membrane of the mouth and tongue" (p.
23). As illustrated in Fig. 8.1, these hints can be interpreted, within a representational approach, to imply that specific sensory features of the US
become capable of eliciting alimentary reflexes through their connection with a system sensitive to the chemosensory stimuli generated on
consummatory contact with food. For want of a better term, this system
is labeled in Fig. 8.1 as the nutritive system (N); that is, a system sensitive to nutritive signals. This connection is, therefore, referred to as an
evaluative connection.

As this analysis suggests, the introduction of an evaluative process appears to add an additional feature to the learning processes that underlie Pavlovian conditioning in contemporary theories and it is easy to see why. Within contemporary theorizing, it is not uncommon to read accounts of Pavlovian processes phrased in informational terms; for example, the CS predicts or signals the US or engenders an expectancy of the US in the animal (cf. Rescorla, 1973). Indeed, it is this kind of analysis that provides much of the basis for discussion of the adaptive significance of Pavlovian processes. However, given Pavlov's own analysis, it is clear that much of this talk of informational variables in Pavlovian conditioning must be predicated on a more fundamental learning process through which the representation of the specific US about which the CS informs the animal is acquired. Evaluative processes can, therefore, be considered critical to the acquisition and expression of predictive relations involving the US representation in Pavlovian conditioning. In fact, as argued in considerably more detail later, they are, perhaps, even more critical in determining what is learned in instrumental conditioning.

Instrumental Conditioning

It is rarely acknowledged that both prediction and control are required for successful adaptation in a changing environment. Although predictive learning provides animals with the capacity to elicit anticipatory responses as a result of learning about associations between events, the adaptive form of these responses is clearly determined by evolutionary processes rather than individual learning. As a consequence, an animal that can engage only in predictive learning is at the mercy of the stability of the causal consequences of these responses. For its responses to remain adaptive in an unstable environment, therefore, the animal must be capable of modifying its behavioral repertoire in the face of changing environmental contingencies; that is, it must be capable of learning to control responses instrumental to gaining access to sources of benefit and avoiding events that can maim or kill. This form of learning is, therefore, often referred to as *instrumental*.

The importance of the distinction between learning processes sensitive to prediction and control was recognized early on in studies of animal learning. Both S. Miller and Konorski (1928) and Skinner (1932) argued that Pavlov's theory of stimulus substitution was unable to account for cases where stimulus control could be demonstrated for responses that were not directly related to the URs to stimulus events. Nevertheless, these authors failed to demonstrate that responses conditioned in these free-operant situations were controlled by the relation to their consequences (i.e., by the instrumental contingency). This was, in fact, first demonstrated by Grindley (1932) using guinea pigs as subjects. He trained his subjects to turn their heads either to the left or the right in the presence of a buzzer to receive access to a carrot. What established that this action was under the control of the action–outcome contingency was the fact that these animals were able to reverse the direction of their head turn when the contingency between direction of head turn and access to the carrot outcome was reversed. Although the relation between the buzzer and carrot delivery was kept constant across phases, the animals were perfectly able to modify their responses during the buzzer in accord with the current contingency between action and outcome.

Grindley (1932) and Skinner (1932) followed Thorndike (1911) in attributing the development of instrumental conditioning to the formation of a stimulus–response (S–R) association, arguing that the presentation of an effective outcome following an action acted to reinforce a connection between a particular environmental stimulus and that action (i.e., between the buzzer and the head turn response). According to this approach, in instrumental conditioning, the outcome of an action does not enter into the associative structure controlling performance of the action. Instead, the outcome acts merely as a catalyst to help cement the association between stimulus and response.

Considerable evidence has accumulated against the S–R conceptualization of what animals learn in instrumental conditioning coming mainly from outcome devaluation studies. The logic behind these demonstrations is straightforward. Animals are first trained to perform an instrumental action for a particular outcome. The evaluation of that outcome is then changed in some way without allowing the animal to experience this change in connection with the action before, finally, the propensity to perform the action is assessed. If initial training merely establishes an S–R association reinforced by the outcome, changing the animals' evaluation of that outcome should have no impact on subsequent performance of the action because the relation between the action and the outcome is not represented within the S–R association. If, however, animals do encode the consequences of their actions during instrumental training, any subsequent change in the animals' evaluation of the outcome should be directly manifest in performance. In fact, in recent years a large number of successful demonstrations of instrumental outcome revaluation have been reported (cf. Colwill & Rescorla, 1986; Dickinson & Balleine, 1994, 1995, for reviews).

The first demonstrations of the outcome devaluation effect used a conditioned taste aversion procedure to change the animals' evaluation of the outcome. For example, Colwill and Rescorla (1985; following Adams & Dickinson, 1981) trained hungry rats to perform two instrumental actions, lever pressing and chain pulling, with one action earning access to food pellets and the other earning access to a sucrose solution. The rats were then given several trials in which they were allowed to consume one of these outcomes with the levers and chains withdrawn and were then made ill by an injection of the emetic agent lithium chloride (LiCl). Over trials this treatment strongly suppresses consumption of the outcome paired with illness, an example of a conditioned taste aversion. All animals were then given a choice test on the levers and chains conducted in extinction, in the absence of either of the outcomes. Although S–R accounts should predict no effect of this treatment, Colwill and Rescorla (1985) found that animals performed fewer of the action whose training outcome was subsequently paired with LiCl than the other action, indicating that the rats indeed encoded the consequences of their actions.

One of the best demonstrations of the potency of the outcome devaluation procedure is Rescorla's (1990, Experiment 1) finding that, in instrumental conditioning, even motivationally incidental features of the instrumental outcome are encoded. In that experiment, thirsty rats were trained to lever press and to chain pull with both actions earning water. For one action, however, the water was made sour through the use of a small quantity of hydrochloric acid. The other action earned water made bitter through the use of a small quantity of quinine. An aversion was then conditioned to either the bitter or sour water by pairing it with LiCl, after which an extinction test was conducted on the levers and chains. In spite of the fact that the critical motivational feature (i.e., the fluidic property) was the same for both of the instrumental outcomes, Rescorla found that animals performed fewer of the action that, in training, had delivered the poisoned outcome, indicating that they encoded the incidental sour and bitter taste features of the water outcomes as consequences of their instrumental actions.

Rescorla's (1990) demonstration is important because it shows that the evaluation of an outcome can be mediated by a motivationally arbitrary feature, its taste. If this devaluation treatment modified the degree of thirst or the animal's encoding of the motivationally relevant properties of fluid outcomes, then the performance of both of the actions should have been reduced on test and to a similar degree. As such, this finding provides evidence for a highly specific encoding of the instrumental outcome, one that allows for the modification of the value of a taste feature while leaving the value of features common to the other fluid outcome (e.g., temperature, texture, visual features, etc.) relatively unaffected.

The importance of these demonstrations of the outcome revaluation effect lies in the fact that together they provide strong evidence that, in instrumental conditioning, animals encode the specific features of the consequences or outcome of their instrumental actions.[2] Furthermore, these studies show that instrumental performance is not only determined by the encoding of the action–outcome relation, but also by the animals' current evaluation of the outcome. In recent years, considerable attention has been paid to the processes that contribute to the encoding of the action–outcome relation and so these processes are not considered further here (cf. Colwill & Rescorla, 1986; Dickinson, 1994; Rescorla, 1991). Instead, in the remainder of this chapter, I focus on the second determinant of instrumental performance: the processes that contribute to the animals' evaluation of the instrumental outcome.

In the next section I begin to address this issue by examining how conditioning a taste aversion to the instrumental outcome works to modify the animals' evaluation of the outcome and so change the course of its instrumental performance.

INSTRUMENTAL OUTCOME DEVALUATION

Perhaps the simplest account of the way taste aversion learning works to devalue the instrumental outcome can be derived from accounts of aversive conditioning generally, according to which pairing the instrumental outcome with illness changes the evaluation of the outcome through the formation of a predictive association between the food or fluid and the aversive state induced by illness. The result of an effective pairing of the outcome with illness is, therefore, that the animal learns that the outcome now signals that aversive consequence. From this perspective, the outcome devaluation effect is the product of a practical inference process through which a previously encoded action–outcome relation is combined with learning that the outcome signals an aversive consequence to reduce subsequent performance of the action.

In contrast, Garcia (1989) introduced a more complex account, according to which the change in the evaluation of the outcome induced by taste aversion learning is not due to changing what the outcome predicts but how it tastes. Garcia related the change in taste to negative

---

[2]It is sometimes argued that devaluation effects of this kind can be explained in terms of Pavlovian associations between cues, such as the context or manipulanda, and specific outcomes and that this effect, therefore, does not provide evidence that, in instrumental conditioning, animals encode the action–outcome relation (cf. Bindra, 1972, 1978; Konorski, 1967; Rescorla & Solomon, 1967; Trapold & Overmier, 1972). By equating exposure to the two outcomes during training, the studies described suggest associations with contextual cues alone cannot explain this kind of effect. Other studies have found devaluation effects when manipulanda cues were controlled in a similar fashion (e.g. Bolles, Holtz, Dunn, & Hill, 1980; Dickinson et al., 1996). As such, these kinds of explanations for the outcome devaluation effect are not considered further here.

feedback from a system sensitive to illness that he identified as inducing a disgust or distaste reaction. It is important to see that this view implies that taste aversion learning involves not one learning process but two: (a) an effective pairing of the outcome with illness initially enables a connection between the sensory properties of the outcome and processes sensitive to illness, and (b) this association is activated when the outcome is subsequently contacted to generate a distaste reaction and allow the animal to associate the outcome representation with disgust or distaste. Importantly, this account predicts that, to induce outcome devaluation, it is not sufficient merely to pair the outcome with an injection of LiCl. Rather, a change in value is not effected until the second process is engaged when the outcome is again contacted.

The procedures that are standardly employed to induce outcome devaluation do not differentiate between these two accounts of taste aversion learning. This is because the conditioning of an aversion to the outcome is usually conducted using multiple pairings of the outcome with illness. Clearly the pairings themselves would be sufficient to establish a signaling relation between the outcome and an aversive consequence. However, the fact that the animals were allowed to contact the outcome on subsequent pairings could have provided the opportunity for the animals to associate the outcome representation with distaste. If a substantial aversion to the outcome could be conditioned with a single pairing of the outcome with illness, however, then these accounts of outcome devaluation make divergent predictions.

A recent experiment designed to test these predictions is used to explain why this is so (cf. Dickinson & Balleine, 1994, for a review of earlier studies). In this experiment, the design of which is illustrated in the top panel of Fig. 8.2, 16 thirsty rats were trained to press two levers, one to left and the other to the right of a central magazine, on a concurrent schedule such that pressing one lever delivered orange-flavored sucrose (i.e., R1→O1 + O2) and pressing on the other lever delivered grape-flavored sucrose (i.e., R2→O1 + O3). Immediately after this session half of the rats, Group D, were given a single injection of LiCl (0.15 M; 20ml/kg) and the other half, Group N, were injected with saline. The day following this treatment all the rats were allowed to drink a small quantity of either the orange- or the grape-flavored sucrose before being given a 10-min choice extinction test on the two levers the next day.

The two accounts of outcome devaluation just presented make opposing predictions as to what the rats in Group D will do during the extinction test. Although some mutual overshadowing might be anticipated, if the injection of LiCl was effective in Group D, the signaling account should predict that both the orange- and the grape-flavored sucrose will become associated with illness. The subsequent extinction of the aversion to one of the two compounds during the reexposure phase should, however, weaken the association between that compound and illness with the effect that rats in Group D should be predicted to perform more responses on the lever that, in training, delivered the reexposed outcome than on the other lever. In contrast, Garcia's (1989) account anticipates that the injection given after initial training establishes a connection between the two outcomes and a structure sensitive to illness but should not, itself, be sufficient to induce outcome devaluation. On this account, devaluation is only accomplished when the outcome is subsequently contacted and so, in Group

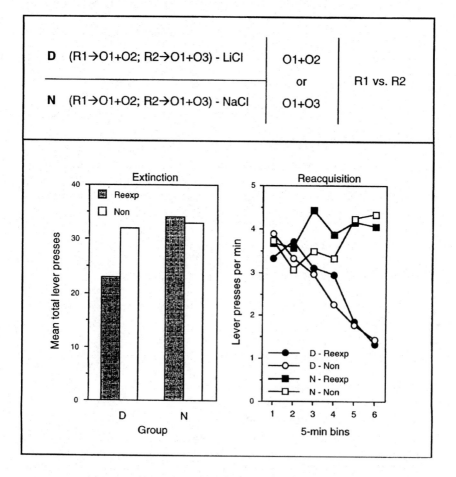

FIG. 8.2.   The design (top panel) and results (lower panels) of a recent experiment conducted to investigate the role of incentive learning in outcome devaluation. R1, R2 = left or right lever press response; O1 = sucrose; O2, O3 = orange or grape flavor; LiCl = lithium chloride injection; NaCl = sodium chloride injection.

D, only the outcome presented during the reexposure phase should be devalued. This account predicts, therefore, that, on test, rats in Group D should perform fewer responses on the lever that, in training, delivered the reexposed outcome than on the other lever.

The results are presented in the lower left panel of Fig. 8.2, which makes clear that the results of this study offer support for Garcia's (1989) position. On test, all eight of the rats in Group D performed fewer responses on the lever that, in training, had delivered the outcome to which they were reexposed. This result was not due merely to reexposure; the performance of rats in Group N did not differ during the test. Finally, this result does not appear to be due to any detectable effect of reexposure on the strength of the association conditioned by the LiCl injection. On the days after the extinction test, rats were given a reacquisition session with water delivered on both levers before a test in which lever pressing again delivered the outcomes assigned during training. As is clear from the right panel of Fig. 8.2, responding on both levers declined to a similar degree in Group D and at a similar rate during that session. Responding in Group N did not decline on either lever.

Together with other similar findings (e.g., Balleine & Dickinson, 1991, 1992), the results of this experiment suggest that outcome devaluation depends on the interaction of two learning processes. The first process involves the conditioning of an association between the outcome and processes that are activated by the induction of illness by LiCl. The failure of this learning process to directly impact on instrumental performance suggests that it alone is not sufficient to induce outcome devaluation. Rather, it appears to be necessary for feedback from this first learning process to become associated with the specific sensory features of the outcome itself for devaluation to occur. It would seem plausible to suppose that the first process is something akin to that derived earlier from Pavlov's analysis of the way animals acquire the US representation in Pavlovian conditioning. As such, this learning process is referred to here as *evaluative conditioning*. The second learning process appears to be critical for animals to establish the current rewarding properties of the instrumental outcome on the basis of evaluative processing of this kind. In the past, this second learning process has been identified as *incentive learning* (Dickinson & Balleine, 1993, 1994, 1995).

The Interaction of Evaluative and Incentive Processes

The kind of structure that the preceding discussion suggests underlies the way that taste aversion learning acts to devalue the instrumental outcome is illustrated in Fig. 8.3. Pairing the instrumental outcome with illness produces an association between a representation of the sensory properties of the outcome (O) and a structure sensitive to the effects of illness. In line with previous analyses (Dickinson & Balleine, 1994; Rozin & Fallon, 1987), this structure is identified as disgust (D). Thus, it is this association between O and D that is referred to here as underlying evaluative conditioning (EC). The conditioning of this association effectively opens a feedback loop that provides the basis for the second learning process proposed to underlie outcome devaluation, that of incentive learning (IL). This learning process is engaged when the outcome is subsequently contacted. This contact activates the representation of the outcome that, through prior evaluative conditioning, increases the activity of the disgust system. This latter activity produces negative feedback, Garcia's disgust or distaste reaction, that is contingent on contact with the outcome. It is this feedback that, in this account of incentive learning, is associated with the representation of the food or fluid itself and acts to change the animal's evaluation of the outcome.[3]

Of the features of this account, one of the more controversial is the suggestion that the pairing of the outcome with illness establishes a connection between the outcome representation and a disgust system; that is, a system that is activated specifically by the detection of gastric malaise. An alternative, and perhaps more parsimonious suggestion would be to bring this analysis into line with analyses of aversive conditioning generally to propose that the outcome representation becomes associated with an aversive system, such as that envisaged by Konorski (1967) and Mowrer (1960). Indeed, in support of this contention, Pelchat, Grill, Rozin, and Jacobs (1983) showed that, when a flavored solution is paired with an electric shock, the consumption of that solution

---

[3]It should be noted that this account differs slightly from other analyses of incentive learning (e.g., Dickinson & Balleine, 1994). Previously it was proposed that pairing the outcome with illness allows the outcome to activate the disgust system but directly and not via the representation of the outcome itself. Incentive learning was proposed as conditioning an association between the representation of the instrumental outcome and the disgust system when the outcome was subsequently contacted that, through a fixed inhibitory connection between the disgust system and the outcome representation, could act to reduce activation of the outcome representation. A problem with this account lies in the fact that, as it stands, the initial connection between the food presentation and disgust could only be formed if food delivery and illness occur contiguously. In fact, taste aversion learning is observed when considerable delays intervene between food presentation and the induction of illness. Indeed, this form of learning is often cited as the strongest evidence that contiguity is not necessary for conditioning to occur (e.g., Rescorla, 1988). As such it would appear to be a requirement that the initial connection is mediated by the outcome representation. As a consequence, the negative feedback induced when the outcome is subsequently contacted is argued here to be mediated by an inhibitory connection, although, as becomes apparent later, this formulation, itself, stands in need of further clarification.

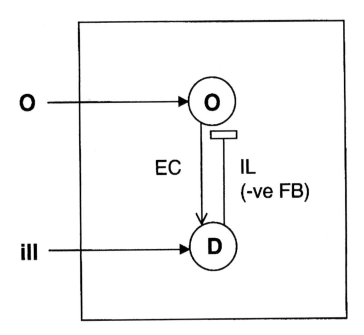

FIG. 8.3. An illustration of a possible structure underlying evaluative (EC) and incentive learning (IL) processes in instrumental outcome devaluation. Fixed excitatory connections are illustrated as blocked arrows (→), acquired excitatory connections as open arrows (→), and acquired inhibitory connections as an open rectangle (—[]). O = outcome; D = disgust system.

is reduced and to a degree comparable to that induced by pairing the solution with illness. There are, however, several reasons for resisting the suggestion that these effects on consumption were induced by the same associative connection.

Grill and Berridge (1985) demonstrated that the ingestive consummatory response patterns elicited by a palatable commodity, such as sucrose, change after it has been paired with illness to resemble the rejection responses produced by unconditionally noxious substances, such as quinine. The same is not true, however, when sucrose is paired with electric shock. Although Pelchat et al. (1983) found that the consumption of a flavor was reduced when it was paired with shock, their animals did not display any rejection reactions when the flavor was subsequently contacted; indeed they continued to display the ingestive reactions produced prior to the pairing. Rejection reactions were, however, produced in their experiments when the flavor was contacted after it had previously been paired with illness together with a reduction in ingestive reactions. This result suggests that, at least in this situation, taste aversion learning is not fully commensurate with other forms of aversive conditioning. In fact, there is also direct evidence that devaluing the instrumental outcome by conditioned taste aversion differs from that induced by other forms of aversive conditioning.

In assessing this issue, we capitalized on the fact that intraperitoneal injections of hypertonic LiCl (i.e., with a concentration greater than 0.18 M) not only produce illness, they also produce somatic pain. Indeed, when thirsty rats were given a single injection of 0.6 M LiCl (5 ml/kg) following a session in which they were trained to press a single lever for a sucrose solution, they reduced their performance on the lever (relative to delay-injected controls) in a subsequent extinction test even if they were not reexposed to the sucrose prior to the test (Balleine & Dickinson, 1992, Experiment 1; Rescorla, 1992). This effect clearly contrasts with that induced when the LiCl is injected in a hypotonic concentration, using which devaluation is generally only observed in rats given reexposure to the sucrose prior to the test (cf. Balleine & Dickinson, 1991). As such, it might be concluded that devaluation induced by somatic pain is mediated by a different process to that induced by illness.

To assess this interpretation, a second experiment was conducted using six groups of thirsty rats. All of the groups were trained in a single session to press a lever for sucrose solution. After this session, four of the groups were injected with the hypertonic concentration of LiCl, but two of these groups were given the injection when they were anesthetized with halothane. The other two groups served as unpaired controls and were anesthetized immediately following the training session but were given the injection of LiCl after a 6-hr delay. The day following this treatment, three of the groups—one immediately injected, one immediately injected under anesthesia, and one delay injected—were given brief reexposure to the sucrose in the operant chambers, whereas the other groups were given exposure to water. The next day all the rats were given a 30-min extinction test on the lever.

If the immediate devaluation effect induced by the hypertonic injection was induced by pairing the sucrose with somatic pain and the anesthesia acted to mitigate that pain, then an outcome devaluation effect should not be anticipated in the absence of reexposure to the sucrose. This is, in fact, exactly what was found. Irrespective of the reexposure condition, the groups given the hypertonic injection without anesthesia showed a comparable reduction in performance on the lever relative to the delay-injected controls, which did not differ. Of the groups given the injection under anesthesia, however, a devaluation effect was only observed in the group given reexposure to the sucrose. The group exposed to water did not differ from the control groups (cf. Balleine & Dickinson, 1992).

This result confirms that devaluation induced by pairing an outcome with somatic pain involves rather different processes than devaluation induced by conditioning a taste aversion to the outcome and, as such, it seems reasonable to suppose that the two forms of devaluation are not mediated by the same associative structure. If pairing the outcome with illness conditions an association between the outcome representation and a system sensitive to the effect of illness (i.e., disgust) then pairing the outcome with somatic pain might be proposed to condition an association between the outcome representation and a system activated by painful events, often characterized within contemporary theories of aversive conditioning as a fear system (Davis, 1997; Fanselow, 1994; LeDoux, 1995).

If this view is accepted, however, it suggests a further difference between outcome devaluation effects induced by pairing the outcome with illness and by pairing the outcome with a painful consequence relating to the lability of the incentive learning process. If pairing the outcome with pain produces an immediate devaluation effect, this account suggests that it does so by (a) conditioning an association between the outcome representation and a fear system, and (b) generating immediate negative feedback that allows the conditioning of the inhibitory incentive learning connection between the fear system and the outcome. In contrast, in taste aversion learning, the lengthy delay between exposure to the outcome and the induction of illness, although sufficient for the excitatory association between the outcome representation and the disgust system to form, appears to be too long for the inhibitory incentive learning connection to form. This suggests that, in instrumental outcome devaluation, the incentive learning process is more sensitive to event contiguity than the evaluative process. Why this is the case is elaborated in the next two sections.

Incentive Learning as Inhibitory Feedback

Another reason for proposing that pairing the instrumental outcome with illness conditions an association between the outcome representation and a disgust system is provided by evidence that antiemetics attenuate both the conditioning and expression of taste aversions. In one such study (Balleine, Garner, & Dickinson, 1995, Experiment 1), thirsty rats were given two sessions. In one, they were allowed to drink a sucrose solution, whereas in the other session they were allowed to drink a saline solution. After both sessions, all of the rats were given an injection of LiCl (0.15M, 5 ml/kg). However, prior to one injection, rats were injected with ondansetron (100 µg/kg), a 5-Hydoxytryptophan-3 (5-HT3) receptor antagonist reported to have a strong antiemetic profile in both animals (Higgins, Kilpatrick, Bunce, Jones, & Tyers, 1989) and humans (Chaffee & Tankanow, 1991). Prior to the other injection of LiCl the rats were given a control injection of saline vehicle. The rats were then given a series of two-bottle choice tests in which they were free to consume both the sucrose and saline solutions. Before these tests, half of the rats were injected with ondansetron and the remainder were injected with vehicle.

If pairing a taste with illness conditions an association between the taste and disgust, blocking the activity of the disgust system at the time of conditioning using an antiemetic should be predicted to attenuate the formation of that association with the effect that, in the test sessions, rats should prefer the solution poisoned under ondansetron to the other solution. Furthermore, if the expression of a previously conditioned aversion depends on the ability of the taste representation to access the disgust system via an established connection, blocking the activity of the disgust system with ondansetron should increase consumption of the solution poisoned under vehicle on test. The results of this study confirmed both predictions—rats injected with vehicle clearly preferred the solution poisoned under ondansetron to the other solution. More important, this preference was clearly attenuated in rats injected with ondansetron prior to the test.

The finding that ondansetron attenuates the expression of a previously conditioned taste aversion suggests that ondansetron should also attenuate the effect of incentive learning in instrumental outcome devaluation. To assess this prediction, thirsty rats were trained in a single session to perform two actions, lever pressing and chain pulling, with one action delivering the sucrose solution and the other delivering the saline solution on a concurrent schedule. Immediately after this training session all the rats were given an injection of LiCl. Over the next 2 days the rats were reexposed to both the sucrose and the saline solutions. Prior to one reexposure session, rats were injected with ondansetron and prior to the other session they were injected with vehicle. The next day the rats were given a choice extinction test on the lever and chain. If reexposure devalues the instrumental outcome via the ability of the outcome representation to access the disgust system, blocking the activity of that system with ondansetron should be predicted to attenuate the effects of reexposure such that, on test, the action that, in training, delivered the outcome subsequently reexposed under ondansetron should be performed more than the other action. This is, in fact, exactly what was found (cf. Balleine, Garner, & Dickinson, 1995, Experiment 2).

The attenuation of incentive learning by ondansetron offers strong confirmation of the suggestion that incentive learning depends critically on negative feedback generated by an association between the outcome representation and a disgust system. This feedback, it was argued earlier, is provided by the conditioning of an inhibitory connection between the disgust system and the outcome representation when it is contacted during the reexposure phase. As a consequence, when the animal is faced with a choice between the lever press and chain pull actions on test, this account suggests that recollection of the consequences of those responses activates the disgust system and, hence, any previously conditioned inhibitory connection so to reduce the activation of the outcome representation. Inhibition of the outcome representation should be expected to reduce performance of actions that previously gained access to it by reducing the ability of the action to activate the outcome representation through any encoded action–outcome relation.

Careful consideration of this account of the role of associations between the outcome representation and the disgust system in outcome devaluation provides a further prediction. If the impact of outcome devaluation on performance is carried by a feedback loop comprising an excitatory association between the outcome representation and the disgust system and an inhibitory feedback connection from disgust to the outcome representation, then reducing the ability of the outcome representation to activate the disgust system by administering ondansetron on test should be predicted to attenuate the effects of outcome devaluation on performance. The design of the experiment used to test this prediction is illustrated in the top panel of Fig. 8.4. Essentially, this experiment replicated the procedures used in the previously described experiment (Balleine, Garner, & Dickinson, 1995, Experiment 3) except that, prior to the choice extinction test, half of the animals were injected with ondansetron and the remainder were injected with vehicle. Based on the previous study, it was anticipated that the group given the injection of vehicle prior to the test (i.e., Group VEH) would perform more of the action that, in training, delivered the outcome preexposed under ondansetron than the other action. More important, if the disgust system mediates the impact of incentive learning on performance in the test, as argued earlier, then any difference found in the vehicle group should be attenuated in the group injected with ondansetron on test (i.e., Group OND). This is because, by blocking the activity of the disgust system on test using an injection of ondansetron, negative feedback from disgust to the representation of the outcome reexposed under vehicle should be reduced. As such, on this account, the difference in performance of the two actions found in the previous study should be reduced. The results are presented in the lower panel of Fig. 8.4.

The results of this experiment were very clear; contrary to prediction, the injection of ondansetron on test had no impact on performance in the choice extinction test. Thus, in both Group VEH and Group OND, performance of the action that, in training, delivered the outcome reexposed under ondansetron (i.e., O-ond) was greater than the other action (i.e., O-veh). This failure to confirm a critical prediction derived from the account of outcome devaluation developed earlier is informative. It suggests that, although activity in the disgust system determines the effects of incentive learning, the disgust system does not play a role once incentive learning has occurred. If, after incentive learning,

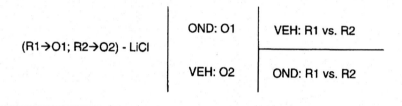

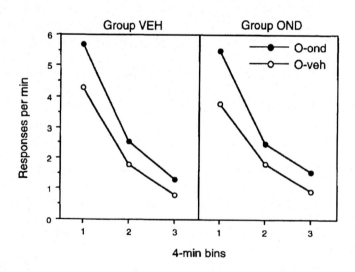

FIG. 8.4. The design (top panel) and results (lower panels) of Balleine, Garner, and Dickinson (1995, Experiment 3). R1, R2 = lever press or chain pull response; O1, O2 = sucrose or saline solution; LiCl = lithium chloride injection; OND = ondansetron injection; VEH = vehicle injection.

changes in instrumental performance are no longer dependent on feedback from the disgust system, the account of outcome devaluation under consideration must be revised.

Incentive Learning as an Emotional Process

If incentive learning is not mediated by a direct inhibitory association between the disgust system and the outcome representation, perhaps it is mediated by an association between the outcome representation and the effects induced by the arousal of disgust. Indeed, this kind of suggestion is not new. Traditional neobehaviorist learning theories argued that conditioned responses could themselves exert a motivating effect on instrumental performance (Hull, 1943, 1952; Spence, 1956). Largely due to the subsequent work of Konorski (1967) and Mowrer (1960), however, it is now widely accepted that these effects reflect the conditioning of an affective state that can exert a direct modulatory influence over consummatory responses and, through a change in the emotional responses elicited during ingestion, on instrumental performance (cf. Dickinson, 1989; Rescorla & Solomon, 1967). With respect to incentive learning, this approach suggests that during reexposure to the poisoned outcome, the reactivation of the outcome representation increases activity in the disgust system to produce an aversive state that is manifest in aversive feedback in the form of an emotional response. If, as a consequence, the outcome representation becomes associated with this aversive emotional response, a ready means is available for the effects of reexposure to transfer to test and in a manner that is independent of activation of the disgust system itself. This structure is illustrated in Fig. 8.5.

On this account, incentive learning depends on two processes: a feedback process and a feed-forward process. Pairing the instrumental outcome with illness conditions an association between the outcome representation and the disgust system (i.e., the evaluative connection) and acts, effectively, to open a feedback loop (fb). When the outcome is reexposed, activation of the outcome representation acts to produce activity in the disgust system to induce activity in aversive (AV) affective structures productive of an aversive emotional response (R_{EM}). On this view, incentive learning is the formation of a feed-forward (ff) association between the outcome representation and this emotional response.

There are several points to make about this account. First, if incentive learning is identified with the conditioning of this feed-forward association, it should be clear why devaluation induced by taste aversion should rely on reexposure whereas devaluation induced by somatic pain should not. In the latter case, the aversive response induced by the injection

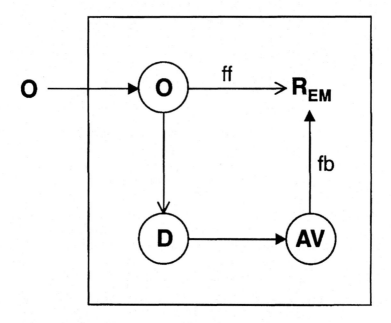

FIG. 8.5.   A revised version of the structure presented in Fig. 8.3 proposed to underlie evaluative (EC) and incentive learning (IL) processes in instrumental outcome devaluation. Fixed excitatory connections are illustrated as blocked arrows (→), acquired excitatory connections as open arrows (→). O = outcome; D = disgust system; AV = aversive system: R_{EM} = emotional response; ff = feed-forward; fb = feedback.

should be relatively contiguous with consumption of the outcome, allowing a stronger feed-forward association to form; that is, one less likely to be overshadowed by other reactions. In the former case, comparable contiguity between contact with the outcome and the aversive emotional reaction induced by disgust will only occur during reexposure. Second, this account can clearly handle transfer of incentive learning to the test situation in the case where the animal has been injected with ondansetron prior to the test. Recalling the outcome reexposed under vehicle during the test should, on this account, recall the aversive emotional response associated with that outcome via the feed-forward connection, in a manner that does not rely on the strength of feedback via the disgust system. In contrast, by virtue of the reduction in disgust activity induced by the drug during reexposure, recall of the outcome reexposed under ondansetron should recall a weaker aversive emotional response that should, as a consequence, interfere less with performance of the action that delivered that outcome in training.

Of course, such an account is predicated on the assumption that the strength of the feed-forward or incentive learning connection can act directly to determine instrumental performance. Such an assumption would appear justified if the change in the value of the outcome (from positive to negative) experienced during incentive learning is encoded via this connection. This account rests, however, on the further assumption that it is the encoded value of the instrumental outcome that is critical in determining instrumental performance. In fact, studies assessing the role that primary motivational processes play in instrumental conditioning provide considerable evidence to support this assumption.

THE MOTIVATIONAL CONTROL OF INSTRUMENTAL CONDITIONING

Pavlov (1927) used the term *signalization* to describe the association formed between representations of the sensory and the chemical properties of foods by hungry dogs and, hence, equated quite directly the way the US representation is acquired with the way animals subsequently associate a signal, such as the sound of a metronome, with the sight of food. Nevertheless, although these processes may have a similar associative structure, psychologically they differ in two important ways. First, at a descriptive level, whereas the relation between the sound of the metronome and the food is extrinsic, holding between two independent events, the relation between the sensory and chemical properties of food is intrinsic, being between the parts of a single event. More important, the sound of the metronome and the sight of the food are both perceptual events and, as such, are similarly represented. In contrast, it is difficult to claim that the sight of food and the chemical or nutrient properties of food are similarly represented. Indeed, it is quite clear that rats, like humans, do not possess the sensory capacities to perceive the chemical properties of the objects that they ingest in any objective sense. For if they did, it would surely be impossible to condition taste aversions to foods using injections of LiCl. The rat would be able directly to perceive that it was LiCl and not the food that caused the illness. As such, it would appear reasonable to claim that, although the sensory properties of foods, fluids, and other commodities is immediately represented by animals, the biological significance of these objects is not.[4]

---

[4]An important aspect of this two-process account of what animals learn in Pavlovian conditioning is that the different perceptual features of an event have an equal propensity to form associations either with each other or with innate structures (e.g., the disgust and nutrient systems) sensitive to changes in internal (continued on next page)

In fact, within psychology, the way in which animals encode the biological significance of commodities like foods and fluids and the role that this process plays in behavior has been the matter of intense debate and, indeed, forms the subject matter of the numerous motivational theories that have been advanced over the course of this century (e.g., Bindra, 1972, 1978; Hull, 1943, 1952; Konorski, 1967; Spence, 1956; Tolman, 1949a, 1949b; Young, 1961). Many of these theories, advanced within S–R psychology, contended that animals encode no such thing. In the absence of any ability directly to represent the consequences of behavior, this view cannot suppose that animals can represent the biological significance of those consequences. It was for this reason that S–R theorists adhered to a general drive theory of motivation (e.g., Hull, 1943) that assumes that specific needs (induced, say, by the deprivation of food or water or by sexual and thermoregulatory demands) do not select specific classes of response suited to meeting those needs but act as different sources of general arousal that potentiate any dominant S–R habit. Any selectivity of responding induced by different needs arises, on this view, from the association of responses with specific internal stimuli produced by the need through the standard S–R process.

In contrast, a number of theorists developed an alternative approach, arguing that animals could represent the biological significance of foods, fluids, and so on, but only indirectly through learning about their rewarding or incentive properties. Thus, rather than describing the animal as being pushed into performing particular behavioral responses by sources of drive, this approach described the influence of motivational processes on behavior as a product of learning to anticipate reward and, therefore, in terms of the way environmental events exert pull. One such approach was that advanced by Tolman (1949a; 1949b) and, as Garcia (1989) explicitly related his conception of taste aversion learning to Tolman's incentive theory, it is perhaps worth pausing to consider this position (see also Dickinson & Balleine, 1994).

---

[4](*continued from previous page*) biochemical conditions. As such, this position implies that biological constraints on learning can be reduced to the constraints on association in the evaluative conditioning process. These constraints might involve, for example, the relative salience of stimuli, the temporal contiguity of the stimulus and changes in biological conditions, as well as generalization between stimuli based on prior experience (cf. Mackintosh, 1983, for discussion). As a consequence, there is no reason to assert that the laws of association differ in evaluative and Pavlovian conditioning. Nevertheless, from this perspective, these conditioning processes may differ in the representational status of the mediating association: Whereas Pavlovian conditioning is the formation of associations between perceptual representations, evaluative conditioning is, from this perspective, essentially nonrepresentational.

Consistent with the results of outcome devaluation studies, Tolman argued, against S–R theory, that in instrumental conditioning, animals encode the consequences of their actions. Indeed, for Tolman, the performance of an instrumental action is a product of an activated instrumental belief, or expectancy, and the value or valence of the goal at that time (cf. Dickinson, 1989). However, Tolman considered a goal's value to be the product of the current motivational state of the animal and the learning of what he called a *cathexis* to the goal; that is, "the acquisition of a connection between a given variety of goal-object or disturbance-object—i.e., a given type of food, a given type of drink, a given type of sex-object or a given type of fear object—and the corresponding drive of hunger, thirst, sex or fright" (Tolman, 1949b, p. 144). The acquisition of cathexes, Tolman (1949b) believed, came about through consummatory contact with new foods, drinks, sex objects, and so on; that is, "by trying out the corresponding consummatory responses upon such objects and finding that they work" (p. 146).

Finally, in a companion paper, Tolman (1949a) set out how he believed the value of a goal is modified by the current motivational state or drive of the animal:

> By a cathexis I shall mean not the resultant loading of a given type of goal-object by drive (this loading I shall call value, see below) but rather the innate or acquired connection (or channel) between the given drive, say a viscerogenic hunger (such as food-hunger or thirst-hunger, or sex-hunger) and the given type of goal-object. The result of such a cathexis (i.e., such a channel) will be that when the given drive is in force and this cathexis channel is deep, that is, highly permeable, there will be a flow of energy from the drive to the compartment for the given type of goal object. And this will result in what I call a corresponding positive value for that type of goal-object. (pp.360–361).

Thus, for Tolman the learning of a cathexis is the acquisition of a connection between a particular motivational state and a given goal object, or outcome, which results in a disposition for that outcome (in the case of positive cathexes). Having formed such a cathexis, the activation of the outcome representation by the motivational system imbues that object with value and it is this value that determines the readiness of the animal to perform actions that lead to that object. It is important to note, however, that for Tolman, the value of a goal object under a particular motivational state is not immediately apprehended by the animal. It is something that is learned when the object is consumed in that motivational state. Thus, in a similar manner to the account developed from Pavlov's comments on the formation of the US representation in conditioning, Tolman's incentive theory suggests that the biological significance of the instrumental outcome is not immediately represented by the animal and must be acquired through consummatory experience.

Posttraining Shifts in Food Deprivation

As far as we can tell, Tolman's incentive theory was not based on experimental observation and was largely derived from conjecture. Nevertheless, in recent years, considerable evidence has emerged that is generally consistent with his position. Much of this evidence comes from studies assessing the effects of a posttraining shift in primary motivation on instrumental performance.

The logic of these studies is again straightforward. If animals have to learn about a change in the incentive value of an instrumental outcome through consummatory contact with the outcome after a change in motivational state (i.e., from Tolman's perspective, establish a cathexis between the outcome representation and drive), then a shift in primary motivation should only affect instrumental performance if the opportunity for such contact is provided.

In fact, in the past, a considerable number of studies were conducted precisely to assess the impact of a shift in motivational state on the performance of a previously acquired instrumental action (cf. Bolles, 1967, for a review). Many of these studies found evidence against the prediction derived from Tolman's account; that is, instrumental performance was found to be immediately modified by a shift in motivation state without the need for consummatory contact in that state. Nevertheless, as argued before and in more detail (cf. Dickinson & Balleine, 1994), the procedures employed in these studies suffer two defects. First, many of these studies employed responses that were only nominally instrumental in nature; that is, for which no attempt was made to assess whether performance was controlled by the instrumental, action–outcome contingency. Second, no attempt was made to control the animals' prior experience with the instrumental outcome. Indeed, consistent with the general practice employed in laboratories at that time (Siegel, 1944), most of these studies manipulated the degree of food deprivation and used as the instrumental outcome a dried pellet molded from the lab chow used to give the rats their daily food ration. As such, it may have been the case that previous exposure allowed to the lab chow during the daily feeding, which would have been consumed initially while food deprived, allowed the opportunity for learning a cathexis between the instrumental outcome and a hunger drive. If the outcome contacted during training was merely a pelletized version of the daily lab chow then it is not surprising, from the point of view of cathexis theory, that performance was found to be a direct function of deprivation state.

A number of studies have, however, been conducted to assess the prediction derived from Tolman's incentive theory using procedures that overcome the limitations of earlier studies (e.g., Balleine, 1992; Balleine, Ball, & Dickinson, 1994). In several studies, for example, undeprived rats were trained to press a lever delivering either novel, high-protein food pellets or a 20% solution of corn starch. After this training the rats were deprived of food with the intention of assessing the effect of this shift in primary motivation on subsequent instrumental performance in an extinction test. In the absence of the opportunity to learn about the biological significance of the training outcomes in the food-deprived state (i.e., to establish a cathexis between the specific outcomes and hunger), Tolman's incentive theory does not anticipate an effect of this posttraining change in deprivation conditions. Indeed, the results of these studies have generally confirmed this prediction (cf. Dickinson & Balleine, 1994, 1995, for review).

According to Tolman's position, allowing animals the opportunity for consummatory contact with the instrumental outcome when they are food deprived allows them to establish a cathexis between the hunger drive and the outcome representation and so to assign a high incentive value to the outcome when hungry. As a consequence, this position predicts that animals given this experience should subsequently increase the performance of instrumental actions that they have learned gain access to that outcome. To test this prediction, groups of rats were given explicit exposure to the instrumental outcome in the food-deprived state either before (Balleine, 1992) or after (Balleine et al., 1994) instrumental training, described earlier, for which the rats were undeprived. Whether consummatory contact was given before or after training, these experiments have confirmed that consummatory contact with the instrumental outcome when food deprived is necessary for the influence of an increase in food deprivation to be observed in instrumental performance. Specifically it was found that, when trained undeprived, only those rats given the opportunity to consume the instrumental outcome when food deprived increased their instrumental performance when food deprived during a subsequent extinction test. The lever press performance of rats that had only ever contacted the instrumental outcome in the undeprived state appeared to be unaffected by the increase in deprivation.

Although these studies confirm predictions derived from Tolman's incentive theory, they do not allow us to assert that these effects depend on the interaction of the effects of consummatory contact with the instrumental action–outcome relation encoded during training. To make this further assertion, evidence is required that the effects of contact with an outcome are specific to the action that delivered that outcome in training. In a number of previous studies evidence has been found that supports this assertion (e.g., Balleine, 1992, Experiment 2), although here the results of a recently conducted experiment that provides a well-controlled illustration of this point are described. In this study, the design of which is presented in the top panel of Fig. 8.6, undeprived rats (i.e., maintained with free access to food) were trained, in separate sessions, to press two levers, one delivering high-protein food pellets and the other a 20% solution of polycose (i.e., corn starch), on a random ratio schedule. After this initial training, the rats were divided into two groups. Both groups were given a series of six sessions for which they were, in alternation, deprived of food for 23 hr or undeprived as in training across successive days in a counterbalanced order. The groups differed with respect to the outcome that they were exposed to in these sessions. One group was allowed to consume the food pellets on days when they were food deprived and to consume the polycose solution on days when they were undeprived. The other group was allowed to consume the polycose solution on days when they were food deprived and the food pellets on days when they were undeprived. Following these consumption sessions, both groups of rats were given two 10-min tests of performance on each lever in separate sessions conducted in extinction. For one test the animals were food deprived and for the other test they were undeprived with the tests conducted in a counterbalanced order. Thus, each rat was given four brief extinction tests, one on each lever when food deprived and when undeprived. The results of these tests are presented in the bottom panel of Fig. 8.6.

A number of points can be made with reference to Fig. 8.6. First, it is clear that, as predicted by Tolman's incentive theory, in the absence of consummatory contact with the instrumental outcome in the food-deprived state, instrumental performance remained relatively unaffected by the shift in deprivation conditions. Thus, the performance of R2, in the left panel, and R1, in the right panel, was similar whether the test was conducted when the rats were food deprived (DEP) or undeprived (NON). This failure of performance of one action to come under control of the food-deprived state was clearly not general; as predicted by Tolman's account, prior exposure to an instrumental outcome in the food-deprived state acted to increase performance of the action that, in training, had delivered that outcome. Thus, in the food-deprived test, the performance of R1 (left panel) and R2 (right panel) was increased in all rats relative to R2 and R1, respectively. This pattern of results makes clear the most important point resulting from this experiment; the effects of consummatory experience with an outcome when food deprived on instrumental performance when food-deprived were found to be selective for the action with which that outcome was trained. As

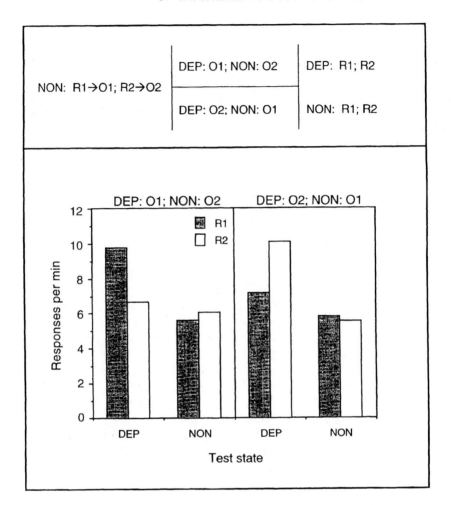

FIG. 8.6.   The design (top panel) and results (lower panels) of a recent experiment conducted to investigate the role of incentive learning in outcome revaluation induced by an increase in food deprivation. R1, R2 = left or right lever press response; O1, O2 = food pellet or starch solution; DEP = 23-hr food deprivation; NON = undeprived.

the effect of contact with the outcome in the food-deprived state on instrumental performance was clearly specific to the action that delivered that outcome in training, it can be concluded that the effect of this contact is determined by the instrumental action–outcome contingency encoded during that training.

Cathexis and Incentive Learning

Tolman's description of the formation of cathexes and their role in the experience of outcome valence and, consequently, the encoded value of the outcome, provides a clear indication of the kind of structure he would suppose underlies the effects of reexposure in this experiment. Consumption of the instrumental outcome while food deprived would, for Tolman, establish a connection between the representation of the outcome and a hunger drive. As a consequence of this connection, an increase in hunger will increase activation of that outcome's representation, an effect that Tolman described as increasing the value of that outcome.

There is a symmetry between Tolman's account and the account of taste aversion learning considered in Fig. 8.3. In that case, the reduction in value induced by conditioning a taste aversion to the outcome was carried by an inhibitory disgust–outcome connection, whereas for Tolman, the increase in the value of a food outcome is carried by an excitatory hunger–outcome connection. Nevertheless, the inadequacy of the inhibitory feedback account of decreases in outcome value, described earlier, must raise questions about an excitatory feedback account of increases in value. There are, in fact, several good reasons to reject the structure of incentive learning that Tolman proposed.

The account of incentive learning as inhibition in outcome devaluation studies was found to inaccurately predict the results of experiments that employed posttraining treatment with the antiemetic ondansetron. In similar fashion, Tolman's account of increases in value has been found to inaccurately predict the results of studies in which incentive value is manipulated by posttraining administration of the so-called satiety peptide cholecystokinin (CCK). Peripheral administration of CCK reduces food intake in a number of species including humans, primates, and rats (Cooper, 1985; Gibbs, Falasco, & McHugh, 1976; Gibbs, Young, & Smith, 1973; Stacher, 1985), an effect that is accompanied by a behavioral sequence characteristic of spontaneously occurring satiety (Antin, Gibbs, Holt, Young, & Smith, 1975; Antin, Gibbs, & Smith, 1978; Dourish, 1992). By contrast, the consumption of water (Bartness & Waldbillig, 1984; Kraly, Carty, Resnick, & Smith, 1978; Kulkosky, 1984) and nonnutritive solutions (Fedorchak & Bolles, 1988) is unaffected by CCK. Finally, CCK has also been reported to reduce instrumental performance for food outcomes. For example, Gosnell and Hsiao (1981) found that, in food-deprived animals, lever pressing for food pellets on a fixed ratio schedule was reduced by intraperitoneal injections of the synthetic octapeptide of CCK (CCK-8).

Tolman's incentive theory provides a straightforward explanation of these effects of CCK; if the valence of a specific food commodity is mediated by establishing an excitatory association between the representation of the food and hunger and subsequent increases in hunger cause an increase in the value of the food, then CCK could reduce consumption by either (a) blocking the formation of the food–hunger association, or (b) reducing the value of the food by reducing activity in the hunger system.

Given the role of incentive learning in the effect of a posttraining increase in food deprivation on instrumental performance described previously, this account makes two testable predictions: First, the administration of CCK should block the effect of consummatory contact with the instrumental outcome when food deprived. Second, if CCK reduces hunger (and hence, for Tolman, incentive value), its administration should act in a similar fashion to normal satiety and so attenuate the performance of actions that deliver food outcomes in an extinction test in food-deprived rats. In a test of these predictions (Balleine, Davies, & Dickinson, 1995, Experiment 1), undeprived rats were trained to lever press and to chain pull with one action earning food pellets and the other a starch solution. Following training the rats were deprived of food and allowed consummatory contact with the food pellets and the starch solution in separate sessions. Prior to one session rats were injected with CCK (CCK-8s, 4 μg/kg) and prior to the other session they were injected with saline vehicle. The rats were then divided into two groups and a choice extinction test was conducted on the levers and the chains. Prior to the test, one of the groups was injected with CCK and the other group was injected with vehicle. The results of this experiment are presented in Fig. 8.7.

The group injected with vehicle (Group VEH) showed a clear difference in performance at test, preferring the action that, in training, had delivered the outcome subsequently contacted when food deprived after the injection of the vehicle. Thus, in confirmation of the first prediction derived earlier, CCK acted to attenuate the effect of consummatory contact with one of the food outcomes when the rats were food deprived. More important, however, this effect of CCK during the reexposure phase was not influenced by the injection of CCK on test. The rats in Group CCK showed a comparable effect to that observed in Group VEH. In stark contrast to the effects of normal satiety (cf. Fig. 8.6), the performance of the two actions was not detectably affected by the administration of CCK.[5] This latter result stands contrary to the sec-

---

[5]Indeed, despite claims to the contrary (e.g., Smith & Gibbs, 1992), it is clear that, although CCK has similar effects on outcome value to those induced by a reduction in food deprivation, it does not induce the full complement of these effects. In a series of studies, for example, CCK was used to model the effects of a posttraining reduction in food deprivation. In one experiment, food-deprived rats were trained to lever press and chain pull for the food pellet and starch solution outcomes as previously described. After training, the rats were allowed to consume one outcome after an injection of CCK and the other outcome after an injection (continued on next page)

ond prediction derived from Tolman's account of incentive learning. Indeed, in similar fashion to the effects of ondansetron on outcome devaluation by conditioned taste aversion, the valence of the outcome encoded during incentive learning was impervious to subsequent changes in the internal conditions of the animal induced by CCK.

A second reason for rejecting Tolman's account of incentive learning comes from studies assessing the effects of a posttraining reduction in food deprivation. In the past, considerable resistance to the effects of reductions in deprivation on instrumental performance have been reported (cf. Morgan, 1974 for review). The problem here is that Tolman's account predicts that, in contrast to an increase, a reduction in food deprivation will act immediately to reduce instrumental performance without the need for consummatory contact with the outcome in this reduced deprivation state. This is because once a cathexis has been established between the outcome representation and the hunger drive, the value of the instrumental outcome should be directly determined by the strength of the hunger drive. As a consequence, a reduction in food deprivation should produce an immediate reduction in outcome value that, as a consequence, should then directly reduce the performance of actions that gain access to that outcome.

In a number of experiments assessing this issue, direct evidence has been found against this prediction. In these studies, food-deprived rats were trained to lever press for a food outcome. In some studies this outcome was the high-protein food pellets and in others a starch solution (cf. Balleine, 1992, Experiments 3A and 3B; Balleine & Dickinson, 1994, Experiment 1A). After this training, half of the rats were shifted to an undeprived state and the remainder were maintained food deprived with the intention of assessing the effect of the shift in deprivation on instrumental performance in an extinction test. The predictions from Tolman's incentive theory derived earlier suggest that this shift in deprivation should have an immediate effect on instrumental performance with animals tested undeprived pressing less in the extinction test than those tested while food deprived. Contrary to this prediction, however, in all of the studies cited earlier, no immediate effect of a reduction in food deprivation on lever press performance was detected.

---

[5] *(con't.)* of vehicle before the rats were given an extinction test on lever and chain after an injection of CCK. If CCK acts in a similar manner to a reduction in food deprivation, consummatory contact under CCK will act both to change the animals' evaluation of the outcome and to control that evaluation such that it should transfer to the test conducted under CCK to reduce the performance of the action that, in training, delivered the outcome reexposed under CCK. In fact, we found no such effect. Although the choice test situation provides a highly sensitive assay of the motivational control of instrumental performance, we could not detect any impact of the incentive learning treatment on test (cf. Balleine & Dickinson, 1994).

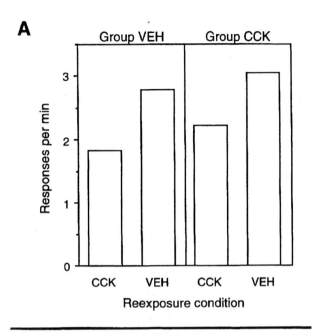

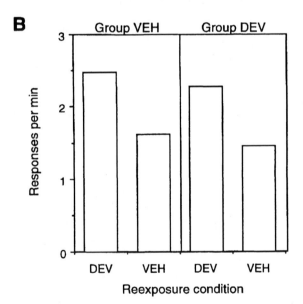

FIG. 8.7 (a) The results of Balleine, Davies, and Dickinson (1995, Experiment 1) and (b) of Balleine and Dickinson (1994, Experiment 5). Copyright © 1994, 1995 by the American Psychological Association. Reprinted with permission.

Whether animals were food deprived or were undeprived, they pressed the lever at a comparable rate during the extinction session.

This failure to find an effect of the shift in deprivation was not due to any general insensitivity to this shift. In each of these studies, a subsequent test was conducted in which the food reward used in training was delivered contingent on lever pressing. In this test it was found that undeprived rats persistently pressed the lever at a lower rate than food-deprived rats. As this finding suggests, an interaction between the change in deprivation conditions and consummatory contact seems to be required for the effects of that change to be manifest in instrumental performance. In fact, these studies provided evidence for this suggestion. In these studies, two further groups were added to those already described to assess the effect of consummatory contact with the outcome in the undeprived state. Both groups were also trained to lever press when food deprived but, in contrast to the groups described previously, these groups were given the opportunity to consume the instrumental outcome in the undeprived state before the test either before (Balleine, 1992) or after (Balleine & Dickinson, 1994) the training phase. For the extinction test, one group of rats given this treatment was undeprived and the other was food deprived. The results indicated that the group tested when undeprived and given the opportunity to consume the instrumental outcome when in the undeprived state lever pressed at a lower rate than the group tested when they were food deprived. Indeed, this latter group did not differ from the other two groups.

Finally, in a number of studies (Balleine, 1992, Experiment 5; Balleine & Dickinson, 1994, Experiment 2), it was confirmed that this effect of contact with the outcome when undeprived is specific to the action that delivered the reexposed outcome during training. For these studies, food-deprived rats were trained to lever press and to chain pull with one action delivering the food pellets and the other action earning the starch solution. Animals were given a choice extinction test when undeprived, prior to which they were allowed the opportunity to consume one of the instrumental outcomes when undeprived. On test, it was found that the action in training that had delivered the outcome consumed undeprived prior to the test was performed at a lower rate than the other action. This selective effect of exposure on instrumental performance could only have emerged if the rats were able to integrate the effect of exposure to one of the outcomes when undeprived with the action–outcome relations encoded during training.

The finding that a reduction in food deprivation only influences instrumental performance when the opportunity to consume the outcome in this new deprivation state is given provides perhaps the strongest evidence against Tolman's description of incentive learning. Clearly, following the formation of a cathexis between the outcome and hunger, incentive value, and, hence, instrumental performance, is not simply a direct function of the animal's degree of food deprivation. Indeed, if any further evidence were required, as with posttraining increases in food deprivation, there is evidence that, after incentive learning in the undeprived state has been given, instrumental performance following a reduction in food deprivation is largely independent of the conditions that support that learning.

This evidence comes from manipulations of endogenous CCK using the CCK antagonist devazepide (MK329), which binds selectively at alimentary CCK (CCK-A) receptors and has been reported both to block the effects of exogenous CCK on feeding (Dourish, Ruckert, Tattersall, & Iversen, 1989; Hanson & Strouse, 1987; Khosla & Crawley, 1988) and, in undeprived animals, to increase food consumption (cf. Dourish, 1992). In one study (Balleine & Dickinson, 1994, Experiment 5), food-deprived rats were again trained to lever press and chain pull with one action delivering the food pellets and the other the starch solution. After this training, the rats were given free access to their maintenance diet and then allowed consummatory contact with both the pellet and starch outcomes while in that undeprived state. Prior to contact with one outcome, however, the rats were injected with devazepide in the hope that the drug would block endogenous CCK activity and so block learning about the reduced valence of the outcome while undeprived. Prior to contact with the other outcome, the rats were injected with vehicle. The rats were then divided into two groups with both groups given a choice extinction test while in the undeprived state. Prior to the test, one group was injected with vehicle (Group VEH) and the other group was given an injection of devazepide (Group DEV). The results of the test are presented in Fig. 8.7.

As this figure shows, the reduction in performance induced by consummatory contact with the outcome in the undeprived state was clearly attenuated by the administration of devazepide prior to the exposure session. In Group VEH, rats performed more of the action the training outcome of which was exposed under devazepide than of the other action. Importantly, the effect of devazepide during reexposure was not affected by the injection of devazepide on test and a comparable effect was observed in Group DEV to that observed in Group VEH. Thus, just as was observed when CCK was used to block the increase in valence induced by an increase in food deprivation, the conditions that supported the change in the rats' evaluation of the outcome during the reexposure phase were clearly not responsible for the transfer of this evaluation to the extinction test. As a consequence, just as was found necessary in assessing the factors that contribute to outcome devaluation by taste aversion learning, reference to a direct connection between hunger and the outcome representation is not, in itself, sufficient to explain the motivational control of instrumental performance.

The Determination of Incentive Value

When pressing a lever delivers food, a hungry rat presses at a higher rate than a sated rat. The question is why. As already described, historically this question has provoked two seemingly opposing answers: Hull (1943) argued that hunger generates more drive and, hence, more performance, whereas Tolman (1949a, 1949b) proposed that hunger increases the incentive value of food and so increases the performance of actions that gain access to it. We have seen that neither of these positions is satisfactory. Reference to drive alone does not explain why shifts in the level of hunger have only an indirect effect on lever press performance, whereas the supposition that hunger directly determines the value of food does not explain why reductions in hunger fail to alter performance or, when hunger is increased, why CCK is effective in attenuating increases in value but not increases in performance.

The problem lies, perhaps, in the fact that these positions are not entirely independent. Although Tolman regarded hunger as determining incentive value, the way value influenced performance was based, as in Hull's theory, on the energetic functions of hunger as a drive. In essence, the connection between a specific food representation and hunger allowed "a flow of energy from the drive to the compartment for the given type of goal object" (Tolman, 1949a, p. 361) and it was this energy that increased the performance of any actions with which the outcome was associated. It would appear, therefore, that it is the role of the energetic component of drive in determining instrumental performance that is in need of reconsideration.

This is not a task that can be lightly undertaken and it is certainly beyond the scope of this chapter to provide a thorough analysis of this issue. Nevertheless, it is possible to give a flavor of the kind of account that is demanded based on several features of the experiments already described. The fact that instrumental performance is only indirectly influenced by shifts in food deprivation suggests that the way hunger controls lever pressing for food is also indirect. One reason can be derived from Pavlov's (1927) analysis of the way dogs come to salivate at the sight of food, according to which the sensory properties of food were not associated with hunger directly but with the chemical properties of the food itself. As described earlier, this can be interpreted as suggesting that one learning process engaged by the consumption of food involves the formation of an association between a representation of these sensory properties and a system activated by the detection of nutrients. If it is this association on which learning about the biological significance of food is based, then perhaps the energetic functions of hunger and the influence of hunger on incentive value may be mediated by different, if interdependent, processes.

There is, in fact, a considerable literature documenting the complex relation between hunger and the detection of nutrients as it emerges from studies assessing the physiological bases of hunger. Importantly, with regard to the analysis here, the results of these studies have largely converged on the view that this relation determines the acceptance or palatability of food, what Le Magnen (1985) referred to as the development of a "nutrient-specific appetite" (p. 28). In general, the claim is that changes in food deprivation modify food consumption and the performance of instrumental responses for food because they modify the palatability of food. Evidence for this claim can be drawn from Cabanac's (1971) study of the effects of nutrient repletion on ratings of palatability in humans. He asked two groups of participants to rate how much they liked the taste of a mildly sweet-tasting glucose solution. Both groups were allowed to taste 50 ml of solution every 3-min. One group was asked to swallow the solution, the other was asked to spit it out. Initially, both groups gave high ratings of pleasure. By the time 1,000 ml of solution had been consumed, however, the ratings had diverged, with the ratings of participants asked to swallow the solution changing from highly pleasant to highly unpleasant. In the group that was asked to spit the solution out, the rating remained highly pleasant throughout the test. Thus, the participants positive affective reactions decreased not because of taste-related processes alone, but as they became increasingly sated on the sugar solution.

The corresponding motivational modulation of affective responses can also be observed in rats. For example, the incidence of ingestive fixed-action patterns elicited by a sweet solution increases with the level of food deprivation (Berridge, 1991). Moreover, if rats are given a prior intragastric infusion of 5 ml of glucose, their orofacial responses change from ingestive to those associated with rejection, just as the hedonic ratings of humans changed from positive to negative (Cabanac, 1990). This pattern of results in rats can also be observed using deprivation states other than hunger. A hypertonic sodium chloride solution, saltier than sea water, produces mainly rejection responses in rats. If, however, the rats are deprived of salt to induce a sodium appetite, the hypertonic solution elicits an increase in ingestive responses and a reduction in rejection responses (Berridge, Flynn, Schulkin, & Grill, 1984). Sodium-depleted humans also report that salty foods are more pleasant (cf. Rolls, 1990).

These observations suggest that shifts in primary motivation act to change the incentive value of instrumental outcomes by changing the way the outcome tastes. It should, therefore, be clear why incentive learning is required for shifts in primary motivation to affect instrumental performance; without the opportunity to contact the outcome after the shift and so discover that its palatability has changed, the rats would have no grounds on which to modify the incentive value of the outcome and, hence, the performance of actions that gain access to it.

Careful consideration of this point suggests that, as was argued for changes in incentive value induced by taste aversion learning, the motivational control of instrumental performance may also depend on two processes: a feedback process through which the palatability of the outcome is changed, and a feed-forward process through which animals associate the outcome representation with the experienced palatability of the outcome to encode its current incentive value. The fact that food deprivation acts indirectly to modify incentive value suggests that this treatment modulates affective processing through its influence on activity in a nutrient system. On this view, a shift in food deprivation modifies the activation of this system induced by nutrients and so, through affective feedback, can influence the palatability of the outcome—ranging from highly positive when food deprived to relatively neutral when undeprived. In accord with the analysis of devaluation by taste aversion learning, this view supposes that incentive learning following a shift in primary motivation is mediated by a change in the way the outcome tastes rather than what consumption of the outcome predicts.

Direct evidence that incentive learning following a shift in food deprivation is mediated by changes in palatability can be drawn from the finding that incentive learning can be mediated by a single taste feature. This evidence comes from studies that have used a specific satiety treatment to modify the incentive value of the instrumental outcome (Balleine & Dickinson, 1998b; 1998c; Colwill & Rescorla, 1985; Dickinson, Campos, Varga, & Balleine, 1996). In one study (Balleine & Dickinson, 1998c, Experiment 1), food-deprived rats were trained to press two levers on a concurrent schedule, with one lever delivering a sour-tasting starch solution and the other delivering a salty-tasting starch solution. After this training the food-deprived rats were given free access to either the sour or salty starch in drinking tubes in their home cage for 1 hr immediately prior to a choice extinction test conducted on the two levers. The design and results of this test are presented in Fig. 8.8. As is clear from Fig 8.8a, in spite of the fact that the instrumental outcomes differed only with respect to their taste features and were identical with respect to their motivationally relevant (i.e., nutrient) properties, on test the rats clearly reduced their performance of the action that, in training, delivered the outcome that they were allowed to consume prior to the test.

The analysis of devaluation effects induced by a reduction in food deprivation presented earlier suggests that this example of the instrumental outcome devaluation effect should rely on incentive learning. It remains, however, to be demonstrated whether the same is true of the case where outcome devaluation is achieved through a specific satiety treatment using outcomes that differ only in a single taste feature. Assessing this account, however, presents special difficulties because, using this devaluation procedure, the satiety treatment (the period of free consumption) and the opportunity for incentive learning are confounded. Consumption of the starch solution should be expected, over time, to induce a progressive reduction in food deprivation, while consummatory contact with the outcome should provide the opportunity to learn about the reduction in the palatability of the outcome as deprivation is reduced.

To overcome this problem, the opportunity for incentive learning was provided independently of the induction of satiety prior to the test using the design presented in Fig. 8.8b. In this study (Balleine & Dickinson, 1998c, Experiment 2), food-deprived rats were again trained to press two levers, with one lever delivering the sour starch and the other delivering the salty starch. Over the next 2 days, the rats were given the opportunity to consume one of the instrumental outcomes for a 1-hr period. On the third day after training, the rats were given 1 hr exposure to unadulterated starch without the accompanying taste feature before their performance on the two levers was assessed in an extinction test. If extended contact with one of the outcomes allows animals to learn about the reduced incentive value of the taste features of that outcome when in the reduced deprivation state induced by the consumption of starch, then, on incentive learning theory, starch consumption prior to the choice extinction test should selectively reduce the value of the taste presented with the starch during incentive learning. As such, performance of the action that, in training, delivered the starch solution containing that taste should be reduced relative to the other action. As is shown in Fig. 8.8b, this is exactly what was found.

This demonstration is important for two reasons. First, it confirms that outcome devaluation by a specific satiety treatment depends on incentive learning. During the satiety treatment, the rats clearly learned about the reduction in incentive value of a specific, motivationally irrelevant feature of the instrumental outcome, a value that controlled performance when the rats were sated on the starch solution prior to the test. Second, this finding provides clear evidence for the suggestion that shifts in food deprivation can modify the incentive value of nutritive commodities by altering their palatability. Thus, the effect of exposure to the salt or sour taste when sated on the starch clearly modified the

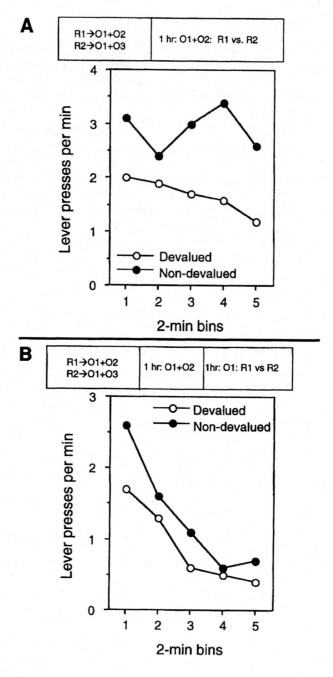

FIG. 8.8. The design and results of Balleine and Dickinson (1998c) Experiment 1 and Experiment 2.

value of these unique taste features despite the fact that they were motivationally irrelevant. Indeed, the finding that changes in outcome value following a shift in food deprivation can be mediated solely by taste suggests that, generally speaking, incentive learning consists primarily in associating an emotional response with the outcome representation (or specific, salient features of it), however that is achieved. It does not appear to be necessary, therefore, for an outcome itself to initiate the feedback process on which incentive value is based for the incentive value of that outcome to be modified.

Together with the studies described in previous sections, these conclusions provide a strong indication of the kind of structure that underlies the way primary motivational states determine the incentive value of the instrumental outcome. This structure is illustrated in Fig. 8.9. This account generally assumes that the outcome represented by the animal has a number of sensory features (i.e., s1, s2, s3 etc.) and that the incentive value of these features is determined by two interacting learning processes. The first involves the conditioning of a direct connection between the outcome representation (or its most salient features) and a nutrient system (N). This connection is modulated by hunger (H) which, it is assumed, determines the degree to which the nutrient system is activated when nutrients are detected to establish the biological significance of the outcome. This connection is what was referred to earlier as underlying evaluative conditioning. This evaluative connection opens a feedback loop through a fixed connection between the nutrient system and a presumably appetitive affective system, the activity of which provides feedback via an emotional response (R_{EM}); that is, the palatability reaction elicited on consummatory contact with the food. The second learning process involves the conditioning of a feed-forward (ff) connection between the outcome representation and the emotional response (R_{EM}). It is this connection that is proposed to underlie incentive learning and to determine the incentive value of the outcome encoded by the animal.

To this analysis may be added the assumption that, of the features of the outcome, those that best predict nutrient activity become more strongly associated with the nutrient system and overshadow other features. In the specific satiety studies considered earlier, for example, the best predictor of nutrients should be the starch taste present in both outcomes. Now, during the specific satiety treatment, the reduction in hunger produced by consumption of the starch will reduce the activity of the nutrient system induced by the starch taste and hence modify the emotional response elicited by affective feedback. As each of the features of the outcome presented in the incentive learning phase are equally good predictors of this change in emotional response, the salt or sour taste features could become associated with that response even though they may

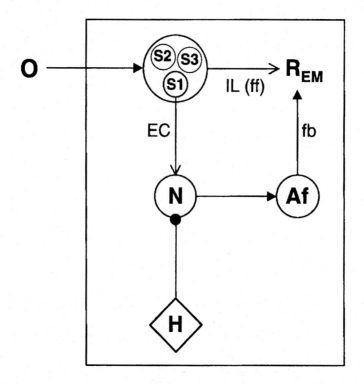

FIG. 8.9. An illustration of a possible structure underlying the evaluative (EC) and incentive learning (IL) processes argued to mediate the motivational determination of the incentive value of the instrumental outcome. Fixed excitatory connections are illustrated as blocked arrows (→), acquired excitatory connections as open arrows (→), modulatory connection (—•). O = outcome; S1, S2, S3 = sensory features of O; N = nutritive system; H = hunger system; Af = affective system: R_EM = emotional response; ff = feed-forward; fb = feedback.

not, themselves, have any direct association with the nutrient system. Pairing the detection of these tastes with the emotional reaction elicited during consummatory contact with the outcome may, therefore, be regarded as sufficient to change the value of those features.

There are two sources of evidence that bear on this account of incentive learning. The first comes from the finding that components of an instrumental chain of actions are differentially sensitive to shifts in food deprivation. The second comes from studies in which affective feedback was manipulated by pharmacological agents independently of shifts in primary motivation. These sources of evidence are presented in the next two sections.

Variations in Outcome Encoding

Although incentive learning was required before a shift in primary motivation was effective in modifying instrumental performance in the preceding experiments, it must be conceded that this is not true of all the responses an animal performs in the instrumental situation. For example, in a number of studies, we have found evidence suggesting that the animals' tendency to approach the location of food delivery (the food magazine) was directly affected by shifts in food deprivation, that is, without the need for animals to experience the food in the new motivational state following the shift (cf. Balleine, 1992; Balleine et al., 1994; Balleine & Dickinson, 1994; Dickinson & Balleine, 1995). To explain this difference in sensitivity to the effects of shift in deprivation we have at various points argued that this could reflect a difference in the contingency that controls the performance of these responses, suggesting that instrumental actions, such as lever pressing, are controlled by the action–outcome relation, whereas anticipatory approach is elicited by Pavlovian stimulus–outcome associations (Dickinson & Balleine, 1993).

In a series of experiments designed to assess this issue, however, we have found evidence that when rats were trained on a heterogeneous chain of actions, in an attempt to model the situation where lever pressing is followed by magazine approach, the performance of actions proximal to outcome delivery was also directly affected by a reduction in food deprivation (Balleine, Garner, Gonzalez, & Dickinson, 1995). In contrast, more distal actions were not affected by the shift and only came under the control of the reduction in deprivation state when the opportunity for incentive learning was given. For example, in one study (Balleine, Garner, Gonzalez, & Dickinson, 1995, Experiment 1), food-deprived rats were trained such that they had to perform two actions (designated R1 and R2) in sequence to gain access to the instrumental outcome, in this case food pellets (i.e., R1 → R2 → pel). Half the rats were required to press a lever then pull a chain, whereas for the other animals this relation was reversed. Rats had no great difficulty acquiring this relation and, indeed, the conditional probability of the performance of R2 following R1 was found to be significantly higher than for R1 following R2. After this training, we examined the sensitivity of the performance of R1 and R2 to a reduction in food deprivation by shifting half of the rats to an undeprived state (Group NON) whereas the remainder were maintained food deprived (Group DEP) before assessing the performance of R1 and R2 in an extinction test. The results of this test are presented in Fig. 8.10a.

It is clear from this figure that the performances of R1 and R2 were differentially affected by the shift in primary motivation. Whereas the performance of the two responses did not differ in Group DEP, the performance of R2 (i.e., of the action proximal to the delivery of the pellets) was immediately and directly reduced by the shift relative to R1 in Group NON. In a second study we assessed the role of incentive learning in bringing the performance of the distal action, (i.e., R1) under the control of the animals' test deprivation state. To achieve this, we (Balleine, Garner, et al., 1995, Experiment 2) trained food-deprived rats on the heterogeneous chain for food pellets as previously described and then, on the 4 days following the training phase, we shifted the rats between a food-deprived and an undeprived state on successive days. During this phase, half of the animals were allowed to consume the food pellets when they were undeprived (Exp-non) and the remainder were only allowed to consume the pellets when they were food deprived (Exp-dep). Both groups were then given an extinction test on the levers and chains when they were undeprived, the results of which are presented in Fig. 8.10b. As is clear from this figure, the rats in Group Exp-dep again showed differential performance of the two actions, performing more of the distal (R1) than of the proximal action (R2). This effect was, however, mitigated by exposure to the outcome when undeprived prior to the test. In Group Exp-non, the performance of the distal action (R1) was clearly reduced compared with Group Exp-dep, whereas the performance of the proximal action (R2) was not. As such, the impact of incentive learning was most clearly observed in performance of the action distal to outcome delivery and, in this study, was not observed in the performance of the action proximal to outcome delivery.

The differential effectiveness of shifts in deprivation on the performance of actions in an instrumental chain is similar to that observed in devaluation studies conducted in Pavlovian conditioning. For example, Holland and Rescorla (1975) found that when a food US was devalued by a shift in food deprivation, the performance of CRs to a CS that predicted food delivery were immediately reduced by this shift. In contrast, as was found with responses distal to outcome delivery in the current study, CRs conditioned to a second-order CS (CS_2) were left unaffected by this devaluation treatment. Mackintosh (1983) interpreted differences in the susceptibility of CRs to the effects of changes in the value of the US as suggesting that first- and second-order CSs become associated with different attributes of the US. For example, the relative proximity of the first-order CS (CS_1) to US delivery may allow CS_1 to become associated with both the salient sensory and affective attributes of the US. When CS_2 is paired with CS_1, however, the sensory properties of that CS may be less salient than the emotional reactions that it elicits with the effect that CS_2 becomes predominantly associated with the affective attributes of the US.

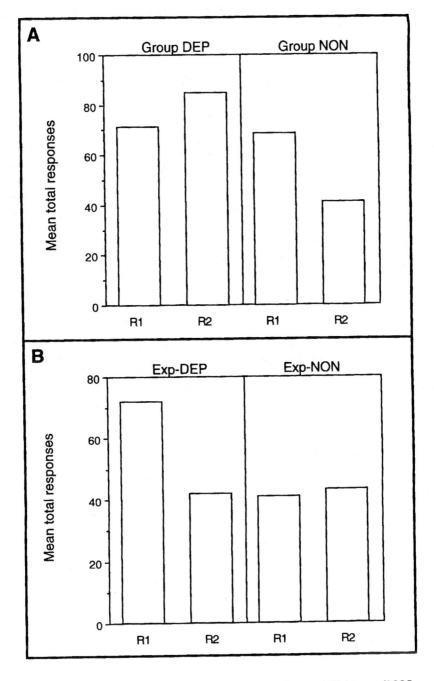

FIG. 8.10. The results of Balleine, Garner, Gonzales, and Dickinson (1995, Experiment 1 and Experiment 2). Copyright © 1995 by the American Psychological Association. Reprinted with permission.

Although there is no evidence to suggest that incentive learning after a shift in deprivation modifies the performance of CRs conditioned to CS_2 it is possible, following Mackintosh (1988), that similar variations in the outcome that is encoded as a consequence of performing R1 and R2 underlie the differences in the sensitivity of these responses to a shift in deprivation. For example, the proximal action may overshadow the distal action in the formation of an association with the most salient, motivationally relevant features of the instrumental outcome, that is, those sensory features that form a direct association with the nutrient system. As a consequence, the distal action may be predominantly associated with motivationally irrelevant features. On this account, illustrated in Fig. 8.11, the actions distal (i.e., R1) and proximal (i.e., R2) to outcome delivery in a chain of actions become associated with different features of the outcome representation due to differences in the salience of specific features of the outcome (here represented as S1, S2, and S3). When food deprivation is reduced, the tendency to perform R2 will, predominantly, recall S1 and, if only to a limited degree, the reduction in the activation of the nutrient system induced by S1 may produce sufficient change in affective feedback to reduce the motivational support for that action. In contrast, if R1 is associated with motivationally irrelevant features of the outcome, and the incentive value of these features is determined solely by the feed-forward connection, then the tendency to perform R1 cannot directly modify the motivational support for that action through the feedback process. Thus, without the opportunity to attach a new emotional state to these features of the outcome through incentive learning, the features of the outcome representation with which the distal action is associated should provide sufficient incentive feedback (through the feed-forward connection) to maintain a similar level of performance to food-deprived rats. In essence, therefore, this account accords with Mackintosh's (1983) account of devaluation effects in first- and second-order conditioning: Whereas performance of the proximal action is largely determined by the sensory properties of the outcome with which it becomes related, the performance of more distal action is largely determined by the emotional reactions associated with the consequences of performance.

The Motivational Control of Incentive Value

By way of summary, in the analysis of the way food deprivation determines the incentive value of nutritive outcomes presented earlier it was suggested that associating the representation of the sensory features of the instrumental outcome with an emotional response is sufficient to establish the incentive value of that outcome. This emotional response, it

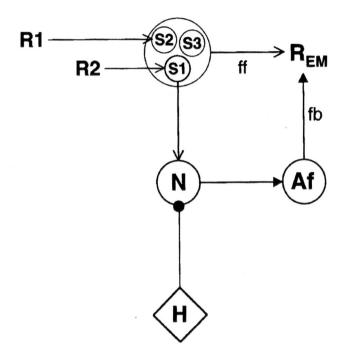

FIG. 8.11. An illustration of a possible structure underlying the differential sensitivity of distal (R1) and proximal (R2) actions in a heterogeneous instrumental chain to the effects of a shift in food deprivation and to incentive learning. Fixed excitatory connections are illustrated as blocked arrows (→), acquired excitatory connections as open arrows (→), and modulatory connection (—●). S1, S2, S3 = sensory features of the instrumental outcome; N = nutritive system; H = hunger system; Af = affective system: R_{EM} = emotional response; ff = feed-forward; fb = feedback.

was argued, functions as feedback elicited by affective activity produced by (hunger modulated) activation of a nutrient system through either the detection of nutrients or stimuli associated with nutrients through evaluative conditioning. Thus, when a rat is trained to lever press for a food outcome, contact with the outcome is sufficient for it to assign a high incentive value to that outcome and, when food deprivation is reduced, contact with the outcome is required before the reduced value of the outcome can be encoded. It is important to note, however, that—as it stands—the rat has now encoded two separate outcome values, one high and one low. However, if this is true, then surely the value of the outcome is now ambiguous. Which of these two values will control subsequent lever press performance?

In fact, an important feature of studies assessing posttraining shifts in primary motivation is the finding that the value of the instrumental outcome is not only determined by the current motivational state, it also comes under the conditional control of that state. As an example, recall the effects of reexposure to the instrumental outcome when the rats were food deprived in the study illustrated in Fig. 8.6. In that study, rats were trained undeprived and then exposed to one of the instrumental outcomes when food deprived. Importantly, the two deprivation states were found to exert control over subsequent performance; the action that, in training, delivered the outcome reexposed when food deprived was increased, but only when the rats were tested when food deprived. Likewise, in other studies, rats trained food deprived and given incentive learning in the undeprived state were found to reduce their instrumental performance in an extinction test, but only when they were tested undeprived. As a consequence, it is clear that the current value of the instrumental outcome is, to some degree, disambiguated by the way in which a particular motivational state acts to control the value encoded through incentive learning. It is equally clear, however, that motivational processes do not immediately exert control over outcome value and do so only when the experienced value of an outcome is changed; that is, when it has more than one value.

Bouton's studies assessing the way contexts control the predictive value of a CS offer some insight into the way motivational control might be accomplished. The association between a CS and US is often not immediately controlled by the context in which conditioning is conducted. Bouton (1989, 1994) argued, however, that when the predictive value of the CS is altered, say following a period of extinction, animals will often use contextual cues to disambiguate what that CS predicts. Thus, in one demonstration (Bouton & Peck, 1989) a tone was paired with pellets in one context and extinguished either in the same context or in a discriminably different context. Although the course of extinction did not differ in the two contexts, a test of conditioned responding to the CS conducted in the conditioning context following extinction found evidence of robust renewal of responding when the CS was extinguished in the nontraining context.

There are considerable similarities between the way contexts control the predictive value of the CS and the way motivational states control the incentive value of the instrumental outcome. Both contexts and motivational states only exert conditional control when the value of the CS or outcome is changed, whether by extinction or by shifts in deprivation. Perhaps, then, motivational states control outcome value by providing an internal contextual cue on which that value can become conditional. There is, in fact, an extensive literature documenting the stimulus effects induced by shifts in deprivation state (cf. Bolles, 1967). Indeed, Davidson (1987, 1993) showed that the states induced by increases and decreases in food deprivation can be used to control the predictive value of CSs. Furthermore, in his assessments of renewal, Bouton found that internal cues induced by an injection of various benzodiazepine (BZ) agonists can act like external contexts to control the predictive value of the CS and to induce renewal (Bouton, Kenney, & Rosengard, 1990).

The argument that state cues induced by shifts in deprivation can control incentive value in this way provides an account of how the value of the outcome is disambiguated by supposing that the rats learn that the outcome has different values under different internal conditions. Nevertheless, it is not clear whether the ability to exert control over incentive value should be regarded as the exclusive province of internal states induced by shifts in primary motivation. Surely, by this account, any discriminable internal cue could act to control incentive value in this way. This prediction has much in common with the suggestion that the motivational determination of incentive value is indirect. Indeed, the motivational control of instrumental performance may well be accomplished by two very general functions of motivational systems: The first is the way motivational processes act to modulate affective feedback and the second is the influence that these systems have on the internal state of the animal. However, if this is true, it should be clear that primary motivational systems do not have any privileged access to the processes that underlie either the determination or the control of incentive value. As such, this position makes the strong claim that anything that alters appetitive feedback and produces a unique state cue should exert control over instrumental performance similar to that induced by shifts in primary motivation.

We have tested this prediction in a series of experiments in which we assessed the ability of the BZ agonist midazolam to model the motivational control of instrumental performance (Balleine et al., 1994). It has for some time been known that BZ agonists act to modify the affective state of humans and other animals, acting both to reduce anxiety (Blanchard & Blanchard, 1988; Leonard, 1999) and to elevate positive emotional states (Cooper, 1986). Indeed, BZ agonists have been reported to increase food intake in rats in conditions where that increase cannot readily be explained in terms of the removal of an inhibitory influence through their anxiolytic effect (see Cooper, 1989, for review).

Furthermore, Wise and Dawson (1974) found that the BZ agonist diazepam increased lever pressing for food pellets in a dose-dependent manner in undeprived rats, a result that suggests that BZ agonists increase the value of food as an instrumental outcome. On the basis of this and other evidence, Cooper and Higgs (1994) recently put forward a strong case supporting the claim that BZ agonists cause increases in consumption and in instrumental performance by increasing the palatability of commodities contacted while under the influence of the drug.

In addition to their effects on outcome value, BZ agonists have also been reported to elicit a novel and discriminable internal state in humans and animals, something Bouton and his colleagues used to effect in his study of renewal (Bouton et al., 1990). Using operant discrimination procedures, for example, it has been demonstrated that the state elicited by BZ agonists, such as midazolam (Garcha, Rose, & Stolerman, 1985; Woudenberg & Slangen, 1989), diazepam (Shannon & Herling, 1983), and chlordiazepoxide (De Vry & Slangen, 1986) are all discriminated from injections of vehicle. Further, the state elicited by a BZ agonist is highly specific, generalizing to other BZ agonists (Shannon & Herling, 1983; Woudenberg & Slangen, 1989) but not to similar compounds such as the non-BZ anxiolytic buspirone (Ator & Griffiths, 1986). As a consequence, there appear to be good reasons to anticipate that BZ agonists can act both to determine and control the incentive value of the instrumental outcome.

To assess this prediction, we (Balleine et al., 1994) first trained undeprived rats to lever press for either food pellets (Experiment 2b) or for a .05% saccharin solution (Experiment 2c). Following this training we allowed half of the rats to consume the training outcome after an injection of midazolam (1 mg/kg, i.p.), whereas the remainder were given this experience after an injection of vehicle before an extinction test was conducted on the lever. For the test, half of the rats exposed to the outcome under midazolam and half of those exposed under vehicle were tested after an injection of midazolam. The remaining animals were tested under vehicle. If midazolam models the way primary motivational states control instrumental performance, we should anticipate that, on test, animals exposed to the training outcome under midazolam and tested under midazolam should increase their instrumental performance relative to the other groups. As presented in the top panel of Fig. 8.12, this is exactly what we found.

As is clear from Fig. 8.12, exposure to the instrumental outcome under midazolam acted to increase subsequent instrumental performance, but only when the rats were tested under midazolam. Furthermore, this effect was found when midazolam was used to re-

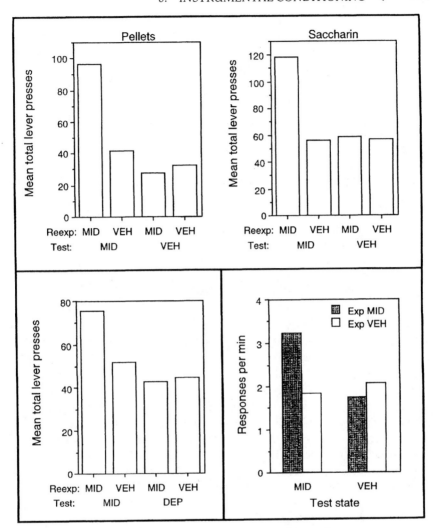

FIG 8.12.   The results of Balleine et al. (1994). Experiments 2b and 2c are presented in the top panels; Experiment 3 is presented in the lower left and Experiment 4 in the lower right panel. Copyright © 1994 by American Psychological Association. Reprinted with permission.

value either a nutritive (i.e., food pellets; left panel) or a nonnutritive (i.e., saccharin; right panel) outcome, suggesting that this effect was not mediated by any ability of midazolam to induce a state similar to food deprivation. To confirm that this was indeed the case, in a subsequent study we trained undeprived rats to lever press for food pellets before allowing half of them to consume the pellets under midazolam (MID) and the remainder were exposed under vehicle (VEH). On test, half of each of the rats in each exposure condition were tested under midazolam (MID) and the remainder were tested food deprived (DEP). If midazolam induces effects similar to those of food deprivation, we should anticipate that the effects of exposure to the pellets under midazolam will transfer to the test conducted when the rats were food deprived. In fact, as is shown in the lower lefthand panel of Fig. 8.12, we found that, although the effects of exposure to pellets under midazolam transferred to the test under midazolam, they did not transfer in rats tested food deprived.

Finally, we (Balleine et al., 1994, Experiment 4) were also able to show that this effect of midazolam on instrumental performance depended on integration of the change in outcome value with the instrumental action–outcome relation encoded during training. Undeprived rats were trained to lever press and to chain pull with one action delivering food pellets and the other a starch solution. The rats were then given several exposure sessions in which they were allowed to consume one outcome under midazolam (Exp MID) and the other outcome under vehicle (Exp VEH), following which they were given a choice extinction test on the levers and chains. For the test, half of the rats were injected with midazolam, Group MID, and the remainder were tested under vehicle, Group VEH. If the effects of midazolam observed in the previous studies depended on the integration of the change in the value of the outcome with the action–outcome relation encoded during training and that value is controlled by the state cue induced by the injection of midazolam, we anticipated that, whereas rats in Group VEH should not show an effect of exposure on test, rats in Group MID should perform more of the action that, in training, delivered the outcome subsequently consumed under midazolam. As shown in the lower right panel of Fig. 8.11, that is exactly what we found.

These studies provide consistent evidence that the motivational control of incentive value is not direct or based on a privileged connection with primary motivational states. Furthermore, the effects of midazolam on incentive value suggest that changes in the value of an instrumental outcome can be accomplished solely by modifying the affective feedback associated with those outcomes and does not depend on the relevance of the outcome itself (or features of it) to the current motivational state. As a consequence, this analysis of the motivational control of instrumental action provides the basis for suggesting that instrumental performance is determined by the value of the outcome that is encoded when that outcome is contacted. The ascription of value appears to be based on the emotional responses experienced at the time of that contact and can be controlled by internal state cues prevalent at that time in the case of an outcome that, under different internal conditions, has been found to have different incentive values.

GENERALITY

The case for the nature of the incentive processes that mediate the representation of the outcome that is encoded during instrumental conditioning has been made with reference to the effects of posttraining revaluation of the outcome by (a) taste aversion procedures, (b) increases in food deprivation, (c) reductions in food deprivation, (d) a specific satiety treatment, and (e) the administration of BZ agonist. As such, we feel that this evidence already provides a strong case for the generality of these processes across a wide range of instrumental training situations. Indeed, the fact that much the same pattern of results is found whether the incentive value of the instrumental outcome is devalued by aversive conditioning or is revalued by increases in appetitive motivational states suggests that this proposed structure is general across all the primary motivational systems that affect conditioned responding. In fact, there is already considerable converging evidence to support this suggestion. As we have summarized this evidence elsewhere in considerable detail, it is only briefly described here (cf. Dickinson, 1989; Dickinson & Balleine, 1994).

In one series of studies conducted with Lopez (Lopez, Balleine, & Dickinson, 1992), we were able to show that, when rats were trained to lever press for fluid outcomes while fluid deprived, a posttraining reduction in fluid deprivation was only effective in reducing instrumental performance if the animals were given the opportunity to consume the fluid in the undeprived state prior to the test. More recently, Lopez and Paredes-Olay (1999) have found evidence that, in similar fashion, a posttraining increase in fluid deprivation only increases the instrumental performance of rats trained to lever press for a fluid outcome when undeprived, in rats given the opportunity to consume the outcome when fluid deprived. Thus, the incentive processes that control instrumental performance following a shift in fluid deprivation appear to be similar in nature to those that control performance following a shift in food deprivation. The only difference would presumably be that, rather than becoming directly associated with a nutrient system, fluid outcomes would become associated with a system sensitive to the fluidic properties of the outcome with the latter gated or thresholded by a system, such as thirst, that is sensitive to the deprivation of fluids.

The same case can be made for shifts between, as opposed to within, motivational state (cf. Dickinson, 1989; Dickinson & Balleine, 1994, for review). In one such study (cf. Dickinson & Dawson, 1988), food deprived rats were trained to lever press and chain pull with one action earning dry food pellets and the other a sucrose solution. When the rats were fluid deprived following this training, they selectively increased their performance of the action that, in training, delivered the sucrose solution, but only if they were previously allowed to consume the sucrose when fluid deprived prior to the test.

There is also evidence for the involvement of incentive learning in a situation where male rats are trained to lever press for a signal that has been associated with access to an estrous female. Everitt and Stacey (1987) subsequently reduced the sexual motivation of the males by castration. Nevertheless, this treatment, which strongly reduces circulating testosterone, had no impact on the tendency of their rats to lever press for the signal until they were given the opportunity to engage in sexual activity with the female. Once this opportunity for incentive learning experience was given, however, the castrated subjects pressed significantly less than controls.

Finally, Hendersen and Graham (1979) found evidence that changes in the value of thermal stimuli are not directly controlled by the thermoregulatory system and depend on incentive learning. Rats were trained to avoid a heat source in a warm environment. The performance of the avoidance response was then assessed either in the same warm environment or in one where the ambient temperature was sharply reduced. In spite of the fact that the avoidance response would have denied the rats access to a source of warmth when the ambient temperature was reduced, Hendersen and Graham found no impact of the change in ambient temperature on avoidance responding. If, however, the rats were previously given noncontingent exposure to the heat lamp when the ambient temperature was reduced, they subsequently showed a reduction in avoidance responding. Thus, in a similar fashion to the effects of shifts in hunger, thirst, and sexual motivation, a shift in thermoregulatory demands had no effect on instrumental performance unless the animals were given the opportunity to learn about the incentive value of the heat source when ambient temperature was reduced.

Taken together with the evidence described earlier, these studies provide evidence to suggest that the role of incentive processes in instrumental conditioning has considerable generality. Indeed, it appears reasonable to conclude that instrumental performance is determined by the encoded representation of the consequences of an action, a representation that is both determined and controlled by primary motivational systems through their effects on incentive processes. Nevertheless, the fact that the motivational control of instrumental performance is largely indirect and can be modeled using pharmacological agents, such as BZ, suggests that the generality of the processes specified in this chapter may extend further than the operation of primary motivational systems. Motivational theories have, in the past, been criticized for the rather limited range of motives that they have ascribed to animals. However, if incentive learning is largely mediated by associating a sensory representation with an emotional response, then a very broad range of goals could be acquired by this means, whether the emotional basis for the ascription of value to those goals is causally related to primary motivational systems or some other process. Careful consideration of this point raises interesting questions about the motivational support for actions that seek drugs of abuse, such as alcohol, nicotine, opiates, and the like as well as for social goals and more abstract goals that humans have been argued to pursue (cf. Balleine & Dickinson, 1998a).

Whatever the role of incentive processes in these situations turns out to be, the general position that can be derived from the evidence presented in this chapter is that the representation of the outcome in instrumental conditioning is strongly determined by two interacting learning processes. This position is summarized in Fig. 8.13. From Pavlov's (1927) discussion of signalization, together with Tolman's (1949a, 1949b) cathexis theory and Garcia's (1989) description of latent associative connections in taste aversion learning, we proposed that the biological significance of the instrumental outcome is composed of two interacting associative connections. The first is derived from evaluative conditioning and involves the formation of an association between the representation of salient sensory features of the instrumental outcome (Se) with innate systems sensitive to the detection of chemical, perhaps hormonal, signals induced by nutrients, fluids, toxins, and the like; that is, the biological objects of primary motivational states (B). This connection opens a feedback loop to provide the basis for the second associative connection between the outcome representation (as a sensory event—Se) and emotional feedback (Se$\rightarrow$R$_{EM}$), the latter being induced by connections between the innate biological systems and affective systems (that determine valence; B$\rightarrow$Af). It is the acquisition of this second associative connection that I have referred to as incentive learning.

It is difficult to characterize incentive learning in signaling terms or in the language of predictive learning. This is because the associative connection formed appears to generate an evaluation of the outcome as if the emotional response associated with it is intrinsic to that outcome. Thus, just as animals treat an outcome paired with LiCl as if it, itself, is disgusting, they treat specific foods, fluids, and frightening events as if their emotional consequences are intrinsic to these events, whether these emotional effects are pleasant or unpleasant. From this perspec-

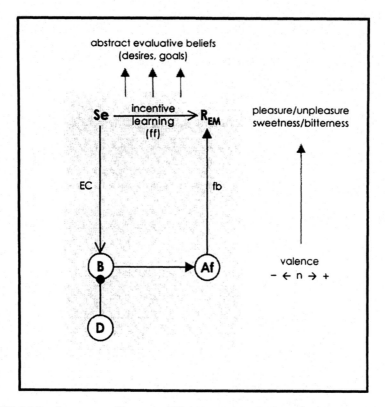

FIG. 8.13.   A summary illustration of the structures and connections that are proposed to underlie incentive processes in instrumental conditioning. Fixed excitatory connections are illustrated as blocked arrows (→), acquired excitatory connections as open arrows (→); and modulatory connection (—•). Se = representation of sensory events; B = biological structures sensitive to the detection of primary incentive such as nutrients, fluids, hormonal signals, etc; D = primary drive structures; Af = affective system; R_{EM} = emotional response; ff = feed-forward; fb = feedback.

tive, predictive learning differs from both evaluative conditioning and incentive learning because it is based on the formation of associations between the representation of sensory events. When this learning produces a change in behavior, such as that observed when a CS is paired with a US in Pavlovian conditioning, I contend that this is because it is predicated on associative processes that make contact with the biological significance of the US such as those specified as underlying the formation of the outcome representation in instrumental conditioning.

Naturally enough, different response systems are likely to be influenced by different aspects of this underlying structure, and so will likely depend to a different extent upon the evaluative and incentive learning processes described. Nevertheless, the undeniable and very general role that has been established for incentive processes in instrumental conditioning suggests that studies assessing the involvement of basic motivational processes in conditioning, for all their resonance with issues over half a century old, are of considerable relevance to contemporary theories of learning.

ACKNOWLEDGMENTS

The preparation of this chapter and the research that it reports was supported by grants from the National Institute of Mental Health (NIMH Grant No. MH 56446) and the U.K. Biotechnology and Biological Sciences Research Council. I am indebted to Tony Dickinson for the many insightful discussions of the ideas contained in this chapter and for his comments on a draft version of the chapter.

REFERENCES

Adams, C. D., & Dickinson, A. (1981). Instrumental responding following reinforcer devaluation. *Quarterly Journal of Experimental Psychology, 33B,* 109–122.

Antin, J., Gibbs, J., Holt, J., Young, R. C., & Smith, G. P. (1975). Cholecystokinin elicits the complete behavioural sequence of satiety in rats. *Journal of Comparative and Physiological Psychology, 89,* 784–790.

Antin, J., Gibbs, J., & Smith, G. P. (1978). Cholecystokinin interacts with pregastric food stimulation to elicit satiety in the rat. *Physiology and Behavior, 20,* 67–70.

Ator, N. A., & Griffiths, R. R. (1986). Discriminative stimulus effect of atypical anxiolytics in baboons and rats. *Journal of Pharmacology and Experimental Therapeutics, 237,* 393–403.

Balleine, B. W. (1992). The role of incentive learning in instrumental performance following shifts in primary motivation. *Journal of Experimental Psychology: Animal Behavior Processes, 18,* 236–250.

Balleine, B. W., Ball, J., & Dickinson, A. (1994). Benzodiazepine-induced outcome revaluation and the motivational control of instrumental action. *Behavioral Neuroscience, 108,* 573–589.

Balleine, B. W., Davies, A., & Dickinson, A. (1995). Cholecystokinin attenuates incentive learning in rats. *Behavioral Neuroscience, 109,* 312–319.

Balleine, B. W., & Dickinson, A. (1991). Instrumental performance following reinforcer devaluation depends upon incentive learning. *Quarterly Journal of Experimental Psychology, 43B,* 279–296.

Balleine, B. W., & Dickinson, A. (1992). Signalling and incentive processes in instrumental reinforcer devaluation. *Quarterly Journal of Experimental Psychology, 45B,* 285–301.

Balleine, B. W., & Dickinson, A. (1994). The role of cholecystokinin in the motivational control of instrumental action. *Behavioral Neuroscience, 108,* 590–605.

Balleine, B. W., & Dickinson, A. (1998a). Consciousness: The interface between affect and cognition. In J. Cornwell (Ed.), *Consciousness and human identity* (pp. 57–85). Oxford, UK: Oxford University Press.

Balleine, B. W., & Dickinson, A. (1998b). Goal-directed instrumental action: Contingency and incentive learning and their cortical substrates. *Neuropharmacology, 37*, 407–419.

Balleine, B. W., & Dickinson, A. (1998c). The role of incentive learning in instrumental outcome revaluation by specific satiety. *Animal Learning & Behavior, 26*, 46–59.

Balleine, B. W., Garner, C., & Dickinson, A. (1995). Instrumental outcome devaluation is attenuated by the anti-emetic ondansetron. *Quarterly Journal of Experimental Psychology, 48B*, 235–251.

Balleine, B. W., Garner, C., Gonzalez, F., & Dickinson, A. (1995). Motivational control of heterogeneous instrumental chains. *Journal of Experimental Psychology: Animal Behavior Processes, 21*, 203–217.

Bartness, T. J., & Waldbillig, R. J. (1984). Cholecystokinin-induced suppression of feeding: An evaluation of the generality of gustatory-cholecystokinin interactions. *Physiology and Behavior, 32*, 409–415.

Berridge, K. C. (1991). Modulation of taste affect by hunger caloric satiety, and sensory-specific satiety in the rat. *Appetite, 16*, 103–120.

Berridge, K. C., Flynn, F. W., Schulkin, J., & Grill, H. J. (1984). Sodium depletion enhances salt palatability in rats. *Behavioral Neuroscience, 98*, 652–660.

Bindra, D. (1972). A unified account of Pavlovian conditioning and operant training. In A. H. Black & W .F. Prokasy (Eds.), *Classical conditioning II: Current research and theory* (pp. 453–482). New York: Appleton-Century-Crofts.

Bindra, D. (1978). How adaptive behavior is produced: A perceptual motivational alternative to response-reinforcement. *Behavior & Brain Sciences, 1*, 41–52.

Blanchard, D. C., & Blanchard, R. J. (1988). Etho-experimental approaches to the biology of emotion. *Annual Review of Psychology, 39*, 43–68.

Bolles, R. C. (1967). *Theory of motivation*. New York: Harper & Row.

Bolles, R. C., Holtz, R., Dunn, T., & Hill, W. (1980). Comparison of stimulus learning and response learning in a punishment situation. *Learning & Motivation, 11*, 78–96.

Bouton, M. E. (1989). Context and retrieval in extinction and in other examples of interference in simple associative learning. In L. Dachowski & C. F. Flaherty (Eds.), *Current topics in animal learning: Brain emotion and cognition* (pp. 25–53). Hillsdale, NJ: Lawrence Erlbaum Associates.

Bouton, M. E. (1994). Conditioning, remembering and forgetting. *Journal of Experimental Psychology: Animal Behavior Processes, 20*, 219–231.

Bouton, M. E., Kenney, F. A., & Rosengard, C. (1990). State-dependent fear extinction with two benzodiazepine tranquilizers. *Behavioral Neuroscience, 104*, 44–55.

Bouton, M. E., & Peck, C. A. (1989). Context effects on conditioning, extinction and reinstatement in an appetitive conditioning paradigm. *Animal Learning & Behavior, 17*, 188–98.

Cabanac, M. (1990). Taste: The maximization of multidimensional pleasure. In E. D. Capaldi and T. L. Powley (Eds.), *Taste Experience and Feeding* (pp. 28–42). Washington, D.C.: American Psychological Association.

Cabanac, M. (1971). Physiological role of pleasure. *Science, 173*, 1103–1107.

Chaffee, B. J., & Tankanow, R. M. (1991). Ondansetron—The first of a new class of anti-emetic agents. *Clinical Pharmacy, 10*, 430–446.

Colwill, R. M., & Rescorla, R. A. (1985). Postconditioning devaluation of a reinforcer affects instrumental responding. *Journal of Experimental Psychology: Animal Behavior Processes, 11*, 120–132.

Colwill, R. C., & Rescorla, R. A. (1986). Associative structures in instrumental learning. In G. H. Bower (Ed.), *The psychology of learning and motivation* (Vol. 20, pp. 55–104). New York: Academic Press.

Cooper, S. J. (1985). Neuropeptides and food and water intake. In M. Sandler, & T. Silverstone (Eds.), *Psychopharmacology and food* (pp. 17–58). Oxford, UK: Oxford University Press.

Cooper, S. J. (1986). β-carbolines characterized as benzodiazepine receptor agonists and inverse agonists produce bi-directional changes in palatable food consumption. *Brain Research Bulletin, 17*, 627–637.

Cooper, S. J. (1989). Benzodiazepine receptor-mediated enhancement and inhibition of taste reactivity, food choice and intake. *Annals of the New York Academy of Sciences, 575*, 321–337.

Cooper, S. J. & Higgs, S. (1994). Neuropharmacology of appetite and taste preferences. In C. R. Legg & D. A. Booth (Eds.), *Appetite: Neural and behavioural bases* (pp. 212–242). Oxford, UK: Oxford University Press.

Davidson, T. L. (1987). Learning about deprivation intensity stimuli. *Behavioral Neuroscience, 101*, 198–208.

Davidson, T. L. (1993). The nature and function of interoceptive signals to feed: Towards integration of physiological and learning perspectives. *Psychological Review, 100*, 640–657.

Davis, M. (1997). Neurobiology of fear responses: The role of the amygdala. *Journal of Neuropsychiatry & Clinical Neurosciences, 9*, 382–402.

De Vry, J., & Slangen, J. L. (1986). Effects of chlordiazepoxide training dose on the mixed agonist–antagonist properties of benzodiazepine receptor antagonist Ro15-1788 in a drug discrimination procedure. *Psychopharmacology, 88*, 177–183.

Dickinson, A. (1989). Expectancy theory in animal conditioning. In S. B. Klein & R. R. Mowrer (Eds.), *Contemporary learning theories* (pp. 279–308). Hillsdale, NJ: Lawrence Erlbaum Associates.

Dickinson, A. (1994). Instrumental conditioning. In N. J. Mackintosh (Ed.), *Animal learning and cognition* (pp. 45–79). San Diego, CA: Academic Press.

Dickinson, A., & Balleine, B. W. (1993). Actions and responses: The dual psychology of behaviour. In N. Eilan, R. McCarthy, & M. W. Brewer (Eds.), *Spatial representation* (pp. 277–293). Oxford, UK: Basil Blackwell.

Dickinson, A., & Balleine, B. W. (1994). Motivational control of goal-directed action. *Animal Learning & Behavior, 22*, 1–18.

Dickinson, A., & Balleine, B. W. (1995). Motivational control of instrumental action. *Current Directions in Psychological Science, 4*, 162–167.

Dickinson, A., Campos, J., Varga, Z., & Balleine, B. W. (1996). Bidirectional control of instrumental conditioning. *Quarterly Journal of Experimental Psychology, 49B*, 289–306.

Dickinson, A., & Dawson, G. R. (1988). Motivational control of instrumental performance: The role of prior experience with the reinforcer. *Quarterly Journal of Experimental Psychology, 40B*, 113–134.

Dourish, C. T. (1992). Behavioural analysis of the role of CCK-A and CCK-B receptors in the control of feeding by rodents. In C. T. Dourish, S. J. Cooper, S. D. Iversen, & L. L. Iversen (Eds.), *Multiple cholecystokinin receptors in the CNS* (pp. 234–253). Oxford, UK: Oxford University Press.

Dourish, C. T., Ruckert, A. C., Tattersall, F. D., & Iversen, S. D. (1989). Evidence that decreased feeding induced by systemic injection of cholecystokinin is mediated by CCK-A receptors. *European Journal of Pharmacology, 173*, 233–234.

Everitt, B. J., & Stacey, P. (1987). Studies of instrumental behavior with sexual reinforcement in male rats (Rattus norvegicus): II. Effects of preoptic area lesions, castration and testosterone. *Journal of Comparative Psychology, 101*, 407–419.

Fanselow, M. S. (1994). Neural organization of the defensive behavior system responsible for fear. *Psychonomic Bulletin & Review, 1,* 429–438.

Fedorchak, P. M., & Bolles, R. C. (1988). Nutritive expectancies mediate cholecystokinin's suppression-of-intake effect. *Behavioral Neuroscience, 102,* 451–455.

Gallistel, C. R. (1990). *The organization of learning.* Cambridge, MA: MIT Press.

Garcha, H. S., Rose, I. C., & Stolerman, I. P. (1985). Midazolam cue in rats: Generalization tests with anxiolytic and other drugs. *Psychopharmacology, 87,* 233–237.

Garcia, J. (1989). Food for Tolman: Cognition and cathexis in concert. In T. Archer & L.-G. Nilsson (Eds.), *Aversion, avoidance and anxiety* (pp. 45–85). Hillsdale, NJ: Lawrence Erlbaum Associates.

Gibbs, J., Falasco, J. D., & McHugh, P. R. (1976). Cholecystokinin-decreased food intake in rhesus monkeys. *American Journal of Physiology, 230,* 15–18.

Gibbs, J., Young, R. C., & Smith, G. P. (1973). Cholecystokinin decreases food intake in rats. *Journal of Comparative and Physiological Psychology, 84,* 488–495.

Gosnell, B. A., & Hsiao, S. (1981). Cholecystokinin satiety and orosensory feedback. *Physiology and Behavior, 27,* 153–156.

Grill, H. J., & Berridge, K. C. (1985). Taste reactivity as a measure of the neural control of palatability. In J. M. Sprague & A. N. Epstein (Eds.), *Progress in psychobiology and physiological psychology* (Vol. 11, pp. 1–61). Orlando, FL: Academic Press.

Grindley, G. C. (1932). The formation of a simple habit in guinea pigs. *British Journal of Psychology, 23,* 127–147.

Hall, W. G., Arnold, H. M., & Myers, K. P. (2000). The acquisition of an appetite. *Psychological Science, 68,* 603–610.

Hanson, H., & Strouse, J. (1987). Effects of the CCK antagonist L-364,718 on food intake and on the blockade of feeding produced by exogenous CCK in the rat. *Federation Proceedings, 46,* 1480.

Hendersen, R. W., & Graham, J. (1979). Avoidance of heat by rats: Effects of thermal context on the rapidity of extinction. *Learning & Motivation, 10,* 351–363.

Higgins, G. A., Kilpatrick, G. J., Bunce, K. T., Jones, B. J., & Tyers, M. B. (1989). 5-HT3 receptor antagonists injected into the area postrema inhibit cisplatin-induced emesis in the ferret. *British Journal of Pharmacology, 97,* 247–255.

Holland, P. C., & Rescorla, R. A. (1975). The effects of two ways of devaluing the unconditioned stimulus after first- and second-order appetitive conditioning. *Journal of Experimental Psychology: Animal Behavior Processes, 1,* 355–363.

Hull, C. L. (1943). *Principles of behavior.* New York: Appleton.

Hull, C. L. (1952). *A behavior system.* New Haven, CT: Yale University Press.

Khosla, S., & Crawley, J. N. (1988). Potency of L-364,718 as an antagonist of the behavioural effects of peripherally administered cholecystokinin. *Life Sciences, 42,* 153–160.

Konorski, J. (1967). *Integrative activity of the brain: An interdisciplinary approach.* Chicago: University of Chicago Press.

Kraly, F. S., Carty, W., Resnick, S., & Smith, G. P. (1978). Effect of cholecystokinin on meal size and intermeal interval in the sham feeding rat. *Journal of Comparative and Physiological Psychology, 92,* 697–707.

Kulkosky, P. J. (1984). Effect of cholecystokinin octapeptide on ethanol intake in the rat. *Alcohol, 1,* 125–128.

LeDoux, J. E. (1995). Emotion: Clues from the brain. *Annual Review of Psychology, 46,* 209–235.

Le Magnen, J. (1985). *Hunger.* Cambridge, UK: Cambridge University Press.

Leonard, B. E. (1999). Therapeutic applications of benzodiazepine receptor ligands in anxiety. *Human Psychopharmacology Clinical & Experimental, 14,* 125–135.

Lopez, M., Balleine, B. W., & Dickinson, A. (1992). Incentive learning and the motivational control of instrumental performance by thirst. *Animal Learning & Behavior, 20*, 322–328.

Lopez, M., & Paredes-Olay, C. (1999). Sensitivity of instrumental responses to a upshift in water deprivation. *Animal Learning and Behavior, 27*, 280–287.

Mackintosh, N. J. (1975). A theory of attention: Variations in the associability of stimuli with reinforcement. *Psychological Review, 82*, 276–298.

Mackintosh, N. J. (1983). *Conditioning and associative learning*. Oxford, UK: Oxford University Press.

McLaren, I. P. L., Kaye, H., & Mackintosh, N. J. (1989). An associative theory of the representation of stimuli: Applications to perceptual learning and latent inhibition. In R. G. M. Morris (Ed.), *Parallel distributed processing—Implications for psychology and neurobiology* (pp. 102–130). Oxford, UK: Oxford University Press.

Miller, R. R., & Matzel, L. D. (1988). The comparator hypothesis: A response rule for the expression of associations. In G. H. Bower (Ed.), *The psychology of learning and motivation* (Vol. 22, pp. 51–92). San Diego, CA: Academic Press.

Miller, S., & Konorski, J. (1928). Sur une forme particulière des reflex conditionnels [On a particular form of conditioned reflexes]. *Les Compte Rendus des Seances de la Société Polonaise de Biologie, 49*, 1155–1157.

Morgan, M. J. (1974). Resistance to satiation. *Animal Behaviour, 22*, 449–466.

Mowrer, O. H. (1960). *Learning theory and symbolic processes*. New York: Wiley.

Pavlov, I. P. (1927). *Conditioned reflexes*. Oxford, UK: Oxford University Press.

Pearce, J. M. (1994). Similarity and discrimination: A selective review and a connectionist model. *Psychological Review, 94*, 61–73.

Pearce, J. M., & Hall, G. (1980). A model for Pavlovian learning: Variations in the effectiveness of conditioned but not of unconditioned stimuli. *Psychological Review, 87*, 532–552.

Pelchat, M. L., Grill, H. J., Rozin, P., & Jacobs, J. (1983). Quality of acquired responses to taste by Rattus norvegicus depends upon type of associated discomfort. *Journal of Comparative Psychology, 97*, 140–153.

Rescorla, R. A. (1973). Informational variables in Pavlovian conditioning. In G. H. Bower (Ed.), *The psychology of learning and motivation* (Vol. 10, pp. 1–46). San Diego, CA: Academic Press.

Rescorla, R. A. (1988). Pavlovian conditioning: It's not what you think it is. *American Psychologist, 43*, 151–160.

Rescorla, R. A. (1990). Instrumental responses become associated with reinforcers that differ in one feature. *Animal Learning & Behavior, 18*, 206–211.

Rescorla, R. A. (1991). Associative relations in instrumental learning: The eighteenth Bartlett memorial lecture. *Quarterly Journal of Experimental Psychology: Comparative & Physiological Psychology, 43*, 1–23.

Rescorla, R. A. (1992). Depression of an instrumental response by a single devaluation of its outcome. *Quarterly Journal of Experimental Psychology, 44B*, 123–136.

Rescorla, R. A., & Solomon, R. L. (1967). Two-process learning theory: Relationship between Pavlovian conditioning and instrumental learning. *Psychological Review, 74*, 151–182.

Rescorla, R. A., & Wagner, A. R. (1972). A theory of Pavlovian conditioning: variations in the effectiveness of reinforcement and non-reinforcement. In A. H. Black & W. F. Prokasy (Eds.), *Classical conditioning II: Current research and theory* (pp. 64–99). New York: Appleton-Century-Crofts.

Rolls, B. J. (1990). The role of sensory-specific satiety in food intake and food selection. In E. D. Capaldi and T. L. Powley (Eds.). *Taste Experience and Feeding* (pp. 197–209). Washington, D.C.: American Psychological Association.

Rozin, P., & Fallon, A. E. (1987). A perspective on disgust. *Psychological Review, 94*, 23–41.

Shannon, H. E., & Herling, S. (1983). Discriminative stimulus effects of diazepam in rats: Evidence for a maximal effect. *Journal of Pharmacology and Experimental Therapeutics, 227,* 160–166.

Siegel, P. S. (1944). A note on the construction of Skinner box pellets. *Journal of Comparative Psychology, 37,* 233–234.

Skinner, B. F. (1932). On the rate of formation of a conditioned reflex. *Journal of General Psychology, 7,* 274–285.

Smith, G. P., & Gibbs, J. (1992). The development and proof of the CCK hypothesis of satiety. In C. T. Dourish, S. J. Cooper, S. D. Iversen, & L. L. Iversen (Eds.), *Multiple cholecystokinin receptors in the CNS* (pp. 166–182). Oxford, U: Oxford University Press.

Spence, K. W. (1956). *Behavior theory and conditioning.* New Haven, CT: Yale University Press.

Stacher, G. (1985). Satiety effects of cholecystokinin and ceruletide in lean and obese man: Neuronal cholecystokinin. *Annals of the New York Academy of Science, 448,* 431–436.

Sutton, R. S., & Barto, A. G. (1981). Toward a modern theory of adaptive networks: Expectation and prediction. *Psychological Review, 88,* 135–171.

Thorndike, E. L. (1911). *Animal intelligence: Experimental studies.* New York: Macmillan.

Tolman, E. C. (1949a). The nature and functioning of wants. *Psychological Review, 56,* 357–369.

Tolman, E. C. (1949b). There is more than one kind of learning. *Psychological Review, 56,* 144–155.

Trapold, M. A., & Overmier, J. B. (1972). The second learning process in instrumental learning. In A. H. Black & W. F. Prokasy (Eds.), *Classical conditioning II: Current research and theory* (pp. 427–452). New York: Appleton-Century-Crofts.

Wagner, A. R. (1981). SOP: A model of automatic memory processing in animal behavior. In N. E. Spear & R. R. Miller (Eds.), *Information processing in animals: Memory mechanisms* (pp. 5–47). Hillsdale, NJ: Lawrence Erlbaum Associates.

Wise, R. A. & Dawson, V. (1974). Diazepam-induced eating and lever pressing for food in sated rats. *Journal of Comparative and Physiological Psychology, 86,* 930–941.

Woudenberg, F., & Slangen, J. L. (1989). Discriminative stimulus properties of midazolam: Comparison with other benzodiazepines. *Psychopharmacology, 97,* 466–470.

Young, P. T. (1961). *Motivation and emotion.* New York: Wiley.

chapter 9

Perceptual Learning:
Association and Differentiation

Geoffrey Hall
University of York

*A*n animal (or person) trained to respond in a given way to one stimulus will tend to show the same behavior (although usually with reduced vigor) when confronted with another similar stimulus. The standard explanation for this phenomenon of *generalization* is, in principle, very simple. It is acknowledged that the event or object that the experimenter refers to, for convenience, as a stimulus will always be, in fact, a complex made up of many features or elements. The simplest of tones, such as might be used in the animal conditioning laboratory, has a definable intensity, duration, frequency, site of origin, and so on. All of these features may be presumed to be capable of entering into associations and thus of contributing to a conditioned response (CR) that the tone can come to elicit as a result of training. Another stimulus such as a clicker may appear to be quite different from the tone but it will hold some features in common with the latter. The situation is shown in Fig. 9.1. Each circle represents the set of features that constitutes a stimulus. Each of the stimuli, A and B, possesses certain unique and defining features (represented by the areas marked *a* and *b*). However, A and B also have some features in common (the overlapping area marked *c*). Establishing a CR to A will mean conditioning both *a* and *c* elements. Generalization to B will occur because presentation of this stimulus will activate some elements (the *c* elements) that have been conditioned when presented as parts of Stimulus A.

The degree to which generalization occurs between a pair of stimuli can be modified by prior experience of them. Some forms of prior training can enhance generalization; others can reduce it (i.e., enhance the ease with which the two stimuli are discriminated), resulting in what has sometimes been termed a *perceptual learning effect*. There is nothing in what has been said so far about the nature of generalization that would lead us to expect this. If the set of elements activated by a given stimulus is fixed and defined by the nature of that stimulus, and if our conditioning procedures are effective in endowing its elements with associative strength, then it might be supposed that generalization to

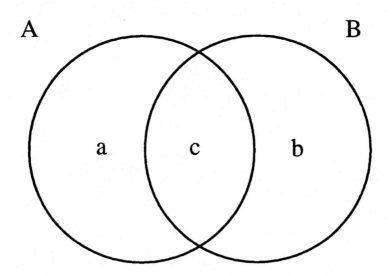

FIG. 9.1. Diagrammatic representation of two stimuli, A and B. The area of the circle represents the set of stimulus elements activated by a stimulus. Those in the segment marked *a* are elements unique to Stimulus A; those in the *b* segment are unique to B. The area marked *c* corresponds to a set of elements held in common by the two stimuli.

some other stimulus would occur automatically, to a degree determined solely by the number of elements held in common. The fact that prior experience with the stimuli can influence the extent to which generalization will occur needs explanation. Certain possibilities come to mind immediately. Some are consistent with the framework just outlined—pretraining procedures might have their effects because they modulate the associative strength acquired by common elements or because they establish other associations that also contribute to the strength of the observed CR. Other possibilities may require a more radical revision of the framework—perhaps we are wrong to take the set of elements evoked by a stimulus as a given; perhaps the constituents of this set vary as a result of experience. The essence of the notion of *stimulus differentiation*, as employed by Gibson (1969) in her influential account of perceptual learning, is that, with experience, events or objects become able to activate the central representations of elements that were not activated on first presentation; also that some elements (principally those that are not unique features of the stimulus) may become less readily activated.

In what follows I attempt a review of the major categories of procedure in which generalization (or discrimination) has been shown to be modulated by prior training in animal subjects. For convenience of exposition I divide these procedures into two main groups—those in which pretraining is given with just one of the critical stimuli (i.e., just to A, the reinforced stimulus, or just to B, the test stimulus) and those in which pretraining is given to both. Each of these sections is further subdivided according to whether the pretraining involves reinforcement or not. The central question in each case is whether the phenomena can be accommodated by amendments to associative theory as applied to the framework depicted in Fig. 9.1, or whether a more radical revision, which might involve the operation of a special process of perceptual learning, needs to be accepted. The topics to be discussed were considered in detail by Hall (1991), who dealt with the work published before 1990. Only an outline of the conclusions reached then is presented here, and the focus is on research conducted since that date.

PRETRAINING WITH ONE STIMULUS

Reinforced Training With Stimulus A

A test of generalization requires that A receive some reinforced training to establish the response under study. However, we may compare the generalization produced by a standard amount of initial training with that obtained after more extensive reinforced training with A. Extended training can be expected to ensure that all the elements of A, both type *a* and type *c* will become strongly associated with the reinforcer. If no other processes are operating, generalization to B should occur readily and be more marked than that obtained when less training with A is given. It is of interest, therefore, that it has been repeatedly reported that, in some training preparations, generalization gradients appear to grow sharper after prolonged initial training (e.g., Hearst & Koresko, 1968; Hoffeld, 1962; Hovland, 1937). This result prompts the speculation that prolonged exposure to Stimulus A might allow differentiation to occur, with the stimulus becoming increasingly likely to activate *a* elements, and the *c* elements becoming unresponsive. If the presentation of B on test is also unable to activate the *c* elements fully, then generalized responding will be weak. An obvious problem for this account is that it is difficult to see how the system could "know" which elements were the *c* elements, in advance of experience with test stimulus B. I do not consider possible solutions to this problem at this stage, however, in view of other, more basic issues that arise in connection with these data.

First, at the empirical level, there is the mundane point that the sharpening of the gradient observed in at least some experiments may be more apparent than real. Generalization gradients are often expressed in relative terms (i.e., the responding shown to B is given as a proportion of that shown to A). Extended reinforcement of A can thus produce a sharpening of the relative gradient not because of any real reduction in the vigor of the response elicited by B, but because it produces a disproportionate increase in the vigor of that evoked by A. Even for those few cases in which there appears to be a sharpening of the gradient when measured in absolute terms, it is possible to construct a perfectly adequate alternative account without departing from the tenets of standard associative learning theory. When a subject is first reinforced in the presence of A, other aspects of the training situation will also acquire associative strength and will thus be able to contribute to the responding shown to B on test. However, standard associative learning principles (e.g., Rescorla & Wagner, 1972) predict that these background cues, being less well correlated with reinforcement than Stimulus A, will lose strength as training proceeds. This loss may be enough to explain why the response to the test stimulus, B, should be reduced.

We must conclude, then, that the classical body of work on simple generalization provides only weak support for the notion that stimulus differentiation goes on during extended training, and recent work using this procedure has done little to change the picture (see, e.g., Walker & Branch, 1998). There are, however, some recent experiments, using a rather different procedure and directed, ostensibly, at a rather different issue, that turn out to be relevant to the basic theoretical question. Todd and Mackintosh (1990) trained pigeons on a successive discrimination in which, on every session, the birds saw 20 pictorial stimuli, each presented twice, usually several trials apart. The birds were given a recognition memory task in that they were rewarded for pecking at a picture on its first presentation but not on the second. There were two conditions of training. In one, the same pictures were used on every session, and thus a relative recency discrimination was required—all the pictures were familiar and the bird's job was to refrain from pecking at a picture that it had seen earlier in the same session. In the other, the absolute novelty version of the task, a new set of pictures was used on each session so that the bird could solve the problem simply by pecking at any picture that it had never seen before. Rather surprisingly, given that proactive interference effects might be expected to disrupt performance on the relative recency discrimination, Todd and Mackintosh found that this version of the task was learned more readily than the absolute novelty discrimination. (This result has been confirmed and extended by Macphail, Good, & Honey, 1995, whose experimental results are presented in Fig. 9.2.) Todd and Mackintosh concluded that any proactive interference effects occurring in their experiment must have been outweighed by the operation of another, more powerful process.

The relevance of these experiments to the issue of the effect of extended training on generalization is as follows. First, an important feature of the relative recency task is that the subjects are faced with the same set of stimuli on every session and thus can become fully familiar with them; to this extent, the relative recency task constitutes a parallel to the extended training procedure. Second, generalization between the stimuli used will play an important part in determining the outcome. Accurate performance depends not only on an ability to recognize a picture as being the same as one seen before, but also on the ability to discriminate this picture from others that are similar but not identical—a reduction in the tendency to generalize between similar pictures would facilitate performance. The superior performance of subjects in the relative recency condition can thus be taken to support the view that generalization gradients are sharpened after extensive training. This is essentially the conclusion reached by Todd and Mackintosh (1990), who argued that repeated exposure to a stimulus will be needed if the birds are to acquire "a representation of the stimulus … sufficiently precise and durable for it to be discriminated from the numerous other stimuli to which the birds are being exposed" (p. 398). Proactive interference effects in the relative recency condition, they suggested, are outweighed by the operation of the perceptual learning processes that result in the formation of such representations. Their results do not speak, however, to the exact nature of the process involved.

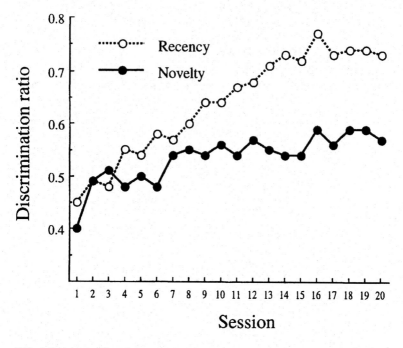

FIG. 9.2. Mean discrimination ratios (ratio of responses in the first 10 sec of positive trials to responses in the first 10 sec of all trials) over 20 days of training for two groups of pigeons in the experiment by Macphail et al. (1995). All animals saw 12 pictures twice on each session and were rewarded for responding to the first presentation of a picture. In the recency condition the same pictures were used in every session; in the novelty condition a new set of pictures was used in each session.

Nonreinforced Preexposure to Stimulus A

When reinforcement is given during preexposure to A, effects based simply on the animal's growing familiarity with this stimulus are likely to be obscured by the enhanced generalization that will be a consequence of A's elevated level of associative strength. It may seem sensible, then, to look at the effects of nonreinforced preexposure to A. Does this procedure result in reduced generalization to B once a CR has subsequently been established to A? Unfortunately, this question yields no simple answer—some experiments (e.g., Honey, 1990, Experiment 1) have found generalization to be reduced; others (e.g., Symonds & Hall, 1995, Experiment 1) have found no difference between subjects given preexposure to A and those for whom A was novel at the time of conditioning. No doubt a close analysis of the procedural details of these experiments would throw up suggestions about the source of this discrepancy, but to pursue such an analysis seems unlikely to be fruitful for the following reason. Whatever else may have happened during nonreinforced preexposure in the experiments just cited, we can be fairly sure that Stimulus A would have suffered latent inhibition and thus have been rendered less effective as a conditioned stimulus (CS) when it came to conditioning. This in itself would be enough to reduce the extent to which Stimulus B was capable of evoking generalized responding, thus rendering ambiguous the result of prime theoretical importance. Reduced generalization to B will be of interest only if we can be reasonably confident that the groups being compared do not differ in the associative strength acquired by A. The simple absence of a difference in a direct test of A will not be enough to convince (such a test may simply be less sensitive than one given with Stimulus B). We should focus our attention, therefore, on the small group of experiments in which, in spite of what might expected from considerations of latent inhibition, preexposure to A has been found to facilitate conditioning with this stimulus.

These experiments are characterized by the fact that exposure to A, both during preexposure and on the conditioning trial, is kept to a minimum, and also by the use of stimuli substantially more complex than those usually employed in standard conditioning procedures. Thus, Bennett, Tremain, and Mackintosh (1996) conducted a flavor-aversion experiment with rats in which the CS was a solution of monosodium glutamate to which were added sucrose and quinine. Only 1 ml of the compound was given on the conditioning trial and preexposure consisted of a single presentation of 3 ml of the compound given several days before conditioning. On a test given after conditioning, animals given this preexposure showed a more substantial aversion than control subjects given no preexposure. The other experiments that revealed a similar facilitation of conditioning as a result of preexposure all used a context conditioning procedure in which the CS is the set of cues that constitute an experimental chamber and the CR is the freezing response that develops in rats that have received an electric shock in that chamber. In these experiments, by Fanselow (1990) and by Kiernan and Westbrook (1993), rats were given brief exposure to the context (for 2 min in Fanselow's experiments, for four 2-min trials in those by Kiernan & Westbrook) prior to a conditioning session in which a single shock was given after the rat had been in the context for about a minute. On a subsequent test session, these subjects showed more freezing in the context than did control subjects that had received no preexposure (or preexposure to a different context).

Before turning to the issue of how the CR established by these training procedures generalizes to other stimuli, we should consider why it might be that these procedures yield a facilitation of conditioning rather than the usual latent inhibition effect. The explanation offered in one form or another by all the experimenters supposes that preexposure allows the animal to form an integrated representation of the complex of features that will be used as the CS. With extended preexposure, latent inhibition will begin to develop, but before this happens (i.e., when preexposure is brief) the beneficial effects on conditioning of having a preformed representation can be observed. Bennett et al. (1996) referred to the formation of a representation as a process of unitization, and provided an associative account of the mechanism, based on that suggested by McLaren, Kaye, and Mackintosh (1989). Preexposure to a complex stimulus, they pointed out, allows the animal to experience the cooccurrence of its various features, and thus allows the formation of associative links among these features. On a subsequent, brief, conditioning trial, only some of these features will be sampled (the stimulus is complex and the animal's processing capacity is limited), and only these will become associated with the reinforcer. A different set may be sampled on the test trial but, for animals given preexposure, a CR should still occur as the associative links established during preexposure will mean that those sampled on test will be able to activate those that formed links with the reinforcer during conditioning. The basic explanatory principle will be familiar as a form of sensory preconditioning.

The issue of generalization in animals given minimal preexposure to A prior to conditioning was addressed by Kiernan and Westbrook (1993, Experiment 3; see also Killcross, Kiernan, Dwyer, & Westbrook, 1998, Experiments 1b and 2). The experimental group in the Kiernan and Westbrook study received four 2-min preexposures to Context A followed by a conditioning session in which a shock was given 60 sec after the animals had been put into this same context. Control subjects experienced the same conditioning regime but received their preexposure in a different context, C. All subjects then received test sessions in which freezing was measured in A and also in the generalization test context, B. The results of this test are summarized in Fig. 9.3. The results for the test in A confirm those already discussed—the preexposed subjects showed significantly more freezing than did the controls. On the test in Context B, the levels of freezing were somewhat less, as might be expected of a generalization test. Critically, the pattern was now reversed with the control subjects showing more freezing than the experimental subjects.

The results presented in Fig. 9.3 show that nonreinforced preexposure to A can limit the degree of generalization to B. This effect is not to be explained away in terms of poor acquisition of strength by A—the preexposure procedure used was one that actually facilitated conditioning to A. The conclusion suggested by this pattern of results is

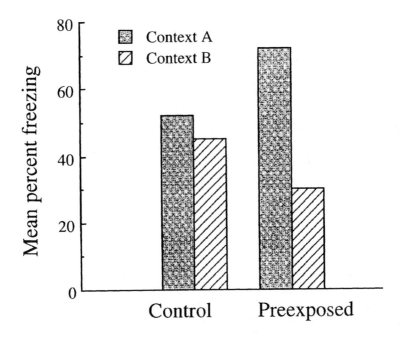

FIG. 9.3. Mean percentage of observations scored as freezing in a context previously paired with shock (Context A) and a different test context (B), for control rats given no preexposure to A and for rats given four 2-min preexposure trials with A (preexposed). From Kiernan and Westbrook (1993, Experiment 3).

that, whatever else happens during preexposure, some perceptual learning process is brought into play that acts to increase the discriminability of A and B and outweighs the effect to be expected on the basis of the magnitude of the CR governed by A. These results are silent as to the nature of this process, but Kiernan and Westbrook (1993) suggested that the associative processes proposed as the basis of unitization may play a role. Central to their argument is the assumption that the features most likely to be sampled during brief exposure to the context given on the conditioning trial are those that it will hold in common with other similar contexts (the c elements of Fig. 9.1). For control subjects, therefore the c elements will be strongly conditioned and the presence of these elements on test with B (or with A for that matter) will allow a fairly strong CR to be evoked. For animals given preexposure to A, the features that compose this stimulus will undergo latent inhibition to some extent, the c elements will be less strongly conditioned, and the CR evoked by B will be weaker. However, preexposure will also give the animal a chance to sample the less salient a elements and to form a–c

associations (the unitization process). When tested with A, the c elements may be sampled first, but as the test proceeds, a elements will also be sampled and, by virtue of their ability to activate the conditioned c elements, they will contribute to the CR observed. This effect could be enough to outweigh those of latent inhibition. With its assumption that the initial perception of the A stimulus is likely to be dominated by c elements, this ingenious explanation has something in common with the notion of stimulus differentiation. It differs, however, in that it does not suppose that exposure to A produces some permanent change in which elements are activated, in the way that the event is perceived. All it needs to assume is that c elements are more salient than a elements and that the limited capacity of the animal's processing system means that only salient elements are sampled when exposure to the stimulus is brief.

Nonreinforced Preexposure to Stimulus B

As preexposure to A can enhance the discriminability of A and B, it will come as no surprise that preexposure to B appears to be able to produce the same effect. Experiments using the flavor-aversion technique have routinely found that an aversion conditioned to A generalizes poorly to B in rats given prior exposure to B (e.g., Bennett, Wills, Wells, & Mackintosh, 1994; Best & Batson, 1977; Burch-Vernon & Riccio, 1997; Honey & Hall, 1989b; but see also Symonds & Hall, 1995). An experiment using quite a different training procedure (imprinting techniques with domestic chicks as the subjects) has generated essentially the same result (Honey, Horn, & Bateson, 1993).

It seems likely that latent inhibition plays a major role in generating this effect. During preexposure to B, the b and c stimulus elements will undergo latent inhibition and thus conditioning to A (a stimulus composed of a and c elements) will be largely a consequence of the acquisition of strength by the novel a elements. Generalized responding to B, which will depend on the strength acquired by c elements, will therefore be weak. Support for this interpretation comes from the fact that Burch-Vernon and Riccio (1997), who found a particularly strong effect, used stimuli that were very similar (milk and chocolate milk) and thus, presumably, had a high proportion of c elements. Further, Bennett et al. (1994), who explicitly manipulated the common elements of the stimuli by adding a salient extra flavor to both A and B (i.e., they preexposed to BX, conditioned with AX, and tested with BX), found a potent effect only in these conditions. In other circumstances (e.g., when animals were preexposed to BY, i.e., to a compound made up of B and some other salient flavor), generalization from AX to BX was profound. Finally, a feature of the experiment by Symonds and Hall (1995), which found no effect of preexposure to B on generalization, was that very extensive conditioning was given with Stimulus A—such training might well have been enough to overcome the latent inhibition engendered during the preexposure phase.

There is one experiment, however, for which an interpretation in terms of latent inhibition seems not to be viable. Using auditory stimuli as A and B (a tone and white noise, counterbalanced), Honey (1990) investigated the effects of giving preexposure to A (48 trials), to B (48 trials), to both (48 trials with each), or to neither of these stimuli on the generalization to B of an appetitive response conditioned to A. The results of the test session with B are presented in Fig. 9.4. They show, first, that animals given preexposure to A generalize less than those given no preexposure, a result already mentioned and one consistent with the supposition that this preexposure endows the c elements, on which generalization will depend, with latent inhibition. Strikingly, however, the subjects given preexposure to B showed even less test responding than those given preexposure to A in spite of having received approximately equivalent exposure to the c elements. Those animals given preexposure to both stimuli, and who therefore had exposure to the c elements twice as often as animals in the other preexposed groups, showed the highest level of test performance. Considerations of latent inhibition require that this group should show the lowest level of response of all. Some process other than, or in addition to, latent inhibition must be at work in this experiment.

In explaining his findings, Honey (1990) turned to a suggestion, originally made by Best and Batson (1977), that the novelty (or familiarity) of a stimulus might be a feature that can acquire associative strength and thus mediate generalization. When the CS and the test stimulus have the same degree of novelty or familiarity, generalization will occur readily. Thus test responding will be vigorous both in the control group (for which both stimuli are novel) and in the group exposed to both A and B (for which both will be familiar). Generalization will be less in those groups for whom the stimuli do not share a common feature of this sort—that is, in the group preexposed to B (trained with a novel CS but given a familiar test stimulus) and in the group preexposed to A (who received a familiar CS and a novel test stimulus). This is an intriguing notion that might have general relevance in the explanation of perceptual learning effects (see Hall, 1991). It should be acknowledged, however, that other interpretations of Honey's results are available. A feature of Honey's procedure was that the trial durations during preexposure were different for the two stimuli, that for B being longer than that for A. It follows that the c elements had more opportunity to acquire latent inhibition in B-preexposed animals, and this may be

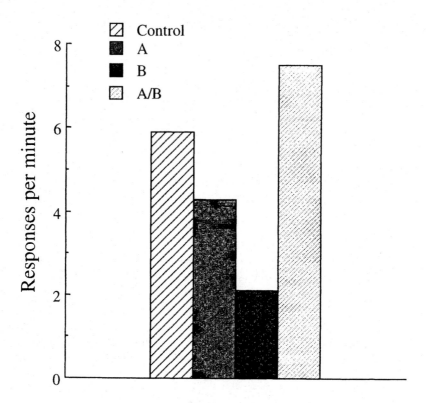

FIG. 9.4. Group mean response rates for a generalization test with Stimulus B for rats previously given food-reinforced conditioning with A. Before conditioning, different groups had received exposure to A, to B, to both stimuli (A/B), or to neither (control). After Honey (1990).

enough to explain their low level of test responding. It remains the case that the group given preexposure to both stimuli must have suffered the most latent inhibition of all, but here another factor may have come into play. These subjects received pretraining in which A and B occurred together in the same session, separated by only a fairly brief intertrial interval. This experience could have allowed the development of excitatory association between the stimuli and, if so, the high level of responding shown to B on test would be explicable in terms of the familiar associative principle of sensory preconditioning. Until this matter is resolved, it would be prudent to withhold judgment on the role played by novelty and familiarity in generalization.

PRETRAINING WITH BOTH STIMULI

Differential Pretraining

Discrimination training in which the animal experiences reinforcement in association with A (A+) but not with B (B−) will establish differential responding so that the animal performs the CR to A and not to B. Standard associative theory (e.g., Rescorla & Wagner, 1972) explains this by adopting a mechanism that ensures that excitatory associative strength accrues to the *a* elements, inhibitory strength to the *b* elements, and that the *c* elements, which do not reliably predict an outcome, become neutralized. There is no need to suppose what has sometimes been proposed, that such training also enhances the discriminability of the stimuli. It may do so, but the formation of a discrimination in itself is not enough to prove the point. Relevant evidence on this matter comes from experiments in which the subjects are required to learn some new discrimination task involving the same stimuli. If this second task is chosen with care it is possible to ensure that direct transfer based on the responses acquired during training on the first does not contribute to the discriminative performance required in the second. In these circumstances, positive transfer has been taken to indicate that the first stage of training has led to an increase in the discriminability of the stimuli, a phenomenon referred to as the *acquired distinctiveness* of cues.

A Demonstration of the Effect

In a recent study, conducted in collaboration with Ward-Robinson (Ward-Robinson & Hall, 1999), I attempted to demonstrate this phenomenon. The design of the experiment, based in part on one reported by Honey and Hall (1989a), is summarized in Table 9.1. In Phase 1, rats received training with three auditory stimuli. For one group, two stimuli (A and C) signaled the delivery of a sucrose pellet and the third (B) was not reinforced. For a second group, B was reinforced and A and C were not. After the animals had learned their Phase 1 discriminations, all received a second phase of training in which Stimulus A was paired with a new reinforcer, an electric shock. Generalization of the conditioned fear established by this training was assessed in a test of the ability of B and of C to suppress a baseline instrumental response supported by the delivery of a standard food pellet reinforcer.

The results of the generalization test are shown in Fig. 9.5. In neither group was suppression very profound, and what suppression there was tended to diminish over the course of the three test trials given with

TABLE 9.1   Design of Experiment by Ward-Robinson and Hall (1999)

Group	Phase 1	Phase 2	Generalization Test	Mediated Conditioning Test
	A → +			
A+/B–/C+	B–			
	C → +			
		A → shock	B vs. C	Lever → +
	A–			
A–/B+/C–	B → +			
	C–			

Note. A, B, and C refer to auditory stimuli that either signaled delivery of a sucrose pellet, → +, or were nonreinforced, –. Stimulus A was paired with a shock reinforcer during Phase 2. The effect of this training on the rat's willingness to earn sucrose pellets by lever pressing was assessed during the mediated conditioning test. The generalization test examined the ability of Stimuli B and C to suppress a different instrumental response.

each stimulus. In both groups, however, Stimulus C evoked more suppression than Stimulus B. The effect was more marked in Group A+/B–/C+ than in Group A–/B+/C–, but statistical analysis confirmed that the difference was reliable in both. This result may be summarized as showing that generalization occurs more readily between stimuli that have shared a common training history in Phase 1 (A and C, for both groups) than between stimuli that have been treated differently (A and B). The particular design used here allows us to avoid some of the problems that have complicated previous attempts to demonstrate such an effect (see Hall, 1991). First, all subjects received discrimination training in Phase 1. In some previous experiments comparison has been made between separate groups, one given discrimination training and one not, leaving open the possibility that any effect obtained might be a consequence of the general effects of discrimination training rather than one based on changes in the effectiveness of specific cues. Next, in experiments using a between-groups design, it is possible that differences on test arise, not because of differences in generalization between A and the test stimulus, but because of differences in the ease with which A acquires associative strength in the second phase of training. The within-subjects comparisons allowed by the present design (be-

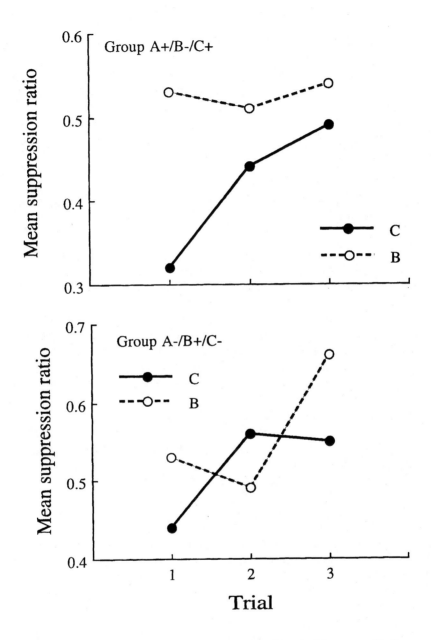

FIG. 9.5.   Group mean suppression scores for each trial of the generalization test in the experiment by Ward-Robinson and Hall (1999). For both groups, Stimulus C had received the same Phase 1 treatment as Stimulus A and Stimulus B had received a different treatment (see Table 9.1).

tween B and C for each group) rule out this possibility. Finally, the pattern of results shown in Fig. 9.5 cannot be the product of the transfer of CRs acquired in the first phase of training. It might be thought, for instance, that the enhanced suppression in the presence of C in Group A+/B−/C+ is simply a consequence of the interfering effects of the food-reinforced CR carried over from Phase 1 training. If this were so, however, Group A−/B+/C− should show more marked suppression to B than to C, the opposite of the result obtained.

Acquired Equivalence and Representation-Mediated Conditioning

Although this experimental design allows us to say that there is less generalization between A and B (stimuli that have undergone differential training in Phase 1) than between A and C, it does not allow us to conclude that this effect is the consequence of the acquisition of distinctiveness by A and B—it could reflect a reduction in the animal's ability to discriminate A from C (the stimuli that were trained in the same way in Phase 1). The notion that a common training history might result in the *acquired equivalence* of cues has a long history and a possible associative basis for the phenomenon was proposed by Hull (1939). The essence of Hull's proposal (expressed, of course, in rather different terminology) was that the associate of a stimulus might be capable of acquiring associative strength and could thus mediate generalization to some other different event that shared the same associate. It is as if an extra c element has been added to both the stimuli. Applied to the results shown in Fig. 9.5 (see also Honey & Hall, 1989a) the argument runs as follows. In Phase 1 of training, Stimulus A (for Group A+/B−/C+) forms an excitatory association with the sucrose reinforcer. In Phase 2, therefore, the sucrose representation will be associatively activated in the presence of the shock reinforcer, allowing the possibility that a sucrose–shock association will be formed (see Hall, 1996). On the generalization test, Stimulus C, but not Stimulus B, will be able to activate the sucrose representation and thus contact the shock reinforcer by way of the chain C–sucrose–shock. Some suppression can therefore be expected in the presence of C. A similar analysis can be applied to Group A−/B+/C− where the mediating event (the associate shared by A and C) will be the state (of frustration, say) engendered by the fact that neither stimulus was paired with sucrose in Phase 1.

Central to this interpretation is the assumption that the associatively activated representation of an event can serve as a CS, forming excitatory associations with a reinforcer. Hall (1996) reviewed the evidence for this assumption. Perhaps the strongest comes from the work of Holland (e.g., 1981, 1983, 1990), who showed that pairing the presentation of a tone with a nausea-inducing injection will create an aversion to a distinctively flavored food pellet that has previously been signaled by the tone. This result, he argued, reflected the formation of an association between the associatively activated representation of the flavor and the state of nausea. My analysis of the acquired equivalence effect assumes exactly this process, but with shock rather than nausea serving as the reinforcer. Unfortunately, for present purposes, Holland (1981) extended his work to investigate the effect of a shock reinforcer and found no evidence of representation-mediated conditioning in these circumstances. That is, rats that had experienced tone–pellet pairings followed by tone–shock pairings showed no evidence of an aversion to the food pellets in a final consumption test.

Although Holland's (1981) results were not encouraging, we (Ward-Robinson & Hall, 1999) thought it possible that his failure to find an effect might be a consequence of the insensitivity of the test procedure that was used. Holland (1981) used a simple consumption test, but there is some evidence to suggest (Jackson & Delprato, 1974) that a test in which the animals must perform an instrumental response to earn the pellet may give a more sensitive measure. Accordingly, we extended the experiment outlined in Table 9.1 to include a further test (the mediated conditioning test) in which a lever was made available for the first time, responding on which produced the sucrose pellets that had been used in Phase 1 of training. (For half the animals this test followed the generalization test; for the remainder the order of the tests was reversed.) For animals in Group A+/B–/C+, pairings of the representation of the sucrose pellet with shock will have occurred during Phase 2 training. This might be revealed in their showing an unwillingness to lever press for these pellets. The performance of this group can be conveniently assessed by comparison with that shown by Group A–/B+/C–, for whom no such pairings will have occurred. Any effect produced by this test will be a consequence of training procedures that are known to result in an acquired equivalence effect.

In the mediated conditioning test, the rats were permitted to perform 11 lever presses, each of which caused the delivery of a single sucrose pellet. The first response started a timer so that the latency of the subsequent 10 responses (those performed after a sucrose pellet had been encountered) could be recorded. Group mean latencies are presented in Fig. 9.6. As would be expected of rats learning a new instrumental response, latencies tended to decline over the course of the test. This decline occurred steadily in Group A–/B+/C–. Strikingly, however, Group A+/B–/C+ showed very long latencies early in the test. (Statistical analysis showed that the groups differed reliably in their latencies for Responses 2 and 3.) This difference indicates that the sucrose pellet was a less effective reinforcer for the latter group than for the former, the outcome that would be expected if the pairing of A with shock in Phase 2 endowed A's associate (sucrose for Group A+/B–/C+) with some degree of aversiveness. Although the simple cooccurrence of two phenomena cannot prove the existence of a causal relation between them, the demonstration of acquired equivalence and mediated conditioning in the same experiment adds support to the argument that the former is a consequence of the latter.

Acquired Distinctiveness and Attentional Factors

The conclusion merited by the evidence discussed so far is that results of the sort depicted in Fig. 9.5 can be explained perfectly well in terms of acquired equivalence between Stimuli A and C. This does not prove, however, that the discrimination training given to A and B was without effect—equivalence and distinctiveness could be acquired concurrently. To prove the reality of acquired distinctiveness, however, it is necessary to compare the performance of subjects given initial discrimi-

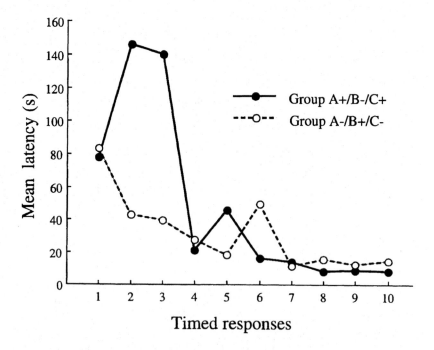

Fig. 9.6. Group mean latency data from the mediated conditioning test of the experiment by Ward-Robinson and Hall (1999). Scores represent the interval between successive responses after the first response.

nation training with that of control subjects who have not had the opportunity to build up an acquired equivalence between the stimuli but who are matched to the discrimination-trained subjects in other relevant respects (e.g., in their exposure to the stimuli and their general experience of the training situation). As Hall (1991) pointed out, a control condition that meets these criteria has been very hard to find. There is a recent series of experiments by Delamater (1998), however, that makes some progress in this direction.

Delamater's (1998) basic procedure involved the use of two sets of stimuli, an auditory pair (tone and white noise; A1 and A2) and a visual pair (steady and flashing light; V1 and V2), and two reinforcers, sucrose and standard food pellets (S and F). Animals can thus be given differential pretraining in which both stimuli of a given modality are followed by (different) reinforcers (e.g., A1→F; A2→S) and transfer to a new task can easily be arranged by omitting one of the reinforcers (i.e., A1→F; A2→0). The dependent variable is the rate at which this second discrimination is formed. Control subjects receive the same reinforcer in association with the two stimuli in the first phase of training (A1→F; A2→F). The use of the second set of stimuli makes it possible to equate the two groups in terms of their experience of the reinforcers. With these stimuli the control subjects experience V1→S and V2→S and the experimental subjects V1→F and V2→S. Using these procedures, Delamater demonstrated that the transfer discrimination is acquired more readily in subjects given differential training in the first phase than in control subjects.

This basic result can be accommodated, as Delamater (1998) acknowledged, by an interpretation in terms of mediated conditioning and acquired equivalence. When control subjects experience a nonreinforced (A2→0) trial in the test discrimination, the A2 cue, as a result of the first stage of training, will be able to activate the F representation. Thus the possibility arises that associative activation of the representation of food will become a signal for its omission. Such learning can only detract from performance on A1 trials because on these trials the event that has previously signaled food continues to do so. For experimental subjects, on the other hand, it will be the representation of S that becomes associated with nonreinforcement. Performance to A1 (supported by a different reinforcer, F) will accordingly suffer less. In a further experiment, however, Delamater modified his basic design to produce a result that cannot be explained in this way.

The design of the critical experiment is outlined in Table 9.2. As before, animals in the experimental condition (the distinctiveness group of the table) were trained initially with one auditory and one visual cue followed by S, the other cues being followed by F. Animals in the control

TABLE 9.2   Design of Experiment by Delamater (1998)

Group	Training	Test
Distinctiveness (within modality)	A1 →F / A2 → S	
	V1 → F / V2 → S	
		A1 → F / A2 → 0
		V1 → 0 / V2 → S
Equivalence (within modality)	A1 → F / A2 → F	
	V1 → S / V2 → S	

Note. A1 and A2 = auditory cues (tone and noise); V1 and V2 = visual cues (steady and flashing light); F = food; S = sucrose pellets. Only specimen groups are portrayed (the full design was counterbalanced). After 16 sessions of training on the test, the animals were trained on the reversal of this discrimination.

(equivalence) group experienced one reinforcer type along with the auditory cues and the other with the visual cues. It should be noted that the group labels refer to the condition that applies within a modality; between modalities the position is reversed. We may assume, however, that when it comes to the test, the animal's chief task is to discriminate one auditory cue from the other and one visual cue from the other. The form of the test is shown on the right of Table 9.2. Its novel feature is that the subjects were required to learn two discriminations concurrently: A1 continued to be reinforced as before but the reinforcer for A2 was omitted; V2 continued to be reinforced as before but the reinforcer for V1 was omitted. Performance on this test (pooled over both discriminations) and on a subsequent reversal of the discriminations is shown in Fig. 9.7. It is evident that performance was superior in the distinctiveness group.

It is difficult to explain the results of Fig. 9.7 in terms of acquired equivalence produced by representation-mediated conditioning. As before, an association formed on A2→0 trials, for example, between the expectancy of F and its omission will tend to detract from performance in the equivalence group on A1 trials on which the stimulus continues to lead to F. However, something of the same sort will also be true of the distinctiveness group. For these animals the A2→0 trials might result in the formation of an association between the expectancy of sucrose and reinforcer omission. This may not interfere with the food-reinforced A1 trials, but it can be expected to cause a problem on the other discrimination in which V2 trials continue to lead to sucrose. Thus, by requiring the animals to learn two discriminations concurrently, the postulated interference from acquired equivalence is equated in the two groups. The advantage shown by the distinctiveness group must be the consequence of some other acquired distinctiveness process.

Delamater's (1998) suggestion was that differential pretraining enhances the tendency of the animal to attend to distinctive features of the stimuli. Standard associative theory can readily be extended to accommodate such a process. We have already noted that the associative account of discrimination learning (A+/B−) assumes that the *a* elements of the stimuli become associated with one outcome, the *b* elements become associated with the other, and that the *c* elements become neutralized. In Delamater's experiments, the outcomes are F and S rather than reinforcement and nonreinforcement, but the same principle applies. That the associations formed in the distinctiveness condition involve

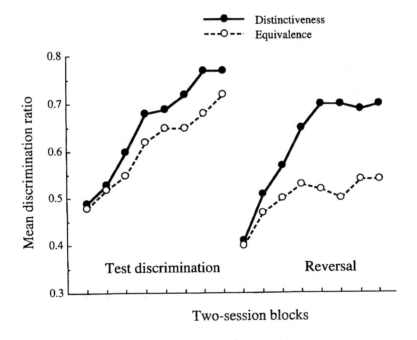

FIG. 9.7. Mean discrimination ratios (rate on positive trials / rate on all trials) for the test discrimination and its reversal in the experiment by Delamater (1998, Experiment 2). One group had previously received within-modality distinctiveness training; the other group had received within-modality equivalence training (see Table 9.2).

just *a* and *b* elements and not *c* elements does not, in itself, predict that a subsequent discrimination involving A and B will be advantaged. However, if we add the assumption that, in addition to the mechanism responsible for association formation, there also exists an attentional learning mechanism that selectively boosts the associability of predictive stimuli, then the result follows. The formal theory of attention in animal conditioning proposed by Mackintosh (1975) has just this property (but see also Hall, 1991; Pearce & Hall, 1980).

Before accepting these results as proof of the operation of an attentional learning mechanism, a possible alternative interpretation should be considered. Although associative learning principles are more comfortable with the notion of equivalence than that of distinctiveness, it is not beyond their scope to supply an explanation of the latter. Hall (1991) discussed a number of possibilities, one of which may be applicable here. Discrimination training is assumed to establish associations between cues and their (different) consequences (e.g., A1→F and A2→S in the experiments just described). This means that on subsequent presentation, each cue will elicit activity in the representation of its associate. It has long been accepted that the simultaneous presentation of another cue may modify the way in which a target cue is perceived (the principle of generalization decrement). Hall suggested that such effects might also operate when the added cue is not itself physically present, but is the associatively activated representation of an event. An untrained A stimulus may be perceived in one way, one that evokes the representation of F in a different way, and one that evokes the representation of S in a different way again. Establishing A1–F and A2–S associations could mean that the perception of A1 is changed in one way and the perception of A2 is changed in different way. These effects will operate on all features of the stimuli, including those that are common to both. Thus the number of *c* elements may be reduced, and discrimination between the stimuli will be enhanced, resulting in the acquired distinctiveness effect. This account is frankly speculative and there is little independent evidence to support it. It is presented here simply to make clear that we cannot yet accept, as undisputed truth, the idea that discrimination training increases the attention paid to distinctive features of the stimuli.

Nonreinforced and Nondifferential Pretraining

To accept that acquired distinctiveness may occur because of an increase in the attention paid to features that distinguish between stimuli and a reduction in attention to nondistinguishing features is to accept an important aspect of Gibson's (1969) notion of stimulus differentiation. However, the two interpretations are not identical. In the attentional account just described, changes in attention are taken to be a consequence of associative changes—in Mackintosh's (1975) theory, a stimulus (or stimulus feature) has its associability boosted because, as a good predictor of reinforcement, it gains associative strength more readily than other stimuli. Differential reinforcement is necessary to produce attentional learning. Gibson, by contrast, denied this necessity. Discrimination training may be helpful because it maintains attention generally (the animal stays awake during pretraining) and thus ensures that the stimuli are properly experienced; but the differentiation process does not depend on differential reinforcement—mere exposure to the stimuli will suffice. To investigate this suggestion, it is necessary to look at experimental procedures in which animals are required to learn an A+/B– discrimination after preexposure in which neither stimulus is reinforced or, if reinforcement is present in pretraining, it is given equally in association with both stimuli.

Some Examples of the Effect

The classic study of exposure learning is that described by Gibson and Walk (1956) in which young rats were given prolonged preexposure in the home cage to two geometrical objects that later were presented as the stimuli in a simultaneous discrimination task conducted in a conventional choice apparatus. Preexposure was found to facilitate discrimination learning (see also Hall, 1979, 1980). This procedure has not been used much recently, but related experiments using a range of different procedures have been conducted over the last decade and they have largely confirmed the reliability of this perceptual learning effect.

An example of the effect in maze learning comes from an experiment by Trobalon, Sansa, Chamizo, and Mackintosh (1991; see also Chamizo & Mackintosh, 1989). Rats in the preexposed condition were allowed to explore, on separate trials, the two maze arms (arms differing in the nature of the floor covering, rubber or sandpaper) that subsequently they would be required to discriminate between. Control subjects were given equivalent exposure to the apparatus, but encountered an unrelated stimulus (a maze arm covered in plastic) on each trial. In the test phase, access to two arms was possible for the first time, with food available at the end of one of them. This rubber–sandpaper discrimination was learned more rapidly by the subjects that had been preexposed to these stimuli.

A further example using very different procedures is found in a study reported by Honey and Bateson (1996, Experiment 1). This experiment made use of imprinting procedures with domestic chicks as the subjects. In the first phase of training, experimental subjects were given, on separate trials, exposure to two objects, A and B. This training was effective in establishing imprinting (i.e., the tendency to emit filial responses) to both objects. Control subjects were exposed to the apparatus, but A and B were not presented. On the following day, all subjects received training in which they were placed in a cool cabinet with Object A displayed at one end and Object B at the other. Approach to one of the objects was rewarded by the delivery of a stream of warm air. Experimental subjects were found to learn this discrimination more readily than the controls.

For the most part, however, modern studies of the perceptual learning effect have made use of the flavor-aversion learning procedure (e.g., Honey & Hall, 1989b; Mackintosh, Kaye, & Bennett, 1991; Symonds & Hall, 1995). An experiment by Symonds and Hall (1995, Experiment 1) serves as an example. All subjects in this study received the same test procedure in which an aversion was established to Flavor A followed by a generalization test to Flavor B. Over the preceding 8 days, subjects in the experimental condition (Group A/B) had experienced four trials with each of these flavors presented on alternate days. Control subjects (Group W) received only water on these pretraining trials. The experiment also included two further groups: Group B, given four presentations of Flavor B during pretraining, and Group A given four presentations of A. The results of the test are shown in Fig. 9.8. Generalization was profound in Group W, was slightly less in Group A and Group B, but was dramatically attenuated in Group A–B. It appears that the A/B discrimination is facilitated in animals given nonreinforced preexposure to both stimuli.

Before turning to a discussion of explanations for this effect, the contrast between these results and those reported by Honey (1990; see Fig. 9.4) requires comment. Honey found a significant attenuation of generalization in the equivalents of Groups A and B. The failure to find this effect here may simply be a consequence of the fact, already mentioned, that the experiment by Symonds and Hall (1995) used a very potent conditioning regime for the A+ stage (three trials with a high concentration of lithium as the reinforcer), a procedure that established a strong aversion to A in all groups. This regime could have been enough to obscure differences produced by latent inhibition effects that were operating in Honey's (1990) experiment. Perhaps more significant is the fact that Honey found enhanced generalization in his equivalent of Group A/B. In my earlier discussion of this result, I speculated that it might be the consequence of excitatory associations formed between A and B. The fact that the reverse result is obtained in a procedure in which such associations are unlikely to form (for Group A/B in this experiment there was an interval of 24 hr between successive presentations of A and B

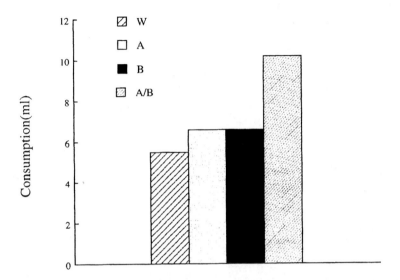

FIG. 9.8. Group mean scores for consumption of Flavor B after conditioning with Flavor A in the experiment by Symonds and Hall (1995, Experiment 1). Before conditioning, different groups had received exposure to A, to B, to both stimuli (A/B), or to neither (W).

during preexposure) lends support to this speculation. However this may be, we will take as the central finding in need of explanation the observation that prior exposure to A and B usually enhances discrimination, or reduces generalization, between these stimuli.

The Role of Latent Inhibition

That preexposure to both stimuli should be especially effective in producing the perceptual learning effect is anticipated by Gibson's (1969) concept of differentiation. Although the mechanism is not specified, it seems clear that the process of differentiation (which involves an increased sensitivity to *a* and *b* elements and a reduction in the attention paid to the *c* elements) will be fostered by giving the animal a chance to compare the stimuli and thus detect which elements are common and which are unique (see Gibson, 1969). There is, however, an alternative explanation available that has no need to assume the existence of a special process of stimulus comparison. As we have already acknowledged, preexposure to one of the stimuli (either A or B) will result in latent inhibition of *c* stimulus elements and thus can be expected to attenuate generalization to some extent. However, as McLaren et al. (1989) pointed out, preexposure to both A and B will mean that the *c* elements receive twice as much preexposure (they will be present on both A and B trials); the latent inhibition suffered by the *c* elements will be particularly profound in this case, and generalization will be even less, producing the pattern of results seen in Fig. 9.8.

Symonds and Hall (1995, Experiment 2) conducted an experiment using the flavor-aversion procedure that was designed to allow a choice between these alternative interpretations. There were three groups of rats differing in the pretraining they received. One group received the standard preexposure treatment—trials with Flavors A and B presented in alternation (Group A/B–I, where I denotes intermixed presentations of A and B). Control subjects (Group W) received only unflavored water in this stage. The third group (A/B–B, for Blocked) received the same amount of preexposure to A and B as did Group A/B–I but the different trial types were arranged in separate blocks. That is, these subjects received a block of A trials followed by a block of B trials, or vice versa. All subjects then received conditioning with A as the CS, followed by a generalization test with B. In both preexposed groups the *c* elements will have suffered latent inhibition during preexposure, and, to the extent to which this factor determines generalization, the aversion to B should be less in these groups than in Group W. However, as the total amount of exposure to the stimuli is equated in the B and I conditions, the extent to which latent inhibition accrues to the *c* elements in Groups A/B–I and A/B–B should be the same; on the basis of latent inhibition, therefore, there are no grounds to expect a difference between the two preexposed groups.

The results of the test phase of this experiment are presented in Fig. 9.9. Generalization was profound in Group W but was markedly attenuated in the group given intermixed preexposure; that is, the basic perceptual learning effect was reproduced here. This result is not a consequence of latent inhibition. Group A/B–B, which had the same amount of exposure to the stimuli as Group A/B–I, showed almost as much generalization as the control group.[1]

Simply giving the *c* stimulus elements the opportunity to undergo latent inhibition is not enough to reduce generalization—it is critical that the subjects also experience the other elements of the stimuli (the *a* and *b*

---

[1]The lack of a difference between these two groups suggests that latent inhibition effects probably played only a minor role in this experiment (I have already suggested that conditioning parameters employed by Symonds & Hall, 1995, were sufficiently powerful that even preexposed stimulus elements might have acquired a full measure of associative strength). However, the critical point, for present purposes, is not the absolute size of any latent inhibition effect but the fact that it should be the same size in the two preexposed groups.

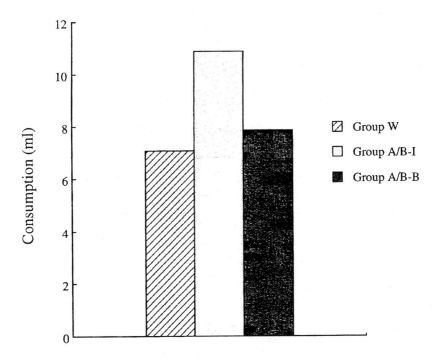

FIG. 9.9.   Group mean scores for consumption of Flavor B after conditioning with Flavor A in the experiment by Symonds and Hall (1995, Experiment 2). Before conditioning, different groups had received exposure to A and B presented in an intermixed fashion (A/B–I), to A and B presented on separate blocks of trials (A/B–B), or to only unflavored water (W).

elements) in an intermixed schedule (see also Symonds & Hall, 1997). Results from experiments using the imprinting procedure with chicks confirm this conclusion. Honey, Bateson, and Horn (1994; see also Honey & Bateson, 1996) compared chicks given blocked exposure (100 presentations of Object A in one session and 100 of Object B in a separate session) with chicks given intermixed exposure (50 presentations of each stimulus in each session). When the objects used as A and B were similar, the subjects given intermixed preexposure were found to learn a subsequent discrimination between A and B more rapidly than those given blocked preexposure.

Symonds and Hall (1995) concluded that the superior discrimination evident in the intermixed condition was consistent with the suggestion that the perceptual learning effect depends on the operation of a process of stimulus comparison. Although we were unable to specify the mechanism by which comparison might operate, we felt reasonably comfortable with the assumption that, whatever the mechanism might be, comparison was more likely in the intermixed case than in the blocked case.

The Role of Associations Within and Between Stimuli

In their analysis of perceptual learning, McLaren et al. (1989) pointed out that giving nonreinforced preexposure does not preclude the operation of associative processes. Although they do not become associated with an orthodox reinforcer, stimuli given such preexposure are likely to form associations with other events, such as the context in which they occur and, if they are presented close enough together in space and time, with each other. Accepting that the event or object referred to as "a stimulus" should be construed as consisting of a set of elements, each of which can enter into associations, opens up a range of other possibilities. In my discussion of unitization I have already noted that mere exposure to a stimulus should allow excitatory associations to form among its constituent elements (i.e., within-stimulus associations will develop). Put simply, exposure to A should allow $a–c$ links to form; exposure to B should allow $b–c$ links to form. Furthermore, for animals exposed to both A and B, the formation of these within-stimulus links can be expected to contribute to the formation of between-stimulus associations, even when A and B are presented on quite separate occasions. In this case, however, the associations will be inhibitory. Once presentations of A have established the excitatory $a–c$ association, presentation of B, a stimulus containing c elements, will be able to activate the representation of a. According to standard theory (e.g., Wagner, 1981; Wagner & Rescorla, 1972) this combination of events will result in inhibition forming between the stimulus that is present and the representation that is activated only associatively. If the excitatory $a–c$ association is maintained by continued presentation of A, it can be predicted that inhibitory power will accrue chiefly to the unique, b, elements of Stimulus B. Similarly, on A trials, a will acquire an inhibitory connection with b. In short, mutually inhibitory links will be formed between the unique elements of each compound as a occurs only on trials when b does not, and vice versa.

McLaren et al. (1989) argued that these various associations may play an important role in determining generalization between A and B. For animals given no preexposure to the stimuli, an excitatory $a–c$ link will form for the first time during reinforced trials with A, at the same time as associations are being formed between these stimulus elements and the reinforcer. Generalized responding to B will presumably depend largely on the associative strength acquired by c elements, but the a–c link will also make a contribution—the reinforcer representation will be activated not only directly by c but also by way of the associative chain, c–a–reinforcer. Preexposure to A and B, at least when these stimuli are presented on an intermixed schedule, will eliminate this extra source of generalization. Such preexposure will establish mutually inhibitory connections between a and b with the result that the c elements of Stimulus B will be unable to activate the a representation on the test. In the absence of the contribution from the associatively activated a elements, generalization will be less. Thus the basic perceptual learning effect can be accommodated.

This analysis also provides an explanation for the differing effects of intermixed and blocked preexposure schedules. An inhibitory link between a and b will be formed on an A (i.e., an ac) preexposure trial only when the excitatory c–b link already has some strength; similarly B (bc) trials will be effective in producing inhibition only when the excitatory c–a link already exists. The alternation of A and B trials of the intermixed procedure is ideal for ensuring that the relevant connections have strength on each trial. With the blocked procedure, on the other hand, there is only a single transition from one trial type to the other; excitatory associations established during the first block will extinguish during the second, and there will be little opportunity for inhibitory links to form. Accordingly, the c–a association will be able to contribute to test performance in animals given blocked preexposure, and generalization to B should be greater than that seen after intermixed preexposure.

We thus have two explanations available for the differing effects on generalization produced by blocked and intermixed preexposure schedules. One proposes that the differing opportunities for stimulus comparison afforded by the two schedules result in differing amounts of stimulus differentiation; the other explains the effect purely in associative terms. Alonso and Hall (1999) conducted the following experiment in an attempt to decide between these alternatives. The procedures used were modeled on those of Symonds and Hall (1995) but differed in that two drinking bottles were made available to the rat on each exposure trial. For rats in the blocked preexposure condition, both bottles contained the same flavored solution, Flavor A for the first block of preexposure trials and Flavor B for the second block (or vice versa). For rats in the concurrent preexposure condition, however, the two bottles contained different flavors (A and B) throughout preexposure. A control group received access only to unflavored water at this stage. All animals then received aversion conditioning with A, followed by a generalization test with B.

The concurrent procedure of this experiment was intended to equate to the intermixed procedure of the earlier studies in allowing the animals the opportunity to compare the stimuli—indeed, we may suppose that comparison processes are likely to be more effective with this procedure, in which the flavors will be sampled in quick succession, than in the intermixed procedure when they are presented several hours apart. On these grounds a substantial perceptual learning effect can be expected, with group concurrent showing less generalization than group blocked. The associative theory, by contrast, predicts no such effect—concurrent preexposure to A and B will preclude the possibility of inhibitory connections forming between them and, if no other factors operate, the degree of generalization should be the same in the two preexposed groups. The results of the generalization test, shown in Fig. 9.10, lend no support to the stimulus comparison theory. Both preexposed groups showed less aversion to B than did the control group

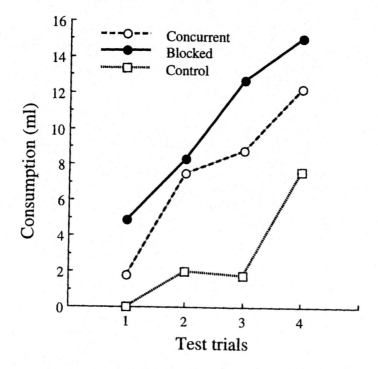

FIG. 9.10. Group mean consumption of B over four generalization test trials in the experiment by Alonso and Hall (1999). Group Concurrent had received preexposure in which Flavors A and B were made available at the same time; Group Blocked received preexposure consisting of a block of A trials and a separate block of B trials; Group Control received no preexposure to the flavors.

(as might be expected from considerations of latent inhibition), and although these two groups differed, it was not in the way predicted by the comparison theory—group concurrent showed significantly more generalization than group blocked.

The associative theory can easily be extended to deal with the superior generalization shown by group concurrent. Not only will presenting A and B concurrently preclude the formation of inhibitory *a–b* links of the sort discussed earlier, it might actually allow the formation of direct excitatory associations between the two flavors—an animal that samples both drinking bottles during a preexposure trial will frequently be exposed to A–B pairings. The familiar principle of sensory preconditioning leads to the conclusion that Stimulus B will then be rendered capable of eliciting a CR conditioned to its associate, A. Alonso and Hall (1999) conducted a further experiment that produced results entirely consistent with this interpretation. Rats given the concurrent preexposure treatment initially were subjected to a second phase of preexposure (a block of trials in which A was presented alone followed by a block of trials in which B was presented alone) designed to extinguish any associations between A and B that might have formed in the first phase. Generalization in these subjects was found to be much the same as that shown by subjects in a comparable blocked- preexposure condition. Significantly, there was no indication that eliminating these associative effects allowed the effects of a stimulus comparison to show themselves. We must conclude that experiments using flavor-aversion learning procedures with rats produce no results that cannot be accommodated by a version of standard associative learning theory. For results that seem to indicate the operation of a distinct perceptual learning process it is necessary to turn to a quite different experimental paradigm—visual discrimination learning in the pigeon.

Nondifferential Preexposure and Discrimination Learning in Pigeons

In a recent series of experiments (conducted in collaboration with Mondragón) I attempted an exploration of the role played by stimulus comparison in the discrimination learning of pigeons (Hall & Mondragón, 1999). In these experiments two pairs of stimuli were used: two shapes (call them A and B) and two colors (X and Y). Our preexposure procedure made use of the fact that it is possible to present two stimuli simultaneously on the side keys of a three-key pigeon chamber. In the first experiment to be reported here, two groups of pigeons received preexposure in this way. One group (Group C, for comparison) received 12 sessions of preexposure each consisting of 40 trials.

On 20 of these trials the two shapes (A and B) were presented, on the others, the two colors (X and Y) were presented. These birds thus had the opportunity to compare the members of each pair of similar stimuli. The other group (Group NC, for noncomparison) received the same number of preexposure trials, but the stimulus pairings were different; on some trials they saw A and Y together and on others they saw, X and B. They thus had no opportunity to make a direct comparison between the two shapes or the two colors. To ensure that the birds attended to the keys during preexposure, (nondifferential) reinforcement was given. A peck at either of the keys turned off that keylight and resulted in the delivery of grain. The other key remained lit until it too had been pecked. A response to this key again turned off the keylight, produced food reinforcement, and initiated the intertrial interval. The design of the experiment is presented schematically in Fig. 9.11.

In the test phase of the experiment (see Fig. 9.11), all birds were trained with a successive discrimination procedure, the stimuli being presented on the center key. One of the shapes (A) and one of the colors (X) continued to be associated with food reward; the other stimuli (B and Y) were nonreinforced. There were 80 trials per session in this stage, 20 with each stimulus. Positive stimuli were presented for up to 10 sec, but were turned off and reinforcement was delivered if the bird responded to them. Negative stimuli were presented for a minimum of 10 sec and were terminated only after the bird had refrained from pecking for a period of 2 sec. We assume that discrimination between the colors and shapes is easy but that there may be considerable generalization between the two colors and between the two shapes. The test task can thus be construed as involving two concurrent discriminations, A+/B− and X+/Y−. It follows that a preexposure procedure that enhances discrimination between the colors and between the shapes should be particularly effective in promoting acquisition in the test phase.

Presenting stimuli simultaneously on two keys during preexposure allows the possibility that excitatory associations will form between them (see, e.g., Zentall, Sherburne, Roper, & Kraemer, 1996). With this experimental design, however, these associations should not contribute to any difference between the groups in their test performance. Birds in Group C will form associations between A and B and between X and Y; birds in Group NC will form associations between A and Y and between X and B. In each group, therefore, associations will exist between each positive test stimulus and one of the negative stimuli. Such associations might retard acquisition of the discrimination, but they will do so in both groups. With this factor controlled for, we hoped to be able to demonstrate that the opportunity for stimulus comparison during preexposure would facilitate subsequent discrimination learning. The results obtained (see Fig. 9.12) revealed no such effect. The groups did

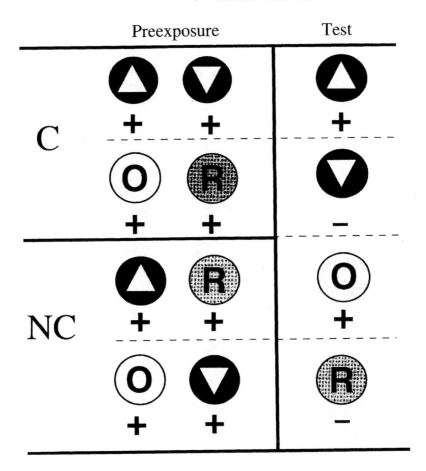

FIG. 9.11. Design of experiment on discrimination learning in the pigeon. In preexposure, all subjects were presented with two illuminated keys on each trial, Group C (for comparison) saw two shapes or two colors on each trial; Group NC (noncomparison) saw one shape and one color. Example trials are shown in the figure (the full design was counterbalanced). The test consisted of a successive discrimination with four trial types. R = red keylight; O = orange keylight; + = food reward; − = no reward.

not differ over the first five sessions of the test, but thereafter, Group NC pulled ahead of Group C. The difference was small but proved to be statistically reliable, $p < .05$ (see also Hall, 1976; Hall & Channell, 1980).

Why should Group NC show better test performance than Group C? One possible explanation can be derived from the associative account of perceptual learning effects, described in the preceding section of this chapter. Consider the stimulus pair, A and B (similar arguments will ap-

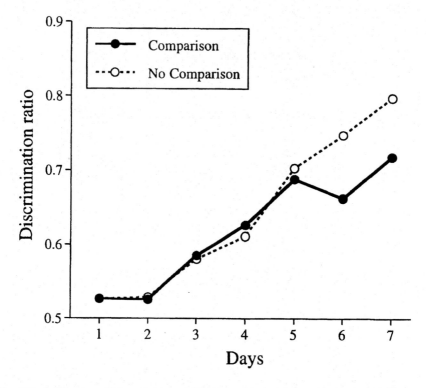

FIG. 9.12. Acquisition of the test discrimination by pigeons trained according to the procedures outlined in Fig. 9.11. The score used is the number of positive trials on which a response occurred over the total number of trials on which at least one response occurred.

ply to X and Y). These are taken to consist of the compounds *ac* and *bc* and, as before, it may be assumed that preexposure allows the formation of excitatory associations between *a* and *c* and between *b* and *c*. Inhibitory learning will then become possible. For Group NC, which sees A on trials when B is absent and B on trials when A is absent, *a* will signal the absence of *b* and *b* will signal the absence of *a*; mutually inhibitory associations will form between these stimulus elements. No such associations will form in Group C, which sees A and B together on the same trial. In the latter group, therefore, the excitatory *a–c* and *b–c* associations will be able to contribute to generalization between A and B. However, for Group NC the inhibitory associations between *a* and *b* will eliminate this source of generalization and discrimination learning will proceed more readily.

The notion of comparison-induced stimulus differentiation suggests an alternative explanation. Suppose that, in the absence of an opportunity for comparison, subjects in Group NC tend to perceive Stimuli A and B simply as "colors" whereas Group C, given the opportunity to compare, becomes sensitive to the distinguishing features of these stimuli, *a* and *b*. Only in the latter group, therefore, will it be possible for an excitatory association to be formed between *a* and *b*, and only this group will suffer the negative transfer that this association will bring to the discrimination task. The relatively poor performance of Group C can thus be explained on these grounds alone, without any need to postulate an additional inhibitory learning process.

In a further experiment, Mondragón and I (Hall & Mondragón, 1999) attempted to discriminate between these alternatives. As in the previous experiment, pigeons in Groups C and NC were given nondifferentially reinforced preexposure to colors and shapes (see Fig. 9.13) and were subsequently tested on a successive discrimination task in-

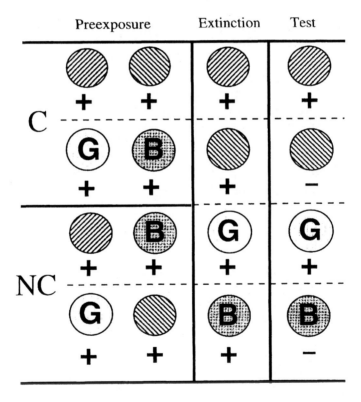

FIG. 9.13. Experimental design, modified from that shown in Fig. 9.11, in which a further phase of training was inserted between preexposure and the test. In this (extinction) phase, all four stimuli were presented singly on the center key and all four were associated with reward. (The term *extinction* refers to the notion that within-display associations formed during preexposure might be expected to extinguish during this phase.) G = green keylight; B = blue keylight; + = food reward; – = no reward.

volving these same stimuli. Between these two stages, however, a further phase of training (labeled *extinction* in Fig. 9.13) was given. This consisted of four sessions each of which contained 20 (reinforced) presentations of each of the four stimuli presented individually on the center key. This procedure was intended to bring about the extinction of excitatory associations formed between the simultaneously presented stimuli during preexposure. It should, however, be without effect on any inhibitory associations formed during preexposure (see Zimmer-Hart & Rescorla, 1974); it may, indeed, even strengthen inhibitory associations between the unique elements of A and B and of X and Y, as a will still predict the absence of b (and vice versa) and x the absence of y (and vice versa). If the superiority of Group NC observed in the previous experiment depends on these inhibitory associations, then the same result should be obtained in this study. However, if the previous result depends on the existence of excitatory associations between A and B and between X and Y, the extinction treatment introduced in this version of the experiment should abolish the effect.

The results of the test discrimination, shown in Fig. 9.14, are quite the reverse of those of our first experiment. We now find that Group C learns the discrimination more readily than Group NC. The number of trials necessary to reach an overall criterion of .75 was 260 for Group C and 450 for Group NC, a difference that was statistically reliable ($p <$ .05). This outcome is not that predicted by the inhibitory associations theory. It can, however, be accommodated by the alternative account. According to that account, excitatory associations are able to form between the unique features of simultaneously presented similar stimuli in Group C precisely because this mode of presentation allows differentiation to occur, rendering the animal sensitive to these features. Extinguishing these associations will not only eliminate their deleterious effect on the performance of Group C; it will also allow the facilitatory effects of the differentiation process to show through. The results shown in Fig. 9.14 reflect the operation of a stimulus differentiation process in perceptual learning.

CONCLUSIONS

The various experimental findings summarized in this chapter allow the general conclusion (admittedly with a large number of qualifications) that prior exposure to one or both of a pair of similar stimuli can reduce generalization (or facilitate discrimination) between them. Many of these findings can be explained in terms of standard associative mechanisms (including among these subsidiary but related processes like latent inhibition). There remains, however, a stubborn

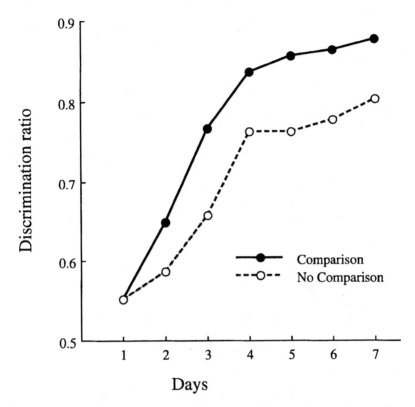

FIG. 9.14. Acquisition of the test discrimination by pigeons trained according to the procedures outlined in Fig. 9.13. The score used is the number of positive trials on which a response occurred over the total number of trials on which at least one response occurred.

residue of observations that resists explanation in these terms. These seem to indicate that mere exposure to a stimulus can allow differentiation to occur, so that the animal becomes more sensitive to unique features of that stimulus and less sensitive to features that it holds in common with other similar stimuli.

We (the work is being done in collaboration with Killcross) recently started to attempt to develop an account of the mechanism by which differentiation might occur. Our starting point is the phenomenon of habituation, which we interpret as showing that exposure to a stimulus will reduce its effectiveness, making that stimulus less able to elicit responding and also less likely to be learned about. Next we assume that the animal's processing system is of limited capacity so that often not all the elements that constitute a stimulus will be sampled when that stimulus is presented. We further assume that, for stimuli of the sort used in the experiments discussed here, the common (c) elements are likely to be more salient than the unique (a or b) elements. On the first presentation of A (or B), therefore, it is the c elements that will be sampled. If the trial with A is reinforced, generalization to B in these circumstances will be substantial. Exposure to a stimulus will allow habituation to occur, but for any given element to undergo habituation, it must first be sampled. It follows that the c elements will undergo habituation before the unique elements. It then becomes a simple matter, given certain assumptions about the limited capacity of the animal's processing system, to predict that the effectiveness of the unique elements can come to exceed that of the initially more salient common elements. Preexposure to A will thus mean that its a elements are especially likely to be learned about on a subsequent conditioning trial, and generalization to B (which depends on the c elements acquiring strength) will be limited (e.g., Honey, 1990). Preexposure to B will mean that its c elements are less likely to be sampled on the test trial and generalization will again be restricted (e.g., Honey & Hall, 1989b). With preexposure to A and B, both these effects will operate and little generalization should occur (e.g., Symonds & Hall, 1995). Evidently a theory of this general sort can be made to encompass the basic facts of perceptual learning with relative ease.

We are currently attempting to develop a formal theory of perceptual learning along the lines outlined in the preceding paragraph. This is not the place to go into details of the formalization and several matters still remain to be resolved (e.g., how the phenomenon referred to as unitization should be dealt with; why the effects of preexposure to two stimuli should depend on the way in which they are scheduled). The point of presenting this brief outline is not to offer a precise explanation of any particular phenomenon. Rather, it is to make clear (in spite of the impression sometimes generated by Gibson's [1969] pronouncements on the topic) that there is not necessarily anything mysterious about the notion of stimulus differentiation. The differentiation process can be modeled by a mechanism that does little more than combine standard notions of habituation with the widely accepted tenets of stimulus-sampling theory. We have reason to hope that this simple model, when appropriately developed, will prove able to accommodate more than just the basic facts of perceptual learning—the attempt to extend the model to more complex phenomena is currently at the focus of our theoretical endeavors.

ACKNOWLEDGMENTS

The new experimental work reported here was supported by a grant from the U.K. Biotechnology and Biological Sciences Research Council.

Discussions with C. Bonardi, S. Graham, S. Killcross, S. Leonard, E. Mondragón, and J. Ward-Robinson contributed much to the ideas put forward in this chapter.

REFERENCES

Alonso, G., & Hall, G. (1999). Stimulus comparison and stimulus association processes in the perceptual learning effect. *Behavioural Processes, 48,* 11–23.

Bennett, C. H., Tremain, M., & Mackintosh, N. J. (1996). Facilitation and retardation of flavour aversion following prior exposure to the CS. *Quarterly Journal of Experimental Psychology, 49B,* 220–230.

Bennett, C. H., Wills, S. J., Wells, J. O., & Mackintosh, N. J. (1994). Reduced generalization following preexposure: Latent inhibition of common elements or a difference in familiarity. *Journal of Experimental Psychology: Animal Behavior Processes, 20,* 232–239.

Best, M. R., & Batson, J. D. (1977). Enhancing the expression of flavor neophobia: Some effects of the ingestion-illness contingency. *Journal of Experimental Psychology: Animal Behavior Processes, 3,* 132–143.

Burch-Vernon, A. S., & Riccio, D. C. (1997). The effects of CS- preexposure in conditioned taste aversion: Enhanced flavor discrimination. *Learning and Motivation, 28,* 170–187.

Chamizo, V. D., & Mackintosh, N. J. (1989). Latent learning and latent inhibition in maze discriminations. *Quarterly Journal of Experimental Psychology, 41B,* 21–31.

Delamater, A. R. (1998). Associative mediational processes in the acquired equivalence and distinctiveness of cues. *Journal of Experimental Psychology: Animal Behavior Processes, 24,* 467–482.

Fanselow, M. S. (1990). Factors governing one-trial contextual conditioning. *Animal Learning & Behavior, 18,* 264–270.

Gibson, E. J. (1969). *Principles of perceptual learning and development.* New York: Appleton-Century-Crofts.

Gibson, E. J., & Walk, R. D. (1956). The effect of prolonged exposure to visually presented patterns on learning to discriminate them. *Journal of Comparative and Physiological Psychology, 49,* 239–242.

Hall, G. (1976). Learning to ignore irrelevant stimuli: Variations within and between displays. *Quarterly Journal of Experimental Psychology, 28,* 247–253.

Hall, G. (1979). Exposure learning in young and adult laboratory rats. *Animal Behaviour, 27,* 586–591.

Hall, G. (1980). Exposure learning in animals. *Psychological Bulletin, 88,* 535–550.

Hall, G. (1991). *Perceptual and associative learning.* Oxford, UK: Clarendon.

Hall, G. (1996). Learning about associatively activated stimulus representations: Implications for acquired equivalence and perceptual learning. *Animal Learning & Behavior, 24,* 233–255.

Hall, G., & Channell, S. (1980). A search for perceptual differentiation produced by nondifferential reinforcement. *Quarterly Journal of Experimental Psychology, 32,* 185–195.

Hall, G., & Mondragón, E. (1999). *Positive and negative transfer to discrimination learning after preexposure to the stimuli.* Paper presented at the third meeting of the Associative Learning Group, Gregynog, Wales.

Hearst, E., & Koresko, M. B. (1968). Stimulus generalization and amount of prior training on variable-interval reinforcement. *Journal of Comparative and Physiological Psychology, 66,* 133–138.

Hoffeld, D. R. (1962). Primary stimulus generalization and secondary extinction as a function of strength of conditioning. *Journal of Comparative and Physiological Psychology, 55,* 27–31.

Holland, P. C. (1981). Acquisition of representation mediated food aversions. *Learning and Motivation, 12,* 1–18.

Holland, P. C. (1983). Representation-mediated overshadowing and potentiation of conditioned aversions. *Journal of Experimental Psychology: Animal Behavior Processes, 9,* 1–13.

Holland, P. C. (1990). Event representation in Pavlovian conditioning: Image and action. *Cognition, 37,* 105–131.

Honey, R. C. (1990). Stimulus generalization as a function of stimulus novelty and familiarity in rats. *Journal of Experimental Psychology: Animal Behavior Processes, 16,* 178–184.

Honey, R. C., & Bateson, P. (1996). Stimulus comparison and perceptual learning: Further evidence and evaluation from an imprinting procedure. *Quarterly Journal of Experimental Psychology, 49B,* 259–269.

Honey, R. C., Bateson, P., & Horn, G. (1994). The role of stimulus comparison in perceptual learning: An investigation with the domestic chick. *Quarterly Journal of Experimental Psychology, 47B,* 83–103.

Honey, R. C., & Hall, G. (1989a). Acquired equivalence and distinctiveness of cues. *Journal of Experimental Psychology: Animal Behavior Processes, 15,* 338–346.

Honey, R. C., & Hall, G. (1989b). Enhanced discriminability and reduced associability following flavor preexposure. *Learning and Motivation, 20,* 262–277.

Honey, R. C., Horn, G., & Bateson, P. (1993). Perceptual learning during filial imprinting: Evidence from transfer of training studies. *Quarterly Journal of Experimental Psychology, 46B,* 253–270.

Hovland, C. I. (1937). The generalization of conditioned responses IV: The effect of varying amounts of reinforcement upon the degree of generalization of conditioned responses. *Journal of Experimental Psychology, 21,* 261–276.

Hull, C. L. (1939). The problem of stimulus equivalence in behavior theory. *Psychological Review, 46,* 9–30.

Jackson, D. E., & Delprato, D. J. (1974). Aversive CSs suppress lever pressing for food but not the eating of free food. *Learning and Motivation, 5,* 448–458.

Kiernan, M. J., & Westbrook, R. F. (1993). Effects of exposure to a to-be-shocked environment upon the rat's freezing response: Evidence for facilitation, latent inhibition, and perceptual learning. *Quarterly Journal of Experimental Psychology, 46B,* 271–288.

Killcross, A. S., Kiernan, M. J., Dwyer, D., & Westbrook, R. F. (1998). Effects of a retention interval on latent inhibition and perceptual learning. *Quarterly Journal of Experimental Psychology, 51B,* 59–74.

Mackintosh, N. J. (1975). A theory of attention: Variation in the associability of stimuli with reinforcement. *Psychological Review, 82,* 276–298.

Mackintosh, N. J., Kaye, H., & Bennett, C. H. (1991). Perceptual learning in flavour aversion learning. *Quarterly Journal of Experimental Psychology, 43B,* 297–322.

Macphail, E. M., Good, M., & Honey, R. C. (1995). Recognition memory in pigeons for stimuli presented repeatedly: Perceptual learning or reduced associative interference? *Quarterly Journal of Experimental Psychology, 48B,* 13–31.

McLaren, I. P. L., Kaye, H., & Mackintosh, N. J. (1989). An associative theory of the representation of stimuli: Applications to perceptual learning and latent inhibition. In R. G. M. Morris (Ed.), *Parallel distributed processing: Implications for psychology and neurobiology* (pp. 102–130). Oxford, UK: Clarendon.

Pearce, J. M., & Hall, G. (1980). A model for Pavlovian learning: Variations in the effectiveness of conditioned but not of unconditioned stimuli. *Psychological Review, 87*, 532–552.

Rescorla, R. A., & Wagner, A. R. (1972). A theory of Pavlovian conditioning: Variations in the effectiveness of reinforcement and nonreinforcement. In A. H. Black & W. F. Prokasy (Eds.), *Classical conditioning II: Current research and theory* (pp. 64–99). New York: Appleton-Century-Crofts.

Symonds, M., & Hall, G. (1995). Perceptual learning in flavor aversion conditioning: Roles of stimulus comparison and latent inhibition of common elements. *Learning and Motivation, 26*, 203–219.

Symonds, M., & Hall, G. (1997). Stimulus preexposure, comparison, and changes in the associability of common stimulus features. *Quarterly Journal of Experimental Psychology, 50B*, 317–331.

Todd, I. A., & Mackintosh, N. J. (1990). Evidence for perceptual learning in pigeon's recognition memory for pictures. *Quarterly Journal of Experimental Psychology, 42B*, 385–400.

Trobalon, J. B., Sansa, J., Chamizo, V. D., & Mackintosh, N. J. (1991). Perceptual learning in maze discriminations. *Quarterly Journal of Experimental Psychology, 43B*, 389–402.

Wagner, A. R. (1981). SOP: A model of automatic memory processing in animal behavior. In N. E. Spear & R. R. Miller (Eds.), *Information processing in animals: Memory mechanisms* (pp. 5–47). Hillsdale, NJ: Lawrence Erlbaum Associates.

Wagner, A. R., & Rescorla, R. A. (1972). Inhibition in Pavlovian conditioning: Application of a theory. In R. A. Boakes & M. S. Halliday (Eds.), *Inhibition and learning* (pp. 301–336). London: Academic Press.

Walker, D. J., & Branch, M. N. (1998). Effects of variable-interval value and amount of training on stimulus generalization. *Journal of the Experimental Analysis of Behavior, 70*, 139–163.

Ward-Robinson, J., & Hall, G. (1999). The role of mediated conditioning in acquired equivalence. *Quarterly Journal of Experimental Psychology, 52B*, 335–350.

Zentall, T. R., Sherburne, L. M., Roper, K. L., & Kraemer, P. J. (1996). Value transfer in a simultaneous discrimination appears to result from within-event Pavlovian conditioning. *Journal of Experimental Psychology: Animal Behavior Processes, 22*, 68–75.

Zimmer-Hart, C. L., & Rescorla, R. A. (1974). Extinction of Pavlovian conditioned inhibition. *Journal of Comparative and Physiological Psychology, 86*, 837–845.

chapter 10

Autoshaping and Drug-Taking

Arthur Tomie
Rutgers University

A ddiction researchers have long noted that Pavlovian conditioned responses (CRs) develop as a result of repeated paired presentations of an environmental stimulus (conditioned stimulus; CS) with an abused drug (unconditioned stimulus; US). For example, Pavlovian conditioned physiological reflexes and Pavlovian conditioned subjective, motivational, or emotional states are reported to develop as a function of CS–US pairings, and these physiological and emotional reactions have been proposed to account for various aspects of the drug abuse syndrome including urges, cravings, euphoria, withdrawal, and tolerance (for reviews, see Robinson & Berridge, 1993; Siegel, 1989; Tomie, 1995, 1996). It remains unclear, however, how Pavlovian conditioning of physiological reactions and subjective, emotional, and motivational states are transcribed into the narrow and repetitive motor responses that comprise the specific actions performed in consuming the drug (Robinson & Berridge, 1993). Recently, Tomie

(1995, 1996) proposed that autoshaping, a particular form of Pavlovian conditioning, may provide a more precise and unified account of how the pairing of environmental stimuli with drug reward leads to directed motor and consummatory features of the abuse syndrome.

AUTOSHAPING MODEL OF DRUG ABUSE

Tomie (1995, 1996) noted that Pavlovian autoshaping and drug abuse share in common aspects of procedures as well as properties of the constellation of behavioral symptoms induced. In Pavlovian autoshaping procedures, the presentation of a localized visual stimulus (CS) is followed by the response-independent presentation of a rewarding substance (US). Repeated CS–US pairings lead to the acquisition of the Pavlovian autoshaping CR, which is a complex sequence of motor responses directed at the CS (Brown & Jenkins, 1968; Tomie, Brooks, & Zito, 1989). For example, several studies reporting lever press autoshaping in rats have employed procedures wherein the brief insertion of a retractable lever CS preceded the response-independent delivery of the liquid solution US. The topography of the autoshaping CR includes lever CS-directed approach responses culminating in the expression of consummatory-like responding (i.e., grasping, nose touching, mouthing, and licking of the lever), typically recorded as Pavlovian lever press autoshaping CRs (Davey & Cleland, 1982; Davey, Phillips, & Cleland, 1981; Myer & Hull, 1974; Poplawsky & Phillips, 1986; for review see Tomie et al., 1989).

In both autoshaping and drug abuse, repeated pairings of a small object CS (i.e., lever or drug-taking implement) with a rewarding substance US (i.e., food or abused drug) leads to CS-directed approach, contact, and manipulation responses, culminating in the expression of consummatory-like responses directed at the CS. In both autoshaping and drug abuse, the induced responding is highly reflexive, triggered by the CS, difficult to restrain or control (Locurto, 1981; Tomie, 1996), and exhibits recurrent relapse-like effects, including spontaneous recovery and rapid reacquisition (Tomie, Hayden, & Biehl, 1980; Tomie & Kruse, 1980; Tomie, Rohr-Stafford, & Schwam, 1981). Autoshaping CRs, therefore, may provide an account of several prominent features of the drug abuse syndrome, and those subjects that readily acquire autoshaping CRs may be particularly vulnerable to drug abuse (Tomie, 1995, 1996).

It is interesting that procedures typically employed in human and animal drug self-administration procedures are particularly conducive to the development of Pavlovian autoshaping CRs. In humans, for example, drugs of abuse are typically self-administered with the aid of a drug delivery system (i.e., drug-taking implement) employed as a conduit to facilitate the consumption of the drug. The drug-taking implement is a small object (CS) that is paired repeatedly with the drug's rewarding effects (US). Repeated acts of voluntary drug taking provide for repeated CS–US pairings, setting the stage for the development of Pavlovian autoshaping CRs. Although the induced autoshaping CRs resemble voluntary drug taking, they are Pavlovian and additive with voluntary or operant drug taking (e.g., Hearst & Jenkins, 1974; Schwartz & Gamzu, 1977), resulting in an increase in the frequency of expression of drug-taking behavior. The induction of autoshaping CRs, therefore, will result in an increase in drug taking, and the excessive drug-taking will be reflexive and involuntary.

Procedures employed in studies of drug taking by animals are also conducive to the development of Pavlovian autoshaping CRs (Tomie, 1995, 1996). For example, a rat licks a sipper tube to drink a fluid solution containing an abused drug (i.e., ethanol or amphetamine). The sipper tube is, therefore, a small object CS that is paired repeatedly with the drug's rewarding effects (US). The induction of Pavlovian autoshaping CRs increases licking responses directed at the sipper tube CS, resulting in additional consumption of the drug solution. Thus, the induction of Pavlovian autoshaping CRs is accompanied by an increase in drug taking, and this effect is expressed in those subjects that tend to acquire and perform autoshaping CRs.

Evidence of Autoshaping In Drug-Taking Procedures

The issue of whether self-administered drugs of abuse actually function as effective USs in Pavlovian autoshaping procedures was recently addressed by Carroll and her associates, who engendered lever press autoshaping CRs by pairings of lever CS with intravenous drug self-administration of either amphetamine (Carroll & Lac, 1997) or cocaine (Carroll & Lac, 1993, 1997; Gahtan, Labounty, Wyvell, & Carroll, 1996; Specker, Carroll, & Loc, 1994). In addition, these investigators reported that lever pressing autoshaping CR performance is dose dependent, and substantial individual differences in the rate of acquisition of lever press autoshaping CR performance are observed. Although there are no published studies evaluating the effectiveness of ethanol solutions as the US in autoshaping procedures, there are data showing that a small object (illumination of a small light above the sipper) can function as an effective signal for ethanol availability, engendering light signal-directed approach responses that control responding more than the location of the ethanol solution itself (Falk, 1994; Falk & Lau, 1993, 1995).

There is some indirect evidence suggesting that autoshaping and eth-anol drinking are linked phenomena. In a recent study performed in our lab, rats given training with lever CS–food US autoshaping procedures were subsequently tested for their tendency to choose small immediate reward instead of large delayed reward (i.e., to behave impulsively). There were large and stable differences between subjects in both autoshaping and in impulsivity; moreover, the individual differences were closely linked, such that more impulsive rats were those that per-formed more autoshaping CRs. The link between autoshaping and impulsivity has implications for ethanol drinking, as higher levels of impulsivity in rats have been correlated with greater consumption of ethanol (Poulos, Le, & Parker, 1995; Poulos, Parker, & Le, 1998). In addi-tion, impulsivity was increased by acute presession intraperitoneal in-jections of a moderate (0.5 g/kg) dose of ethanol (Tomie, Aguado, Pohorecky, & Benjamin, 1998), a result that is consistent with the effects of presession injections of 0.5 mg/kg ethanol on autoshaping main-tained by food US in rats (Tomie, Cunha, et al., 1998).

Although the autoshaping model of drug abuse (Tomie, 1995, 1996) provides a unique theoretical perspective on the origins of excessive and uncontrolled drug taking, direct empirical support for the pre-dicted relation between Pavlovian autoshaping CRs and drug taking has been unavailable in the literature. The studies presented here are designed to assess predictions derived from the autoshaping model by evaluating the relation between the tendency to perform autoshaping CRs and the propensity for drug taking in rats.

EXPERIMENTAL FINDINGS

Experiment 1: Correlations Between Saccharin/ Ethanol Drinking and Lever CS–Food US Autoshaping

Previous research (already described) suggests that autoshaping in-duced by lever CS–food US pairings may be a form of impulsive re-sponding (Tomie, Aguado, et al., 1998). Whereas other researchers (Poulos et al., 1995; Poulos et al., 1998) have found that impulsiveness for food predicts ethanol drinking, this study asks if autoshaping in-duced by lever CS–food US pairings predicts individual differences in the tendency to drink ethanol.

On Session 1, male Long–Evans hooded rats ($n = 12$) were trained to eat from the food receptacle, then given the first of 12 daily autoshaping sessions. Each autoshaping trial consisted of the insertion of a retract-able stainless steel lever for 5 sec, and then, independently of responding, the pellet dispenser was operated, resulting in the delivery of one 45 mg food pellet. Each autoshaping session consisted of 25 autoshaping trials, separated by a mean intertrial interval of 60 sec (minimum interval = 45 sec, maximum interval = 75 sec).

On the day following the completion of the 12th autoshaping session, subjects received the first of 20 daily sessions of testing in their home cage for consumption of a solution consisting of 6% ethanol (v/v) diluted in 0.1% saccharin. The solution was made available for 30 min per day, beginning at approximately 1430 hr. For each subject, the water bottle was removed from the home cage and replaced with a 70-ml Plexiglas tube containing approximately 50 ml of the saccharin/ethanol solution. A stainless steel sipper tube was inserted into the home cage and provided access to the saccharin/ethanol solution. Fluid consumption was estimated by weighing the Plexiglas tube before and after each drinking session.

The number of lever press autoshaping CRs per session increased as a function of autoshaping sessions, and on the 12th autoshaping session, the mean number of CRs for the group was 67.49. Variability between subjects was considerable. The range of the number of CRs on Session 12 was 0 to 139, and the standard error of the mean was 31.73. Drinking of the saccharin/ethanol solution increased as a function of drinking sessions, and during the last 10 sessions (11–20), mean grams consumed was 15.85. Variability between subjects was considerable. The range of the mean grams of solution consumed during Sessions 11 through 20 was 1.92 to 27.99, and the standard error of the mean was 13.02. The relation between autoshaping CR performance on the 12th autoshaping session and consumption of the saccharin/ethanol solution on drinking Sessions 11 through 20 was evaluated by correlation regression technique (SYSTAT). Pearson's product–moment correlation coefficient revealed that the positive correlation between autoshaping and ethanol drinking was significant, $r(11) = +.527, p < .05$.

Because the test solution consisted of saccharin and ethanol, the degree to which these differences in drinking were attributable to each component of the solution is unclear. There is evidence that saccharin drinking is positively correlated with ethanol drinking (Bell, Gosnell, Krahn, & Meisch, 1994; Gahtan et al., 1996; Gosnell & Krahn, 1992; Overstreet et al., 1993), and therefore, drinking of the two components of the solution would likely covary within subjects. This prediction was supported by the results of the saccharin fading procedure, wherein the concentration of saccharin was gradually reduced by .01% after every fifth drinking session. There was an overall decrease in the amount of solution consumed, but the rats that performed more autoshaping CRs continued to drink more, and when saccharin fading was completed (solution = 6% ethanol diluted in tap water), the four rats that consumed on average more than 12 g of solution per session were the four highest responders in the autoshaping test.

Rats that performed more lever press autoshaping CRs on autoshaping Session 12 consumed more saccharin/ethanol solution on drinking Sessions 11 through 20. This result is consistent with the hypothesis that autoshaping and saccharin/ethanol drinking are linked. There are several possible mediators of this apparent link between autoshaping and ethanol drinking. For example, experience with autoshaping CR performance may create a state that enhances the rewarding properties of ethanol, or, alternatively, both performances may be due to a common preexisting, perhaps genetically determined, trait such as impulsivity (i.e., Poulos et al., 1995). Or, as suggested by Tomie (1995, 1996), operant licking of the sipper (CS) to obtain ethanol (US) reward may induce sipper-directed autoshaping CRs. According to this view, the link between autoshaping and ethanol drinking is due to the environmental features common to both procedures—the repeated Pavlovian pairing of object CS with rewarding substance US. According to this view, the trait linked to autoshaping is not specific to a particular US. Subjects prone to autoshaping with food US are also more likely to exhibit autoshaping with ethanol US; therefore, the tendency to consume more ethanol solution derives, at least in part, from the tendency to express autoshaping behavior per se. Although it is beyond the scope of this chapter to evaluate all possible interpretations of the positive correlation between autoshaping and ethanol drinking, it is appropriate to ask if this relation is observed in each of the remaining studies.

Experiment 2: Correlations Between Saccharin/ Ethanol Drinking and Lever CS–Food US Autoshaping Omission Training (Negative Automaintenance) Procedures

The premise that autoshaping CRs are difficult to control or suppress is supported by data from autoshaping studies employing instrumental omission training procedures (Atnip, 1977; Davey, Oakley, & Cleland, 1981; Picker, Blakely, & Poling, 1986; Poling & Appel, 1978). In these studies, autoshaping procedures are employed with the added stipulation that contacting the CS results in the cancellation of the food US that would otherwise be delivered. Despite the omission contingency many rats acquire the autoshaping CR and persist in maintaining CR performance despite contingent nonreinforcement. This phenomenon, called *negative automaintenance* (for reviews, see Locurto, 1981; Tomie, 1996;

Tomie et al., 1989) reveals that autoshaping CRs are reflexive, involuntary, and difficult to control. They are intractable to instrumental contingency and persist despite extensive experience with their maladaptive consequences. These properties augur well for their suitability as mediators of the drug abuse syndrome.

There are substantial individual differences in autoshaping CR performance during autoshaping procedures with the omission training contingency. Some rats persist in performing autoshaping CRs and consequently lose a large percentage of the available food, whereas other rats respond only occasionally (Locurto, 1981). This experiment asks if higher levels of autoshaping CR performance in these omission training procedures predict higher levels of drinking of a saccharin/ethanol solution. Presumably, rats that perform autoshaping CRs despite the omission contingency are especially prone to capitulate to the Pavlovian autoshaping contingency, and these rats may be especially vulnerable to drinking larger amounts of ethanol. The autoshaping model predicts that those rats that perform more autoshaping CRs despite the omission training contingency will subsequently consume more saccharin/ethanol solution.

Male Long–Evans hooded rats (n = 12) received autoshaping procedures similar to those described in Experiment 1, except that pressing the lever CS during the autoshaping trial canceled the delivery of the food US that would otherwise have been delivered. Thus, rats received autoshaping with omission (negative automaintenance) training procedures. As in Experiment 1, the rats were then tested for drinking of a solution consisting 6% ethanol diluted in 0.1% saccharin.

The number of lever press autoshaping CRs per session decreased as a function of three-session blocks, and on the fourth block of three sessions, mean number of lever press CRs for the group was 14.62. Variability between subjects was considerable. The range of the number of lever press CRs on the fourth block was 0 to 112, and the standard error of the mean was 19.90. Drinking of the saccharin/ethanol solution increased as a function of drinking sessions, and during the last 10 sessions (11 through 20), mean grams consumed was 17.34. Variability between subjects was considerable. The range of the mean grams of solution consumed during Sessions 11 to 20 was 0.71 to 31.32, and the standard error of the mean was 11.94. The relation between lever press autoshaping CR performance on the fourth block (Sessions 10–12) and consumption of the saccharin/ethanol solution on drinking Sessions 11–20 was evaluated by correlation regression technique (SYSTAT). Pearson's product–moment correlation coefficient revealed that the positive correlation between autoshaping and ethanol drinking was significant, $r(11)= +.585, p < .05$.

Those rats that performed more lever press autoshaping CRs on Sessions 10 through 12 of autoshaping with omission training subsequently consumed more saccharin/ethanol solution on drinking Sessions 11 through 20. This replicates and extends the findings of Experiment 1 that lever press autoshaping CR performance maintained by food US predicts subsequent drinking of saccharin/ethanol solution in the home cage. This study provides particularly compelling evidence of a link between lever press autoshaping CR expression and ethanol drinking because lever pressing during omission training is unlikely due to adventitious operant reinforcement contingencies (Locurto, 1981). The data also reveal the poorly controlled nature of the autoshaping CR, a feature that is consistent with the hypothesis that autoshaping CRs may contribute to the uncontrollable nature of ethanol taking.

Experiment 3: Lever CS–Saccharin/Ethanol US Pairings Induce Lever-directed Autoshaping CRs

The purpose of this study is to ask if lever press autoshaping CRs are acquired and maintained when the insertion of a retractable lever CS precedes the insertion of a sipper tube of a bottle containing a saccharin/ethanol solution US. In addition, this study asks if individual differences in lever press autoshaping CR performance are correlated with individual differences in saccharin/ethanol drinking during the autoshaping procedure. The autoshaping model of drug abuse (Tomie, 1995, 1996) predicts that the saccharin/ethanol solution US will be effective in producing lever press autoshaping CR performance, and that there will be a positive relation between lever press autoshaping CR performance and the tendency to consume the saccharin/ethanol solution US.

An additional concern relates to the possibility that the lever press performance observed in this study may be due to pseudoconditioning rather than to Pavlovian conditioning. It is possible, for example, that ethanol-induced psychostimulation increases directed motor responding per se, resulting in an increase in the probability of lever pressing, and particularly in the rats that consume more ethanol. This possibility is addressed by comparing lever press performance in the paired group that receives lever CS–bottle US pairings to lever press performance in the random group that receives lever CS randomly with respect to bottle US. Pavlovian autoshaping CRs will be differentiated from psychostimulation-induced lever pressing by comparing the lever press performance of the paired versus the random group. The autoshaping hypothesis predicts that far fewer lever press responses will be performed by rats in the random group, and individual differences in lever press performance in the random group will be less highly correlated with the volume of ethanol consumed.

Male Long–Evans hooded rats ($n = 12$) were randomly divided into two groups of six rats each. On Session 1, rats in the lever–bottle paired group were placed in the autoshaping chambers, trained to lick the sipper tube connected to a bottle containing 6% ethanol (v/v) diluted in 0.1% saccharin, then given the first of 10 daily autoshaping sessions. Each autoshaping trial consisted of the insertion of the retractable lever for 8 sec (CS), and then, independent of responding, the saccharin/ethanol solution US was made available by inserting the sipper tube into the chamber for 16 sec. During each session, the rat received 25 autoshaping trials, separated by a mean intertrial interval of 60 sec (minimum interval = 45 sec, maximum interval = 75 sec). Subjects in the lever–bottle random group received similar training, except that the availability of the saccharin/ethanol solution US occurred randomly with respect to the insertion of the lever CS. For each subject in both groups, the number of lever press CRs during each lever CS presentation and the number of milliliters of saccharin/ethanol solution consumed during each session was recorded. Subjects were run once daily, 5 days per week, for a total of 10 autoshaping sessions.

Mean number of lever press CRs increased as a function of sessions for the lever–bottle paired group, but remained at a low level across sessions for the lever–bottle random group (Fig. 10.1). Thus, repeated pairings of the lever CS with the saccharin/ethanol solution US produced the acquisition and maintenance of lever press autoshaping CR performance. Moreover, the induction of lever pressing is not due to pseudoconditioning, as little lever pressing was observed in the lever–bottle random control group. Mixed-design two-way multivariate analysis of variance (MANOVA) with groups and sessions as factors revealed a reliable main effect of groups, $F(1, 10) = 9.02, p < .01$, a reliable main effect of sessions, $F(9, 90) = 5.63, p < .01$, and reliable Groups × Sessions interaction, $F(9, 90) = 4.81, p < .01$. Fisher's LSD ($\alpha = .05$) revealed that the groups differed reliably on Sessions 6 through 10.

For both the lever–bottle paired and the lever–bottle random groups, the mean volume of saccharin/ethanol solution consumed during the first six autoshaping sessions was approximately 7.0 ml +/– (1.3 ml). However, during the last three (8–10) autoshaping sessions, mean volume of saccharin/ethanol solution consumed increased in the lever–bottle paired group, but did not change appreciably across sessions for the lever–bottle random group (Fig. 10.2). A mixed-design two-way MANOVA with groups and sessions as factors revealed no reliable main effect of groups, $F(1, 10) = 3.17, p > .05$, no reliable main effect of sessions, $F(9, 90) = 1.84, p > .05$, but a reliable Groups × Sessions interaction,

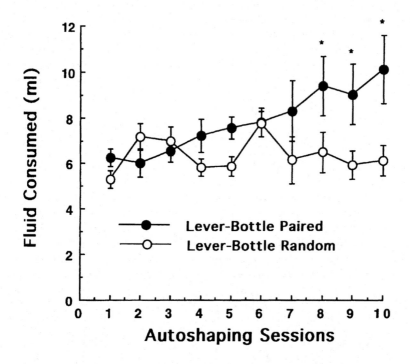

FIG. 10.1. Mean ml of 0.1% saccharin–6% ethanol consumed by the lever–bottle paired and the lever–bottle random groups, as a function of 10
autoshaping sessions. The vertical bars represent the standard errors of the
means. The asterisk (*) indicates that the groups differed reliably (Fisher's LSD,
p < .05).

$F(9, 90) = 2.16, p < .05$. Fisher's LSD ($\alpha = .05$) revealed that the groups differed reliably on Sessions 8 through 10.

These data reveal that the saccharin/ethanol solution US was effective in producing lever press autoshaping CR performance, although
the frequency of autoshaping CRs were considerably lower than has
typically been observed in studies employing food US. The form of the
autoshaping CRs induced by saccharin/ethanol solution US included
lever CS-directed approach and contact responses, culminating in sniffing, nose touching, and licking of the lever CS. These topographies are
similar to those reported by previous investigators who have employed
fluid solutions as the US in autoshaping procedures with rats (Atnip,
1977; Davey, Phillips, & Cleland, 1981; Picker et al., 1986; Poling & Appel, 1978). The vigorous gnawing and chewing of the lever CS, typically
observed in studies employing food US, was not observed in any rats.

Variability between subjects in autoshaping CR performance and in drinking the saccharin/ethanol solution was considerable, and although the two rats that provided the most autoshaping CRs also drank the most saccharin/ethanol solution, there were too few subjects in the lever–bottle paired group to verify this effect by statistical correlation analyses. The tendency of the lever–bottle paired group to increase drinking of the saccharin/ethanol solution across autoshaping sessions was largely attributable to increased drinking in the two rats that performed the most autoshaping CRs; however, a larger number of subjects are required to evaluate the reliability of this effect. The two rats that performed the most autoshaping CRs also consumed the most saccharin/ethanol solution. These two rats were observed to be substantially impaired in motor coordination by the end of each session. The impairment was accompanied by cessation of lever pressing and ethanol drinking. Thus, these procedures produce rapid intake of ethanol solution, at least in some rats, and the re-

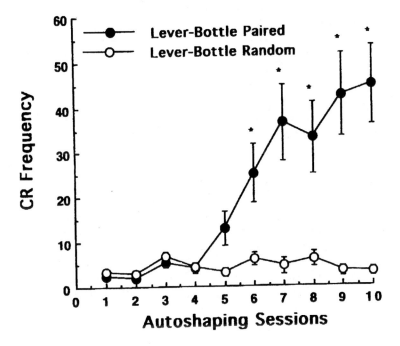

FIG. 10.2. Mean number of lever pressing responses for rats in the lever–bottle paired group and the lever–bottle random group as a function of 10 autoshaping sessions. The vertical bars represent the standard errors of the means. The asterisk (*) indicates that the groups differed reliably (Fisher's LSD, $p < .05$).

sulting motor impairment places a ceiling on the performance of both lever pressing and ethanol drinking.

Experiment 4: Autoshaping Procedures Employing Saccharin/Ethanol Solution as the US: Autoshaping Maintained Despite Saccharin Fading

The six rats in the lever–bottle paired group received 64 additional sessions of autoshaping, during which time the saccharin concentration was systematically reduced across sessions (Table 10.1). Although the mean volume of fluid consumed decreased somewhat as a function of the lowering of the concentration of saccharin, when the 6% ethanol was dissolved in tap water (i.e., 0% saccharin) all of the rats drank on average at least 2.0 ml of the solution during those 10 sessions, and the average volume consumed across those 10 sessions was 5.8 ml. In addition, mean lever press autoshaping CRs per session was maintained at a level that was only slightly lower than those observed before the saccharin was eliminated.

These data reveal that a solution of ethanol without saccharin is an effective US in a lever press autoshaping procedure. Substantial volumes of 6% ethanol diluted in tap water are consumed, and moderate levels of lever press autoshaping CR performance are maintained for at least 10 sessions. The two rats that provided the most autoshaping CRs were the two that drank the most 6% ethanol solution when the saccharin was eliminated. Although this suggests that vulnerability to autoshaping predicts excessive ethanol drinking, data from more subjects are needed to evaluate this trend using statistical analyses.

Three rats were placed on free feeding and then received 10 additional autoshaping sessions with the 6% ethanol (0% saccharin) solution US. The mean number of autoshaping CRs performed and the mean volume (in ml) of ethanol consumed by each of these three rats under the nondeprived condition was at least as high as the level of responding recorded when these rats were run at 80% of their free-feeding weights. Thus, once ethanol consumption has been initiated and maintained for several weeks, food deprivation is not required to maintain either ethanol drinking or lever press autoshaping CR performance.

In two pilot studies conducted in these autoshaping chambers, we attempted to bypass the saccharin fading procedures by offering naive rats a solution of 0% saccharin and 6% ethanol. In both of these studies very low volumes of this fluid were consumed, even though training was given for more than 20 daily sessions, and few lever press autoshaping CRs were recorded. Thus, it appears that in highly trained and experienced rats, autoshaping CR performance can be sustained by

TABLE 10.1 Saccharin Fading

Percentage Saccharin in 6% Ethanol Solution	Number of Autoshaping Sessions	Fluid Consumed (ml)	Autoshaping CRs
.10	20	9.3	42.4
.09	8	9.1	38.1
.08	8	10.1	39.1
.07	6	8.7	34.2
.06	6	8.2	36.4
.05	4	9.0	34.9
.04	3	9.2	28.1
.03	3	8.3	29.4
.02	3	7.0	25.4
.01	3	7.2	26.1
.00	10	5.8	24.7

6% ethanol solution as the US even after the saccharin has been eliminated; however, in naive rats, the saccharin solution is an essential component of the US solution that is effective in producing stable and reliable ethanol intake.

Experiment 5: Lever CS–Saccharin/Amphetamine US Pairings Induce Lever-Directed Autoshaping CRs

This study asks if lever press autoshaping CRs are acquired and maintained when lever insertion (CS) precedes saccharin/amphetamine solution (US). There are several earlier reports of oral self-administration of amphetamine solutions by rats (Janicke, Heil, & Cooper, 1989; Kanarek & Marks-Kauffman, 1988; Kanarek, Marks-Kauffmann, D'Anci, & Przypek, 1995; Kanarek, Mathes, & Przypek, 1996; Kongyingyoes, Janicke, & Cooper, 1988; see also Macenski & Meisch, 1994). These studies indicate that amphetamine is a nonpreferred solution for rats, and stringent fluid deprivation conditions are typically imposed to induce oral intake of unadulterated amphetamine solutions. The palatability of nonpreferred drug solutions may be dramatically improved by initially offering the drug in combination with saccharin (Samson, 1988). This strategy has been successfully employed to induce rats to drink saccharin/amphetamine solution US (Experiment 5) and to sustain some levels of drinking of higher amphetamine concentrations (Experiment 6).

Male Long–Evans hooded rats ($n = 12$), were food-deprived to 80% of their free-feeding weights and given free access to water in their home cages. Rats were run for 28 daily 1-hr sessions in autoshaping chambers sessions wherein the insertion of a retractable lever CS for 8 sec preceded the response-independent insertion of a sipper tube of a bottle containing amphetamine in a concentration of 12.5 mg/l of 0.1% saccharin for 16 sec. For each subject, the number of lever press autoshaping CRs during each trial and the volume (in ml) of saccharin/amphetamine solution consumed during each session was recorded. To test for the retention of lever press autoshaping CR performance, all subjects were maintained on food deprivation, but received no additional autoshaping sessions for 16 days (retention interval), followed by the 29th autoshaping session (retention test).

Mean volume (in ml) of the saccharin/amphetamine solution consumed during the 28 autoshaping sessions was calculated for each of the 12 rats. Seven rats consumed on average more than 4 ml of the saccharin/amphetamine solution per session and were designated high drinkers. The remaining five rats consumed on average less than 4 ml of the saccharin/amphetamine solution per session and were designated low drinkers (Fig. 10.3). Statistically reliable group differences in fluid consumption are indicated by the asterisk (*), MANOVA, and Fisher's LSD ($p < .05$). During Block 7, mean milligrams of amphetamine consumed per kilograms of body weight per session was 0.293 for the high drinkers and 0.127 for the low drinkers.

Mean lever press autoshaping CR acquisition functions for the high drinkers and low drinkers reveal that the rats that consumed more saccharin/amphetamine solution (high drinkers) performed more lever press autoshaping CRs (Fig. 10.4). Statistically reliable group differences in mean number of lever press autoshaping CRs per session are indicated by the asterisk (*), MANOVA, and Fisher's LSD ($p < .05$). All 12 rats performed lever press autoshaping CRs on at least 2 of the 28 sessions. The topography of the autoshaping CR included lever CS-directed approach and contact responses culminating in nosing and licking of the lever CS. The vigorous gnawing and chewing of the lever CS, typically observed with food US, was not observed in any rats.

Pavlovian autoshaping procedures yielded stable and reliable daily consumption of the saccharin/amphetamine solution US in all rats; however, individual differences between rats in the amount of saccharin/amphetamine solution consumed was substantial. Between-sub-

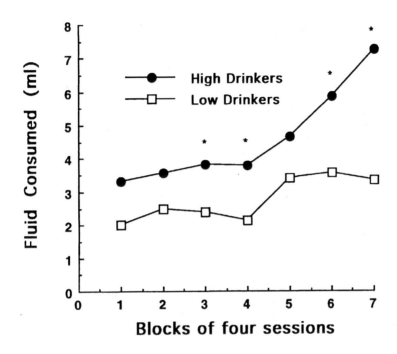

FIG. 10.3. Mean ml of fluid solution US consumed per session by the high drinkers and low drinkers as a function of seven blocks of four autoshaping sessions. Fluid solution US was 12.5 mg of amphetamine per liter of 0.1% saccharin.

ject differences in drinking of the saccharin/amphetamine solution US were reliably related to lever press autoshaping CR performance. High drinkers acquired the lever press autoshaping CR more rapidly and achieved higher asymptotic levels of responding than low drinkers. Moreover, the form of the autoshaping CR acquisition function (Fig. 10.3) is similar to the form of the function relating fluid consumption to session blocks (Fig. 10.4). The data are consistent with the hypothesis that higher levels of consumption of saccharin/amphetamine solution US may be due to the induction of autoshaping CRs.

Retention of lever press autoshaping CR performance was revealed by performance on the autoshaping session (Session 29) following the 16-day retention interval. For both the high drinkers and low drinkers, group mean lever press autoshaping CR frequency varied from the levels observed during Block 7 by less than 10%. For both the high drinkers and low drinkers, group mean volume (in ml) consumption of the saccharin/amphetamine solution varied from the levels observed during Block 7 by less than 10%. Thus, despite the absence of autoshaping

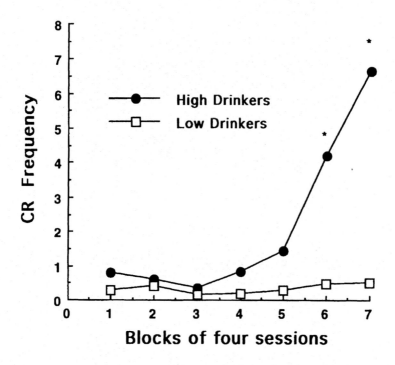

FIG. 10.4.   Mean number of lever press autoshaping CRs per session by high drinkers and low drinkers as a function of seven blocks of four autoshaping sessions.

training sessions for 16 days, lever press autoshaping CR performance and saccharin/amphetamine fluid consumption were maintained by both groups at the levels observed prior to the suspension of daily autoshaping training sessions. This suggests that once responding is established, continued training with autoshaping CS–US pairings or the opportunity to practice performance of lever press autoshaping CRs are not necessary to maintain high levels of autoshaping CR performance. The results are consistent with previous reports of long-term retention of autoshaping CR performance reported in studies employing food US (Rescorla, Durlach, & Grau, 1985; Tomie, 1976, 1981), and, as noted previously, the long-term retention of well-established autoshaping CR performance in procedures employing drug US is reminiscent of the drug abuse phenomenon of relapse.

The saccharin/amphetamine solution was an effective US, producing CS-directed patterns of consummatory responding, which were recorded as lever press autoshaping CRs. The topography of the response was similar to that observed when saccharin/ethanol solution was employed as the US–lever CS-directed approach responses, followed by lever sniffing and lever licking. These topographies are similar to those reported by previous investigators employing various fluid solutions as US (Davey & Cleland, 1982; Davey, Phillips, & Cleland, 1981). The autoshaping model suggests that autoshaping CRs will also develop to the sipper tube CS paired with the amphetamine solution US. Autoshaping CRs directed at the sipper tube CS are difficult to distinguish from voluntary drinking responses, as both types of responses consist of approach, sniffing, and licking the sipper tube. However, the induction of autoshaping CRs directed at the sipper tube CS provides an additional source of consumption of the fluid US, which contributes to the total volume of the fluid US consumed. Consequently, there should be a positive relation between sipper tube CS-directed autoshaping CRs and the volume of fluid consumed. Our procedures provide another measure of autoshaping CRs induced by amphetamine solution US, namely lever pressing, and lever pressing autoshaping CRs do not result in consumption of the fluid solution US. To the extent, therefore, that an increase in consumption of the fluid solution US is due to autoshaping, then we expect that the increase in drinking will be accompanied by an increase in autoshaping CR performance directed at the lever (i.e., lever pressing).

This relation is observed in comparisons between subjects. Those rats that tend to perform more lever press autoshaping CRs should also perform more sipper tube CS-directed autoshaping CRs, and consequently, should consume more of the fluid solution US. The data of Experiment 5 confirm this prediction. There were large differences between individual rats in the tendency to drink the amphetamine solution US, and, in addition, large differences between subjects in the performance of lever press autoshaping CRs. High drinkers performed more Pavlovian lever press autoshaping CRs than did the low drinkers, and increased drinking presaged the initiation of lever pressing, suggesting that autoshaping first develops to the sipper tube, then to the lever. An additional concern relates to the possibility that the lever press performance observed in this study may be due to pseudo-conditioning rather than to Pavlovian conditioning. It is possible, for example, that amphetamine-induced psychostimulation increases directed motor responding per se, resulting in an increase in the probability of lever pressing, and particularly in the rats that consume more amphetamine.

This possibility is being addressed by a study currently underway in this laboratory. This study compares lever press performance in the paired group, receiving lever CS–bottle US pairings, to performance in the random group that receives lever CS randomly with respect to bottle

US. Pavlovian autoshaping CRs are differentiated from psychostimulation-induced lever pressing by comparing the lever press performance of the paired versus the random groups. Although the study is not yet complete, there is little evidence of lever pressing in the random group, suggesting that the lever pressing observed in the paired group is not due to the direct psychostimulant effects of amphetamine (i.e., amphetamine-induced motor activation). In addition, in the random group there is less variability between subjects in consumption of the saccharin/amphetamine solution, and between-subject differences in drinking appear to be unrelated to lever pressing.

Experiment 6: Lever CS–Saccharin/Amphetamine US Pairings Induce Lever-directed Autoshaping CRs: Effects of Amphetamine Concentration

The effects of increasing the concentration of amphetamine in the saccharin/amphetamine solution US on consumption of the fluid solution US and performance of lever press autoshaping CRs was evaluated in 6 Long–Evans rats. The concentration of amphetamine was 6.25 mg/l during the first 16 sessions, 12.5 mg/l during the next 16 sessions, and 18.75 mg/l during the last 16 sessions. During all sessions, the amphetamine was per liter of 0.1% saccharin.

As in Experiment 5, all rats consumed the saccharin/amphetamine solution and performed lever press autoshaping CRs. Individual differences in drinking of the saccharin/amphetamine solution US were substantial, as were individual differences in lever press autoshaping CR performance. Three rats drank more of the fluid solution US when the amphetamine was in a concentration of 6.25 mg/l of 0.1% saccharin (high drinkers) than did the remaining three rats (low drinkers). The group mean drinking data for the last four sessions of training with each amphetamine concentration are plotted in Fig. 10.5. During the last four sessions, mean milligrams of amphetamine consumed per kilograms of body weight per session was 0.168 for the high drinkers and 0.074 for the low drinkers. The group mean lever press data for the last four sessions of training with each amphetamine concentration are plotted in Fig. 10.6. During training with the amphetamine concentration of 6.25 mg/l of 0.1% saccharin, lever press autoshaping CR performance was positively related to drinking, as revealed by the higher number of lever press autoshaping CRs performed by the high drinkers relative to the low drinkers (Fig. 10.6).

The same three rats (high drinkers) also consumed more of the fluid solution US than did the low drinkers when the amphetamine concen-

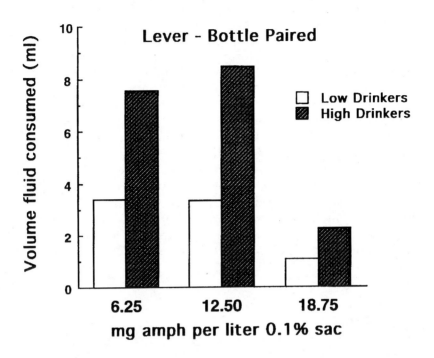

FIG. 10.5. Mean ml of fluid solution US consumed per session by the high drinkers and low drinkers as a function of mg amphetamine per liter 0.1% saccharin in the fluid solution US.

tration was 12.5 mg/l of 0.1% saccharin (Fig. 10.5). During the last four sessions, mean milligrams of amphetamine consumed per kilograms of body weight per session was 0.367 for the high drinkers and 0.142 for the low drinkers. During training with the amphetamine concentration of 12.5 mg/l of 0.1% saccharin, lever press autoshaping CR performance was positively related to drinking, as revealed by the higher number of lever press autoshaping CRs performed by the high drinkers relative to the low drinkers (Fig. 10.6).

These same three rats (high drinkers) continued to consume more of the fluid solution US than did the low drinkers when the amphetamine concentration was 18.75 mg/l of 0.1% saccharin. During the last four sessions, mean milligrams of amphetamine consumed per kilograms of body weight per session was 0.141 for the high drinkers and 0.065 for the low drinkers. During training with the amphetamine concentration of 18.75 mg/l of 0.1% saccharin, lever press autoshaping CR performance was positively related to drinking, as revealed by the higher number of lever press autoshaping CRs performed by the high drinkers relative to the low drinkers (Fig. 10.6).

Thus, rats that consumed more of the amphetamine solution US also perform more lever press autoshaping CRs and this effect is observed across a threefold range (6.25 mg–18.75 mg) of concentrations of amphetamine. These data reveal that those rats that are more susceptible to the induction of autoshaping CRs drink more amphetamine solution US. This relation between autoshaping and drinking is consistent with the hypothesis that the tendency to drink more of the fluid solution US is mediated by autoshaping CRs directed at the sipper tube CS. For the high drinkers, the form of the function relating lever press autoshaping CR performance to amphetamine concentration (Fig. 10.6) is an inverted U-shape, with the highest level of CR performance observed with the 12.5 mg/l concentration of amphetamine. This reveals that lever press autoshaping CRs are due, at least in part, to the amphetamine concentration of the fluid solution US, as the concentration of saccharin was invariant during this study.

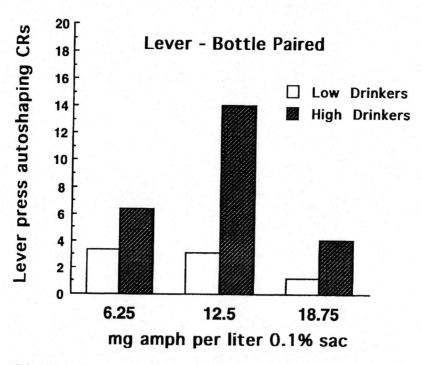

FIG. 10.6. Mean number of lever press autoshaping CRs per session by high drinkers and low drinkers as a function of mg amphetamine per liter 0.1% saccharin in the fluid solution US.

The increase in autoshaping CR performance of the high drinkers when the amphetamine concentration was increased to 12.5 mg/l is important. It shows that on the ascending limb of the function, where the dose of amphetamine consumed is also ascending, lever press autoshaping CRs increase and the magnitude of the increase in lever pressing is proportional to the difference in amount of amphetamine consumed (.168 mg/kg vs. 367 mg/kg) rather than to the difference in the amount of saccharin consumed (negligible). These data reveal that for amphetamine concentrations between 6.25 mg/l and 12.5 mg/l there is a positive relation between amphetamine concentration and lever press autoshaping CR performance that is proportional to the amount of amphetamine consumed, and most notably, this relations is observed only in the high drinkers.

The low drinkers showed no increase in drinking or in lever press autoshaping CRs when the amphetamine concentration was increased to 12.5 mg/l. Thus, for the low drinkers, the additional amphetamine consumed as a result of drinking the higher amphetamine concentration fluid solution US (.074 mg/kg for 6.25 mg/l amphetamine vs. 142 mg/kg for 12.5 mg/kg amphetamine) did not yield increases in either lever press autoshaping CR performance or in drinking of the fluid solution US. For the low drinkers, lever pressing and drinking more closely approximated the amount of saccharin consumed rather than the amount of amphetamine consumed.

In summary, the lever press and drinking performance of the high drinkers appears to be more closely related to the amount of amphetamine consumed, whereas the lever press and drinking performance of the low drinkers appears to be more closely related to the amount of saccharin consumed. The autoshaping model suggests that those rats that respond to the consumption of amphetamine by increasing the performance of autoshaping CRs will perform more lever press autoshaping CRs and, in addition, more sipper tube CS-directed autoshaping CRs. Thus, the tendency to engage in autoshaping CR performance in response to amphetamine consumption will lead to even higher levels of consumption of the amphetamine solution. These predicted relations are evident in these data and they support the hypothesis that susceptibility to the induction of autoshaping CRs contributes to the tendency to increase drug consumption.

In Experiment 6, the concentration of amphetamine was increased during successive blocks of autoshaping sessions across a three-fold range (6.25 mg/l–18.75 mg/l), resulting in a function relating autoshaping CR performance to amphetamine concentration that was an inverted U-shape in form. The amphetamine concentration that produced the most drinking (12.5 mg/l) also produced the most lever press autoshaping CR performance, and the amphetamine concentration that produced the least drinking (18.75 mg/l) also produced the lowest level of lever press autoshaping CR performance. The positive relation between drinking and lever press autoshaping was also observed at the level of the individual subject. Each of the three concentrations of amphetamine employed resulted in high drinkers performing more autoshaping CRs than low drinkers. The similarity in the forms of the functions relating drinking and lever press autoshaping CR performance to amphetamine concentrations is consistent with the hypothesis that excessive drinking is due to autoshaping.

Experiment 7: Correlations Between Lever CS–Food US Autoshaping Performance and Stress-Induced Pathophysiological Markers of Vulnerability to Drug Abuse

This study asks if individual differences in lever press autoshaping CR performance in rats predict individual differences in neurochemical indexes proposed to indexes vulnerability to drug taking. Rats prone to self-administer amphetamine have been reported to exhibit more novelty stress-induced release of corticosterone (Lucas, Angulo, Le Moal, McEwen, & Piazza, 1998; Piazza, Deminiere, Le Moal, & Simon, 1989; Piazza & Le Moal, 1996; Piazza et al., 1991). Individual differences in the pattern of endogenous corticosterone secretion also predict individual differences in ethanol intake. For example, rats with high basal levels of corticosterone together with an attenuated rise in corticosterone output during stress are predisposed to consume more alcohol in a two-bottle choice test (Prasad & Prasad, 1995). In adult nonhuman primates, plasma cortisol concentrations are positively correlated with alcohol consumption rate (Higley & Linnoila, 1997). These results are consistent with the finding that adrenalectomy attenuates voluntary ethanol intake in rats (Fahlke, Engel, Eriksson, Hard, & Soderpalm, 1994; Hansen, Fahlke, Hard, & Thomasson, 1995; Lamblin & De Witte, 1996; Morin & Forger, 1982) and short-term treatment with corticosterone reverses these effects (Fahlke, Engle, et al., 1994, Fahlke, Hard, Thomasson, Engel, & Hansen, 1994).

Rats prone to self-administer amphetamine have been reported to exhibit higher levels of dopamine activity in nucleus accumbens and striatum (Lucas et al., 1998; Rouge-Pont, Piazza, Kharouby, Le Moal, & Simon, 1993) but not in prefrontal cortex (Piazza et al., 1991; Simon et al., 1988), and lower levels of serotonergic activity in the mesolimbic dopamine tract (Piazza et al., 1991). In addition, individual differences in the tendency to express nonregulatory ingestive-like responding, which, like autoshaping is consummatory-like, poorly controlled, and highly variable between subjects, have also been positively correlated with forebrain dopamine (Mittleman, Castaneda, Robinson, & Valenstein, 1985; Mittleman, & Valenstein, 1986).

This study asks if individual differences in lever press autoshaping CR performance induced by lever CS–food US pairings predict stress-induced corticosterone release and tissue levels of monoamines and metabolites in rats. Fourteen food-deprived Long-Evans hooded male rats were given 20 daily sessions of autoshaping wherein the insertion of a retractable lever CS preceded the response-independent delivery of food US. Immediately before and after the 20th session of autoshaping, each rat's tail was cut and a 50 μl sample of tail blood was drawn. Twenty-four hours after the 20th autoshaping session, each rat was sacrificed by rapid decapitation. Brains were removed, and tissue samples of prefrontal cortex (PFC), nucleus accumbens (NAC), caudate putamen (CP), and ventral tegmental area (VTA) were dissected out and later assayed for tissue levels of dopamine, serotonin, and their metabolites by high-pressure liquid chromatography with electrochemical detection (DeVito & Wagner, 1989).

There were large between-subject differences in the acquisition and maintenance of autoshaping CR performance. For each subject, the mean number of lever press autoshaping CRs (CR frequency) performed during Sessions 1 through 10 provided an estimate of CR acquisition rate, and the mean number of lever press autoshaping CRs performed during Sessions 15 through 19 provided an estimate of asymptotic levels of CR performance. Relations between tissue monoamine levels and autoshaping performance during Sessions 1 through 10 was evaluated using multiple regression techniques (Table 10.2). These analyses reveal that rats that performed more lever press autoshaping CRs during sessions 1 through 10 had higher levels of dopamine in NAC ($p < .05$), lower (dihydroxphenylacetic acid) DOPAC/DA turnover ratios in CP ($p < .01$), and lower levels of 5-hydroxyindoleacetic acid) 5-HIAA in VTA ($p<.05$). Similar analyses were performed to evaluate the relation between tissue monamine levels and autoshaping performance during Sessions 15 to 19 (Table 10.3). These analyses reveal that rats that performed more lever press autoshaping CRs during Sessions 15 through 19 had higher levels of dopamine in NAC ($p < .05$), higher levels of DOPAC in NAC ($p < .05$), lower DOPAC/DA turnover ratios in CP ($p < .01$), and lower levels of 5-HIAA in VTA ($p < .05$). Multiple regression analyses relating autoshaping performance to corticosterone levels are presented in Table 10.4. These analyses reveal that rats that performed more autoshaping CRs during Sessions 1 through 10 had higher postsession corticosterone levels and higher changes in corticosterone level (postsession minus presession corticosterone levels); however, CR frequency during Sessions 15

TABLE 10.2 Monoamine–Autoshaping Pearson Product–Moment Correlations in Autoshaping Sessions 1 Through 10

	Brain Region			
Monoamine	NAC	PFC	CP	VTA
DA	.671*	−.417	.213	−.022
DOPAC	.519	−.322	−.429	−.183
DOPAC/DA	.037	.294	−.704**	−.387
HVA	.274	−.299	−.132	.031
HVA/DA	−.171	−.069	−.333	−.134
5-HT	.164	−.176	.031	−.413
5-HIAA	−.334	−.415	−.250	−.586*
5-HIAA/5-HT	−.525	−.521	−.408	−.630*

Note. NAC - nucleus accumbens; PFC = prefrontal cortex; CP = caudate putamen; VTA = ventral tegmental area; DA = dopamine; DOPAC = dihydroxyphenylacetic acid; HVA = homovanillic acid; 5-HT = serotonin; 5-HIAA = 5-hydroxyindoleacetic acid. The DOPAC/DA turnover ratio was derived by dividing for each subject the tissue level of DOPAC by the tissue level of DA. The 5-HIAA/5-HT turnover ratio was derived by dividing for each subject the tissue level of 5-HIAA by the tissue level of 5-HT.

*$p = .05.$ **$p = .01.$

through 19 was not significantly correlated with any measures of corticosterone level.

Stepwise multiple regression analysis (SYSTAT) revealed that three factors accounted for 87% of the variance in autoshaping performance during Sessions 1 through 10. The neurochemical profiles of the rats that performed more autoshaping CRs were high in postsession levels of corticosterone, with low DOPAC/DA turnover ratios in CP, and high levels of DA in NAC. Two factors accounted for 94% of the variance in autoshaping performance during Sessions 15 through 19. The neurochemical profiles of the rats that performed more autoshaping CRs during these sessions were low in DOPAC/DA turnover ration in CP and low in 5-HIAA/5-HT (serotonin) turnover ratio in CP.

Although those rats that acquired lever press autoshaping CR performance more rapidly were also those that provided higher asymptotic levels of autoshaping performance, the neurochemical correlates of autoshaping CR acquisition were not identical to the correlates of asymptotic CR maintenance. The most notable distinction between the neurochemical correlates of acquisition and asymptotic performance is the clear evidence that stress-induced corticosterone release is positively correlated with CR acquisition but not significantly correlated with asymptotic CR performance. In addition, 5-HIAA/5-HT turnover is significantly correlated with the acquisition of lever press autoshaping CRs but not related to asymptotic maintenance of CR frequency. Finally, higher levels of DOPAC in NAC are significantly negatively related to higher levels of asymptotic CR maintenance, but not to CR acquisition performance.

There are similarities between the neurochemical profile of autoshaping and pathophysiological markers of vulnerability to amphetamine self-administration. Both are positively correlated with stress-induced corticosterone release, increases in indexes of DA functioning in NAC, and decreases in indexes of 5-HT functioning in VTA. Nevertheless, the neurochemical profiles differ in several regards. Notably, autoshaping is negatively related to DA functioning in CP,

TABLE 10.3 Monoamine–Autoshaping Pearson Product–Moment Correlations Autoshaping Sessions 15 Through 19

Monoamine	Brain Region			
	NAC	PFC	CP	VTA
DA	.674*	−.367	.335	−.264
DOPAC	.732**	−.307	−.473	−.404
DOPAC/DA	.199	.159	−.836**	−.452
HVA	.404	−.295	−.015	−.297
HVA/DA	−.133	−.173	−.253	−.368
5-HT	.189	−.276	.067	−.574
5-HIAA	−.196	−.375	−.289	−.624*
5-HIAA/5-HT	−.413	−.147	−.513	−.461

Note. NAC = nucleus accumbens; PFC = prefrontal cortex; CP = caudate putamen; VTA = ventral tegmental area; DA = dopamine; DOPAC = dihydroxyphenylacetic acid; HVA = homovanillic acid; 5-HT = serotonin; 5-HIAA = 5-hydroxyindoleacetic acid. The DOPAC/DA turnover ratio was derived by dividing for each subject the tissue level of DOPAC by the tissue level of DA. The 5-HIAA/5-HT turnover ratio was derived by dividing for each subject the tissue level of 5-HIAA by the tissue level of 5-HT.

$p = .05.$ $p = .01.$

TABLE 10.4 Corticosterone–Autoshaping Pearson Product–Moment
Correlations

Corticosterone	Autoshaping Sessions	
	1–10	15–19
Presession	.132	.031
Postsession	.658*	.283
Change (Post – Pre)	.599*	.275

Note. Presession corticosterone levels were determined from samples taken immediately before the 20th autoshaping session. Postsession corticosterone levels were determined from samples taken immediately after the 20th autoshaping session. Change (post – pre) in corticosterone levels was derived by subtracting each subject's presession corticosterone level from that subject's postsession corticosterone level.

$p = .05$.

whereas, in contrast, rats that self-administer amphetamine show higher levels of DA functioning in CP (Piazza et al., 1991). In addition, autoshaping was not significantly negatively correlated with DA functioning in PFC, whereas lower levels of DA activity in PFC have been related to amphetamine self-administration (Piazza et al., 1991; Simon et al., 1988), and, in contrast to our results, other investigators (Izaki, Hori, Nomura, 1998) have reported elevation in extracellular DA as measured by in vivo microdialysis in medial prefrontal cortex during operant lever press acquisition. Finally, although autoshaping was significantly negatively correlated with 5-HIAA/5-HT turnover in VTA, a similar effect has been documented with 5- HIAA but not with 5-HIAA/5-HT turnover in rats that self-administer abused drugs (Piazza et al., 1991).

CONCLUSION

These data support the following conclusions:

1. Drugs of abuse (ethanol and amphetamine) function as effective USs in Pavlovian autoshaping procedures, inducing lever CS-directed autoshaping CRs.
2. This effect is not due to pseudo-conditioning, as far more lever pressing is observed in lever–drug paired groups, as compared to lever–drug random groups.
3.

Individual differences in the volume of drug solutions consumed are positively correlated with individual differences in autoshaping of lever pressing. This supports the hypothesis that sipper tube-directed autoshaping CRs may develop as a result of sipper tube–drug pairings.

4. The neurochemical profile of rats that perform more lever press autoshaping CRs includes several features of the pathophysiological profile of vulnerability to drug abuse.

These data support the hypothesis that two types of autoshaping CRs develop as a result of repeated acts of voluntary drug taking. Sipper tube–drug pairings induce sipper tube-directed autoshaping CRs (approach, contact, manipulation, and licking of the sipper tube), increasing the volume of the drug solution consumed. This interpretation is supported by lever–drug pairings inducing lever press autoshaping CRs even though lever pressing does not obtain access to the drug, and the observed positive correlation between sipper tube licking and lever pressing. The lever pressing data reveal that autoshaping develops to objects paired with a drug, even when the object itself (i.e., lever) is not employed as a conduit to consume the drug. This type of autoshaping may play an important role in animal drug self-administration procedures, which typically require operant lever pressing to obtain drug reward. As noted by Tomie (1995, 1996), animal models of voluntary operant responding for oral self-administration of abused drugs also typically provide for experience that may be conducive to the development of Pavlovian autoshaping CRs. For example, a well-developed animal model of ethanol seeking provides for oral self-administration of ethanol, which serves as a positive reinforcer for rats in operant lever press tasks (e.g., Meisch, 1977; Meisch & Thompson, 1974a; Rassnick, D'Amico, Riley, & Koob, 1993; Samson, 1988; Weiss, Mitchiner, Bloom, & Koob, 1990). Rats that lever press for the opportunity to drink ethanol will experience Pavlovian pairings of lever CS–ethanol US, allowing for the development of Pavlovian lever-directed autoshaping CRs, which would serve to increase further lever pressing for ethanol reinforcement.

The autoshaping model (Tomie, 1995, 1996) provides a unique theoretical perspective on the environmental determinants of the drug abuse syndrome. These data support the premise that autoshaping CRs are induced by abused drugs and suggest that individual differences in the tendency to perform autoshaping CRs may play a vital role in predisposing vulnerability to drug abuse. Although the validity of this novel theoretical approach requires more extensive experimental analysis, it is notable that autoshaping, although fundamental, is largely counterintuitive (at least to me). In this regard, it shares much in common with the befuddling perplexities of drug abuse.

REFERENCES

Atnip, G. W. (1977). Stimulus- and response-reinforcer contingencies in autoshaping, operant, classical, and omission training procedures in rats. *Journal of the Experimental Analysis of Behavior, 28,* 59–69.

Bell, M. S., Gosnell, B. A., Krahn, D. D., & Meisch, R. A. (1994). Ethanol reinforcement and its relationship to saccharin preference in rats. *Alcohol, 11,* 141–145.

Brown, P. L., & Jenkins, H. M. (1968). Auto-shaping the pigeon's key-peck. *Journal of the Experimental Analysis of Behavior, 11,* 1–8.

Carroll, M. E., & Lac, S. T. (1993). Autoshaping i.v. cocaine self-administration in rats: Effects of nondrug alternative reinforcers on acquisition. *Psychopharmacology, 110,* 5–12.

Carroll, M. E., & Lac, S. T. (1997). Acquisition of IV amphetamine and cocaine self-administration in rats as a function of dose. *Psychopharmacology, 129,* 206–214.

Davey, G. C., & Cleland, G. G. (1982). Topography of signal-centered behavior: Effects of deprivation state and reinforcer type. *Journal of the Experimental Analysis of Behavior, 38,* 291–304.

Davey, G., Oakley, C. L., & Cleland, G. G. (1981). Autoshaping in the rat: Effects of omission on the form of the response. *Journal of the Experimental Analysis of Behavior, 36,* 75– 91.

Davey, G. C., Phillips, S., & Cleland, G. G. (1981). The topography of signal-centered behaviour in the rat: The effects of solid and liquid food reinforcers. *Behaviour Analysis Letters, 1,* 331–337.

DeVito, M. J., & Wagner, G. C. (1989). Methamphetamine-induced neuronal damage: A possible role for free radicals. *Neuropharmacology, 28,* 1145–1150.

Fahlke, C., Engel, J. A., Eriksson, C. J. P., Hard, E., & Soderpalm, B. (1994). Involvement of corticosterone in the modulation of ethanol consumption in the rat. *Alcohol, 11,* 195–202.

Fahlke, C., Hard, E., Thomasson, R., Engel, J. A., & Hansen, S. (1994). Meyrapone-induced suppression of corticosterone synthesis reduces ethanol consumption in high-preferring rats. *Pharmacology, Biochemistry & Behavior, 48,* 977–981.

Falk, J. L. (1994). The discriminative stimulus and its reputation: Role in the instigation of drug abuse. *Experimental & Clinical Psychopharmacology, 2,* 43–52.

Falk, J. L., & Lau, C. E. (1993). Oral cocaine as a reinforcer: Acquisition conditions and importance of stimulus control. *Behavioural Pharmacology, 4,* 597–609.

Falk, J. L., & Lau, C. E. (1995). Stimulus control of addictive behavior: Persistence in the presence and absence of a drug. *Pharmacology, Biochemistry and Behavior, 50,* 71–75.

Gahtan, E., Labounty, L. P., Wyvell, C., & Carroll, M. E. (1996). The relationships among saccharin consumption, oral ethanol, and IV cocaine self-administration. *Pharmacology, Biochemistry and Behavior, 53,* 919–925.

Gosnell, B. A., & Krahn, D. D. (1992). The relationship between saccharin and alcohol intake in rats. *Alcohol, 9,* 203–206.

Hansen, S., Fahlke, C., Hard, E., & Thomasson, R. (1995). Effects of ibotenic-acid lesions of the ventral striatum and the medial prefrontal cortex on ethanol consumption in the rat. *Alcohol, 12,* 397–402.

Hearst, E., & Jenkins, H. M. (1974). *Sign tracking: The stimulus–reinforcer relation and directed action.* Austin, TX: Psychonomic Society

Higley, J. D., & Linnoila, M. (1997). A nonhuman primate model of excessive alcohol intake (personality and neurbiological parallels of type I- and type II-like alcoholism). In M. Galanter (Ed.), *Recent developments in alcoholism* (Vol. 13, pp. 191–219). New York: Plenum.

Izaki, Y., Hori, K., & Nomura, M. (1998). Dopamine and acetylcholine elevation on lever-press acquisition in rat prefrontal cortex. *Neuroscience Letters, 258*, 33–36.

Janicke, B., Heil, T., & Cooper H. (1989). P-hydroxy-norephedrine as a possible mediator causing the reduction of oral intake of d-amphetamine in rats. *Drug & Alcohol Dependence, 23*, 247–253.

Kanarek, R. B., & Marks-Kauffman, R. (1988). Dietary modulation of oral amphetamine intake in rats. *Physiology & Behavior, 44*, 501–505.

Kanarek, R. B., Marks-Kauffman, R., D'Anci, K. E., & Przypek, J. (1995). Exercise attenuates oral intake of amphetamine in rats. *Pharmacology, Biochemistry and Behavior, 51*, 725–729.

Kanarek, R. B., Mathes, W. F., & Przypek, J. (1996). Intake of dietary sucrose or fat reduced amphetamine drinking in rats. *Pharmacology, Biochemistry and Behavior, 54*, 719–723.

Kongyingyoes, B., Janicke, B., & Coper, H. (1988). The influence of brain catecholamines on "drug taking behaviour" relative to oral self-administration of d-amphetamine by rats. *Drugs & Alcohol Dependence, 22*, 223–233.

Lamblin, F., & De Witte, P. (1996). Adrenalectomy prevents the development of alcohol preference in male rats. *Alcohol, 13*, 233–238.

Locurto, C. M. (1981). Contributions of autoshaping to the partitioning of conditioned behavior. In C. M. Locurto, H. S. Terrace, & J. Gibbon (Eds.), *Autoshaping and conditioning theory* (pp. 101–135). New York: Academic Press.

Lucas, L. R., Angulo, J. A., Le Moal, M., McEwen, B. S., & Piazza, P. V. (1998). Neurochemical characterization of individual vulnerability to addictive drugs in rats. *European Journal of Neuroscience, 10*, 3153–3163.

Macenski, M. J., & Meisch, R. A. (1994). Oral drug reinforcement studies with laboratory animals: Applications and implications for understanding drug-reinforced behavior. *Current Directions in Psychological Science, 3*, 22–27.

Meisch, R. A. (1977). Ethanol self-administration: Infra-human studies. In T. Thompson & P. B. Dews (Eds.), *Advances in behavioural pharmacology* (Vol. 1, pp. 35–84). New York: Academic Press.

Meisch, R. A., & Thompson, T. (1974). Ethanol intake as a function of concentration during food deprivation and satiation. *Pharmacology, Biochemistry and Behavior, 2*, 589–596.

Mittleman, G. M., Castaneda, E., Robinson, T. E., & Valenstein, E. S. (1986). The propensity for non-regulatory ingestive behavior is related to differences in dopamine systems: Behavioral and biochemical evidence. *Behavioral Neuroscience, 100*, 213–220.

Mittleman, G., & Valenstein, E. S. (1985). Individual differences in non-regulatory ingestive behavior and catecholamine systems. *Brain Research, 348*, 112–117.

Morin, L. P., & Forger, N. G. (1982). Endocrine control of ethanol intake by rats or by hamsters: Relative contributions of the ovaries, adrenals and steroids. *Pharmacology, Biochemistry & Behavior, 17*, 529–537.

Myer, J. S., & Hull, J. H. (1974). Autoshaping and instrumental learning in the rat. *Journal of Comparative and Physiological Psychology, 86*, 724–729.

Overstreet, D. H., Kampov-Polevoy, A. B., Rezvani, A. H., Murrelle, L., Halikas, J. A., & Janowsky, D. S. (1993). Saccharin intake predicts ethanol intake in genetically heterogeneous rats as well as different rat strains. *Alcoholism: Clinical & Experimental Research, 17*, 366–369.

Piazza, P. V., Deminiere, J. M., Le Moal, M., & Simon, H. (1989). Factors that predict individual vulnerability to amphetamine self-administration. *Science, 245*, 1511–1513.

Piazza, P. V., & Le Moal, M. (1996). Pathophysiological basis of vulnerability to drug abuse: Role of an interaction between stress, glucocorticoids, and dopaminergic neurons. *Annual Review of Pharmacology and Toxicology, 36*, 359–378.

Piazza, P. V., Rouge-Pont, F., Deminiere, J. M., Kharoubi, M., Le Moal, M., & Simon, H. (1991). Dopaminergic activity is reduced in the prefrontal cortex and increased in the nucleus accumbens of rats predisposed to develop amphetamine self-administration. *Brain Research, 567,* 169–174.

Picker, M., Blakely, E., & Poling, A. (1986). Effects of anticonvulsant drugs under automaintenance and negative automaintenance procedures. *Pharmacology, Biochemistry and Behavior, 24,* 555–560.

Poling, A. D., & Appel, J. B. (1978). Drug effects under automaintenance and negative automaintenance procedures. *Pharmacology, Biochemistry and Behavior, 9,* 315–318.

Poplawsky, A., & Phillips, C. L. (1986). Autoshaping a leverpress in rats with lateral, medial, or complete septal lesions. *Behavioral and Neural Biology, 45,* 319–328.

Poulos, C. X., Le, A. D., & Parker, J. L. (1995). Impulsivity predicts individual susceptibility to high levels of alcohol self-administration. *Behavioural Pharmacology, 6,* 810–814.

Poulos, C. X., Parker, J. L., & Le, A. D. (1998). Increased impulsivity after injected alcohol predicts later alcohol consumption in rats: Evidence for "loss-of-control drinking" and marked individual differences. *Behavioral Neuroscience, 112,* 1247–1257.

Prasad, C., & Prasad, A. (1995). A relationship between increased voluntary alcohol preference and basal hypercorticosteronemia associated with an attenuated rise in corticosterone output during stress. *Alcohol, 12,* 59–63.

Rassnick, S., D'Amico, E., Riley, E., & Koob, G. F. (1993). GABA antagonist and benzodiazepine partial inverse agonist reduce motivated responding for ethanol. *Alcoholism: Clinical and Experimental Research, 17,* 124–130.

Rescorla, R. A., Durlach, P. J., & Grau, J. W. (1985). Contextual learning in Pavlovian conditioning. In P. D. Balsam & A. Tomie (Eds.), *Context and learning* (pp. 23–56). Hillsdale, NJ: Lawrence Erlbaum Associates.

Robinson, T. E., & Berridge, K. C. (1993). The neural basis of drug craving: An incentive sensitization theory of addiction. *Brain Research Reviews, 18,* 247–291.

Rouge-Pont, F., Piazza, P. V., Kharouby, M., Le Moal, M., & Simon, H. (1993). Higher and longer stress-induced increase in dopamine concentrations in the nucleus accumbens of animals predisposed to amphetamine self-administration. A microdialysis study. *Brain Research, 602,* 169–174.

Samson, H. H. (1988). Oral ethanol self-administration in rats: Models of alcohol-seeking behavior. *Alcoholism: Clinical and Experimental Research, 12,* 591–597.

Schwartz, B., & Gamzu, E. (1977). Pavlovian control of operant behavior. An analysis of autoshaping and its implications for operant conditioning. In W. K. Honig & J. E. R. Staddon (Eds.), *Handbook of operant behavior.* (pp. 53–79). Englewood Cliffs, NJ: Prentice-Hall.

Siegel, S. (1989). Pharmacological conditioning and drug effects. In A. J. Goudie & M. Emmett-Oglesby (Eds.), *Psychoactive drugs* (pp. 115–180). Clifton, NJ: Humana.

Simon, H., Gabhzouti, K., Gozlan, H., Studler, J. M., Louilot, A., Herve, D., Glowinski, J., Tassin, J. P., & Le Moal, M. (1988). Lesion of dopaminergic terminals in the amygdala produces enhanced locomotor response to D-amphetamine and opposite changes in dopaminergic activity in prefrontal cortex and nucleus accumbens. *Brain Research, 447,* 335–340.

Specker, S., Carroll, M. E., & Lac, S. T. (1994). Food deprivation history and cocaine self-administration: An animal model of binge eating. *Pharmacology, Biochemistry and Behavior, 48,* 1025–1029.

Tomie, A. (1976). Interference with autoshaping by prior context conditioning. *Journal of Experimental Psychology: Animal Behavior Processes, 2,* 323–334.

Tomie, A. (1981). Effects of unpredictable food upon the subsequent acquisition of autoshaping: Analysis of the context blocking hypothesis. In C. M. Locurto, H. S. Terrace, & J. Gibbon (Eds.), *Autoshaping and conditioning theory* (pp. 181–215). New York: Academic Press.

Tomie, A. (1995). CAM: An animal learning model of excessive and compulsive implement-assisted drug-taking in humans. *Clinical Psychology Review, 15,* 145–167.

Tomie, A. (1996). Locating reward cue at response manipulandum (CAM) induces symptoms of drug abuse. *Neuroscience and Biobehavioral Reviews, 20,* 505–535.

Tomie, A., Aguado, A. S., Pohorecky, L. A., & Benjamin, D. (1998). Ethanol induces impulsive-like responding in a delay-of-reward operant choice procedure: Impulsivity predicts autoshaping. *Psychopharmacology, 139,* 376–382.

Tomie, A., Brooks, W., & Zito, B. (1989). Sign-tracking: The search for reward. In S. B. Klein & R. R. Mowrer (Eds.), *Contemporary learning theory: Pavlovian conditioning and the status of traditional learning theory* (pp. 191–223). Hillsdale, NJ: Lawrence Erlbaum Associates.

Tomie, A., Cunha, C., Mosakowski, E. M., Quartarolo, N. M., Pohorecky, L. A., & Benjamin, D. (1998). Effects of ethanol on Pavlovian autoshaping in rats. *Psychopharmacology, 139,* 154–159.

Tomie, A., Hayden, M., & Biehl, D. (1980). Effects of response elimination procedures upon the subsequent reacquisition of autoshaping. *Animal Learning & Behavior, 11,* 117–134.

Tomie, A., & Kruse, J. M. (1980). Retardation tests of inhibition following discriminative autoshaping. *Animal Learning & Behavior, 8,* 402–408.

Tomie, A., Rhor-Stafford, I., & Schwam, K. T. (1981). The retarding effects of the TRC response elimination procedure upon the subsequent reacquisition of autoshaping: Comparison of between- and within-subjects assessment procedures and evaluation of the role of background contextual stimuli. *Animal Learning & Behavior, 9,* 230–238.

Weiss, F., Mitchiner, M., Bloom, F. F., & Koob, G. F. (1990). Free-choice responding for ethanol versus water in alcohol-preferring (P) and unselected Wistar rats is differentially altered by naloxone, bromocriptine and methysergide. *Psychopharmacology, 101,* 178–186.

chapter **11**

Neurobiology of Reinforcement:
Interaction Between Dopamine and Cholecystokinin Systems

Norberto J. DeSousa
Franco J. Vaccarino
University of Toronto

*T*horndike (1911) laid the foundation for reinforcement theory. He stated in the law of effect that actions that lead to a "satisfying state of affairs" are repeated. According to this rather subjective notion, reinforcing stimuli strengthen certain behaviors by virtue of the fact that they produce a satisfying, or rewarding, state of affairs. This raises the question of what a satisfying state of affairs is. According to the law of effect, a satisfying state of affairs is produced by any stimulus that will reinforce behavior. Fortunately, this definitional circularity did not produce a satisfying state of affairs amongst reinforcement theorists. Over time, alternative conceptualizations of reinforcement emerged. For example, Hull (1943) focused not on subjective internal states, but rather on internal drive states (i.e., hunger). Within

441

this framework, reinforcers reduce this drive state and establish internal homeostasis. Alternatively, the Skinnerian view (Skinner, 1958) is one of simple empiricism that does not rely on internal states. Rather, a reinforcer is a stimulus that increases the probability of an organism repeating a behavior that preceded the reinforcer's presentation. Another approach involves Meehl's (1950) principle of transsituationality. This principle assumes that reinforcers are effective at increasing the probability of responses across a broad range of behavioral situations. In contrast, Pavlov's (1927) writings on reinforcement focused not on the behavioral responses that precede the reinforcing event, but rather on the elicitation of an unconditioned behavioral response by an unconditioned reinforcing stimulus. Pavlov further added that a conditioned response can be elicited by a previously neutral stimulus that has been paired with an unconditioned reinforcing stimulus. Finally, Bindra (1968, 1974) proposed an incentive-motivational model that incorporated many of the previous notions regarding reinforcement. This model asserts that both unconditioned and conditioned reinforcing stimuli are endowed with response eliciting and response strengthening properties that are characterized by approach, contact, and consummatory behaviors.

The roots for a biological basis of reinforcement may be found in the writings of Schneirla (1959), who focused not on reinforcement, but instead on approach and withdrawal behaviors. All motivated behavior, he suggested, involves basic motor responses consisting of either approach or withdrawal. He further believed that the brain mechanisms mediating these two fundamental processes are dissociable. In a similar vein, Glickman and Schiff (1967) proposed that a common feature of all natural reinforcers is their ability to facilitate approach-related behavior and that this facilitation is specifically mediated by the medial forebrain bundle (MFB) system. Over the past decade, a number of authors have further extended this idea to unconventional reinforcers, such as drugs of abuse, and suggested that their capacity to serve as positive reinforcers is intimately associated with their locomotor approach activating properties (Koob, 1996; Vaccarino, 1994; Vaccarino, Schiff, & Glickman, 1989; Wise & Bozarth, 1987). Today, there is a vast body of data that suggests that these behavioral processes are critically dependent on activation of a subcomponent of the MFB, the mesolimbic dopamine (DA) system.

GENERAL OVERVIEW

Consistent with the conceptualization of Bindra (1968, 1974), this chapter focuses on the activational (eliciting), primary (unconditioned), and secondary (conditioned) rewarding (incentive) properties of conventional and unconventional reinforcing stimuli. As discussed, previously neutral stimuli that have been paired with unconditioned reinforcers may come to function as conditioned reinforcers capable of eliciting approach, contact, and consummatory responses. In this chapter, we review the literature concerning the delineation of the neurochemical mechanisms that contribute to unconditioned behaviors associated with reinforcement from animal studies utilizing approach-related activation, feeding, brain stimulation reward (BSR), and psychostimulant reward techniques. These studies are consistent in highlighting the importance of mesolimbic DA neurotransmission, particularly within the nucleus accumbens (NAC) terminal region. Further, we review data from studies utilizing conditioned reinforcement models that also implicate NAC–DA in the establishment and possibly the expression of secondary reward.

Anatomical results have shown that the mesolimbic DA system is surrounded by a network of endogenous neuropeptides. For example, neurotensin, met-enkephalin, and substance P systems have all been shown to exert important modulatory effects on mesolimbic neurons (Deutch et al., 1985; Johnson, Sar, & Stumpf, 1980; Ljungdahl, Hokefelt, Nilsson, & Goldstein, 1978; Uhl, Kuhar, & Snyder, 1977). Of particular interest here, the neuropeptide cholecystokinin (CCK) also coexists with DA in a significant subset of mesolimbic neurons that originate in the ventral mesencephalon and terminate in the NAC. A review of data that demonstrate functional interactions between DA and CCK systems at the pharmacological, neurochemical, and electrophysiological level are presented. Furthermore, we explore results from numerous studies suggesting that CCK is also critically involved in processes associated with the mediation of both conventional and unconventional reinforcement.

DOPAMINE AND UNCONDITIONED REINFORCEMENT

Olds and Milner (1954) discovered that rats could be easily trained to perform an operant response to receive trains of electrical stimulation into discrete brain regions. This finding sparked a multitude of studies that were aimed at characterizing the nature of the neural substrates mediating BSR. The fact that the reinforcer in this case was the electrical stimulation of discrete brain areas, rather than a natural reinforcer, indicated that the brain possesses groups of neurons that, when stimulated, represent a reward to the animal. Because the activation of these neurons is rewarding to the animal it has been suggested that, under normal conditions, the activation of reward neurons by conventional stimuli could, in principle, reinforce behavior. Consistent with the general principles suggested by Schneirla (1959) and Glickman and Schiff (1967), this represented a possible neural substrate for mediation of reinforcement. The fact that BSR was only observed in certain brain regions further suggested that reward neurons are not a general brain phenomenon and that reinforcement may be dependent on the activation of specific neural systems.

Although BSR can be obtained from a number of brain regions, much of the research aimed at characterizing neural substrates of BSR has focused on stimulation of the MFB. Further, although research indicates that the directly stimulated MFB reward neurons are small, myelinated neurons that travel in a descending direction (see Yeomans, 1988), numerous pharmacological studies investigating the neurochemical characteristics of BSR provide strong support for the involvement of ascending mesolimbic DA neurons in the expression of MFB BSR.

Before discussing these data, a brief anatomical overview of the mesolimbic DA system follows. This is followed by a discussion of the involvement of this system in mediating the activational and rewarding properties of conventional and unconventional reinforcers.

Mesolimbic DA System

Classically, three main dopaminergic cell bodies have been described in the central nervous system (Dahlstrom & Fuxe, 1964; Ungerstedt, 1971). Grouped into small clusters, these cell bodies originate in the substantia nigra and ventral tegmental area of the mesencephalon and are labeled A8, A9, and A10. Cells from A8, in the caudolateral-most extent of the substantia nigra pars lateralis, and those of A9, in the more rostromedial substantia nigra pars compacta, form the nigrostriatal pathway innervating the striatum as well as the central nucleus of the amygdala and dorsal NAC. Closer to the midline, the A10 cell bodies originate mainly in the medial ventral tegmentum and course rostrally joining with the MFB. Recipients of these dopaminergic fibers include limbic structures such as the NAC, as well as the central amygdala, lateral septum, olfactory tubercle, interstitial nucleus of the stria terminalis, ventral striatum (Moore & Bloom, 1978; Ungerstedt, 1971), and frontal cortex (Lindvall & Bjorklund, 1974). The term *mesolimbic system* refers generally to the A10 DA cells that project to all limbic structures, but is used here to denote DA tegmental-NAC cells.

Approach-Related Locomotor Activity

As discussed earlier, a key component of reinforcing stimuli is their capacity to elicit approach behavior (Glickman & Schiff, 1967; Vaccarino et al., 1989; Wise & Bozarth, 1987). In the laboratory, researchers have attempted to quantify approach using the exploratory locomotor activity paradigm. Although there are some interpretive difficulties associated with these assumptions (DeSousa & Vaccarino, 1998), the locomotor activity technique has nevertheless proved an important research tool for examining approach-related behaviors associated with reinforcing stimuli.

The involvement of DA systems in forward locomotor behavior has been demonstrated by studies manipulating DA neurotransmission. Some of the first such studies utilized neuronal lesion techniques. These studies showed that destruction of NAC, but not striatal terminals using either electrolytic or 6-hydroxydopamine (6-OHDA) lesions reduce hyperlocomotion induced by systemically injected DA agonists (Creese & Iversen, 1972; Kelley, Sevoir, & Iversen, 1975; Ungerstedt, 1979; Uretsky & Schoenfeld, 1971). Similarly, bilateral injection of the dopaminergic antagonist haloperidol directly into the NAC, but not the striatum, blocks the locomotor activity elicited by systemic injections of the indirect DA agonist amphetamine (Pijnenburgh, Honig, & van Rossum, 1975). Results from studies utilizing intracerebral microinjections of DA agonists further support the findings from these studies. For example, a number of researchers have shown that localized injections of DA or dopaminergic agonists, such as amphetamine, directly into the NAC facilitate locomotor activity (Pijnenburgh & van Rossum, 1973; Pijnenburgh, Honig, van der Heyden, & van Rossum, 1976). Interestingly, injections into caudal NAC sites produce more pronounced effects than injections into rostral NAC sites (Essman, McGonigle, & Lucki, 1993). However, injections of amphetamine into the cortex, the ventrolateral and anteromedial striatum, and other regions are without effect on locomotor activity (Carr & White, 1987).

The involvement of endogenously released DA in these effects is further highlighted by in vivo microdialysis studies that have shown that administration of dopaminergic agonists, such as cocaine and amphetamine, at doses that stimulate forward locomotion preferentially increase extracellular DA in the NAC, but not the striatum (Carboni, Imperato, Perezzani, & Di Chiara, 1989; Di Chiara, Tanda, Frau, & Carboni, 1993; and Sharp, Zetterstrom, Ljungberg, & Ungerstedt, 1987). More interestingly, in untreated animals the circadian pattern of NAC DA release correlates with the circadian profile of forward locomotor activity such that both peak during the night cycle (O'Neill & Fillenz,

1985). Additional microdialysis studies have demonstrated that individual variability across animals in NAC dihydroxyphenylacetic acid (DOPAC)/DA ratios and DA release are positively correlated with individual differences in approach-related activity elicited by a novel environment or psychostimulant administration (Hooks, Jones, Smith, Neill, & Justice, 1991; Piazza et al., 1991). Taken together, these studies demonstrate that approach-related behaviors are critically mediated via the NAC DA system.

Primary Reward

This section focuses on primary reward associated with both conventional and unconventional reinforcers. The following findings from studies utilizing feeding, BSR, intravenous (IV) self-administration, and conditioned place preference procedures provide a summary of the evidence supporting the involvement of mesolimbic DA function in mediating the primary rewarding properties of both conventional and unconventional reinforcers.

Feeding

Consistent with an excitatory role for DA in feeding behavior are numerous studies that demonstrate that interference of dopaminergic transmission inhibits feeding. Wise and Raptis (1986) found that the dopaminergic antagonist pimozide increases the latency and decreases the rate of feeding. These effects have been taken to suggest that blockade of DA transmission causes a motivational deficit and that the progressive decrease in food intake is related to an attenuation of the reinforcing value of food reward as pimozide-treated animals are capable of responding at control levels and show a progressive decrease in their feeding behavior with repeated trials (Wise, 1982; Wise & Colle, 1984; Wise & Raptis, 1986). Interestingly, DA antagonist treatment is more effective at decreasing intake of sweetened solutions than water (Sclafani, Aravich, & Xenakis, 1982).

A number of studies have highlighted the facilitory role of DA in feeding. For example, low doses but not high doses of systemically administered amphetamine have been shown to increase feeding (Evans & Vaccarino, 1987, 1990; Grinker, Drewnowski, Enns, & Kisseleff, 1980; Holtzman, 1974; Winn, Williams, & Herberg, 1982). Intracerebroventricular administration of low doses of amphetamine or the DA agonist bromocriptine also facilitate food intake (Evans & Eikelboom, 1987; Morley, Levine, Grace, & Kneip, 1982). Studies aimed at identifying the central site of action for these effects have shown that microinjections of low doses of amphetamine into the NAC produce stimulatory effects on food intake (Colle & Wise, 1988; Evans & Vaccarino, 1986, 1990). Further, Evans and Vaccarino (1990) showed that this effect is most pronounced in feeding associated with highly palatable foods. Together with previous results, this suggests that palatability may be an important factor in DA's mediation of food intake.

The link between mesolimbic DA and feeding has been further explored by studies utilizing neurophysiological, postmortem, and microdialysis techniques. For example, neurophysiological studies have shown that presentation of both food and fluid stimuli increase the firing rates of DA neurons originating in the mesencephalon (Ljungberg, Apicella, & Schultz, 1992; Romo & Schultz, 1990; Schultz, 1986). Similarly, reports from post mortem and microdialysis studies demonstrate that food-rewarded operant responding produces elevations in the concentration of extracellular DA (Hernandez & Hoebel, 1988a, 1988b). Using microdialysis, Radhakishun, van Ree, and Westerink (1988) reported that during the initiation of feeding there is a concomitant increase in the release of endogenous DA neurotransmission within the NAC. Interestingly, individual differences in sucrose intake predict the degree of amphetamine-induced NAC–DA overflow as measured by online in vivo microdialysis (Sills & Crawley, 1996). Taken together, there is strong evidence implicating mesolimbic DA in feeding processes.

Electrical Brain Stimulation and Psychostimulants

As discussed, there is substantial evidence implicating mesolimbic DA in electrical BSR. Additionally, it has been proposed that drugs of abuse derive their primary rewarding properties by acting as biochemical surrogates, tapping into neuronal motivational systems that are normally activated by conventional primary reinforcing stimuli such as food (Di Chiara & Imperato, 1988; DiChiara, 1995; Vaccarino, 1994; Wise & Bozarth, 1987). In this context, psychostimulant drugs, such as amphetamine and cocaine, are of particular interest here as they possess high abuse potential in humans and are potent facilitators of mesolimbic DA transmission.

Psychostimulant drugs have been shown to support robust responding for IV self-administration in both primates (Deneau, Yanagita, & Seevers, 1969; Griffiths, Findley, Brady, Dolan-Gutcher, & Robinson, 1975) and rats (Collins, Weeks, Cooper, Good, & Russell, 1984; Pickens, 1968) and potentiate bar pressing for BSR (Crow 1972). Further, in the conditioned place preference paradigm, rats will demonstrate approach and contact responses for a place in which they have previously been exposed to amphetamine or cocaine (Reicher & Holman, 1977; Spyraki, Fibiger, &

Phillips, 1982a, 1982b). Consistent with a role for the NAC in these effects are observations that intra-NAC injections of psychostimulant drugs support IV self-administration, potentiate BSR, and induce place preference (Carr & White, 1986; Colle & Wise, 1986; Hoebel et al., 1983; Monaco, Hernandez, & Hoebel, 1981). Finally, manipulations that severely compromise the integrity of mesolimbic DA function attenuate the rewarding properties of BSR and psychomotor stimulant drugs. Thus, studies utilizing 6-OHDA lesions of mesolimbic neurons or NAC antagonist administrations have consistently shown decreases in reward associated with electrical brain stimulation, psychostimulant self-administration, and conditioned place preference paradigms (Fibiger, Le Piane, Jakubovic, & Phillips, 1987; Lyness, Friedle, & Moore, 1979; Mackey & van der Kooy, 1985; Morency & Beninger, 1986; Roberts & Koob, 1982).

Individual Differences

Over the last decade, numerous studies have focused on individual differences related to reinforcement. Generally, these studies are consistent with the notion that mesolimbic DA is critically involved in mediating the effects of conventional and unconventional reinforcers. More specifically, this research has shown that individual differences in approach-related novelty exploration and sucrose feeding are predictive of the activational and rewarding effects of psychostimulant drugs and that these effects are positively correlated with mesolimbic DA neurotransmission.

In one of the first such studies, individuals from a random population of rats were designated as either low responders (LRs) or high responders (HRs) based on a median split of their forward locomotor response during exposure to a novel environment (Piazza, Deminiere, Le Moal, & Simon, 1989). This study reported greater locomotor activation in HRs than in LRs following an acute systemic injection of amphetamine. Other studies have confirmed the relation between novel exploration and the psychomotor stimulant properties of drugs of abuse, including amphetamine (Hooks, Jones, Neill, & Justice, 1991) and cocaine (Hooks, Jones, Smith, et al., 1991). Piazza et al. (1989) further linked these activational differences to reward. Thus, when animals are allowed the opportunity to self-administer IV amphetamine, HRs more readily acquire self-administration behavior than do LRs. As discussed, microdialysis studies report that these behavioral differences are associated with variability in the activation of mesolimbic DA projections that terminate within the NAC. For example, postmortem tissue homogenate studies have reported that following exposure to a novel environment, HRs have a higher DOPAC/DA ratio than LRs (Piazza et al., 1991). Similarly, in vivo microdialysis studies show a positive relation between response to novelty and extracellular DA release within the NAC during both basal and psychostimulant-induced test conditions (Bradberry, Gruen, Berridge, & Roth, 1991; Hooks, Colvin, Juncos, & Justice, 1992). Thus, individual differences in natural approach-related responding are predictive of the psychomotor stimulating, rewarding, and mesolimbic DA activating effects of psychostimulant drugs.

Studies from our lab have shown similar effects related to individual differences in the intake of a conventional reinforcer such as sucrose. We have reported that rats exhibit considerable individual variability in their consumption of granulated sucrose (DeSousa, Wunderlich, de Cabo, & Vaccarino, 1998; Sills & Vaccarino, 1991). Based on a median split of sucrose intake in sucrose-habituated rats, Sills and Vaccarino (1996) categorized animals as either low sucrose feeders (LSFs) or high sucrose feeders (HSFs). Following administration of various systemic or intra-accumbens doses of amphetamine, HSFs are more sensitive than LSFs to the inhibitory effects of amphetamine on sucrose intake. These feeding data are consistent with those from locomotor activity studies and show that HSFs display higher levels of exploratory activity compared to LSFs following an acute injection of amphetamine (Sills & Vaccarino, 1994). Further, recent data suggest that the rewarding value of amphetamine may also be augmented in HSFs compared to LSFs (DeSousa, Bush, & Vaccarino, 2000). For example, IV amphetamine acquisition is significantly greater in HSFs than LSFs. Additionally, when animals are given access to different doses of IV amphetamine, HSFs demonstrate an exaggerated dose self-administration response function compared to LSFs. As mentioned, research suggests a role for the mesolimbic DA system in the mediation of these effects. Specifically, results from microdialysis studies showed that HSFs exhibit greater NAC–DA release than LSFs during access to sucrose and following acute treatment with amphetamine (Sills & Crawley, 1996; Sills, Onalaja, & Crawley, 1998). Taken together with results from studies examining approach-related individual differences, these data support the notion that mesolimbic DA is critically involved in mediating both the activational and rewarding effects of both conventional and unconventional reinforcing stimuli.

DA AND CONDITIONED REINFORCEMENT

Motivationally neutral stimuli associated with primary reinforcers may themselves acquire reinforcing properties through incentive-motivational learning (Bindra, 1968, 1974). Studies directed at examining incentive-motivational learning have been organized into two broad, temporally based categories. The first category concerns the mechanisms of acquisition, or development, of incentive learning and the second involves the expression, or maintenance, of previously established incentive learning.

Two main paradigms have been used to assess the acquisition and expression of incentive learning: the conditioned activity (CA) and conditioned reward (CR) paradigms. CA studies typically involve placing animals in a distinct test environment following a specific drug treatment over a series of trials. On the test day animals are returned to that environment following vehicle treatment. Incentive learning is said to take place if the previously neutral environmental stimuli elicit approach responses, measured as an increase in locomotor activity relative to untreated controls. CR studies involve pairing of neutral cues with food delivery over a series of trials. On the test day, two levers are presented; depression of one lever results in cue presentation and depression of the other has no consequences. CR is said to occur if rates of responding are greater for the paired lever. Results from studies using these and related paradigms have been instrumental in implicating NAC–DA in incentive learning. The following section provides a summary of the evidence linking NAC–DA to the acquisition and expression of conditioned learning.

Acquisition of Incentive Learning

Behavioral studies have established that environmental stimuli paired with systemically injected psychostimulants condition hyperlocomotion in the CA paradigm (Pickens & Crowder, 1967; Post & Rose, 1976). Pairing of environmental stimuli with conventional reinforcers such as food have also been shown to condition activity (Jones & Robbins, 1992). Additional studies have revealed that microinfusion of psychostimulant drugs directly into the NAc produce a similar effect (Carr & Phillips, 1988; Hemby, Jones, Justice, & Neill, 1992).

Numerous studies demonstrate that blockade of DA neurotransmission during conditioning trials impairs the establishment of incentive learning. For example, 6-OHDA lesions of the NAC prevent the acquisition of psychostimulant-induced CA (Gold, Swerdlown, & Koob, 1988). Further, animals treated with DA antagonists prior to conditioning trials do not demonstrate psychostimulant- induced CA (Beninger & Hahn, 1983; Fontana, Post, Weiss, & Pert, 1993). Similar manipulations also block the establishment of food CR behavior (Beninger & Phillips, 1980; Hoffman & Beninger, 1985).

Recent neurophysiological evidence further supports the results of CA and CR paradigms that suggest a role for mesolimbic DA in the acquisition of incentive learning. Ljungberg et al. (1992) investigated the responses of monkey DA neurons during reaction time tasks that involved the pairing of reinforcing stimuli with behaviorally neutral stimuli. They found that initially DA neurons respond preferentially to the unconditioned reinforcer. However, during the course of training, these responses are transferred to the conditioned stimulus. This research, together with that from previous studies, suggests that increased DA neurotransmission is associated with the acquisition of incentive learning.

Expression of Incentive Learning

Interestingly, in the study conducted by Ljungberg et al. (1992) described earlier, the responses of DA neurons strongly diminish with overtraining, suggesting that DA may be less critical to the expression of incentive learning than it is to the acquisition of incentive learning. This conclusion is supported by numerous other studies. For example, several studies have reported that DA metabolites in tissue do not reflect conditioned behavioral changes induced by DA agonists (Barr et al., 1983; Moller, Nowak, & Kuschinsky, 1987). Microdialysis studies fail to show concomitant elevations of extracellular DA concentrations in animals showing a cocaine-induced CA response (Brown & Fibiger, 1992). Consistent with this work, Brown, Robertson, and Fibiger (1992) elegantly demonstrated that whereas acute injections of cocaine elevate Fos expression in the NAC, exposure to a cocaine-paired environment fails to stimulate similar neuronal activation. Lesion studies show that 6-OHDA injection into mesolimbic DA neurons does not affect established preferences for a CR lever previously paired with a food reinforcer (Taylor & Robbins, 1984, 1986). Further, a systemically injected moderate dose of *cis*-flupenthixol, a DA antagonist, does not block the expression of an established CR (Robbins, Watson, Gaskin, & Ennis, 1983). However, higher doses have been shown to have some inhibitory effect (Cador, Taylor, & Robbins, 1991). Consistent with these observation, systemic administration of doses of the DA antagonists that block the acquisition of CA do not block its expression (Beninger & Hahn, 1983; Beninger & Herz, 1986; Fontana, Post, Weiss, & Pert, 1993; Poncelet, Dangoumau, Soubrie, & Simon, 1987).

Although it is clear that mesolimbic DA neurotransmission is not necessary for the expression of incentive learning, a number of studies suggest that it can nevertheless modulate the expression of incentive learning. Thus, numerous pharmacological studies have reported that systemic and intra-NAC administration of DA agonists selectively augment responding for cues paired with primary reward (Beninger,

Hanson, & Phillips, 1981; Beninger & Ranaldi, 1992; Chu & Kelley, 1992; Robbins et al., 1983; Taylor & Robbins, 1984, 1986).

CCK–DA INTERACTIONS

CCK, a neuropeptide found throughout the mammalian brain and periphery, is of critical interest here as it coexists with DA in a subset of mesolimbic neurons (Hokfelt et al., 1987, 1980). Given the prominence of the mesolimbic system in the mediation of primary and secondary reinforcement, the possibility that colocalized CCK might modulate DA-dependent reinforcement is tenable. In this next section we explore this idea by reviewing pharmacological, anatomical, neurochemical, and behavioral studies examining the interaction between CCK and DA systems.

Pharmacology

Although many forms of CCK exist in abundance throughout the mammalian brain, the principal active type is sulfated CCK_8 (Beinfeld, Meyer, Eskay, Jensen, & Brownstein, 1981). In this chapter, the more general term *CCK* is used to refer to sulfated CCK_8. CCK is synthesized de novo (Golterman, Stengarrd-Pedersen, Rehfeld, & Christensen, 1981), released via calcium-dependent mechanisms (Emson, Lee, & Rehfeld, 1980), and active at two subreceptors: the CCK_A and CCK_B receptors (Moran, Robinson, Goldrich, & McHugh, 1986). The CCK_A (peripheral-type) receptor has been found primarily in the periphery, but it is also localized in several brain regions including the NAC (Abercrombie, Keefe, DiFrischia, & Zigmond, 1989; Barrett, Steffey, & Wolfram, 1989). CCK_A receptors exhibit a high affinity for sulfated CCK_8 (Hill, Campbell, Shaw, & Woodruff, 1987), but not for unsulfated CCK_8 or CCK_4. In contrast, the CCK_B (central-type) receptor is distributed throughout the central nervous system including the NAC (Gaudreau, St.-Pierre, Pert, & Quinon, 1985) and binds to sulfated and unsulfated CCK_8 as well as unsulfated CCK_4 with approximately equimolar affinity (Lotti & Chang, 1989). Evidence indicates that CCK may act either as a neurotransmitter or neuromodulator in many areas within the central nervous system, including the NAC (Vanderhaeghen, Deschepper, Lostra, Vierendeels, & Schoenen, 1982).

Anatomy

Classically, distribution of CCK-containing fibers terminating in the NAC have been viewed within the context of a rostral-to-caudal dichotomy (Hokfelt et al., 1987; Hokfelt et al., 1980; Studler et al., 1981). It was reported originally that although both the rostral and caudal NAC are innervated by mesolimbic neurons from the ventral tegmentum, a subset of these cells (over 40%) contain both CCK and DA. These CCK and DA containing cells in the ventral tegmental area were reported to project predominantly to the medial caudal NAC (Hokfelt et al., 1980). Data from other anatomical studies suggest that although the rostral NAC is also CCK immunoreactive, these fibers are non-mesolimbic (Studler et al., 1981) and it has been suggested that CCK in this region derives from non-DA neurons.

The NAC can be divided into a central core surrounded by a peripheral shell on anatomical, pharmacological, and functional grounds (Heimer & Alheid, 1991). Recent data from our laboratory suggest that, in the context of NAC–CCK, this distinction is a useful one (Lanca, de Cabo, Arifuzzaman, & Vaccarino, 1998). Our immunocytochemical results indicate that, in the context of CCK and DA fibers, the tegmentum primarily projects to the shell (medial caudal NAC), and the medial substantia niagra projects primarily to the core of the NAC (rostral NAC). These results suggest that the rostral-caudal differences in NAC–CCK organization may overlap core–shell differences. Therefore, the level of CCK and DA colocalization in the NAC may be more extensive than previously thought.

Neurochemistry

Results from studies measuring DA-stimulated adenylate cyclase (AC) activity have provided insights regarding DA interactions with both mesolimbic and nonmesolimbic CCK. DA acts on a receptor linked to AC, such that DA, or DA agonists, stimulate its activity, whereas DA antagonists inhibit AC activity (Kebabian & Calne, 1979). Thus, Studler et al. (1986) showed CCK potentiated and CCK inhibited DA-stimulated AC activity in tissue homogenates from rat caudal and rostral NAC, respectively. These data suggest that endogenously released CCK in the caudal NAC may act in a fashion directly opposite to CCK released in the rostral NAC.

Other neurochemical studies have reported conflicting results, demonstrating increases (Ruggeri et al., 1987), decreases (Lane, Blaha, & Phillips, 1986; Voight, Wang, & Westfall, 1986), and no effect (Hamilton,

Sheehan, De Belleroche, & Herberg, 1984) of CCK on DA release. However, these studies failed to incorporate anatomical information concerning NAC CCK heterogeneity. Acknowledging such a distinction, Marshall, Barnes, Hughes, Woodruff, and Hunter (1991) reported data that are concurrent with those of Studler et al. (1986). Using in vitro release techniques, they demonstrated that CCK potentiated and attenuated K^+-stimulated DA release in tissue slices from rat caudal and rostral NAC, respectively. These effects were reversible with a CCK_A antagonist in the caudal NAC, and a CCK_B antagonist in the rostral NAc. Other investigators have presented concurrent data. For example, Voight, Wang, and Westfall (1985) reported increased or decreased in vivo release of DA following intra-NAC administration of either unsulfated or sulfated CCK_8, respectively. Further, Vickroy and Bianchi (1989) demonstrated that in vitro release of DA was potentiated by sulfated CCK_8 in rat caudal NAC slices, and that this effect was reversible following application of the CCK_A antagonist CR-1409. In agreement with these data are reports of increased DA and DA metabolite levels in the caudal NAC, specifically in the shell region, following caudal NAC and peripheral administration of sulfated CCK_8 (Kariya, Tanaka, & Nomura, 1994; Ladurelle, Durieux, Roques, & Dauge, 1994; Ladurelle, Keller, Roques, & Dauge, 1993;). Conversely, peripherally administered CCK_4 produced no DA-related effect in the caudal NAC.

Taken together with anatomical data, these results suggest that in the caudal NAC, DA activity is potentiated by CCK via a CCK_A receptor mechanism. In contrast, in the rostral NAC, DA activity is inhibited by CCK via a CCK_B receptor mechanism.

Behavior

Consistent with neurochemical results, behavioral studies have demonstrated that CCK is a powerful modulator of DA-mediated behaviors. Moreover, the behavioral studies are also consistent with the notion that CCK_A and CCK_B receptors have opposing effects that may be dependent on rostral–caudal differences in NAC–CCK function. The following section provides an overview of studies that illustrate the effects of CCK manipulations on DA-mediated locomotion, unconditioned reward, and CR.

Approach-Related Locomotor Activity

Exogenous CCK. CCK administration into the caudal NAC potentiates hyperlocomotion induced by DA agonists (Crawley, 1992; Crawley, Hommer, & Skirboll, 1985; Crawley, Stivers, Blumstein, &

Paul, 1985; Vaccarino & Rankin, 1989). This effect is reversed by intracaudal NAC devazepide, a CCK_A antagonist (Crawley, 1992). In contrast, injections of CCK into the rostral NAC inhibit DA agonist-induced hyperlocomotion (Crawley, 1992; Crawley, Hommer, & Skirboll, 1985; Vaccarino & Rankin, 1989). This effect is reversed by intracaudal NAC CCK_B antagonism (Crawley, 1992).

Endogenous CCK: CCK_A Receptor. Administration of the CCK antagonists proglumide and benzotript and CCK antiserum into the caudal NAc does not affect baseline locomotion (Crawley, Stivers, Hommer, Skirboll, & Paul, 1986). However, dark-induced locomotion was inhibited by administration of proglumide into the medial caudal NAC (Crawley, 1988). Several studies have failed to replicate this finding in conjunction with various manipulations including baseline, dark-environment, dark-phase, and DA and amphetamine treatments (Crawley, 1992; DeSousa, Lanca, Coscina, & Vaccarino, 1994; DeSousa, Wunderlich, de Cabo, & Vaccarino, 1999; Higgins, Sills, Tomkins, Sellers, & Vaccarino, 1994). However, recent data indicate that both systemic (DeSousa, Wunderlich, deCabo, & Vaccarino, 1999), and intra-NAC (Wunderlich, DeSousa, & Vaccarino, 1997) blockade of CCK_A receptors blocks the expression of context-independent amphetamine sensitization following a 10-day withdrawal period. These results suggest that, in the context of locomotor activity, endogenous activation of CCK_A receptors may occur only under circumstances in which DA neurotransmission has been sensitized.

Endogenous CCK: CCK_B Receptor. Although no effect was found following systemic, rostral, or caudal NAC administration of several doses of the CCK_B antagonists L-365,260 and CI-988 on light-, dark-, and DA-induced activity (Crawley, 1992), results from our laboratory have shown positive results by incorporating individual differences in amphetamine responsivity in our analyses (Higgins et al., 1994). In this study, we reported that systemic injection of L-365,260 potentiates amphetamine-induced activity in animals demonstrating low locomotor responsivity, but not high locomotor responsivity, to amphetamine. Similarly, antagonism of CCK_B receptors in the rostral NAC in low responder rats, defined according to baseline exploratory activity levels, also potentiated amphetamine-induced activity (Vaccarino, Westwood, & Lanca, 1994).

Taken together, these studies suggest that endogenous CCK may act, via CCK_A receptors in the caudal NAC, to potentiate DA-mediated locomotion only during conditions producing high levels of NAC–DA neurotransmission. This idea is in line with the frequency coding hypothesis that states that corelease of peptides and classical neurotransmitters may occur only under conditions associated with high levels of neurotransmission (Bartfai, Iverfeldt, Fisone, & Serfozo, 1988; Iversen, 1995). Additionally, these results indicate that under conditions associated with low levels of NAC–DA neurotransmission, endogenous CCK may inhibit DA-mediated locomotion via CCK_B receptors in the rostral NAC.

Primary Reward

CCK_A Receptors. Microinjections of CCK into the caudal NAC potentiate responding for BSR (De Witte, Heidbreder, Roques, & Vandernaeghen, 1987; Heidbreder, Gewiss, DeMot, Mertens, & DeWitt, 1992). In contrast to these results, research from our lab has shown that systemic administration of a wide dose range of the CCK_A antagonist devazepide did not affect sucrose feeding (Sills & Vaccarino, 1996b). Similarly, blockade of CCK_A receptors with PD-140548 across a broad dose range did not affect IV cocaine self-administration (DeSousa, Smith, & Vaccarino, 1998).

CCK_B Receptors. Central studies demonstrate that infusions into the rostral NAC of CCK or the CCK antagonist proglumide, respectively, reduce or potentiate responding for BSR (De Witte et al., 1987; Heidbreder et al., 1992; Vaccarino & Vaccarino, 1989; Vaccarino & Koob, 1985). Further, systemic administration of high doses of the CCK_B antagonist L-365, 260 have been shown to produce a place preference (Higgins, Nguyen, & Sellers, 1992). Interestingly, systemic administration of morphine and the CCK_B antagonist L365,260 produce a place preference at doses where neither drug alone produces an effect.

Recent data from our laboratory are consistent with previous reports suggesting a DA antagonist-like profile associated with CCK_B receptor activation. For example, sucrose feeding experiments show that both systemic and intra-NAC injections of CCK_B antagonists have DA-agonist-like effects, increasing sucrose consumption of LSFs and decreasing consumption of HSFs (Sills & Vaccarino, 1996b). Similarly, injections of the CCK_B agonist pentagastrin into the rostral NAC dose-dependently increase IV amphetamine self-administration under a fixed ratio schedule (Bush, DeSousa, & Vaccarino, 1999), and decrease IV amphetamine self-administration under a progressive ratio schedule (DeSousa, Bush, Smith, & Vaccarino, 1997). These self-administration results are consistent with a neuroleptic-like effect.

Taken together, the data reviewed in the preceding section indicate that endogenous CCK_A receptor activation in the caudal NAC may potentiate approach- and reward-related mechanisms under very specific conditions. However, it is clear that further research is required to further elucidate the role of CCK_A receptors in such processes. With respect to the CCK_B system, the data summarized here are consistent with the notion that endogenous CCK_B receptor activation, likely in the rostral NAC, acts to inhibit DA-mediated approach and primary reward. These results provide converging evidence for the hypothesized distinction between CCK_A and CCK_B receptor function, as well as the rostral–caudal NAC.

Secondary Reward

CCK_A Receptors. Numerous studies have suggested a role for the CCK_A receptor in DA-dependent incentive learning. For example, Higgins, Nguyen, and Sellers (1991, 1992) showed that systemic administration of the CCK_A antagonist devazepide during the conditioning phase of the conditioned place preference paradigm blocks the acquisition of a morphine-induced place preference—an effect consistent with that seen following DA antagonist treatment (Mackey & van der Kooy, 1985). In line with these results, we have recently demonstrated that systemic administration of devazepide during the pairing of environmental stimuli with either amphetamine or cocaine blocks the subsequent expression of CA (Josselyn, Franco, & Vaccarino, 1996a; Josselyn, DeCristafaro, & Vaccarino, 1997). Additional research has shown that devazepide treatments during the expression of CA produce no behavioral effects (Josselyn et al., 1997). In studies conducted using the CR paradigm, animals were treated systemically with devazepide during the pairing of a light–tone stimulus complex with sucrose reward. This manipulation reduces the subsequent expression of CR (Josselyn et al., 1996a). Importantly, control studies have confirmed that this effect is not attributable to a decrease in food consumption or to a conditioned taste aversion (Josselyn et al., 1996a). Additionally, studies have shown that intra-NAC administration of the CCK_A antagonist PD-140548 also blocks the acquisition of cocaine-induced CA and sucrose-pellet CR (Josselyn & Vaccarino, 1996; Josselyn et al., 1997)

Consistent with the notion that a CCK_A receptor blockade impairs incentive learning are recent results from a cued cocaine relapse study conducted in our laboratory (DeSousa, Smith, & Vaccarino, 1998). In this study, animals were allowed to self-administer IV cocaine or saline daily during alternate trials. Each infusion type was paired with a distinct light–tone stimulus complex across a series of 14 daily sessions. Later, following a 21-day extinction period, control animals showed cued relapse of cocaine-seeking behavior in the presence of cocaine-paired but not saline-paired cues. In treatment animals, it was further demonstrated that this effect was abolished in a dose-dependent manner by systemic treatment with a CCK_A receptor antagonist during the initial cocaine self-administration conditioning sessions. The selective effect of CCK_A blockade on incentive learning is highlighted by the observation that these manipulations had no direct effect on cocaine self-administration itself.

   CCK_B Receptors.   Whereas CCK_A receptors contribute to the establishment, but not expression, of incentive learning, CCK_B receptors appear to produce opposite effects. Thus, we have shown that when injected systemically, or into the NAC, CCK_B antagonists potentiate the facilitory effect of intra-NAC amphetamine on responding for sucrose CR (Josselyn & Vaccarino, 1995; Josselyn, Franco, & Vaccarino, 1996b). Conversely, we have recently shown that systemic administration of the CCK_B antagonist L-365,260 does not affect either the acquisition or expression of cocaine-induced CA or baseline sucrose CR (Josselyn & Vaccarino, 1995; Josselyn et al., 1996a; Josselyn et al., 1997).

   Together, these results showing disruption of incentive learning following CCK_A antagonist treatment suggest that the acquisition of DA-mediated reward-related learning involves endogenous activation of NAC–CCK_A receptors. Moreover, potentiation by CCK_B receptor antagonists of amphetamine's facilitory effect on CR suggests that endogenous activation of CCK_B receptors may act in a modulatory way, thereby dampening the facilitory effects of DA on the expression of incentive conditioning. Taken together, these results demonstrate that CCK is intimately involved in incentive-motivational learning.

GENERAL CONCLUSIONS

As evidenced in the preceding discussion, mesolimbic DA is critically involved in the mediation of reinforcement. The behavioral significance of CCK–DA interactions in this context are complex and depend on a number of factors including CCK receptor subtype, NAC subregion, and the specific behavior in question. Previous inconsistencies in this area were related to limitations in our understanding of functional, anatomical, and behavioral processes associated with CCK subreceptors. When these factors are taken into account, it is clear that CCK exerts powerful effects on DA-dependent processes related to reinforcement.

   Our work, and that of others, suggests that CCK_A and CCK_B receptors in the NAC mediate very different (and in most cases opposing) behavioral effects. Specifically, CCK_A receptor activation potentiates DA neurotransmission in the medial caudal (shell) portion of the NAC. Behaviorally, endogenous activation of this system may be critically involved in facilitating the acquisition of DA-dependent incentive-motivational learning. In contrast, CCK_B receptor activation inhibits DA neurotransmission in the rostral compartment of the NAC. In terms of behavioral significance, this system may function as a dampening mechanism, thereby regulating DA neurotransmission associated with the mediation of the activational and rewarding properties of reinforcing stimuli.

This chapter has merged several different lines of evidence to arrive at an integrated view of the nature of CCK–DA interactions and their role in the mediation of reinforcement. CCK is introduced here as a key neuropeptide to consider in motivated behaviors as defined by the activational and rewarding effects of conventional and unconventional reinforcing stimuli. Future research directed at examining the role of CCK–DA interactions should further our theoretical understanding of motivated behaviors and may have profound implications for human disease states such as Parkinson's disease, schizophrenia, depression, anxiety, and drug dependence.

ACKNOWLEDGMENT

This chapter was prepared with support from a Medical Research Council of Canada grant (20001961) to Franco J. Vaccarino.

REFERENCES

Abercrombie, E. D., Keefe, K. A., DiFrischia, D. S., & Zigmond, M. J. (1989). Differential effect of stress on in vivo dopamine release in striatum, nucleus accumbens, and medial frontal cortex. *Journal of Neurochemistry, 52,* 1655–1658.

Barr, G. A., Sharpless, N. S., Cooper, S., Schiff, S. R., Parades, W., & Bridger, W. H. (1983). Classical conditioning, decay and extinction of cocaine-induced hyperactivity and stereotypy. *Life Sciences, 33,* 1341–1351

Barrett, R. W., Steffey, M. E., & Wolfram, C. A. W. (1989). Type-A cholecystokinin binding sites in cow brain: Characterization using (-)-[^{3}H] L-365,718 membrane binding assays. *Molecular Pharmacology, 36,* 285–290

Bartfai, T., Iverfeldt, K., Fisone, G., & Serfozo, P. (1988). Regulation of the release of co-existing neurotransmitters. *Annual Review of Pharmacology and Toxicology, 28,* 285–310

Beinfeld, M. C., Meyer, D. K., Eskay, R. L., Jensen, R. T., & Brownstein, M. J. (1981). The distribution of CCK immunoreactivity in the CNS of the rat as determined by radioimmunoassay. *Brain Research, 212,* 51–57

Beninger, R. J., & Hahn, B. L. (1983). Pimozide blocks establishment but not expression of amphetamine-produced environment-specific conditioning. *Science, 220,* 1304–1306.

Beninger, R. J., Hanson, D. R., & Phillips, A. G. (1981). The acquisition of responding with conditioned reinforcement: Effects of cocaine, (+)-amphetamine and pipradrol. *British Journal of Pharmacology, 74,* 149–154

Beninger, R. J., & Herz, R. S. (1986). Pimozide blocks establishment but not expression of cocaine-produced environment-specific conditioning. *Life Sciences, 38,* 1425–1431.

Beninger, R. J., & Phillips, A. G. (1980). The effects of pimozide on the establishment of conditioned reinforcement. *Psychopharmacology, 68,* 147–153.

Beninger, R. J., & Ranaldi, R. (1992). The effects of amphetamine, apomorphine, SKF 38393, quinpirole and bromocriptine on responding for conditioned rewards in rats. *Behavioral Pharmacology, 3,* 155–163.

Bindra, D. (1968). Neuropsychological interpretation of the effects of drive and incentive motivation on general activity and instrumental behavior. *Psychological Review, 75,* 1–22.

Bindra, D. (1974) A motivational view of learning, performance and behavior modification. *Psychological Review, 81,* 199–213.

Bradberry, C. W., Gruen, R. J., Berridge, C. W., & Roth, R. H. (1991). Individual differences in behavioral measures: Correlations with nucleus accumbens dopamine measured by microdialysis. *Pharmacology, Biochemistry, and Behavior, 39,* 877–882.

Brown, E. E., & Fibiger, H. C. (1992). Cocaine-induced conditioned locomotion: Absence of increases in dopamine release. *Neuroscience, 48,* 621–629.

Brown, E. E., Robertson, G. S., & Fibiger, H. C. (1992). Evidence for conditional neuronal activation following exposure to a cocaine-paired environment: Role of forebrain limbic structures. *Journal of Neuroscience, 12,* 4112–4121.

Bush, D. E. A., DeSousa, N. J., & Vaccarino, F. J. (1999). Self-administration of intravenous amphetamine: Effect of nucleus accumbens CCK_B receptor activation on fixed ratio responding. *Psychopharmacology, 147,* 331–334.

Cador, M., Taylor, J. R., & Robbins, T. W. (1991). Potentiation of the effects of reward-related stimuli by dopaminergic-dependent mechanisms in the nucleus accumbens. *Psychopharmacology, 104,* 377–385.

Carboni, E., Imperato, A., Perezzani, L., & Di Chiara, G. (1989). Amphetamine, cocaine, phencyclidine and nomifensine increase extracellular dopamine concentrations preferentially in nucleus accumbens of freely moving rats. *Neuroscience, 28,* 653–661.

Carr, G. D., & Phillips, A. G. (1988). Conditioned locomotion following micro-injections of amphetamine into the nucleus accumbens. *Society for Neuroscience Abstracts, 14,* 662.

Carr, G. D., & White, N. M. (1986). Anatomical disassociation of amphetamine's rewarding and aversive effects: An intracranial microinjection study. *Psychopharmacology, 89,* 340–346.

Carr, G. D., & White, N. M. (1987). Effects of systemic and intracranial amphetamine injections on behavior in an open field: A detailed analysis. *Pharmacology, Biochemistry, and Behavior, 27,* 113–122.

Chu, B., & Kelley, A. E. (1992). Potentiation of reward-related responding by psychostimulant infusion into nucleus accumbens: Role of dopamine receptor subtypes. *Psychobiology, 20,* 153–162.

Colle, L. M., & Wise, R. A. (1986). Facilitation of lateral hypothalamic self-stimulation by amphetamine injections into the nucleus accumbens. *Society of Neuroscience Abstracts, 12,* 930.

Colle, L. M., & Wise, R. A. (1988). Facilitory and inhibitory effects of nucleus accumbens amphetamine on feeding. *Annals of the New York Academy of Sciences, 537,* 491–492.

Collins, R. J., Weeks, J. R., Cooper, M. M., Good, P. I., & Russell, R. R. (1984). Prediction of abuse liability of drugs using iv self-administration by rats. *Psychopharmacology, 82,* 6–13.

Crawley, J. N. (1988). Attenuation of dark-induced hyperlocomotion by a cholecystokinin antagonist in the nucleus accumbens. *Brain Research, 473,* 398–400.

Crawley, J. N. (1992). Subtype-selective cholecystokinin receptor antagonists block cholecystokinin modulation of dopamine-mediated behaviors in the rat mesolimbic pathway. *Journal of Neuroscience, 12,* 3380–3393.

Crawley, J. N., Hommer, D. W., & Skirboll, L. R. (1985). Topographical analysis of nucleus accumbens sites at which cholecystokinin potentiates the dopamine induced hyperlocomotion in the rat. *Brain Research, 335,* 337–341.

Crawley, J. N., Stivers, J. A., Blumstein, L. K., & Paul, S. M. (1985). Cholecystokinin potentiates dopamine-mediated behaviors: evidence for modulation specific to a site of coexistence. *Journal of Neuroscience, 5,* 1972–1983.

Crawley, J. N., Stivers, J. A., Hommer, D. W., Skirboll, L. R., & Paul, S. M. (1986). Antagonists of central and peripheral behavioral effects of cholecystokinin octapeptide. *Journal of Pharmacology and Experimental Therapeutrics, 236,* 320–330.

Creese, I., & Iversen, S. (1972). Amphetamine response in rat after dopamine neuron destruction. *Nature New Biology, 238,* 247–248.

Crow, T. J. (1972). Catecholamine-containing neurons and electrical self-stimulation: A review of some data. *Psychological Medicine, 2,* 414–421.

Dahlstrom, A., & Fuxe, K. (1964). Evidence for the existence of monoamine-containing neurons in the central nervous system: I. Demonstration of monoamines in the cell bodies of brain stem neurons. *Acta Physiologica Scandinavia, 247 (Suppl),* 1–55.

Deneau, G., Yanagita, T., & Seevers, M. H. (1969). Self-administration of psychoactive substances by the monkey. *Psychopharmacologia, 16,* 30–48.

DeSousa, N. J., Bush, D. E. A., Smith, M. A., & Vaccarino, F. J. (1997). The effects of nucleus accumbens CCK_B receptor activation: A behavioural dissociation. *Society for Neuroscience Abstracts, 23,* 630.

DeSousa, N. J., Bush, D. E. A., & Vaccarino, F. J. (2000). Self-administration of intravenous amphetamine is predicted by individual differences in sucrose feeding in rats. *Pharmacology, Biochemistry, and Behavior, 148,* 52–58.

DeSousa, N. J., Lanca, A. J., Coscina, D. V., & Vaccarino, F. J. (1994). Blockade of CCK_A receptors does not affect amphetamine- or dark phase-induced locomotor activity. *Society for Neuroscience Abstracts, 20,* 163.

DeSousa, N. J., Smith, M. A., & Vaccarino, F. J. (1998). Relapse of cocaine-seeking behaviour: Involvement of CCK_A receptor mechanisms. *Society for Neuroscience Abstracts, 24,* 192.

DeSousa, N. J., & Vaccarino, F. J. (1998). Preclinical behavioral approaches for assessing the reinforcing properties of drugs of abuse. In A. A. Boulton, G. B. Baker, & A. N. Bateson (Eds.), *In vivo neuromethods* (pp. 227–252). Clifton, NJ: Humana.

DeSousa, N. J., Wunderlich, G. R., de Cabo, C., & Vaccarino, F. J. (1998). Individual differences in sucrose intake predict behavioural reactivity in rodent models of anxiety. *Pharmacology, Biochemistry, and Behavior, 60,* 841–846.

DeSousa, N. J., Wunderlich, G. R., de Cabo, C., & Vaccarino, F. J. (1999). The expression of behavioral sensitization to amphetamine: Role of CCK_A receptors. *Pharmacology, Biochemistry, and Behavior, 62,* 31–37.

Deutch, A. Y., Maggio, J. E., Bannon, M., Kalivas, P. W., Tam, S. Y., Goldstein, M., & Roth, R. H. (1985) Substance K and substance P differentially modulate mesolimbic and mesocortical systems. *Peptides, 6,* 113–122.

De Witte, P., Heidbreder, C., Roques, B., & Vanderhaeghen, J. J. (1987). Opposite effects of cholecystokinin octapeptide (CCK-8) and tetrapeptide (CCK-4) after injection into the caudal part of the nucleus accumbens or into its rostral part and the cerebral ventricles. *Neurochemistry International, 10,* 473–479.

Di Chiara, G. (1995). The role of dopamine in drug abuse viewed from the perspective of its role in motivation. *Drug and Alcohol Dependence, 38,* 95–137.

Di Chiara, G., Imperato, A. (1988). Drugs abused by humans preferentially increase synaptic dopamine concentrations in the mesolimbic system of freely moving rats. *Proceedings of the National Academy of Sciences USA, 85,* 5274–5278.

Di Chiara, G., Tanda, G., Frau, R., & Carboni, E. (1993). On the preferential release of dopamine in the nucleus accumbens by amphetamine: Further evidence obtained by vertically implanted concentric dialysis probes. *Psychopharmacology, 112,* 398–402.

Emson, P. C., Lee, C. M., & Rehfeld, J. F. (1980). Cholecystokinin octapeptide: Vesicular localization and calcium-dependent release from rat brain in vitro. *Life Sciences, 26,* 2157–2163.

Essman, W. D., McGonigle, P., & Lucki, I. (1993). Anatomical differentiation within the nucleus accumbens of the locomotor stimulatory actions of selective dopamine agonists and d-amphetamine. *Psychopharmacology, 112,* 233–241.

Evans, K. R., & Eikelboom, R. E. (1987). Feeding induced by ventricular bromocriptine and amphetamine: A possible excitatory role for dopamine in eating behavior. *Behavioral Neuroscience, 101,* 591–593.

Evans, K. R., & Vaccarino, F. J. (1986). Intra-nucleus accumbens amphetamine: Dose-dependent effects on food intake. *Pharmacology, Biochemistry, and Behavior, 25,* 1149–1151.

Evans, K. R., & Vaccarino, F. J. (1987). Effects of d- and l-amphetamine on food intake: Evidence for a dopaminergic substrate. *Pharmacology, Biochemistry, and Behavior, 27,* 649–652.

Evans, K. R., & Vaccarino, F. J. (1990). Amphetamine- and morphine-induced feeding: evidence for involvement of reward mechanisms. *Neuroscience, Biobehavioral Reviews, 14,* 9–22.

Fibiger, H. C., Le Piane, F. G., Jakubovic, A., & Phillips, A. G. (1987). The role of dopamine in intracranial self-stimulation of the ventral tegmental area. *Journal of Neuroscience, 7,* 3888–3896.

Fontana, D., Post, R. M., Weiss, S. R. M., & Pert, A. (1993). The role of D1 and D2 dopamine receptors in the acquisition and expression of cocaine-induced conditioned increases in locomotor behavior. *Behavioral Pharmacology, 4,* 375–387.

Gaudreau, P., St.-Pierre, S., Pert, C., & Quinon, R. (1985). Cholecystokinin receptors in mammalian brain: A comparative characterization and visualization. *Annals of the New York Academy of Sciences, 448,* 198–219.

Glickman, S. E., & Schiff, B. B. (1967). A biological theory of reinforcement. *Psychological Review, 74,* 81–109.

Gold, L. H., Swerdlow, N. R., & Koob, G. R. (1988). The role of mesolimbic dopamine in conditioned locomotion produced by amphetamine. *Behavioral Neuroscience, 102,* 544–552.

Golterman, N. R., Stengaard-Pedersen, H., Rehfeld, J. F., & Christensen, N. J. (1981). Newly synthesized cholecystokinin in subcellular fractions of rat brain. *Journal of Neurochemistry, 36,* 859–865.

Griffiths, R. R., Findley, J. D., Brady, J. V., Dolan-Gutcher, K., & Robinson, W. W. (1975). Comparison of progressive-ratio performance maintained by cocaine, methylphenidate and secobarbital. *Psychopharmacologia, 43,* 81–83.

Grinker, J. A., Drewnowski, A., Enns, M., & Kisseleff, H. (1980). The effects of d-amphetamine and fenfluramine on feeding patterns and activity of obese and lean Zucker rats. *Pharmacology, Biochemistry, and Behavior, 12,* 265–275.

Hamilton, M., Sheehan, M. J., De Belleroche, J., & Herberg, L. J. (1984). The cholecystokinin analogue cerulin does not modulate dopamine release or dopamine-induced locomotor activity in the nucleus accumbens. *Neuroscience Letters, 44,* 77–82.

Heidbreder, C., Gewiss, M., DeMot, B., Mertens, I., & DeWitte, P. (1992). Balance of glutamate and dopamine in the nucleus accumbens modulates self-stimulation behavior after injection of cholecystokinin and neurotensin in the rat brain. *Peptides, 13,* 441–449.

Heimer, L., & Alheid, G. F. (1991). Piecing together the puzzle of basal forebrain anatomy. *Advances in Experimental Medicine and Biology, 295,* 1–42.

Hemby, S. E., Jones, G. H., Justice, J. B. J., & Neill, A. B. (1992). Conditioned locomotor activity but not conditioned place preference following intra-accumbens infusions of cocaine. *Psychopharmacology, 106*(3), 330–336.

Hernandez, L., & Hoebel, B. G. (1988a). Feeding and hypothalamic stimulation increase dopamine turnover in the accumbens. *Physiology and Behavior, 44,* 599–608.

Hernandez, L., & Hoebel, B. G. (1988b). Food reward and cocaine increase extracellular dopamine in the nucleus accumbens as measured by microdialysis. *Life Sciences, 42,* 1705–1712.

Higgins, G. A., Nguyen, P., & Sellers, E. M. (1991). Blockade of morphine place conditioning by the CCK$_A$ receptor antagonist devazepide. *European Journal of Pharmacology, 197,* 229–230.

Higgins, G. A., Nguyen, P., & Sellers, E. M. (1992). Morphine place conditioning is differentially affected by CCK$_A$ and CCK$_B$ receptor antagonists. *Brain Research, 572,* 208–215.

Higgins, G. A., Sills, T. L., Tomkins, D. M., Sellers, E. M., & Vaccarino, F. J. (1994). Evidence for the contribution of CCK-B receptor mechanisms to individual differences in amphetamine-induced locomotion. *Pharmacology, Biochemistry, and Behavior, 48,* 1019–1024.

Hill, D. R., Campbell, N. J., Shaw, T. M., & Woodruff, G. N. (1987). Autoradiographic localization and biochemical characterization of peripheral type CCK receptors in rat CNS using highly selective nonpeptide CCK antagonists. *Journal of Neuroscience, 7,* 2967–2976.

Hoebel, B. G., Monaco, A. P., Hernandez, L., Aulisi, E. F., Stanley, B. G., & Lenard, L. (1983). Self-injection of amphetamine directly into the brain. *Psychopharmacology, 81,* 158–163.

Hoffman, D. C., Beninger, R. J. (1985). The effects of pimozide on the establishment of conditioned reinforcement as a function of the amount of conditioning. *Psychopharmacology, 87,* 454–460.

Hokfelt, T., Millhorn, D., Seroogy, K., Tsuruo, Y., Cellatelli, S., Lindith, B., Meister, B., & Melander, T. (1987). Coexistence of peptides with classical neurotransmitters. *Experientia, 43,* 768–776.

Hokfelt, T., Skirboll, L., Rehfeld, J. F., Goldstein, M., Markey, K., & Dann, O. (1980). A subpopulation of mesencephalic dopamine neurons projecting to limbic areas contain a cholecystokinin-like peptide: Evidence from immunohistochemistry combined with retrograde tracing. *Neuroscience, 5,* 2093–2124.

Holtzman, S. G. (1974). Behavioral effects of separate and combined administration of naloxone and d-amphetamine. *Journal of Pharmacology and Experimental Therapy, 189,* 51–60.

Hooks, M. S., Colvin, A. C., Juncos, J. L., & Justice, J. B., Jr. (1992). Individual differences in basal and cocaine-stimulated extracellular dopamine in the nucleus accumbens using quantitative microdialysis. *Brain Research, 587,* 306–312.

Hooks, M. S., Jones, G. H., Neill, D. B., & Justice, J. B., Jr. (1991a). Individual differences in amphetamine sensitization: Dose-dependent effects. *Pharmacology, Biochemistry, and Behavior, 41,* 203–210.

Hooks, M. S., Jones, G. H., Smith, A. D., Neill, D. B., & Justice, J. B., Jr. (1991b). Response to novelty predicts the locomotor and nucleus accumbens dopamine response to cocaine. *Synapse, 9,* 121–128.

Hull, C. L. (1943). *Principles of behavior.* New York: Appleton.

Iversen, L. L. (1995). Neuropeptides: Promise unfulfilled? *Trends in Neuroscience, 18,* 49–50.

Johnson, R. P., Sar, M., & Stumpf, W. E. (1980). A topographical localization of enkephalin on the dopamine neurons of the rat substantia nigra and ventral tegmental area demonstrated by combined histofluorescence-immunochemistry. *Brain Research, 194,* 566–571.

Jones, G. H., & Robbins, T. W. (1992). Differential effects of mesocortical, mesolimbic and mesostriatal dopamine depletion on spontaneous, conditioned and drug-induced locomotor activity. *Pharmacology, Biochemistry, and Behavior, 43,* 887–895.

Josselyn, S. A., De Cristafaro, A., & Vaccarino, F. J. (1997). Evidence for CCK_A receptor involvement in the acquisition of conditioned activity produced by cocaine in rats. *Brain Research, 763,* 93–102.

Josselyn, S. A., Franco, V., & Vaccarino, F. J. (1996a). Devazepide, a CCK_A receptor antagonist, impairs the acquisition of conditioned reward and conditioned activity. *Psychopharmacology, 123,* 131–143.

Josselyn, S. A., Franco, V. P., & Vaccarino, F. J. (1996b). PD-135158, a CCK_B receptor antagonist, microinjected into the nucleus accumbens and the expression of conditioned rewarded behavior. *Neuroscience Letters, 209,* 85–88.

Josselyn, S. A., & Vaccarino, F. J. (1995). Blockade of CCK_B receptor interacts with intra-accumbens amphetamine to potentiate responding for conditioned rewards. *Peptides, 16,* 959–964.

Josselyn, S. A., & Vaccarino, F. J. (1996). Acquisition of conditioned reward blocked by intra-accumbens infusion of PD-140548, a CCK_A receptor antagonist. *Pharmacology, Biochemistry, and Behavior, 55,* 439–444.

Kariya, K., Tanaka, J., & Nomura, M. (1994). Systemic administration of CCK-8S but not CCK-4, enhances dopamine turnover in the posterior nucleus accumbens: A microdialysis study in freely moving rats. *Brain Research, 657,* 1–6.

Kebabian, J. W., & Calne, D. B. (1979). Multiple receptors for dopamine. *Nature, 277,* 93–96.

Kelley, P. H., Sevoir, P. W., & Iversen, S. D. (1975). Amphetamine and apomorphine responses in the rat following 6-OHDA lesions of the nucleus accumbens septi and corpus striatum. *Brain Research, 94,* 501–522.

Koob, G. F. (1996). Hedonic valence, dopamine and motivation. *Molecular Psychiatry, 1;* 186–189.

Ladurelle, N., Durieux, C., Roques, V. P., & Dauge, V. (1994). Differential modification of dopamine metabolism in the core and shell parts of the nucleus accumbens following CCK-A receptor stimulation in the shell region. *Neuroscience Letters, 178,* 5–10.

Ladurelle, N., Keller, G., Roques, B. P., & Dauge, U. (1993). Effects of CCK-8 and of the CCK_B-selective agonist BC264 on extracellular dopamine content in the anterior and posterior nucleus accumbens: A microdialysis study in freely moving rats. *Brain Research, 628,:* 254–262.

Lanca, A. J., de Cabo, C., Arifuzzaman, A. I., Vaccarino, F. J. (1998). Cholecystokinergic innervation of nucleus accumbens subregions. *Peptides, 19*, 859–868.

Lane, R. F., Blaha, C. D., & Phillips, A. G. (1986). In vivo electrochemical analysis of cholecystokinin-induced inhibition of dopamine release in the nucleus accumbens. *Brain Research, 397*, 200–204.

Lindvall, O., & Bjorklund, A. (1974). The organization of the ascending catecholamine neurons in the rat brain as revealed by the gloxylic acid fluorescence method. *Acta Physiologica Scandinavia 412, (Suppl.)*, 1–48.

Ljungberg, T., Apicella, P., & Schultz, W. (1992). Responses of monkey dopamine neurons during learning of behavioral reactions. *Journal of Neurophysiology, 67*, 145–163.

Ljungdahl, A., Hokefelt, T., Nilsson, G., & Goldstein, M. (1978). Distribution of substance P-like immunoreactivity in the central nervous system of the rat. II. Light microscopic localization in relation to catecholamine containing neurones. *Neuroscience, 3*, 945–976.

Lotti, V. J., & Chang, R. S. L. (1989). A new potent and selective non-peptide gastrin antagonist and brain cholecystokinin receptor (CCK-B) ligand: L-365, 260. *European Journal of Pharmacology, 162*, 273–280.

Lyness, W. H., Friedle, N. M., & Moore, K. E. (1979). Destruction of dopaminergic nerve terminals in nucleus accumbens: effect on *d*-amphetamine self-administration. *Pharmacology, Biochemistry, and Behavior, 11*, 553–556.

Mackey, W. B., & van der Kooy, D. (1985). Neuroleptics block the positive reinforcing effects of amphetamine but not of morphine as measured by place conditioning. *Pharmacology, Biochemistry, and Behavior, 22*, 101–105.

Marshall, F. H., Barnes, S., Hughes, J., Woodruff, G. N., & Hunter, J. C. (1991). Cholecystokinin modulates the release of dopamine from the anterior and posterior nucleus accumbens by two different mechanisms. *Journal of Neurochemistry, 56*, 917–922.

Meehl, P. E. (1950). On the circularity of the law of effect. *Psychological Bulletin, 47*, 52–75.

Moller, H. G., Nowak, K., & Kuschinsky, K. (1987). Conditioning of pre- and postsynaptic behavioral responses to the dopamine receptor agonist apomorphine in rats. *Psychopharmacology, 91*, 50–55.

Monaco, A. P., Hernandez, L., & Hoebel, B. G. (1981). Nucleus accumbens: Site of amphetamine self-injection: Comparison with the lateral ventricle. In R. B. Chronister and J. F. DeFrance (Eds.), *The neurobiology of the nucleus accumbens* (pp 338–342). Brunswick, ME: Haer Institute for Electrophysiology.

Moore, T. H., & Bloom, F. E. (1978). Central catecholamine neuron systems: anatomy and physiology of the dopamine system. *Annual Review of Neuroscience, 1*, 129–169.

Moran, T. H. , Robinson, P., Goldrich, M. S., & McHugh, P. R. (1986). Two brain cholecystokinin receptors: Implications for behavioral actions. *Brain Research, 362*, 175–179.

Morency, M. A., & Beninger, R. J. (1986). Dopaminergic substrates of cocaine-induced place conditioning. *Brain Research, 399*, 33–41.

Morley, J. E., Levine, A. S., Grace, M., & Kneip, J. (1982). Dynorphin (1, 13), dopamine, and feeding in rats. *Psychopharmacology, Biochemistry, and Behavior, 16*, 701–705.

Olds, J., & Milner, P. M. (1954). Positive reinforcement produced by electrical stimulation of septal area and other regions of rat brain. *Journal of Comparative and Psyiological Psychology, 47*, 419–427.

O'Neill, R. D., & Fillenz, M. (1985). Simultaneous monitoring of dopamine release in rat frontal cortex, nucleus accumbens and striatum: Effect of drugs, circadian changes and correlations with motor activity. *Neuroscience, 16*, 49–55.

Pavlov, I. P. (1927). *Conditioned reflexes.* London: Oxford University Press.

Piazza, P. V., Deminiere, J. M., Le Moal, M., & Simon, H. (1989). Factors that predict individual vulnerability to AMPH self-administration. *Science, 245,* 1511–1513.

Piazza, P. V., Rogué-Pont, F., Deminière, J. M., Kharouby, M., Le Moal, M., & Simon, H. (1991). Dopaminergic activity is reduced in the prefrontal cortex and increased in the nucleus accumbens of rats predisposed to develop amphetamine self-administration. *Brain Research, 567,* 169–174.

Pickens, R. (1968). Self-administration of stimulants by rats. *International Journal of Addictions, 3,* 215–221.

Pickens, R. W., & Crowder, W. F. (1967). Effects of CS–US interval on conditioning of drug response, with assessment of speed of conditioning. *Psychopharmacology, 11,* 88–94.

Pijnenburgh, A. J. J., Honig, W. M. M., van der Heyden, J. A. M., & van Rossum, J. M. (1976). Effects of chemical stimulation of the mesolimbic dopamine system upon locomotor activity. *European Journal of Pharmacology, 35,* 45–58.

Pijnenburgh, A. J. J., Honig, W. M. M., & van Rossum, J. M. (1975). Inhibition of *d*-amphetamine-induced locomotor activity by injection of haloperidol into the nucleus accumbens of the rat. *Psychopharmacology, 41,* 87–95.

Pijnenburgh, A. J. J., & van Rossum, J. M. (1973). Stimulation of locomotor activity following injection of dopamine into the nucleus accumbens. *Journal of Pharmacology, 25,* 1003–1005.

Poncelet, M., Dangoumau, L., Soubrie, P., & Simon, P. (1987). Effects of neuroleptic drugs, clonidine and lithium on the expression of conditioned behavioral excitation in rats. *Psychopharmacology, 92,* 393–397.

Post, R. M., & Rose, H. (1976). Increasing effects of repetitive cocaine administration. *Nature, 260,* 731–732.

Radhakishun, F. S., van Ree, J. M., & Westerink, B. H. C. (1988). Scheduled eating increases dopamine release in the nucleus accumbens of food-deprived rats as assessed with on-line brain dialysis. *Neuroscience Letters, 35,* 351–356.

Reicher, M. A., & Holman, E. W. (1977). Location preference and flavor aversion reinforced by amphetamine in rats. *Animal Learning and Behavior, 5,* 343–356.

Robbins, T. W., Watson, B. A., Gaskin, M., & Ennis, C. (1983). Contrasting interactions of pipradol, d-amphetamine, cocaine, cocaine analogues, apomorphine and other drugs with conditioned reinforcement. *Psychopharmacology, 84,* 113–119.

Roberts, D. C. S., & Koob, G. F. (1982). Disruption of cocaine self-administration following 6-hydroxydopamine lesions of the ventral tegmental area in rats. *Pharmacology, Biochemistry, and Behavior, 17,* 901–904.

Romo, R., & Schultz, W. (1990). Dopamine neurons of the monkey midbrain: Contingencies of responses to active touch during self-initiated arm movements. *Journal of Neurophysiology, 63,* 592–606.

Ruggeri, M., Ungerstedt, U., Agnati, L. F., Mutt, V., Harfstrand, A., & Fuxe, K. (1987). Effects of cholecystokinin peptides and neurotensin on dopamine release and metabolism in the rostral and caudal part of the nucleus accumbens using intracerebral dialysis in the anaesthetized rat. *Neurochemistry International, 10,* 509–520.

Schneirla, T. C. (1959). An evolutionary and developmental theory of biphasic processes underlying approach and withdrawal. In M. R. Jones (Ed.). *Nebraska symposium on motivation* (pp 1–42). Lincoln: University of Nebraska Press.

Schultz, W. (1986). Responses of midbrain dopamine neurons to behavioral trigger stimuli in the monkey. *Journal of Neurophysiology, 56,* 1439–1462.

Sclafani, A., Aravich, P. F., & Xenakis, S. (1982). Dopaminergic and endorphinergic mediation of a sweet reward. In B. G. Hoebel, & D. Novin (Eds.), *The neural basis of feeding and rewards* (pp. 507–515). Brunswick, ME: Haer Institute.

Sharp, K. M., Zetterstrom, T., Ljungberg, T., & Ungerstedt, U. (1987). A direct comparison of amphetamine-induced behaviors and regional brain dopamine release in the rat using intracerebral dialysis. *Brain Research, 401,* 322–330.

Sills, T. L., & Crawley, J. N. (1996). Individual differences in sugar consumption predict amphetamine-induced dopamine overflow in nucleus accumbens. *European Journal of Pharmacology, 303,* 177–181.

Sills, T. L., Onalaja, A. O., & Crawley, J. N. (1998). Mesolimbic dopamine mechanisms underlying individual differences in sugar consumption and amphetamine hyperlocomotion in Wistar rats. *European Journal of Neuroscience, 10,* 1895–1902.

Sills, T. L., & Vaccarino, F. J. (1991). Facilitation and inhibition of feeding by a single dose of amphetamine: Relationship to baseline intake and accumbens CCK. *Psychopharmacology, 105,* 329–334.

Sills, T. L., & Vaccarino, F. J. (1994). Individual differences in sugar intake predict the locomotor response to acute and repeated amphetamine administration. *Psychopharmacology, 116,* 1–8.

Sills, T. L., & Vaccarino, F. J. (1996a). Individual differences in sugar consumption following systemic or intraccumbens administration of low doses of amphetamine in nondeprived rats. *Pharmacology, Biochemistry, and Behavior, 54,* 665–670

Sills, T. L., & Vaccarino, F. J. (1996b). Individual differences in the feeding response to CCKB antagonists: role of the nucleus accumbens. *Peptides, 17,* 593–599.

Skinner, B. F. (1958). Reinforcement today. *American Psychologist, 13,* 94–99.

Spyraki, C., Fibiger, H. C., & Phillips, A. G. (1982a). Cocaine-induced place preference conditioning: Lack of effects of neuroleptics and 6-hydroxydopamine lesions. *Brain Research, 253,* 195–203.

Spyraki, C., Fibiger, H. C., & Phillips, A. G. (1982b). Dopaminergic substrates of amphetamine-induced place preference conditioning. *Brain Research, 253,* 185–193.

Studler, J. M., Reibaud, M., Herve, D., Blanc, G., Glowinski, J., & Tassin, J. P. (1986). Opposite effects of sulfated cholecystokinin on DA-sensitive adenylate cyclase in two areas of the rat nucleus accumbens. *European Journal of Pharmacology, 126,* 125–128.

Studler, J. M., Simon, H., Ceselin, F., Legrand, J. C., Glowinski, J., & Tassin, J. P. (1981). Biochemical investigation of the localization of CCK octapeptide in dopaminergic neurons originating from the ventral tegmental area of the rat. *Neuropeptides, 2,* 131–139.

Taylor, J. R., & Robbins, T. W. (1984). Enhanced behavioral control by conditioned reinforcers following microinjection of d-amphetamine into the nucleus accumbens. *Psychopharmacology, 84,* 405–412.

Taylor, J. R., & Robbins, T. W. (1986). 6-hydroxydopamine lesions of the nucleus accumbens, but not the caudate nucleus, attenuate enhanced responding with reward-related stimuli produced by intra-accumbens d-amphetamine. *Psychopharmacology, 90,* 390–397.

Thorndike, E. L. (1911). *Animal intelligence.* New York: Macmillan.

Uhl, G. R., Kuhar, M. J., & Snyder, S. H. (1977). Neurotensin: immunohistochemical localization in rat central nervous system. *Proceedings of the National Academy of Sciences United States of America, 74,* 4059–4063.

Ungerstedt, U. (1971). Stereotaxic mapping of the monoamine pathway in the rat brain. *Acta Physiologica Scandinavia, 367 (Suppl.),* 1–48.

Ungerstedt, U. (1979). Central dopamine mechanisms and behavior. In A. S. Horn, J. Korf, & B. H. C. Westerink (Eds.), *The neurobiology of dopamine* (pp. 577–596). London: Academic Press.

Uretsky, N. J., & Schoenfeld, R. I. (1971). Effect of L-DOPA on the locomotor activity of rats pretreated with 6-hydroxydopamine. *Nature New Biology, 234,* 157–159.

Vaccarino, F. J. (1994). Nucleus accumbens dopamine-CCK interactions in psychostimulant reward and related behaviors. *Neuroscience and Biobehavioral Review, 18,* 207–214.

Vaccarino, F. J., & Koob, G. F. (1985). Microinjections of nanogram amounts of sulfated cholecystokinin octapeptide into the rat nucleus accumbens attenuates brain stimulation reward. *Neuroscience Letters, 52,* 61–66.

Vaccarino, F. J., & Rankin, J. (1989). Nucleus accumbens cholecystokinin (CCK) can either attenuate or potentiate amphetamine-induced locomotor activity: Evidence for rostral-caudal differences in accumbens CCK function. *Behavioral Neuroscience, 103,* 831–836.

Vaccarino, F. J., Schiff, B. B., & Glickman, S. E. (1989). A biological view of reinforcement. In S. B. Klein & R. R. Mowrer (Eds.), *Contemporary learning theories* (pp. 111–142). Hillsdale, NJ: Lawrence Erlbaum Associates.

Vaccarino, F. J., & Vaccarino, A. L. (1989). Antagonism of cholecystokinin function in the rostral and caudal nucleus accumbens: Differential effects on brain stimulation reward. *Neuroscience Letters, 97,* 151–156.

Vaccarino, F. J., Westwood, R. P., & Lanca, A. J. (1994). The effects of blockade of CCK_B receptors in the nucleus accumbens on amphetamine-induced locomotor activity. *Society of Neuroscience Abstracts, 20,* 380.

Vanderhaeghen, J. J., Deschepper, C., Lostra, F., Vierendeels, G., & Schoenen, J. (1982). Immunohistochemical evidence for cholecystokinin-like peptides in neuronal cell bodies of the rat spinal cord. *Cell Tissue Research, 223,* 463–467.

Vickroy, T. W., & Bianchi, B. R. (1989). Pharmacological and mechanistic studies of CCK-facilitated [^{3}H]dopamine efflux from rat nucleus accumbens. *Neuropeptides, 13,* 43–50.

Voight, M., Wang, R. Y., & Westfall, I. C. (1985). The effects of cholecystokinin on the in vivo release of newly synthesized [^{3}H]-dopamine from the nucleus accumbens of the rat. *Journal of Neuroscience, 5,* 2744–2749.

Voight, M., Wang, R. Y., & Westfall, T. C. (1986). Cholecystokinin octapeptide alters the release of endogenous dopamine from the rat nucleus accumbens in vivo. *Journal of Pharmacology and Experimental Therapeutics, 237,* 147–153.

Winn, P., Williams, S. F., & Herberg, L. J. (1982). Feeding stimulated by very low doses of d-amphetamine administered systemically or by microinjection into the striatum. *Psychopharmacology, 78,* 336–341.

Wise, R. A. (1982). Neuroleptics and operant behavior: The anhedonia hypothesis. *Behavioral Brain Sciences, 5,* 39–87.

Wise, R. A., & Bozarth, M. A. (1987). A psychomotor stimulant theory of addiction. *Psychological Review, 94,* 469–492.

Wise, R. A., & Colle, L. M. (1984), Pimozide attenuates free feeding: Best scores analysis reveals a motivational deficit. *Psychopharmacology, 84,* 446–451.

Wise, R. A., & Raptis, L. (1986). Effects of naloxone and pimozide on initiation and maintenance of free feeding. *Brain Research, 368,* 62–68.

Wunderlich, G. R., DeSousa, N. J., Vaccarino, F. J. (1997). Microinjection of PD-140, 548, a CCK_A antagonist, into the caudal nucleus accumbens attenuates the locomotor response to amphetamine in amphetamine-sensitized animals. *Society of Neuroscience Abstracts, 23,* 630.

Yeomans, J. S. (1988). Mechanisms of brain stimulation reward. In A. N. Epstein & A. Morrison (Eds.), *Progress in psychobiological and physiological psychology* (pp. 227–266). San Diego, CA: Academic Press.

chapter 12

Effects of Uncontrollable Aversive Events:
Some Unsolved Puzzles

Vincent M. LoLordo
Tracy L. Taylor
Dalhousie University

INESCAPABLE SHOCKS PRODUCE AN ESCAPE LEARNING DEFICIT

A generation ago, while testing some predictions derived from the two-process theory of avoidance learning, researchers in Richard Solomon's laboratory at the University of Pennsylvania discovered a dramatic effect of exposure to inescapable aversive events. Dogs were restrained in a hammock and given many painful, inescapable foot shocks. A day later they were placed in a shuttlebox, a chamber with two compartments separated by a shoulder-high barrier, and given electric shocks through the grid floor that would be turned off when they crossed from one side to the other. These dogs showed a marked impairment in learning to escape shock in the shuttlebox. Most of them failed to learn to escape. This was an impressive effect, because nearly all of the control dogs that had simply been restrained in the hammock on the preceding day readily learned to escape (Overmier & Seligman, 1967).

Overmier and Seligman (1967) proposed that the inescapabilty of shock in the hammock was responsible for the failure to escape in the shuttlebox and suggested that an experiment comparing the proactive effects of escapable and inescapable shocks on subsequent escape learning should be done to test that hypothesis. Seligman and Maier (1967) conducted such an experiment, using the three-group or triadic design that has become the standard for research in this area. Plexiglas panels were placed on both sides of the dogs' heads as they lay in the hammock. Dogs in the escapable shock group could terminate shocks by pressing either panel once. Dogs in the inescapable shock group had nonfunctional panels. The duration of each shock for a dog in the inescapable shock group was matched or yoked to that of a dog in the escape group, so that the two dogs received the same pattern of shock durations across trials. Thus operationally only the escapability of shocks distinguished the two groups. Dogs in the third group were simply restrained in the hammock. When the dogs were tested in the shuttlebox the next day, escape learning of the previously inescapably shocked dogs was profoundly impaired. Most failed to learn, receiving the full 30 sec of shock on 9 or more of the 10 trials. In contrast, the escape response was learned quickly by nearly all the dogs in the other two groups, which did not differ.

LEARNED HELPLESSNESS

Although the sheer magnitude of this interference effect was impressive, it was the experimenters' theoretical account of the phenomenon that has made it such an important part of contemporary psychology. The learned helplessness hypothesis (Maier, Seligman, & Solomon, 1969; Overmier & Seligman, 1967; Seligman & Maier, 1967; Seligman, Maier, & Solomon, 1971) asserted that during the first phase of the experiment the inescapably shocked dogs made many different responses, none of which was consistently followed by shock termination, and so learned that none of those responses turned off shock. This led them to expect that none of their behaviors would turn off shock, and when they received the first shock in the shuttlebox the next day this expectation was activated. Two sorts of deficits were hypothesized to arise from learned helplessness. First, there was a motivational or response initiation deficit; active attempts to escape were impaired. This follows from the expectation of lack of control over shock termination. Second, there was an associative, later called a cognitive, deficit. If a previously inescapably shocked dog happened to cross the barrier, thus turning off shock, it would learn little from this coincidence, because it had already learned that there was no relation between its responses and shock offset. It should be noted that if the motivational deficit is very strong, so that the animals never escape, and thus never are exposed to the escape contingency, then the result can provide no evidence for the proposed associative deficit (Klosterhalfen & Klosterhalfen, 1983). In any case, dogs that pressed a panel to escape shock during the first phase could not have learned that they were helpless, and thus should have exhibited neither motivational nor associative deficits.

Research arising from the interference effect and the learned helplessness hypothesis has gone in three directions (Maier, 1989). First, it has radiated outward to other areas of psychology, where the hypothesis has had a substantial impact, and has been modified as it confronted a broader range of phenomena (e.g., Mikulincer, 1994; Peterson, Maier, & Seligman, 1993). These developments are beyond the scope of this chapter.

Second, research in a "downward" direction, aimed at understanding the physiological and biochemical bases of the interference effect and related sequelae of exposure to inescapable shock, has burgeoned in recent years. Most of the current animal research on the interference effect is of this sort. Again, a thorough review of this area is beyond the scope of this chapter. However, because efforts to understand the physiology of the interference effect through pharmacological and physiological manipulations have cast some light on the psychology of the effect, they are considered here.

Third, there have been many experiments directed "inward"; that is, designed to elucidate the psychological mechanisms of the interference effect and related phenomena. Although this enterprise continues today, relatively few investigators are engaged in it, and progress has been slow. This chapter focuses on unsolved problems in this area.

Why was the learned helplessness hypothesis important within the context of learning theory? Maier (1989; see also Maier & Jackson, 1979; Maier & Seligman, 1976) has written at length on this question, and only the bare bones of an answer are presented here. The learned helplessness hypothesis account of the interference effect attracted considerable attention because it was fundamentally different from, and at odds with, the sorts of account that the dominant views of instrumental learning would have generated. It maintained that the source of the escape learning deficit is not to be found in the acquisition of some response during the inescapable shock phase that transfers to the escape training phase and competes with the required response of crossing from one side to the other. Rather, the deficit is to be understood as arising from the acquisition of knowledge, the knowledge that there is no contingency between any response and shock offset. The learned helplessness hypothesis not only held that the contingency between response and reinforcer, rather than response–reinforcer contiguity, is fundamental, but went further to assert that animals learn the fact that there is a contingency, or none, between their behaviors and exteroceptive stimuli. It appeared in print at roughly the same time as Rescorla's (1967) contingency view of Pavlovian conditioning, and their shared emphasis on contingency increased the impact of both views. However, the learned helplessness hypothesis went beyond Rescorla's position which stated that when there was no contingency between conditioned stimuli (CS) and unconditioned stimuli (US), the CS would not acquire any associative strength, by asserting that learning occurs even when there is no contingency between any response and the reinforcer, in this case shock termination, and that what is learned is the lack of response–reinforcer contingency.

In the years since publication of Rescorla's contingency view, research in Pavlovian conditioning has demonstrated that animals exposed to uncorrelated CS and US are: (a) slower to condition than CS-alone or US-alone controls when CS and US are subsequently paired (Baker & Mackintosh, 1979; Mackintosh, 1973), and (b) also slower to condition than groups given a block of CS-alone trials followed by a block of US-alone trials or the reverse (Bennett, Maldonado, & Mackintosh, 1995). Bennett et al. (1995) have argued that the latter result reflects learning of the lack of contingency between CS and US, called *learned irrelevance*, over and above the sum of latent inhibition and US preexposure (context-blocking) effects, but this claim has been questioned (Bonardi & Hall, 1996).

Note that learned irrelevance would not be truly analogous to learned helplessness unless the former were generalized learned irrelevance; that is, learning that CSs in general are uncorrelated with a US. There are even fewer data bearing on this possibility. However, Linden, Savage, and Overmier (1997) recently observed deficits in Pavlovian conditioning when some target CS was paired with a US following uncorrelated presentations of nontarget CSs and that US, and in their autoshaping situation there was no generalized latent inhibition. This result suggests that animals can learn that CSs in general are uncorrelated with a US, but more work is needed before a strong conclusion can be drawn. Moreover, for the claim of generalized learned irrelevance to parallel the claim of learned helplessness, there would have to be generality across USs as well as CSs. In any case, the learned helplessness hypothesis was ahead of its time, and therefore controversial, but not so far ahead as to be easily dismissed.

ALTERNATIVE ACCOUNTS OF THE INTERFERENCE EFFECT

From the very start, the proponents of the learned helplessness hypothesis were aware that plausible alternative accounts of the interference effect would be generated. They anticipated the hypothesis that the interference effect is the result of the occurrence of some instrumental response that is acquired during inescapable shocks in the hammock, transfers to shock in the shuttlebox, and is incompatible with shuttling. Such an instrumental response might be reinforced directly because its occurrence makes the inescapable shock hurt less. Alternatively, it might occur just before, and be adventitiously reinforced by, shock termination.

Overmier and Seligman (1967) argued that it was unlikely that the dogs could have done anything to reduce the effectiveness of the contact between the footpads of their hind feet and the brass plate electrodes that were taped to them, but allowed the possibility that tensing the muscles or moving a certain way might reduce the severity of the shocks. To rule out this possibility, before the session in the hammock they immobilized the skeletal muscles of two groups of dogs by injecting them with the neuromuscular blocking agent tubocurarine chloride. One group received 64 intense, 5-sec shocks and the other received no shocks. Twenty-four hours later, after the dogs had recovered from the effects of the curare, the curarized, inescapably shocked dogs showed a large escape deficit in the shuttlebox compared with curarized controls. This outcome rules out the possibility that the interference effect was the result of competing responses that were acquired because they made the shock hurt less (but see Bracewell & Black, 1974; Maier & Seligman, 1976, for discussion of a related possibility).

Maier (1970) attempted to rule out competing response accounts of the interference effect in a different way. He reasoned that the most effective competing response would be remaining motionless during shock, and so he trained dogs to remain motionless, or at least not to contact two panels very close to their heads for a few seconds, to escape shock. Inescapably shocked controls were yoked to the experimental animals. In the subsequent shuttlebox escape test, the experimental dogs showed negative transfer, relative to restrained controls, but learned the escape response better than the yoked controls, most of which failed to learn. Because the "worst possible competing response" resulted in less interference than did inescapable shock, Maier reasoned that the effect of the latter was not the result of a competing response. He concluded that lack of control, as specified by the learned helplessness hypothesis, was responsible for the interference effect.

RAT MODELS OF THE INTERFERENCE EFFECT

By the mid-1970s dogs were no longer the favored animal in learned helplessness research, which uses large numbers of animals, primarily because they were so much more expensive to purchase, house, and feed than rodents. Much of the research by proponents of the learned helplessness hypothesis had shifted to rats. Maier, Albin, and Testa (1973) and Seligman and Beagley (1975) developed rat models of the interference effect. The former found that although prior exposure to a large number of inescapable tail shocks failed to interfere with subsequent escape learning in a shuttlebox when only a single crossing was required to terminate shock, a profound interference effect was obtained when the rats were required to cross to the other side and back again (a Fixed Ratio-2 [FR-2] requirement). This became the most widely used procedure for studying the interference effect in rats. Seligman and Beagley found that preexposure to inescapable shocks to the back, between a subcutaneous electrode and the grid floor, resulted in interference with subsequent lever press escape learning on an FR-3 schedule.

LEARNED INACTIVITY

With the shift to research with rats and mice, competing response hypotheses of the interference effect reemerged (e.g., Anisman, deCatanzaro, & Remington, 1978; Bracewell & Black, 1974; Glazer & Weiss, 1976a; Levis, 1976), despite Overmier and Seligman's (1967) and Maier's (1970) earlier evidence against such hypotheses. The primary strategy of opponents of the learned helplessness hypothesis was to show that exposure to inescapable shocks would result in subsequent escape deficits only insofar as the animals became inactive during the inescapable shocks, and subsequently were inactive in response to escapable shocks. This strategy manifested itself in experiments that varied one or more parameters that were expected to affect the animals' activity during inescapable shocks. Then the correlation between activity during those shocks and measures of performance during the subsequent escape learning test was examined. In general, relative inactivity was positively correlated with escape learning deficits, usually in the form of longer escape latencies than were shown by controls.

Anisman and his colleagues conducted a long series of experiments in which mice were given inescapable foot shocks, and then were given shock escape training in the shuttlebox a day later. Unlike dogs, Anisman's mice failed to show an interference effect unless on each escape trial they were confined to one side of the shuttlebox during shock for 4 or 6 sec before a gate was raised and they were permitted to escape by crossing to the other side (Anisman et al., 1978). In one experiment, groups of mice received 60 inescapable foot shocks at intervals of 60 sec in a circular field. Groups received shock durations of 2, 4, 6, or 8 sec. Mean activity per second of shock declined across shocks in all groups, but the decline was much steeper, and to a much lower level, in the 6-sec group than in the 2-sec group (Anisman et al., 1978). In a related experiment, the 2-sec shocks caused no interference with subsequent shuttlebox escape learning, but the 6-sec shocks resulted in a profound interference effect, whether the training-test interval was 24 hr or 96 hr (but see Altenor, Volpicelli, & Seligman, 1979, who found no effect of inescapable foot shock duration in rats).

A further experiment looked at second-by-second activity during the inescapable shocks. For the 2-sec shocks there was a slight decline in activity between the first and second five-trial block, and no further change. There was no decline in activity from the first to the second second. The pattern was very different for the 6-sec shocks. Overall activity during shock declined across the first three blocks, by which time it was much lower than activity during the 2-sec shocks. Moreover, within about 15 trials, activity declined markedly from the first to the second second of each shock and declined further to the end of the shock. Again subsequent shuttlebox escape latencies of the 6-sec group were much longer than those of the 2-sec and no-shock groups, which did not differ. Finally, for the 6-sec group, average activity during inescapable shocks and activity during just the first 2 sec of those shocks were significantly negatively correlated with escape latency.

In a later experiment Anisman, Grimmer, Irwin, Remington, and Sklar (1979) found that among lines of mice selectively bred for general locomotor activity, prior inescapable shock resulted in large escape deficits in some lines, but had little or no effect on others. Moreover, the lines that had the lowest levels of shock-evoked activity showed the greatest escape deficits.

Anisman et al. (1978) interpreted the escape learning deficit as a deficit in maintaining motor activity in the presence of shock. Six-second shocks evoke an initial burst of activity followed by a decline in running and jumping. Nonpreshocked mice are still active enough to escape readily when the gate is raised after 6-sec exposure to shock on the first escape trial, but mice that have received 60 6-sec inescapable preshocks have become much less active after 6 sec of shock, and do not escape readily. Anisman and his colleagues proposed several mechanisms of this effect. First, they noted that a learned competing response view was compatible with their findings. According to such a view, inactivity during inescapable shocks is either directly reinforced (e.g., because it makes the foot shock hurt less; Bracewell & Black, 1974) or it is adventitiously reinforced by the termination of the 6-sec shocks.

Anisman and Sklar (1979) also proposed an account at another level. Inescapable but not escapable shock resulted in a decline in brain catecholamines, in particular in hypothalamic norepinephrine (NE), that was correlated with the magnitude of the escape deficit. Anisman and Sklar suggested that the decline in catecholamines would result in the decline in activity during inescapable shocks, paving the way for adventitious reinforcement of inactivity. At the start of a shuttlebox escape test a day or two later, the catecholamine level would no longer be reduced, but the learned inactivity would result in fairly long shocks, only a small number of which would be required to redeplete catecholamines. In support of this view, administration of L-dopa, which increases whole brain levels of dopamine (DA) and NE, shortly before the inescapable shocks antagonized the decline in shock-elicited activity (Anisman, Remington, & Sklar, 1979), and this treatment also prevented the escape deficit (Anisman & Sklar, 1979).

These results are compatible with outcomes obtained by Glazer and Weiss (1976a, 1976b), who administered inescapable tail shocks to rats and then assessed their learning to avoid or escape shock by jumping a barrier between the two sides of a shuttlebox. When 60 1-mA, 6-sec shocks were administered in 1 hr, the rats showed an escape deficit when tested 72 hr later. Glazer and Weiss (1976a) suggested that when the inescapable tail shocks came on, the rats struggled and thrashed about for 3 or 4 sec, and then became less active. Moreover, the activity burst became shorter as the shock session progressed. These observations suggested that long shocks, which ended when the rat was inactive, would be more likely than short shocks to reinforce inactivity in the presence of shock and thus lead to an inactivity-mediated escape deficit.

Results of a subsequent experiment were consistent with this conclusion; 5-sec or 6-sec shocks resulted in an escape deficit, whereas 2-, 3-, or 4-sec shocks did not, even with total seconds of shock equated. The escape deficit following long shocks was observed even when a week separated inescapable shock and testing. Moreover, the deficit was as large after 10 sessions of inescapable shock as it was after a single session. The last two results also are compatible with the view that the deficit was the result of learning.

Glazer and Weiss (1976b) pointed out that their view predicts that inescapable shock would facilitate, rather than impair, escape performance if the escape response was one that would be easier to perform when the rat was inactive. Such an outcome would not be predicted by the learned helplessness hypothesis. The avoidance/escape task required the rat, which was restrained within a tube, to poke its nose through a hole in the tube to terminate the warning signal or both the signal and tail shock. Latency of the nose-poke response declined more sharply for inescapably shocked rats than for no-shock controls, supporting the prediction. After the first few trials, most of the nose-poke responses for previously inescapably shocked rats were avoidance responses, rather than escapes. Moreover, this happened with the same inescapable shock parameters and 72-hr training–test interval that produced escape deficits in Weiss's laboratory when the escape learning test was (a) FR-3 lever press escape, the dependent variable used in Seligman's laboratory (e.g., Seligman & Beagley, 1975); (b) FR-1 barrier jumping in the shuttlebox, the procedure used by Glazer and Weiss (1976a); or (c) 5 FR-1 trials followed by 25 FR-2 trials in the shuttlebox, the procedure used in Maier's laboratory (e.g., Maier et al., 1973). Finally, the impairment of lever press escape responding and facilitation of nose poking depended on the preshocks being inescapable; rats trained to turn a wheel with their paws to escape shock in the first phase subsequently behaved like no-shock controls.

These last findings constitute a strong challenge to the learned helplessness hypothesis. In describing the performance of their inescapably shocked rats, Glazer and Weiss (1976b) noted that

> as trials progressed, such an animal would come to remain with its nose pressed against the door so that when the door was drawn back at the beginning of the trial its head followed the door forward, accomplishing a rapid correct response. Following this response, the door moved forward to cover the hole, simply pushing the animal's nose back into the tube for a similar correct response on the next trial. (p. 205)

On the basis of this quotation, Maier and Jackson (1979) suggested that the nose-poke response of the inescapably shocked rats might not have been learned. However, it should be noted that the door was drawn back at the start of the warning signal, and so the initial escape responses, occurring as they did 6 to 7 sec later, could not have resulted simply from the rat's head following the door forward.

Glazer and Weiss did not measure activity during the inescapable shocks, but there are several studies using rat subjects that have done so. In general, within-experiment comparisons of several inescapable shock treatments revealed that the amount of activity evoked by the inescapable shocks in the various treatments was negatively correlated with escape latencies during a subsequent test (e.g., Balleine & Job, 1991; Crowell & Anderson, 1981; Crowell, Lupo, Cunningham, & Anderson, 1978; Lawry et al., 1978; Steenbergen, Heinsbroek, van Haaren, & van de Poll, 1989). However, several dissociations between inactivity during inescapable shocks and escape deficits have been observed. Lawry et al. (1978) found that activity remained high during intense pulsed shocks, whether they were alternating current or direct current, but the alternating current shocks nonetheless resulted in a subsequent escape latency deficit in the shuttlebox. Crowell and Anderson (1979) found that a series of increasingly long inescapable shocks resulted in a marked decline in the mean activity per second during shock without resulting in a subsequent escape deficit in the shuttlebox.

Moreover, none of the studies cited as showing a correlation between inactivity and escape deficits in rats has reported the sorts of within-shock decline in activity that Anisman et al. (1978) showed with mice. Drugan and Maier (1982) used a motion detector to monitor rats' activity during 5-sec, 1-mA tail shocks. Within any 10-trial block of the 80-trial session, the level of activity was constant within a given shock. Thus Drugan and Maier argued that there were no reductions in activity within shock that could have been adventitiously reinforced by shock termination. However, the overall amount of activity during shock declined markedly across blocks of trials. Drugan and Maier pointed out that this decline might have resulted from depletion of a neurochemical necessary for the maintenance of activity, from some reinforcement mechanism other than adventitious reinforcement of inactivity, from the development of analgesia, or of a reduced incentive to respond as proposed by the learned helplessness hypothesis, or a combination of these.

In the 1970s there were several conceptual replications, using rat subjects, of Maier's (1970) experiment (Anderson, Crowell, Cunningham, & Lupo, 1979; Crowell & Anderson, 1979; Nation & Matheny, 1980). These experiments invariably found a result opposite Maier's: Rats trained to remain inactive during the pretreatment stage showed greater deficits in shuttlebox escape responding than yoked, inescapably shocked controls. Balleine and Job (1991) noted that in these experiments rats were required to remain inactive for much longer than the 3-sec criterion used by Maier. For example, Anderson et al. (1979) had a final requirement of 15 sec of inactivity for shock termination.

Balleine and Job (1991) compared the effects of brief and long inactivity requirements; separate groups of rats were required to be inactive for 2 continuous sec to turn off shock (short criterion), or to engage in an average of seven such bouts of inactivity to turn off shock (long criterion). A triadic design was used in each case. The FR-2 escape training in the shuttlebox occurred on the next day. In the first phase, the short criterion groups received progressively shorter shocks, but the long criterion groups received progressively longer ones. The test data reconciled the results of the earlier studies: The inescapably shocked, short (IS–S) criterion and escapably shocked, long (ES–L) criterion rats had longer escape latencies than the escapably shocked, short (ES–S) criterion and inescapably shocked, long (IS–L) criterion rats, which in turn had longer latencies than controls. Inactivity was also measured during pretreatment; at the end of training the number of seconds of inactivity per minute was greater for IS–S and ES–L rats than for IS–L and ES–S rats. The pretreatment shock contingency was of little use in predicting test stage performance, but the relative amount of inactivity during pretreatment shocks was a strong predictor, accounting for 77% of the variance in test stage performance. These data are compatible with a competing response account of the FR-2 escape deficit, although they do not demand the conclusion that the rats in the IS groups instrumentally learned to be inactive during the inescapable shock phase. However, it should be noted that freely moving rats and grid shock were used in both stages of this experiment, and it remains to be seen whether the results would generalize to the case where rats are restrained or semirestrained in the first stage and receive tail shock. Moreover, Prabhakar and Job (1996) subsequently gave two groups of rats inescapable shocks of variable durations. For one group, the shocks were progressively longer, and for the other they were progressively shorter. The two groups showed equal freezing during the inescapable shock session. Furthermore, fear of the inescapable shock context, as determined in a subsequent passive avoidance test, was greater in rats that had received progressively longer shocks than in rats that had received progressively shorter ones. The authors argued that these results contradicted Balleine and Job's (1991) predictions; the longer escape latencies in Balleine and Job's Group IS–S than in Group IS–L lead one to expect more fear of the inescapable shock context in Prabhakar and Job's group that, like Group IS–S, received progressively shorter shocks.

Alloy and Ehrman (1981) took a different approach to the question of whether the effects of inescapable shock can be explained in terms of learned inactivity. They asked whether exposure to inescapable shocks interfered with Pavlovian aversive conditioning, as reflected by conditioned suppression of licking (see Baker, 1976; Jackson, Maier, & Rapaport, 1978). If the inescapable shocks induced a generalized associative deficit (Linden et al., 1997), then the previously inescapably shocked rats would be expected to acquire less conditioned suppression than the two control groups of a triadic design. Learned inactivity should not produce such a result, as interference with conditioned suppression would be reflected by a relative increase in licking during the CS.

After rats had been pretrained to lick a tube for sucrose, in a triadic design they received inescapable, escapable, or no foot shocks in a shuttlebox. Pavlovian aversive conditioning occurred several days later in a different chamber, and lasted 4 days. Two days after the end of Pavlovian conditioning the CSs were superimposed on the licking baseline. Groups did not differ in baseline lick rate, but previously inescapably shocked rats showed much less conditioned suppression of licking than those given escapable or no shocks in Phase 1, a result compatible with the claim that inescapable shocks induced an associative deficit.

ESCAPE DEFICITS, INACTIVITY, AND ANALGESIA

By the late 1970s their own data, along with some of the findings just mentioned, had persuaded Maier's group (Maier & Jackson, 1979) that the most widely used measure of the interference effect in rats, long escape latencies on a test of FR-2 escape responding in the shuttlebox, might reflect activity deficits. Jackson et al. (1978) had shown that the escape deficit that was observed when 0.6 mA foot shock was used in the test phase disappeared when a 1.0 mA shock was used, and that this effect reflected improved performance in previously inescapably shocked rats rather than any change in the performance of the restrained controls. Moreover, when in a second experiment the FR-2 escape trials were replaced by 30-sec inescapable shocks in the shuttlebox, and the number of trials on which two or more crosses occurred was measured, an activity deficit was found with 0.6 mA foot shock, but not with 1.0 mA shock. Furthermore, the escape and activity deficits had the same time course. Both were present, and substantial, when 24 hr elapsed between inescapable shock and test, but neither was found when that interval was extended to 48 or 168 hr.

Maier and Jackson (1979) considered possible mechanisms of the activity deficit. Jackson, Maier, and Coon (1979) suggested that the deficit might be mediated by analgesia. Rats exposed to the triadic design received five FR-1 trials in the shuttlebox 24 hr later and then, instead of receiving FR-2 trials, were tested for analgesia on either the hot plate or tail-flick test. The latter, which entails measurement of the latency of a discrete tail twitch in response to heat applied to the tail, was especially useful for the analysis of the relation of analgesia and inactivity because it required little activity, and so latency differences would not be primarily a reflection of activity differences. Only the yoked, inescapably shocked rats had longer tail-flick latencies than restrained controls; escapably shocked rats showed no analgesia. This result suggested that the long shocks in the shuttlebox evoke less activity in previously inescapably shocked rats than in controls because the shocks hurt the former less. To further analyze this possibility, in a between-subjects design with six groups, Maier and Jackson examined analgesia on the tail-flick test right after five FR-1 shuttlebox escape trials that occurred 24, 48, or 168 hr after restraint or inescapable shocks. Relative to controls, rats were quite analgesic when tested 24 hr after inescapable shock, somewhat analgesic after 48 hr, and showed no analgesia after 168 hr.

This result, along with a correlation of $r = -.52$ between tail-flick latency and total number of crosses during twenty-five 30-sec shocks given in the shuttlebox immediately after the analgesia test, suggested, although they do not require, the conclusion that the activity deficits are at least partially mediated by analgesia. Subsequently Moye, Coon, Grau, and Maier (1981) found that a prior history of escaping shock by turning a wheel immunizes the rat against the long-term analgesic effects of inescapable shock, just as that treatment immunizes the rat against the shuttlebox escape deficit that otherwise results from inescapable shock (Williams & Maier, 1977). It seems likely that the same pretreatment also would have immunized the rat against the reduction in shock-evoked activity that results from prior inescapable shock. However, Moye et al. noted that even if that were the case, neither such data nor the other observed correlations between analgesia and activity deficits would require the conclusion that the change in analgesia caused the change in activity. The two effects would also be positively correlated if they were common consequences of some neurochemical change produced by inescapable shocks.

Subsequent research further analyzed the relations between analgesia, activity deficits, and the escape deficit. Maier, Sherman, Lewis, Terman, and Liebeskind (1983) showed that several inescapable shock procedures that produce hormonally mediated, long-term analgesia also produce the escape learning deficit, whereas other inescapable shock procedures that do not result in the former also do not produce the latter. Procedures that resulted in both analgesia and the escape deficit included: (a) the procedure used in most of the experiments from Maier's laboratory; that is, 80 5-sec, 1-mA tail shocks at intervals averaging 1 min, and (b) 20 min of 2.5-mA foot shock on a 1-sec on, 5-sec off schedule. Procedures that resulted in neither effect included (a) 3 min of continuous foot shock, and (b) 40 tail shocks. Maier et al. (1983) argued that some factor that activates processes that produce interference with escape learning seems also to activate processes leading to long-term opioid analgesia, and further suggested that learning of uncontrollability might be that factor.

THE ESCAPE DEFICIT IS NOT CAUSED BY ANALGESIA OR INACTIVITY

Maier et al. (1983) did not argue that the analgesia caused the escape learning deficit. This is because a year earlier MacLennan et al. (1982) demonstrated that both hypophysectomy, or removal of the pituitary, and injection of dexamethasone, which blocks the stress-induced release of adrenocorticotrophic hormone (ACTH) and beta-endorphin from the anterior pituitary, a few hours before inescapable shocks completely eliminated the long-term analgesia that otherwise would have resulted from those shocks. However, neither manipulation had any effect on the escape learning deficit. Thus long-term analgesia is not a necessary condition of (i.e., does not cause) the escape deficit.

In a subsequent experiment Drugan and Maier (1983) showed that dexamethasone reduced the activity deficit shown by inescapably preshocked rats. The activity test occurred in an open field, rather than the shuttlebox, and the test shocks during which activity was measured were tail shocks rather than shocks administered through a grid floor. On the somewhat risky assumption that these differences make no difference, Drugan and Maier concluded that the activity deficit does not cause the escape learning deficit.

In any case, Maier and Jackson (1979) noted that even if (a) the FR-2 escape deficit in the shuttlebox was the result of an activity deficit, and (b) the activity deficit was not the consequence of learning that responses and shock termination are independent, it could still be asserted that inescapable shock also resulted in such learning. However, because crossing twice was so influenced by activity deficits, their FR-2 shuttlebox escape test was a poor choice when the goal was to demonstrate an associative or cognitive deficit. Consequently, they attempted to develop test tasks in which evidence for a cognitive deficit could not be reinterpreted as reflecting an activity deficit.

EVIDENCE FOR AN ASSOCIATIVE DEFICIT

Jackson et al. (1978) trained rats to press a lever for food in an operant chamber and then restrained them in a tube and gave them either 80 inescapable, 5-sec, 1-mA tail shocks or no shocks. A day later the rats were returned to the operant chamber and given discriminative punishment training. Eight 3-min discriminative stimuli were presented, during each of which a variable interval punishment schedule was in effect. Previously inescapably shocked rats showed significantly less suppression of responding during the signal than restrained controls. To determine whether this outcome was specific to learning about response–shock contingencies, in a subsequent experiment the test procedure was changed from discriminative punishment to the conditioned emotional response procedure (Annau & Kamin, 1961). In this procedure the shocks, which occurred only during the 3-min stimuli, were administered in a response-independent fashion as soon as they were programmed to occur, rather than being administered following the first response to occur after they had been programmed. The preshocked and restrained groups acquired conditioned suppression of responding at equivalent rates. This result suggests that it was a deficit in learning of the response–reinforcer contingency, rather than impaired learning of the stimulus–reinforcer contingency, that was responsible for the greater resistance to punishment in preshocked than control rats. This outcome, like that of Alloy and Ehrman (1981) discussed earlier, cannot be the result of an activity deficit, because the latter would result in greater suppression of instrumental responding in preshocked rats than controls, not less. Unfortunately, there was no group that had received escapable shocks during the first phase of this experiment, so it is not certain that this greater resistance to punishment was caused by the inescapability of the shocks. In any case, the discriminative punishment procedure has not been widely used, perhaps because it involves learning about the relation of a response to shock onset, rather than shock termination, and thus has been seen as a step removed from the prediction made by the learned helplessness hypothesis.

Jackson, Alexander, and Maier (1980) attempted to provide unequivocal evidence for an associative deficit by using as the test task choice escape in a y-maze. The rationale for this procedure was that an organism with a deficit in associating its behaviors with the termination of shock would have difficulty learning to make the correct choice. In the test, rats were placed in one arm of a small y-maze in the dark, so that there were few extramaze cues, and were required to turn in a particular direction to escape the shock. If a rat was required to turn right, and it instead turned left, it would then have to make a right turn to end the shock. Thus response learning rather than place learning was required. In such a task relative inactivity would not necessarily lead to fewer correct choices.

In a series of experiments Jackson et al. (1980) showed that inescapably shocked rats made more errors in the y-maze than restrained controls or escapably shocked rats from a triadic design, and that neither increasing the shock intensity in test nor increasing the interval between training and test to 168 hr decreased the number of errors made by previously inescapably shocked rats. As we have seen, the last two manipulations eliminate the FR-2 escape deficit in the shuttlebox, and both are known to increase the rat's activity in the presence of shock (Maier & Jackson, 1979). These facts, and the fact that the effects on choice remained significant when latency was used as a covariate in a multiple regression, suggested that the choice escape test was tapping an associative or cognitive deficit. Rosellini, DeCola, and Shapiro's (1982) finding that inescapably shocked rats were slower than controls or escapably shocked rats to learn a food-reinforced position discrimination also suggests that the inescapable shock produces a cognitive deficit.

In a paper submitted at roughly the same time as Jackson et al. (1980), Irwin, Suissa, and Anisman (1980, Experiment 4) used the triadic design to study the effects of preshock on acquisition of a position discrimination in a water filled, gray T-maze. Subjects were mice. Several measures of discrimination accuracy failed to reveal differences among the three groups, although late in testing choice latencies were slower for previously inescapably shocked mice.

In research stimulated by that report and several unpublished failures to replicate the findings of Jackson et al. (1980), Minor, Jackson, and Maier (1984) demonstrated that the deficit in choice accuracy only occurs if there is a short, variable delay of shock termination following the correct response, say turning left, and task-irrelevant external cues are present. They used lights coming on behind one or another of the end walls of the y-maze as irrelevant cues; irrelevant because the location of the light was uncorrelated with the location of the arm into which a correct left turn would take the rat. Again previously inescapably shocked rats had a higher percentage of trials with error than the other two groups. Minor, Pelleymounter, and Maier (1988) replicated this effect.

ATTENTIONAL SHIFTS

Minor et al. (1984) proposed a mechanism of the choice escape deficits following inescapable shock, arguing that inescapable shock led to a decline in attention to response-produced stimuli and a consequent enhancement of attention to external stimuli. This account is substantially different from the original learned helplessness hypothesis: Inescapable shocks change the organism cognitively, but that change cannot simply be described as a deficit. Results of an experiment by Lee and Maier (1988), in which rats were tested on choice escape from room-temperature water after being exposed to escapable, inescapable, or no shock are compatible with this conclusion. Inescapable shock resulted in an interference effect on choice accuracy if the rats had to learn a position discrimination with brightness cues irrelevant. On the other hand, inescapable shock resulted in facilitation of performance if they had to learn a brightness discrimination with position irrelevant. Because the rats in the latter experiment began by responding to position rather than brightness, the results are not readily explained by

Anisman, Hamilton, and Zacharko's (1984) suggestion that exposure to inescapable shock restricts the rat's defensive responses to ones high in its hierarchy (also see Szostak & Anisman, 1985). Such an account would predict interference with discriminations in which the dimension on which solution must be based is not the one initially controlling performance (e.g., brightness in the case of the third experiment of Lee & Maier, 1988).

Maier, Jackson, and Tomie (1987) observed that the escape latency deficit found in the shuttlebox was eliminated when each of the two required crosses was followed by brief auditory and visual feedback stimuli. They argued that this outcome was compatible with the claim that one effect of the inescapable shocks was to make the rats pay less attention to their own responses and response-produced stimuli; the feedback might draw attention to the response-produced stimuli and make them more available for association with shock termination, just as seems to happen with rats with caudate putamen lesions (Mitchell, Channell, & Hall, 1985).

Irwin et al.'s (1980) failure to observe impaired choice accuracy in mice following inescapable shock does not directly contradict Lee and Maier's (1988) result, because the maze used by the former contained no obvious task-irrelevant exteroceptive cues. Indeed, when Lee and Maier eliminated the irrelevant brightness cues in their position discrimination by making both arms the same brightness on a trial, previously inescapably shocked rats no longer learned more slowly than the other two groups. However, there is an unresolved discrepancy between Lee and Maier's results and those of Anisman et al. (1984). The latter, using mice, conducted an experiment formally similar to Lee and Maier's third experiment: The test task was a cue discrimination, with position irrelevant. Inescapably shocked mice, unlike Lee and Maier's rats, were not more accurate than controls. If the grid shock used in the mouse experiments allowed the mice to reduce pain by becoming inactive, then there is no reason to expect their attention to have shifted away from response-produced to exteroceptive cues.

Rodd, Rosellini, Stock, and Gallup (1997) attempted to test the hypothesis that exposure to inescapable shock results in increased attention to exteroceptive cues by using the duration of an unconditioned response as the measure of attention. When a young chick is manually restrained, it struggles a bit and then becomes motionless, remaining so even when released. This is called *tonic immobility* (TI). The duration of TI is affected by the presence of exteroceptive stimuli. The presence of artificial eyes potentiates TI, whereas the presence of conspecifics attenuates it. The authors reasoned that if a history of inescapable shocks enhances attention to exteroceptive cues, then the effects of artificial eyes and conspecifics should be greater in inescapably shocked chicks than in escapably shocked controls.

The first phase used the triadic design. Chicks in the escapably shocked group (Group ES) could escape foot shocks by jumping up to a perch that was introduced 2 sec after each shock began. The inescapably shocked group (Group IS) was yoked to Group ES, and a third group was placed in the apparatus for as long as the other two groups stayed there. The TI test occurred a day after the fourth session of Phase 1. Each of the three groups was divided in three. In one test condition, TI was induced in the presence of artificial eyes, and in a second condition the artificial eyes were covered with tape. In the third condition three mobile conspecifics were placed where they could be seen by the subject as TI was induced. For each bird up to five attempts were made to induce TI.

Results provided some support for the attentional shift hypothesis. For duration of TI, there was an interaction of pretreatment and test condition, which resulted primarily from much briefer TI in inescapably shocked than escapably shocked chicks in the conspecifics-present condition, along with the opposite trend, longer TI in the inescapably shocked group, in the eyes-absent condition. This result is consistent with Lee and Maier's (1988) finding. However, eyes present versus absent had no effect, contrary to the attentional shift hypothesis.

Recent research on Pavlovian aversive conditioning following inescapable shocks may also bear on the attentional shift hypothesis. Shors and her colleagues (Beylin & Shors, 1998; Servatius & Shors, 1994; Shors & Mathew, 1998; Shors & Servatius, 1997; Shors, Weiss, & Thompson, 1992) found that exposure to at least 30 1-mA, 1-sec inescapable tail shocks resulted in enhanced Pavlovian eye-blink conditioning in freely moving rats a day later. Shors and Mathew (1998) suggested that the inescapable shocks led to enhanced attention to exteroceptive cues, in their case the paired weak auditory CS and shock to the eyelid, resulting in faster associative learning. There were no escapable shock controls in these experiments, so we do not know whether the tail shocks had to be inescapable to produce the facilitation of conditioning.

Maier and Minor (1993) used pharmacological manipulations to dissociate the interference effects on the speed and accuracy of escape responding. Rats were injected with vehicle, or 5mg/kg or 10mg/kg of the benzodiazepine diazepam just before inescapable shock or restraint, and the next day received 100 trials of the y-maze choice escape task, with task-irrelevant visual cues present. Percentage trials with an error revealed a big interference effect and no drug effect. However, the marked increase in latency in the inescapably shocked vehicle group was completely eliminated by both doses of diazepam (also see Drugan, Ryan, Minor, & Maier, 1984).

In a second experiment restrained rats were given vehicle, or 5mg/kg or 10mg/kg of the anxiogenic drug FG-7142 (a benzodiazepine receptor inverse agonist, which antagonizes the inhibitory effects of gamma aminobutyric acid (GABA) at the GABA A receptor; benzodiazepines facilitate these effects) and were tested the next day. Error scores revealed no drug effect; all three groups learned rapidly. Yet the higher dose of drug markedly slowed escape latencies. In the third experiment 3.5, 7.0, or 14.0 mg/kg of the opioid antagonist naltrexone or vehicle was administered just before inescapable shock or restraint. Errors in the y-maze the next day revealed a big interference effect, which was unaffected by drug. Inescapable shock also produced long escape latencies, but this effect was reversed by the two highest doses of naltrexone. Therefore, all three drugs affected escape latency but failed to affect choice.

Although they admitted that it is possible that the error measure was simply less sensitive to drug effects than the latency measure, the authors instead argued that the two effects are mediated by different processes: the escape latency deficit perhaps by intense fear resulting from inescapable shock (e.g., Minor & LoLordo, 1984; but see Maier, 1990), and the increased proportion of errors by decreased attention to behavior-related cues and a consequent increased attention to task-irrelevant external stimuli (see Lee & Maier, 1988). It is not obvious that the latter view should predict no interference with choice escape accuracy in the absence of task-irrelevant exteroceptive cues in test; that is, should predict that a reduction in attention to response-produced cues is not sufficient for the deficit. Peterson et al. (1993) suggested that the deficit might fail to occur when the response–reinforcer contingency was very obvious and there was nothing else to attend to. This aspect of the theory needs further development.

In any case, the attentional shift account will have difficulty explaining several findings. Testa, Juraska, and Maier (1974) found that when rats that had been exposed to inescapable shocks, escapable shocks, or no shocks in a wheel-turn apparatus and then had acquired an FR-1 escape response in a shuttlebox were switched to extinction (i.e., long, inescapable shocks in the shuttlebox) the previously inescapably shocked rats were less persistent in shuttling than the other groups. In a formally similar experiment that examined food-reinforced responding in the last two phases, Rosellini, DeCola, Plonsky, Warren, and Stilman (1984) obtained an analogous result. When rats were shifted from a response-contingent, random interval schedule of food reinforcement for poking their noses into a hole to a response-independent, random time schedule, previously inescapably shocked rats showed more rapid extinction of the instrumental response. It is hard to see how reduced attention to response-produced cues would make an animal more sensitive to a change from a contingent to a noncontingent relation between such cues and shock termination or food. On the other hand, the learned helplessness hypothesis correctly predicts the results of these two experiments, arguing that if animals have learned in one situation that their behaviors are uncorrelated with the occurrence of an important event, then they should more readily learn that their behaviors are uncorrelated with the same or a different important event in another situation.

One can gain another perspective on the attentional shift hypothesis by considering the convergence of research on the physiology of attention and research on physiological effects of inescapable shocks. Inescapable shocks result in the depletion of NE from several brain regions, most notably from the locus coeruleus (LC), which is a large nucleus of the rostral pontine tegmentum that, via the ascending dorsal tegmental bundle, is the sole source of noradrenergic innervation of the rat hippocampus and neocortex (e.g., Anisman, Pizzino, & Sklar, 1980; Weiss et al., 1981). Weiss and his colleagues (for a review see Weiss, 1991) showed that this depletion of NE in the LC is strongly associated with behavioral depression, as manifested by inactivity in the forced swim test. A consequence of the depletion in NE is that the amount available for release will decline, and so too will the amount of NE released into the synapse. This results in decreased stimulation of the alpha-2 adrenergic autoreceptors on the cell bodies and dendrites of neurons in the LC. These receptors are inhibitory, so a further consequence is that the firing of cells in the LC will increase, so that there will be excessive stimulation of postsynaptic receptors in the projection fields of the LC.

Pharmacological blockade of the alpha-2 receptors is in a sense a model of the effects of inescapable shock. Both a session of inescapable shocks and the infusion of the alpha-2 antagonist idazoxan into the LC result in an increase in the firing rate of the LC neurons in response to exteroceptive stimuli (Weiss, 1991). Moreover, there is evidence that administration of idazoxan has effects on attention.

DeVauges and Sara (1990) activated the noradrenergic system of rats via injection of idazoxan. Animals were appetitively trained to traverse a fixed path in a linear maze by making a set series of six turns to pass barriers placed along the length of the maze. After five trials, cards were placed over the barriers to indicate the correct path: Black cards indicated a barrier and white cards indicated no barrier. Rats were then injected with idazoxan or saline. Results indicated that the increased concentration of NE resulting from idazoxan injection facilitated the shift from position to luminance cues.

Further supporting the view that activation of the noradrenergic system facilitated the shift of attention, in a second experiment DeVauges and Sara (1990) showed that idazoxan also increases sensitivity to novelty and change in a nose-poke task. Rats were placed in a box that had nine holes cut in the floor. Photoelectric cells enabled the measurement of the number of holes visited and the time spent at each hole. Following 3 days of habituation, objects (e.g., plastic toys) were placed behind four of the holes. Thirty minutes before the trial, subjects were injected with idazoxan or saline. No differences emerged in the total time spent exploring empty holes as a function of treatment condition and all animals spent more time at the holes containing objects than at those that did not contain objects. The idazoxan treatment, however, did result in greater time spent visiting holes with objects relative to the saline treatment. This difference between groups was particularly marked for the most complex object (a plastic horse).

In another experiment, rats that had been trained to asymptote in a radial maze were given either idazoxan or saline prior to being placed in the maze in a new environment with new extramaze cues. Both groups showed a marked decrement in performance, but on the next day, when no drug was given, performance of the idazoxan group recovered completely and was superior to performance of controls (Sara, Vankov, & Herve, 1994). On the basis of these and other results Sara, Dyon-Laurent, and Herve (1995) concluded that the NE released in target forebrain areas as a result of the injection of idazoxan served to direct attention to novel exteroceptive stimuli, which would facilitate learning when such stimuli are relevant but impair learning when they are irrelevant.

Thus far our argument is that inescapable shocks that result in a choice escape deficit do so because they have an effect on the LC that results in increased attention to task-irrelevant cues. However, Weiss's (1991) dependent variable was not errors in a choice escape task, but reduced activity in the forced swim test. Moreover, the findings of the one paper that has reported changes in NE levels accompanying the choice escape deficit are not easily reconciled with those from Weiss's and Sara's laboratories. Minor et al. (1988) exposed groups of rats to varying numbers of inescapable tail shocks and a day later gave them a test of choice escape learning in the y-maze in the presence of task-irrelevant visual cues. Rats exposed to at least 80 shocks showed significant impairment in choice escape learning relative to those exposed to 40 shocks or no shocks. In a second similar experiment, instead of the choice escape test rats received either five shocks on a response-independent Variable Time (VT) 45-sec schedule in the y-maze or none, and then NE levels in hippocampus and the rest of the forebrain were examined. In controls NE levels had recovered over the 24 hr since the inescapable shocks, but rats that received the five shocks showed a pattern of redepletion of NE that mirrored the behavioral data. Significant depletion was observed in forebrain for the groups that received 80 or 120 inescapable shocks, and was observed in hippocampus for the 120-shock group.

In a third experiment, Minor et al. (1988) asked whether depletion of NE was sufficient for the choice escape deficit. Two groups of rats received chemical (6-hydroxydopamine) lesions of the dorsal adrenergic bundle and two received saline. A day later they were given the choice escape test. Half were tested in the presence of task-irrelevant cues and half were tested without such cues. Lesioned rats showed a marked deficit in choice behavior only in the presence of irrelevant cues. There was no effect on escape latency. Lesions resulted in an 85% reduction in hippocampal NE and a 63% reduction in NE in the rest of the forebrain.

The authors argued that although increased NE activity in forebrain may be responsible for the activity deficit, it is decreased NE activity in forebrain that is responsible for the choice escape deficit. They noted that this analysis predicts that stimulation and blockade of alpha-1 and beta-adrenergic receptors in forebrain should have opposite effects on measures of activity and accuracy of choice escape. Agonists should produce activity deficits, as has been shown by Weiss and Simson (1985), but should have no effect on choice accuracy. On the other hand, receptor antagonists should impair choice escape accuracy, but should have no effect on activity or escape latency. There are no reports of the effects of forebrain beta-adrenergic receptor antagonists on accuracy in choice escape. However, Sara et al. (1995) showed that the beta-receptor antagonist propranolol reduces attention to novel exteroceptive cues, suggesting that, contrary to the prediction, it would have no effect on choice accuracy. To sum up, on the basis of the physiological data reviewed here, it makes sense to think that inescapable shocks do enhance attention to exteroceptive cues, and that changes in adrenergic functioning somehow mediate this effect. The nature of this mediation remains unclear.

REINTERPRETING THE EFFECTS OF ESCAPABILITY

Recently Minor, Dess, and Overmier (1991; see Overmier, 1988) proposed a new way of thinking about the interference effect and other sequelae of exposure to inescapable shocks. Exposure to unpredictable, uncontrollable shocks is considered the baseline stress condition, and the effect of controllability is analyzed by adding an escape contingency to the baseline and comparing the effects of the two treatments. If the effects of the two differ, then the added contingency is said to modulate the baseline reaction to the shocks. Considering the problem in these terms, a strong challenge to the learned helplessness hypothesis arose more than a decade ago from the suggestion that adding the escape contingency to the sheer presentation of shock prevents the interference effects that would have resulted, not by adding controllability of shock termination per se, but by adding the stimuli that result from the escape response and thereby accompany shock termination. First backward CSs, which began when shocks ended and lasted for a few seconds, were added to the inescapable shocks in an attempt to mimic the escape contingency. Volpicelli, Ulm, and Altenor (1984) found that adding a 3-sec backward CS to inescapable shocks at least partially attenuated the deficit in subsequent lever press escape responding caused by inescapable shock pretreatment (also see Anderson, Crowell, Boyd, & Hantula, 1995). Maier and Warren (1988) found a similar effect using the more common FR-2 shuttlebox escape test, as did DeCola, Rosellini, and Warren (1988).

One interpretation of this outcome was that it was mediated by a reduction in contextual fear, because just as adding an escape contingency results in less fear in the pretreatment context, so does adding a backward CS (see Mineka, Cook, & Miller, 1984). Consequently both manipulations should result in less generalized fear in the test context, and thus better escape performance. Maier and Keith (1987), using a lick suppression measure of context fear, found that the presence of such backward CSs did result in less fear in the pretreatment context, so long as they followed the end of shock by no more than a few seconds (see also Anderson et al., 1995; DeCola et al., 1988; Jackson & Minor, 1988). Backward CSs were known to become conditioned inhibitors of fear, and it was thought that the inhibitory property was necessary for their ability to reduce context fear. Some support for this notion came from the fact that backward CSs do not become conditioned inhibitors of fear when the minimum interval before the next shock is short (Moscovitch & LoLordo, 1968), and do not reduce context fear under those conditions either (Rosellini, DeCola, & Warren, 1986). The conditioned inhibitory property of a backward CS seems to be acquired in somewhat fewer trials than the diminution in context fear (Rosellini, Warren, & DeCola, 1987), which makes sense if the backward CS is counterconditioning and thus functionally weakening the shock or producing inhibitory conditioning of the context through its pairing with that context (Mineka et al., 1984). Warren, Rosellini, and Maier (1989) added a third alternative mechanism of the effects of the backward CS. Perhaps the backward CS, because it is a conditioned inhibitor, is actively inhibiting the activation or rehearsal of the representation of the shock, thereby reducing the amount of joint rehearsal of context and shock and weakening their association (Wagner, 1978, 1981).

In any case, before it could be concluded that the addition of an escape contingency and the addition of backward CSs to inescapable shocks attenuate contextual fear or prevent escape deficits for the same reason, it had to be ascertained that the effects of escapability and backward CSs respond in the same way to other manipulations. Sometimes they do not. Rosellini et al. (1987) demonstrated one dissociation: Inclusion of a very short minimum time to the next shock wiped out the attenuation of contextual fear resulting from the addition of backward CSs, but had no effect on the attenuation of fear resulting from escapability (but see Anderson et al., 1995).

Another dissociation was demonstrated by Maier and Warren (1988), who found that, in a three-stage immunization experiment, administration in the first stage of inescapable shocks followed by a CS, unlike escapable shocks, failed to immunize the shuttlebox escape response against the effects of inescapable shock. Thus even when the addition of backward CSs reduced the impact of the shock session in which they were presented (i.e., reduced context fear), this manipulation did not proactively interfere with the effects of subsequent shock (also see Murison & Isaksen, 1982; Overmier, Murison, Skoglund, & Ursin, 1985). Yet another dissociation was observed by DeCola et al. (1988) in a noncontingent appetitive test, in which rats that had been pressing a lever for food on a response-contingent Random Interval 30-sec schedule were switched to a response-independent Random Time 30-sec schedule. Previously escapably shocked rats continued lever pressing much longer than previously inescapably shocked rats, whether the inescapable shocks had been followed by brief CSs or not. Taken together, these dissociations indicate that the effects, whether on context fear, on the impact of a subsequent inescapable shock treatment, or on performance of an instrumental response, of adding an escape contingency to shock cannot be reduced to the effects of adding a backward CS or safety signal.

CESSATION SIGNALS

The argument that the effects of adding controllability can be mimicked by adding a stimulus took a new turn when Minor, Trauner, Lee, and Dess (1990) compared the effects of backward CSs and cessation signals; that is, stimuli that are present only during the last few seconds of each shock, and thus might come to signal the end of the shock. Because an escape response is initiated before shock ends, it makes sense to assert that escape responding supplies a cessation signal, and thus to ask whether addition of that signal to inescapable shock mimics the effect of escapability. Moscovitch (1972) had shown that cessation CSs become potent conditioned inhibitors of fear, and thus there was reason to expect that they might attenuate context fear and the escape deficit.

In several experiments Minor et al. (1990) showed that the presence of a brief cessation signal during inescapable shocks resulted in at least partial alleviation of the shuttlebox escape deficit resulting from those shocks. Moreover, the addition of brief shocks 5 sec after the end of some of the trials had no effect on this outcome, whereas such shocks erased the ameliorating effects of backward CSs. The ameliorating effects of a cessation signal were significantly diminished if it continued for the 3 sec following the end of shock, but were unaffected if a different stimulus played the role of backward CS. The latter outcome may be the result of a ceiling effect; it would be useful to know whether a backward CS would add to the ameliorating effect of a cessation signal in the case of relatively brief shocks that result from yoking in the triadic design, where the cessation signal by itself produces only a partial alleviation of the escape deficit.

Finally, although backward CSs failed to produce an immunization effect, cessation signals produced a partial one, and a combination of a cessation signal and a backward CS resulted in complete immunization. Thus controllability of shocks in the first phase of the experiment is not necessary for immunization. We do not know whether the addition of cessation signals, like the addition of the escape contingency, enhances persistence when response-contingent food becomes response independent, nor do we know whether the addition of such signals to inescapable shocks would attenuate the deficit in choice escape. An experiment on the last point would be especially useful, for if addition of a cessation signal and addition of escapability do have the same effect on subsequent choice escape performance, then it will be very difficult to maintain that shock's inescapability produces the cognitive deficit. Instead, that outcome will have to be attributed to the absence of a reliable predictor of shock termination. Moreover, Lee and Maier's (1988) account of the choice escape deficit in terms of reduced attention to response-produced cues and enhanced attention to task-irrelevant external stimuli would hardly predict that adding an external cessation signal to the inescapable shocks would eliminate the deficit.

Minor et al. (1990) suggested that the cessation signal was having its effect through counterconditioning the shock, and therefore making it less aversive. Segundo, Galeano, Sommer-Smith, and Roig (1961) reported that tones that signaled that long shocks to the paw would end in a few seconds acquired the power to evoke relaxed postures similar to those the cats displayed when the shocks were turned off. Thus the effect of adding the cessation signal can be construed as functionally like reducing the duration of the shock, thereby reducing the strength of fear conditioning to context. Minor et al. further argued that this effect in turn would result in attenuation of the intense, chronic fear response shown in the test context by inescapably shocked rats that had not been given cessation signals (Minor, 1990). If such intense, chronic fear is necessary for the escape deficits, then the addition of cessation signals should attenuate or eliminate those deficits.

EXCESSIVE FEAR IS NOT THE CAUSE
OF THE ESCAPE DEFICIT

Maier (1990) noted that even if the fear hypothesis just described is correct in stating that more fear is evoked by inescapable shocks without signals than by escapable ones or inescapable ones accompanied by a cessation signal, and that these different amounts of fear transfer to the test task, it still remained to be seen whether the greater fear in previously inescapably shocked rats is the cause of the escape deficits. Therefore Maier concurrently measured fear and shuttlebox escape responding. In the test, freezing was assessed for 10 min, then there were two FR-1 escape trials, then freezing was assessed for an additional 20 min, and finally there were three more FR-1 and 25 FR-2 trials. In the first experiment rats had been pretreated with escapable shock (Group E), inescapable shock (Group I), or restraint (Group R). The Group I rats froze more than the other two groups at the start of the test. This result very likely reflects greater generalized conditioned fear in Group I. After the occurrence of shocks on the two FR-1 trials, the amount of freezing increased in all groups, with Group I showing the largest, most persistent increase, and Group R the smallest. Maier suggested that such differential postshock freezing reflects shock interacting with a sensitized fear system in Group I. In a later paper, Maier and Watkins (1998) identified the sensitization of the fear system by inescapable shocks with a state of unconditioned anxiety, which acted to enhance the amount of fear conditioned to the test context by the shocks that occurred on the first two FR-1 escape trials. Finally, the Group I rats showed a marked escape deficit on the FR-2 trials, relative to the other groups. Therefore, increased fear and anxiety in the test environment were positively correlated with the escape deficit.

In a second experiment, a 72-hr delay separated pretreatment and test; this is known to eliminate the escape deficit (Maier, Coon, McDaniel, & Jackson, 1979). This manipulation had no effect on freezing at the start of the test session, but did reduce inescapably shocked rats' freezing after the first two FR-1 trials to the level of Group R. This finding that anxiety induced by inescapable shock dissipates in 3 days is consistent with results obtained with the social interaction test of rat anxiety (File, 1980), in which two male rats are placed in an unfamiliar, brightly lit environment and their interactions are monitored. Drugs and other stimuli that increase anxiety reduce social interaction. Short and Maier (1993) found that inescapable shocks, but not escapable ones, reduced interactions, and that the reduction was blocked by known anxiolytics. Moreover, they found that this effect of inescapable shock on social interaction was no longer significant 72 hr after the inescapable shocks.

This finding that extending the delay between phases from 24 to 72 hr has no effect on freezing at the start of the test session but eliminates both the enhanced freezing following two FR-1 trials and the escape deficit indicates that the greater fear at the start of the test in Group I is not sufficient for the escape deficit, but leaves open the possibility that the freezing resulting from the sensitized fear substrate reacting to the first two shocks is sufficient for the escape deficit. To assess this possibility, in a third experiment Maier administered either diazepam or naltrexone, an opiate antagonist, just before the test session. Diazepam reduced both preshock and postshock freezing to control levels, but had no effect on the escape deficit. Naltrexone, on the other hand, had no effect on freezing, but wiped out the escape deficit.

This double dissociation indicates that the more intense fear in the test situation resulting from prior inescapable shocks is neither necessary nor sufficient for the shuttlebox FR-2 escape deficit. It may be important for other sequelae of exposure to inescapable shocks. Again choice escape would be important to look at. These are important findings, because they suggest that even if adding cessation signals to inescapable shocks attenuates the level of fear displayed in the shuttlebox, the attenuation of the shuttlebox escape deficit that results from adding cessation signals may not be mediated by such attenuation.

In a subsequent experiment using the same test procedure Maier et al. (1993) found that lesions of the basolateral and central nuclei of the amygdala prior to inescapable shock virtually eliminated both the freezing at the start of the test session and that which followed the first two shocks, but had no effect on the FR-2 escape deficit. These results support Maier's (1990) effect of diazepam in suggesting that intense fear during test is not necessary for the escape deficit. Moreover, as the lesions were made before the first phase of the experiment, the results also suggest that intense fear during the inescapable shock session is not a necessary condition of the escape deficit.

Lesions of the dorsal raphe nucleus (DRN), which contains the largest cluster of serotonergic neurons in the brain and is a major source of innervation of the forebrain, had no effect on freezing at the start of the test session, but eliminated both the exaggerated freezing that follows two shocks and the FR-2 escape deficit. Maier et al. (1993) suggested that the inescapable shocks sensitize the DRN for 2 to 3 days, so that it is highly activated by the first two shocks in the test. Then through projections from the DRN to the lateral and basal amygdala, and then to the central nucleus of the amygdala and finally to the ventral periaqueductal gray, this activation results in the exaggerated fear conditioned to the test context. Maier and Watkins (1998) described this sequence as anxiety modulating the neural circuitry that mediates fear.

However, because DRN but not amygdala lesions eliminate the FR-2 escape deficit, the DRN projection to basolateral amygdala cannot be responsible for the escape deficit. It is known that lesions of the dorsal periaqueductal gray (dPAG) reduce unconditioned motor responses to shock (Fanselow, 1991). Moreover, simultaneous stimulation of the DRN inhibits running and jumping in response to dPAG stimulation (Kiser, Brown, Sanghera, & German, 1980), and this inhibition is known to be mediated by serotonin receptors in the dPAG (Schutz, DeAguiar, & Graeff, 1985). Assuming that the shuttlebox escape response is mediated by activity in the dPAG, Maier et al. (1993) hypothesized that the escape deficit might be caused by inhibition of activity in the dPAG mediated by the serotonin pathway between the sensitized DRN and the dPAG. In support of this hypothesis, Maier, Busch, Maswood, Grahn, and Watkins (1995) found that microinjection into the DRN of the benzodiazepine inverse agonist Methyl 6, 7-Dimethoxy-4-ethyl—β carboline-3-carboxylate (DMCM), which activates the DRN, has the effect of producing anxiety and the escape deficit in the absence of inescapable shocks.

This discussion of the physiological basis of the escape deficit resulting from prior inescapable shocks has interesting implications for the mechanisms by which adding cessation CSs to inescapable shocks attenuates the effects of those shocks. Perhaps the presence of a signal for the end of shock eliminates or reduces the sensitization of the DRN otherwise produced by inescapable shocks. If this happens, then the DRN should have a weaker or no inhibitory effect on dPAG, and the vigorous shock escape responding normally mediated by activation of that structure should be relatively unaffected. As noted earlier, it is not known whether adding cessation CSs attenuates the intense, chronic fear in the test situation resulting from inescapable shock, but that should happen, because reduced sensitization of DRN should also result in reduced activation of structures in the amygdala that mediate fear and freezing. Given this argument, the effect of cessation signals on the escape deficit should be dissociable from their effect on fear and freezing, just as the effect of escapability is. Consequently, it makes sense to give up the fear hypothesis of the effects of cessation signals on the escape deficit, even if one maintains that it is the lack of a signal for shock termination, rather than the lack of control over shock termination, that is responsible for the escape deficit.

As was noted earlier, on the basis of dissociative effects of several drugs, Maier and Minor (1993) argued that different mechanisms were responsible for the escape latency deficit and the choice escape accuracy deficit. They suggested that the latter resulted from the rats learning that their behaviors did not produce or predict termination of shock, so that in aversive situations their attention shifted from response-produced to exteroceptive cues. Combining this conclusion with those drawn by Maier et al. (1993), in terms of underlying physiology, the argument is either that sensitization of the DRN is not responsible for the accuracy deficit, or that it is responsible but has its effect by way of a third pathway beyond the DRN. Which view, if either, is correct remains to be determined.

In any case, the mechanism based on serotonin and the DRN proposed by Maier and his colleagues should not be considered an exclusive alternative to Weiss's account based on NE and the LC. Maier and Watkins (1998) noted that a midbrain structure like the DRN is unlikely to mediate the differential effects of inescapable and escapable shocks. Moreover, they pointed out that LC and DRN project to each other, leaving open the possibility that both are in the circuit. Space does not permit discussion of the physiological mechanisms of inescapable shock effects proposed by other groups and their relation to the preceding (e.g., Anisman, Zalcman, Shanks, & Zacharko, 1991; Martin & Puech, 1996; Neumaier, Petty, Kramer, Szot, & Hamblin, 1997; Woodson, Minor, & Job, 1998).

CONCLUSIONS

The initial experiments on the interference effect set in motion an interplay of theory building and data collection that has resulted in the development of diverse psychological explanations, among them the learned helplessness hypothesis itself, the attentional shift hypothesis, the claim that the effects of escapability can be modeled by the presence of cessation and safety signals, and notions about the relation among fear, anxiety, and escape failures.

The escape latency deficit in the shuttlebox does not require that inescapably shocked rats be more fearful than controls during the test, or less active during shock, or more analgesic, although all those sequelae might covary in intact rats. Whether the escape latency deficit can best be thought of as arising from the absence of control of shock termination or from the absence of stimuli that predict shock termination remains to be seen, but the latter possibility is certainly worthy of further investigation. Strongly supportive of the learned helplessness hypothesis, and contrary to the attentional shift hypothesis, has been the finding that inescapably shocked animals give up instrumental responding sooner when in test they are switched from response-contingent to noncontingent reinforcement. Thus it would be useful to know whether adding both cessation and safety signals to inescapable shocks would alter this outcome. Such a result would undermine the learned helplessness hypothesis.

Less is known about the choice escape deficit. It does seem to be unaffected by manipulations that eliminate the latency deficit. The learned helplessness hypothesis says little about the importance of task-irrelevant cues for this outcome. The modal interpretation of the effect is in terms of reduced attention to response-produced stimuli and consequent increased attention to task-irrelevant exteroceptive cues, although this interpretation needs to be fleshed out. If addition of a cessation signal to inescapable shock happens to eliminate the choice escape deficit, then the interpretation will have to be expanded, perhaps to say that when there is a stimulus predicting shock offset, the animal does not sample the contingency between its various behaviors and shock offset, and so does not learn to pay less attention to its behaviors and more to exteroceptive cues.

ACKNOWLEDGMENTS

This chapter is based in part on LoLordo, V. M. (1998). Desesperanza aprendida; el estado actual de la investigacion con animales. In R. Ardila, W. Lopez Lopez, A. Perez-Acosta, R. Quiñones, & F. Reyes (Eds.), *Manual de analisis experimental del comportamiento.* (pp. 447–472). Madrid: Biblioteca Nueva.

The authors would like to thank Bob Boakes and Fred Westbrook for their helpful suggestions.

■ REFERENCES

Alloy, L. B., & Ehrman, R. N. (1981). Instrumental to Pavlovian transfer: Learning about response–reinforcer contingencies affects subsequent learning about stimulus–reinforcer contingencies. *Learning & Motivation, 12,* 109–132.

Altenor, A., Volpicelli, J., & Seligman, M. E. P. (1979). Debilitated shock escape is produced by both short- and long-duration inescapable shock: Learned helplessness vs. learned inactivity. *Bulletin of the Psychonomic Society, 14,* 337–339.

Anderson, D. C., Crowell, C. R., Boyd, N. R., & Hantula, D. A. (1995). Fixed-duration shock treatment: Pre- and posttreatment stimulation, activity, and skin resistance as predictors of escape performance. *Animal Learning & Behavior, 23,* 329–344.

Anderson, D. C., Crowell, C. R., Cunningham, C. L., & Lupo, J. V. (1979). Behavior during shock exposure as a determinant of subsequent interference with shuttlebox escape-avoidance learning in the rat. *Journal of Experimental Psychology: Animal Behavior Processes, 5,* 243–257.

Anisman, H., deCatanzaro, D., & Remington, G. (1978). Escape performance following exposure to inescapable shock: Deficits in motor response maintenance. *Journal of Experimental Psychology: Animal Behavior Processes, 4,* 197–218.

Anisman, H., Grimmer, L., Irwin, J., Remington, G., & Sklar, L. (1979). Escape performance after inescapable shock in selectively bred lines of mice: Response maintenance and catecholamine activity. *Journal of Comparative and Physiological Psychology, 93,* 229–241.

Anisman, H., Hamilton, M., & Zacharko, R. M. (1984). Cue and response-choice acquisition and reversal after exposure to uncontrollable shock: Induction of response perseveration. *Journal of Experimental Psychology: Animal Behavior Processes, 10,* 229–243.

Anisman, H., Pizzino, A., & Sklar, L. S. (1980). Coping with stress, norepinephrine depletion and escape performance. *Brain Research, 191,* 538–588.

Anisman, H., Remington, G., & Sklar, L. S. (1979). Effect of inescapable shock on subsequent escape performance: Catecholaminergic and cholinergic mediation of response initiation and maintenance. *Psychopharmacology, 61,* 107–124.

Anisman, H., & Sklar, L. S. (1979). Catecholamine depletion in mice upon reexposure to stress: Mediation of the escape deficits produced by inescapable shock. *Journal of Comparative and Physiological Psychology, 93,* 610–625.

Anisman, H., Zalcman, S., Shanks, N., & Zacharko, R. M. (1991). Multi-system regulation of performance deficits induced by stressors: An animal model of depression. In A. Boulton, G. Baker, & M. T. M. Iverson (Eds.), *Animal models in psychiatry II.* (pp. 1–60). Clifton, NJ: Humana.

Annau, Z., & Kamin, L. J. (1961). The conditioned emotional response as a function of intensity of the US. *Journal of Comparative and Physiological Psychology, 54,* 428–432.

Baker, A. G. (1976). Learned irrelevance and learned helplessness: Rats learn that stimuli, reinforcers, and responses are uncorrelated. *Journal of Experimental Psychology: Animal Behavior Processes, 2,* 130–141.

Baker, A. G., & Mackintosh, N. J. (1979). Preexposure to the CS alone, US alone, or CS and US uncorrelated: Latent inhibition, blocking by context, or learned irrelevance? *Learning & Motivation, 10,* 278–294.

Balleine, B., & Job, R. F. S. (1991). Reconsideration of the role of competing responses in demonstrations of the interference effect (learned helplessness). *Journal of Experimental Psychology: Animal Behavior Processes, 17,* 270–280.

Bennett, C. H., Maldonado, A., & Mackintosh, N. J. (1995). Learned irrelevance is not the sum of exposure to CS and US. *Quarterly Journal of Experimental Psychology, 48B,* 117–128.

Beylin, A., & Shors, T. J. (1998). Stress enhances excitatory trace eyeblink conditioning and opposes acquisition of inhibitory conditioning. *Behavioral Neuroscience, 112,* 1327–1338.

Bonardi, C., & Hall, G. (1996). Learned irrelevance: No more than the sum of CS and US preexposure effects? *Journal of Experimental Psychology: Animal Behavior Processes, 22,* 183–191.

Bracewell, R. J., & Black, A. H. (1974). The effects of restraint and noncontingent preshock on subsequent escape learning in the rat. *Learning & Motivation, 5,* 53–69.

Crowell, C. R., & Anderson, D. C. (1979). Shuttle interference effects in the rat depend upon activity during prior shock: A replication. *Bulletin of the Psychonomic Society, 14,* 413–416.

Crowell, C. R., & Anderson, D. C. (1981). Influence of duration and number of inescapable shocks on intrashock activity and subsequent interference effects. *Animal Learning & Behavior, 9,* 28–37.

Crowell, C. R., Lupo, J. V., Cunningham, C. L., & Anderson, D. C. (1978). Temporal form of shock is a determinant of magnitude of interference with escape-avoidance learning produced by exposure to inescapable shock. *Bulletin of the Psychonomic Society, 12,* 407–410.

DeCola, J. P., Rosellini, R. A., & Warren, D. A. (1988). A dissociation of the effects of control and prediction. *Learning & Motivation, 19,* 269–282.

DeVauges, V., & Sara, S. J. (1990). Activation of the noradrenergic system facilitates an attentional shift in the rat. *Behavioural Brain Research, 39,* 19–28.

Drugan, R. C., & Maier, S. F. (1982). The nature of the activity deficit produced by inescapable shock. *Animal Learning & Behavior, 10,* 401–406.

Drugan, R. C., & Maier, S. F. (1983). Analgesic and opioid involvement in the shock-elicited activity and escape deficits produced by inescapable shock. *Learning & Motivation, 14,* 30–47.

Drugan, R. C., Ryan, S. M., Minor, T. R., & Maier, S. F. (1984). Librium prevents the analgesia and shuttlebox escape deficit typically observed following inescapable shock. *Pharmacology, Biochemistry, & Behavior, 21,* 749–754.

Fanselow, M. S. (1991). The midbrain periaqueductal gray as a coordinator of action in response to fear and anxiety. In A. Depaulis & R. Bandler (Eds.), *The midbrain PAG* (pp. 151–173). New York: Plenum.

File, S. E. (1980). The use of social interaction as a method for detecting anxiolytic activity of chlordiazepoxide-type drugs. *Journal of Neuroscience Methods, 2,* 219–238.

Glazer, H. I., & Weiss, J. M. (1976a). Long-term and transitory interference effects. *Journal of Experimental Psychology: Animal Behavior Processes, 2,* 191–201.

Glazer, H. I., & Weiss, J. M. (1976b). Long-term interference effect: An alternative to "learned helplessness." *Journal of Experimental Psychology: Animal Behavior Processes, 2,* 202–213.

Irwin, J., Suissa, A., & Anisman, H. (1980). Differential effects of inescapable shock on escape performance and discrimination learning in a water escape task. *Journal of Experimental Psychology: Animal Behavior Processes, 6,* 21–40.

Jackson, R. L., Alexander, J. H., & Maier, S. F. (1980). Learned helplessness, inactivity, and associative deficits: Effects of inescapable shock on response choice escape learning. *Journal of Experimental Psychology: Animal Behavior Processes, 6,* 1–20.

Jackson, R. L., Maier, S. F., & Coon, D. J. (1979). Long-term analgesic effects of inescapable shock and learned helplessness. *Science, 206,* 91–94.

Jackson, R. L., Maier, S. F., & Rapaport, P. M. (1978). Exposure to inescapable shock produces both activity and associative deficits in the rat. *Learning & Motivation, 9,* 69–98.

Jackson, R. L., & Minor, T. R. (1988). Effects of signaling inescapable shock on subsequent escape learning: Implications for theories of coping and "learned helplessness." *Journal of Experimental Psychology: Animal Behavior Processes, 14,* 390–400.

Kiser, R. S., Brown, C. A., Sanghera, M. K., & German, D. C. (1980). Dorsal raphe nucleus stimulation reduces centrally-elicited fearlike behavior. *Brain Research, 191,* 265–272.

Klosterhalfen, W., & Klosterhalfen, S. (1983). A critical analysis of the animal experiments cited in support of learned helplessness. *Psychologische Beitrage, 25,* 436–458.

Lawry, J. A., Lupo, V., Overmier, J. B., Kochevar, J., Hollis, K. L., & Anderson, D. C. (1978). Interference with avoidance behavior as a function of qualitative properties of inescapable shocks. *Animal Learning & Behavior, 6,* 147–154.

Lee, R. K. K., & Maier, S. F. (1988). Inescapable shock and attention to internal versus external cues in a water escape discrimination task. *Journal of Experimental Psychology: Animal Behavior Processes, 14,* 302–311.

Levis, D. J. (1976). Learned helplessness: A reply and alternative S-R interpretation. *Journal of Experimental Psychology: General, 105,* 47–65.

Linden, D. R., Savage, L. M., & Overmier, J. B. (1997). General learned irrelevance: A Pavlovian analogue to learned helplessness. *Learning & Motivation, 28,* 230–247.

Mackintosh, N. J. (1973). Stimulus selection: Learning to ignore stimuli that predict no change in reinforcement. In R. A. Hinde & J. S. Hinde (Eds.), *Constraints on learning* (pp. 75–96). London: Academic Press.

MacLennan, A. J., Drugan, R. C., Hyson, R. L., Maier, S. F., Madden, J., IV, & Barchas, J. D. (1982). Dissociation of long-term analgesia and the shuttlebox escape deficit caused by inescapable shock. *Journal of Comparative and Physiological Psychology, 96,* 904–913.

Maier, S. F. (1970). Failure to escape traumatic electric shock: Incompatible skeletal motor response or learned helplessness? *Learning & Motivation, 1,* 157–169.

Maier, S. F. (1989). Learned helplessness: Event covariation and cognitive changes. In S. B. Klein & R. R. Mowrer (Eds.), *Contemporary learning theories: Instrumental conditioning theory and the impact of biological constraints on learning* (pp. 73–110). Hillsdale, NJ: Lawrence Erlbaum Associates.

Maier, S. F. (1990). The role of fear in mediating the shuttle escape learning deficit produced by inescapable shock. *Journal of Experimental Psychology: Animal Behavior Processes, 16,* 137–150.

Maier, S. F., Albin, R. W., & Testa, T. J. (1973). Failure to learn to escape in rats previously exposed to inescapable shock depends on nature of escape response. *Journal of Comparative and Physiological Psychology, 85,* 581–592.

Maier, S. F., Busch, C. R., Maswood, S., Grahn, R. E., & Watkins, L. R. (1995). The dorsal raphe nucleus is a site of action mediating the behavioral effects of the benzodiazepine receptor inverse agonist DMCM. *Behavioral Neuroscience, 109,* 759–766.

Maier, S. F., Coon, D. J., McDaniel, M. A., & Jackson, R. L. (1979). Time course of learned helplessness, inactivity, and nociceptive deficits in rats. *Learning & Motivation, 10,* 467–488.

Maier, S. F., Grahn, R. E., Kalman, B. A., Sutton, L. C., Wiertelak, E. P., & Watkins, L. R. (1993). The role of the amygdala and dorsal raphe nucleus in mediating the behavioral consequences of inescapable shock. *Journal of Behavioral Neuroscience, 107,* 377–388.

Maier, S. F., & Jackson, R. L. (1979). Learned helplessness: All of us were right (and wrong): Inescapable shock has multiple effects. In G. H. Bower (Ed.), *The psychology of learning and motivation,* (Vol. 13, pp. 155–218). New York: Academic Press.

Maier, S. F., Jackson, R. L., & Tomie, A. (1987). Potentiation, overshadowing, and prior exposure to inescapable shock. *Journal of Experimental Psychology: Animal Behavior Processes, 13,* 260–270.

Maier, S. F., & Keith, J. R. (1987). Shock signals and the development of stress-induced analgesia. *Journal of Experimental Psychology: Animal Behavior Processes, 13,* 226–238.

Maier, S. F., & Minor, T. R. (1993). Dissociation of interference with the speed and accuracy of escape produced by inescapable shock. *Behavioral Neuroscience, 107,* 139–146.

Maier, S. F., & Seligman, M. E. P. (1976). Learned helplessness: Theory and evidence. *Journal of Experimental Psychology: General, 103,* 3–46.

Maier, S. F., Seligman, M. E. P., & Solomon, R. L. (1969). Pavlovian fear conditioning and learned helplessness. In B. A. Campbell & R. M. Church (Eds.), *Punishment* (pp. 299–342). New York: Appleton.

Maier, S. F., Sherman, J. E., Lewis, J. W., Terman, G. W., & Liebeskind, J. C. (1983). The opioid/nonopioid nature of stress-induced analgesia and learned helplessness. *Journal of Experimental Psychology: Animal Behavior Processes, 9,* 80–90.

Maier, S. F., & Warren, D. A. (1988). Controllability and safety signals exert dissimilar proactive effects on nociception and escape performance. *Journal of Experimental Psychology: Animal Behavior Processes, 14,* 18–25.

Maier, S. F. , & Watkins, L. R. (1998). Stressor controllability, anxiety, and serotonin. *Cognitive Therapy and Research, 22,* 595–613.

Martin, P., & Puech, A. J. (1996). Antagonism by benzodiazepines of the effects of serotonin-, but not norepinephrine-, uptake blockers in the learned helplessness paradigm in rats. *Biological Psychiatry, 39,* 882–890.

Mikulincer, M. (1994). *Human learned helplessness.* New York: Plenum.

Mineka, S., Cook, M., & Miller, S. (1984). Fear conditioned with escapable and inescapable shock: Effects of a feedback stimulus. *Journal of Experimental Psychology: Animal Behavior Processes, 10,* 307–323.

Minor, T. R. (1990). Conditioned fear and neophobia following inescapable shock. *Animal Learning & Behavior, 18,* 212–226.

Minor, T. R., Dess, N. K., & Overmier, J. B. (1991). Inverting the traditional view of "learned helplessness." In M. R. Denny (Ed.), *Fear, avoidance, and phobias: A fundamental analysis* (pp. 87–134). Hillsdale, NJ: Lawrence Erlbaum Associates.

Minor, T. R., Jackson, R. L., & Maier, S. F. (1984). Effects of task irrelevant cues and reinforcement delay on choice escape learning following inescapable shock: Evidence for a deficit. *Behavior Processes, 10,* 543–556.

Minor, T. R., & LoLordo, V. M. (1984). Escape deficits following inescapable shock: The role of contextual odor. *Journal of Experimental Psychology: Animal Behavior Processes, 10,* 168–181.

Minor, T. R., Pelleymounter, M. A., & Maier, S. F. (1988). Uncontrollable shock, forebrain norepinephrine, and stimulus selection during choice escape learning. *Psychobiology, 16,* 135–145.

Minor, T. R., Trauner, M. A., Lee, C., & Dess, N. K. (1990). Modeling signal features of escape response: Effects of cessation conditioning in "learned helplessness" paradigm. *Journal of Experimental Psychology: Animal Behavior Processes, 16,* 123–136.

Mitchell, J. A., Channell, S., & Hall, G. (1985). Response-reinforcer associations after caudate-putamen lesions in the rat: Spatial discrimination and overshadowing-potentiation effects in instrumental learning. *Behavioral Neuroscience, 99,* 1074–1088.

Moscovitch, A. (1972). *Pavlovian cessation conditioning.* Unpublished doctoral dissertation, University of Pennsylvania, Philadelphia.

Moscovitch, A., & LoLordo, V. M. (1968). Role of safety in the Pavlovian backward fear conditioning procedure. *Journal of Comparative and Physiological Psychology, 66,* 673–678.

Moye, T. B., Coon, D. J., Grau, J. W., & Maier, S. F. (1981). Therapy and immunization of long-term analgesia in rats. *Learning & Motivation, 12,* 133–148.

Murison, R., & Isaksen, E. (1982). Gastric ulceration and adrenocortical activity after inescapable and escapable pre-shock in rats. *Scandanavian Journal of Psychology, 1,* 133–137.

Nation, J. R., & Matheny, J. L. (1980). Instrumental escape responding after passive avoidance training: Support for an incompatible response account of learned helplessness. *American Journal of Psychology, 93,* 299–308.

Neumaier, J. F., Petty, F., Kramer, G. L., Szot, P., & Hamblin, M. W. (1997). Learned helplessness increases 5-hydroxytryptamine 1B receptor mRNA levels in the rat dorsal raphe nucleus. *Biological Psychiatry, 41,* 668–674.

Overmier, J. B. (1988). Psychological determinants of when stressors stress. In D. Hellhammer, I. Florin, & H. Weiner (Eds.), *Neurobiological approaches to human disease* (pp. 236–259). Toronto: Hans Huber.

Overmier, J. B., Murison, R., Skoglund, E., & Ursin, H. (1985). Safety signals can mimic responses in reducing the ulcerogenic effects of prior shock. *Physiological Psychology, 13,* 243–247.

Overmier, J. B., & Seligman, M. E. P. (1967). Effects of inescapable shock upon subsequent escape and avoidance behavior. *Journal of Comparative and Physiological Psychology, 63,* 23–33.

Peterson, C., Maier, S. F., & Seligman, M. E. P. (1993). *Learned helplessness.* Oxford, UK: Oxford University Press.

Prabhakar, T., & Job, R. F. S. (1996). The effects of order of shock durations on helplessness in rats. *Animal Learning & Behavior, 24,* 175–182.

Rescorla, R. A. (1967). Pavlovian conditioning and its proper control procedures. *Psychological Review, 74,* 71–80.

Rodd, Z. A., Rosellini, R. A., Stock, H. S., & Gallup, G. A. (1997). Learned helplessness in chickens (Gallus gallus): Evidence for attentional basis. *Learning & Motivation, 28,* 43–55.

Rosellini, R. A., DeCola, J. P., Plonsky, M., Warren, D. A., & Stilman, A. J. (1984). Uncontrollable shock proactively increases sensitivity to response–reinforcer independence in rats. *Journal of Experimental Psychology: Animal Behavior Processes, 10,* 346–359.

Rosellini, R. A., DeCola, J. P., & Shapiro, N. R. (1982). Cross-motivational effects of inescapable shock are associative in nature. *Journal of Experimental Psychology: Animal Behavior Processes, 8,* 376–388.

Rosellini, R. A., DeCola, J. P., & Warren, D. A. (1986). The effect of feedback stimuli on contextual fear depends upon the length of the intertrial interval. *Learning & Motivation, 17,* 229–242.

Rosellini, R. A., Warren, D. A., & DeCola, J. P. (1987). Predictability and controllability: Differential effects upon contextual fear. *Learning & Motivation, 18,* 392–420.

Sara, S. J., Dyon-Laurent, C., & Herve, A. (1995). Novelty seeking behavior in the rat is dependent upon the integrity of the noradrenergic system. *Cognitive Brain Research, 2,* 181–187.

Sara, S. J., Vankov, A., & Herve, A. (1994). Locus coeruleus-evoked responses in behaving rats: A clue to the role of noradrenaline in memory. *Brain Research Bulletin, 35,* 457–465.

Schutz, M. T. B., DeAguiar, J. C., & Graeff, F. G. (1985). Antiaversive role of serotonin in the dorsal periaqueductal gray matter. *Psychopharmacology, 85,* 340–345.

Segundo, J. P., Galeano, C., Sommer-Smith, J. A., & Roig, J. A. (1961). Behavioral and EEG effects of tones reinforced by cessation of painful stimuli. In A. Fessard, R. W. Gerard, & J. Konorski (Eds.), *Brain mechanisms and learning* (pp. 347–401). Oxford, UK: Blackwell Scientific.

Seligman, M. E. P., & Beagley, G. (1975). Learned helplessness in the rat. *Journal of Comparative and Physiological Psychology, 88,* 534–541.

Seligman, M. E. P., & Maier, S. F. (1967). Failure to escape traumatic shock. *Journal of Experimental Psychology, 74,* 1–9.

Seligman, M. E. P., Maier, S. F., & Solomon, R. L. (1971). Unpredictable and uncontrollable aversive events. In F. R. Brush (Ed.), *Aversive conditioning and learning* (pp. 347–401). New York: Academic Press.

Servatius, R. J., & Shors, T. J. (1994). Exposure to inescapable stress persistently facilitates associative and nonassociative learning in rats. *Behavioral Neuroscience, 108,* 1101–1106.

Shors, T. J., & Mathew, P. R. (1998). NMDA receptor antagonism in the lateral/basolateral but not central nucleus of the amygdala prevents the induction of facilitated learning in response to stress. *Learning & Memory, 5,* 220–230.

Shors, T. J., & Servatius, R. J. (1997). The contribution of stressor intensity, duration, and context to the stress-induced facilitation of associative learning. *Neurobiology of Learning and Memory, 67,* 92–96.

Shors, T. J., Weiss, C., & Thompson, R. F. (1992). Stress-induced facilitation of classical conditioning. *Science, 257,* 537–539.

Short, K. R., & Maier, S. F. (1993). Stressor controllability, social interaction, and benzodiazepine systems. *Pharmacology, Biochemistry, & Behavior, 45,* 1–9.

Steenbergen, H. L., Heinsbroek, R. P. W., van Haaren, F., & van de Poll, N. E. (1989). Sex-dependent effects of inescapable shock administration on behavior and subsequent escape performance in rats. *Physiology & Behavior, 45,* 781–787.

Szostak, C., & Anisman, H. (1985). Stimulus perseveration in a water maze following exposure to controllable and uncontrollable shock. *Behavioral and Neural Biology, 43,* 178–198.

Testa, T. J., Juraska, J. M., & Maier, S. F. (1974). Prior exposure to inescapable electric shock in rats affects extinction behavior after the successful acquisition of an escape response. *Learning & Motivation, 5,* 380–392.

Volpicelli, J. R., Ulm, R. R., & Altenor, A. (1984). Feedback during exposure to inescapable shocks and subsequent shock-escape performance. *Learning & Motivation, 15,* 279–286.

Wagner, A. R. (1978). Expectancies and the priming of STM. In S. H. Hulse, H. Fowler, & W. K. Honig (Eds.), *Cognitive processes in animal behavior* (pp. 177–209). Hillsdale, NJ: Lawrence Erlbaum Associates.

Wagner, A. R. (1981). SOP: A model of automatic memory processing in animal behavior. In N. E. Spear & R. R. Miller (Eds.), *Information processing in animals: Memory mechanisms* (pp. 5–47). Hillsdale, NJ: Lawrence Erlbaum Associates.

Warren, D. A., Rosellini, R. A., & Maier, S. F. (1989). Controllability and predictability of stress. In G. H. Bower (Ed.), *The psychology of learning and motivation* (pp. 167–207). San Diego, CA: Academic Press.

Weiss, J. M. (1991). Stress-induced depression: Critical neurochemical and electrophysiological changes. In J. Madden IV (Ed.), *Neurobiology, of learning, emotion, and affect* (pp. 123–154). New York: Raven.

Weiss, J. M., Goodman, P. A., Losito, B. G., Corrigan, S., Charry, J. M., & Bailey, W. H. (1981). Behavioral depression produced by an uncontrollable stressor: Relationship to norepinephrine, dopamine, and serotonin levels in various regions of the rat brain. *Brain Research Review, 3,* 167–205.

Weiss, J. M., & Simson, P. G. (1985). Neurochemical basis of stress-induced depression. *Psychopharmacological Bulletin, 21,* 447–457.

Williams, J. L., & Maier, S. F. (1977). Transituational immunization and therapy of learned helplessness in the rat. *Journal of Experimental Psychology: Animal Behavior Processes, 3,* 240–252.

Woodson, J. C., Minor, T. R., & Job, R. F. S. (1998). Inhibition of adenosine deaminase by erythro-9-(2-hydroxy-3-nonyl)adenine (EHNA) mimics the effect of inescapable shock on escape learning in rats. *Behavioral Neuroscience, 112,* 399–409.

chapter 13

The Attenuating Effects of Drug Preexposure on Taste Aversion Conditioning:

Generality, Experimental Parameters, Underlying Mechanisms, and Implications for Drug Use and Abuse

Anthony L. Riley
Gregory R. Simpson
American University

CONDITIONED TASTE AVERSIONS

*I*f consumption of a novel solution or food is followed by one of a number of illness-inducing compounds, the rat will avoid consumption of that solution or food on a subsequent exposure (Garcia & Ervin, 1968; Revusky & Garcia, 1970; Rozin & Kalat, 1971; for additional reviews, see Klosterhalfen & Klosterhalfen, 1985; Logue, 1979; Riley, 1998; Spiker, 1977; for a bibliography on taste aversion learning, see Riley & Tuck, 1985a). This avoidance is rapidly acquired and very robust, resulting in a dramatic suppression of consumption of the illness-associated substance (see Fig. 13.1). Given that the avoidance appears dependent on the learned association between the ingested substance and the resulting illness it has been termed a *conditioned taste* or *conditioned food aversion* (Garcia & Ervin, 1968; however, see Mitchell, Scott, & Mitchell, 1977).

As described by Garcia and his colleagues, conditioned taste aversion learning occurs with few conditioning trials (in some instances learning is evident after only a single pairing of the solution with

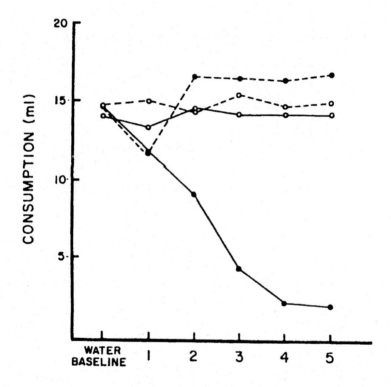

FIG. 13.1. Mean consumption (ml) of saccharin over repeated taste aversion conditioning trials for rats receiving pairings of saccharin and 0.18 mEq, 0.15 M LiCl (closed circles, solid lines). Control rats received pairings of saccharin and the saline vehicle (closed circles, dashed lines), of water and saline (open circles, dashed lines), or of water and LiCl (open circles, solid lines).

toxicosis; see Garcia, McGowan, & Green, 1972) and when extremely long delays intervene between consumption of the solution and administration of the illness-inducing drug (see Garcia, Ervin, & Koelling, 1966). Such characteristics (among others) established aversion learning as an instance of a violation of traditional laws of learning. Along with a number of other experimental preparations (e.g., bird song learning, tonic immobility, schedule-induced drinking, species-specific defense reactions; see Seligman, 1970; Shettleworth, 1972), conditioned taste aversion learning altered the long-accepted view of the arbitrary nature of learning and forced a reconceptualization of the role of evolution and adaptation in the acquisition and display of behavior (for discussions, see Garcia & Ervin, 1968; Rozin & Kalat, 1971; see also Domjan, 1983; Domjan & Galef, 1983).

Although conditioned taste aversion learning was initially examined within the context of constraints on learning and its implications for general learning theory, subsequent to its introduction taste aversion learning was soon examined empirically for the parameters under which such learning did or did not occur (Barker, Best, & Domjan, 1977; Braveman & Bronstein, 1985; Bures, Bermudez-Rattoni, & Yamamoto, 1998; Milgram, Krames, & Alloway, 1977). Accordingly, a wide variety of parameters were defined as being important for the acquisition of aversion learning (Riley & Baril, 1976). For example, the type and concentration of the to-be-conditioned taste (or food), the amount of solution or food consumed during conditioning (and prior to the drug), and its ambient temperature have all been reported to impact aversion learning. Similarly, the variety and intensity of the illness-inducing agent and its route of administration and spacing also affect the acquisition of taste aversions. Factors related to the association or pairing of the taste and toxicosis are important as well. Such factors include the temporal interval separating exposure to the taste and administration of the illness-inducing agent and the number of conditioning trials. In addition to these parameters that affect the taste, toxicosis, and their pairing, a number of other manipulations have also been reported to influence the rate and level of aversion conditioning, including the method by which the aversion is trained or tested (e.g., one- vs. two-bottle exposure), the level of fluid or food deprivation during conditioning or testing, the delay from training to testing, the age and sex of the subject, the strain and species of the subject, the social context in which the aversion is acquired or displayed, the circadian cycle during which the aversion is established or tested, the level of sleep deprivation, whether subjects are group or individually housed and whether or not the subjects are drug dependent (for a review of these factors, see Klosterhalfen & Kosterhalfen, 1985; Riley, 1998). Thus, although aversion learning is robust and rapidly acquired, similar to other learning preparations it is parameter dependent and can be strengthened or weakened by variations in these parameters (see Mackintosh, 1983).

UNCONDITIONED STIMULUS PREEXPOSURE

One parameter extensively examined in this context of factors affecting aversion learning is the familiarity of the to-be conditioned taste and of the aversive or illness-inducing agent. One of the most well-documented findings in aversion learning is the fact that familiarity of the taste or food prior to conditioning attenuates the acquisition of the aversion (Elkins, 1973; Fenwick, Mikulka, & Klein, 1975; Nachman & Jones, 1974; Riley, Jacobs, & Mastropaolo, 1983). Specifically, such familiarity can totally attenuate aversion acquisition such that subjects might drink the poison-associated solution at control levels or consume this solution (relative to another concurrently presented solution) even when the preexposed taste was more temporally contiguous with poison (Ahlers & Best, 1971). Subsequent to these demonstrations, similar analyses appeared assessing the effects of preexposure to the aversion-inducing agent on aversion learning[1] (see Fig. 13.2; see also Brookshire & Brackbill, 1971; Elsmore, 1972; Gamzu, 1974; Vogel, 1974). In one of the initial published reports of the effects of unconditioned stimulus (US) preexposure in aversion learning, Elkins (1974) exposed different groups of rats to either saline or the toxin cyclophosphamide (12.5 mg/kg; one, three, or six times) prior to presenting the subjects with a single pairing of a novel saccharin solution and cyclophosphamide (at the same dose administered

---

[1]For the purposes of this review, the US preexposure effect refers to the attenuation of taste aversion learning produced by exposure to an aversion-inducing agent given days prior to aversion training with that agent (or a second agent also effective in inducing aversions). This attenuation has been termed the *distal* or *durable US preexposure effect*. There are other pharmacological manipulations that may also attenuate aversion learning that are not included in this specific discussion. Specifically, under somewhat different conditions animals may be exposed to the aversion-inducing agent minutes or hours prior to aversion conditioning with that same agent. This has been termed the *proximal US preexposure effect* (see Domjan & Best, 1980). Although procedurally similar to the distal US preexposure effect, there appear to be considerable differences in the mechanisms underlying the two, as well as the effects of various manipulations on their display. Attenuated aversions can also be produced by treatment with a myriad of compounds prior to aversion conditioning that antagonize (either pharmacologically or physiologically) the effects of the aversion-inducing agent (see Riley & Baril, 1976). These studies reflect pharmacological and physiological interactions between the pretreatment and conditioning drugs as opposed to changes in aversiveness with simple exposure to the drug (as with the US preexposure effect). Again, for this review only the effects of exposure to an aversion-inducing agent given days prior to aversion conditioning with that drug (or a second agent effective in inducing taste aversions) are discussed.

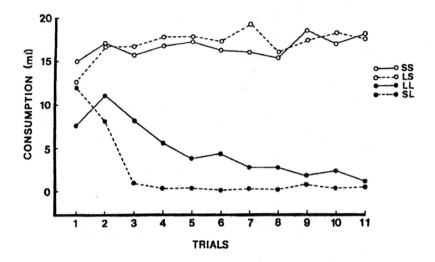

FIG. 13.2. Mean consumption (ml) of saccharin over repeated conditioning trials for rats receiving pairings of saccharin and LiCl (1.8 mEq, 0.15 M) or saline (the LiCl vehicle). The first letter in each group designation refers to the injection given during preexposure, that is, LiCl (L) or saline (S). The second letter refers to the injection given during conditioning (i.e., L or S). From Riley et al. (1976). Reprinted with permission of American Psychological Association.

during preexposure; i.e., 12.5 mg/kg). Subsequent to the conditioning session, all subjects were given a two-bottle choice between saccharin and water for 60 days with no further conditioning sessions (i.e., the subjects were tested in extinction). Subjects preexposed to saline (the drug vehicle) and conditioned with cyclophosphamide displayed typical taste aversion learning, drinking less than 10% saccharin on the initial extinction sessions. With repeated nonpoisoned exposures to saccharin, these subjects eventually consumed saccharin at levels comparable to water (although still less than nonconditioned subjects). Subjects preexposed to and conditioned with cyclophosphamide displayed varying degrees of attenuated aversions, dependent on the number of preexposures. Specifically, subjects receiving only a single preexposure displayed no clear effects of drug preexposure. On the other hand, subjects receiving three preexposures, although avoiding saccharin to the same degree as nonpreexposed subjects on the initial extinction trials, extinguished the aversion to saccharin faster and to a greater degree (and to the level of nonconditioned subjects). Finally, subjects given six preexposures to cyclophosphamide displayed significantly less aversion to saccharin on

the initial extinction trials and more rapid and greater extinction than nonpreexposed subjects. Thus, similar to the effects of preexposure to the to-be-conditioned taste, preexposure to the aversion-inducing agent dramatically attenuated taste aversion learning with the degree of attenuation apparently a direct function of the number of drug preexposures. Subsequent reports that Lithium Chloride (LiCl) preexposure attenuated LiCl-induced aversions suggested that the preexposure effect might be a general phenomenon in aversion learning that could be extended to a number of toxins traditionally reported to produce taste aversions (see Braveman, 1975; Cannon, Berman, Baker, & Atkinson, 1975).

Concurrent with these reports with classical toxins (e.g., cyclophosphamide and LiCl), the preexposure effect was also being demonstrated with other compounds as well, compounds not traditionally described as toxic but effective in inducing taste aversion learning (e.g., recreational drugs such as ethanol, morphine, and amphetamine). For example, Berman and Cannon (1974) exposed different groups of rats to either water or ethanol (95% ethanol in a decarbonated beer solution; up to 5%) for 35 days prior to taste aversion conditioning in which subjects were given five pairings of a novel saccharin solution and an intragastric injection of 2 or 5 g/kg ethanol. Naive subjects (i.e., those exposed to water prior to conditioning) displayed clear dose-dependent aversions to the ethanol-associated saccharin solution. Subjects preexposed to ethanol, however, displayed attenuated aversions with the degree of attenuation dependent on the concentration of ethanol given during conditioning. Specifically, subjects conditioned with the higher concentration of ethanol displayed the least attenuation (although aversions were still weaker than in naive subjects conditioned at this dose). Preexposed subjects conditioned at the lower ethanol concentration displayed no aversion to the ethanol-associated solution, drinking at levels comparable to subjects receiving the ethanol vehicle during conditioning. LeBlanc and Cappell (1974) extended these findings with the demonstration that exposure to either morphine (either 40 or 200 mg/kg for 16 consecutive days) or amphetamine (4 or 20 mg/kg for 15 consecutive days) attenuated subsequent aversion learning with these same drugs (at 20 mg/kg and 1 mg/kg, respectively). Further, for both of these drugs the degree of attenuation appeared to be a function of the amount of drug given during preexposure; that is, the higher the dose of the preexposure drug, the greater the attenuation (although see Experiment 1 with the highest dose of morphine). Thus, similar to the work with cyclophosphamide (Elkins, 1974) and LiCl (Braveman, 1975; Cannon et al., 1975), the work by Berman and Cannon (1974) and LeBlanc and Cappell (1974) suggested that the US preexposure effect was a general finding that may be evident with both toxins and recreational drugs.

GENERALITY AND EXPERIMENTAL PARAMETERS
OF US PREEXPOSURE

Subsequent to these initial demonstrations, a wide variety of compounds have been shown to produce the US preexposure effect in taste aversion learning, including amobarbital (Vogel & Nathan, 1976), amphetamine (Goudie, Taylor, & Atherton, 1975), apomorphine (Brookshire & Brackbill, 1976), chlordiazepoxide (Gamzu, 1977), cocaine (Riley & Diamond, 1998), delta-9-THC (Fisher & Vail, 1980), diazepam (Switzman, Fishman, & Amit, 1981), estradiol (Merwin & Doty, 1994), fenfluramine (Goudie et al., 1975), fluvoxamine (Gommans et al., 1998), LiCl (Riley, Jacobs, & LoLordo, 1976), meprobamate (Gamzu, 1977), methamphetamine (Goudie, Thornton, & Wheeler, 1976), morphine (Cappell, LeBlanc, & Herling, 1975), nicotine (Iwamoto & Williamson, 1984), N-tert-butyl-a-phenyl nitrone (PBN; Rabin, 1996) and 2,4,5-trichlorophenoxyacetic acid (Sjoden, Archer, & Carter, 1979). Further, preexposure to nondrug aversion-inducing agents such as radiation (Rabin, Hunt, & Lee, 1988), area postrema cooling (Wang, Lavond, & Chambers, 1997), and rotation (Braveman, 1975) also attenuates subsequent aversion learning to these same agents. These attenuating effects on aversion learning occur across a variety of preexposure conditions, again indicating the generality of this phenomenon. To date, such effects have been reported in both male and female subjects; in both rats and mice (and in several different strains of each); across a variety of ages; under deprived and nondeprived conditions; when the preexposed and conditioned drugs are different (see later); and following oral, intraperitoneal, intragastric, subcutaneous, and in utero administration (for instances in which drug preexposure fails to attenuate taste aversion learning, see Elsmore, 1972; Ferrari & Riley, 1994; for cases in which such preexposure facilitates aversion learning, see Aguado, del Valle, & Perez, 1997; Batsell & Best, 1994; see also Bienkowski, Koros, Piasecki, & Kostowski, 1998; Bowers, Gingras, & Amit, 1996; Ellenbroek, Knobbout, & Cools, 1997). Table 13.1 summarizes the variety of manipulations assessed in studies on the US preexposure effect in taste aversion learning.

Although displayed across this range of conditions, the US preexposure effect in aversion learning is, nonetheless, affected by these and other parametric variations, some of which may be important to an understanding of the mechanism underlying the effect (see later). For example, the age (Misanin, Hoefel, Riedy, & Hinderliter, 1997), sex (Fisher & Vail, 1980), and strain (Risinger & Cunningham, 1995) of the subject, the deprivation state (Barker & Johns, 1978; Suarez & Barker, 1976), and changes in the route of administration of the drug from preexposure to conditioning (Domjan & Best, 1980; Riley & Diamond,

TABLE 13.1 Studies Assessing the Effects of Drug Preexposure on Taste Aversion Learning

Reference	Preexposure			Conditioning		Study Focus
	Drug	Dose	No.	Drug	Dose	
Aguado, De Brugada, & Hall (1997)	LiCl	10 ml/kg, 0.3 M (IP)	3 (daily)	LiCl	10 ml/kg 0.3 M (IP)	Examined effect of PRE–COND interval
Aguado, del Valle, & Perez (1997)	Ketamine LiCl	25 ml/kg (IP) 10 ml/kg, 0.15 M (IP)	3 (48 hr.)	LiCl	10 ml/kg 0.15 M (IP)	Examined cross-drug effect
Aragon et al. (1986)	Acetaldehyde Ethanol	0.2, 0.3 g/kg (5, 7% v/v) (IP) 1.2 g/kg (IP)	3 (72 hr.)	Acetaldehyde Ethanol	0.2, 0.3 g/kg (5, 7% v/v) (IP) 1.2 g/kg (IP)	Examined cross-drug effect
Barker & Johns (1978)	Ethanol	3–6 g/kg, (30% w/v) (intubation)	14 (over 21 days)	Ethanol	6 g/kg (5, 7% v/v) (IP) (intubation)	Examined effect of PRE–COND interval
Batsell & Best (1994)	LiCl	12 mg/kg, 0.15 M (IP)	1	LiCl	12 mg/kg, 0.15 M (IP)	Examined effect of COND–test interval
Batson (1983)	LiCl	12 cc/kg, 0.15 M (IP)	8 (48 hr)	LiCl	12 cc/kg, 0.15 M (IP)	Examined US PRE effect and effect of LiCl PRE on temperature and activity
Batson & Best (1979)	LiCl	10–20 cc/kg, 0.15 M (IP)	4, 8 (daily)	LiCl	5–10 cc/kg, 0.15 M (IP)	PRE and COND in same and/or different environment
Berman & Cannon (1974)	Ethanol-beer	3–5 (oral) Ethanol 95% (w/w)	35 (daily)	Ethanol	2, 5 g/kg (5 ml) (intubation)	Examined US PRE effect
Bienkowski, Iwinska, et al. (1998)	Ethanol mCPBG	1.5 g/kg, (10% v/v) (IP) 50 ug (ICV)	4 (daily)	Ethanol	1.5 g/kg (10% v/v) (IP)	Examined cross-drug effect

Reference	Drug	Dose	No.	Drug	Dose	Study Focus
Bienkowski, Koros, et al. (1998)	MK-801	0.1, 0.2 mg/kg (IP)	6 (daily)	Ethanol	1.5 g/kg (10% v/v) (IP)	Examined cross-drug effect
Bienkowski, Piasecki, et al. (1998)	Ethanol Nicotine Mecamylamine	1.5 g/kg (10% v/v) 0.1, 0.6 mg/kg (SC) 1, 3 mg/kg (SC)	6 (daily)	Ethanol	1.5 g/kg (10% v/v) (IP)	Correlated PRE effects with drug discrimination effects; cross-drug effect
Bowers et al. (1996)	Shock	30 min (1 mA, 1.5 s, 60 s ITI)	2 (48 hr)	Amphetamine	2 mg/kg (IP)	Examined cross-drug effect
Braveman (1975)	LiCl Methylscopolamine Amphetamine Rotation	1% bw, 0.3 M (IP) 1 mg/kg (IP) 2 mg/kg (IP) 15 min (60 rpm)	1, 3, 5, 7 (120 hr)	LiCl Methylscopolamine Amphetamine Rotation	0.5% bw, 0.3 M (IP) 1 mg/kg (IP) 2 mg/kg (IP) 15 min (60 rpm)	Examined cross-drug effect
Braveman (1977)						Review
Braveman (1978)	LiCl	1% bw, 0.15 M (IP)	4 (72 hr)	LiCl	1% bw, 0.15 M (IP)	Examined effect of handling cues
Braveman (1979)	LiCl Amphetamine	1% bw, 0.3 M (IP) 2 mg/kg (IP)	7 (96 hr) 4 (96 hr)	LiCl	1% bw, 0.3 M (IP)	Examined cross-drug effect; PRE and COND in same and/or different environment
Brookshire & Brackbill (1976)	Apomorphine	15 mg/kg (n/a)	10 (daily)	Apomorphine	15 mg/kg (n/a)	Examined US PRE effect
Brown et al. (1979)	Morphine Diazepam	9 mg/kg (IP) 4 mg/kg (IP)	1	Morphine Diazepam	9 mg/kg (IP) 4 mg/kg (IP)	Examined cross-drug effect
Cain & Baenninger (1977)	LiCl	6 ml, 0.15 M (intubation)	5 (48 hr)	LiCl	6 ml, 0.15 M (intubation)	Examined UCS PRE effect; examined tolerance to locomotor activity

513

	Preexposure			Conditioning		Study Focus
Reference	Drug	Dose	No.	Drug	Dose	
Cannon et al. (1977)	LiCl	0.02 ml/g, 0.06–0.12 M (intubation)	4, 14 (daily)	LiCl	0.02 ml/g, 0.10 M (intubation)	Examined cross-drug effect; examined behavioral tolerance using rotarod
	Ethanol	3 (22.5%), 5 (37.5%), 6 g/kg (45% v/v) (intubation)		Ethanol	5 g/kg (37.5% v/v) (intubation)	
Cannon et al. (1975)	Ethanol	4 g/kg (30%) (intubation)	1, 3, 5 (daily)	Ethanol	4 g/kg (30%) (intubation)	PRE and COND in same and/or different environments; examined effect of PRE–COND interval
	LiCl	0.02 ml/g (0.12, 0.36 M (intubation)	1	LiCl	0.02 ml/g, (0.12, 0.36 M) (intubation)	
Cappell & LeBlanc (1975a)	Amphetamine	7.5 mg/kg (IP)	1, 5, 20 (daily)	Amphetamine	1 mg/kg (IP)	Examined effects of PRE–COND interval
Cappell & LeBlanc (1975b)						Review
Cappell & LeBlanc (1977a)						Review
Cappell & LeBlanc (1977b)	Morphine	20–40 mg/kg (IP)	15 (daily, 120 hr)	Morphine	10 mg/kg (IP)	Examined effects of massed vs. spaced pretreatment; examined effects of PRE–COND interval
	Amphetamine	4 mg/kg (IP)		Amphetamine	1 mg/kg (IP)	
Cappell et al. (1975)	Amphetamine	10–20 mg/kg (IP)	20 (daily)	Amphetamine	1 mg/kg (IP)	Examined cross-drug effect
	Morphine	5–40 mg/kg (IP	21 (daily)	Morphine	6 mg/kg (IP)	
	Chlordiazepoxide	5–25 mg/kg (IP)	15 (daily)			
Cappell & Poulos (1979)	Amphetamine	7.5 mg/kg (IP)	15 (120 hr)	Amphetamine	1 mg/kg (IP)	Examined cross-drug effect; PRE and COND in same and/or different environments
	Morphine	12 mg/kg (IP)				

Reference	Drug	Dose	No.	Drug	Dose	Study Focus
Cole et al. (1993)	LiCl	2 ml/kg, 1 M (IP)	3 (daily)	LiCl	2 ml/kg, 0.25 M (IP)	Examined effect of COND–test interval
Cole et al. (1996)	LiCl	2 ml/kg, 1 M (IP)	3 (daily)	LiCl	2 ml/kg, 0.25 M (IP)	PRE and COND in same and/or different environments
Corcoran (1973)	Hashish	1, 10, 30 mg/kg (IP)	1, 2 (240 hr)	Hashish	1, 10, 30 mg/kg (IP)	Related Study
Cunningham & Linakis (1980)	Ethanol + LiCl	0.6 g/kg, (30.4% v/v (IP) + 5 ml/kg, 0.6 M (IP)	5 (48 hr)	Ethanol	1.8 g/kg (30.4% v/v) (IP)	Examined effect of handling cues; examined cross-drug effect
Dacanay & Riley (1982)	LiCl Morphine	1.8 mEq, 0.15 M (IP) 40 mg/kg (IP)	5 (72 hr)	LiCl Morphine	1.8 mEq, 0.15 M (IP) 40 mg/kg (IP)	PRE and COND in same and/or different environments
Danguir & Nicolaidis (1977)	LiCl	2% bw, 0.15 M (IP)	1, 3 (daily)	LiCl	2% bw, 0.15 M (IP)	Examined effect of CS
DeBeun et al. (1996)	Ethanol Ipsapirone	500, 750, 1,000, 1,500 mg/kg (12.5% w/v) (IP) 1, 3, 10, 30 mg/kg (IP)	4 (daily)	Ethanol	1,000 mg/kg (12.5% w/v) (IP)	Examined cross-drug effect; correlated PRE effects with drug discrimination effects
DeBeun, Peeters, & Broekkamp (1993)	Estradiol Progesterone Testosterone LiCl Apomorphine	2–50 ug/kg (SC) 50–200 ug/kg (SC) 250–1,000 ug/kg (SC) 22 mg/kg (SC) 0.1–0.2 mg/kg (SC)	4 (daily)	Estradiol	50 ug/kg (SC)	Examined cross-drug effects

	Preexposure			Conditioning		
Reference	Drug	Dose	No.	Drug	Dose	Study Focus
DeBeun, Rijk, & Broekkamp (1993)	Variety of serotonergic and nonserotonergic drugs (e.g., 8-OH-DPAT, Ipsapirone, Amphetamine, Apomorphine, LiCl, Diazepam)	Varied with PRE drug (SC)	4 (daily)	8-OH-DPAT	0.22 mg/kg (SC)	Examined cross-drug effects
Domjan & Best (1980)	LiCl	3.0 mEq/kg, 0.15 M (IP infusion or injection)	1, 8 (over 20 days)	LiCl	1.8 mEq/kg, 0.15 M (IP infusion or injection)	Examined effect of route of administration; PRE and COND in same and/or different environment
Domjan & Siegel (1983)	Morphine	8 mg/kg (IP) 40 mg/kg (IP)	5 (48 hr)	Morphine	8 mg/kg (IP) 40 mg/kg (IP)	PRE and COND in same and/or different environment; assessed analgesic tolerance
Elkins (1974)	Cyclophosphamide	12.5 mg/kg (IP)	1, 3, 6 (48 hr)	Cyclophosphamide	12.5 mg/kg (IP)	Examined dose effects
Ellenbroek et al. (1997)	Amphetamine	0.1, 0.25, 0.5 mg/kg (IP)	3 (daily)	LiCl	75 mg/kg (IP)	Examined cross-drug effect
Ferrari & Riley (1994)	Cocaine	20 mg/kg (SC)	13 (GD 7–19)	Cocaine	18, 32, 50 mg/kg (SC)	Examined effect of prenatal US exposure
Fischer et al. (1987)	Nitrous oxide	80% N2: 20% O2 (1 hr) (inhalation)	3, 4 (72 hr)	Nitrous oxide	80% N2: 20% O2 (1 hr) (inhalation)	Examined US PRE effect
Fischer & Vail (1980)	Delta-9-THC	1, 2 mg/kg (IP)	4 (72 hr)	Delta-9-THC	1, 2 mg/kg (IP)	Examined gender differences

Reference	Drug	Dose	No.	Drug	Dose	Study Focus
Ford & Riley (1984)	LiCl	1.8 mEq, 0.15M (IP)	5 (72 hr)	Amphetamine	2 mg/kg (IP)	Examined cross-drug effect; PRE and COND in same and/or different environment
Gaiardi et al. (1991)	Morphine	20 mg/kg (IP)	21 (daily)	Morphine	10, 20 mg/kg (IP)	Examined US PRE in CTA and CPP
Gamzu (1977)	Chlordiazepoxide Apomorphine Diazepam Amphetamine Meprobamate	15 mg/kg (IP) 10 mg/kg (IP) 7.5 mg/kg (IP) 2 mg/kg (IP) (n/a)	1, 3, 4 (daily)	Chlordiazepoxide Apomorphine Amphetamine Meprobamate	15 mg/kg (IP) 10 mg/kg (IP) 2 mg/kg (IP) (n/a)	Review; examined cross-drug effect
Glowa & Williams (1992)	Cocaine	0.13–0.3 mg/kg (IV)	(n/a)	Cocaine	0.3 mg/kg (IM)	Examined US PRE effect (PRE was self-administered)
Gommans et al. (1998)	Fluvoxamine Fluoxetine 8-OH-DPAT Flesinoxan DOI MK-212	5, 15, 50 mg/kg (SC) 1, 3, 10 mg/kg (SC) 0.06, 0.2, 0.6 mg/kg (SC) 0.03, 0.1, 0.3 mg/kg (SC) 0.5, 1.5, 5 mg/kg (SC) 1, 3, 10 mg/kg (SC)	4 (daily)	Fluvoxamine Fluoxetine Flesinoxan	50 mg/kg (SC) 10 mg/kg (SC) 0.1 mg/kg (SC)	Examined cross-drug effect
Goudie et al. (1975)	Amphetamine Fenfluramine	2 mg/kg (IP) 9 mg/kg (IP)	1, 4 (daily) 4, 8 (daily)	Amphetamine Fenfluramine	2 mg/kg (IP) 9 mg/kg (IP)	Examined effect of no. of PRE on CTA
Goudie & Thornton (1975)	Amphetamine Fenfluramine	2 mg/kg (IP) 6 mg/kg (IP)	9 (daily)	Amphetamine Fenfluramine	2 mg/kg (IP) 9 mg/kg (IP)	Examined cross-drug effect
Goudie et al. (1976)	Methamphetamine	3 mg/kg (IP)	2, 4, 6, 9, 14 (daily)	Methamphetamine Fenfluramine Chloramphetamine Morphine	3, 10 mg/kg (IP) 5 mg/kg (IP) 5 mg/kg (IP) 20 mg/kg (IP)	Examined cross-drug effect

Reference	Preexposure			Conditioning		Study Focus
	Drug	Dose	No.	Drug	Dose	
Holman (1976)	LiCl	5 ml, 0.15 M (IP)	8 (daily)	LiCl	5 ml, 0.15 M (IP)	Examined US PRE effect
Hunt et al. (1985)	Morphine	0.3, 1.25, 2.5, 5, 15 mg/kg (IP)	3 (48 hr)	Morphine	2.5, 5, 15 mg/kg (IP)	Examined dose effect
W. A. Hunt & Rabin (1988)	Ethanol	4–6 g/kg (20% w/v) (oral)	10 (over 5 days)	Ethanol Radiation	4 g/kg (20%) (oral) ^{60}Co, 40 rad/min	Examined cross-effect; examined behavioral tolerance in a righting reflex procedure
Iwamoto & Williamson (1984)	Nicotine	0.5 mg/kg (SC)	2, 4 (daily)	Nicotine	0.5 mg/kg (SC)	Examined effect of PRE–COND interval
June et al. (1992)	Ethanol	2 g/kg (20% v/v) (IP)	5 (daily)	Ethanol	2 g/kg (20% v/v) (IP)	Examined effect of antagonist and US and PRE effect
Kiefer et al. (1977)	Apomorphine	20 mg/kg (IP)	1	Apomorphine	20 mg/kg (IP)	Examined both US and CS PRE effect
Klein et al. (1986)	LiCl	0.5, 0.75, 1.5, 2.25, 3, 3.75 mEq, 0.3 M (n/a)	2, 4 (48 hr)	LiCl	0.5, 1.25, 1.5, 3 mEq, 0.3 M (n/a)	Examined dose effects
LeBlanc & Cappell (1974)	Morphine Amphetamine	20–200 mg/kg (IP) 2–4, 10–20 mg/kg (IP) 15 (daily)	5, 16 (daily)	Morphine Amphetamine	20 mg/kg (IP) 1 mg/kg (IP)	Examined different levels of drug dependence on CTA
Marfaing-Jallat & LeMagnen (1979)	Ethanol	11.36–13.75% (v/v) 1.33 kcal/ml (oral) (free access)	15 (daily)	Ethanol	1.5, 3, 4.5 g/kg (20% w/v) (IP)	Examined effect of COND dose
Merwin & Doty (1994)	Estradiol	0.3, 0.75, 1.5 ug (SC)	8 (daily)	Estradiol	0.1 mg (SC)	Examined US PRE effect in ovariectomized rats
Mikulka et al. (1977)	LiCl	3 mEq/2% bw, 0.15 M (IP)	1, 4 (48 hr)	LiCl	3 mEq/2% bw, 0.15 M (IP)	Examined US PRE effect

Reference	Drug	Dose	No.	Drug	Dose	Study Focus
Miranda & Vila (1985)	LiCl	2 ml/kg, 0.7, 0.15 M (IP)	6 (daily)	LiCl	2 ml/kg, 0.7, 0.15 M (IP)	Spanish; Examined dose effect
Misanin et al. (1997)	LiCl	1% bw, 0.15 M (IP)	6 (daily)	LiCl	1% bw, 0.15 M (IP)	Examined effect of age on US PRE effect
Opitz et al. (1997)	Ethanol	3.16 g/kg (oral)	5 (GD 14–18)	LiCl	0.01 ml/g, 0.15 M (oral)	Examined effect of prenatal US exposure; examined radial maze performance; examined cross-drug effect
Parker et al. (1973)	Morphine	20–140 mg/kg (IP) (+ 5 mg/kg daily)	25 (daily)	Morphine	95 mg/kg (IP)	Examined "unnatural need state"
Poulos & Cappell (1979)	Amphetamine	7.5 mg/kg (IP)	12 (over 15 days)	Amphetamine	1 mg/kg (IP)	Examined effect of handling cues
Preston et al. (1984)	Methamphetamine Mehtylphenidate	50 mg/kg (IP) 50, 100 mg/kg (SC)	4 (daily)	Atropine	2.5, 5, 10 mg/kg (IP)	Examined cross-drug effect
Rabin (1996)	PBN Amphetamine	20 mg/kg (IP) 3 mg/kg (IP)	3 (72 hr)	PBN Radiation Amphetamine	20 mg/kg (IP) 1 Gy, ^{60}CO 3 mg/kg (IP)	Examined cross-manipulation
Rabin et al. (1988)	Ethanol LiCl Radiation	4 g/kg (PO) 3 mEq/kg (IP) ^{60}CO: 100 rad, 40 rad/min	3 (72 hr)	Ethanol LiCl Radiation	4 g/kg (PO) 1.5, 3 mEq/kg (IP) ^{60}CO: 100 rad, 40 rad/min	Examined cross-manipulation
Randich & LoLordo (1979)						Review
Revusky et al. (1982)	LiCl	2.5–3 ml (2% w/v) (IP)	7 (48 hr)	LiCl	1.5–2.5 ml (2% w/v) (IP)	Examined "poisoned partner effect"

| | Preexposure | | No. | Conditioning | | Study Focus |
Reference	Drug	Dose		Drug	Dose	
Revusky & Taukulis (1975)	Ethanol LiCl	10% (v/v) (IP) 1.2 ml, 2% (w/v) (IP)	8 (48 hr)	LiCl	1.2 ml, 2% (w/v) (IP)	Examined cross-drug effect
Riley, Dacanay, & Mastropaolo (1984)	Morphine	6 mg/kg (IP)	5 (72 hr)	Morphine	6 mg/kg (IP)	PRE and COND in same and/or different environments; examined dose for behavioral effects
Riley & Diamond (1998)	Cocaine	32 mg/kg (SC or IP)	5 (daily or 96 hr)	Cocaine	32 mg/kg (SC)	Examined effect of route of administration; examined spaced vs. massed PRE
Riley et al. (1976)	LiCl	1.8 mEq (12 ml/kg), 0.15 M (IP)	6 (96 hr)	LiCl	1.8 mEq (12 ml/kg), 0.15 M (IP)	Examined US PRE effect
Riley & Simpson (1999)	Cocaine	10, 40 mg/kg (IP)	1, 10 (daily)	Cocaine	32 mg/kg (SC)	Examined sensitization
Riley, Barron, et al. (1984)	Ethanol	35% ethanol-derived calories (oral)	15 (GD 6–20)	LiCl	n/a	Examined effect of prenatal US exposure; examined effects of age; cross-drug effect
Risinger & Cunningham (1995)	Ethanol	2, 4 g/kg (20% v/v) (IP)	4 (48 hr)	Ethanol	2, 4 g/kg (20% v/v) (IP)	Examined genetic differences
Rudy et al. (1977)	LiCl	1 cc/100 g, 0.15 M (IP)	4 (daily)	LiCl	1 cc/100 g, 0.15 M (IP)	PRE and COND in same and/or different environments
Shoaib & Stolerman (1996)	Nicotine MK801	0.4 mg/kg (SC) 0.3 mg/kg (IP)	7 (daily)	Nicotine	0.4 mg/kg (SC)	Examined cross-drug effect; examined locomotor tolerance

Reference	Drug	Dose	No.	Drug	Dose	Study Focus
Sjoden et al. (1979)	2,4,5-trichlorophen-oxy-acetic acid	100 mg/kg (intubation)	2 (72 hr)	2,4,5-trichlorophen-oxy-acetic acid	100 mg/kg (intubation)	Examined US PRE effect
J. Stewart & Eikelboom (1978)	Morphine	10 mg/kg (IP)	4 (48 hr)	Morphine	10 mg/kg (IP)	PRE and COND in same and/or different environments; examined analgesic tolerance
Stewart et al. (1991)	Ethanol	10% (v/v) (oral) ad lib	33 (daily)	Ethanol	0.5, 1, 1.5 g/kg (7.5% w/v) (IP)	Examined US PRE effect with alcohol-preferring rats
Suarez & Barker (1976)	LiCl	20 ml/kg, 0.12 M (IP)	6 (96 hr)	LiCl	20 ml/kg, 0.12 M (IP)	Examined effect of PRE–COND interval; examined effect of deprivation state
Switzman et al. (1981)	Morphine Diazepam Delta-9-THC	9 mg/kg (IP) 10 mg/kg (IP) 4 mg/kg (IP)	3 (48 hr)	Morphine Diazepam Delta-9-THC	9 mg/kg (IP) 10 mg/kg (IP) 4 mg/kg (IP)	Examined cross-drug effect
Ton & Amit (1983)	Ethanol Morphine	1.2 g/kg (20%) (IP) 12 mg/kg (IP)	3, 6 (48 hr)	Morphine Ethanol	12 mg/kg (IP) 1.2 g/kg (20%, E) (IP)	Examined cross-drug effect
Ton & Amit (1985a)	Acetaldehyde Morphine	0.2 g/kg (IP) 12 mg/kg (IP)	3 (48 hr)	Morphine Acetaldehyde	12 mg/kg (IP) 0.2 g/kg (IP)	Examined cross-drug effect
Ton & Amit (1985b)	Levorphanol Dextrorphan	5 mg/kg (IP) 5 mg/kg (IP)	3 (48 hr)	Morphine Ethanol	12 mg/kg (IP) 1.2 g/kg (20%)	Examined cross-drug effect
Vogel & Nathan (1976)	Amobarbital Amphetamine	73.4, 120 mg/kg (IP) 2 mg/kg (IP)	1, 3 (96 hr) 5 (daily)	Amobarbital Amphetamine	73.4 mg/kg (IP) 2 mg/kg (IP)	Examined cross-drug effect; examined behavioral tolerance
Wang et al. (1997)	Cooling Area Postrema	HFC-134a (10–60 min)	7 (daily)	Cooling LiCl	HFC-134a (60 min) 2 ml/kg, 0.15 M (IP)	Examined cross manipulation

Reference	Drug	Dose	No.	Drug	Dose	Study Focus
Whaley et al. (1966)	Drum-trauma (shock)	200–3000 rev (40 rpm)	4 (daily)	X-Irradiation	250 kV; 15 mA 60 r (6 r/min)	Examined cross manipulation
Wilner (1978)	LiCl	1.8 mEq/kg, 0.15 M (IP)	5 (120 hr)	LiCl	1.8 mEq/kg, 0.15 M (IP)	PRE and COND in same and/or different environments; examined effect of handling cues

Note. For each preexposure manipulation (*Preexposure*), the drug administered, its dose (and route of administration), and the number of times it was administered (and its temporal spacing) are presented. For each conditioning manipulation (*Conditioning*), both the drug and its dose (and route of administration) are presented. Where multiple drugs and their parameters are listed, the specific preexposure–conditioning relation is not indicated. Finally, the table also lists the specific focus of each study. Throughout the table, PRE = preexposure; COND = conditioning.

1998) have all been reported to affect the degree of attenuation produced by drug preexposure. Factors receiving the most attention in terms of modulating the effects of drug preexposure on aversion learning have been the number of drug preexposures, the dose of the preexposed drug (or its relation to the conditioning dose), the length of time separating drug preexposure and conditioning, and the specific compound used during preexposure and conditioning.

In relation to the number of drug preexposures, several investigators have reported that the degree of the attenuation following drug preexposure is a direct function of the number of such preexposures (see Braveman, 1977; Cannon et al., 1975; Elkins, 1974; Gamzu, 1977; Goudie et al., 1975; Goudie et al., 1976). For example, Cannon et al. (1975) noted that subjects given any preexposure to ethanol (one, three, or five exposures of 4 g/kg of 30% ethanol) displayed weaker ethanol-induced taste aversions (at 4 g/kg) than nonpreexposed subjects and that subjects receiving either three or five preexposures displayed aversions weaker still than subjects receiving only a single preexposure. There was no differential effect for the three and five preexposure conditions (see also Braveman, 1977; Elkins, 1974; Goudie et al., 1976; Vogel & Nathan, 1976). Although the degree of attenuation does vary with the number of preexposures, not all studies report a graded effect of such preexposure. For example, Cappell and LeBlanc (1975a) reported that although amphetamine preexposure (7.5 mg/kg) attenuated amphetamine-induced taste aversions (at 1 mg/kg) this effect was not evident until 20 drug preexposures had been given. Subjects receiving either one or five preexposures displayed no significant preexposure effect. A similar absence of a graded effect with multiple preexposures has been reported with amphetamine and fenfluramine (see Goudie et al., 1975), with nicotine (see Iwamoto & Williamson, 1984), and with LiCl (see Braveman, 1975). The basis for these absences of a graded attenuation with variations in the number of drug preexposures is not known, although it may reflect in part the absolute difference between the specific number of drug preexposures assessed within the individual studies (i.e., whether the differences were large enough to allow for a demonstration of a graded effect) as opposed to the fact that for some drugs under some conditions the nature of the effects of drug preexposure is quantal and not continuous.

A second variable that has received considerable attention in the assessments of drug preexposure on aversion learning has been the effects of variation in the intensity (or dose) of the preexposed drug. Generally, the degree of attenuation is a direct function of the dose of the preexposed drug. For example, Miranda and Vila (1985) assessed the effects of variations in the dose of LiCl given during preexposure on subsequent taste aversion conditioning with a fixed dose of LiCl.

Specifically, they administered either saline (LiCl vehicle), a low dose of LiCl (0.15 M; 2 ml/kg), or a high dose of LiCl (0.7 M; 2 ml/kg) to different groups of subjects prior to taste aversion conditioning in which a novel saccharin solution was paired with LiCl (0.7 M; 2 ml/kg). Although both LiCl-preexposed groups displayed weaker taste aversions than vehicle-preexposed subjects, those preexposed to the lower dose of LiCl displayed the weakest attenuation, eventually drinking the saccharin solution at levels comparable to the vehicle-preexposed subjects after two conditioning trials (for similar graded effects of ethanol preexposure on ethanol-induced taste aversions and estradiol preexposure on estradiol-induced taste aversions; see DeBeun, Lohmann, Schneider, & de Vry, 1996; Merwin & Doty, 1994). Although the attenuating effects of drug preexposure are typically dependent on drug dose, this attenuation is not always a graded function of the intensity of the preexposed drug. For example, LeBlanc and Cappell (1974) exposed rats to either saline (amphetamine vehicle), a low dose of amphetamine (up to 4 mg/kg after 15 days), or a high dose of amphetamine (up to 20 mg/kg after 15 days) during drug preexposure and then assessed the effects of this preexposure on amphetamine-induced taste aversions (at 1 mg/kg). Both amphetamine-preexposed groups displayed attenuated taste aversions; however, there was no differential effect of amphetamine dose during preexposure on the degree of attenuation. This lack of a graded effect of preexposure dose has also been demonstrated with morphine. In an analysis of the effects of exposure to weak (and reinforcing) effects of morphine on morphine-induced taste aversions, T. Hunt, Spivak, and Amit (1985) exposed different groups of rats to 2.5, 5, or 15 mg/kg morphine (every other day for three injections) prior to aversion training with morphine (during which subjects receiving each preexposure dose were conditioned at either 2.5, 5, or 15 mg/kg). There was no effect of the dose of the preexposed drug on morphine-induced taste aversions. That is, all three preexposure doses equally attenuated morphine-induced taste aversions. This absence of a graded effect of preexposure dose was evident at all three conditioning doses of morphine (for similar findings with LiCl, estradiol, and ethanol preexposure, see Cannon et al., 1975; DeBeun, Peeters, & Broekkamp, 1993; Risinger & Cunningham, 1995).

It is not clear why under some conditions variations in the dose of the preexposed drug produce graded attenuation of subsequent aversion learning, whereas under other conditions the attenuation is either present or absent (i.e., it is dependent on some minimally effective dose; see T. Hunt et al., 1985), but some of these differences may be related to the relation between the doses of the preexposed and conditioning drug. As described earlier, Berman and Cannon (1974) exposed rats for 35 consecutive days to a fixed dose of ethanol (5% of a 95% ethanol/decarbonated beer solution) prior to taste aversion conditioning with one of two doses (2 or 5 g/kg) of ethanol. The effects of ethanol preexposure were dependent on the conditioning dose. Specifically, although attenuation was evident under both conditions it was greater (and more complete) at the lower conditioning dose. Taste aversion learning was only partially attenuated for the animals conditioned with the highest dose of ethanol (see also Marfaing-Jallat & LaMagnen, 1979). Similarly, Klein, Mikulka, and Lucci (1986) demonstrated that when the preexposure dose of LiCl was less than (or slightly above) the conditioning dose, the US preexposure effect was weak or not evident. When the preexposure dose was equal to or substantially higher than the conditioning dose, the US preexposure effect was strong (although not different for the varying preexposure doses). These findings simply reveal that there is a relation between preexposure and conditioning doses in terms of the occurrence of the US preexposure effect (see also Cannon et al., 1975). Such a relation may account in part for the differing effects of drug preexposure on taste aversion learning; that is, whether (and the degree to which) it occurs.

In addition to the aforementioned effects of number and intensity of the preexposed drug on the attenuation of taste aversion learning, another variable reported to affect the display of the US preexposure effect is the time between drug preexposure and conditioning. In general, the attenuating effect of drug preexposure is an inverse function of the interval separating preexposure and conditioning (although the specific temporal window varies with the specific drug given during preexposure). In one of the initial assessments of this issue, Cannon et al. (1975) examined the effects of a single exposure to LiCl (0.12 M; 0.02 ml/g) on LiCl-induced taste aversion training (at the same dose used during preexposure) administered 1, 4, and 8 days following LiCl preexposure. Under these conditions, only the subjects conditioned within a single day following preexposure displayed attenuated taste aversions. Subjects conditioned 4 and 8 days following the drug exposure drank at levels comparable to nonpreexposed subjects, indicating a clear loss of the effects of drug preexposure with time. Similar effects were reported with LiCl by Aguado, De Brugada, and Hall (1997). Specifically, they demonstrated that the attenuating effects of LiCl exposure (0.3 M, 10 ml/kg LiCl once a day for 3 days) on LiCl-induced taste aversions (at the same dose given during preexposure) were greatest when conditioning occurred 2 days following drug preexposure. Subjects conditioned after a 15-day delay did not differ from nonpreexposed, conditioned subjects. That is, the 15-day delay completely eliminated the effects of LiCl preexposure (see Experiment 2; see also Cappell & LeBlanc, 1975a, 1977a). Although the attenuation following drug preexposure appears to vary with the interval between preexposure and conditioning, it should be noted that the effect is often weak (see Barker & Johns, 1978; Cappell & LeBlanc, 1977a) or not evident (see Iwamoto & Williamson, 1984, for an assessment of the effects of nicotine preexposure given 1 or 7 days prior to aversion training with nicotine, see Suarez & Barker, 1976, for an assessment of the effects of LiCl preexposure given 2 or 15 days prior to aversion training with LiCl).

The focus of this discussion thus far has been the effect of exposure to a specific compound on subsequent aversion conditioning with that same compound. It should be noted, however, that the US preexposure effect in taste aversion learning has not been limited to such assessments. In fact, shortly after the initial demonstrations that preexposure to a drug affected its ability to condition aversions, others began assessing the cross-drug preexposure effect; that is, where preexposure and conditioning were with two different compounds (the basis for such assessments is discussed later). For example, Braveman (1975) reported that exposure to methylscopolamine (1mg/kg) attenuated LiCl-induced taste aversion learning. Interestingly, this attenuation was a function of the number of preexposures to methylscopolamine (discussed earlier). In the same series of experiments, Braveman extended this cross-drug preexposure effect to other compounds. For example, methylscopolamine preexposure also attenuated amphetamine-induced taste aversions, again as a function of the number of preexposures. In one of the most extensive assessments of cross-drug attenuation, Braveman reported that preexposure to LiCl, methylscopolamine, amphetamine, or mechanical rotation attenuated rotation-induced taste aversions. Interestingly, the attenuation produced by all of the preexposure manipulations was comparable; that is, there were no differential attenuating effects dependent on which compound (or manipulation) was administered during preexposure. Subsequent to these initial demonstrations, a variety of cross-drug preexposure assessments have been made (see Aguado, del Valle, & Perez, 1997; Aragon, Abitol, & Amit, 1986; Bienkowski, Iwinska, et al., 1998; Bienkowski, Piasecki, Koros, Stefanski, & Kostowski, 1998; Brown, Amit, Smith, & Rockman, 1979; Cannon, Baker, & Berman, 1977; Cappell et al., 1975; Cappell & Poulos, 1979; Cunningham & Linakis, 1980; DeBeun et al., 1996; DeBeun, Peeters, & Broekkamp, 1993; DeBeun, Rijk, & Broekkamp, 1993; Ford & Riley, 1984; Gamzu, 1977; Gommans et al., 1998; Goudie & Thornton, 1975; Goudie et al., 1976; W. A. Hunt & Rabin, 1988; Opitz, Mothes, & Clausing, 1997; Preston, Wagner, Seiden, & Schuster, 1984; Rabin, 1996; Rabin et al., 1988; Riley, Barron, Driscoll, & Chen, 1984; Switzman et al., 1981; Ton & Amit, 1985a, 1985b; Vogel & Nathan, 1976; Wang et al., 1997).

Although cross-drug attenuation is often reported, it should be noted that the attenuation is not always symmetrical; that is, preexposure to one drug attenuates aversions induced by another, but not vice versa. For example, Braveman (1975) reported that although methylscopolamine attenuated subsequent amphetamine-induced aversions, amphetamine preexposure did not affect aversions induced by methylscopolamine. Similar asymmetry has been reported for a number of other drug combinations, including amphetamine–fenfluramine (Goudie & Thornton, 1975); foot shock–LiCl (Braveman, 1977); morphine–diazepam (Brown et al., 1979); diazepam–Δ^9 Tetrahydrocannabinol (THC), morphine–diazepam, and morphine–THC (Switzman et al., 1981); radiation–LiCl, ethanol–LiCl, and ethanol–radiation (Rabin et al., 1988); and PBN–amphetamine (Rabin, 1996, where preexposure to the first drug listed fails to attenuate aversion learning to the second drug, but preexposure to the second drug attenuates aversion learning to the first). In other drug combinations, there is no evidence of cross-drug attenuation: chlordiazepoxide–amphetamine and chlordiazepoxide–meprobamate (Gamzu, 1977); methamphetamine–fenfluramine, methamphetamine–morphine and methamphetamine–p-chloramphetamine (Goudie et al., 1976); chlordiazepoxide–d-amphetamine and chlordiazepoxide–morphine (Cappell & LeBlanc, 1975b; Cappell et al., 1975); methylphenidate–atropine (Preston et al., 1984); dextrorphan–morphine and dextrorphan–ethanol (Ton & Amit, 1985b); progesterone–estradiaol and testosterone–estradiaol (DeBeun, Peeters, & Broekkamp, 1993); ipsapirone–ethanol (DeBeun et al., 1996); 1-[meta-chlorophonyl]-piperazine (mCPP)–8-Hydroxy-2-[di-n-propylamino]tetralin (8-OHDPAT), quipazine–8-OHDPAT, pindolol–8-OHDPAT, umespirone–8-OHDPAT, and haloperidol–8-OHDPAT (DeBeun, Rijk, & Broekkamp, 1993); PBN–radiation (Rabin, 1996); ketamine–LiCl (Aguado, del Valle, & Perez, 1997); 1-[m-chlorophenyl]-biguanide (mCPBG)–ethanol (Bienkowski, Iwinska, et al., 1998); and mecamylamine–ethanol (Bienkowski, Piasecki, et al., 1998), where preexposure to the first drug listed fails to attenuate aversion learning to the second drug.

MECHANISMS UNDERLYING THE US PREEXPOSURE EFFECT

In addition to the focus of research assessing the parameters of (or limiting conditions for) the US preexposure effect in aversion learning, considerable attention has been devoted to determining its basis. Although a variety of positions have been presented to account for the attenuating effects of drug preexposure, they generally form two classes of explanations: nonassociative and associative (for reviews, see Cappell & LeBlanc, 1977a; Gamzu, 1977; Randich & LoLordo, 1979). Among the nonassociative processes that have been suggested to occur during drug preexposure are habituation to drug novelty (Brookshire & Brackbill, 1976; Gamzu, 1977), habituation to drug-induced illness (Cain & Baenninger, 1977; Elkins, 1974), the creation of an unnatural need state (dependence; see Parker, Failor, & Weidman, 1973), reward sensitization (Gaiardi et al., 1991), activation of an opponent B process (for a discussion, see Randich & LoLordo, 1979), and development of drug tolerance (LeBlanc & Cappell, 1974; Riley et al., 1976). Associative processes include the acquisition of stimulus associations during preexposure that subsequently interfere with taste aversion learning (i.e., associative blocking; see Batson & Best, 1979; Mikulka, Leard, & Klein, 1977; Rudy, Iwens, & Best, 1977; Willner, 1978) and the development of learned helplessness (or learned irrelevance; for a discussion, see Gamzu, 1977; Randich & LoLordo, 1979) that interferes with learning the subsequently presented consumption–illness or taste–illness association. Of course, these two general accounts do not necessarily preclude each other in that other positions such as the acquisition and display of compensatory conditioning and conditioned tolerance and sensitization combine elements of both the nonassociative and associative models (see Braveman, 1979; Cappell & Poulos, 1979; Poulos & Cappell, 1979).

Nonassociative

Although a wide range of nonassociative processes have been invoked as explanations of the US preexposure effect, they have at least one characteristic in common: They all assume that as a result of drug preexposure the property of the US that is effective in inducing the aversion is lessened or weakened. This change in the efficacy of the US to induce an aversion may result from habituation (or adaptation) to this property (drug novelty or illness); the sensitization of the drug's rewarding effect that masks, interferes, or summates with its aversive effect; the creation of a need state (e.g., morphine dependence) that may change the affective response to the drug; or the development of tolerance to the drug such that the drug itself produces a smaller effect. Although each of these positions has been addressed in assessments of the drug preexposure effect, the one position that has received the most systematic examination has been that of drug tolerance. Consequently, it is the focus of the discussion on nonassociative mechanisms. This is not to suggest that the other nonassociative positions have been systematically tested and rejected. In fact, few empirical assessments have been made of the remaining positions. The current focus on drug tolerance is based on the fact that this position has been more systematically evaluated and the fact that many of the arguments against the remaining nonassociative positions are the same as those that are applied to drug tolerance. Thus, its evaluation provides in part an assessment of the nonassociative positions in general.

Drug tolerance (whether behavioral, pharmacokinetic, or pharmacodynamic) is said to occur when the response to a drug diminishes with repeated exposures to that drug (or to maintain the same response level with repeated administrations of the drug, one has to increase its dose). In some of the initial demonstrations of the US preexposure effect, it was suggested that during preexposure the animal became tolerant to the aversive effects of the drug, thereby reducing its ability to establish taste aversion learning (see Cannon et al., 1975; LeBlanc & Cappell, 1974; Riley et al., 1976). As noted by a number of investigators, although such attenuation was consistent with a tolerance interpretation, this consistency was not support for the tolerance position and amounted to little more than a redescription of the data (see Cappell & LeBlanc, 1977a; Randich & LoLordo, 1979). In fact, in the initial study providing an independent assessment of tolerance (by examining the effects of the preexposed drug on a second behavioral endpoint, sleep) Vogel and Nathan (1976) reported that although five preexposures to the barbiturate amobarbital (73.4 mg/kg) markedly attenuated amobarbital-induced taste aversions (at 73.4 mg/kg) and reduced amobarbital-induced sleep (an index of tolerance), there was no relation between the degree of attenuation and changes in amobarbital-induced sleep. Although it could be argued that rates of tolerance development differ for different indexes (e.g., amobarbital-induced illness and amobarbital-induced sleep), the fact that there was no relation between these two measures seemed problematic for a tolerance interpretation of the US preexposure effect (see also Brookshire & Brackbill, 1976). Subsequent to this report, other investigators began assessing the role of tolerance in the US preexposure effect, either indirectly by assessing tolerance to other behavioral measures during and following the drug preexposure or directly by varying the parameters of drug preexposure in a manner known to affect the development of tolerance. For example, Cannon et al. (1977) demonstrated that ethanol preexposure (up to 6 g/kg daily for 14 consecutive days) attenuated ethanol-induced taste aversions (at 5 g/kg). Following conditioning, the same animals were given a single injection of ethanol and assessed for the amount of time spent on a rotarod (to evaluate ethanol-induced suppression of motor performance). Animals with no history of ethanol spent little time on the rotarod (indicative of ethanol's effect on motor behavior). On the other hand, subjects receiving ethanol during preexposure (and those that displayed attenuated ethanol-induced taste aversions) spent significantly longer times on the rotarod, indicative of tolerance to ethanol's debilitating effects on motor behavior (see also Berman & Cannon, 1974; Fischer, Gilman, & Blank, 1987; W. A. Hunt & Rabin, 1988; Shoaib & Stolerman, 1996, for similar assessments of tolerance development; see also Barker & Johns, 1978; Risinger & Cunningham, 1995; R. B. Stewart, McBride, Lumeng, Li, & Murphy, 1991). As noted earlier, although such independent assessments indicate that tolerance can develop to the drug during preexposure, they do not directly test whether tolerance has occurred to the illness-inducing effects of the compound.

More direct assessments have been provided by investigators who have varied the parameters of the drug preexposure in a manner known to affect the development of tolerance. Such parameters include the number of drug preexposures, the dose of the preexposed drug, and the time between preexposure and conditioning. In relation to the effects of temporal parameters on the US preexposure effect, such parametric variations do affect the degree of attenuation produced by the preexposed drug (see Generality and Experimental Parameters of US Preexposure). For example, Cappell and LeBlanc (1975b) exposed rats to amphetamine (up to 20 mg/kg daily for 25 consecutive days) prior to taste aversion conditioning with amphetamine (at 1 mg/kg). The subjects differed in terms of the number of days separating the last preexposure injection and the first day of conditioning (0, 1, 7, or 14 days). Subjects conditioned immediately following preexposure or following a delay of 1 day displayed attenuated aversions, drinking at levels comparable to nonconditioned subjects. Subjects conditioned 7 and 14 days following preexposure also displayed attenuated aversions; however, as the time increased between preexposure and conditioning, the attenuating effects of amphetamine preexposure weakened. Specifically, both of these latter two groups differed from nonconditioned subjects with the degree of the difference greater with increased delays. Further, with repeated conditioning trials, subjects conditioned following a 14-day delay drank at levels comparable to nonpreexposed, conditioned subjects; that is, there was no evidence of amphetamine preexposure after repeated conditioning trials (see Cannon et al., 1975, and Cappell & LeBlanc, 1977a for similar temporal analyses with LiCl and morphine preexposure, respectively; see also Aguado, De Brugada, & Hall, 1997; Barker & Johns, 1978; cf. Iwamoto & Williamson, 1984; Suarez & Barker, 1976). Although such investigations directly manipulate parameters that affect tolerance, they do not rule out the possibility that other processes (both nonassociative and associative) are similarly affected (discussed later). As such, results from these investigations do not provide unequivocal support for the tolerance position.

The development of tolerance to the illness-inducing effects of the drug during preexposure does appear adequate to account for the US preexposure effect; however, it should be noted that this position cannot be the explanation for all instances of drug preexposure. As noted earlier, when independent assessments of tolerance have been made within the drug preexposure preparation, not all investigators have reported changes in response to the drug (other than attenuated aversions; see Batson, 1983; Brookshire & Brackbill, 1976; Suarez & Barker, 1976; Vogel & Nathan, 1976). Further, not all manipulations known to produce (or modulate the development of) tolerance affect the US preexposure effect. For example, Cappell and LeBlanc (1977b) gave different groups of rats 15 exposures to morphine (up to 40 mg/kg) or amphetamine (4 mg/kg) either massed (once a day) or spaced (every fourth day) prior to taste aversion conditioning with either morphine (at 10 mg/kg) or amphetamine (at 1 mg/kg). For both drugs, preexposure attenuated subsequent taste aversion learning with the preexposed drug. However, there were no differential attenuating effects of the massed or spaced administration. This finding is somewhat at odds with a tolerance interpretation in that tolerance is known to be affected by the spacing or the frequency of the repeated drug injections (see Goldstein, Aronov, & Kalman, 1974). One might argue that in the Cappell and LeBlanc study, maximal tolerance had occurred. That is, because of the extended number of preexposure injections, the rate at which they were given could produce no greater tolerance. However, in a similar analysis of the effects of massed versus spaced cocaine, Riley and Diamond (1998) reported that five cocaine preexposures (32 mg/kg; once a day or every fourth day) produced equal attenuation of cocaine-induced taste aversions (at 32 mg/kg; see also Riley & Simpson, 1999). Thus, under less extensive preexposure conditions there was still no evidence of any effect of the frequency of drug preexposure (see Fig. 13.3). One final concern with the tolerance account of drug preexposure comes from the finding that preexposure to one drug may attenuate aversions induced by another (i.e., the cross-drug preexposure effect). The major difficulty that this finding has for the tolerance account concerns the issue of cross-tolerance; that is, to account for the cross-drug preexposure effect by the tolerance position, it must be assumed that drug preexposure produces tolerance to both the preexposed and conditioning drugs. Although possible, such cross-tolerance has not been empirically assessed (but see W. A. Hunt & Rabin, 1988; see also Braveman, 1977). The issue becomes even more difficult when one considers that not all cross-drug preexposure effects are symmetrical in nature. That is, although preexposure to one drug may attenuate aversion learning to another, exposure to this second drug may have no attenuating effects on aversions induced by the first drug (as discussed earlier). To account for this asymmetry, it must be as-

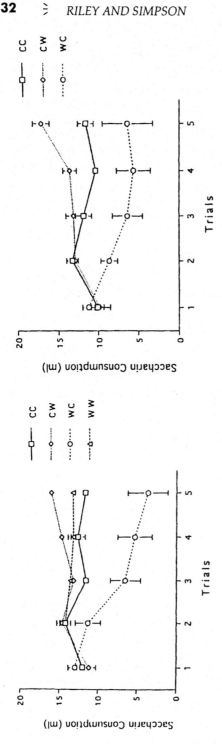

FIG. 13.3.   The left panel depicts the mean (+/− SEM) saccharin consumption by rats receiving saccharin–cocaine (32 mg/kg; Groups CC and WC) or saccharin–distilled water (Groups CW and WW) pairings during taste aversion conditioning. The first letter in each group designation refers to the injection given during preexposure, that is, cocaine (C) or water (W). The second letter refers to the injection given during conditioning. All preexposures were given subcutaneously every fourth day for a total of five preexposures. The right panel depicts saccharin consumption for similarly treated rats except that all preexposures were given daily for 5 consecutive days. From Riley and Diamond (1998). Reprinted with permission of Elsevier Science.

sumed that cross-tolerance is not bidirectional. Again, although cross-tolerance may be dependent on the specific drug to which the animal has first been exposed, there are no independent assessments of the differential development of tolerance within the cross-drug preexposure preparation. One is left with data that may be consistent with the tolerance account but may not necessarily empirically test (or substantiate) this explanation.

Associative

Concurrent with the investigations into the role of nonassociative factors such as tolerance in the US preexposure effect, others were assessing the contribution of associative factors (i.e., conditioning). Although several associative models have been assessed for their mediation of the US preexposure effect in aversion learning, only associative blocking has been systematically evaluated. Given this and the fact that many assessments of associative blocking also apply to other associative models, only blocking is discussed in this analysis (for discussions of associative models, see Braveman, 1977; Randich & LoLordo, 1979).

The basis for assuming a role for blocking arose from the fact that a substantial literature existed demonstrating that preexposure to a nondrug stimulus (e.g., shock) interfered with subsequent conditioning with that US. One account of this interference was that environmental or contextual cues in which the shock was given became associated with the shock and subsequently blocked the establishment of other cue–shock associations when conditioning was attempted in the presence of these previously conditioned cues (given the limited amount of associative strength that could be supported by a single US, in this case shock; Rescorla & Wagner, 1972). The application of such an analysis to the US preexposure effect in taste aversion learning seemed clear. During preexposure, a variety of stimuli such as handling cues, the injection per se, the specific environment in which the animal receives the drug preexposure, and deprivation-related stimuli (see Peck & Ader, 1974) become associated with the drug. When a taste is then paired with the drug during conditioning in the presence of these same drug-associated cues, taste aversion conditioning is blocked, an attenuation based on the animal's prior associative history. If the US preexposure effect in aversion learning is due to associative blocking, several predictions can be made about the strength or display of this attenuation. First, the attenuating effects of drug preexposure should only be evident when taste aversion conditioning is attempted in the presence of these previously conditioned cues (those associated with the preexposed drug). Only under these conditions should the previously acquired associations interfere with taste aversion conditioning. If aversion conditioning is attempted in the absence of these cues, there should be no attenuating effects of preexposure on conditioning. Second, manipulations known to affect associative blocking (e.g., familiarization to the stimuli that will be paired with the US during preexposure, changes in the predictive relation of the US-associated stimuli during preexposure, or nonreinforced presentations of the US-associated stimuli following preexposure but prior to conditioning) should similarly affect the attenuating effects of drug preexposure on taste aversion learning. Both of these general predictions have been tested.

For example, in relation to the importance of the similarity of the preexposure and conditioning cues a variety of researchers have assessed the effects of training animals in one specific context (or under one specific set of conditions) and conditioning the subjects under these or different conditions. In one of the initial studies assessing the contribution of blocking, Mikulka et al. (1977) demonstrated that animals exposed to LiCl (3 mEq, 0.15 M LiCl every other day for a total of four injections) prior to aversion conditioning (sucrose paired with the same dose of LiCl) displayed the US preexposure effect (i.e., weaker aversions than nonpreexposed subjects conditioned with LiCl). This attenuation, however, was not evident in subjects for which LiCl had been explicitly paired with a novel sodium chloride (NaCl) solution during preexposure. That is, signaling the LiCl exposures with one taste eliminated the US preexposure effect with LiCl. Given that blocking should only be evident when conditioning was attempted in the presence of the stimuli paired with the drug during preexposure, these results were consistent with a blocking interpretation of the US preexposure effect (see also Danguir & Nicolaidis, 1977; although for reports of no differences between signaled and unsignaled preexposures, see Cannon et al., 1975; Riley et al., 1976; see also Corcoran, 1973).

In a related study, Rudy et al. (1977) reported that animals given four exposures to LiCl (0.15 M; 1 cc/100 g) in a black chamber prior to aversion training (LiCl at the same dose) in that same black chamber displayed attenuated taste aversions, again an effect consistent with a blocking interpretation. Interestingly, subjects exposed to the drug in the black chamber and conditioned in the home cages (i.e., a different environment from that in which the drug preexposures had been given) also showed attenuated aversions, not drinking significantly different amounts from those consumed by animals preexposed and conditioned in the same environment. Although this latter result seems at odds with an associative interpretation, Rudy et al. suggested that the stimulus associated with the drug during preexposure was not the actual chamber in which exposure occurred but the handling cues that accompanied the injection (however, see Braveman, 1978). All subjects had experience with such handling and consequently should not have readily associated these cues with the drug during preexposure (because of latent inhibition; see Lubow, 1973). However, the fact that those exposed to the drug in the novel black chamber displayed the attenuated aversions suggests that placement into the novel environment disrupted this latent inhibition to the handling cues, allowing them to be associated with the drug. When subsequent taste aversion conditioning was then attempted, the previously conditioned handling cues blocked the saccharin–LiCl association, thereby attenuating taste aversion learning. Animals preexposed and conditioned in the home cage displayed significantly less attenuation than that displayed by subjects preexposed in the black chambers, an effect likely due to the fact that the latently inhibited handling cues were not able to be associated with the drug (or not as much as in the subjects preexposed in the chambers) and as such did not block aversion conditioning.

Subsequent to this work, others have demonstrated that the environmental context itself can become associated with the drug during preexposure and block taste aversion conditioning. For example, Willner (1978) exposed rats to LiCl (five exposures of 1.8 mEq, 0.15 M LiCl) in a distinctive environment prior to taste aversion conditioning with LiCl (at the same dose) in the distinctive environment or the home cage. Consistent with blocking, only the subjects preexposed and conditioned in the distinctive environment displayed attenuated aversions. Those subjects preexposed in the distinctive environment and conditioned in the home cages avoided the LiCl-associated saccharin solution at the same level as nonpreexposed, conditioned subjects. Such an environment-specific US preexposure effect has now been widely reported (see Batson & Best, 1979; Braveman, 1979; Cole, VanTilburg, Burch-Vernon, & Riccio, 1996; Dacanay & Riley, 1982; Domjan & Best, 1980).

In addition to the previously mentioned work assessing the role of blocking in the US preexposure effect by changing the preexposure and conditioning environments, a variety of manipulations known to affect associative blocking have been tested for their ability to modulate the attenuating effects of drug preexposure on aversion learning. For example, Cappell and Poulos (1979) exposed rats to injections of saline for 4 days prior to amphetamine preexposure (7.5 mg/kg) as well as on days between each exposure to amphetamine (a total of 15 such preexposures given every fifth day) in an attempt to reduce the ability of handling and injection cues to be associated with the drug during preexposure. Subjects were then given pairings of saccharin and amphetamine (at 1 mg/kg) during aversion conditioning. If handling and injection cues do become associated with the drug during preexposure and subsequently block taste aversion conditioning, such familiarization should reduce their ability to become associated with the drug. As predicted, subjects handled and injected with saline prior to (and during) drug preexposure displayed less of a preexposure effect than subjects that were not handled or injected. Similarly, Willner (1978) demonstrated that subjects receiving LiCl exposure (1.8 mEq 0.15 M; every fifth day for a total of five exposures) prior to aversion conditioning with LiCl (at the same dose) displayed attenuated aversions to an LiCl-associated saccharin solution. However, subjects that received saline injections on days intervening between the multiple drug preexposures displayed significantly less attenuation than subjects that did not receive the intervening saline injections. According to Willner, the intervening saline injections degraded the association between the handling and injection cues and the drug. When aversion conditioning was subsequently attempted, these cues were less able to block the saccharin–LiCl association. Finally, Batson and Best (1979) demonstrated that nonreinforced exposures to the environment in which LiCl preexposures (eight injections of 0.15 M; 10 ml/kg) had been given eliminated the US preexposure effect. That is, reducing the previously established association between the environment and the drug by placing the animals in the environment without subsequent drug injections prevented these environmental cues from subsequently blocking taste aversion conditioning with LiCl (at the same dose) in that environment. Again, such an effect is consistent with an associative account of the US preexposure effect (see also Cunningham & Linakis, 1980; Poulos & Cappell, 1979).

Although blocking appears to be able to account for the US preexposure effect in aversion learning and has received considerable empirical support, it is not a sufficient account of the attenuating effects of drug preexposure. Specifically, a variety of findings seem inexplicable by this associative account. First, as noted earlier, signaled versus unsignaled drug preexposures do not always result in differential attenuation. For example, Cannon et al. (1975) found only marginal differences in the degree of attenuation between groups of subjects receiving a single LiCl preexposure (0.12 M; 0.02 ml/g) signaled by a taste different from that given during subsequent conditioning. Given that a blocking interpretation would predict that animals conditioned in the absence of the drug-associated stimulus (in the case of Cannon et al., 1975, an NaCl solution) should display no attenuation, these results argue against an associative mechanism. Similar nondifferential effects have also been reported with LiCl by Riley et al. (1976).

Further, the attenuating effects of drug preexposure are not always environment dependent (see Cannon et al., 1975; Dacanay & Riley, 1982; Domjan & Siegel, 1983; Ford & Riley, 1984; Stewart & Eikelboom, 1978). For example, Dacanay and Riley (1982) reported that animals preexposed to morphine (five injections of 40 mg/kg morphine) in a distinctive environment displayed attenuated morphine-induced taste aversions (at 40 mg/kg), independent of whether aversion conditioning occurred in the distinctive environment or the home cage (an environment different from that in which the drug was preexposed; see Fig. 13.4; see also Domjan &

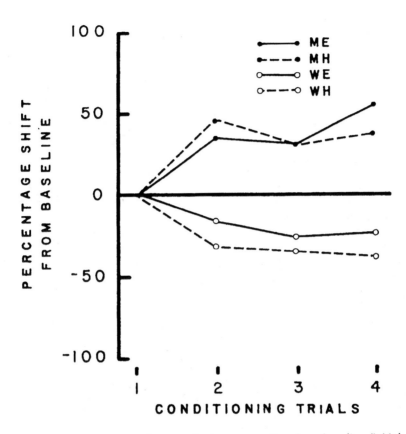

FIG. 13.4. Percentage shift in saccharin consumption from baseline (initial conditioning trial) over repeated conditioning trials for rats receiving saccharin–morphine (40 mg/kg) pairings during taste aversion conditioning in a distinctive environment (ME and WE) or the home cage (Groups MH and WH). Preexposures—morphine (M) or water (W)—were given in the distinctive environment for all groups. From Dacanay and Riley (1982). Reprinted with permission of Psychonomic Society.

Siegel, 1983; Stewart & Eikelboom, 1978). This failure to see an environment-specific preexposure effect was not likely a result of other stimuli being associated with the drug during preexposure (e.g., injection, handling, or deprivation cues) that subsequently blocked taste aversion learning in animals conditioned in both the distinctive and home cage environments. Specifically, animals exposed to LiCl (1.8 mEq; 0.15 M) in the distinctive environment during preexposure (as opposed to morphine) and injected with the same dose of LiCl during conditioning displayed a clear environment-specific US preexposure effect (see Fig. 13.5). Clearly, the environmental context (in this case the distinctive en-

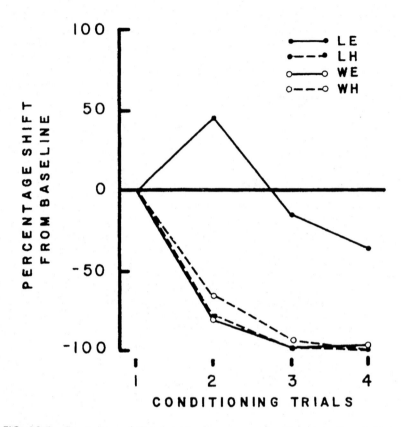

FIG. 13.5. Percentage shift in saccharin consumption from baseline (initial conditioning trial) over repeated conditioning trials for rats receiving saccharin–LiCl (1.8 mEq, 0.15M) pairings during taste aversion conditioning in a distinctive environment (LE and WE) or the home cage (Groups LH and WH). Preexposures, that is, LiCl (L) or water (W), were given in the distinctive environment for all groups. From Dacanay and Riley (1982). Reprinted with permission of Psychonomic Society.

vironment) was associable with LiCl. The failure of its becoming associated with morphine and selectively attenuating aversion learning is unclear (discussed later).

Finally, it is uncertain how blocking can account for the cross-drug preexposure effect (and its often-reported asymmetry). In assessments of blocking with other USs (e.g., shock), variations in the intensity of the shock from preexposure to conditioning result in "unblocking." Under such conditions, stimuli paired with the changed shock intensity acquire associative strength. The fact that exposure to a specific drug can attenuate aversions to different drugs, thus, would assume that the aversive effects of the two drugs are similar (for a related discussion with different doses of the same drug, see T. Hunt et al., 1985). It should be noted, however, that this is only an assumption in that there have been few independent assessments of their similarity (outside of the fact that exposure to one drug attenuates aversions to a second; see Bienkowski, Plasecki, et al., 1998; DeBeun et al., 1996; for related discussions, see Gaiardi, Bartoletti, Gubellini, Bacchi, & Babbini, 1998; Goudie, Leathley, McNally, & West, 1989).

It is interesting in this context that although the work on the cross-drug preexposure effect is quite extensive, only a single study has examined whether this effect is environment specific. In that single study, Ford and Riley (1984) examined the effects of LiCl preexposure (exposure to 1.8 mEq; 0.15 M LiCl every fourth day for five injections) on amphetamine-induced aversions (at 2 mg/kg). The preexposures occurred in a distinctive environment (different from the animal's home cage), whereas taste aversion conditioning occurred in either the distinctive environment or the home cage. Under these conditions, LiCl preexposure attenuated amphetamine-induced taste aversions, independent of the similarity of the preexposure and conditioning environments, arguing against an associative interpretation of this specific cross-drug attenuation (see Fig. 13.6).

Blocking may also have difficulties with the asymmetry often noted in assessments of the cross-drug US preexposure effect. As described earlier, it is often the case that preexposure to one drug attenuates aversions induced by a second drug; however, this attenuation is not evident when the positions of the two drugs are reversed; that is, the attenuation is unidirectional (discussed earlier). If it is argued that the attenuation obtained when Drug A is given prior to conditioning with Drug B is due to blocking (which is a function of the similarity of the two drugs), it is difficult to explain the failure to obtain similar attenuation when Drug B is given prior to Drug A. To account for the absence of attenuation in this latter case in a manner consistent with a blocking interpretation, it has to be argued that the two drugs are not identical or that they differ in ways sufficient for them to be seen as different compounds. Their perceived similarity, therefore, would have to be dependent on the order of presentation. Although possible, such suggestions have not been empirically tested within the aversion design.

Interaction of Associative and Nonassociative Processes

In the examination of tolerance and blocking as processes mediating the US preexposure effect in aversion learning, it becomes clear that neither

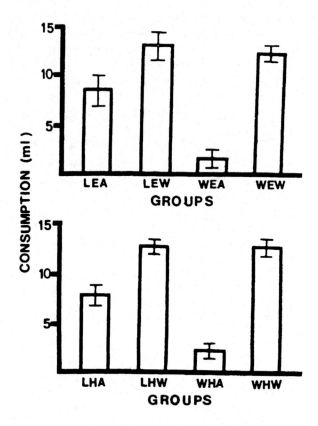

FIG. 13.6. Mean consumption (+/– SEM) of saccharin for rats receiving saccharin–amphetamine (2 mg/kg) or saccharin–water pairings during aversion conditioning. The first letter in each group designation refers to the injections given during preexposure, that is, lithium (L) or water (W). Preexposures were given in a distinctive environment for all groups. The second letter refers to the conditioning environment, that is, distinctive environment (E) or home cage (H). The third letter refers to the drug given during conditioning, i.e., amphetamine (A) or water (W). From Ford and Riley (1984). Reprinted with permission of Elsevier Science.

of the two can provide a complete account of the attenuating effects of drug preexposure. As described earlier, although a substantial set of data can be explained by each of the two processes, another set of data, equally substantial, seems inconsistent with each account. What becomes difficult is attempting to determine the basis for the fact that under some conditions the effects of drug preexposure appear nonassociative in nature, whereas under others the effects appear to be due to an associative mechanism. In an earlier attempt at determining the nature of the US preexposure effect, Dacanay and Riley (1982) argued that the basis for the US preexposure effect was drug specific. This position was based on the fact that under identical preexposure and conditioning procedures, the attenuating effects of LiCl preexposures on LiCl-induced taste aversions were environment specific (i.e., associative), whereas the attenuating effects of morphine preexposure on morphine-induced taste aversions were independent of the preexposure and conditioning environments (nonassociative; discussed earlier). Suggesting that different mechanisms mediated the US preexposure effect with LiCl and morphine was consistent with other taste aversion work with these two compounds in which aversions induced by LiCl and morphine differed in other respects, such as, rate of acquisition of the aversion, strength of the aversion, variability, physiological mechanism, and changes in hedonic reactivity (see T. Hunt, Segal, & Amit, 1987; Parker, 1995; Riley, Jacobs, & LoLordo, 1978; Siegel, Parker, & Moroz, 1995; Sklar & Amit, 1977).

Although the apparently different bases for the preexposure effect with LiCl and morphine are consistent with these other findings, there are several concerns with concluding that the nature of the US preexposure effect is drug dependent. First, this is simply descriptive and provides no basis for any differential mechanisms. Second, such a conclusion would be based on only a handful of drugs for which an associative or nonassociative mechanism has been examined, specifically LiCl, morphine, amphetamine, and ethanol. That is, although the US preexposure effect has been extensively examined, conclusions regarding the nature of this effect are limited to these four drugs. Any conclusions regarding the nature of the US preexposure effect would have to be cautiously made. Third, even for these four drugs that have been examined, the conclusions about underlying mechanisms are not always consistent. For example, the attenuating effects with LiCl are generally concluded as being associative in nature (due primarily to the blocking of taste aversion conditioning by drug-associated contextual cues). However, several studies have shown that LiCl's attenuating effects occur when LiCl is signaled (Cannon et al., 1975; Riley et al., 1976), when preexposure and conditioning occur in different environments (Cannon et al., 1975), and when the LiCl-associated handling cues are latently inhibited (Braveman, 1978). This is not to argue that the preexposure effect with LiCl is not associative in nature, only that blocking does not unequivocally account for LiCl's attenuating effects under all conditions. Conversely, morphine's effects are generally described as nonassociative in nature (due primarily to the development of tolerance). However, several studies have shown that nonreinforced exposures to morphine-associated contextual cues (either before, during, or after drug preexposure; see Cappell & Poulos, 1979; Poulos & Cappell, 1979) abate the effects of morphine preexposure on morphine-induced taste aversions. Again, these data do not argue that the US preexposure effect with morphine is not nonassociative, only that tolerance does not unequivocally account for morphine's attenuating effects under all conditions. Support for both associative and nonassociative accounts has also been provided for the attenuating effects of ethanol (see Barker & Johns, 1978; Berman & Cannon, 1974; Cannon et al., 1977; Cunningham & Linakis, 1980) and amphetamine (Cappell & LeBlanc, 1975a, 1977b; Cappell & Poulos, 1979; LeBlanc & Cappell, 1974; Poulos & Cappell, 1979) preexposure.

Although these different conclusions for the same drug can possibly be a result of different procedures used in the assessment of the US preexposure effect across different studies, we have reported that under similar experimental conditions both associative and nonassociative mechanisms mediate the attenuating effects of methadone on methadone-induced taste aversions (see Dacanay, Mastropaolo, & Riley, 1986). Specifically, rats were given either 5 or 10 exposures to methadone (12 mg/kg every fourth day) in a distinctive environment prior to taste aversion conditioning with methadone (at 12 mg/kg) in either the distinctive environment or the home cage. Animals receiving the 5 methadone preexposures displayed environment-specific attenuation; that is, the US preexposure effect appeared to be due to blocking for this group of subjects (see Fig. 13.7). On the other hand, animals receiving the 10 preexposures to methadone displayed attenuated aversions independent of the similarity of the preexposure and conditioning environments; that is, the US preexposure effect appeared to be due to tolerance for this group of subjects (see Fig. 13.8). Dacanay et al. (1986) suggested that during methadone preexposure contextual stimuli did in fact become associated with methadone. Further, tolerance was also occurring during the drug preexposure. When 10 preexposures were given, this tolerance was complete, and as such the drug was ineffective in inducing aversions, independent of where conditioning was attempted (distinctive environment or home cage). On the other hand, with 5 preexposures, tolerance was not complete and the drug-associated stimuli were able to block the ability of methadone to induce an aversion in an environment-specific manner. This study clearly argues that any conclusions regarding the drug-specific nature of the US preexposure effect can only be made after systematic evaluation of the conditions under which the effect is being demonstrated. It further suggests that an interaction between associative and nonassociative processes may be important for understanding the basis of the attenuating effects of

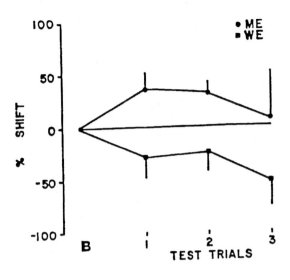

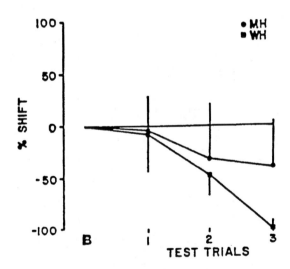

FIG. 13.7. The top panel depicts percentage shift (+/− SD) in saccharin consumption from baseline (B) over repeated conditioning trials for rats receiving
saccharin–methadone (12 mg/kg) pairings during aversion conditioning. The
first letter in each group designation refers to the injections given during
preexposure, that is, methadone (M) or water (W) every fourth day for a total of
five injections. Preexposure and conditioning were given in the distinctive environment (E) for all groups. The bottom panel depicts data for rats preexposed in
the distinctive environment but conditioned in the home cage (H).

543

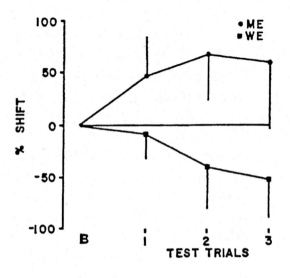

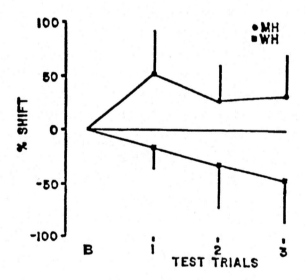

FIG. 13.8. The top panel depicts percentage shift (+/− SD) in saccharin consumption from baseline (B) over repeated conditioning trials for rats receiving
saccharin–methadone (12 mg/kg) pairings during aversion conditioning following preexposure to either methadone (M) or water (W) every fourth day for a
total of 10 injections. Preexposure and conditioning were given in the distinctive
environment (E) for all groups. The bottom panel depicts data for rats
preexposed in the distinctive environment but conditioned in the home cage
(H).

drug preexposure on taste aversion learning. Whether this interaction can account for the apparent discrepencies noted for the aforementioned compounds awaits empirical test.

IMPLICATIONS FOR DRUG USE AND ABUSE

The focus of this chapter to this point has been exploring the attenuating effect of drug preexposure on aversion learning and in so doing its generality, the experimental conditions under which it occurs, and its possible bases. The title of the chapter, however, offered a promissory note about its implications for drug use and abuse. The literature on the preexposure effect, although extensive, has not directly addressed these possible implications, but other work on taste aversion learning suggests that the aversive effects of a drug may directly impact drug-taking behavior (discussed later). Manipulations that affect a drug's aversiveness (e.g., drug preexposure) thus, may in turn affect drug taking.

Although taste aversion learning was initially demonstrated with compounds (and manipulations) known to be toxic or aversive as indexed in other preparations (see Riley & Tuck, 1985b), the range of compounds reported to induce taste aversions rapidly extended beyond these known agents. Some of these latter compounds included known recreational drugs, such as alcohol, morphine, marijuana, amphetamine, and cocaine. The finding that recreational drugs induced taste aversion learning initially seemed paradoxical in that by virtue of their use it was presumed that these compounds were reinforcing (see Goudie, 1979, 1985; T. Hunt & Amit, 1987; for a recent discussion of this issue, see Grigson, 1997).

This apparent paradox was initially noted based on findings from separate and procedurally very different studies. For example, the reinforcing properties of compounds like morphine and amphetamine were demonstrated in a variety of preparations known to assess such properties, such as self-administration, conditioned place preferences, electrical brain stimulation, and reinstatement (see Bozarth, 1987), whereas their aversive properties were demonstrated within the conditioned taste aversion design (see Cappell & LeBlanc, 1977a; Riley & Tuck, 1985b). That these differential properties were evident under such different parametric conditions suggested that these variations (or some facet of the procedures themselves) may be responsible in part for the specific effect demonstrated. However, others have reported that the aversive and reinforcing properties of such compounds could be demonstrated within the same preparation. For example, in one of the initial examinations of the aversive and reinforcing properties of drugs under similar experimental conditions, Wise, Yokel, and DeWitt (1976) reported that rats trained to press a lever for intravenous injections of apomorphine or amphetamine acquired an aversion to a novel taste available during the presentation of the self-administered drugs. That is, under identical experimental conditions, both apomorphine and amphetamine appeared to have both reinforcing and aversive properties. Why the reinforcing properties appeared to become associated with the operant response and the aversive properties associated with the taste of the concurrently available solution has been the subject of considerable debate (see Gamzu, 1977; Goudie, 1985). The fact remains, however, that both affective responses (reward and aversion) occurred to the same drug (and presumably at the same time). Similar demonstrations of both rewarding and aversive effects have been reported when subjects run down a runway for morphine-adulterated food (see White, Sklar, & Amit, 1977). Under these conditions, animals tend to run faster to get to the food (an index of morphine's rewarding effects), but suppress consumption of the food upon entering the goal box in which the morphine-adulterated food is located (an index of morphine's aversive effects). When the food is adulterated with LiCl, both the running speed and the amount consumed decrease, effects consistent with the position that LiCl is only aversive (see also Corrigall, Linesman, D'Onofrio, & Lei, 1986; Sherman, Pickman, Rice, Liebeskind, & Holman, 1980; Stefurak, Martin, & van der Kooy, 1990; Turenne, Miles, Parker, & Siegel, 1996).

The importance of a drug producing both rewarding and aversive effects may lie in how these effects interact to affect drug taking. As suggested by many (see Baker & Cannon, 1982; Berman & Cannon, 1974; Cannon & Carrell, 1987a, 1987b; Ettenberg, Sgro, & White, 1982; Gaiardi et al., 1991; Gaiardi et al., 1998; Gauvin & Holloway, 1992; Gorman, De Obaldia, Scott, & Reid, 1978; Goudie, 1979; Goudie et al., 1975; Goudie & Thornton, 1975; Sanudo-Pena et al., 1997; R. B. Stewart et al., 1991; Stolerman & D'Mello, 1981; Swtzman et al., 1981), the degree to which each of these two effects occur for any specific drug may impact the likelihood of subsequent use, that is, if the aversive effects are dominant over the rewarding effects, the likelihood of subsequent use may be reduced (see Goudie, 1979, 1985; Stolerman & D'Mello, 1981). As described earlier, exposure to a drug prior to aversion conditioning attenuates subsequent aversion learning. Independent of the specific mechanism thought to underlie this attenuation (either associative or nonassociative), the drug's aversiveness (or the ability of its aversive effects to be associated with concurrently administered stimuli) appears reduced as a result of the preexposure. If the probability of drug taking is a function of the interaction of the drug's aversive and reinforcing effects, any reduction in its aversive effects may result in a relative increase in its perceived rewarding effects and an increase in its use (for related discussions, see Ettenberg et al., 1982; Pizzi & Cook, 1996; Siegel et al., 1995).

Support for this possibility has been reported by several investigators assessing the effects of drug exposure on the reinforcing and aversive effects of a variety of recreational compounds. For example, R. B. Stewart et al. (1991) reported that rats given continuous access to both ethanol (10% v/v) and water for 33 days increased consumption of ethanol over the exposure period. Following this free-choice exposure to ethanol and water, the subjects were given access to a polycose solution and then injected with one of a number of doses of ethanol (0.5, 1, or 1.5 g/kg). Consumption of the ethanol-associated polycose solution by the ethanol-preexposed subjects was then compared to that of subjects given only water access during preexposure but which also received the polycose–ethanol pairings (as well as to control subjects that received polycose alone). At the highest dose of ethanol paired with polycose, all conditioned subjects avoided the ethanol-paired flavor, independent of preexposure condition (i.e., ethanol and water vs. water). At the two lower doses of ethanol, however, rats preexposed to ethanol drank significantly more than the ethanol-naive subjects (those receiving water alone during preexposure). In fact, at the lowest dose of ethanol there was evidence of a preference for the ethanol-associated polycose solution (relative to nonconditioned subjects). These findings suggest that chronic ethanol exposure weakens the aversive effects of ethanol, a reduction that may be underlying the increased consumption of ethanol during its free choice (see Gauvin & Holloway, 1992; see also Gorman et al., 1978, for a similar analysis of changes in the free-choice consumption of a sweetened morphine solution; but see Shoaib & Almeida, 1996). Consistent with this interpretation that the waning of ethanol's aversive effects may mediate an increase in its reinforcing value (and acceptability) is the fact that for selected strains of rats the preference for ethanol in a free-choice situation is correlated with the ability of ethanol to induce a taste aversion, again suggesting that the aversive effects of ethanol may initially limit its acceptance (see Cannon & Carrell, 1987b; but see Cannon, Leeka, & Block, 1994).

In a related experiment to that of R. B. Stewart et al. (1991), Gaiardi et al. (1991) assessed the effects of morphine preexposure on the ability of morphine to condition both place preferences and aversions. Specifically, animals receiving morphine exposure (20 mg/kg daily for 12 consecutive days) prior to place preference conditioning with morphine (2.5 mg/kg) displayed a significantly greater conditioned place preference relative to drug-naive subjects. Conversely, animals receiving morphine exposure (20 mg/kg daily for 21 consecutive days) prior to taste aversion conditioning with morphine (10 or 20 mg/kg) displayed significantly weaker taste aversions relative to drug-naive subjects. Thus, preexposure affected both measures, albeit in opposite ways. Given that the aversive effects of morphine are reduced with exposure (as indexed by an attenuated taste aversion), it is possible that this reduction increased the relative reinforcing value of morphine, an increase that was reflected in the facilitated acquisition of a conditioned place preference to morphine (see Gaiardi et al., 1991, for an alternative interpretation). Such changes in the aversive properties of morphine with repeated exposures clearly may be involved in the affective response to morphine and may facilitate its use (for similar analysis with phencyclidine, see Kitaichi, Noda, Hasegawa, Furukawa, & Nabeshima, 1996; but see Gaiardi, Bartoletti, Bacchi, Gubellini, & Babbini, 1997).

Similar support for changes in the aversive (and reinforcing) properties of alcohol with chronic exposure has been reported by Kiefer, Bice, and Badia-Elder (1994). Specifically, Kiefer et al. used a taste reactivity preparation (see Grill & Norgren, 1978) in which the animals' orofacial ingestive and rejection responses were measured to infusions of ethanol into the mouth to index the rewarding and aversive properties of the ethanol solution, respectively. Using this preparation, they reported that rats given continuous access to 10% ethanol and water (for 6 weeks) displayed a decrease in rejection responses to infused ethanol (at concentrations ranging from 10% to 40%). They further showed an increase in ingestive responses to the same ethanol concentrations. Animals without the chronic ethanol exposure showed no changes in taste reactivity to ethanol over repeated taste reactivity tests. As discussed earlier, the affective responses to ethanol appear to have changed with exposure from aversive to reinforcing, a change that may have modulated its acceptance during its continuous access. Similar decreases in the rejection responses to infusions of a cocaine-associated saccharin solution have recently been demonstrated in our laboratory in animals exposed to cocaine (32 mg/kg, every fourth day for five injections) prior to taste aversion conditioning with 32 mg/kg cocaine (Simpson, Parker, & Riley, 1997).

Although the aversiveness of a variety of recreational compounds appears reduced by drug preexposure, it should be noted that the suggestion that this reduction is responsible even in part for the change in the affective response to the drug and its increased likelihood of self-administration must remain speculative. To date, the number of drugs for which changes in the aversive and reinforcing reactions have been assessed with chronic exposure are quite limited. Further, there have been no concurrent assessments of the effects of drug preexposure on the ability of the same animals to display taste aversions and to self-administer the preexposed drug. Finally, although the findings mentioned here are consistent with the position that changes in a drug's aversiveness increase the reinforcing properties of that drug, it is certainly possible that an increase in the drug's reinforcing effects (e.g., directly by sensitization; see Lett, 1989; Schenk & Partridge, 1997) produces a decrease in the perceived aversiveness of the drug (see Gaiardi et al., 1991) or that concurrent (and independent) changes occur to both the drug's aversive and reinforcing effects. Thus, how an animal's affective response to a drug changes with exposure is not known. Although speculative, the fact that preexposure to drugs such as alcohol, morphine, and cocaine clearly attenuates their aversiveness raises the possibility of its involvement in drug use and abuse. The fact that preexposure to a range of recreational drugs also attenuates taste aversions to other recreational compounds suggests that this influence of drug preexposure on drug intake (use or abuse) may not necessarily be limited only to the preexposed drug (see Fig. 13.9; see also Bienkowski, Piasecki, et al., 1998; Brown et al., 1979; Cappell & LeBlanc, 1975b; Gamzu, 1977; Switzman et al., 1981; Ton & Amit, 1983; Vogel & Nathan, 1976).

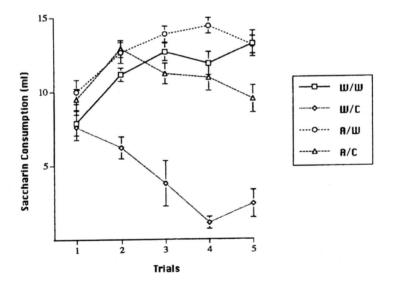

FIG. 13.9. Mean consumption (+/- SEM) of saccharin for rats receiving saccharin–cocaine (C; 32 mg/kg) or saccharin–water (W) pairings during taste aversion conditioning. Rats received preexposures to either alcohol (A; 3.5 g/kg) or the water vehicle (W) every fourth day for a total of five injections prior to conditioning. From Grakalic and Riley (unpublished data, 1999).

CONCLUSIONS

In this chapter we described the phenomenon of the US preexposure effect in taste aversion learning, whereby such preexposure attenuates the subsequent acquisition of aversions induced by the preexposed drug. This effect is robust and has been reported with a wide variety of compounds and under an equally varied range of conditions. The attenuating effects of drug preexposure may be mediated by nonassociative and associative processes (tolerance and blocking, respectively) and for some drugs its basis may be a function of both processes depending on the conditions of the preexposure. Independent of the mechanism underlying the US preexposure effect, the aversive effects of the preexposed drugs do appear to be diminished with exposure (or less associable with concurrently presented tastes). This reduction in the aversiveness of the preexposed compound may contribute to the use and abuse of recreational drugs by affecting the perceived rewarding effects of that drug (either alone or in conjunction with direct changes in the reinforcing effects of the compound). A phenomenon that began as a simple parameter (among many) affecting the acquisition of taste aversion learning has subsequently been useful in both pharmacological and learning preparations when assessing the pharmacological and physiological properties of drugs and the role of drug-related stimuli in the associative control of behavior and in clinical psychopharmacology when assessing its contribution to drug use and abuse.

■ REFERENCES

Aguado, L., De Brugada, I., & Hall, G. (1997). Effects of a retention interval on the US-preexposure phenomenon in flavor aversion learning. *Learning and Motivation, 28*, 311–322.

Aguado, L., del Valle, R., & Perez, L. (1997). The NMDA-receptor antagonist ketamine as an unconditioned stimulus in taste aversion learning. *Neurobiology of Learning and Memory, 68*, 189–196.

Ahlers, R. H., & Best, P. J. (1971). Novelty vs. temporal contiguity in taste aversions. *Psychonomic Science, 25*, 34–36.

Aragon, C. M. G., Abitol, M., & Amit, Z. (1986). Acetaldehyde may mediate reinforcement and aversion produced by ethanol. *Neuropharmacology, 25*, 79–83.

Baker, T. B., & Cannon, D. S. (1982). Alcohol and taste-mediated learning. *Addictive Behaviors, 7*, 211–230.

Barker, L. M., Best, M. R., & Domjan, M. (Eds.). (1977). *Learning mechanisms in food selection.* Waco, TX: Baylor University Press.

Barker, L. M., & Johns, T. (1978). Effect of ethanol preexposure on ethanol-induced conditioned taste aversion. *Journal of Studies on Alcohol, 39*, 39–46.

Batsell, W. R., & Best, M. R. (1994). The role of US novelty in retention interval effects in single-element taste-aversion learning. *Animal Learning & Behavior, 22*, 332–340.

Batson, J. D. (1983). Effects of repeated lithium injections on temperature, activity, and flavor conditioning in rats. *Animal Learning & Behavior, 11*, 199–204.

Batson, J. D., & Best, P. J. (1979). Drug-preexposure effects in flavor-aversion learning: Associative interference by conditioned environmental stimuli. *Journal of Experimental Psychology: Animal Behavior Processes, 5*, 273–283.

Berman, R. F., & Cannon, D. S. (1974). The effect of prior ethanol experience on ethanol-induced saccharin aversions. *Physiology & Behavior, 12*, 1041–1044.

Bienkowski, P., Iwinska, K., Koros, E., Panocka, I., Piasecki, J., & Kostowski, W. (1998). Prior repeated exposure to a 5-HT3 receptor agonist does not alter the ethanol-induced conditioned taste aversion in rats. *Pharmacology, Biochemistry and Behavior, 59*, 975–980.

Bienkowski, P., Koros, E., Piasecki, J., & Kostowski, W. (1998). Prior exposure to MK-801 sensitizes rats to ethanol-induced conditioned taste aversion. *Alcohol & Alcoholism, 33*, 116–120.

Bienkowski, P., Piasecki, J., Koros, E., Stefanski, R., & Kostowski, W. (1998). Studies on the role of nicotinic acetylcholine receptors in the discriminative and aversive stimulus properties of ethanol in the rat. *European Neuropharmacology, 8*, 79–87.

Bowers, W. J., Gingras, M. A., & Amit, Z. (1996). Time-dependent exacerbation of amphetamine-induced taste aversions following exposure to footshock. *Psychopharmacology, 125*, 43–49.

Bozarth, M. (Ed.). (1987). *Methods of assessing the reinforcing properties of abused drugs.* New York: Springer-Verlag.

Braveman, N. S. (1975). Formation of taste aversions in rats following prior exposure to sickness. *Learning and Motivation, 6*, 512–534.

Braveman, N. S. (1977). What studies on pre-exposure to pharmacological agents tell us about the nature of the aversion-inducing treatment. In L. M. Barker, M. R. Best, & M. Domjan (Eds.), *Learning mechanisms in food selection* (pp. 511–530). Waco, TX: Baylor University Press.

Braveman, N. S. (1978). The role of handling cues in the treatment preexposure effect in taste aversion learning. *Bulletin of the Psychonomic Society, 12*, 74–76.

Braveman, N. S. (1979). The role of blocking and compensatory conditioning in the treatment preexposure effect. *Psychopharmacology, 61*, 177–189.

Braveman, N. S., & Bronstein, P. (Eds.). (1985). *Experimental assessments and clinical applications of conditioned food aversions.* New York: New York Academy of Sciences.

Brookshire, K. H., & Brackbill, R. M. (1971, November). *Habituation to illness: Effects on acquisition and retention of a conditioned taste aversion.* Paper presented at the meeting of the Psychonomic Society, St. Louis, MO.

Brookshire, K. H., & Brackbill, R. M. (1976). Formation and retention of conditioned taste aversions and UCS habituation. *Bulletin of the Psychonomic Society, 7*, 125–128.

Brown, Z. W., Amit, Z., Smith, B., & Rockman, G. (1979). Disruption of taste aversion learning by pretreatment with diazepam and morphine. *Pharmacology, Biochemistry and Behavior, 10*, 17–20.

Bures, J., Bermudez-Rattoni, F., & Yamamoto, T. (1998). *Conditioned taste aversion: Memory of a special kind.* New York: Oxford University Press.

Cain, N. W., & Baenninger, R. (1977). Habituation to illness: Effects of prior experience with the US on the formation of learned taste aversions in rats. *Animal Learning & Behavior, 5*, 359–364.

Cannon, D. S., Baker, T. B., & Berman, R. F. (1977). Taste aversion disruption by drug pretreatment: Dissociative and drug-specific effects. *Pharmacology, Biochemistry and Behavior, 6*, 93–100.

Cannon, D. S., Berman, R. F., Baker, T. B., & Atkinson, C. A. (1975). Effect of preconditioning unconditioned stimulus experience on learned taste aversions. *Journal of Experimental Psychology: Animal Behavior Processes, 104*, 270–284.

Cannon, D. S., & Carrell, L. E. (1987a). Effect of taste aversion learning on ethanol self-administration. *Pharmacology, Biochemistry and Behavior, 28,* 53–56.

Cannon, D. A., & Carrell, L. E. (1987b). Rat strain differences in ethanol self-administration and taste aversion learning. *Pharmacology, Biochemistry and Behavior, 28,* 57–63.

Cannon, D. S., Leeka, J. K., & Block, A. K. (1994). Ethanol self-administration patterns and taste aversion learning across inbred rat strains. *Pharmacology, Biochemistry and Behavior, 47,* 795–802.

Cappell, H. D., & LeBlanc, A. E. (1975a). Conditioned aversion by amphetamine: Rates of acquisition and loss of the attenuating effects of prior exposure. *Psychopharmacologia, 43,* 157–162.

Cappell, H. D., & LeBlanc, A. E. (1975b). Conditioned aversion by psychoactive drugs: Does it have significance for an understanding of drug dependence? *Addictive Behaviors, 1,* 55–64.

Cappell, H. D., & LeBlanc, A. E. (1977a). Gustatory avoidance conditioning by drugs of abuse. In N. W. Milgram, L. Krames, & T. M. Alloway (Eds.), *Food aversion learning* (pp. 133–167). New York: Plenum.

Cappell, H., & LeBlanc, A. E. (1977b). Parametric investigations of the effects of prior exposure to amphetamine and morphine on conditioned gustatory aversion. *Psychopharmacology, 51,* 265–271.

Cappell, H., LeBlanc, A. E., & Herling, S. (1975). Modification of the punishing effects of psychoactive drugs in rats by previous drug experience. *Journal of Comparative and Physiological Psychology, 89,* 347–356.

Cappell, H., & Poulos, C. X. (1979). Associative factors in drug pretreatment effects on gustatory conditioning: Cross-drug effects. *Psychopharmacology, 64,* 209–213.

Cole, K. C., Bakner, L., Vernon, A., & Riccio, D. C. (1993). The effect of US preexposure on conditioned taste aversion: Lack of postconditioning recovery of the aversion. *Behavioral and Neural Biology, 60,* 271–273.

Cole, K. C., VanTilburg, D., Burch-Vernon, A., & Riccio, D. C. (1996). The importance of context in the US preexposure effect in CTA: Novel versus latently inhibited contextual stimuli. *Learning and Motivation, 27,* 362–374.

Corcoran, M. E. (1973). Role of drug novelty and metabolism in the aversive effects of hashish injections in rats. *Life Sciences, 12,* 63–72.

Corrigall, W. A., Linseman, M. A., D'Onofrio, R., & Lei, H. (1986). An analysis of the paradoxical effect of morphine on runway speed and food consumption. *Psychopharmacology, 89,* 327–333.

Cunningham, C. L., & Linakis, J. G. (1980). Paradoxical aversive conditioning with ethanol. *Pharmacology, Biochemistry and Behavior, 12,* 337–341.

Dacanay, R. J., Mastropaolo, J., & Riley, A. L. (1986, November). *Effects of the number of preexposures on the methadone-induced preexposure effect in taste aversion learning in the rat.* Paper presented at the meeting of the Society for Neuroscience, Washington, DC.

Dacanay, R. J., & Riley, A. L. (1982). The UCS preexposure effect in taste aversion learning: Tolerance and blocking are drug specific. *Animal Learning & Behavior, 10,* 91–96.

Danguir, J., & Nicolaidis, S. (1977). Lack of reacquisition in learned taste aversions. *Animal Learning & Behavior, 5,* 395–397.

DeBeun, R., Lohmann, A., Schneider, R., & de Vry, J. (1996). Ethanol intake-reducing effects of ipsapirone in rats are not due to simple stimulus substitution. *Pharmacology, Biochemistry and Behavior, 53,* 891–898.

DeBeun, R., Peeters, B. W. M. M., & Broekkamp, C. L. E. (1993). Stimulus characterization of estradiol applying a crossfamiliarization taste aversion procedure in female mice. *Physiology & Behavior, 53,* 715–719.

DeBeun, R., Rijk, H. W., & Broekkamp, C. L. E. (1993). Cross-familiarisation conditioned taste aversion procedure as a method to reveal stimulus resemblance between drugs: Studies on the 5-HT1A agonist 8-OHDPAT. *Psychopharmacology, 112*, 121–128.

Domjan, M. (1983). Biological constraints on instrumental and classical conditioning: Implications for general process theory. In G. Bower (Ed.), *The psychology of learning and motivation* (Vol. 17, pp. 215–277). New York: Academic Press.

Domjan, M., & Best, M. R. (1980). Interference with ingestional aversion learning produced by preexposure to the unconditioned stimulus: Associative and nonassociative aspects. *Learning and Motivation, 11*, 522–537.

Domjan, M., & Galef, B. G. (1983). Biological constraints in instrumental and classical conditioning: Retrospect and prospect. *Animal Learning & Behavior, 11*, 151–161.

Domjan, M., & Siegel, S. (1983). Attenuation of the aversive and analgesic effects of morphine by repeated administration: Different mechanisms. *Physiological Psychology, 11*, 155–158.

Elkins, R. L. (1973). Attenuation of drug-induced baitshyness to a palatable solution as an increasing function of its availability prior to conditioning. *Behavioral Biology, 9*, 221–226.

Elkins, R. L. (1974). Bait-shyness acquisition and resistance to extinction as functions of US exposure prior to conditioning. *Physiological Psychology, 2*, 341–343.

Ellenbroek, B. A., Knobbout, D. A., & Cools, A. R. (1997). The role of mesolimbic and nigrostriatal dopamine in latent inhibition as measured with the conditioned taste aversion paradigm. *Psychopharmacology, 129*, 112–120.

Elsmore, T. F. (1972). *Saccharin aversion induced by Δ⁹-tetrahydrocannabinol: Effects of repeated doses prior to pairing with saccharin.* Proceedings of the 80th Annual Convention of the American Psychological Association, 7, 817–818.

Ettenberg, A., Sgro, S., & White, N. (1982). Algebraic summation of the affective properties of a rewarding and aversive stimulus in the rat. *Physiology & Behavior, 28*, 873–877.

Fenwick, S., Mikulka, P. J., & Klein, S. B. (1975). The effect of different levels of pre-exposure to sucrose on the acquisition and extinction of a conditioned aversion. *Behavioral Biology, 14*, 231–235.

Ferrari, C. M., & Riley, A. L. (1994). Effect of prenatal cocaine on the acquisition of cocaine-induced taste aversions. *Neurotoxicology and Teratology, 16*, 17–23.

Fischer, G. J., Gilman, S. C., & Blank, C. (1987). Corticosterone response underlying tolerance to stress induced by a gaseous (nitrous oxide) environment. *Perceptual and Motor Skills, 64*, 799–808.

Fischer, G. J., & Vail, B. J. (1980). Preexposure to delta-9-THC blocks THC-induced conditioned taste aversion in rats. *Behavioral and Neural Biology, 30*, 191–196.

Ford, K. A., & Riley, A. L. (1984). The effects of LiCl preexposure on amphetamine-induced taste aversions: An assessment of blocking. *Pharmacology, Biochemistry and Behavior, 20*, 643–645.

Gaiardi, M., Bartoletti, M., Bacchi, A., Gubellini, C., & Babbini, M. (1997). Motivational properties of buprenorphine as assessed by place and taste conditioning in rats. *Psychopharmacology, 130*, 104–108.

Gaiardi, M., Bartoletti, M., Bacchi, A., Gubellini, C., Costa, M., & Babbini, M. (1991). Role of repeated exposure to morphine in determining its affective properties: Place and taste conditioning studies in rats. *Psychopharmacology, 103*, 183–186.

Gaiardi, M., Bartoletti, M., Gubellini, C., Bacchi, A., & Babbini, M. (1998). Modulation of the stimulus effects of morphine by d-amphetamine. *Pharmacology, Biochemistry and Behavior, 59*, 249–253.

Gamzu, E. (1974, November). *Pre-exposure to a unconditioned stimulus alone may eliminate taste-aversions.* Paper presented at the meeting of the Psychonomic Society, Boston, MA.

Gamzu, E. (1977). The multifaceted nature of taste-aversion-inducing agents: Is there a single common factor? In L. M. Barker, M. R. Best, & M. Domjan (Eds.), *Learning mechanisms in food selection* (pp. 477–509). Waco, TX: Baylor University Press.

Garcia, J., & Ervin, F. R. (1968). Gustatory-visceral and telereceptor-cutaneous conditioning: Adaptation in internal and external milieus. *Communications in Behavioral Biology, 1,* 389–415.

Garcia, J., Ervin, F. R., & Koelling, R. A. (1966). Learning with prolonged delay of reinforcement. *Psychonomic Science, 5,* 121–122.

Garcia, J., McGowan, B. K., & Green, K. F. (1972). Biological constraints on conditioning. In A. H. Black & W. F. Prokasy (Eds.), *Classical conditioning II: Current research and theory* (pp. 21–43). New York: Appleton-Century-Crofts.

Gauvin, D. V., & Holloway, F. A. (1992). Ethanol tolerance developed during intoxicated operant performance in rats prevents subsequent ethanol-induced conditioned taste aversion. *Alcohol, 9,* 167–170.

Glowa, J. R., & Williams, A. N. (1992). Effects of prior exposure to cocaine: Interaction of reinforcing and suppressant effects. *Life Sciences, 51,* 987–994.

Goldstein, A., Aronov, L., & Kalman, S. M. (1974). *Principles of drug action: The basis of pharmacology.* New York: Wiley.

Gommans, J., Bouwknecht, J. A., Hijzen, T. H., Berendsen, H. H. G., Broekkamp, C. L. E., Maes, R. A. A., & Olivier, B. (1998). Stimulus properties of fluvoxamine in a conditioned taste aversion procedure. *Psychopharmacology, 140,* 496–502.

Gorman, J. E., De Obaldia, R. N., Scott, R. C., & Reid, L. D. (1978). Morphine injections in the taste aversion paradigm: Extent of aversions and readiness to consume sweetened morphine solutions. *Physiological Psychology, 6,* 101–109.

Goudie, A. J. (1979). Aversive stimulus properties of drugs. *Neuropharmacology, 18,* 971–979.

Goudie, A. J. (1985). Aversive stimulus properties of drugs: The conditioned taste aversion paradigm. In A. Greenshaw & C. Dourish (Eds.), *Experimental approach in psychopharmacology* (pp. 341–381). Clifton, NJ: Humana.

Goudie, A. J., Leathley, M., McNally, J., & West, C. R. (1989). Individual differences in cocaine discrimination. *Drug Development Research, 16,* 123–131.

Goudie, A. J., Taylor, M., & Atherton, H. (1975). Effects of prior drug experience on the establishment of taste aversions in rats. *Pharmacology, Biochemistry and Behavior, 3,* 947–952.

Goudie, A. J., & Thornton, E. W. (1975). Effects of drug experience on drug induced conditioned taste aversions: Studies with amphetamine and fenfluramine. *Psychopharmacologia, 44,* 77–82.

Goudie, A. J., Thornton, E. W., & Wheeler, T. J. (1976). Drug pretreatment effects in drug induced taste aversions: Effects of dose and duration of pretreatment. *Pharmacology, Biochemistry and Behavior, 4,* 629–633.

Grakalic, I. & Riley, A. L. (1999). [Cross-drug preexposure in taste aversion learning: Assessment of cocaine and alcohol]. Unpublished data.

Grigson, P. S. (1997). Conditioned taste aversions and drugs of abuse: A reinterpretation. *Behavioral Neuroscience, 111,* 129–136.

Grill, H. J., & Norgren, R. (1978). The taste reactivity test: I. Mimetic responses to gustatory stimuli in neurologically normal rats. *Brain Research, 143,* 263–279.

Holman, E. W. (1976). The effect of drug habituation before and after taste aversion learning in rats. *Animal Learning & Behavior, 4,* 329–332.

Hunt, T., & Amit, Z. (1987). Conditioned taste aversion induced by self-administered drugs: Paradox revisited. *Neuroscience and Biobehavioral Reviews, 11,* 107–130.

Hunt, T., Segal, R., & Amit, Z. (1987). Differential involvement of central cholinergic mechanisms in the aversive stimulus properties of morphine and amphetamine. *Pharmacology, Biochemistry & Behavior, 28,* 335–339.

Hunt, T., Spivak, K., & Amit, Z. (1985). Aversive stimulus properties of morphine: Evaluation using the drug preexposure conditioned taste aversion paradigm. *Behavioral and Neural Biology, 44,* 60–73.

Hunt, W. A., & Rabin, B. M. (1988). Attenuation of a radiation-induced conditioned taste aversion after the development of ethanol tolerance. *Life Sciences, 43,* 59–66.

Iwamoto, E. T., & Williamson, E. C. (1984). Nicotine-induced taste aversion: Characterization and preexposure effects in rats. *Pharmacology, Biochemistry and Behavior, 21,* 527–532.

June, H. L., June, P. L., Domangue, K. R., Hicks, L. H., Lummis, G. H., & Lewis, M. J. (1992). Failure of Ro15-4513 to alter an ethanol-induced taste aversion. *Pharmacology, Biochemistry and Behavior, 41,* 455–460.

Kiefer, S. W., Bice, P. J., & Badia-Elder, N. (1994). Alterations in taste reactivity to alcohol in rats given continuous alcohol access followed by abstinence. *Alcoholism: Clinical and Experimental Research, 18,* 555–559.

Kiefer, S. W., Phillips, J. A., & Braun, J. J. (1977). Preexposure to conditioned and unconditioned stimuli in taste-aversion learning. *Bulletin of the Psychonomic Society, 10,* 226–228.

Kitaichi, K., Noda, Y., Hasegawa, T., Furukawa, H., & Nabeshima, T. (1996). Acute phencyclidine induces aversion, but repeated phencyclidine induces preference in the place conditioning test in rats. *European Journal of Pharmacology, 318,* 7–9.

Klein, S. B., Mikulka, P. J., & Lucci, K. (1986). Influence of lithium chloride intensity on unconditioned stimulus-alone interference in a flavor aversion paradigm. *Learning and Motivation, 17,* 76–90.

Klosterhalfen, S., & Klosterhalfen, W. (1985). Conditioned taste aversion and traditional learning. *Psychological Research, 47,* 71–94.

LeBlanc, A. E., & Cappell, H. (1974). Attenuation of punishing effects of morphine and amphetamine by chronic prior treatment. *Journal of Comparative and Physiological Psychology, 87,* 691–698.

Lett, B. T. (1989). Repeated exposures intensify rather than diminish the rewarding effects of amphetamine, morphine, and cocaine. *Psychopharmacology, 98,* 357–362.

Logue, A. W. (1979). Taste aversion and the generality of the laws of learning. *Psychological Bulletin, 86,* 276–296.

Lubow, R. E. (1973). Latent inhibition. *Psychological Bulletin, 79,* 398–407.

Mackintosh, N. J. (1983). *Conditioning and associative learning.* Oxford, UK: Oxford University Press.

Marfaing-Jallat, P., & LeMagnen, J. (1979). Ethanol-induced taste aversion in ethanol-dependent and normal rats. *Behavioral and Neural Biology, 26,* 106–114.

Merwin, A., & Doty, R. L. (1994). Early exposure to low levels of estradiol (E_2) mitigates E_2-induced conditioned taste aversions in prepubertally ovariectomized female rats. *Physiology & Behavior, 55,* 185–187.

Mikulka, P. J., Leard, B., & Klein, S. B. (1977). Illness-alone exposure as a source of interference with the acquisition and retention of a taste aversion. *Journal of Experimental Psychology: Animal Behavior Processes, 3,* 189–201.

Milgram, N. W., Krames, L., & Alloway, T. M. (Eds.). (1977). *Food aversion learning.* New York: Plenum.

Miranda, F., & Vila, R. A. y J. (1985). Efectos de la preexposicion al LiCl sobre el subsecuente aprendizaje de la aversion gustativa [Effect of LiCl pre-exposure on subsequent acquisition of a flavour aversion]. *Revista Mexicana de Analisis de la Conducta, 11,* 91–97.

Misanin, J. R., Hoefel, T. D., Riedy, C. A., & Hinderliter, C. F. (1997). Remote and proximal US preexposure and aging effects in taste aversion learning in rats. *Physiology & Behavior, 61,* 221–224.

Mitchell, D., Scott, D. W., & Mitchell, L. K. (1977). Attenuated and enhanced neophobia in the taste-aversion "delay of reinforcement" effect. *Animal Learning & Behavior, 5,* 99–102.

Nachman, M., & Jones, D. R. (1974). Learned taste aversions over long delays in rats: The role of learned safety. *Journal of Comparative and Physiological Psychology, 86,* 949–956.

Opitz, B., Mothes, H. K., & Clausing, P. (1997). Effects of prenatal ethanol exposure and early experience on radial maze performance and conditioned taste aversion in mice. *Neurotoxicology and Teratology, 19,* 185–190.

Parker, L. A. (1995). Rewarding drugs produce taste avoidance, but not taste aversion. *Neuroscience and Biobehavioral Reviews, 19,* 143–151.

Parker, L., Failor, A., & Weidman, K. (1973). Conditioned preferences in the rat with an unnatural need state: Morphine withdrawal. *Journal of Comparative and Physiological Psychology, 82,* 294–300.

Peck, J. H., & Ader, R. (1974). Illness-induced taste aversion under states of deprivation and satiation. *Animal Learning & Behavior, 2,* 6–8.

Pizzi, W. J., & Cook, D. F. (1996). Conditioned taste aversion is a confound in behavioral studies that report a reduction in the reinforcing effects of drugs. *Pharmacology, Biochemistry, and Behavior, 53,* 243–247.

Poulos, C. X., & Cappell, H. (1979). An associative analysis of pretreatment effects in gustatory conditioning by amphetamine. *Psychopharmacology, 64,* 201–207.

Preston, K. L., Wagner, G. C., Seiden, L. S., & Schuster, C. R. (1984). Effects of methamphetamine on atropine-induced conditioned gustatory avoidance. *Pharmacology, Biochemistry and Behavior, 20,* 601–607.

Rabin, B. M. (1996). Free radicals and taste aversion learning in the rat: Nitric oxide, radiation and dopamine. *Progress in Neuro-psychopharmacology & Biological Psychiatry, 20,* 691–707.

Rabin, B. M., Hunt, W. A., & Lee, J. (1988). Attenuation and cross-attenuation in taste aversion learning in the rat: Studies with ionizing radiation, lithium chloride and ethanol. *Pharmacology, Biochemistry and Behavior, 31,* 909–918.

Randich, A., & LoLordo, V., M. (1979). Associative and nonassociative theories of the UCS preexposure phenomenon: Implications for Pavlovian conditioning. *Psychological Bulletin, 86,* 523–548.

Rescorla, R. A., & Wagner, A. R. (1972). A theory of Pavlovian conditioning: Variations in the effectiveness of reinforcement and nonreinforcement. In A. H. Black & W. F. Prokasy (Eds.), *Classical conditioning II: Current theory and research* (pp. 64–99). New York: Appleton-Century-Crofts.

Revusky, S., Coombes, S., & Pohl, R. W. (1982). US preexposure: Effects on flavor aversions produced by pairing a poisoned partner with ingestion. *Animal Learning & Behavior, 10,* 83–90.

Revusky, S. H., & Garcia, J. (1970). Learned associations over long delays. In G. H. Bower & J. J. Spence (Eds.), *The psychology of learning and motivation: Advances in research and theory,* (Vol. 4, pp. 1–83) New York: Academic Press.

Revusky, S., & Taukulis, H. (1975). Effects of alcohol and lithium habituation on the development of alcohol aversions through contingent lithium injection. *Behaviour Research and Therapy, 13*, 163–166.

Riley, A. L. (1998). Conditioned flavor aversions: Assessment of drug-induced suppression of food intake. In J. Crawley (Ed.), *Current protocols in neuroscience, Supplement 5, pp. 8.6E.1–8.6E.10.* New York: Wiley.

Riley, A. L., & Baril, L. L. (1976). Conditioned taste aversions: A bibliography. *Animal Learning & Behavior, 4*, 1S–13S.

Riley, A. L., Dacanay, R. J., & Mastropaolo, J. P. (1984). The effect of morphine preexposure on the acquisition of morphine-induced taste aversions: A nonassociative effect. *Animal Learning & Behavior, 12*, 157–162.

Riley, A. L., & Diamond, H. F. (1998). The effects of cocaine preexposure on the acquisition of cocaine-induced taste aversions. *Pharmacology, Biochemistry and Behavior, 60*, 739–745.

Riley, A. L., Jacobs, W. J., & LoLordo, V. M. (1976). Drug exposure and the acquisition and retention of a conditioned taste aversion. *Journal of Comparative and Physiological Psychology, 90*, 799–807.

Riley, A. L., Jacobs, W. J., & LoLordo, V. M. (1978). Morphine-induced taste aversions: A consideration of parameters. *Physiological Psychology, 6*, 96–100.

Riley, A. L., Jacobs, W. J., & Mastropaolo, J. P. (1983). The effects of extensive taste preexposure on the acquisition of conditioned taste aversions. *Bulletin of the Psychonomic Society, 21*, 221–224.

Riley, A. L., & Simpson, G. R. (1999). Cocaine preexposure fails to sensitize the acquisition of cocaine-induced taste aversions. *Pharmacology, Biochemistry and Behavior, 63*, 193–199.

Riley, A. L., & Tuck, D. L. (1985a). Conditioned food aversions: A bibliography. *Annals of the New York Academy of Sciences, 443*, 381–437.

Riley, A. L., & Tuck, D. L. (1985b). Conditioned taste aversions: A behavioral index of toxicity. *Annals of the New York Academy of Sciences, 443*, 272–292.

Riley, E. P., Barron, S., Driscoll, C. D., & Chen, J.-S. (1984). Taste aversion learning in preweanling rats exposed to alcohol prenatally. *Teratology, 29*, 325–331.

Risinger, F. O., & Cunningham, C. L. (1995). Genetic differences in ethanol-induced conditioned taste aversion after ethanol preexposure. *Alcohol, 12*, 535–539.

Rozin, P., & Kalat, J. W. (1971). Specific hungers and poison avoidance as adaptive specializations of learning. *Psychological Review, 78*, 459–486.

Rudy, J. W., Iwens, J., & Best, P. J. (1977). Pairing novel exteroceptive cues and illness reduces illness-induced taste aversions. *Journal of Experimental Psychology: Animal Behavior Processes, 3*, 14–25.

Sanudo-Pena, M. C., Tsou, K., Delay, E. R., Hohman, A. G., Force, M., & Walker, J. M. (1997). Endogenous cannabinoids as an aversive or counter-rewarding system in the rat. *Neuroscience Letters, 223*, 125–128.

Schenk, S., & Partridge, B. (1997). Sensitization and tolerance in psychostimulant self-administration. *Pharmacology, Biochemistry and Behavior, 57*, 543–550.

Seligman, M. E. P. (1970). On the generality of the laws of learning. *Psychological Review, 77*, 406–418.

Sherman, J. E., Pickman, C., Rice, A., Liebeskind, J. C., & Holman, E. W. (1980). Rewarding and aversive effects of morphine: Temporal and pharmacological properties. *Pharmacology, Biochemistry & Behavior, 13*, 501–505.

Shettleworth, S. J. (1972). Constraints on learning. *Advances in the Study of Behavior, 4*, 1–68.

Shoaib, M., & Almeida, O. F. X. (1996). Absence of tolerance to the aversive stimulus properties of ethanol following oral self-administration. *Alcohol, 13*, 175–180.

Shoaib, M., & Stolerman, I. P. (1996). The NMDA antagonist dizocilpine (MK801) attenuates tolerance to nicotine in rats. *Journal of Psychopharmacology, 10,* 214–218.

Siegel, S., Parker, L. A., & Moroz, I. (1995). Morphine-induced taste avoidance is attenuated with multiple conditioning trials. *Pharmacology, Biochemistry and Behavior, 50,* 299–303.

Simpson, G. R., Parker, L. A., & Riley, A. L. (1997). [The effect of US preexposure on Cocaine-Induced CTA and Taste Reactivity responses: Tolerance or Sensitization?] Unpublished data.

Sjoden, P.-O., Archer, T., & Carter, N. (1979). Conditioned taste aversion induced by 2,4,5-trichlorophenoxyacetic acid: Dose-response and preexposure effects. *Physiological Psychology, 7,* 93–96.

Sklar, L. S., & Amit, Z. (1977). Manipulations of catecholamine systems block the conditioned taste aversion induced by self-administered drugs. *Neuropharmacology, 16,* 649–655.

Spiker, V. A. (1977). Taste aversion: A procedural analysis and an alternative paradigmatic classification. *The Psychological Record, 27,* 753–769.

Stefurak, T. L., Martin, G., & van der Kooy, D. (1990). The representation in memory of morphine's unconditioned motivational effects depends on the nature of the conditioned stimulus. *Psychobiology, 18,* 435–442.

Stewart, J., & Eikelboom, R. (1978). Pre-exposure to morphine and the attenuation of conditioned taste aversion in rats. *Pharmacology, Biochemistry & Behavior, 9,* 639–645.

Stewart, R. B., McBride, W. J., Lumeng, L., Li, T.-K., & Murphy, J. M. (1991). Chronic alcohol consumption in alcohol-preferring P rats attenuates subsequent conditioned taste aversion produced by ethanol injections. *Psychopharmacology, 105,* 530–534.

Stolerman, I. P., & D'Mello, G. D. (1981). Oral self-administration and the relevance of conditioned taste aversions. *Advances in Behavioral Pharmacology, 3,* 169–214.

Suarez, E. M., & Barker, L. M. (1976). Effects of water deprivation and prior LiCl exposure in conditioning taste aversions. *Physiology & Behavior, 17,* 555–559.

Switzman, L., Fishman, B., & Amit, Z. (1981). Pre-exposure effects of morphine, diazepam and Δ⁹-THC on the formation of conditioned taste aversions. *Psychopharmacology, 74,* 149–152.

Ton, J. M. N. C., & Amit, Z. (1983). Symmetrical effect of pre-exposure between alcohol and morphine on conditioned taste aversion. *Life Sciences, 33,* 665–670.

Ton, J. M. N. C., & Amit, Z. (1985a). Acetaldehyde and morphine interaction in the preexposure conditioned taste aversion paradigm in the rat. *Neuroscience Letters, 61,* 131–134.

Ton, J. M. N. C., & Amit, Z. (1985b). Receptor stereospecificity in opiate–ethanol interaction using the preexposure-conditioned taste aversion (CTA) paradigm. *Pharmacology, Biochemistry and Behavior, 22,* 255–259.

Turenne, S. D., Miles, C., Parker, L. A., & Siegel, S. (1996). Individual differences in reactivity to the rewarding/aversive properties of drugs: Assessment by taste and place conditioning. *Pharmacology, Biochemistry and Behavior, 53,* 511–516.

Vogel, J. R. (1974, November). *Prior exposure to a drug (US) attenuates learned taste aversions.* Paper presented at the meeting of the Psychonomic Society, Boston, MA.

Vogel, J. R., & Nathan, B. A. (1976). Reduction of learned taste aversions by pre-exposure to drugs. *Psychopharmacology, 49,* 167–172.

Wang, Y., Lavond, D. G., & Chambers, K. C. (1997). Cooling the area postrema induces conditioned taste aversions in male rats and blocks acquisition of LiCl-induced aversions. *Behavioral Neuroscience, 111,* 768–776.

Whaley, D. L., Scarborough, B. B., & Reichard, S. M. (1966). Traumatic shock, x-irradiation and avoidance behavior. *Physiology and Behavior, 1,* 93–95.

White, N., Sklar, L., & Amit, Z. (1977). The reinforcing action of morphine and its paradoxical side effect. *Psychopharmacology, 52,* 63–66.

Willner, J. A. (1978). Blocking of a taste aversion by prior pairings of exteroceptive stimuli with illness. *Learning and Motivation, 9,* 125–140.

Wise, R. A., Yokel, R. A., & DeWitt, H. (1976). Both positive reinforcement and conditioned aversion from amphetamine and from apomorphine in rats. *Science, 191,* 1273–1275.

chapter 14

The Neurotic Paradox:
Attempts by Two-Factor Fear Theory and Alternative Avoidance Models to Resolve the Issues Associated With Sustained Avoidance Responding in Extinction

Donald J. Levis
Karen E. Brewer
State University of New York at Binghamton

O ne of the most common behaviors correlated with the occurrence of aversive events is the tendency of organisms to escape from stimuli associated with that aversive event. Escape from the presenting stimuli permits avoidance of other current and impending aversive stimuli. As such, avoidance models of learning have developed from a vast historical research literature with animals. This literature was embraced early on for its potential to advance theoretical generality to human psychopathology, as it became clear that avoidance behavior generated by feared aversive events in the animal laboratory could provide a systematic database for investigating the complex development and maintenance of human symptomatic behavior (Brown, 1961; Dollard & Miller, 1950; Mowrer, 1939; Shaw, 1946; Shoben, 1949; Skinner, 1953, 1954; Stampfl, 1961; Wolpe, 1958). Thus, principles derived mainly from animal research became regarded as important foundations from which behavioral laws could be developed and applied to clinical human psychopathology.

Throughout the years, many major investigators of animal learning have alluded to the relevance of their interpretations of a wide variety of human psychological disorders in terms of the learning process. Rivers (1920) analyzed the behavior and treatment of World War I battle casualties from a fear-avoidance extinction model, as did Hollingworth (1928) in his treatment of a soldier suffering "traumatic neurosis." Hull (1929) described some "dilemmas" of Pavlovian extinction relevant to human phobias. He later presented a translation of psychoanalytic concepts into learning theory terms (Hull, 1939), and went so far as to suggest that all practitioners involved in human mental disorders might benefit from the study of animal learning as a means of determining causal factors in etiology and treatment (Hull, 1945). Guthrie (1938) interpreted a number of human mental disorders using learning theory terms in his book, *The Psychology of Human Conflict* (Stampfl, 1991).

Thus, it was quite clear to these and many others working in the field in the early 20th century that an understanding of the behavior of humans could be facilitated through scientific, controlled study of other organisms. Through this process, it soon became obvious that behavior, human or otherwise, is manifestly subject to modification and change, and that an understanding of the basic laws of the learning process could facilitate an understanding of exactly how and why such behavioral flexibility could come about (Mowrer, 1960).

The earlier explorations of the mechanisms of behavior change facilitated by the contribution of Pavlov (1927) and Thorndike (1898) gained considerable impetus in the 1940s and 1950s from the incorporation of a neobehaviorism philosophy of science (see Fiegl & Brodbeck, 1953; Marx, 1963) into theory construction, as illustrated by Hull-Spence and other contributors during this period of development (see Hilgard & Bower, 1966). Neobehaviorism, following the lead of Watsonian behaviorism (Watson, 1913, 1930), strove to move the field of psychology away from the study of mentalistic phenomenon to the study of behavior that was deemed public and confirmable rather than private and nonconfirmable. This approach linked the field of psychology with the goals of natural sciences in their emphasis on objectivism, measurement, and verification. This goal was achieved at a theoretical level of analysis by operationally defining each construct within a theory with a definitional structure that was orthogonal to the dependent measures used to assess the degree of learning. As a result, the predictive power of behavioral theories was greatly enhanced by eliminating surplus meaning concepts and untestable mentalistic terms. Further, consistent with evolutionary theory, the laws of behavior were believed to be operating across the phylogenetic spectrum. This assumption gave infrahuman researchers a sense of purpose and relevance that the knowledge gained from their research might be generalizable to the more complex human situation (Levis, 1989).

During this period of theoretical development in the field of learning, relatively little attention was given to the empirical finding that animals could learn a response that prevented the presentation of electric shock. It did not appear, at first, to be a mystery as to why a child avoided touching a flame after he or she was burned. The explanation for this behavior seems straightforward. The child, like the rat, avoids to prevent exposure to further pain (Hilgard & Marquis, 1940). However, this teleological "expectancy" interpretation of avoidance did not sit well with neobehaviorists like Mowrer (1939, 1947), who recognized the complexity of the avoidance paradigm and the need for any theory of avoidance to resolve two critical paradoxes that confronted the area.

THE AVOIDANCE LEARNING PARADOXES

The first paradox centered on the question of how the avoidance response could show signs of being strengthened over trials when the response, by definition, occurred in the absence of the reinforcement, electric shock. Further, how could this response continue to manifest signs of increased strength over trials once the reinforcement was discontinued? Schoenfeld (1950) also raised the critical question reflecting this paradox: How can the nonoccurrence of an unconditioned stimulus (shock) act as a reinforcement?

The second, related paradox centered on the teleological issues raised by Hilgard and Marquis's (1940) commonsense interpretation. The critical question reflecting this paradox was this: How did the animal ever make its first avoidance response? Prior to the occurrence of the first avoidance response, the animal was never exposed to the contingency that an avoidance response terminated the conditioned stimulus (CS) and prevented the occurrence of shock. A simple random occurrence explanation of the first avoidance response seemed unlikely given the finding that rats can quickly learn the response, even following exposure to one shock trial (Levis, 1971b; Stampfl, 1991).

Although a number of theorists (e.g., Miller, 1948; Sheffield, 1948) made significant contributions to help resolve these paradoxes, it was Mowrer's (1939, 1947) rather simple, yet ingenious theoretical solution that stimulated the most attention and led to the development of his now well-known two-factor theory of avoidance learning. Mowrer, in developing his avoidance theory, was influenced by Freud's (1936) signal theory interpretation of symptom development. Freud first conceptualized symptom formations as a direct outgrowth of psychopathology development. He later rejected this interpretation, realizing that symptom occurrence was a response elicited by the presence of a danger signal (internal or external) and enacted by the patient's unconscious (memory). In other words, Freud posited that all anxiety (fear) reactions were probably learned, such that the anxiety is the conditioned form of the pain reaction, which according to Mowrer (1939) "has the highly useful function of motivating and reinforcing behaviors that tend to avoid or prevent the recurrence of the pain-producing (unconditioned) stimulus" (p. 555). However, Freud's conceptualization proposed that a danger signal may come to elicit an infinite variety of reactions that may be completely unlike the reaction that occurs to the actual trauma being signaled (response substitution). He further assumed that the initial response to the danger signal is not, as Pavlov would hold, a complete overt reflexive behavioral reaction, but rather a covert, internal state of tension and increased preparedness for action—a state of anxiety. This state then produces a source of discomfort that can motivate innumerable random acts or responses, of which some, by virtue of the law of effect, will be selected and fixated as the behaviors that most effectively reduce the anxiety. As such, Freud reasoned that human symptoms of psychopathology were essentially learned avoidance behaviors enacted by the patient to remove danger signals linked to the patient's unconscious memory; aversive cues eliciting symptom behavior were considered to be generalized cues associated with earlier traumatic learning situations.

Recognizing the importance of Freud's contributions regarding symptom elicitation and maintenance, Mowrer (1939, 1947) set out to resolve these paradoxes by combining into a single theory the principles associated with Pavlov's (1927) classical conditioning learning and Thorndike's (1898) law of effect learning. To achieve this objective, Mowrer's explanation required the introduction of a theoretical construct between the stimulus and the response that reflected some process occurring within the organism. He concluded that the process was emotional, involving the conditioning of the autonomic nervous system, and that it possessed both motivational and reinforcing properties. Consistent with Freud's analysis, Mowrer introduced the construct of fear. Thus, he hypothesized that two types of learning were involved in the development of avoidance learning. The first factor, fear learning, was governed by the Pavlovian laws of classical conditioning and simply resulted from the pairing of a nonaversive stimulus with a US that produces a pain reaction (e.g., electric shock). The elicitation of pain produces an unconditioned response (UR) of fear via the principle of contiguity. As a result of this pairing procedure, fear becomes associated with or conditioned to the nonfear stimulus, which then becomes capable of functioning as a CS. Following the Hullian tradition, Mowrer viewed the fear construct as a drive stimulus, and, as such, its onset acted as an energizing or motivating stimulus for the elicitation of the avoidance response. Further, the offset of the fear stimulus, which resulted in the termination or decrease in the presence of the fear stimuli, provided a reinforcing effect for strengthening the avoidance behavior. This latter factor, Mowrer's second factor, was believed to be governed by Thorndike's laws of trial and error or instrumental learning.

To explain the first avoidance paradox of how the initial instrumental response occurs, Mowrer drew on the motivating properties of fear. Following the conditioning of fear to the CS, its subsequent presentations activate or energize the organism, resulting in the emitting of various behaviors in an attempt to escape the aversive CS until the desired response occurs. Because the desired response is followed by a reduction in fear, it becomes strengthened. Repeated trials will elicit additional avoidance responses and subsequent reinforcement of these responses as long as the drive stimuli conditioned to the CS are still present, thus resolving the second paradox of how avoidance learning can produce an acquisition and maintenance function in the absence of any further US presentation (see Mowrer, 1939, 1947, 1960).

It is not surprising given Mowrer's objective to develop a stimulus–response (S–R) theory of avoidance behavior that he (Mowrer, 1960) expressed concern over the term *avoidance* which implies a teleological or "purposeful" intent on behalf of the animal. Rather he preferred the term *escape* from the CS to describe the animal's behavior. Thus, from Mowrer's perspective, the animal does not avoid to prevent the presentation of the US, but rather it responds to escape the aversive properties of the CS.

Mowrer's (1947) theory generated considerable research activity in support of it (see Mowrer, 1960). For example, Mowrer maintained that fear is initially elicited by the onset of the US, whereas a Hullian interpretation (Sheffield, 1948) argued that it is the offset of the US that reinforces fear via the principle of drive reduction. Mowrer conducted a series of studies (Mowrer & Lamoreaux, 1946; Mowrer & Solomon, 1954; Mowrer & Viek, 1948) that provided a differential test of the preceding positions. The results of these studies confirmed the onset of the US as the critical element. In a similar vein, Mowrer's contention that the offset of the aversive CS resulted in a reinforcing state of affairs was also confirmed by the results of a number of studies (Brown & Jacobs, 1949; Goldstein, 1960; Hoffman & Fleshler, 1962; Kalish, 1954; Ley, 1965;

D. E. McAllister & W. R. McAllister, 1964; W. R. McAllister & D. E. McAllister, 1971; Miller, 1948).

Perhaps the most compelling support for Mowrer's fear theory account of avoidance behavior came from Miller's (1948) classic study that demonstrated that a previously conditioned aversive CS can provide reinforcement for the learning of a new response once the US had been discontinued. Miller not only achieved this objective, but the study was replicated by Brown and Jacobs (1949) to rule out potential effects of frustration or conflict to which the results might be attributed instead of fear. We know of no other construct offered as a substitute for fear (e.g., a cognitive construct) that is capable of empirically producing this effect. Even Seligman and Johnston's (1973) cognitive theory of avoidance required the addition of a fear construct to account for the acquisition of the avoidance response.

Although a number of competing theories have challenged two-factor and related fear theories' account of avoidance learning (e.g., Bolles, 1969; Dinsmoor, 1950, 1954; Herrnstein, 1969; Seligman & Johnston, 1973; Sidman & Boren, 1957) fear theory has withstood these challenges and still remains the dominant theory within the field some 30 years after Mowrer's (1947) paper (Levis, 1989). Attempts by Rachman (1976), Silva and Rachman (1981), and others to announce the passing of two-factor theory have been, to say the least, premature.

As D. E. McAllister and W. R. McAllister (1991) noted, perhaps the most frequently cited criticism of fear theory is the apparent lack of parallelism between levels of fear of the CS and of avoidance performance (see Domjan & Burkhard, 1986). Critics of fear theory often cite the Kamin, Brimer, and Black (1963) study to support their position. Briefly, these researchers reported that after 27 consecutive two-way avoidance responses there was less fear of the CS (as measured by the suppression of an appetitively reinforced instrumental response) than there was after nine consecutive avoidance responses. The authors then concluded that variables other than the CS must be responsible for the sustained avoidance behavior. However, the Kamin et al. conclusion regarding what fear theory would predict represents a gross misunderstanding of the detail of the theory, as those most familiar with the details of fear theory would not expect that such parallelism would be found in this study. Unfortunately Kamin et al. failed to make a distinction between learning and performance and to take into account the effects of contextual fear cues. If they had, the Kamin et al. results would be consistent with what fear theory would predict (see Levis, 1989; D. E. McAllister & W. R. McAllister, 1991; Mowrer, 1960). Over the years, considerable support for the concordance between fear and avoidance responding has been obtained at both the animal (e.g., Boyd & Levis, 1976; Brush, 1957; Callen, McAllister, & McAllister, 1984; Levis & Boyd, 1979; W. R.

McAllister, D. E. McAllister & Benton, 1983; W. R. McAllister, D. E. McAllister, Scoles, & Hampton 1986; Quartermain & Judge, 1983; Smith & Levis, 1991; Spear, Hamberg, & Bryan, 1980) and at the human level of analysis (e.g., Kaloupek & Levis, 1980, Kaloupek & Levis, 1983; Malloy & Levis, 1988; Peterson & Levis, 1985).

The intricacies of two-factor and related fear theories, along with a review of supporting research, have already been provided in recent years (see Ayres, 1998; Denny, 1991; Levis, 1989, 1991; D. E. McAllister & W. R. McAllister, 1991; W. R. McAllister & D. E. McAllister, 1971), as has a discussion of the criticisms leveled against a fear-theory approach (see Levis, 1989; D. E. McAllister & W. R. McAllister, 1991). Therefore, the remainder of this chapter focuses on the implications of fear theory for the area of psychopathology. In preparing for this objective we need to first address what some critics maintain represents the Achilles heel of fear theory, the issue of sustained avoidance responding in extinction.

It is important to recognize that while acquisition of avoidance learning is occurring, so is the concurrent process of extinction, as the CS occurs in the absence of the US presentation. This state of affairs also exists for clinical patients when they emit a symptom (avoidance behavior). Thus, one may legitimately ask, why is psychotherapy necessary if patients are in an extinction mode of responding, and why do they persist in repeating their symptom over long periods of time? This is the question Freud raised and one that is central to any attempt by avoidance theorists to extrapolate to the clinical situation. In the following section we review those theories that have addressed this critical issue of sustained avoidance responding in extinction, along with an account extrapolated from a two-factor theory position.

THE NEUROTIC PARADOX

In 1926, Freud (see Freud, 1936) pondered over a theoretical issue that perplexed him and defied attempts at solution. In his words:

> We consider it entirely normal that a little girl should weep bitterly at the age of four if her doll is broken, at the age of six if her teacher reprimands her, at the age of sixteen if her sweetheart neglects her, at the age of twenty-five perhaps, if she buries her child. Each of these grief-occasioning situations has its proper time and vanishes with its passing; but the later and more definite ones remain operative throughout life. We should be rather surprised, in fact, if this girl, after she had become a wife and mother, should weep over some knickknack getting broken. Yet this is how the neurotics behave. Although in their mental apparatus there have long since developed all the agencies necessary for dealing with a wide range of stimuli, although

they are mature enough to be able to gratify the greater part of their needs themselves ... they nevertheless behave as though the old danger situation still existed, they remain under the spell of all the old courses of anxiety.... But how does this situation come about? Why are not all neuroses merely episodes in the individual's development which become a closed chapter when the next stage of development is reached? Whence comes the element of permanency in these reactions to danger? ... In other words, we find ourself abruptly confronted once again by the oft-repeated riddle: What is the source of neurosis, what is the ultimate, its specific, underlying principle? After decades of analytic effort this problem arises up before us, as untouched as at the beginning. (pp. 89–92)

Mowrer (1948) later referred to this phenomenon described by Freud as the neurotic paradox. As Stampfl (1987) reported, Mowrer acknowledged that the paradox poses severe difficulties for learning-based explanations of neurotic behavior: "It is the question as to why so-called neurotic behavior is at one time self-defeating and yet self-perpetuating, instead of self-eliminating" (Mowrer, 1950, p. 351). Mowrer (1952) like Freud, questioned, "Why is it then, that in neuroses we have fears which appear to have long outlived any real justification but which stubbornly persist or which may even augment to the point of seriously incapacitating the individual?" (p. 679).

Clinical experience does attest to the finding that exposure to traumatic events rarely produces transient effects on behavior and emotional reactivity, but rather generates effects that have prolonged and even lifetime consequences (Potts, 1994; Schnurr, Aldwin, Spiro, Stukel, & Keane, 1993). A learning theory analysis would predict that once the traumatic situation is removed, the stimulus situations eliciting the onset of symptomatology would eventually be unlearned via the principle of experimental extinction, nonreinforced CS exposure. Eysenck (1976) also reached the conclusion that neurotic behavior does not follow Thorndike's law of effect or Skinner's law of reinforcement. As Eglash (1952) concluded, "We stand today where Freud stood, with the problem unsolved" (p. 378). Clearly, the neurotic paradox and its resolution remains a major nemesis for both the fields of learning and psychopathology. The following section describes attempts by learning theorists to resolve this paradox.

Solomon and Wynne's Principles of Anxiety Conservation and Partial Irreversibility

Cognizant of the need to address this issue, Solomon and Wynne (1954) attempted to theoretically enhance Mowrer's two-factor theory of avoidance based on the results of two studies conducted in Solomon's laboratory (Solomon, Kamin, & Wynne, 1953; Solomon & Wynne, 1953). Prior to the publication of these studies, few laboratory demonstrations were available in the animal laboratory that reflected the extreme resistance to extinction reported with human symptomatic behavior. Unlike the maintenance of human symptoms, animal avoidance learning was reported to extinguish fairly rapidly following the removal of the US (Mackintosh, 1974).

If a learning analysis is to be successfully applied in an attempt to resolve this paradox, a reliable laboratory procedure needs to be developed for producing extreme avoidance maintenance in extinction. Once this is achieved, the underlying principles responsible for maintaining the behavior hopefully can be isolated. Solomon and Wynne (1954) reasoned that if Freud were correct in his analysis that psychopathology is an outgrowth of being exposed to traumatic experiences, then extreme resistance to extinction of avoidance responding may be achieved via the use of a traumatic US. Solomon et al. (1953) appeared to achieve this objective. They found that following exposure to traumatic US presentations during acquisition of a shuttlebox avoidance task, dogs' mean latency of responding following the removal of shock was still getting shorter 200 trials later.

That study, in combination with the results of the Solomon and Wynne (1953) study, led Solomon and Wynne (1954) to highlight three behavioral observations that they believed required explanation in addition to their finding of extreme avoidance maintenance in extinction. The first reported observation under consideration was their finding that the avoidance latencies of the dogs shortened considerably with training, with response latencies under 4 sec being common. Second, they reported that overt signs of anxiety rapidly disappeared with training and seemed nonexistent as responding during the extinction phase continued. Third, if a dog happened to produce a long-latency response on a given extinction trial, behavioral signs of anxiety reportedly reemerged and were followed by a return to short-latency avoidance responding for the next few trials.

In an attempt to reconcile these observations within a two-factor theory framework, Solomon and Wynne (1954) hypothesized that the observation that overt signs of fear rapidly disappeared with continued avoidance regarding occurred because the short-latency responses did not permit the time required for the elicitation of the classically conditioned fear reaction. Without fear elicitation and subsequent fear reduction, the habit strength of the fear response was weakened, resulting in longer latency responses. To account for the reemergence of fear to these long-latency responses, Solomon and Wynne introduced their well-known principle of anxiety conservation, which states that fear conditioned to a previously unexposed part of the CS–US interval will remain intact or be conserved until repeated nonreinforced exposures weaken the previously unexposed segment of the CS. This hypothesis explained their observation that fear reemerged following exposure to the previous unexposed part of the CS–US interval. To account for the animals' return to short-latency responding following a long-latency response, the authors argued that the resulting fear reduction following the long-latency response reinforced the habit strength of the avoidance response, resulting in progressively shorter response latencies. To account for the final observation that some of their dogs failed to show any sustained signs of extinction after 200 extinction trials, Solomon and Wynne concluded that the traumatic conditioning procedure employed in this study produced a functional autonomy state of responding similar to Freud's reported clinical observations.

To account for these observations, Solomon and Wynne proposed their principle of partial irreversibility. This hypothesis is predicated on the premise that a very intense (traumatic) pain–fear reaction conditioned to a given CS pattern will result in some kind of brain alteration that facilitates a permanent fear reaction to the conditioned CS pattern that is capable of sustaining long-term avoidance. The implications of partial irreversibility are profound as, under certain circumstances, fear and symptom elicitation in patients does appear to be a permanent state of affairs, defying the laws of extinction.

Although Solomon and Wynne's (1954) attempt to resolve the neurotic paradox was not completely successful, it did have a major impact on the field of psychopathology. Because their experimental procedure provided a laboratory example of extreme resistance to extinction of discrete trial avoidance behavior, a renewed interest in the clinical field emerged regarding the value of extrapolating principles based on animal research. Clinical symptoms that are viewed by most theorists in the clinical field as avoidance behavior do appear to resist extinction for long periods of time. Furthermore, like Solomon's dogs, patients who have overlearned their symptoms also appear to be performing in the absence of observable overt signs of fear. However, if the symptoms are blocked or ineffective in avoiding the fear-eliciting stimulus, overt signs of fear do appear to reemerge such as was the case for Solomon's dogs and their return to faster symptomatic response time.

Solomon and Wynne's (1954) paper also inadvertently had a major impact on the theoretical rethinking of the merits of Mowrer's fear construct account of avoidance learning. Rather than clarifying issues within the theory, this paper, along with a subsequent paper by Kamin et al. (1963), became a catalyst for generating a host of new avoidance theories within both the experimental and clinical literature that resulted in the reactivation of the classical debate between nonmotivational cognitive and S–R fear interpretations. This ongoing debate continues to remain an issue confronting the field today (e.g., Bandura, 1986; Bolles, 1970, 1972a, 1972b; Herrnstein, 1969; Levis, 1989; D. E. McAllister & W. R. McAllister, 1991; Rachman & Hodgson, 1974; Rescorla & Solomon, 1967; Seligman & Johnston, 1973).

The impetus for some theorists to abandon an S–R analysis of avoidance behavior resides, in part, in Solomon and Wynne's contention that short-latency avoidance responses appear to be elicited in the absence of fear, as is the case for asymptotic avoidance responding generated by procedures that produce extreme resistance to extinction. What Solomon and Wynne implied, and later made explicit as previously discussed by Kamin et al. (1963), is that there exists a lack of parallelism between the presence of the CS and a fear-eliciting response. A fear position requires that fear stimuli be present to elicit avoidance behavior and if present they should obey the laws of fear extinction (Levis, 1989).

It is somewhat mystifying to us that Solomon and Wynne's unsystematic observations regarding the presence or absence of fear were not put to a direct experimental assessment until some 25 years later (see Levis & Boyd, 1979). Yet somehow these observations became assumed as representative of a scientifically established fact. For example, Gray (1971, 1975) accepted Solomon and Wynne's contention that avoidance responding can continue in the absence of fear. Rachman and Hodgson (1974) stated dogmatically that it is well established that avoidance behavior can persist in the absence of fear with no decrease in response strength. A similar conclusion was reached by Bandura (1986) and by Seligman and Johnston (1973). One can only agree with the conclusion reached by D. E. McAllister and W. R. McAllister (1991) that this stated misrepresentation of the literature gives credence to their assertion that Lewis Carroll's Bellman in *The Hunting of the Snark* formulated a powerful law when he stated, "What I tell you three times is true," or as Thomson (1988) asserted, "Repetition is the mother of acceptance" (pp. 59–61).

Rescorla and Solomon's Central State Fear Hypothesis

Rescorla and Solomon (1967) advanced a central state fear hypothesis opposed to Mowrer's (1947) assertion that fear is an emotional state resulting from conditioning involving the autonomic nervous system. Their position maintains that the observed relation between instrumental behavior and peripheral CSs associated with the conditioning of fear may be mediated by a common central state. Although they did not acknowledge the theoretical difficulties the Solomon and Wynne (1954) article presented for fear theory, they were aware that at the time of their article, Solomon and Wynne's principle of partial irreversibility had been seriously weakened by subsequent research conducted in Solomon's laboratory (Brush, 1957).

Unfortunately, the research cited by Solomon and Wynne in support of the effectiveness of traumatic shock failed to include a nontraumatic shock level control group to establish the relation between the traumatic shock level and the finding of extreme resistance to avoidance extinction. When Brush (1957) conducted the necessary study with a lower intensity shock level, he found that the data reported in the preceding studies were not dependent on the use of traumatic shock, thus relegating this principle to obscurity. Although Rescorla and Solomon's (1967) central state hypothesis does provide fear theory an opportunity to "wiggle out" of thorny theoretical issues raised by critics of fear theory, it has the distinct disadvantage of removing one key strength of fear theory, its ability to be tested and disproven. Fear theory maintains that a peripheral fear response must be present to elicit an avoidance response. Rescorla and Solomon provided no direct test or supporting data for their central state hypothesis, nor did they offer a differential prediction between Mowrer's and their concepualizations. Our position is in agreement with the critical assessment of the Rescorla and Solomon paper made by Seligman and Johnston (1973). Therefore, let us proceed in our quest to find a satisfactory theoretical resolution of the neurotic paradox and sustained avoidance responding in extinction.

Since the publication of the Solomon et al. (1953) study, numerous other studies have appeared that have provided examples of extreme resistance to extinction of avoidance behavior both with animals (e.g., Kostanek & Sawrey, 1965; Levis, 1966a, 1966b; Levis, Bouska, Eron, & McIlhon, 1970; Levis & Boyd, 1979; W. R. McAllister et al., 1986; Oliverio, 1967; Stampfl, 1987) and with humans (e.g., Levis, 1971a; Malloy & Levis, 1988; Williams & Levis, 1991).

Eysenck's Fear Incubation Hypothesis

Eysenck's (1968, 1976, 1979, 1985) attempt to resolve the neurotic paradox and issues related to sustained avoidance and symptom maintenance resulted in his advancing a conditioning model of neurosis. At the center of his theory is the theoretical construct of *fear incubation*. Eysenck's use of this term differs from the traditional usage that refers to a growth of fear following fear conditioning over time in the absence of any further exposure to the CS or US. W. R. McAllister and D. E. McAllister (1971) provided a comprehensive critical review of the supporting data for this concept. We are in agreement with their conclusion that although the "incubation-of-fear-hypothesis has been tested in a wide variety of situations, the phenomenon has yet to be convincingly demonstrated" (p. 189).

Eysenck's concept of fear incubation, on the other hand, refers to an increment in the fear response over a period of time that results from additional exposure or exposures to short nonreinforced CS presentations. To account for this increment in fear over time, Eysenck (1968) postulated that the CRs of fear and pain, which he referred to as *novice response* (NRs), themselves have reinforcing properties. According to his theory, when NRs are paired with CSs during extinction trials, the habit strength associating CSs and NRs is capable of being increased, especially when the NRs are particularly strong. In other words, the NRs, in a sense, function as USs, resulting in a continued increase and maintenance of the learned fear response.

In support of his theory, Eysenck cited animal experiments by Napolkov (1963), Lickenstein (1950), and Dykman, Mack, and Ackerman (1965), which he maintained illustrate the presence of autonomic CRs that persisted or even increased in strength over trials following CS exposure. He found additional support for this theory from the reported animal literature on the "paradoxical enhancement" of fear effect (Boyd, 1981; Rohrbaugh & Riccio, 1970; Rohrbaugh, Riccio, & Arthur, 1972; Silvestri, Rohrbaugh, & Riccio, 1970). Human studies cited by Eysenck in support of his incubation theory include those by Campbell, Sanderson, and Laverty (1964), Miller and Levis (1971), Stone and Borkovec (1975), and Sandin and Chorot (1989).

It is argumentative as to how strongly the previously cited studies by Eysenck have a direct bearing on supporting Eysenck's incubation hypothesis. For example, the Napalkov (1963) study that had a major influence on stimulating Eysenck's theory (see Eysenck, 1968, 1979) represents questionable data that have failed an attempt at replication (Kimmel, Kearns, Anderson, 1988). The first author of this chapter has been a persistent critic of Eysenck's supporting data arguing that enhanced fear responding following short CS exposure is related to uncontrolled CS duration effects (Levis, 1979, 1981, 1990; Levis & Malloy, 1982). Levis was not alone in being critical of Eysenck's theory, with 25 leading experts in the area expressing their concerns following the publication of Eysenck's (1979) article.

In fairness to an evaluation of Eysenck's theory, no direct experimental test of his theory was made prior to the preceding criticisms, despite the theory's (Eysenck, 1979) attempt to clearly specify the necessary experimental conditions for the favorable development of fear incubation. The necessary conditions specified by Eysenck (1968, 1979) are: (a) a Pavlovian fear conditioning procedure in which the CR is a drive; (b) a strong US; (c) short exposure of the CS only; and (d) control for individual differences in neuroticism and introversion.

Malloy and Levis (1990) provided a direct test of Eysenck's incubation theory by meeting all four of these conditions for enhancing the incubation effect. First, human participants were presented a single trial of Pavlovian aversive conditioning utilizing either a moderate (2.0 mA) electric shock or an intense US level (6.0 mA). Conditioning trials were equated for all participants, which is a critical requirement in any test of fear incubation. A single conditioning trial was believed desirable to approximate conditions leading to the development of clinical fears of phobias, a point raised by Eysenck (1979) in his criticism of other traditional theories. A single conditioning trial was also used because the "Napalkov effect" reported by Eysenck occurred only for participants receiving a single strong shock presentation. Second, the importance of short CS-only exposure presentations in extinction was examined by presenting individuals either with no postconditioning CS exposure or with exposure of various lengths (2-, 5-, 10-, or 50-sec trials). Total CS exposure was controlled for, which is another critical requirement in any test of differential fear levels. Third, individual differences were examined by assigning participants to blocks based on responses to the Eysenck Personality Inventory (Eysenck & Eysenck, 1968). Eysenck's model predicts individuals who have been rated as having high-neuroticism and low-extraversion personality traits are best suited to demonstrate the effects of fear incubation. Once conditioned fear should increase in these individuals and persist with continued repeated trials of short, nonreinforced CS exposure. Individual differences were also addressed in this study by dividing participants into high and low arousal groups based on spontaneous galvanic skin responses during baseline. This index was examined because Eysenck (1979) stated that electrodermal fluctuation is correlated both with introversion and with neuroticism-anxiety levels. Skin conductance, heartrate, and self-report measures of fear were monitored throughout the experiment.

The results of this experiment lend themselves to the following conclusions. Contrary to the predictions of incubation theory, it was found that (a) neuroticism and introversion levels had no effect on initial conditionability; (b) the fear level for participants defined as being high in neuroticism and introversion did not increase or persist in those receiving high shock and repeated short-CS exposures; and (c) monotonic fear extinction occurred for all participants as a direct function of total CS exposure, a finding predicted by traditional fear theory (Levis, 1989). In conclusion, it appears that both the traditional concept of fear incubation and the concept offered by Eysenck represent phenomena that have yet to be convincingly demonstrated.

Kimble and Perlmuter's Theory of Automatization

The repeated attempts of theorists to account for the finding of sustained avoidance maintenance in extinction by rejecting the established laws of experimental extinction is a puzzling development within the field. It is equally surprising that there appears to be a need to replace these laws with some kind of functional autonomy concept of responding like that proposed by Solomon and Wynne's (1954) principle of partial irreversibility or Eysenck's (1968) principle of incubation. The latest attempt to achieve this objective was provided by Kimble and Perlmuter (1970) when they introduced their principle of automatization. *Automatization*, according to these authors, refers to the process by which well-practiced responses become self-perpetuating at asymptotic performance. Apparently these repetitive responses are initiated and maintained without any direct motivational antecedents. From a fear theory perspective it is unclear how their theory would explain the avoidance paradoxes outlined by Mowrer (1947), the establishment of an orderly process of response latency changes in extinction (e.g., Levis & Boyd, 1979), or the effects of a response prevention procedure in extinguishing the response (e.g., Shipley, Mock, & Levis, 1971), to name but a few areas that represent difficulty for this theory (see Seligman & Johnston's, 1973, critical review of this principle).

COGNITIVE EXPECTANCY THEORIES OF AVOIDANCE MAINTENANCE

Seligman and Johnston's Expectancy Theory

As previously noted in our review of the Solomon and Wynne (1954) article, their observation concerning the relation between fear and sustained avoidance responding failed to clarify fear theory's position regarding this issue. Seligman and Johnston (1973) reached a similar conclusion suggesting that fear theory could not reconcile the findings of sustained avoidance responding in extinction. Their concern was centered on the Solomon et al. (1953) reported observation that behavioral signs of fear were not present in extinction following short-latency asymptotic responding and 200 consecutive avoidance trials. They even noted that one of Solomon's dogs responded for 490 consecutive responses without extinguishing. They bolstered their argument that fear in the Solomon studies had extinguished long before avoidance responding was terminated by citing the Annau and Kamin (1961) study. These investigators reported that rats exposed to a classical fear-conditioning procedure extinguished within 40 trials following high levels of shock.

Seligman and Johnston (1973) then reasoned that another construct was needed to explain this apparent absence of fear. In their attempt to replace fear theory with their own comprehensive theory of avoidance, they proposed that two constructs were needed to explain the findings of the Solomon studies. They retained the fear construct to explain the initial acquisition of avoidance behavior and then added a cognitive component that relies on the constructs of expectancies and preferences to serve as the primary mechanism supporting the maintenance of the avoidance response. The theory postulates that in an avoidance situation the animal or human prefers no shock following a response over shock. They also can develop one of two expectancies: Either a response will be followed by a US if it does not occur within a given time period (CS–US interval) or a nonresponse will not be followed by a US. Expectancies are strengthened when they are confirmed and weakened when they are disconfirmed. In a sense, Seligman and Johnston's theory appears to be an extension to the avoidance area of Maier and Seligman's (1976) learned helplessness theory (see Levis, 1976, for a critical review of this theory). Unfortunately, no new supporting data were offered by Seligman and Johnston in their article, but they did indirectly provide a differential test between an expectancy theory and a fear position. They argued that fear indexed by autonomic responses and conditioned emotional responses (CERs) would not be present to the CS eliciting a short-duration response during asymptotic responding. It would also follow that a fear index would not be present to the CS following extended avoidance responding in extinction. Fear theory, on the other hand, maintains fear must be present to the CS whenever an avoidance response is emitted.

The Expectancy Hypothesis of Bolles and Herrnstein

Other theories by Bolles (1972a, 1972b) and Herrnstein (1969) have also introduced an expectancy construct into their theories. For example, Bolles (1972b) hypothesized that two expectancies are involved in avoidance tasks. The first expectancy learned is that the CS will be followed by shock and, as a result, it serves as a danger signal. The other expectancy is that a certain response will lead to safety. Initially, Bolles (1970, 1972a) regarded this latter expectancy as unlearned and resulting from innate species-specific defense responses like fleeing, freezing, or fighting, which predict safety. Later, Bolles (1972b) argued that these innate species-specific behaviors are modifiable. For example, if the expectancy that freezing leads to safety is disconfirmed by being punished by shock, it will be replaced by the expectancy that running leads to safety if this behavior is confirmed. If both of these species-specific behaviors are learned not to produce safety, the next response in the hierarchy or an alternative species-specific behavior will be made until safety is achieved by either a species-specific behavior or some arbitrary response. Bolles (1975) later modified this theory, suggesting that the learning in an aversive situation consists entirely of species-specific defensive responses determined in part by the organism's expectancies of danger and safety and in part by the structure of environmental supporting stimuli.

It is unclear how the theories of Bolles directly relate to the issue of sustained avoidance maintenance in extinction. Bolles (1972a), who linked his theory to that of Denny (1971), did conclude that safety signals were capable of creating a relaxation state that may produce an abatement of species-specific and learned defensive behavior. Although Bolles did not himself imply it, one could argue (see Seligman & Johnston, 1973) that once safety signals have become well established, they may provide positive reinforcement for maintaining avoidance responding as Denny suggested (see Denny, 1991, for a review of this theory). However, both Denny's and Bolles's theories need to overcome the obstacle of how positively reinforced safety signals are capable of maintaining their reinforcing properties over extended periods of time, as is the case with extreme avoidance responding and with patients who engage in avoidance (symptom) behavior over periods of years. Would not one expect that repeated exposure to the safety stimuli would eventually lead to an extinction of the reinforcing properties of these cues? This same problem exists for Herrnstein's (1969) theory that dispenses with fear and aversion as well (see Seligman & Johnston's, 1973, critical analysis of these theories, and D. E. McAllister & W. R. McAllister's, 1991, review of these theories from a fear theory framework).

THE SOLOMON AND WYNNE DATA RECONSIDERED: A FEAR THEORY'S RESPONSE TO COGNITIVE EXPECTANCY THEORIES

From the authors' perspective, the previously reviewed expectancy theories do not account for the details of behavior reported in the established avoidance literature. Validated dependent measures of the construct of expectancy have not been forthcoming, which prevents any assessment of the laws governing the acquisition and extinction of a given expectancy. For example, at what point does an expectancy develop and at what point does it change? Is the learning of an expectancy an all-or-none or a gradual process such as suggested by Bolles? Can the presence or absence of the construct only be determined after the fact when the behavior has already changed? These questions represent only a few of the issues that are left unresolved. The ability of fear theory to achieve this objective is the very reason the model has persisted. Nevertheless, fear theorists need to address the issues raised by Seligman and Johnston (1973) and other fear critics. To achieve this objective, we need to reconsider the Solomon and Wynne (1954) reported findings from a fear theory perspective.

The Absence of Fear Hypotheses Reconsidered

D. E. McAllister and W. R. McAllister (1991), in their review of the Solomon et al. (1953) study, took issue with Solomon and Wynne's (1954) statement that "overt signs of anxiety rapidly disappeared" (p. 359) during the extinction trials. They argued that the data from the Solomon et al. (1953) study do not support this claim. In this study, observational data were obtained concerning overt behavior such as vocalizing, excreting, salivating, trembling, and so on, to assess the presence of fear. Although these authors did report that some dogs showed no overt emotional signs of fear during the latter part of ordinary extinction, they also reported that despite the findings that some of these fear indexes displayed a decrease in magnitude across extinction trials, others also persisted throughout the 200 trials (see Solomon et al., 1953). D. E. McAllister and W. R. McAllister (1991) concluded, "it is clear that the data as a whole do not support the blanket assertion that overt signs of fear were not present when avoidance responding was at asymptote" (pp. 144–145). They also noted that in related studies (Brush, Brush, & Solomon, 1955; Kamin, 1954) these authors reported that some emotional behavior persisted through the first 100 or 200 extinction trials.

To argue for the need to incorporate a cognitive construct like expectancy, it is essential that the presence or absence of fear to short-latency asymptotic avoidance behavior be established experimentally rather than simply assuming fear is absent as Seligman and Johnston did. Therefore, following the experimental analysis of fear testing suggested by Seligman and Johnston (1973), Levis and Boyd (1979, Experiment 2) trained rats to a criterion of 50 consecutive, short-latency (less than 4 sec) avoidance responses. Following this phase, the CS used to elicit avoidance responding was transferred to a CER paradigm to test the presence or absence of fear at a level of asymptotic responding. Previously conducted CER studies (e.g., Kamin et al., 1963) do not have any direct bearing on the question raised in this study because they either failed to equate groups on total nonreinforced CS exposure experienced prior to suppression testing or they permitted exposure to longer CS durations, which could, in turn, re-reinforce short-latency avoidance responding differentially. This same problem of uncontrolled CS exposure periods also existed in the Solomon studies. To reduce both of these problems, a trace procedure was used to control for the maximum length of CS exposure on each trial and to provide a CS–US interval long enough to produce 50 consecutive short-latency responses within the 200 avoidance trial imposed limit. The control sensitization group subjects were exposed during suppression testing to an alternate CS that had been used during conditioning.

The mean number of trials required to reach the learning criterion of 50 consecutive avoidance trials with response latency of less than 4 sec was 51.38 with the mean per-trial response latency being 1.85 sec, which clearly supports the contention that the avoidance response latency was at an asymptotic performance level. Three days of suppression testing to the CS was then conducted. All subjects in the experimental group displayed reliable suppression effects across the 3 test days, with most subjects displaying complete suppression to the first CS exposure at Day 1 testing. These findings argued for the presence of fear to the CS following short-latency asymptotic avoidance responding in direct disconfirmation of the Seligman and Johnston (1973) prediction.

Levis and Boyd (1979) also criticized Seligman and Johnston's (1973) use of the Solomon et al. (1954) data in providing a rationale for their expectancy construct. They noted that one of Solomon's dogs responded for 490 trials without showing signs of extinction. In addition, they argued that in the Annau and Kamin (1961) study the conditioned fear response extinguished within 40 trials, suggesting that fear to the CS had also extinguished in the Solomon studies long before avoidance responding was terminated. However, when the issue of total CS exposure between studies is evaluated, a different conclusion is reached. The average response latency for Solomon's dog that responded for 490 trials probably varied from 1 to 4 sec. If this were the case, total CS exposure would be around 1,000 sec (assuming an average per-trial exposure of 2 sec (490 × 2). Total CS exposure before extinction occurred in the Annau and Kamin study was 2,400 sec (60 sec per trial × 40). It would then follow that 1,000 sec of CS exposure in the dog that emitted 490 responses would be insufficient for complete fear extinction to have occurred given the data from Annau and Kamin (1961).

The Levis and Boyd (1979) data supporting fear theory's contention that fear is present to the CS following asymptotic avoidance responding was recently confirmed by a Smith and Levis (1991) replication study. Additional evidence has also been developed, demonstrating the presence of fear following extreme resistance to extinction of avoidance behavior in both animals and human conditioning studies (e.g., Levis & Boyd, 1979, Experiment 1; Malloy & Levis, 1988; Williams & Levis, 1991). In addition, a number of studies have reported a sizable amount of fear of the CS is present following the conditioning of a well-learned avoidance response (e.g., W. R. McAllister et al., 1983; Mineka & Gino, 1980; Morris, 1974; Starr & Mineka, 1977).

Finally, we would like to briefly describe an unpublished study with humans conducted by Unger (1988) that provided an additional test of Seligman and Johnston's (1973) expectancy theory by investigating the classically conditioned fear component of a CS. On Day 1, participants received the presentation of one classical fear conditioning trial of a relatively mild electric shock (2.5 mA) of .2 sec duration. This was followed by an avoidance procedure for five additional trials in which a failure to respond resulted in the onset of the US. Therefore the maximum number of shocks received by any participant was six. Avoidance trials were continued until participants met a criterion of 10 consecutive short-latency asymptotic avoidance responses. At the end of this phase of the experiment, each participant's electric shock electrodes were removed, as was the hand dynamometer avoidance apparatus. Five classical fear extinction trials to the CS were then administered in which no avoidance response was possible. On Day 2, 10 additional classical fear extinction test presentations of the CS were administered in the absence of any shock electrode attachment or in the presence of the hand dynamometer avoidance apparatus. The test CS presentations permitted the assessment of the presence of fear as indexed by the magnitude of the skin conductance response (SCR) measure. The results indicated that a conditioned fear response was still present to the CS as indexed by the SCR data and the responses to a self-report fear thermometer. These findings occurred despite the fact that 96% of the participants reported that on Day 2 they had no, or at best only a very low expectation that the test trials would be followed by shock.

Taken collectively, these studies support fear theory's contention that fear is the motivating stimulus for sustained avoidance responding in extinction. At asymptotic responding, overt behavior signs of fear would not be expected to occur as only a minimum level of fear would be needed to elicit the response at this point. Further, both clinical and animal data suggest that if an asymptotic avoidance response is blocked, strong levels of fear can be observed. Thus, we believe the weight of evidence is very damaging to Seligman and Johnston's (1973) cognitive theory of expectancy as well as to the other expectancy theories reviewed.

Stampfl's Two-Factor Theory Resolution of the Neurotic Paradox

The foregoing cognitive accounts of avoidance maintenance not only represent theoretical attempts to replace an S–R behavioral fear interpretation of avoidance learning, but also reflect a position that essentially returns the field to an interpretative framework proposed by

Hilgard and Marquis (1940). Further, the focus on a cognitive, as opposed to emotional, mediator reduces the impact of the area to affect the field of psychopathology that has historically held the belief that the motivation for symptom maintenance is emotional (Alexander, 1965). Despite the tremendous impact animal learning data have had on the development of the behavioral field of psychotherapy (Levis, 1970), recent trends in the behavioral movement have been more influenced by developments in the cognitive area of psychology than in the literature being generated within the animal area (see Levis, 1999a). A number of animal psychologists have also reached the conclusion that the value of extrapolation from the learning laboratory to the human situation is limited. Domjan (1987), for example, in commenting on the power of extrapolating laboratory research stated, "Such enthusiastic embrace of animal research has been discouraged by increasing evidence of the complexity of various forms of human behavior" (pp. 558–559). In a similar vein, Mineka (1985) reached the conclusion that animal research fails to manifest phenomena related to human psychopathology. However, we agree with Stampfl's (1983) defense of such extrapolations when he stated:

> Learning-based behavioral treatment techniques received most of their impetus and development from experimental research with lower animals. The major theories of learning and conditioning were products of decades of research efforts that generated a wealth of various formulations that explicated central phenomena of the learning laboratory. As Teasdale aptly remarks, "The single most important theoretical exercise in the development of the behavioral treatments was the imaginative leap of regarding aspects of the clinical problems as similar to behaviors studied within established paradigms." (p. 528)

In the late 1950s Stampfl himself made such an advance. His familiarity with the existing animal avoidance literature coupled with his experience with severe child and adult human psychopathology led him to develop, from a two-factor avoidance theory framework, the clinical treatment technique of implosive (flooding) therapy (Stampfl, 1961). He recognized that despite the obvious complexity and multiplicity of stimuli involved in the conditioning and maintenance of clinical symptoms representing human psychopathology, and despite the tendency of animal researchers to omit such complexities in conducting their research, that the basic established laws of learning were generalizable.

In summary, some of the key variables that he hypothesized as playing a central role in the development and maintenance of human psychopathology included the complexity of the CS patterns conditioned, the sequencing and ordering of these patterns in memory from least to most aversive, the role of context (external and internal), the unique combination of multiple CSs and USs, the presence of multiple contexts, the inclusion of a wide variety of sensory modalities, the multiple sensory correlates involved in the conditioned pain and fear CSs, and the unique form of pain associated with a traumatic US. The established principles of behavior that Stampfl incorporated within his theory include those associated with secondary intermittent reinforcement, work requirement or response cost, time-out from avoidance, alternative responding, associative cue reactivation, and overlapping generalization of extinction gradients for both CSs and contexts. In addition, other standard principles of conditioning, such as higher order conditioning, secondary conditioning and reinforcement, stimulus generalization, and generalization of extinction and intermittent primary reinforcement are included in the analysis (see Levis, 1985; Stampfl, 1970, 1991).

His goal of extending some of these principles, which he found operating in clinical patients, to laboratory research led to the development of his theoretical resolution of the neurotic paradox.

The Extension of the Principle of Conservation of Anxiety

Recall that Solomon and Wynne's principle of anxiety conservation refers to the notion that the animal's avoidance behavior prevents full exposure to the total CS and that the part of the CS that the avoidance response prevents from being exposed is in turn protected from fear extinction. In other words, fear conditioned to a given CS will be conserved to the unexposed part of the CS complex until it undergoes an extinction process from subsequent nonreinforced exposure. In the same vein, human clinical symptoms (avoidance behaviors) prevent full exposure to the CS patterns (internal and external) eliciting their symptomatology. Stampfl (1961; Stampfl & Levis, 1967) reasoned from his observations of human symptom maintenance that the neurotic paradox could be conceptually understood by extending the conservation of anxiety principle. He assumed that the traumatic conditioning events responsible for maintaining human symptomology occur to a complex network of cues that are presumably stored sequentially in memory in order of their aversive loading and in terms of their accessibility to reactivation. Stampfl reasoned that if avoidance behavior conserved the fear to longer CS segments by preventing their exposure, then the principle of anxiety conservation could be maximized even further by dividing the CS–US interval into distinctive stimulus components arranged in a serial order. This procedure should, in theory, enhance the conservation of anxiety effects from a short CS exposure to a long CS exposure and from one component of the serial CS to the next and so forth, resulting in a procedure that substantially increases avoidance maintenance and resistance to extinction. He then conducted his own animal research and found this to be the case. For example, consider the presentation of an 18-sec CS–US interval in which the first 6 sec of the CS involved the presentation of a tone (S1), the next 6 sec consisted of the presentation of flashing lights (S2), and the last segment of the CS–US interval involved the presentation of a low-intensity buzzer (S3). Once avoidance responding is established to the S1 component in the CS chain, S2 and S3 are prevented from exposure. The fear level to the S2 and S3 components of the serial CS should be conserved because any extinction effects from exposure to the S1 component would be unlikely to generalize to these latter components due to their stimulus dissimilarity to the exposed part of the interval. Thus, it would follow that the greater the reduction in generalization of extinction effects from the early exposed part of the CS–US interval to the unexposed parts, the greater would be the degree of anxiety conservation to the components closer to the US onset, the S2 and S3 components.

However, as long as both the animal and the human are exposed to part of the CS complex condition, the laws of experimental extinction are operating. Nevertheless, the serial CS procedure should retard the extinction process in the following manner. As the exposure to the S1 stimulus weakens the fear level to this stimulus, longer latency responses will gradually occur, resulting in more exposure to the protected part of the CS. Eventually exposure to the S2 component will occur. At this point, the level of fear activation will change from a relatively low level as elicited by the S1 component to a high state as elicited by the S2 component, whose fear level has been protected from infrequent exposure. Upon the exposure of S2 an increase in the behavioral signs of fear should be apparent. Once exposed, the S2 component then becomes capable of functioning as a second-order conditioning stimulus (see Rescorla, 1980). The pairing of the S1 with the S2 component should result in a reconditioning effect of the S1 component, producing a return to short-latency avoidance responses, which in turn, prevents further exposure to the S2 component, ultimately conserving the remaining fear level to this stimulus. This process will be repeated until the S1 component is extinguished, leading to responding being under the control of the S2 component. With the eventual weakening of the fear level to the S2 component, the S3 component, the stimulus with the highest loading of fear due to its proximity to the US during the original conditioning, will be exposed. Upon exposure of the S3 component, the S2 components will be reconditioned secondarily, which in turn, if the fear level is high enough, will result in the reconditioning of the S1 component. The overall effect of this process is to produce a distribution of avoidance latencies in extinction that manifest a see-saw appearance (see Levis, 1979, 1989). Thus, by adding components in a serial fashion, one both maximizes the conservation of anxiety principle and the principle of secondary intermittent reinforcement resulting in a procedure that produces extreme resistance to extinction. The authors agree with Stampfl's contention that these two principles in combination with others provides ample support for an S–R fear interpretation of the neurotic paradox.

Experimental support for the principle of anxiety conservation using a nonserial procedure (Delude & Carlson, 1964; Weinberger, 1965), as well as the enhancement of this principle via the use of a serial CS procedure in nonhumans (Boyd & Levis, 1976; Levis, 1966a, 1966b; Levis et al., 1970; Levis & Boyd, 1979; Levis & Stampfl, 1972) and in humans (Levis, 1971a; Malloy & Levis, 1988; Williams & Levis, 1991) has been obtained.

Clinical data (Levis, 1995) obtained from hundreds of decoded memories of patients who reportedly have been exposed to extensive childhood traumatic conditioning trials involving repeated occurrences of physical and sexual abuse also support Stampfl's assertion that a complex set of conditioned sequential stimuli are involved in maintenance of human psychopathology. Further, an analysis of the decoding process supports Stampfl's assertion that the aversive loading of these traumatic events are ordered in terms of their accessibility along a dimension of severity, with the least aversive cues being reactivated first.

However, as Stampfl (1987) observed, laboratory research frequently omits essential requirements in the analysis of behavior. If laboratory research is to have an impact on explaining complex human behavior, the principles derived from such an analysis must be combined to conform to known features of human psychopathology. As Kimble (1961) concluded over 35 years ago,

> It may, some day, be known whether the laws of conditioning do or do not explain (say) psychological behavior. But that day is still in the future. For the time being all that is possible is to attempt the explanation of complex phenomena in simpler terms. It is to be expected that the resulting explanation will be incomplete and imperfect. Complex behavior, if it is explainable at all in these terms, certainly involves the simultaneous operation of many principles of conditioning. Unfortunately, these principles are not exactly known, and we know even less about the way in which they interact and function together. (p. 436)

Stampfl (1987) attempted to achieve this objective by combining the principles associated with serial CS presentations with those associated with time-out from avoidance. More specifically, he increased the power of a serial CS procedure by introducing contextual changes along a spatial–temporal dimension in which avoidance responses made to stimuli early in the sequence required less work than those made to stimuli later in the serial sequence. Therefore, avoidance responses made to stimuli early in the sequence received more differential reinforcement than responses made to stimuli later in the sequence. Following an initial single-shock trial, animals made more than 1,000 successive responses over five 2-hr sessions, demonstrating that increased time-out from avoidance serves as another critical variable in producing sustained avoidance maintenance. In total, this research provides laboratory data for an animal model of one-trial fear conditioning, complete avoidance of the "phobic" CS, and persistent avoidance responding that is consistent with observations of human phobic behavior, thereby supplementing his theoretical attempt to resolve the neurotic paradox.

Stampfl's Technique of Implosive Therapy

Stampfl's model of treatment incorporated a response prevention procedure of extinction (see Page, 1955; Shipley et al., 1971) based on the principle of direct experimental extinction. At first his approach to treatment involved the presentation of in vivo CS cues. This approach is sometimes referred to as *flooding therapy*. He later modified the technique to incorporate an imagery procedure to enhance the ability to include a wider range of historical, contemporary, and hypothesized fear stimuli (Stampfl, 1961; Stampfl & Levis, 1967).

Implosive therapy has been used successfully to treat a wide range of clinical symptoms including phobic behavior, obsessive–compulsive behavior, depression, pervasive anxiety, hysteria, hallucinations, delusions, and other types of maladaptive behaviors that occur in patients labeled neurotic or psychotic (see Levis & Boyd, 1985; Levis & Hare, 1977). Further, the technique has been clinically used for more than 30 years and its safety has been firmly established (Boudewyns & Shipley, 1983). Details of the treatment procedure and its implementation can be found in several references (Boudewyns & Shipley, 1983; Levis, 1980, 1985, 1995; Stampfl, 1970; Stampfl & Levis, 1967, 1969, 1973, 1976).

The Memory Reactivation Component

Early in the development of implosive therapy, Stampfl (see Stampfl & Levis, 1967) recognized that the technique was capable of reactivating previously nonreportable memories of historical conditioning events that apparently were not, prior to treatment, in conscious awareness. These reactivated memories were reported during and following scene presentation. The emphasis of the technique on presenting context cues (e.g., detailed description of the patient's childhood house) and on imagining the presence of multiple stimulus sensations (e.g., visual, auditory, tactile) represents the critical variables believed to be responsible for the enhanced memory reactivation (see Riccio & Spear, 1991; Spear, 1978).

Following a slight modification in Stampfl's procedure, Levis (1988) was able to enhance the memory reactivation component of implosive therapy to the point where it appears that complete reactivation of all the key traumatic experiences underlying the patient's symptomatic behavior can be recovered. The decoding procedure, which simply involves turning the responsibility from producing the memories over to the patient, appears to be complete, in that all stimuli, internal and external, associated with the beginning, middle, and end of a given traumatic event are reproduced in great detail. This includes: (a) the reactivation of all sensory systems involved in the original conditioning event including the visual, tactual, auditory, kinesthetic, and odoriferous systems; (b) all cognitive components including words spoken and internal thoughts and fears elicited; and most important (c) the release of all autonomic responses conditioned including the memory of pain.

To date, literally hundreds of decoded traumatic memories, collected over a period of some 20 years, have been recorded on audio and videotapes. These traumatic events are associated with a wide range of clinical symptoms. The decoding process appears to be lawful in that the various stages involved in the decoding process have been similar for some 30 patients treated thus far. To the authors' knowledge, these reported memories represent the only database of traumatic memory recovery that is free of any suggestive influences. The therapists rarely speak at all and remain strictly "neutral" as to the reality or accuracy of the decoding content (Levis, 1988, 1995, 1999b). These reported memories are currently being analyzed by a behavioral coding procedure that is designed to map out the details of how the brain releases and inhibits the reportedly stored events. A summary of the procedure used and the preliminary findings reported thus far can be found in Levis (1988, 1991a, 1991b, 1995). It is our belief that once this database is fully analyzed, the results will have a number of important implications for the field. To date, it appears the findings strongly support Stampfl's resolution of the neurotic paradox.

IMPLICATIONS FOR FURTHER LABORATORY RESEARCH

The future of animal research may well depend in part on the ability of the research to shed light on the human situation. Stampfl's (1983) comment regarding the noted decrease in animal research interest by behavior therapists is just as true today as it was then: "It is ironic that this state of affairs should exist precisely at a time when marvelous opportunities of solidly based theoretical innovations to the human condition may readily be inferred from the contemporary learning and conditioning literature" (p. 528).

Both Levis (1991a) and Stampfl (1991) argued that this trend could be reversed if more studies were designed to address clinical interest by conceptually isolating the combination of learning principles operating within complex human situations so they can be brought under controlled laboratory research provided by existing animal paradigms. Stampfl's (1987) previously described study illustrates this point by producing a powerful laboratory effect that is reflective of the clinical situation through his combination of established principles of learning.

In addition to the suggestions offered by Stampfl's (1991) article, it may prove helpful for animal researchers to familiarize themselves with the clinical data obtained from reported recovery of traumatic memories. Our own database in this area suggests that the patient goes through numerous replications of a given traumatic event before it is completely decoded and all of the affectively conditioned cues are fully extinguished. Each replication releases more CS components associated with the traumatic experience. It is also apparent from this data set that the affective loading attached to the various CS components embedded in the memory have differential loading, with the most aversive elements of the context of cues being recovered last. For example, one patient who recovered in considerable detail the context cues associated with her bedroom avoided recalling the presence of a large perfume bottle that sat on her dresser. It turned out that when the memory was fully decoded her father had punished her with this bottle by jamming it into her vagina. Her defense structure prevented her from recalling this object earlier until the other CS components associated with the memory had undergone an extinction effect. Indeed the presence of such highly aversive embedded "hidden cues" within traumatic memories is a common finding (see Levis, 1991a, for a discussion of this finding).

Although laboratory research rarely approaches the kind of complexity reported by clinical researchers who deal with trauma, considerably more work is needed in the laboratory to enhance the specification of the CSs involved in a given conditioned complex, as well as to determine the distribution of fear loading associated with the different components of the complex. This lack of CS specificity is a frequent criticism cited against fear theory (e.g., Herrnstein, 1969), although it should be noted that the problem exists for most conditioning analyses.

Pavlov (1927) was one of the first to recognize this issue. He cautioned that to evaluate the contribution of stimuli in complex situations, it is essential that the independent variables be isolated to permit quantitative evaluation. Hull (1943) reiterated this point when he devoted a whole chapter in his book to discussing the issue of what constitutes the CS. Using Pavlov's classical conditioning study with dogs as an example, Hull, in defining the CS, argued against the misleading suggestion of singularity and simplicity. Following a paragraph in which he attempted to outline all the potential CS components present in Pavlov's experiment, he concluded *"The conditioned stimulus in the experiment under consideration includes all of the immensely complicated stimuli here enumerated and many more besides"* (pp. 205–206).

As D. E. McAllister and W. R. McAllister's (1991) research suggests, it is a mistake of oversimplification to refer to the CS in a given experiment as being the external manipulated stimulus designated by the experimenter (e.g., a tone). For example, the researchers just discussed have already documented the important role that the apparatus cues play in sustaining fear-elicited avoidance behavior. Yet, research has not fully isolated which components of the apparatus complex associated with context conditioning are controlling the animal behavior and if the animal is given forced exposure to these cues, which behaviors are engaged in to reduce the effects of complete CS exposure and subsequent extinction. In a sense, the complexities involved in the conditioning of context cues may prove to be analogues to the clinical example provided in which the patient was able to inhibit the reactivation of hidden cues embedded within the conditioned context cue associated with her traumatic experience.

In an attempt to illustrate this point, an unpublished study conducted in our laboratory by Levis, Smith, Williams, and Zottola (1990) is briefly described. This study modeled after Corriveau and Smith (1978) was designed to more fully assess the role of extended nonreinforced exposure to a previously fear-conditioned box, in which the context cues of the chamber served in the CS. Three experiments were conducted. Each experiment employed the same acquisition procedure, which consisted of a 10-sec exposure period to the contextual apparatus cues of the box followed by a 2-sec duration of a 2 mA level shock to the grid floor. Following the fear acquisition phase of the experiments, rats were exposed to a time-lapse period in which various forced CS exposure time periods were given in the fear-conditioned box to facilitate fear extinction. In Experiment 1, subjects received either a 30-, 60-, or 120-min time-lapsed duration. In Experiments 2 and 3, subjects received 120-min time-lapse duration periods. The third phase of each experiment involved testing for the presence of fear to the conditioned chamber. This was achieved by placing each subject into an adjoining safe box that comprised completely different contextual cues (color and floor surface). Each subject was next provided an opportunity to reenter the shock box. Extinction was defined as entering into the shock compartment and remaining there for a 60-sec period. Various reentry latency measures were also analyzed.

For each experiment, 12 subjects were assigned to each of three groups: (a) a forced-exposure extinction condition (FE), (b) a time control (TC) group that spent their time-lapse period in a carrying cage away from the apparatus, and (c) a nonshock control group (NS) that spent their time-lapse period in the shock compartment in the absence of any shock administration. Subjects in Experiment 1 were tested for the presence of fear following fear conditioning on each of 2 successive days. Subjects in Experiments 2 and 3 were tested for fear on 3 and 5 successive days, respectively.

Experiment 1 subjects' data supported fear theory's contention that the forced CS exposure leads to extinction. Group FE reliably differed from the other groups on both days of testing across each of the fear measures analyzed. However, the analysis of Experiment 2 data, in contrast to the previous study, failed to find any extinction criterion differences between Groups FE and TC on testing Days 1 and 3. Testing Day 2 data, however, revealed considerable extinction effects for Group FE subjects. Experiment 3 findings were similar to those of Experiment 2.

These results may at first appear to be contrary to the expectation of fear theory. However, in each of the experiments fear extinction from forced CS exposure was obtained with a baseline level of responding occurring at some point during testing. The findings in Experiments 2 and 3 that the return to baseline by Group FE subjects would lead to an increase in fear followed by a subsequent reduction was hypothesized based on the assumption that the sole use of context cues as the CS mitigates against complete extinction because of a lack of stimulus control. The organism can crouch in a corner, face the back of the box, and close its eyes to avoid exposing itself to the complete context of the cues conditioned. However, as these avoidance responses extinguish, movement within the box can occur, resulting in exposure to those cue elements that have yet to receive sufficient CS exposure. Thus, if this analysis is correct, one would expect the periodic return of the fear response, which is precisely what the data reflect.

These findings are reflective of what appears to be occurring in the clinical situation. Patients who suffer from posttraumatic stress have a lifelong history of recurring bouts of fear and anxiety as they periodically are exposed to unextinguished conditioned cues associated with their past traumatic experiences. The desire to reduce such prolonged suffering is why we recommend conducting more research on isolating the components of the CS complex and on studies that deal with the reinstatement of fear (D. E. McAllister & W. R. McAllister, 1991), on issues associated with residual fear (Riccio & Silvestri, 1973), on aversive events (Stampfl, 1991), on decoding animals' memory of aversive events (Riccio & Spear, 1991), and on extinction (see Rescorla, chap. 4, this volume) to name only a few areas that have had an impact on the clinical field. In fact we believe that most of the chapters that appear in this volume have important implications for applied areas of research. It is our further belief that the potential in the animal research area for creating functional paradigms to help solve the riddles associated with human problems not only currently exists but is immense. It is our hope that those of you who are inclined will help us achieve this objective.

■ REFERENCES

Alexander, F. (1965). The dynamics of psychotherapy in the light of learning theory. *International Journal of Psychiatry, 1*, 189–197.

Annau, Z., & Kamin, L. J. (1961). The conditioned emotional response as a function of intensity of the US. *Journal of Comparative and Physiological Psychology, 54*, 428–430.

Ayres, J. J. B. (1998). Fear conditioning and avoidance. In W. O'Donohue (Ed.), *Learning and behavior therapy* (pp. 122–145). Boston: Allyn & Bacon.

Bandura, A. (1986). Fearful expectations and avoidant actions as coeffects of perceived self-inefficacy. *American Psychologist, 41*, 1389–1391.

Bolles, R. C. (1969). Avoidance and escape learning: Simultaneous acquisition of different responses. *Journal of Comparative and Physiological Psychology, 68*, 355–358.

Bolles, R. C. (1970). Species-specific defense reactions and avoidance learning. *Psychological Review, 77*, 32–48.

Bolles, R. C. (1972a). The avoidance learning problem. In G. H. Bower (Ed.), *The psychology of learning and motivation* (Vol. 6, pp. 97–145). New York: Academic Press.

Bolles, R. C. (1972b). Reinforcement, expectancy, and learning. *Psychological Review, 79*, 394–409.

Bolles, R. C. (1975). *Theory of motivation,* (2nd ed.). New York: Harper & Row.

Boudewyns, P. A., & Shipley, R. H. (1983). *Flooding and implosive therapy.* New York: Plenum.

Boyd, T. L. (1981). The effects of shock intensity on fear incubation (enhancement): A preliminary investigation of Eysenck's theory. *Behaviour Research and Therapy, 19*, 413–418.

Boyd, T. L., & Levis, D. J. (1976). The effects of single-component extinction of a three-component serial CS on resistance to extinction of the conditioned avoidance response. *Learning and Motivation, 7*, 517–531.

Brown, J. S. (1961). *The motivation of behavior.* New York: McGraw-Hill.

Brown, J. S., & Jacobs, A. (1949). The role of fear in the motivation and acquisition of responses. *Journal of Experimental Psychology, 39*, 747–759.

Brush, F. R. (1957). The effect of shock intensity on the acquisition and extinction of an avoidance response in dogs. *Journal of Comparative and Physiological Psychology, 50*, 547–552.

Brush, F. R., Brush, E. S., & Solomon, R. L. (1955). Traumatic avoidance learning: The effects of CS–US interval with a delayed-conditioning procedure. *Journal of Comparative and Physiological Psychology, 48*, 285–293.

Callen, E. J., McAllister, W. R., & McAllister, D. E. (1984). Investigations of the reinstatement of extinguished fear. *Learning and Motivation, 15*, 302–320.

Campbell, D., Sanderson, R. E., & Laverty, S. G. (1964). Characteristics of a conditioned response in human subjects during extinction trials following a single traumatic conditioning trial. *Journal of Abnormal and Social Psychology, 68*, 627–639.

Corriveau, D. P., & Smith, N. F. (1978). Fear reduction and "safety-test" behavior following response prevention: A multivariate analysis. *Journal of Experimental Psychology: General, 107*, 145–158.

Delude, L. A., & Carlson, N. J. (1964). A test of the conservation of anxiety and partial irreversibility hypothesis. *Canadian Journal of Psychology, 18*, 15–22.

Denny, M. R. (1971). Relaxation theory and experiments. In F. R. Brush (Ed.), *Aversive conditioning and learning* (pp. 235–295). New York: Academic Press.

Denny, M. R. (1991). *Fear, avoidance and phobias: A fundamental analysis.* Hillsdale, NJ: Lawrence Erlbaum Associates.

Dinsmoor, J. A. (1950). A quantitative comparison of the discriminative and reinforcing functions of a stimulus. *Journal of Experimental Psychology, 41*, 458–472.

Dinsmoor, J. A. (1954). Punishment: I. The avoidance hypothesis. *Psychological Review, 61*, 34–36.

Dollard, J., & Miller, N. E. (1950). *Personality and psychotherapy.* New York: McGraw-Hill.

Domjan, M. (1987). Animal learning comes of age. *American Psychologist, 42*, 556–564.

Domjan, M., & Burkhard, B. (1986). *The principles of learning and behavior*, (2nd ed.). Monterey, CA: Brooks/Cole.

Dykman, R. A., Mack, R. L., & Ackerman, P. T. (1965). The evaluation of autonomic and motor components of the conditioned avoidance response in the dog. *Psychophysiology, 1*, 209–230.

Eglash, A. (1952). The dilemma of fear as a motivating force. *Psychological Review, 59*, 376–379.

Eysenck, H. J. (1968). A theory of incubation of anxiety/fear responses. *Behaviour Research and Theory, 6*, 309–322.

Eysenck, H. J. (1976). The learning theory model of neurosis—A new approach. *Behaviour Research and Therapy, 14*, 251–267.

Eysenck, H. J. (1979). The conditioning model of neurosis. *The Behavioral and Brain Sciences, 2*, 155–166.

Eysenck, H. J. (1985). Incubation theory of fear/anxiety. In S. Reiss & R. R. Bootzin (Eds.), *Theortical issues in behavior therapy* (pp. 83–105). New York: Academic Press.

Eysenck, H. J., & Eysenck, S. B. G. (1968). *Eysenck Personality Inventory manual.* San Diego, CA: Educational and Industrial Testing Service.

Fiegl, H., & Brodbeck, M. (1953). *Readings in the philosophy of science.* New York: Appleton-Century-Crofts.

Freud, S. (1936). *The problem of anxiety* (H. A. Bunker, Trans.) (pp. 85–92). New York: Psychoanalytic Quarterly Press/Norton.

Goldstein, M. L. (1960). Acquired drive strength as a joint function of shock intensity and number of acquisition trials. *Journal of Experimental Psychology, 60*, 349–358.

Gray, J. A. (1971). *The psychology of fear and stress.* New York: McGraw-Hill.

Gray, J. A. (1975). *Elements of a two-process theory of learning.* New York: Academic Press.

Guthrie, E. R. (1938). *The psychology of human conflict.* New York: Harper & Row.

Herrnstein, R. (1969). Method and theory in the study of avoidance. *Psychological Review, 76,* 49–69.

Hilgard, E. R., & Bower, G. H. (1966). *Theories of learning.* New York: Appleton-Century-Crofts.

Hilgard, E. R., & Marquis, P. G. (1940). *Conditioning and learning.* New York: Appleton-Century-Crofts.

Hoffman, H. S., & Fleshler, M. (1962). The course of emotionality in the development of avoidance. *Journal of Experimental Psychology, 64,* 288–294.

Hollingworth, H. L. (1928). General laws of reintegration. *Journal of General Psychology, 1,* 79–90.

Hull, C. L. (1929). A functional interpretation of the conditioned reflex. *Psychological Review, 36,* 498–511.

Hull, C. L. (1939). Modern behaviorism and psychoanalysis. *Transactions of the New York Academy of Sciences, 1,* 78–82.

Hull, C. L. (1945). The place of innate individual and species differences in a natural-science theory of behavior. *Psychological Review, 52,* 55–60.

Kalish, H. I. (1954). Strength of fear as a function of the number of acquisition and extinction trials. *Journal of Experimental Psychology, 47,* 1–9.

Kaloupek, D. G., & Levis, D. J. (1980). The relationship between stimulus specificity and self-report indices in assessing fear of heterosexual social interaction: A test of the unitary response hypothesis. *Behavioral Assessment, 2,* 267–281.

Kaloupek, D. G., & Levis, D. J. (1983). Issues in the assessment of fear: Response concordance and the prediction of avoidance behavior. *Journal of Behavior Assessment, 5,* 239–260.

Kamin, L. J. (1954). Traumatic avoidance learning: The effect of CS–US interval with a trace-conditioning procedure. *Journal of Comparative and Physiological Psychology, 47,* 65–72.

Kamin, L. J., Brimer, C. J., & Black, A. H. (1963). Conditioned suppression as a monitor of fear of the CS in the course of avoidance training. *Journal of Comparative and Physiological Psychology, 56,* 497–501.

Kimble, G. A. (1961). *Hilgard and Marquis' conditioning and learning* (2nd ed.). New York: Appleton-Century-Crofts.

Kimble, G. A., & Perlmuter, L. C. (1970). The problem of volition. *Psychological Review, 77,* 361–384.

Kimmel, H. D. Kearns, W. D., & Anderson, D. E. (1988). Extinction instead of incubation following classical aversive conditioning. Unpublished manuscript, University of South Florida.

Kostanek, D. J., & Sawrey, J. M. (1965). Acquisition and extinction of shuttlebox avoidance with complex stimuli. *Psychonomic Science, 3,* 369–370.

Levis, D. J. (1966a). Effects of serial CS presentation and other characteristics of the CS on the conditioned avoidance response. *Psychological Reports, 18,* 755–766.

Levis, D. J. (1966b). Implosive therapy, Part II: The subhuman analogue, the strategy, and the technique. In S. G. Armitage (Ed.), *Behavioral modification techniques in the treatment of emotional Disorders* , (pp. 22–37). Battle Creek, MI: VA Hospital Publications.

Levis, D. J. (1970). Behavioral therapy: The fourth therapeutic revolution? In D. J. Levis (Ed.), *Learning approaches to therapeutic behavior change* (pp. 1–35). Chicago: Aldine.

Levis, D. J. (1971a). Effects of serial CS presentation on a finger-withdrawal avoidance response to shock. *Journal of Experimental Psychology, 87,* 71–77.

Levis, D. J. (1971b). One-trial-a-day avoidance learning. *Behavioral Research Methods and Instrumentation, 3,* 65–67.

Levis, D. J. (1976). Learned helplessness: A reply and an alternative S–R interpretation. *Journal of Experimental Psychology: General, 105,* 47–65.

Levis, D. J. (1979). A reconsideration of Eysenck's conditioning model of neurosis. *The Behavioral and Brain Sciences, 2,* 172–174.

Levis, D. J. (1980). The learned helplessness effect: An expectancy, discrimination deficit or motivational induced persistence? *Journal of Research in Personality, 14,* 158–169.

Levis, D. J. (1981). Extrapolation of two-factor learning theory of infrahuman avoidance behavior to psychopathology. *Neuroscience and Biobehavioral Review, 5,* 355–370.

Levis, D. J. (1985). Implosive theory: A comprehensive extension of conditioning theory of fear/anxiety to psychopathology. In S. Riess & R. R. Bootzin (Eds.), *Theoretical issues in behavior therapy* (pp. 49–82). New York: Academic Press.

Levis, D. J. (1988). Observation and experience from clinical practice: A critical ingredient for advancing behavior theory and therapy. *Behavior Therapist, 11,* 95–99.

Levis, D. J. (1989). The case for a two-factor theory of avoidance: Do non-fear interpretations really offer an alternative. In S. B Klein & R. R. Mowrer (Eds.), *Contemporary learning theories* (pp. 227–277). Hillsdale, NJ: Lawrence Erlbaum Associates.

Levis, D. J. (1990) A human laboratory test of Eysenck's theory of incubation: A search for the resolution of the neurotic paradox. *Journal of Psychopathology and Behavioral Assessment, 12*(4), 309–327.

Levis, D. J. (1991a). A clinician's plea for a return to the development of nonhuman models of psychopathology: New clinical observations in need of laboratory study. In M. R. Denny (Ed.), *Fear, avoidance, and phobias: A fundamental analysis* (pp. 395–427). Hillsdale, NJ: Lawrence Erlbaum Associates.

Levis, D. J. (1991b). The recovery of traumatic memories: The etiological source of psychopathology. In R. G. Kunzendorl (Ed.), *Mental imagery* (pp. 223–240). New York: Plenum.

Levis, D. J. (1995). Decoding traumatic memory: Implosive theory of psychopathology. In W. O'Donohue & L. Krasner (Eds.), *Theories in behavior therapy* (pp. 173–207). Washington, DC: American Psychological Association.

Levis, D. J. (1999a). The negative impact of the cognitive movement on the continued growth of the behavior therapy movement: A historical perspective. *Genetic, social and general psychology monographs, 125*(2), pp. 1–15.

Levis, D. J. (1999b). The traumatic memory debate: A failure in scientific communication and cooperation. *Applied & Preventive Psychology, 8,* 71–76.

Levis, D. J., Bouska, S., Eron, J., & McIlhon, M. (1970). Serial CS presentations and one-way avoidance conditioning: A noticeable lack of delayed responding. *Psychonomic Science, 20,* 147–149.

Levis, D. J., & Boyd, T. L. (1979). Symptom maintenance: An infrahuman analysis and extension of the conservation of anxiety principle. *Journal of Abnormal Psychology, 88,* 107–120.

Levis, D .J., & Boyd, T. L. (1985). The CS exposure approach of Implosive Therapy. In R. McMillan Turner & L. M. Ascher (Eds.), *Evaluation of behavior therapy outcome* (pp. 56–94). New York: Springer.

Levis, D. J., & Hare, N. (1977). A review of the theoretical rationale and empirical support for the extinction approach of implosive (flooding) therapy. In M. Hersen, R. M. Eisler, & P. M. Miller (Eds.), *Progress in behavior modification IV* (pp. 300–376). New York: Academic Press.

Levis, D. J., & Malloy, P. F. (1982). Research in infrahuman and human conditioning. In C. M. Franks & G. T. Wilson (Eds.), *Handbook of behavior therapy* (pp. 65–118). New York: Guilford.

Levis, D. J., Smith, J. E., Williams, R. W., & Zottola, A. (1990). *Problems associated with forced CS exposure following fear conditioning when the context cues of the apparatus serve as the CS.* Unpublished manuscript.

Levis, D. J., & Stampfl, T. G. (1972). Effects of serial CS presentations on shuttlebox avoidance responding. *Learning and Motivation, 3,* 73–90.

Ley, R. (1965). Effects of food and water deprivation on the performance of a response motivated by acquired fear. *Journal of Experimental Psychology, 69,* 583–589.

Lickenstein, C. E. (1950). Studies of anxiety: I. The production of a feeding inhibition in dogs. *Journal of Comparative and Physiological Psychology, 43,* 16–29.

Mackintosh, N. J. (1974). *The psychology of animal learning.* New York: Academic Press.

Maier, S. F., & Seligman, M. E. P. (1976). Learned helplessness: Theory and evidence. *Journal of Experimental Psychology: General, 105,* 3–46.

Malloy, P., & Levis, D. J. (1988). A laboratory demonstration of persistent human avoidance. *Behavior Therapy, 19,* 229–241.

Malloy, P. E., & Levis, D. J. (1990). A human laboratory test of Eysenck's theory of incubation: A search for the resolution of the neurotic paradox. *Journal of Psychopathology and Behavioral Assessment, 12,* 309–327.

Marx, M. H. (1963). *Theories in contemporary psychology.* New York: Macmillan.

McAllister, D. E., & McAllister, W. R. (1964). Second-order conditioning of fear. *Psychonomic Science, 1,* 383–384.

McAllister, D. E., & McAllister, W. R. (1991). Fear theory and aversively motivated behavior: Some controversial issues. In S. D. Klein & R. R. Mowrer (Eds.), *Contemporary learning theory, Pavlovian conditioning and the status of traditional learning theory* (pp. 135–163). Hillsdale, NJ: Lawrence Erlbaum Associates.

McAllister, W. R., & McAllister, D. E. (1971). Behavioral measurement of conditioned fear. In F. R. Brush (Ed.), *Aversive conditioning and learning* (pp. 105–179). New York: Academic Press.

McAllister, W. R., McAllister, D. E., & Benton, M. M. (1983). Measurement of fear of the conditioned stimulus and of situational cues at several stages of two-way avoidance learning. *Learning and Motivation, 14,* 92–106.

McAllister, W. R., McAllister, D. E., Scoles, M. T., & Hampton, S. R. (1986). Persistence of fear-reducing behavior: Relevance for conditioning theory of neurosis. *Journal of Abnormal Psychology, 93,* 365–372.

Miller, B. V., & Levis, D. J. (1971). The effects of varying short visual exposure times to a phobic test stimulus on subsequent avoidance behavior. *Behavior Research and Therapy, 19,* 17–21.

Miller, N. E. (1948). Studies of fear as an acquirable drive: I. Fear as motivation and fear-reduction as reinforcement in the learning of a new response. *Journal of Experimental Psychology, 38,* 89–101.

Mineka, S. (1985). Animal models of anxiety based disorders: The usefulness and limitation. In A. Tuma & J. Maser (Eds.), *Anxiety and anxiety disorders* (pp. 199–244). Hillsdale, NJ: Lawrence Erlbaum Associates.

Mineka, S., & Gino, A. (1980). Dissociation between conditioned emotional response and extended avoidance performance. *Learning and Motivation, 11,* 476–502.

Morris, R. G. M. (1974). Pavlovian conditioned inhibition of fear during shuttlebox avoidance behavior. *Learning and Motivation, 5,* 424–447.

Mowrer, O. H. (1939). A stimulus–response analysis and its role as a reinforcing agent. *Psychological Review, 46,* 553–565.

Mowrer, O. H. (1947). On the dual nature of learning—A re-interpretation of "conditioning" and "problem-solving." *Harvard Educational Review, 17,* 102–148.

Mowrer, O. H. (1948). Learning theory and the neurotic paradox. *American Journal of Orthopsychiatry, 18,* 571–610.

Mowrer, O. H. (1950). Pain, punishment, guilt, and anxiety. *Anxiety,* (pp. 27–40). New York: Grune & Stratton.

Mowrer, O. H. (1952). Learning theory and the neurotic fallacy. *American Journal of Orthopsychiatry, 22,* 679–689.

Mowrer, O. H. (1960). *Learning theory and behavior.* New York: Wiley.

Mowrer, O. H., & Lamoreaux, R. R. (1946). Fear as an intervening variable in avoidance conditioning. *Journal of Comparative and Physiological Psychology, 39,* 29–50.

Mowrer, O. H., & Solomon, L. N. (1954). Contiguity vs. drive-reduction in conditioned fear: The proximity and abruptness of drive-reduction. *American Journal of Psychology, 67,* 15–25.

Mowrer, O. H., & Viek, P. (1948). An experimental analogue of fear from a sense of helplessness. *Journal of Abnormal and Social Psychology, 83,* 193–200.

Napolkov, A. V. (1963). Information process of the brain. In N. Weiner & J. C. Sefade (Eds.), *Progress of brain research, nerve, brain and memory models,* (pp. 59–69). Amsterdam: Elsevier.

Oliverio, A. (1967). Effects of different conditioning schedules based on visual and acoustic conditioned stimulus on avoidance learning of two strains of mice. *Journal of Psychology, 65,* 131–139.

Page, H. A. (1955). The facilitation of experimental extinction by response prevention as a function of the acquisition of a new response. *Journal of Comparative Physiological Psychology, 48,* 14–16.

Pavlov, I. P. (1927). *Conditioned reflexes* (G. V. Anrep, Trans.). London: Oxford University Press.

Peterson, D. A., & Levis, D. J. (1985). The assessment of bodily injury fears via the behavioral avoidance slide-test. *Behavioral Assessment, 7,* 173–184.

Potts, M. K. (1994). Long-term effects of trauma: Post-traumatic stress among civilian internees of the Japanese during World War II. *Journal of Clinical Psychology, 50,* 681–698.

Quartermain, D., & Judge M. E. (1983). Retrieval enhancement in mice by pretest amphetamine injection after a long retention interval. *Physiological Psychology, 11,* 166–172.

Rachman, S. (1976). The passing of the two-stage theory of fear and avoidance: Fresh possibilities. *Behaviour Research and Therapy, 14,* 125–131.

Rachman, S., & Hodgson, R. I. (1974). Synchrony and desynchrony in fear and avoidance. *Behavior Research and Therapy, 12,* 311–318.

Rescorla, R. A. (1980). *Pavlovian second-order conditioning: Studies in associative learning.* Hillsdale, NJ: Lawrence Erlbaum Associates.

Rescorla, R. A., & Solomon, R. L. (1967). Two-process learning theory: Relationships between Pavlovian conditioning and instrumental learning. *Psychological Review, 74,* 151–182.

Riccio, D., & Silvestri, R. (1973). Extinction of avoidance behavior and the problem of residual fear. *Behavior Research and Therapy, 11,* 1–9.

Riccio, D. C., & Spear, N. E. (1991). Changes in memory for aversively motivated learning. In M. R. Denny (Ed.), *Fear, avoidance, and phobias* (pp. 231–258). Hillsdale, NJ: Lawrence Erlbaum Associates.

Rivers, W. H. R. (1920). *Instinct and the unconscious.* London: Cambridge University Press.

Rohrbaugh, M., & Riccio, D. C. (1970). Paradoxical enhancement of learned fear. *Journal of Abnormal Psychology, 75,* 210–216.

Rohrbaugh, M., Riccio, D. C., & Arthur, A. (1972). Paradoxical enhancement of conditioned suppression. *Behaviour Research and Therapy, 10,* 125–130.

Sandin, B., & Chorot, P. (1989). The incubation theory of fear/anxiety: Experimental investigation in a human laboratory model of Pavlovian conditioning. *Behaviour Research and Therapy, 27,* 9–18.

Schnurr, P. P., Aldwin, C. M., Spiro, A., Stukel, T., & Keane, T. M. (1993). *A longitudinal study of PTSD symptoms in older veterans.* Poster session for the Symposium on the Future of VA Mental Health Research, Department of Veterans Affairs Office of Research and Development and National Foundation for Brain Research. Washington, DC.

Schoenfeld, W. N. (1950). An experimental approach to anxiety, escape and avoidance behavior. In P. H. Hock & J. Zubin (Eds.), *Anxiety* (pp. 70–99). New York: Grune & Stratton.

Seligman, M. E. P., & Johnston, J. C. (1973). A cognitive theory of avoidance learning. In F. J. McGuigan & D. B. Lumsden (Eds.), *Contemporary approaches to conditioning and learning* (pp. 69–110). Washington, DC: Winston.

Shaw, F. J. (1946). A stimulus–response analysis of repression and insight in psychotherapy. *Psychological Review, 53,* 36–42.

Sheffield, F. D. (1948). Avoidance training and the contiguity principle. *Journal of Comparative and Physiological Psychology, 47,* 97–100.

Shipley, R. H., Mock, L. A., & Levis, D. J. (1971). Effects of several response prevention procedures on activity, avoidance responding, and conditioned fear in rats. *Journal of Comparative and Physiological Psychology, 77,* 256–270.

Shoben, E. J. (1949). Psychotherapy as a problem in learning theory. *Psychological Bulletin, 46,* 366–392.

Sidman, M., & Boren, J. J. (1957). A comparison of two types of warning stimulus in an avoidance situation. *Journal of Comparative and Physiological Psychology, 50,* 282–287.

Silva, P., & Rachman, S. (1981). Is exposure a necessary condition for fear-reduction? *Behaviour Research, and Therapy, 19,* 227–232.

Silvestri, R., Rohrbaugh, M., & Riccio, D. C. (1970). Conditions influencing the retention of learned fear in young rats. *Developmental Psychology, 2,* 389–395.

Skinner, B. F. (1953). *Science and human behavior.* New York: Macmillan.

Skinner, B. F. (1954). Critique of psychoanalytic concepts and theories. In T. Millon (Ed.), *Theories of psychopathology* (pp. 228–235). Philadelphia: Saunders.

Smith, J. E., & Levis, D. J. (1991). Is fear present following sustained asymptotic avoidance responding? *Behavioural Processes, 24,* 37–47.

Solomon, R. L., Kamin, L. J., & Wynne, L. C. (1953). Traumatic avoidance learning: The outcomes of several extinction procedures with dogs. *Journal of Abnormal and Social Psychology, 48,* 291–302.

Solomon, R. L., & Wynne, L. C. (1953). Traumatic avoidance learning: Acquisition in normal dogs. *Psychological Monographs, 67*(354), 1–19.

Solomon, R. L., & Wynne, L. C. (1954). Traumatic avoidance learning: The principle of anxiety conservation and partial irreversibility. *Psychological Review, 61,* 353–385.

Spear, N. E. (1978). *The processing of memories, forgetting and retention.* Hillsdale, NJ: Lawrence Erlbaum Associates.

Spear, N. E., Hamberg, J. M., & Bryan, R. (1980). Forgetting of recently acquired or recently reactivated memories. *Learning and Motivation, 11,* 456–475.

Stampfl, T. G. (1961). *Acquisition and resistance to extinction of avoidance responses to simple, congruent, and serial-congruent conditioned stimuli.* Unpublished circulated manuscript.

Stampfl, T. G. (1970). Implosive therapy: An emphasis on covert stimulation. In D. J. Levis (Ed.), *Learning approaches to therapeutic behavior change* (pp. 182–204). Chicago: Aldine.

Stampfl, T. G. (1983). Exposure treatment for psychiatrists? *Contemporary Psychology, 28,* 527–529.

Stampfl, T. G. (1987). Theoretical implications of the neurotic paradox as a problem in behavior theory: An experimental resolution. *The Behavior Analyst, 10,* 161–173.

Stampfl, T. G. (1991). Analysis of aversive events in human psychopathology: Fear and avoidance. In M. R. Denny (Ed.), *Fear, avoidance and phobias* (pp. 363–393). Hillsdale, NJ: Lawrence Erlbaum Associates.

Stampfl, T. G., & Levis, D. J. (1967). The essentials of implosive therapy: A learning theory based on psychodynamic behavioral therapy. *Journal of Abnormal Psychology, 72,* 496–503.

Stampfl, T. G., & Levis, D. G. (1969). Learning theory: An aid to dynamic therapeutic practice. In L. D. Eron & R. Callahan (Eds.), *Relationship of theory to practice in psychotherapy* (pp. 85–114). Chicago: Aldine.

Stampfl, T. G., & Levis, D. J. (1973). *Implosive therapy: Theory and technique.* Morristown, NJ: General Learning Press.

Stampfl, T. G., & Levis, D. J. (1976). Implosive therapy: A behavioral therapy. In J. T. Spence, R. C. Carson, & J. W. Thibaut (Eds.), *Behavioral approaches to therapy* (pp. 86–110). Morristown, NJ: General Learning Press.

Starr, M. D., & Mineka, S. (1977). Determinants of fear over the course of avoidance learning. *Learning and Motivation, 8,* 332–350.

Stone, N. M., & Borkovec, T. (1975). The paradoxical effect of brief CS exposure on analogue phobic subjects. *Behaviour Research and Therapy, 13,* 51–54.

Thomson, K. S. (1988). Anatomy of the extinction debate. *American Scientist, 76,* 59–61.

Thorndike, E. L. (1898). Animal intelligence: An experimental study of the associative processes in animals. *Psychology Monograph, 2 (Whole No. 8),* 5, 7, 16, 349–350.

Unger, W. S. (1988). *The evaluation of fear as a motivational variable in short latency avoidance behavior.* Unpublished doctoral dissertation, Binghamton University.

Watson, J. B. (1913). Psychology as the behaviorist views it. *Psychological Review, 20,* 158–177.

Watson, J. B. (1930). *Behaviourism* (rev. ed). New York: Norton.

Weinberger, N. M. (1965). Effects of detainment on extinction of avoidance responses. *Journal of Comparative and Physiological Psychology, 60,* 135–138.

Williams, R. N., & Levis, D. J. (1991). A demonstration of persistent human avoidance in extinction. *Bulletin of the Psychonomic Society, 24(2),* 125–127.

Wolpe, J. (1958). *Psychotherapy and reciprocal inhibition.* Stanford, CA: Stanford University Press.

Author Index

Subject Index